Processes of Constitutional Decisionmaking

2014 Supplement

2014 Supplement

Processes of Constitutional Decisionmaking

Cases and Materials

Fifth Edition

Prepared by Jack M. Balkin

Paul Brest
Professor of Law, Emeritus and Former Dean
Stanford Law School
and President, The William and Flora Hewlett Foundation

Sanford Levinson
W. St. John Garwood & W. St. John Garwood, Jr.
Centennial Chair in Law
University of Texas Law School

Jack M. Balkin
Knight Professor of Constitutional Law
and the First Amendment
Yale Law School

Akhil Reed Amar
Sterling Professor of Law and Political Science
Yale Law School

Reva B. Siegel
Nicholas deB. Katzenbach Professor of Law
Yale Law School

Wolters Kluwer
Law & Business

About Wolters Kluwer Law & Business

Wolters Kluwer Law & Business is a leading global provider of intelligent information and digital solutions for legal and business professionals in key specialty areas, and respected educational resources for professors and law students. Wolters Kluwer Law & Business connects legal and business professionals as well as those in the education market with timely, specialized authoritative content and information-enabled solutions to support success through productivity, accuracy and mobility.

Serving customers worldwide, Wolters Kluwer Law & Business products include those under the Aspen Publishers, CCH, Kluwer Law International, Loislaw, ftwilliam.com and MediRegs family of products.

CCH products have been a trusted resource since 1913, and are highly regarded resources for legal, securities, antitrust and trade regulation, government contracting, banking, pension, payroll, employment and labor, and healthcare reimbursement and compliance professionals.

Aspen Publishers products provide essential information to attorneys, business professionals and law students. Written by preeminent authorities, the product line offers analytical and practical information in a range of specialty practice areas from securities law and intellectual property to mergers and acquisitions and pension/benefits. Aspen's trusted legal education resources provide professors and students with high-quality, up-to-date and effective resources for successful instruction and study in all areas of the law.

Kluwer Law International products provide the global business community with reliable international legal information in English. Legal practitioners, corporate counsel and business executives around the world rely on Kluwer Law journals, looseleafs, books, and electronic products for comprehensive information in many areas of international legal practice.

Loislaw is a comprehensive online legal research product providing legal content to law firm practitioners of various specializations. Loislaw provides attorneys with the ability to quickly and efficiently find the necessary legal information they need, when and where they need it, by facilitating access to primary law as well as state-specific law, records, forms and treatises.

ftwilliam.com offers employee benefits professionals the highest quality plan documents (retirement, welfare and non-qualified) and government forms (5500/PBGC, 1099 and IRS) software at highly competitive prices.

MediRegs products provide integrated health care compliance content and software solutions for professionals in healthcare, higher education and life sciences, including professionals in accounting, law and consulting.

Wolters Kluwer Law & Business, a division of Wolters Kluwer, is headquartered in New York. Wolters Kluwer is a market-leading global information services company focused on professionals.

Contents

Chapter 6.   The Burdens of History:
The Constitutional Treatment of Race   **259**

Chapter 8.   Implied Fundamental Rights:
The Constitution, the Family, and the Body   **339**

Processes of Constitutional Decisionmaking

2014 Supplement

Chapter 4

From Reconstruction to the New Deal: 1866-1934

Insert the following before the Note on p. 309:

SENATOR JACOB HOWARD, SPEECH INTRODUCING THE FOURTEENTH AMENDMENT
Speech delivered in the U.S. Senate, May 23, 1866
Congressional Globe, 39th Cong., 1st Sess. 2764-68

[Senator Jacob Howard of Michigan was a member of the Joint Committee on Reconstruction that drafted the Fourteenth Amendment. He was the floor manager for the Amendment in the Senate. In this speech, he introduces the Amendment on the floor of the Senate and explains its purposes.]

Mr. HOWARD. . . . I can only promise to present to the Senate, in a very succinct way, the views and the motives which influenced th[e] committee, so far as I understand those views and motives, in presenting the report which is now before us for consideration, and the ends it aims to accomplish. . . .

The first section . . . relates to the privileges and immunities of citizens of the several States, and to the rights and privileges of all persons, whether citizens or others, under the laws of the United States. It declares that—

> No State shall make or enforce any law which shall abridge the privileges or immunities of citizens of the United States; nor shall any State deprive any person of life, liberty, or property without due process of law; nor deny to any person within its jurisdiction the equal protection of the laws.

It will be observed that this is a general prohibition upon all the States, as such, from abridging the privileges and immunities of the citizens of the United States. That is its first clause, and I regard it as very important. . . . [It] relates to the privileges and immunities of citizens of the United States as such, and as distinguished from all other persons not citizens of the United States. It is not, perhaps, very easy to define with accuracy what is meant by the expression, "citizen of the United States,"[1] although that expression occurs twice in the Constitution, once in reference to the President of the United States, in which instance it is

---

1. Senator Howard delivered this speech before the first sentence, the Citizenship Clause, which defined citizenship, was added to the proposed amendment.

declared that none but a citizen of the United States shall be President, and again in reference to Senators, who are likewise to be citizens of the United States. Undoubtedly the expression is used in both those instances in the same sense in which it is employed in the amendment now before us. A citizen of the United States is held by the courts to be a person who was born within the limits of the United States and subject to their laws. Before the adoption of the Constitution of the United States, the citizens of each State were, in a qualified sense at least, aliens to one another, for the reason that the several States before that event were regarded by each other as independent Governments, each one possessing a sufficiency of sovereign power to enable it to claim the right of naturalization; and, undoubtedly, each one of them possessed for itself the right of naturalizing foreigners, and each one, also, if it had seen fit so to exercise its sovereign power, might have declared the citizens of every other State to be aliens in reference to itself. With a view to prevent such confusion and disorder, and to put the citizens of the several States on an equality with each other as to all fundamental rights, a clause was introduced in the Constitution declaring that "the citizens of each State shall be entitled to all privileges and immunities of citizens in the several States."

The effect of this clause was to constitute *ipso facto* the citizens of each one of the original States citizens of the United States. And how did they antecedently become citizens of the several States? By birth or by naturalization. They became such in virtue of national law, or rather of natural law which recognizes persons born within the jurisdiction of every country as being subjects or citizens of that country. Such persons were, therefore, citizens of the United States as were born in the country or were made such by naturalization; and the Constitution declares that they are entitled, as citizens, to all the privileges and immunities of citizens in the several States. They are, by constitutional right, entitled to these privileges and immunities, and may assert this right and these privileges and immunities, and ask for their enforcement whenever they go within the limits of the several states of the Union.

I am not aware that the Supreme Court have ever undertaken to define either the nature or extent of the privileges and immunities thus guarantied. . . . But we may gather some intimation of what probably will be the opinion of the judiciary by referring to a case adjudged many years ago in one of the circuit courts of the United States by Judge Washington. . . . It is the case of Corfield vs. Coryell. . . . Judge Washington says:

> "The next question is whether this act infringes that section of the Constitution which declares that 'the citizens of each State shall be entitled to all privileges and immunities of citizens in the several states?'
>
> "The inquiry is, what are the privileges and immunities of citizens in the several States? We feel no hesitation in confining these expressions to those privileges and immunities which are in their nature fundamental, which belong of right to the citizens of all free Governments, and which have at all times been enjoyed by the citizens of the several States which compose this Union from the time of

their becoming free, independent, and sovereign. What these fundamental principles are it would, perhaps, be more tedious than difficult to enumerate. They may, however, be all comprehended under the following general heads: protection by the Government, the enjoyment of life and liberty, with the right to acquire and possess property of every kind, and to pursue and obtain happiness and safety, subject nevertheless to such restraints as the Government may justly prescribe for the general good of the whole. The right of a citizen of one State to pass through or to reside in any other State, for purposes of trade, agriculture, professional pursuits, or otherwise; to claim the benefit of the writ of *habeas corpus*; to institute and maintain actions of any kind in the courts of the State; to take, hold, and dispose of property, either real personal, and an exemption from higher taxes or impositions than are paid by the other citizens of the State, may be mentioned as some of the particular privileges and immunities of citizens which are clearly embraced by the general description of privileges deemed to be fundamental, to which may be added the elective franchise, as regulated and established by the laws or constitution of the State in which it is to be exercised. These, and many others which might be mentioned, are, strictly speaking, privileges and immunities, and the enjoyment of them by the citizens of each State in every other State was manifestly calculated (to use the expressions of the preamble of the corresponding provision in the old Articles of Confederation) 'the better to secure and perpetuate mutual friendship and intercourse among the people of the different States of the Union.'"

Such is the character of the privileges and immunities spoken of in the second section of the fourth article of the Constitution. To these privileges and immunities, whatever they may be—for they are not and cannot be fully defined in their entire extent and precise nature—to these should be added the personal rights guarantied and secured by the first eight amendments of the Constitution; such as the freedom of speech and of the press; the right of the people peaceably to assemble and petition the Government for a redress of grievances, a right appertaining to each and all the people; the right to keep and to bear arms; the right to be exempted from the quartering of soldiers in a house without the consent of the owner; the right to be exempt from unreasonable searches and seizures, and from any search or seizure except by virtue of a warrant issued upon a formal oath or affidavit; the right of an accused person to be informed of the nature of the accusation against him, and his right to be tried by an impartial jury of the vicinage; and also the right to be secure against excessive bail and against cruel and unusual punishments.

Now, sir, here is a mass of privileges, immunities, and rights, some of them secured by the second section of the fourth article of the Constitution, which I have recited, some by the first eight amendments of the Constitution; and it is a fact well worthy of attention that the course of decision of our courts and the present settled doctrine is, that all these immunities, privileges, rights, thus guarantied by the Constitution or recognized by it, are secured to the citizen solely as a citizen of the United States and as a party in their courts. They do not operate in the slightest degree as a restraint or prohibition upon State legislation. States are not affected by them, and it has been repeatedly held[2] that the restriction contained in the Constitution against the taking of private property for public use without just compensation is not a restriction upon State legislation, but applies only to the legislation of Congress.

Now, sir, there is no power given in the Constitution to enforce and to carry out any of these guarantees. They are not powers granted by the Constitution to Congress, and of course do not come within the sweeping clause of the Constitution authorizing Congress to pass all laws necessary and proper for carrying out the foregoing or granted powers, but they stand simply as a bill of rights in the Constitution, without power on the part of Congress to give them full effect; while at the same time the States are not restrained from violating the principles embraced in them except by their own local constitutions, which may be altered from year to year. The great object of the first section of this amendment is, therefore, to restrain the power of the States and compel them at all times to respect these great fundamental guarantees. . . . This is done by the fifth section of this amendment, which declares that "the Congress shall have power to enforce by appropriate legislation the provisions of this article." Here is a direct affirmative delegation of power to Congress to carry out all the principles of all these guarantees, a power not found in the Constitution.

The last two clauses of the first section of the amendment disable a State from depriving not merely a citizen of the United States, but any person, whoever he may be, of life, liberty, or property without due process of law, or from denying to him the equal protection of the laws of the State. This abolishes all class legislation in the States and does away with the injustice of subjecting one caste of persons to a code not applicable to another. It prohibits the hanging of a black man for a crime for which the white man is not to be hanged. It protects the black man in his fundamental rights as a citizen with the same shield which it throws over the white man. Is it not time, Mr. President, that we extend to the black man, I had almost called it the poor privilege of the equal protection of the law? Ought not the time to be now passed when one measure of justice is to be meted out to a member of one caste while another and a different measure is meted out to the member of another caste, both castes being alike citizens of the United States, both bound to obey the same laws, to sustain the burdens of the same Government, and both equally responsible to justice and to God for the deeds done in the body?

But, sir, the first section of the proposed amendment does not give to either of these classes the right of voting. The right of suffrage is not, in law, one of the privileges or immunities thus secured by the Constitution. It is merely the creature of law. It has always been regarded in this country as the result of positive local law, not regarded as one of those fundamental rights lying at the basis of all society and without which a people cannot exist except as slaves, subject to a despotism.

---

2. This is probably a reference to Barron v. City of Baltimore, 32 U.S. 243 (1833).

As I have already remarked, section one is a restriction upon the States, and does not, of itself, confer any power upon Congress. The power which Congress has, under this amendment, is derived, not from that section, but from the fifth section, which gives it authority to pass laws which are appropriate to the attainment of the great object of the amendment. Look upon the first section, taken in connection with the fifth, as very important. It will, if adopted by the States, forever disable every one of them from passing laws trenching upon those fundamental rights and privileges which pertain to citizens of the United States, and to all persons who may happen to be within their jurisdiction. It establishes equality before the law, and it gives to the humblest, the poorest, the most despised of the race the same rights and the same protection before the law as it gives to the most powerful, the most wealthy, or the most haughty. That, sir, is republican government, as I understand it, and the only one which can claim the praise of a just Government. Without this principle of equal justice to all men and equal protection under the shield of the law, there is no republican government and none that is really worth maintaining.

. . .

[Section five] gives to Congress power to enforce by appropriate legislation all the provisions of this article of amendment. Without this clause, no power is granted to Congress by the amendment or any one of its sections. It casts upon congress the responsibility of seeing to it, for the future, that all the sections of the amendment are carried out in good faith, and that no State infringes the rights of persons or property. I look upon this clause as indispensable for the reason that it thus imposes upon Congress this power and this duty. It enables Congress, in case the States shall enact laws in conflict with the principles of the amendment, to correct that legislation by a formal congressional enactment.

Discussion

1. *The Privileges or Immunities Clause and the Privileges and Immunities Clause.* Senator Howard begins his explanation of the Fourteenth Amendment by pointing to the Privileges and Immunities Clause of Article IV, section 2. Like many Republican thinkers of the time, Howard argued that the Privileges and Immunities Clause in Article IV already bound the states to protect fundamental rights of national citizenship. See Michael Kent Curtis, No State Shall Abridge: The Fourteenth Amendment and the Bill of Rights 47-48, 62-91 (1986). In other words, Howard and other Republicans read "of the several states" to mean "of the United States." Nevertheless, the Republican argument went, there was no method in the 1787 Constitution to enforce these guarantees. Hence the Privileges or Immunities Clause of the new Fourteenth Amendment would establish a clear legal obligation enforceable by the courts; moreover Congress could also pass enforcing legislation under its section 5 powers. Thus, it was no accident that what Howard believed to be the central clause in section 1 of the Fourteenth Amendment uses the same language as Article IV, section 2.

The new Privileges or Immunities Clause had another important effect. Just as states had to treat outsiders equally with their own citizens with respect to certain fundamental rights, so too they would now have to treat their own citizens equally with respect to these rights. Thus, the Privileges and Immunities Clause was not only a guarantee of liberty; it was also a guarantee of equality with respect to the basic rights of national citizenship.

As we shall soon see, the Supreme Court quickly robbed the Privileges or Immunities Clause of any importance in the Slaughter-House Cases. As described in Chapter Nine, a century later the Warren Court once again raised the idea that the Fourteenth Amendment protects equal fundamental rights, this time through the Equal Protection Clause.

2. *Incorporation.* According to Senator Howard, the Privileges or Immunities Clause protects the "the personal rights guarantied and secured by the first eight amendments of the Constitution." Thus, Howard believed — and represented to the Senate when he introduced the Amendment — that the Fourteenth Amendment incorporated the personal rights guarantees of the Bill of Rights. As we will see later on in the casebook (pp. 487-489), the Supreme Court did not take up this invitation, and the Bill of Rights (or most of it, at any rate) did not become incorporated until the 20th century. Moreover, incorporation, when it occurred, came through a creative reading of the Due Process Clause, and not the Privileges or Immunities Clause.

3. *Unenumerated rights.* Note Senator Howard's reliance on *Corfield v. Coryell* and his remark that the privileges and immunities of citizens of the United States "are not and cannot be fully defined in their entire extent and precise nature." Howard offers a declaratory theory of privileges or immunities. That is, he assumes that these rights are natural rights that preexist the state, and that the Constitution merely declares their existence and makes them enforceable in positive law. How can courts and legislatures determine what those rights are? We will return to this question in Chapter Eight. (Recall the debate between Justices Chase and Iredell in Calder v. Bull concerning whether courts could protect natural rights against infringements by state governments. How would the inclusion of the Privileges or Immunities Clause change the terms of that debate?)

4. *Class and caste legislation.* When Howard turns to the Equal Protection and Due Process Clauses he argues that they serve a different function: "This abolishes all class legislation in the States and does away with the injustice of subjecting one caste of persons to a code not applicable to another." What does the principle against "caste" legislation mean? One possibility suggested by Howard's speech is simple colorblindness. Another is that "caste" legislation is legislation that subordinates one social group to another.

The related notion of "class legislation" involved singling out a particular group for special burdens or special benefits. Indeed, the expression "equal protection" famously appeared in Andrew Jackson's July 10, 1832 veto message, where he stated:

It is to be regretted that the rich and powerful too often bend the acts of government to their selfish purposes. Distinctions in society will always exist under every just government. Equality of talents, of education, or of wealth can not be produced by human institutions. In the full enjoyment of the gifts of Heaven and the fruits of superior industry, economy, and virtue, every man is equally entitled to protection by law; but when the laws undertake to add to these natural and just advantages artificial distinctions, to grant titles, gratuities, and exclusive privileges, to make the rich richer and the potent more powerful, the humble members of society — the farmers, mechanics, and laborers — who have neither the time nor the means of securing like favors to themselves, have a right to complain of the injustice of their Government. There are no necessary evils in government. Its evils exist only in its abuses. If it would confine itself to equal protection, and, as Heaven does its rains, shower its favors alike on the high and the low, the rich and the poor, it would be an unqualified blessing.

5. *Voting*. Note that Justice Washington included "the elective franchise, as regulated and established by the laws or constitution of the State in which it is to be exercised" in his list of privileges and immunities. Senator Howard, however, takes pains to insist that voting is not one of the rights guaranteed by the new Fourteenth Amendment. In part that was because he and other supporters of the Amendment did not believe it could pass if blacks were given the right to vote. Hence they settled for the compromise measure of section 2, which sought to penalize states that denied black men the vote. As Howard explained in his discussion of section 2:

> Let me not be misunderstood. I do not intend to say, nor do I say, that the proposed amendment, section two, proscribes the colored race. It has nothing to do with that question, as I shall show before I take my seat. I could wish that the elective franchise should be extended equally to the white man and to the black man; and if it were necessary, after full consideration, to restrict what is known as universal suffrage for the purpose of securing this equality, I would go for a restriction; but I deem that impracticable at the present time, and so did the committee.
>
> The colored race are destined to remain among us. They have been in our midst for more than two hundred years; and the idea of the people of the United States ever being able by any measure or measures to which they may resort to expel or expatriate that race from their limits and to settle them in a foreign country, is to me the wildest of all chimeras. The thing can never be done; it is impracticable. For weal or for woe, the destiny of the colored race in this country is wrapped up with our own; they are to remain in our midst, and here spend their years and here bury their fathers and finally repose themselves. We may regret it. It may not be entirely compatible with our taste that they should live in our midst. We cannot help it. Our forefathers introduced them, and their destiny is to continue among us; and the practical question which now presents itself to us is as to the best mode of getting along with them.
>
> The committee were of opinion that the States are not yet prepared to sanction so fundamental a change as would be the concession of the right of suffrage to the colored race. We may as well state it plainly and fairly, so that there shall be no

misunderstanding on the subject. It was our opinion that three-fourths of the states of this Union could not be induced to vote to grant the right of suffrage, even in any degree or under any restriction, to the colored race. We may be right in this apprehension or we may be in error. Time will develop the truth; and for one I shall wait with patience the movements of public opinion upon this great and absorbing question. The time may come, I trust it will come, indeed I feel a profound conviction that it is not far distant, when even the people of the States themselves where the colored population is most dense will consent to admit them to the right of suffrage. Sir, the safety and prosperity of those States depend upon it; it is especially for their interest that they should not retain in their midst a race of pariahs, so circumstanced as to be obliged to bear the burdens of Government and to obey its laws without any participation in the enactment of the laws.

The second section leaves the right to regulate the elective franchise still with the States, and does not meddle with that right. . . .

As it turned out, the Fifteenth Amendment was ratified four years later in 1870. Does this history mean that the Fourteenth Amendment has no application with respect to voting or the right to hold public office?

6. *The status of women.* Women's rights arose during Howard's discussion of black suffrage, since section 2 imposed a penalty only for denying the right to vote to males. In defending his position that blacks should have been given the right to vote, Senator Howard quoted Madison for the "vital principle of free government, that those who are to be bound by the laws ought to have a voice in making them." Howard asserted that this principle was "the vital principle of republican government; it is not representation because of taxation." Responding to a question by Senator Sumner, Howard argued that the principle applied to all persons irrespective of color, and "whether they can read or write or not." When asked by Senator Johnson whether this included women, Howard answered:

Mr. Madison does not say anything about females. . . . I believe Mr. Madison was old enough and wise enough to take it for granted there was such a thing as the law of nature which has a certain influence even in political affairs, and that by that law women and children were not regarded as the equals of men. Mr. Madison would not have quibbled about the question of women's voting or of an infant's voting. He lays down a broad democratic principle, that those who are to be bound by the laws ought to have a voice in making them; and everywhere mature manhood is the representative type of the human race.

In the debates over the Fourteenth Amendment, the proponents of the new Amendment were careful to avoid claiming that it would invalidate any laws regarding women. Although the framers of the Fourteenth Amendment asserted that women and men were civilly equal, they assumed that existing laws and practices—including coverture—did not deny women equal citizenship. See Cong. Globe, 39th Cong. 1st Session, at 1089 (February 28th, 1866) (remarks of Rep. Bingham) (noting that states would retain ability to regulate married women's ownership of property because property rights were governed by local law while "[t]he rights of life and liberty are theirs [i.e., women's] whatever States may enact"); Cong. Globe, 39th Cong., 1st Sess. 1064 (1866) (February 27th, 1866) (remarks of Rep. Stevens) ("When a distinction is made between two married people or two femmes sole, then it is unequal legislation; but where all of the same class are dealt with in the same way then there is no pretense of inequality."). Responding to Stevens, Representative Hale remarked: "[The] argument seems to me to be more specious than sound. The language of the section gives to *all persons* equal protection. Now if that means you shall extend to one married women the same protection you extend to another, and not the same you extend to unmarried women or men, then by parity of reasoning it will be sufficient if you extend to one negro the same rights you do to another, but not those you extend to a white man. . . . The line of distinction is, I take it, quite as broadly marked between negroes and white men as between married and unmarried women."

What weight should we give these remarks in deciding how the Fourteenth Amendment should apply to questions of sex equality today?

Part Two

Constitutional Adjudication in the Modern World

Insert at the end of p. 497:

DISTRICT OF COLUMBIA v. HELLER
554 U.S. 570 (2008)

Justice SCALIA delivered the opinion of the Court.

We consider whether a District of Columbia prohibition on the possession of usable handguns in the home violates the Second Amendment to the Constitution.

I

The District of Columbia generally prohibits the possession of handguns. It is a crime to carry an unregistered firearm, and the registration of handguns is prohibited. See D.C. Code §§7-2501.01(12), 7-2502.01(a), 7-2502.02(a)(4) (2001). Wholly apart from that prohibition, no person may carry a handgun without a license, but the chief of police may issue licenses for 1-year periods. See §§22-4504(a), 22-4506. District of Columbia law also requires residents to keep their lawfully owned firearms, such as registered long guns, unloaded and dissembled or bound by a trigger lock or similar device unless they are located in a place of business or are being used for lawful recreational activities. See §7-2507.02.

Respondent Dick Heller is a D.C. special police officer authorized to carry a handgun while on duty at the Federal Judicial Center. He applied for a registration certificate for a handgun that he wished to keep at home, but the District refused. He thereafter filed a lawsuit in the Federal District Court for the District of Columbia seeking, on Second Amendment grounds, to enjoin the city from enforcing the bar on the registration of handguns, the licensing requirement insofar as it prohibits the carrying of a firearm in the home without a license, and the trigger-lock requirement insofar as it prohibits the use of functional firearms within the home. . . .

II

. . .

A

The Second Amendment provides: "A well regulated Militia, being necessary to the security of a free State, the right of the people to keep and bear Arms, shall not be infringed." In interpreting this text, we are guided by the principle that "[t]he Constitution was written to be understood by the voters; its words and phrases were used in their normal and ordinary as distinguished from technical meaning. Normal meaning may of course include an idiomatic meaning, but it excludes secret or technical meanings that would not have been known to ordinary citizens in the founding generation." . . .

The Second Amendment is naturally divided into two parts: its prefatory clause and its operative clause. . . . The former does not limit the latter grammatically, but rather announces a purpose. The Amendment could be rephrased, "Because a well regulated Militia is necessary to the security of a free State, the right of the people to keep and bear Arms shall not be infringed." . . .

Logic demands that there be a link between the stated purpose and the command. . . . But apart from [its] clarifying function, a prefatory clause does not limit or expand the scope of the operative clause. Therefore, while we will begin our textual analysis with the operative clause, we will return to the prefatory clause to ensure that our reading of the operative clause is consistent with the announced purpose.

1.   Operative Clause.

a. "Right of the People."   The first salient feature of the operative clause is that it codifies a "right of the people." The unamended Constitution and the Bill of Rights use the phrase "right of the people" two other times, in the First Amendment's Assembly-and-Petition Clause and in the Fourth Amendment's Search-and-Seizure Clause. The Ninth Amendment uses very similar terminology ("The enumeration in the Constitution, of certain rights, shall not be construed to deny or disparage others retained by the people"). All three of these instances unambiguously refer to individual rights, not "collective" rights, or rights that may be exercised only through participation in some corporate body. Three provisions of the Constitution refer to "the people" in a context other than "rights"—the famous preamble ("We the people"), §2 of Article I (providing that "the people" will choose members of the House), and the Tenth Amendment (providing that those powers not given the Federal Government remain with "the States" or "the people"). Those provisions arguably refer to "the people" acting collectively—but they deal with the exercise or reservation of powers, not rights. Nowhere else in the Constitution does a "right" attributed to "the people" refer to anything other than an individual right. What is more, in all six other provisions of the Constitution that mention "the people," the term unambiguously refers to all members of the political community, not an unspecified subset. . . . This contrasts markedly with the phrase "the militia" in the prefatory clause. As we will describe below, the "militia" in colonial America consisted of a subset of "the people"—those who were male, able bodied, and within a certain age range. Reading the Second Amendment as protecting only the right to "keep and bear Arms" in an organized militia therefore fits poorly with the operative clause's description of the holder of that right as "the people."

We start therefore with a strong presumption that the Second Amendment right is exercised individually and belongs to all Americans.

b. "Keep and bear Arms."   . . . The 18th-century meaning [of "Arms"] is no different from the meaning today. The 1773 edition of Samuel Johnson's dictionary defined "arms" as "weapons of offence, or armour of defence." . . . The term was applied, then as now, to weapons that were not specifically designed for military use and were not employed in a military capacity. . . . Although one founding-era thesaurus limited "arms" (as opposed to "weapons") to "instruments of offence *generally* made use of in war," even that source stated that all firearms constituted "arms." . . .

Some have made the argument, bordering on the frivolous, that only those arms in existence in the 18th century are protected by the Second Amendment. We do not interpret constitutional rights that way. Just as the First Amendment protects modern forms of communications, and the Fourth Amendment applies to modern forms of search, the Second Amendment extends, prima facie, to all instruments that constitute bearable arms, even those that were not in existence at the time of the founding.

We turn to the phrases "keep arms" and "bear arms." . . . No party has apprised us of an idiomatic meaning of "keep Arms." Thus, the most natural reading of "keep Arms" in the Second Amendment is to "have weapons." . . . Petitioners point to militia laws of the founding period that required militia members to "keep" arms in connection with militia service, and they conclude from this that the phrase "keep Arms" has a militia-related connotation. This is rather like saying that, since there are many statutes that authorize aggrieved employees to "file complaints" with federal agencies, the phrase "file complaints" has an employment-related connotation. "Keep arms" was simply a common way of referring to possessing arms, for militiamen *and everyone else.*

At the time of the founding, as now, to "bear" meant to "carry." When used with "arms," however, the term has a meaning that refers to carrying for a particular purpose—confrontation. . . . Although the phrase implies that the carrying of the weapon is for the purpose of "offensive or defensive action," it in no way connotes participation in a structured military organization.

From our review of founding-era sources, we conclude that this natural meaning was also the meaning that "bear arms" had in the 18th century. In numerous instances, "bear arms" was unambiguously used to refer to the carrying of weapons outside of an organized militia. The most prominent examples are those most relevant to the Second Amendment: Nine state constitutional provisions written in the 18th century or the first two decades of the 19th, which enshrined a right of citizens to "bear arms in defense of themselves and the state" or "bear arms in defense of himself and the state." It is clear from those formulations that "bear arms" did not refer only to carrying a weapon in an organized military unit. . . .

The phrase "bear Arms" also had at the time of the founding an idiomatic meaning that was significantly different from its natural meaning: "to serve as a soldier, do military service, fight" or "to wage war." But it *unequivocally* bore that idiomatic meaning only when followed by the preposition "against," which was in turn followed by the target of the hostilities. (That is how, for example, our Declaration of Independence §28, used the phrase: "He has constrained our fellow Citizens taken Captive on the high Seas to bear Arms against their Country. . . .") . . .

Petitioners justify their limitation of "bear arms" to the military context by pointing out the unremarkable fact that it was often used in that context — the same mistake they made with respect to "keep arms." It is especially unremarkable that the phrase was often used in a military context in the federal legal sources (such as records of congressional debate) that have been the focus of petitioners' inquiry. Those sources would have had little occasion to use it *except* in discussions about the standing army and the militia. And the phrases used primarily in those military discussions include not only "bear arms" but also "carry arms," "possess arms," and "have arms" — though no one thinks that those *other* phrases also had special military meanings. . . .

Justice Stevens places great weight on James Madison's inclusion of a conscientious-objector clause in his original draft of the Second Amendment: "but no person religiously scrupulous of bearing arms, shall be compelled to render military service in person." He argues that this clause establishes that the drafters of the Second Amendment intended "bear Arms" to refer only to military service. It is always perilous to derive the meaning of an adopted provision from another provision deleted in the drafting process. In any case, what Justice Stevens would conclude from the deleted provision does not follow. It was not meant to exempt from military service those who objected to going to war but had no scruples about personal gunfights. Quakers opposed the use of arms not just for militia service, but for any violent purpose whatsoever. . . . Thus, the most natural interpretation of Madison's deleted text is that those opposed to carrying weapons for potential violent confrontation would not be "compelled to render military service," in which such carrying would be required. . . .

c. Meaning of the Operative Clause.   Putting all of these textual elements together, we find that they guarantee the individual right to possess and carry weapons in case of confrontation. This meaning is strongly confirmed by the historical background of the Second Amendment. We look to this because it has always been widely understood that the Second Amendment, like the First and Fourth Amendments, codified a *pre-existing* right. The very text of the Second Amendment implicitly recognizes the pre-existence of the right and declares only that it "shall not be infringed." . . .

Between the Restoration and the Glorious Revolution, the Stuart Kings Charles II and James II succeeded in using select militias loyal to them to suppress political dissidents, in part by disarming their opponents. Under the auspices of the 1671 Game Act, for example, the Catholic James II had ordered general disarmaments of regions home to his Protestant enemies. These experiences caused Englishmen to be extremely wary of concentrated military forces run by the state and to be jealous of their arms. They accordingly obtained an assurance from William and Mary, in the Declaration of Right (which was codified as the English Bill of Rights), that Protestants would never be disarmed: "That the subjects which are Protestants may have arms for their defense suitable to their conditions and as allowed by law." 1 W. & M., c. 2, §7, in 3 Eng. Stat. at Large 441 (1689). This right has long been understood to be the predecessor to our Second Amendment. It was clearly an individual right, having nothing whatever to do with service in a militia. To be sure, it was an individual right not available to the whole population, given that it was restricted to Protestants, and like all written English rights it was held only against the Crown, not Parliament. But it was secured to them as individuals, according to "libertarian political principles," not as members of a fighting force.

By the time of the founding, the right to have arms had become fundamental for English subjects. Blackstone, whose works, we have said, "constituted the preeminent authority on English law for the founding generation," cited the arms provision of the Bill of Rights as one of the fundamental rights of Englishmen. His description of it cannot possibly be thought to tie it to militia or military service. It was, he said, "the natural right of resistance and self-preservation," and "the right of having and using arms for self-preservation and defence." . . . Thus, the right secured in 1689 as a result of the Stuarts' abuses was by the time of the founding understood to be an individual right protecting against both public and private violence.

And, of course, what the Stuarts had tried to do to their political enemies, George III had tried to do to the colonists. In the tumultuous decades of the 1760's and 1770's, the Crown began to disarm the inhabitants of the most rebellious areas. That provoked polemical reactions by Americans invoking their rights as Englishmen to keep arms. A New York article of April 1769 said that "[i]t is a natural right which the people have reserved to themselves, confirmed by the Bill of Rights, to keep arms for their own defence." They understood the right to enable individuals to defend themselves. As the most important early American edition of Blackstone's Commentaries (by the law professor and former Antifederalist St. George Tucker) made clear in the notes to the description of the arms right, Americans understood the "right of self-preservation" as permitting a citizen to "repe[l] force by force" when "the intervention of society in his behalf, may be too late to prevent an injury."

There seems to us no doubt, on the basis of both text and history, that the Second Amendment conferred an individual right to keep and bear arms. Of course the right was not unlimited, just as the First Amendment's right of free speech was not. Thus, we do not read the Second Amendment to protect the right of citizens to carry arms for *any sort* of confrontation, just as we do not read the First Amendment to protect the right of citizens to speak for *any purpose*. Before turning to limitations upon the individual right, however, we must determine whether the prefatory clause of the Second Amendment comports with our interpretation of the operative clause.

2.   Prefatory Clause.

The prefatory clause reads: "A well regulated Militia, being necessary to the security of a free State. . . ."

a. "Well-Regulated Militia."   In *United States v. Miller,* 307 U.S. 174 (1939), we explained that the Militia comprised all males physically capable of acting in concert for the common defense." . . . Petitioners take a seemingly narrower view of the militia, stating that "[m]ilitias are the state and congressionally-regulated military forces described in the Militia Clauses (art. I, §8, cls.15-16)." Although we agree with petitioners' interpretive assumption that "militia" means the same thing in Article I and the Second Amendment, we believe that petitioners identify the wrong thing, namely, the organized militia. Unlike armies and navies, which Congress is given the power to create ("to raise . . . Armies"; "to provide . . . a Navy," Art. I, §8, cls. 12-13), the militia is assumed by Article I already to be *in existence*. Congress is given the power to "provide for calling forth the militia," §8, cl. 15; and the power not to create, but to "organiz[e]" it . . . connoting a body already in existence, *ibid.,* cl. 16. This is fully consistent with the ordinary definition of the militia as all able-bodied men. From that pool, Congress has plenary power to organize the units that will make up an effective fighting force. That is what Congress did in the first militia Act, which specified that "each and every free able-bodied white male citizen of the respective states, resident therein, who is or shall be of the age of eighteen years, and under the age of forty-five years (except as is herein after excepted) shall severally and respectively be enrolled in the militia." Act of May 8, 1792, 1 Stat. 271. To be sure, Congress need not conscript every able-bodied man into the militia, because nothing in Article I suggests that in exercising its power to organize, discipline, and arm the militia, Congress must focus upon the entire body. Although the militia consists of all able-bodied men, the federally organized militia may consist of a subset of them.

Finally, the adjective "well-regulated" implies nothing more than the imposition of proper discipline and training.

b. Security of a Free State.   The phrase "security of a free state" meant "security of a free polity," not security of each of the several States . . . [t]he presence of the term "foreign state" in Article I and Article III shows that the word "state" did not have a single meaning in the Constitution.

There are many reasons why the militia was thought to be "necessary to the security of a free state." First, of course, it is useful in repelling invasions and suppressing insurrections. Second, it renders large standing armies unnecessary—an argument that Alexander Hamilton made in favor of federal control over the militia. The Federalist No. 29 (A. Hamilton). Third, when the able-bodied men of a nation are trained in arms and organized, they are better able to resist tyranny.

3.   Relationship between Prefatory Clause and Operative Clause

We reach the question, then: Does the preface fit with an operative clause that creates an individual right to keep and bear arms? It fits perfectly, once one knows the history that the founding generation knew and that we have described above. That history showed that the way tyrants had eliminated a militia consisting of all the able-bodied men was not by banning the militia but simply by taking away the people's arms, enabling a select militia or standing army to suppress political opponents. This is what had occurred in England that prompted codification of the right to have arms in the English Bill of Rights.

The debate with respect to the right to keep and bear arms, as with other guarantees in the Bill of Rights, was not over whether it was desirable (all agreed that it was) but over whether it needed to be codified in the Constitution. During the 1788 ratification debates, the fear that the federal government would disarm the people in order to impose rule through a standing army or select militia was pervasive in Antifederalist rhetoric. Federalists responded that because Congress was given no power to abridge the ancient right of individuals to keep and bear arms, such a force could never oppress the people. It was understood across the political spectrum that the right helped to secure the ideal of a citizen militia, which might be necessary to oppose an oppressive military force if the constitutional order broke down.

It is therefore entirely sensible that the Second Amendment's prefatory clause announces the purpose for which the right was codified: to prevent elimination of the militia. The prefatory clause does not suggest that preserving the militia was the only reason Americans valued the ancient right; most undoubtedly thought it even more important for self-defense and hunting. But the threat that the new Federal Government would destroy the citizens' militia by taking away their arms was the reason that right—unlike some other English rights—was codified in a written Constitution. Justice Breyer's assertion that individual self-defense is merely a "subsidiary interest" of the right to keep and bear arms, is profoundly mistaken. He bases that assertion solely upon the prologue—but that can only show that self-defense had little to do with the right's *codification;* it was the *central component* of the right itself.

Besides ignoring the historical reality that the Second Amendment was not intended to lay down a "novel principl[e]" but rather codified a right "inherited from our English ancestors," petitioners' interpretation does not even achieve the narrower purpose that prompted codification of the right. If, as they believe, the Second Amendment right is no more than the right to keep and use weapons as a member of an organized militia—if, that is, the *organized* militia is the sole institutional beneficiary of the Second Amendment's guarantee—it does not assure the existence of a "citizens' militia" as a safeguard against tyranny. For Congress retains plenary authority to organize the militia, which must include the authority to say who will belong to the organized force. That is why the first Militia Act's requirement that only whites enroll caused States to amend their militia laws to exclude free blacks. Thus, if petitioners are correct, the Second Amendment protects citizens' right to use a gun in an organization from which Congress has plenary authority to exclude them. It guarantees a select militia of the sort the Stuart kings found useful, but not the people's militia that was the concern of the founding generation.

B

Our interpretation is confirmed by analogous arms-bearing rights in state constitutions that preceded and immediately followed adoption of the Second Amendment. Four States adopted analogues to the Federal Second Amendment in the period between independence and the ratification of the Bill of Rights. Two of them—Pennsylvania and Vermont—clearly adopted individual rights unconnected to militia service. Pennsylvania's Declaration of Rights of 1776 said: "That the people have a right to bear arms *for the defence of themselves, and the state. . . .*" In 1777, Vermont adopted the identical provision, except for inconsequential differences in punctuation and capitalization.

North Carolina also codified a right to bear arms in 1776: "That the people have a right to bear arms, for the defence of the State. . . ." This could plausibly be read to support only a right to bear arms in a militia—but that is a peculiar way to make the point in a constitution that elsewhere repeatedly mentions the militia explicitly. Many colonial statutes required individual arms-bearing for public-safety reasons—such as the 1770 Georgia law that "for the security and *defence of this province* from internal dangers and insurrections" required those men who qualified for militia duty individually "to carry fire arms" to places of public worship. That broad public-safety understanding was the connotation given to the North Carolina right by that State's Supreme Court in 1843.

The 1780 Massachusetts Constitution presented another variation on the theme: "The people have a right to keep and to bear arms for the common defence. . . ." Once again, if one gives narrow meaning to the phrase "common defence" this can be thought to limit the right to the bearing of arms in a state-organized military force. But once again the State's highest court thought otherwise [in 1825].

We therefore believe that the most likely reading of all four of these pre-Second Amendment state constitutional provisions is that they secured an individual right to bear arms for defensive purposes. . . .

Between 1789 and 1820, nine States adopted Second Amendment analogues. Four of them — Kentucky, Ohio, Indiana, and Missouri — referred to the right of the people to "bear arms in defence of themselves and the State." Another three States — Mississippi, Connecticut, and Alabama — used the even more individualistic phrasing that each citizen has the "right to bear arms in defence of himself and the State." Finally, two States — Tennessee and Maine — used the "common defence" language of Massachusetts. That of the nine state constitutional protections for the right to bear arms enacted immediately after 1789 at least seven unequivocally protected an individual citizen's right to self-defense is strong evidence that that is how the founding generation conceived of the right. And with one possible exception . . . 19th-century courts and commentators interpreted these state constitutional provisions to protect an individual right to use arms for self-defense.

The historical narrative that petitioners must endorse would thus treat the Federal Second Amendment as an odd outlier, protecting a right unknown in state constitutions or at English common law, based on little more than an over-reading of the prefatory clause.

C

Justice Stevens relies on the drafting history of the Second Amendment — the various proposals in the state conventions and the debates in Congress. It is dubious to rely on such history to interpret a text that was widely understood to codify a pre-existing right, rather than to fashion a new one. But even assuming that this legislative history is relevant, Justice Stevens flatly misreads the historical record.

It is true, as Justice Stevens says, that there was concern that the Federal Government would abolish the institution of the state militia. That concern found expression, however, *not* in the various Second Amendment precursors proposed in the State conventions, but in separate structural provisions that would have given the States concurrent and seemingly nonpre-emptible authority to organize, discipline, and arm the militia when the Federal Government failed to do so. The Second Amendment precursors, by contrast, referred to the individual English right already codified in two (and probably four) State constitutions. The Federalist-dominated first Congress chose to reject virtually all major structural revisions favored by the Antifederalists, including the proposed militia amendments. Rather, it adopted primarily the popular and uncontroversial (though, in the Federalists' view, unnecessary) individual-rights amendments. The Second Amendment right, protecting only individuals' liberty to keep and carry arms, did nothing to assuage Antifederalists' concerns about federal control of the militia. . . .

Justice Stevens' view . . . relies on the proposition, unsupported by any evidence, that different people of the founding period had vastly different conceptions of the right to keep and bear arms. That simply does not comport with our longstanding view that the Bill of Rights codified venerable, widely understood liberties.

D

We now address how the Second Amendment was interpreted from immediately after its ratification through the end of the 19th century. Before proceeding, however, we take issue with Justice Stevens' equating of these sources with post-enactment legislative history, a comparison that betrays a fundamental misunderstanding of a court's interpretive task. "Legislative history," of course, refers to the pre-enactment statements of those who drafted or voted for a law; it is considered persuasive by some, not because they reflect the general understanding of the disputed terms, but because the legislators who heard or read those statements presumably voted with that understanding. "Postenactment legislative history," a deprecatory contradiction in terms, refers to statements of those who drafted or voted for the law that are made after its enactment and hence could have had no effect on the congressional vote. It most certainly does not refer to the examination of a variety of legal and other sources to determine *the public understanding* of a legal text in the period after its enactment or ratification. That sort of inquiry is a critical tool of constitutional interpretation.

[V]irtually all interpreters of the Second Amendment in the century after its enactment interpreted the amendment as we do. . . . Antislavery advocates routinely invoked the right to bear arms for self-defense. . . . In his famous Senate speech about the 1856 "Bleeding Kansas" conflict, Charles Sumner proclaimed:

> "The rifle has ever been the companion of the pioneer and, under God, his tutelary protector against the red man and the beast of the forest. Never was this efficient weapon more needed in just self-defence, than now in Kansas, and at least one article in our National Constitution must be blotted out, before the complete right to it can in any way be impeached. And yet such is the madness of the hour, that, in defiance of the solemn guarantee, embodied in the Amendments to the Constitution, that "the right of the people to keep and bear arms shall not be infringed," the people of Kansas have been arraigned for keeping and bearing them, and the Senator from South Carolina has had the face to say openly, on this floor, that they should be disarmed — of course, that the fanatics of Slavery, his allies and constituents, may meet no impediment." The Crime Against Kansas, May 19-20, 1856, in American Speeches: Political Oratory from the Revolution to the Civil War 553, 606-607 (2006).

[T]he 19th-century cases that interpreted the Second Amendment universally support an individual right unconnected to militia service. . . . Many early 19th-century state cases indicated that the Second Amendment right to bear arms was an individual right unconnected to militia service, though subject to certain restrictions. . . . In the aftermath of the Civil War, there was an outpouring of discussion of the Second Amendment in Congress and in public discourse, as people debated whether and how to secure constitutional rights for newly free slaves. Since those discussions took place 75 years after the ratification of the Second Amendment, they do not provide as much insight into its original meaning as earlier sources. Yet those born and educated in the early 19th century faced a widespread effort to limit arms ownership by a large number of citizens; their understanding of the origins and continuing significance of the Amendment is instructive.

Blacks were routinely disarmed by Southern States after the Civil War. Those who opposed these injustices frequently stated that they infringed blacks' constitutional right to keep and bear arms. Needless to say, the claim was not that blacks were being prohibited from carrying arms in an organized state militia. . . . Congress enacted the Freedmen's Bureau Act on July 16, 1866. Section 14 stated: "[T]he right . . . to have full and equal benefit of all laws and proceedings concerning personal liberty, personal security, and the acquisition, enjoyment, and disposition of estate, real and personal, including the constitutional right to bear arms, shall be secured to and enjoyed by all the citizens . . . without respect to race or color, or previous condition of slavery. . . ." 14 Stat. 176-177. The understanding that the Second Amendment gave freed blacks the right to keep and bear arms was reflected in congressional discussion of the bill. . . . Similar discussion attended the passage of the Civil Rights Act of 1871 and the Fourteenth Amendment. . . . It was plainly the understanding in the post-Civil War Congress that the Second Amendment protected an individual right to use arms for self-defense. . . .

Every late-19th-century legal scholar that we have read interpreted the Second Amendment to secure an individual right unconnected with militia service. The most famous was the judge and professor Thomas Cooley, who wrote a massively popular 1868 Treatise on Constitutional Limitations. . . . Cooley understood the right not as connected to militia service, but as securing the militia by ensuring a populace familiar with arms. . . . All other post-Civil War 19th-century sources we have found concurred with Cooley. . . .

E

We now ask whether any of our precedents forecloses the conclusions we have reached about the meaning of the Second Amendment. . . . Justice Stevens places overwhelming reliance upon this Court's decision in *United States v. Miller,* 307 U.S. 174 (1939). . . . *Miller* . . . upheld against a Second Amendment challenge two men's federal convictions for transporting an unregistered short-barreled shotgun in interstate commerce, in violation of the National Firearms Act. It is entirely clear that the Court's basis for saying that the Second Amendment did not apply was *not* that the defendants were "bear[ing] arms" not "for . . . military purposes" but for "nonmilitary use." Rather, it was that the *type of weapon at issue* was not eligible for Second Amendment protection: "In the absence of any evidence tending to show that the possession or use of a [short-barreled shotgun] at this time has some reasonable relationship to the preservation or efficiency of a well regulated militia, we cannot say that the Second Amendment guarantees the right to keep and bear *such an instrument*" (emphasis added). "Certainly," the Court continued, "it is not within judicial notice that this weapon is any part of the ordinary military equipment or that its use could contribute to the common defense." . . . This holding is not only consistent with, but positively suggests, that the Second Amendment confers an individual right to keep and bear arms (though only arms that "have some reasonable relationship to the preservation or efficiency of a well regulated militia"). Had the Court believed that the Second Amendment protects only those serving in the militia, it would have been odd to examine the character of the weapon rather than simply note that the two crooks were not militiamen. . . . It is particularly wrongheaded to read *Miller* for more than what it said, because the case did not even purport to be a thorough examination of the Second Amendment. . . . The respondent made no appearance in the case, neither filing a brief nor appearing at oral argument; the Court heard from no one but the Government (reason enough, one would think, not to make that case the beginning and the end of this Court's consideration of the Second Amendment). . . .

We may as well consider at this point (for we will have to consider eventually) *what* types of weapons *Miller* permits. Read in isolation, *Miller*'s phrase "part of ordinary military equipment" could mean that only those weapons useful in warfare are protected. That would be a startling reading of the opinion, since it would mean that the National Firearms Act's restrictions on machineguns (not challenged in *Miller*) might be unconstitutional, machineguns being useful in warfare in 1939. We think that *Miller*'s "ordinary military equipment" language must be read in tandem with what comes after: "[O]rdinarily when called for [militia] service [able-bodied] men were expected to appear bearing arms supplied by themselves and of the kind in common use at the time." The traditional militia was formed from a pool of men bringing arms "in common use at the time" for lawful purposes like self-defense. In the colonial and revolutionary war era, [small-arms] weapons used by militiamen and weapons used in defense of person and home were one and the same. Indeed, that is precisely the way in which the Second Amendment's operative clause furthers the purpose announced in its preface. We therefore read *Miller* to say only that the Second Amendment does not protect those weapons not typically possessed by law-abiding citizens for lawful purposes, such as short-barreled shotguns. That accords with the historical understanding of the scope of the right. . . .

We conclude that nothing in our precedents forecloses our adoption of the original understanding of the Second Amendment. It should be unsurprising that such a significant matter has been for so long judicially unresolved. For most of our history, the Bill of Rights was not thought applicable to the States, and the Federal Government did not significantly regulate the possession of firearms by law-abiding citizens. Other provisions of the Bill of Rights have similarly remained unilluminated for lengthy periods. This Court first held a law to violate the First Amendment's guarantee of freedom of speech in 1931, almost 150 years after the Amendment was ratified, and it was not until after World War II that we held a law invalid under the Establishment Clause. Even a question as basic as the scope of proscribable libel was not addressed by this Court until 1964, nearly two centuries after the founding. See *New York Times Co. v. Sullivan,* 376 U.S. 254 (1964). It is demonstrably not true that, as Justice Stevens claims, "for most of our history, the invalidity of Second-Amendment-based objections to firearms regulations has been well settled and uncontroversial." For most of our history the question did not present itself.

III

Like most rights, the right secured by the Second Amendment is not unlimited. From Blackstone through the 19th-century cases, commentators and courts routinely explained that the right was not a right to keep and carry any weapon whatsoever in any manner whatsoever and for whatever purpose. For example, the majority of the 19th-century courts to consider the question held that prohibitions on carrying concealed weapons were lawful under the Second Amendment or state analogues. Although we do not undertake an exhaustive historical analysis today of the full scope of the Second Amendment, nothing in our opinion should be taken to cast doubt on longstanding prohibitions on the possession of firearms by felons and the mentally ill, or laws forbidding the carrying of firearms in sensitive places such as schools and government buildings, or laws imposing conditions and qualifications on the commercial sale of arms.

We also recognize another important limitation on the right to keep and carry arms. *Miller* said, as we have explained, that the sorts of weapons protected were those "in common use at the time." We think that limitation is fairly supported by the historical tradition of prohibiting the carrying of "dangerous and unusual weapons."

It may be objected that if weapons that are most useful in military service — M-16 rifles and the like — may be banned, then the Second Amendment right is completely detached from the prefatory clause. But as we have said, the conception of the militia at the time of the Second Amendment's ratification was the body of all citizens capable of military service, who would bring the sorts of lawful weapons that they possessed at home to militia duty. It may well be true today that a militia, to be as effective as militias in the 18th century, would require sophisticated arms that are highly unusual in society at large. Indeed, it may be true that no amount of small arms could be useful against modern-day bombers and tanks. But the fact that modern developments have limited the degree of fit between the prefatory clause and the protected right cannot change our interpretation of the right.

IV

We turn finally to the law at issue here. As we have said, the law totally bans handgun possession in the home. It also requires that any lawful firearm in the home be disassembled or bound by a trigger lock at all times, rendering it inoperable.

[T]he inherent right of self-defense has been central to the Second Amendment right. The handgun ban amounts to a prohibition of an entire class of "arms" that is overwhelmingly chosen by American society for that lawful purpose. The prohibition extends, moreover, to the home, where the need for defense of self, family, and property is most acute. Under any of the standards of scrutiny that we have applied to enumerated constitutional rights, banning from the home "the most preferred firearm in the nation to 'keep' and use for protection of one's home and family," would fail constitutional muster.

Few laws in the history of our Nation have come close to the severe restriction of the District's handgun ban. . . . It is no answer to say, as petitioners do, that it is permissible to ban the possession of handguns so long as the possession of other firearms (*i.e.,* long guns) is allowed. It is enough to note, as we have observed, that the American people have considered the handgun to be the quintessential self-defense weapon. There are many reasons that a citizen may prefer a handgun for home defense: It is easier to store in a location that is readily accessible in an emergency; it cannot easily be redirected or wrestled away by an attacker; it is easier to use for those without the upper-body strength to lift and aim a long gun; it can be pointed at a burglar with one hand while the other hand dials the police. Whatever the reason, handguns are the most popular weapon chosen by Americans for self-defense in the home, and a complete prohibition of their use is invalid.

We must also address the District's requirement (as applied to respondent's handgun) that firearms in the home be rendered and kept inoperable at all times. This makes it impossible for citizens to use them for the core lawful purpose of self-defense and is hence unconstitutional. The District argues that we should interpret this element of the statute to contain an exception for self-defense. But we think that is precluded by the unequivocal text, and by the presence of certain other enumerated exceptions: "Except for law enforcement personnel . . . , each registrant shall keep any firearm in his possession unloaded and disassembled or bound by a trigger lock or similar device unless such firearm is kept at his place of business, or while being used for lawful recreational purposes within the District of Columbia." D.C. Code §7-2507.02. The nonexistence of a self-defense exception is also suggested by the D.C. Court of Appeals' statement that the statute forbids residents to use firearms to stop intruders, see *McIntosh v. Washington,* 395 A.2d 744, 755-756 (1978).

Apart from his challenge to the handgun ban and the trigger-lock requirement respondent asked the District Court to enjoin petitioners from enforcing the separate licensing requirement "in such a manner as to forbid the carrying of a firearm within one's home or possessed land without a license." The Court of Appeals did not invalidate the licensing requirement, but held only that the District "may not prevent [a handgun] from being moved throughout one's house." It then ordered the District Court to enter summary judgment "consistent with [respondent's] prayer for relief." Before this Court petitioners have stated that "if the handgun ban is struck down and respondent registers a handgun, he could obtain a license, assuming he is not otherwise disqualified," by which they apparently mean if he is not a felon and is not insane. Respondent conceded at oral argument that he does not "have a problem with . . . licensing" and that the District's law is permissible so long as it is "not enforced in an arbitrary and capricious manner." We therefore assume that petitioners' issuance of a license will satisfy respondent's prayer for relief and do not address the licensing requirement.

Justice Breyer has devoted most of his separate dissent to the handgun ban. He says that, even assuming the Second Amendment is a personal guarantee of the right to bear arms, the District's prohibition is valid. He first tries to establish this by founding-era historical precedent, pointing to various restrictive laws in the colonial period. . . . [These laws did not burden the right of self-defense.] All of them punished the discharge (or loading) of guns with a small fine and forfeiture of the weapon (or in a few cases a very brief stay in the local jail), not with significant criminal penalties. They are akin to modern penalties for minor public-safety infractions like speeding or jaywalking. And although such public-safety laws may not contain exceptions for self-defense, it is inconceivable that the threat of a jaywalking ticket would deter someone from disregarding a "Do Not Walk" sign in order to flee an attacker, or that the Government would enforce those laws under such circumstances. Likewise, we do not think that a law imposing a 5-shilling fine and forfeiture of the gun would have prevented a person in the founding era from using a gun to protect himself or his family from violence, or that if he did so the law would be enforced against him. The District law, by contrast, far from imposing a minor fine, threatens citizens with a year in prison (five years for a second violation) for even obtaining a gun in the first place.

Justice Breyer . . . criticizes us for declining to establish a level of scrutiny for evaluating Second Amendment restrictions. He proposes, explicitly at least, none of the traditionally expressed levels (strict scrutiny, intermediate scrutiny, rational basis), but rather a judge-empowering "interest-balancing inquiry" that "asks whether the statute burdens a protected interest in a way or to an extent that is out of proportion to the statute's salutary effects upon other important governmental interests." After an exhaustive discussion of the arguments for and against gun control, Justice Breyer arrives at his interest-balanced answer: because handgun violence is a problem, because the law is limited to an urban area, and because there were somewhat similar restrictions in the founding period (a false proposition that we have already discussed), the interest-balancing inquiry results in the constitutionality of the handgun ban. QED.

We know of no other enumerated constitutional right whose core protection has been subjected to a freestanding "interest-balancing" approach. The very enumeration of the right takes out of the hands of government—even the Third Branch of Government—the power to decide on a case-by-case basis whether the right is *really worth* insisting upon. A constitutional guarantee subject to future judges' assessments of its usefulness is no constitutional guarantee at all. Constitutional rights are enshrined with the scope they were understood to have when the people adopted them, whether or not future legislatures or (yes) even future judges think that scope too broad. We would not apply an "interest-balancing" approach to the prohibition of a peaceful neo-Nazi march through Skokie. The First Amendment contains the freedom-of-speech guarantee that the people ratified, which included exceptions for obscenity, libel, and disclosure of state secrets, but not for the expression of extremely unpopular and wrong-headed views. The Second Amendment is no different. Like the First, it is the very *product* of an interest-balancing by the people—which Justice Breyer would now conduct for them anew. And whatever else it leaves to future evaluation, it surely elevates above all other interests the right of law-abiding, responsible citizens to use arms in defense of hearth and home.

Justice Breyer chides us for leaving so many applications of the right to keep and bear arms in doubt, and for not providing extensive historical justification for those regulations of the right that we describe as permissible. But since this case represents this Court's first in-depth examination of the Second Amendment, one should not expect it to clarify the entire field. . . . And there will be time enough to expound upon the historical justifications for the exceptions we have mentioned if and when those exceptions come before us.

In sum, we hold that the District's ban on handgun possession in the home violates the Second Amendment, as does its prohibition against rendering any lawful firearm in the home operable for the purpose of immediate self-defense. Assuming that Heller is not disqualified from the exercise of Second Amendment rights, the District must permit him to register his handgun and must issue him a license to carry it in the home.

* * *

We are aware of the problem of handgun violence in this country, and we take seriously the concerns raised by the many *amici* who believe that prohibition of handgun ownership is a solution. The Constitution leaves the District of Columbia a variety of tools for combating that problem, including some measures regulating handguns. But the enshrinement of constitutional rights necessarily takes certain policy choices off the table. These include the absolute prohibition of handguns held and used for self-defense in the home. Undoubtedly some think that the Second Amendment is outmoded in a society where our standing army is the pride of our Nation, where well-trained police forces provide personal security, and where gun violence is a serious problem. That is perhaps debatable, but what is not debatable is that it is not the role of this Court to pronounce the Second Amendment extinct.

. . .

Justice STEVENS, with whom Justice SOUTER, Justice GINSBURG, and Justice BREYER join, dissenting.

The question presented by this case is not whether the Second Amendment protects a "collective right" or an "individual right." Surely it protects a right that can be enforced by individuals. But a conclusion that the Second Amendment protects an individual right does not tell us anything about the scope of that right.

Guns are used to hunt, for self-defense, to commit crimes, for sporting activities, and to perform military duties. The Second Amendment plainly does not protect the right to use a gun to rob a bank; it is equally clear that it *does* encompass the right to use weapons for certain military purposes. Whether it also protects the right to possess and use guns for nonmilitary purposes like hunting and personal self-defense is the question presented by this case. The text of the Amendment, its history, and our decision in *United States v. Miller,* 307 U.S. 174 (1939), provide a clear answer to that question.

The Second Amendment was adopted to protect the right of the people of each of the several States to maintain a well-regulated militia. It was a response to concerns raised during the ratification of the Constitution that the power of Congress to disarm the state militias and create a national standing army posed an intolerable threat to the sovereignty of the several States. Neither the text of the Amendment nor the arguments advanced by its proponents evidenced the slightest interest in limiting any legislature's authority to regulate private civilian uses of firearms. Specifically, there is no indication that the Framers of the Amendment intended to enshrine the common-law right of self-defense in the Constitution.

In 1934, Congress enacted the National Firearms Act, the first major federal firearms law. Upholding a conviction under that Act, this Court held that, "[i]n the absence of any evidence tending to show that possession or use of a 'shotgun having a barrel of less than eighteen inches in length' at this time has some reasonable relationship to the preservation or efficiency of a well regulated militia, we cannot say that the Second Amendment guarantees the right to keep and bear such an instrument." *Miller.* The view of the Amendment we took in *Miller*—that it protects the right to keep and bear arms for certain military purposes, but that it does not curtail the Legislature's power to regulate the nonmilitary use and ownership of weapons—is both the most natural reading of the Amendment's text and the interpretation most faithful to the history of its adoption.

Since our decision in *Miller,* hundreds of judges have relied on the view of the Amendment we endorsed there; we ourselves affirmed it in 1980. See *Lewis v. United States,* 445 U.S. 55, 65-66, n.8 (1980). No new evidence has surfaced since 1980 supporting the view that the Amendment was intended to curtail the power of Congress to regulate civilian use or misuse of weapons. Indeed, a review of the drafting history of the Amendment demonstrates that its Framers *rejected* proposals that would have broadened its coverage to include such uses.

The opinion the Court announces today fails to identify any new evidence supporting the view that the Amendment was intended to limit the power of Congress to regulate civilian uses of weapons. . . .

Even if the textual and historical arguments on both sides of the issue were evenly balanced, respect for the well-settled views of all of our predecessors on this Court, and for the rule of law itself would prevent most jurists from endorsing such a dramatic upheaval in the law. . . .

I

[T]he preamble to the Second Amendment ["A well regulated Militia, being necessary to the security of a free State"] makes three important points. It identifies the preservation of the militia as the Amendment's purpose; it explains that the militia is necessary to the security of a free State; and it recognizes that the militia must be "well regulated." In all three respects it is comparable to provisions in several State Declarations of Rights that were adopted roughly contemporaneously with the Declaration of Independence. Those state provisions highlight the importance members of the founding generation attached to the maintenance of state militias; they also underscore the profound fear shared by many in that era of the dangers posed by standing armies. While the need for state militias has not been a matter of significant public interest for almost two centuries, that fact should not obscure the contemporary concerns that animated the Framers.

The parallels between the Second Amendment and these state declarations, and the Second Amendment's omission of any statement of purpose related to the right to use firearms for hunting or personal self-defense, is especially striking in light of the fact that the Declarations of Rights of Pennsylvania and Vermont *did* expressly protect such civilian uses at the time. Article XIII of Pennsylvania's 1776 Declaration of Rights announced that "the people have a right to bear arms for the defence *of themselves* and the state," (emphasis added); §43 of the Declaration assured that "the inhabitants of this state shall have the liberty to fowl and hunt in seasonable times on the lands they hold, and on all other lands therein not inclosed," *id.,* at 274. And Article XV of the 1777 Vermont Declaration of Rights guaranteed "[t]hat the people have a right to bear arms for the defence *of themselves* and the State" (emphasis added). The contrast between those two declarations and the Second Amendment reinforces the clear statement of purpose announced in the Amendment's preamble. It confirms that the Framers' single-minded focus in crafting the constitutional guarantee "to keep and bear arms" was on military uses of firearms, which they viewed in the context of service in state militias.

The preamble thus both sets forth the object of the Amendment and informs the meaning of the remainder of its text. Such text should not be treated as mere surplusage, for "[i]t cannot be presumed that any clause in the constitution is intended to be without effect." *Marbury v. Madison,* 1 Cranch 137, 174 (1803).

[W]hile the Court makes the novel suggestion that it need only find some "logical connection" between the preamble and the operative provision, it does acknowledge that a prefatory clause may resolve an ambiguity in the text. Without identifying any language in the text that even mentions civilian uses of firearms, the Court proceeds to "find" its preferred reading in what is at best an ambiguous text, and then concludes that its reading is not foreclosed by the preamble. Perhaps the Court's approach to the text is acceptable advocacy, but it is surely an unusual approach for judges to follow. . . .

The centerpiece of the Court's textual argument is its insistence that the words "the people" as used in the Second Amendment must have the same meaning, and protect the same class of individuals, as when they are used in the First and Fourth Amendments. According to the Court, in all three provisions— as well as the Constitution's preamble, section 2 of Article I, and the Tenth Amendment—the term unambiguously refers to all members of the political community, not an unspecified subset. But the Court *itself* reads the Second Amendment to protect a "subset" significantly narrower than the class of persons protected by the First and Fourth Amendments; when it finally drills down on the substantive meaning of the Second Amendment, the Court limits the protected class to "law-abiding, responsible citizens." But the class of persons protected by the First and Fourth Amendments is *not* so limited; for even felons (and presumably irresponsible citizens as well) may invoke the protections of those constitutional provisions. The Court offers no way to harmonize its conflicting pronouncements.

The Court also overlooks the significance of the way the Framers used the phrase "the people" in these constitutional provisions. In the First Amendment, no words define the class of individuals entitled to speak, to publish, or to worship; in that Amendment it is only the right peaceably to assemble, and to petition the Government for a redress of grievances, that is described as a right of "the people." These rights contemplate collective action. While the right peaceably to assemble protects the individual rights of those persons participating in the assembly, its concern is with action engaged in by members of a group, rather than any single individual. Likewise, although the act of petitioning the Government is a right that can be exercised by individuals, it is primarily collective in nature. For if they are to be effective, petitions must involve groups of individuals acting in concert.

Similarly, the words "the people" in the Second Amendment refer back to the object announced in the Amendment's preamble. They remind us that it is the collective action of individuals having a duty to serve in the militia that the text directly protects and, perhaps more importantly, that the ultimate purpose of the Amendment was to protect the States' share of the divided sovereignty created by the Constitution.

As used in the Fourth Amendment, "the people" describes the class of persons protected from unreasonable searches and seizures by Government officials. It is true that the Fourth Amendment describes a right that need not be exercised in any collective sense. But that observation does not settle the meaning of the phrase "the people" when used in the Second Amendment. For, as we have seen, the phrase means something quite different in the Petition and Assembly Clauses of the First Amendment. Although the abstract definition of the phrase "the people" could carry the same meaning in the Second Amendment as in the Fourth

Amendment, the preamble of the Second Amendment suggests that the uses of the phrase in the First and Second Amendments are the same in referring to a collective activity. By way of contrast, the Fourth Amendment describes a right *against* governmental interference rather than an affirmative right *to* engage in protected conduct, and so refers to a right to protect a purely individual interest. As used in the Second Amendment, the words "the people" do not enlarge the right to keep and bear arms to encompass use or ownership of weapons outside the context of service in a well-regulated militia.

[The words "To keep and bear Arms"] describe a unitary right: to possess arms if needed for military purposes and to use them in conjunction with military activities. [T]he Court does not read that phrase to create a right to possess arms for "lawful, private purposes." Instead, the Court limits the Amendment's protection to the right "to possess and carry weapons in case of confrontation." No party or *amicus* urged this interpretation; the Court appears to have fashioned it out of whole cloth. But . . . the Amendment's text *does* justify a different limitation: the "right to keep and bear arms" protects only a right to possess and use firearms in connection with service in a state-organized militia.

The term "bear arms" is a familiar idiom; when used unadorned by any additional words, its meaning is "to serve as a soldier, do military service, fight." It is derived from the Latin *arma ferre,* which, translated literally, means "to bear *[ferre]* war equipment *[arma]*." . . . Had the Framers wished to expand the meaning of the phrase "bear arms" to encompass civilian possession and use, they could have done so by the addition of phrases such as "for the defense of themselves," as was done in the Pennsylvania and Vermont Declarations of Rights. The *unmodified* use of "bear arms," by contrast, refers most naturally to a military purpose, as evidenced by its use in literally dozens of contemporary texts. The absence of any reference to civilian uses of weapons tailors the text of the Amendment to the purpose identified in its preamble. But when discussing these words, the Court simply ignores the preamble.

[T]he Amendment's use of the term "keep" in no way contradicts the military meaning conveyed by the phrase "bear arms" and the Amendment's preamble. To the contrary, a number of state militia laws in effect at the time of the Second Amendment's drafting used the term "keep" to describe the requirement that militia members store their arms at their homes, ready to be used for service when necessary. The Virginia military law, for example, ordered that "every one of the said officers, non-commissioned officers, and privates, shall constantly *keep* the aforesaid arms, accoutrements, and ammunition, ready to be produced whenever called for by his commanding officer." Act for Regulating and Disciplining the Militia, 1785 Va. Acts ch. 1, §3, p. 2 (emphasis added). "[K]eep and bear arms" thus perfectly describes the responsibilities of a framing-era militia member.

This reading is confirmed by the fact that the clause protects only one right, rather than two. It does not describe a right "to keep arms" and a separate right "to bear arms." Rather, the single right that it does describe is both a duty and a right to have arms available and ready for military service, and to use them for military purposes when necessary. Different language surely would have been used to protect nonmilitary use and possession of weapons from regulation if such an intent had played any role in the drafting of the Amendment.

* * *

When each word in the text is given full effect, the Amendment is most naturally read to secure to the people a right to use and possess arms in conjunction with service in a well-regulated militia. So far as appears, no more than that was contemplated by its drafters or is encompassed within its terms. Even if the meaning of the text were genuinely susceptible to more than one interpretation, the burden would remain on those advocating a departure from the purpose identified in the preamble and from settled law to come forward with persuasive new arguments or evidence. The textual analysis offered by respondent and embraced by the Court falls far short of sustaining that heavy burden. . . . Indeed, not a word in the constitutional text even arguably supports the Court's overwrought and novel description of the Second Amendment as "elevat[ing] above all other interests" the right of law-abiding, responsible citizens to use arms in defense of hearth and home.

II

The proper allocation of military power in the new Nation was an issue of central concern for the Framers. The compromises they ultimately reached, reflected in Article I's Militia Clauses and the Second Amendment, represent quintessential examples of the Framers' "splitting the atom of sovereignty."

Two themes relevant to our current interpretive task ran through the debates on the original Constitution. On the one hand, there was a widespread fear that a national standing Army posed an intolerable threat to individual liberty and to the sovereignty of the separate States. . . . On the other hand, the Framers recognized the dangers inherent in relying on inadequately trained militia members "as the primary means of providing for the common defense"; during the Revolutionary War, "[t]his force, though armed, was largely untrained, and its deficiencies were the subject of bitter complaint." In order to respond to those twin concerns, a compromise was reached: Congress would be authorized to raise and support a national Army and Navy, and also to organize, arm, discipline, and provide for the calling forth of "the Militia." U.S. Const., Art. I, §8, cls. 12-16. The President, at the same time, was empowered as the "Commander in Chief of the Army and Navy of the United States, and of the Militia of the several States, when called into the actual Service of the United States." Art. II, §2. But, with respect to the militia, a significant reservation was made to the States: Although Congress would have the power to call forth, organize, arm, and discipline the militia, as well as to govern "such Part of them as may be employed in the Service of the United States," the States respectively would retain the right to appoint the officers and to train the militia in accordance with the discipline prescribed by Congress. Art. I, §8, cl. 16.

But the original Constitution's retention of the militia and its creation of divided authority over that body did not prove sufficient to allay fears about the dangers posed by a standing army. For it was perceived by some that Article I contained a significant gap: While it empowered Congress to organize, arm, and discipline the militia, it did not prevent Congress from providing for the militia's *dis*armament. As George Mason argued during the debates in Virginia on the ratification of the original Constitution:

> "The militia may be here destroyed by that method which has been practiced in other parts of the world before; that is, by rendering them useless — by disarming them. Under various pretences, Congress may neglect to provide for arming and disciplining the militia; and the state governments cannot do it, for Congress has the exclusive right to arm them."

This sentiment was echoed at a number of state ratification conventions; indeed, it was one of the primary objections to the original Constitution voiced by its opponents. The Anti-Federalists were ultimately unsuccessful in persuading state ratification conventions to condition their approval of the Constitution upon the eventual inclusion of any particular amendment. But a number of States did propose to the first Federal Congress amendments reflecting a desire to ensure that the institution of the militia would remain protected under the new Government. The proposed amendments sent by the States of Virginia, North Carolina, and New York focused on the importance of preserving the state militias and reiterated the dangers posed by standing armies. New Hampshire sent a proposal that differed significantly from the others; while also invoking the dangers of a standing army, it suggested that the Constitution should more broadly protect the use and possession of weapons, without tying such a guarantee expressly to the maintenance of the militia. The States of Maryland, Pennsylvania, and Massachusetts sent no relevant proposed amendments to Congress, but in each of those States a minority of the delegates advocated related amendments. While the Maryland minority proposals were exclusively concerned with standing armies and conscientious objectors, the unsuccessful proposals in both Massachusetts and Pennsylvania would have protected a more broadly worded right, less clearly tied to service in a state militia. Faced with all of these options, it is telling that James Madison chose to craft the Second Amendment as he did. . . .

Madison, charged with the task of assembling the proposals for amendments sent by the ratifying States, was the principal draftsman of the Second Amendment. He had before him, or at the very least would have been aware of, all of these proposed formulations. In addition, Madison had been a member, some years earlier, of the committee tasked with drafting the Virginia Declaration of Rights. That committee considered a proposal by Thomas Jefferson that would have included within the Virginia Declaration the following language: "No freeman shall ever be debarred the use of arms [within his own lands or tenements]." But the committee rejected that language, adopting instead the provision drafted by George Mason[, which focused on defense of the state, civilian control of the military and avoidance of standing armies in time of peace].

With all of these sources upon which to draw, it is strikingly significant that Madison's first draft omitted any mention of nonmilitary use or possession of weapons. Rather, his original draft repeated the essence of the two proposed amendments sent by Virginia, combining the substance of the two provisions succinctly into one, which read: "The right of the people to keep and bear arms shall not be infringed; a well armed, and well regulated militia being the best security of a free country; but no person religiously scrupulous of bearing arms, shall be compelled to render military service in person."

Madison's decision to model the Second Amendment on the distinctly military Virginia proposal is therefore revealing, since it is clear that he considered and rejected formulations that would have unambiguously protected civilian uses of firearms. When Madison prepared his first draft, and when that draft was debated and modified, it is reasonable to assume that all participants in the drafting process were fully aware of the other formulations that would have protected civilian use and possession of weapons and that their choice to craft the Amendment as they did represented a rejection of those alternative formulations.

Madison's initial inclusion of an exemption for conscientious objectors sheds revelatory light on the purpose of the Amendment. It confirms an intent to describe a duty as well as a right, and it unequivocally identifies the military character of both. The objections voiced to the conscientious-objector clause only confirm the central meaning of the text. Although records of the debate in the Senate, which is where the conscientious-objector clause was removed, do not survive, the arguments raised in the House illuminate the perceived problems with the clause: Specifically, there was concern that Congress "can declare who are those religiously scrupulous, and prevent them from bearing arms." The ultimate removal of the clause, therefore, only serves to confirm the purpose of the Amendment — to protect against congressional disarmament, by whatever means, of the States' militias.

The Court also contends that because "Quakers opposed the use of arms not just for militia service, but for any violent purpose whatsoever," the inclusion of a conscientious-objector clause in the original draft of the Amendment does not support the conclusion that the phrase "bear arms" was military in meaning. But that claim cannot be squared with the record. [B]oth Virginia and North Carolina included the following language: "That any person religiously scrupulous of bearing arms ought to be exempted, upon payment of an equivalent *to employ another to bear arms in his stead*" (emphasis added). There is no plausible argument that the use of "bear arms" in those provisions was not unequivocally and exclusively military: The State simply does not compel its citizens to carry arms for the purpose of private "confrontation," or for self-defense.

The history of the adoption of the Amendment thus describes an overriding concern about the potential threat to state sovereignty that a federal standing army would pose, and a desire to protect the States' militias as the means by which to guard against that danger. But state militias could not effectively check the prospect of a federal standing army so long as Congress retained the power to disarm them, and so a guarantee against such disarmament was needed. As we explained in *Miller*: "With obvious purpose to assure the continuation and render possible the effectiveness of such forces the declaration and guarantee of the Second Amendment were made. It must be interpreted and applied with that end in view." The evidence plainly refutes the claim that the Amendment was motivated by the Framers' fears that Congress might act to regulate any civilian uses of weapons. And even if the historical record were genuinely ambiguous, the burden would remain on the parties advocating a change in the law to introduce facts or arguments "'newly ascertained'"; the Court is unable to identify any such facts or arguments.

III

Although it gives short shrift to the drafting history of the Second Amendment, the Court dwells at length on four other sources: the 17th-century English Bill of Rights; Blackstone's Commentaries on the Laws of England; postenactment commentary on the Second Amendment; and post-Civil War legislative history. All of these sources shed only indirect light on the question before us, and in any event offer little support for the Court's conclusion. . . .

The Court suggests that by the post-Civil War period, the Second Amendment was understood to secure a right to firearm use and ownership for purely private purposes like personal self-defense. While it is true that some of the legislative history on which the Court relies supports that contention, such sources are entitled to limited, if any, weight. All of the statements the Court cites were made long after the framing of the Amendment and cannot possibly supply any insight into the intent of the Framers; and all were made during pitched political debates, so that they are better characterized as advocacy than good-faith attempts at constitutional interpretation. . . .

IV

The brilliance of the debates that resulted in the Second Amendment faded into oblivion during the ensuing years, for the concerns about Article I's Militia Clauses that generated such pitched debate during the ratification process and led to the adoption of the Second Amendment were short lived.

In 1792, the year after the Amendment was ratified, Congress passed a statute that purported to establish "an Uniform Militia throughout the United States." 1 Stat. 271. The statute commanded every able-bodied white male citizen between the ages of 18 and 45 to be enrolled therein and to "provide himself with a good musket or firelock" and other specified weaponry. The statute is significant, for it confirmed the way those in the founding generation viewed firearm ownership: as a duty linked to military service. The statute they enacted, however, "was virtually ignored for more than a century," and was finally repealed in

1901. . . . In 1901 the President revitalized the militia by creating " 'the National Guard of the several States' "; meanwhile, the dominant understanding of the Second Amendment's inapplicability to private gun ownership continued well into the 20th century. The first two federal laws directly restricting civilian use and possession of firearms—the 1927 Act prohibiting mail delivery of "pistols, revolvers, and other firearms capable of being concealed on the person," and the 1934 Act prohibiting the possession of sawed-off shotguns and machine guns—were enacted over minor Second Amendment objections dismissed by the vast majority of the legislators who participated in the debates. Members of Congress clashed over the wisdom and efficacy of such laws as crime-control measures. But since the statutes did not infringe upon the military use or possession of weapons, for most legislators they did not even raise the specter of possible conflict with the Second Amendment.

Thus, for most of our history, the invalidity of Second-Amendment-based objections to firearms regulations has been well settled and uncontroversial. Indeed, the Second Amendment was not even mentioned in either full House of Congress during the legislative proceedings that led to the passage of the 1934 Act. Yet enforcement of that law produced the judicial decision that confirmed the status of the Amendment as limited in reach to military usage. After reviewing many of the same sources that are discussed at greater length by the Court today, the *Miller* Court unanimously concluded that the Second Amendment did not apply to the possession of a firearm that did not have "some reasonable relationship to the preservation or efficiency of a well regulated militia."

The key to that decision did not, as the Court belatedly suggests, turn on the difference between muskets and sawed-off shotguns; it turned, rather, on the basic difference between the military and nonmilitary use and possession of guns. Indeed, if the Second Amendment were not limited in its coverage to military uses of weapons, why should the Court in *Miller* have suggested that some weapons but not others were eligible for Second Amendment protection? If use for self-defense were the relevant standard, why did the Court not inquire into the suitability of a particular weapon for self-defense purposes? . . .

V

The Court concludes its opinion by declaring that it is not the proper role of this Court to change the meaning of rights "enshrine[d]" in the Constitution. But the right the Court announces was not "enshrined" in the Second Amendment by the Framers; it is the product of today's law-changing decision. The majority's exegesis has utterly failed to establish that as a matter of text or history, "the right of law-abiding, responsible citizens to use arms in defense of hearth and home" is "elevate[d] above all other interests" by the Second Amendment.

Until today, it has been understood that legislatures may regulate the civilian use and misuse of firearms so long as they do not interfere with the preservation of a well-regulated militia. The Court's announcement of a new constitutional right to own and use firearms for private purposes upsets that settled understanding, but leaves for future cases the formidable task of defining the scope of permissible regulations. Today judicial craftsmen have confidently asserted that a policy choice that denies a "law-abiding, responsible citize[n]" the right to keep and use weapons in the home for self-defense is "off the table." Given the presumption that most citizens are law abiding, and the reality that the need to defend oneself may suddenly arise in a host of locations outside the home, I fear that the District's policy choice may well be just the first of an unknown number of dominoes to be knocked off the table.

I do not know whether today's decision will increase the labor of federal judges to the "breaking point" envisioned by Justice Cardozo, but it will surely give rise to a far more active judicial role in making vitally important national policy decisions than was envisioned at any time in the 18th, 19th, or 20th centuries.

The Court properly disclaims any interest in evaluating the wisdom of the specific policy choice challenged in this case, but it fails to pay heed to a far more important policy choice—the choice made by the Framers themselves. The Court would have us believe that over 200 years ago, the Framers made a choice to limit the tools available to elected officials wishing to regulate civilian uses of weapons, and to authorize this Court to use the common-law process of case-by-case judicial lawmaking to define the contours of acceptable gun control policy. Absent compelling evidence that is nowhere to be found in the Court's opinion, I could not possibly conclude that the Framers made such a choice.

For these reasons, I respectfully dissent.

Justice BREYER, with whom Justice STEVENS, Justice SOUTER, and Justice GINSBURG join, dissenting.

I agree with Justice Stevens [that the Second Amendment protects militia-related, not self-defense-related, interests], and I join his opinion. [But] the District's law is consistent with the Second Amendment even if that Amendment is interpreted as protecting a wholly separate interest in individual self-defense. That is so because the District's regulation, which focuses upon the presence of handguns in high-crime urban areas, represents a permissible legislative response to a serious, indeed life-threatening, problem. . . .

II

[Even if] the Second Amendment embodies a general concern about self-defense, [it does not] contain[] a specific untouchable right to keep guns in the house to shoot burglars. . . .

To the contrary, colonial history itself offers important examples of the kinds of gun regulation that citizens would then have thought compatible with the "right to keep and bear arms." . . . [T]hose examples include substantial regulation of firearms in urban areas, including regulations that imposed obstacles to the use of firearms for the protection of the home.

Boston, Philadelphia, and New York City, the three largest cities in America during that period, all restricted the firing of guns within city limits to at least some degree. . . . Furthermore, several towns and cities (including Philadelphia, New York, and Boston) regulated, for fire-safety reasons, the storage of gunpowder, a necessary component of an operational firearm. . . . Even assuming, as the majority does, that this law included an implicit self-defense exception, it would nevertheless have prevented a homeowner from keeping in his home a gun that he could immediately pick up and use against an intruder. Rather, the homeowner would have had to get the gunpowder and load it into the gun, an operation that would have taken a fair amount of time to perform.

Moreover, the law would, as a practical matter, have prohibited the carrying of loaded firearms anywhere in the city, unless the carrier had no plans to enter any building or was willing to unload or discard his weapons before going inside. . . .

This historical evidence demonstrates that a self-defense assumption is the *beginning,* rather than the *end,* of any constitutional inquiry. That the District law impacts self-defense merely raises *questions* about the law's constitutionality. . . .

III

[W]hat kind of constitutional standard should the court use? How high a protective hurdle does the Amendment erect? . . . The majority is wrong when it says that the District's law is unconstitutional "[u]nder any of the standards of scrutiny that we have applied to enumerated constitutional rights." . . . It certainly would not be unconstitutional under, for example, a "rational basis" standard. . . . The law at issue here, which in part seeks to prevent gun-related accidents, at least bears a "rational relationship" to that "legitimate" life-saving objective. . . .

Respondent proposes that the Court adopt a "strict scrutiny" test, which would require reviewing with care each gun law to determine whether it is "narrowly tailored to achieve a compelling governmental interest." But the majority implicitly, and appropriately, rejects that suggestion by broadly approving a set of laws—prohibitions on concealed weapons, forfeiture by criminals of the Second Amendment right, prohibitions on firearms in certain locales, and governmental regulation of commercial firearm sales—whose constitutionality under a strict scrutiny standard would be far from clear.

Indeed, adoption of a true strict-scrutiny standard for evaluating gun regulations would be impossible. That is because almost every gun-control regulation will seek to advance (as the one here does) a "primary concern of every government—a concern for the safety and indeed the lives of its citizens." [In other cases] [t]he Court has deemed that interest, as well as "the Government's general interest in preventing crime," to be "compelling," and the Court has in a wide variety of constitutional contexts found such public-safety concerns sufficiently forceful to justify restrictions on individual liberties, see *e.g., Brandenburg v.*

Ohio, 395 U.S. 444 (1969) (*per curiam*) (First Amendment free speech rights); *Sherbert v. Verner,* 374 U.S. 398 (1963) (First Amendment religious rights); *Brigham City v. Stuart,* 547 U.S. 398 (2006) (Fourth Amendment protection of the home); *New York v. Quarles,* 467 U.S. 649 (1984) (Fifth Amendment rights under *Miranda v. Arizona,* 384 U.S. 436 (1966)); [*United States v.*] *Salerno,* 481 U.S. 739 (1987) (Eighth Amendment bail rights). Thus, any attempt *in theory* to apply strict scrutiny to gun regulations will *in practice* turn into an interest-balancing inquiry, with the interests protected by the Second Amendment on one side and the governmental public-safety concerns on the other, the only question being whether the regulation at issue impermissibly burdens the former in the course of advancing the latter.

I would simply adopt such an interest-balancing inquiry explicitly. [R]eview of gun-control regulation is not a context in which a court should effectively presume either constitutionality (as in rational-basis review) or unconstitutionality (as in strict scrutiny). Rather, "where a law significantly implicates competing constitutionally protected interests in complex ways," the Court generally asks whether the statute burdens a protected interest in a way or to an extent that is out of proportion to the statute's salutary effects upon other important governmental interests. Any answer would take account both of the statute's effects upon the competing interests and the existence of any clearly superior less restrictive alternative. Contrary to the majority's unsupported suggestion that this sort of "proportionality" approach is unprecedented, the Court has applied it in various constitutional contexts, including election-law cases, speech cases, and due process cases.

In applying this kind of standard the Court normally defers to a legislature's empirical judgment in matters where a legislature is likely to have greater expertise and greater institutional factfinding capacity. See *Turner Broadcasting System, Inc. v. FCC,* 520 U.S. 180 (1997). Nonetheless, a court, not a legislature, must make the ultimate constitutional conclusion, exercising its "independent judicial judgment" in light of the whole record to determine whether a law exceeds constitutional boundaries.

[E]xperience as much as logic has led the Court to decide that in one area of constitutional law or another the interests are likely to prove stronger on one side of a typical constitutional case than on the other. Here, we have little prior experience. Courts that *do* have experience in these matters have uniformly taken an approach that treats empirically-based legislative judgment with a degree of deference. See Winkler, Scrutinizing the Second Amendment, 105 Mich. L. Rev. 683 (2007) (describing hundreds of gun-law decisions issued in the last half-century by Supreme Courts in 42 States, which courts with "surprisingly little variation," have adopted a standard more deferential than strict scrutiny). . . .

IV

The present suit involves challenges to three separate District firearm restrictions. . . . Because the District assures us that respondent could obtain . . . a license [for a handgun] so long as he meets the statutory eligibility criteria, and because respondent concedes that those criteria are facially constitutional, I, like the majority, see no need to address the constitutionality of the licensing requirement.

[The District also] requires that the lawful owner of a firearm keep his weapon "unloaded and disassembled or bound by a trigger lock or similar device" unless it is kept at his place of business or being used for lawful recreational purposes. The only dispute regarding this provision appears to be whether the Constitution requires an exception that would allow someone to render a firearm operational when necessary for self-defense (*i.e.,* that the firearm may be operated under circumstances where the common law would normally permit a self-defense justification in defense against a criminal charge). The District concedes that such an exception exists. This Court has final authority (albeit not often used) to definitively interpret District law, which is, after all, simply a species of federal law. And because I see nothing in the District law that would *preclude* the existence of a background common-law self-defense exception, I would avoid the constitutional question by interpreting the statute to include it.

I am puzzled by the majority's unwillingness to adopt a similar approach. It readily reads unspoken self-defense exceptions into every colonial law, but it refuses to accept the District's concession that this law has one. The one District case it cites to support that refusal [does not] say that the statute precludes a self-defense exception of the sort that I have just described. And even if it did, we are not bound by a lower court's interpretation of federal law.

The third District restriction prohibits (in most cases) the registration of a handgun within the District. Because registration is a prerequisite to firearm possession, the effect of this provision is generally to prevent people in the District from possessing handguns. . . . No one doubts the constitutional importance of the statute's basic objective, saving lives. But there is considerable debate about whether the District's statute helps to achieve that objective. . . .

1

First, consider the facts as the legislature saw them when it adopted the District statute. [T]he local council committee that recommended its adoption . . . concluded, on the basis of "extensive public hearings" and "lengthy research," that "[t]he easy availability of firearms in the United States has been a major factor contributing to the drastic increase in gun-related violence and crime over the past 40 years." . . .

The committee informed the Council that guns were "responsible for 69 deaths in this country each day," for a total of "[a]pproximately 25,000 gun-deaths . . . each year," along with an additional 200,000 gun-related injuries. Three thousand of these deaths, the report stated, were accidental. A quarter of the victims in those accidental deaths were children under the age of 14. And according to the committee, [f]or every intruder stopped by a homeowner with a firearm, there are 4 gun-related accidents within the home.

In respect to local crime, the committee observed that there were 285 murders in the District during 1974—a record number. The committee also stated that, "[c]ontrary to popular opinion on the subject, firearms are more frequently involved in deaths and violence among relatives and friends than in premeditated criminal activities." Citing an article from the American Journal of Psychiatry, the committee reported that "[m]ost murders are committed by previously law-abiding citizens, in situations where spontaneous violence is generated by anger, passion or intoxication, and where the killer and victim are acquainted." Twenty-five percent of these murders, "the committee informed the Council," occur within families.

The committee report furthermore presented statistics strongly correlating handguns with crime. Of the 285 murders in the District in 1974, 155 were committed with handguns. This did not appear to be an aberration, as the report revealed that "handguns [had been] used in roughly 54% of all murders" (and 87% of murders of law enforcement officers) nationwide over the preceding several years. Nor were handguns only linked to murders, as statistics showed that they were used in roughly 60% of robberies and 26% of assaults. "A crime committed with a pistol," the committee reported, "is 7 times more likely to be lethal than a crime committed with any other weapon." The committee furthermore presented statistics regarding the availability of handguns in the United States, and noted that they had "become easy for juveniles to obtain," even despite then-current District laws prohibiting juveniles from possessing them.

[I]n the absence of adequate federal gun legislation, the committee concluded, it "becomes necessary for local governments to act to protect their citizens, and certainly the District of Columbia as the only totally urban state-like jurisdiction should be strong in its approach." It recommended that the Council adopt a restriction on handgun registration to reflect "a legislative decision that, at this point in time and due to the gun-control tragedies and horrors enumerated previously" in the committee report, "pistols . . . are no longer justified in this jurisdiction."

The District's special focus on handguns thus reflects the fact that the committee report found them to have a particularly strong link to undesirable activities in the District's exclusively urban environment. The District did not seek to prohibit possession of other sorts of weapons deemed more suitable for an "urban area." Indeed, an original draft of the bill, and the original committee recommendations, had sought to prohibit registration of shotguns as well as handguns, but the Council as a whole decided to narrow the prohibition.

2

Next, consider the facts as a court must consider them looking at the matter as of today. Petitioners, and their *amici*, have presented us with more recent statistics that tell much the same story that the committee report told 30 years ago. At the least, they present nothing that would permit us to second-guess the Council in respect to the numbers of gun crimes, injuries, and deaths, or the role of handguns.

From 1993 to 1997, there were 180,533 firearm-related deaths in the United States, an average of over 36,000 per year. Fifty-one percent were suicides, 44% were homicides, 1% were legal interventions, 3% were unintentional accidents, and 1% were of undetermined causes. Over that same period there were an additional 411,800 nonfatal firearm-related injuries treated in U.S. hospitals, an average of over 82,000 per year. Of these, 62% resulted from assaults, 17% were unintentional, 6% were suicide attempts, 1% were legal interventions, and 13% were of unknown causes.

The statistics are particularly striking in respect to children and adolescents. In over one in every eight firearm-related deaths in 1997, the victim was someone under the age of 20. Firearm-related deaths account for 22.5% of all injury deaths between the ages of 1 and 19. More male teenagers die from firearms than from all natural causes combined. Persons under 25 accounted for 47% of hospital-treated firearm injuries between June 1, 1992 and May 31, 1993.

Handguns are involved in a majority of firearm deaths and injuries in the United States. From 1993 to 1997, 81% of firearm-homicide victims were killed by handgun. In the same period, for the 41% of firearm injuries for which the weapon type is known, 82% of them were from handguns. And among children under the age of 20, handguns account for approximately 70% of all unintentional firearm-related injuries and deaths. In particular, 70% of all firearm-related teenage suicides in 1996 involved a handgun.

Handguns also appear to be a very popular weapon among criminals. In a 1997 survey of inmates who were armed during the crime for which they were incarcerated, 83.2% of state inmates and 86.7% of federal inmates said that they were armed with a handgun. And handguns are not only popular tools for crime, but popular objects of it as well: the FBI received on average over 274,000 reports of stolen guns for each year between 1985 and 1994, and almost 60% of stolen guns are handguns. Department of Justice studies have concluded that stolen handguns in particular are an important source of weapons for both adult and juvenile offenders.

Statistics further suggest that urban areas, such as the District, have different experiences with gun-related death, injury, and crime, than do less densely populated rural areas. A disproportionate amount of violent and property crimes occur in urban areas, and urban criminals are more likely than other offenders to use a firearm during the commission of a violent crime. Homicide appears to be a much greater issue in urban areas; from 1985 to 1993, for example, "half of all homicides occurred in 63 cities with 16% of the nation's population." One study concluded that although the overall rate of gun death between 1989 and 1999 was roughly the same in urban than rural areas, the urban homicide rate was three times as high; even after adjusting for other variables, it was still twice as high. And a study of firearm injuries to children and adolescents in Pennsylvania between 1987 and 2000 showed an injury rate in urban counties 10 times higher than in nonurban counties.

Finally, the linkage of handguns to firearms deaths and injuries appears to be much stronger in urban than in rural areas. "[S]tudies to date generally support the hypothesis that the greater number of rural gun deaths are from rifles or shotguns, whereas the greater number of urban gun deaths are from handguns." And the Pennsylvania study reached a similar conclusion with respect to firearm injuries — they are much more likely to be caused by handguns in urban areas than in rural areas.

3

Respondent and his many *amici* for the most part do not disagree about the *figures* set forth in the preceding subsection, but they do disagree strongly with the District's *predictive judgment* that a ban on handguns will help solve the crime and accident problems that those figures disclose. In particular, they disagree with the District Council's assessment that "freezing the pistol . . . population within the District," will reduce crime, accidents, and deaths related to guns. And they provide facts and figures designed to show that it has not done so in the past, and hence will not do so in the future.

First, they point out that, since the ban took effect, violent crime in the District has increased, not decreased. Indeed, a comparison with 49 other major cities reveals that the District's homicide rate is actually substantially *higher* relative to these other cities than it was before the handgun restriction went into effect. Respondent's *amici* report similar results in comparing the District's homicide rates during that period to that of the neighboring States of Maryland and Virginia (neither of which restricts handguns to the same degree), and to the homicide rate of the Nation as a whole.

Second, respondent's *amici* point to a statistical analysis that regresses murder rates against the presence or absence of strict gun laws in 20 European nations. That analysis concludes that strict gun laws are correlated with *more* murders, not fewer. They also cite domestic studies, based on data from various cities, States, and the Nation as a whole, suggesting that a reduction in the number of guns does not lead to a reduction in the amount of violent crime. They further argue that handgun bans do not reduce suicide rates, or rates of accidents, even those involving children.

Third, they point to evidence indicating that firearm ownership does have a beneficial self-defense effect. Based on a 1993 survey, the authors of one study estimated that there were 2.2-to-2.5 million defensive uses of guns (mostly brandishing, about a quarter involving the actual firing of a gun) annually. Another study estimated that for a period of 12 months ending in 1994, there were 503,481 incidents in which a burglar found himself confronted by an armed homeowner, and that in 497,646 (98.8%) of them, the intruder was successfully scared away. A third study suggests that gun-armed victims are substantially less likely than non-gun-armed victims to be injured in resisting robbery or assault. And additional evidence suggests that criminals are likely to be deterred from burglary and other crimes if they know the victim is likely to have a gun.

Fourth, respondent's *amici* argue that laws criminalizing gun possession are self-defeating, as evidence suggests that they will have the effect only of restricting law-abiding citizens, but not criminals, from acquiring guns. That effect, they argue, will be especially pronounced in the District, whose proximity to Virginia and Maryland will provide criminals with a steady supply of guns.

In the view of respondent's *amici,* this evidence shows that other remedies—such as *less* restriction on gun ownership, or liberal authorization of law-abiding citizens to carry concealed weapons—better fit the problem. They further suggest that at a minimum the District fails to show that its *remedy,* the gun ban, bears a reasonable relation to the crime and accident *problems* that the District seeks to solve.

These empirically based arguments may have proved strong enough to convince many legislatures, as a matter of legislative policy, not to adopt total handgun bans. But the question here is whether they are strong enough to destroy judicial confidence in the reasonableness of a legislature that rejects them. And that they are not. For one thing, they can lead us more deeply into the uncertainties that surround any effort to reduce crime, but they cannot prove either that handgun possession diminishes crime or that handgun bans are ineffective. The statistics do show a soaring District crime rate. And the District's crime rate went up after the District adopted its handgun ban. But, as students of elementary logic know, *after it* does not mean *because of it.* What would the District's crime rate have looked like without the ban? Higher? Lower? The same? Experts differ; and we, as judges, cannot say.

What about the fact that foreign nations with strict gun laws have higher crime rates? Which is the cause and which the effect? The proposition that strict gun laws *cause* crime is harder to accept than the proposition that strict gun laws in part grow out of the fact that a nation already has a higher crime rate. And we are then left with the same question as before: What would have happened to crime without the gun laws—a question that respondent and his *amici* do not convincingly answer.

Further, suppose that respondent's *amici* are right when they say that householders' possession of loaded handguns help to frighten away intruders. On that assumption, one must still ask whether that benefit is worth the potential death-related cost. And that is a question without a directly provable answer.

Finally, consider the claim of respondent's *amici* that handgun bans *cannot* work; there are simply too many illegal guns already in existence for a ban on legal guns to make a difference. In a word, they claim that, given the urban sea of preexisting legal guns, criminals can readily find arms regardless. Nonetheless, a legislature might respond, we want to make an effort to try to dry up that urban sea, drop by drop. And none of the studies can show that effort is not worthwhile.

In a word, the studies to which respondent's *amici* point raise policy-related questions. They succeed in proving that the District's predictive judgments are controversial. But they do not by themselves show that those judgments are incorrect; nor do they demonstrate a consensus, academic or otherwise, supporting that conclusion.

Thus, it is not surprising that the District and its *amici* support the District's handgun restriction with studies of their own. One in particular suggests that, statistically speaking, the District's law has indeed had positive life-saving effects. Others suggest that firearm restrictions as a general matter reduce homicides, suicides, and accidents in the home. Still others suggest that the defensive uses of handguns are not as great in number as respondent's *amici* claim.

Respondent and his *amici* reply to these responses; and in doing so, they seek to discredit as methodologically flawed the studies and evidence relied upon by the District. And, of course, the District's *amici* produce counter-rejoinders, referring to articles that defend their studies.

The upshot is a set of studies and counterstudies that, at most, could leave a judge uncertain about the proper policy conclusion. But from respondent's perspective any such uncertainty is not good enough. That is because legislators, not judges, have primary responsibility for drawing policy conclusions from empirical fact. And, given that constitutional allocation of decisionmaking responsibility, the empirical evidence presented here is sufficient to allow a judge to reach a firm *legal* conclusion.

In particular this Court, in First Amendment cases applying intermediate scrutiny, has said that our "sole obligation" in reviewing a legislature's "predictive judgments" is "to assure that, in formulating its judgments," the legislature "has drawn reasonable inferences based on substantial evidence." *Turner*. And judges, looking at the evidence before us, should agree that the District legislature's predictive judgments satisfy that legal standard. That is to say, the District's judgment, while open to question, is nevertheless supported by "substantial evidence."

There is no cause here to depart from the standard set forth in *Turner*, for the District's decision represents the kind of empirically based judgment that legislatures, not courts, are best suited to make. In fact, deference to legislative judgment seems particularly appropriate here, where the judgment has been made by a local legislature, with particular knowledge of local problems and insight into appropriate local solutions. Different localities may seek to solve similar problems in different ways, and a "city must be allowed a reasonable opportunity to experiment with solutions to admittedly serious problems." The Framers recognized that the most effective democracy occurs at local levels of government, where people with firsthand knowledge of local problems have more ready access to public officials responsible for dealing with them. *Garcia v. San Antonio Metropolitan Transit Authority,* 469 U.S. 528 (1985) (Powell, J., dissenting) (citing The Federalist No. 17 (A. Hamilton). We owe that democratic process some substantial weight in the constitutional calculus. . . .

B

I next assess the extent to which the District's law burdens the interests that the Second Amendment seeks to protect. Respondent and his *amici,* as well as the majority, suggest that those interests include: (1) the preservation of a "well regulated Militia"; (2) safeguarding the use of firearms for sporting purposes, *e.g.,* hunting and marksmanship; and (3) assuring the use of firearms for self-defense. . . .

1

The District's statute burdens the Amendment's first and primary objective [the preservation of a "well regulated Militia"] hardly at all. . . . [T]he present case has nothing to do with *actual* military service. I am aware of no indication that the District either now or in the recent past has called up its citizenry to serve in a militia, that it has any inkling of doing so anytime in the foreseeable future, or that this law must be construed to prevent the use of handguns during legitimate militia activities. Moreover, even if the District were to call up its militia, respondent would not be among the citizens whose service would be requested. The District does not consider him, at 66 years of age, to be a member of its militia. . . . [T]he District's law does not seriously affect military training interests. The law permits residents to engage in activities that will increase their familiarity with firearms. They may register (and thus possess in their homes) weapons other than handguns, such as rifles and shotguns. . . . And while the District law prevents citizens from training with handguns *within the District,* the District consists of only 61.4 square miles of urban area. The adjacent States do permit the use of handguns for target practice, and those States are only a brief subway ride away. . . .

The majority briefly suggests that the "right to keep and bear Arms" might encompass an interest in hunting. But in enacting the present provisions, the District sought "to take nothing away from sportsmen." [T]he District's law does not prohibit possession of rifles or shotguns. . . .

The District's law does prevent a resident from keeping a loaded handgun in his home. And it consequently makes it more difficult for the householder to use the handgun for self-defense in the home against intruders, such as burglars. As the Court of Appeals noted, statistics suggest that handguns are the most popular weapon for self defense. And there are some legitimate reasons why that would be the case: *Amici* suggest (with some empirical support) that handguns are easier to hold and control (particularly for persons with physical infirmities), easier to carry, easier to maneuver in enclosed spaces, and that a person using one will still have a hand free to dial 911. . . .

In weighing needs and burdens, we must take account of the possibility that there are reasonable, but less restrictive alternatives. Are there *other* potential measures that might similarly promote the same goals while imposing lesser restrictions? Here I see none.

The reason there is no clearly superior, less restrictive alternative to the District's handgun ban is that the ban's very objective is to reduce significantly the number of handguns in the District, say, for example, by allowing a law enforcement officer immediately to assume that *any* handgun he sees is an *illegal* handgun. And there is no plausible way to achieve that objective other than to ban the guns.

It does not help respondent's case to describe the District's objective more generally as an "effort to diminish the dangers associated with guns." That is because the very attributes that make handguns particularly useful for self-defense are also what make them particularly dangerous. That they are easy to hold and control means that they are easier for children to use. That they are maneuverable and permit a free hand likely contributes to the fact that they are by far the firearm of choice for crimes such as rape and robbery. That they are small and light makes them easy to steal, and concealable.

This symmetry suggests that any measure less restrictive in respect to the use of handguns for self-defense will, to that same extent, prove less effective in preventing the use of handguns for illicit purposes. If a resident has a handgun in the home that he can use for self-defense, then he has a handgun in the home that he can use to commit suicide or engage in acts of domestic violence. If it is indeed the case, as the District believes, that the number of guns contributes to the number of gun-related crimes, accidents, and deaths, then, although there may be less restrictive, *less effective* substitutes for an outright ban, there is no less restrictive *equivalent* of an outright ban.

Licensing restrictions would not similarly reduce the handgun population, and the District may reasonably fear that even if guns are initially restricted to law-abiding citizens, they might be stolen and thereby placed in the hands of criminals. Permitting certain types of handguns, but not others, would affect the commercial market for handguns, but not their availability. And requiring safety devices such as trigger locks, or imposing safe-storage requirements would interfere with any self-defense interest while simultaneously leaving operable weapons in the hands of owners (or others capable of acquiring the weapon and disabling the safety device) who might use them for domestic violence or other crimes.

The absence of equally effective alternatives to a complete prohibition finds support in the empirical fact that other States and urban centers prohibit particular types of weapons. Chicago has a law very similar to the District's, and many of its suburbs also ban handgun possession under most circumstances. Toledo bans certain types of handguns. And San Francisco in 2005 enacted by popular referendum a ban on most handgun possession by city residents; it has been precluded from enforcing that prohibition, however, by state-court decisions deeming it pre-empted by state law. (Indeed, the fact that as many as 41 States may pre-empt local gun regulation suggests that the absence of more regulation like the District's may perhaps have more to do with state law than with a lack of locally perceived need for them.

In addition, at least six States and Puerto Rico impose general bans on certain types of weapons, in particular assault weapons or semiautomatic weapons. And at least 14 municipalities do the same. These bans, too, suggest that there may be no substitute to an outright prohibition in cases where a governmental body has deemed a particular type of weapon especially dangerous.

D

The upshot is that the District's objectives are compelling; its predictive judgments as to its law's tendency to achieve those objectives are adequately supported; the law does impose a burden upon any self-defense interest that the Amendment seeks to secure; and there is no clear less restrictive alternative. I turn now to the final portion of the "permissible regulation" question: Does the District's law *disproportionately* burden Amendment-protected interests? Several considerations, taken together, convince me that it does not.

First, the District law is tailored to the life-threatening problems it attempts to address. The law concerns one class of weapons, handguns, leaving residents free to possess shotguns and rifles, along with ammunition. The area that falls within its scope is totally urban. That urban area suffers from a serious handgun-fatality problem. The District's law directly aims at that compelling problem. And there is no less restrictive way to achieve the problem-related benefits that it seeks.

Second, the self-defense interest in maintaining loaded handguns in the home to shoot intruders is not the *primary* interest, but at most a subsidiary interest, that the Second Amendment seeks to serve. The Second Amendment's language, while speaking of a "Militia," says nothing of "self-defense." As Justice Stevens points out, the Second Amendment's drafting history shows that the language reflects the Framers' primary, if not exclusive, objective. And the majority itself says that "the threat that the new Federal Government would destroy the citizens' militia by taking away their arms was *the* reason that right . . . was codified in a written Constitution." (emphasis added). The *way* in which the Amendment's operative clause seeks to promote that interest—by protecting a right "to keep and bear Arms"—may *in fact* help further an interest in self-defense. But a factual connection falls far short of a primary objective. The Amendment itself tells us that militia preservation was first and foremost in the Framers' minds.

Further, any self-defense interest at the time of the Framing could not have focused exclusively upon urban-crime related dangers. Two hundred years ago, most Americans, many living on the frontier, would likely have thought of self-defense primarily in terms of outbreaks of fighting with Indian tribes, rebellions such as Shays' Rebellion, marauders, and crime-related dangers to travelers on the roads, on footpaths, or along waterways. Insofar as the Framers focused at all on the tiny fraction of the population living in large cities, they would have been aware that these city dwellers were subject to firearm restrictions that their rural counterparts were not. They are unlikely then to have thought of a right to keep loaded handguns in homes to confront intruders in urban settings as *central*. And the subsequent development of modern urban police departments, by diminishing the need to keep loaded guns nearby in case of intruders, would have moved any such right even further away from the heart of the amendment's more basic protective ends. See, *e.g.*, Sklansky, The Private Police, 46 UCLA L. Rev. 1165 (1999) (professional urban police departments did not develop until roughly the mid-19th century).

Nor, for that matter, am I aware of any evidence that *handguns* in particular were central to the Framers' conception of the Second Amendment. The lists of militia-related weapons in the late 18th-century state statutes appear primarily to refer to other sorts of weapons, muskets in particular. Respondent points out in his brief that the Federal Government and two States at the time of the founding had enacted statutes that listed handguns as "acceptable" militia weapons. But these statutes apparently found them "acceptable" only for certain special militiamen (generally, certain soldiers on horseback), while requiring muskets or rifles for the general infantry.

Third, irrespective of what the Framers *could have thought,* we know what they *did think.* Samuel Adams, who lived in Boston, advocated a constitutional amendment that would have precluded the Constitution from ever being "construed" to "prevent the people of the United States, who are peaceable citizens, from keeping their own arms." Samuel Adams doubtless knew that the Massachusetts Constitution contained somewhat similar protection. And he doubtless knew that Massachusetts law prohibited Bostonians from keeping loaded guns in the house. So how could Samuel Adams have advocated such protection *unless* he thought that the protection was *consistent* with local regulation that seriously impeded urban residents from using their arms against intruders? It seems unlikely that he meant to deprive the Federal Government of power (to enact Boston-type weapons regulation) that he kn[e]w Boston had and (as far as we know) he would have thought constitutional under the Massachusetts Constitution. Indeed, since the District of Columbia (the subject of the Seat of Government Clause, U.S. Const., Art. I, §8, cl. 17) was the only *urban* area under direct federal control, it seems unlikely that the Framers thought about *urban* gun control at all.

Of course the District's law and the colonial Boston law are not identical. But the Boston law disabled an even wider class of weapons (indeed, all firearms). And its existence shows at the least that local legislatures could impose (as here) serious restrictions on the right to use firearms. Moreover, as I have said, Boston's law, though highly analogous to the District's, was not the *only* colonial law that could have impeded a homeowner's ability to shoot a burglar. Pennsylvania's and New York's laws could well have had a similar effect. And the Massachusetts and Pennsylvania laws were not only thought consistent with an *unwritten* common-law gun-possession right, but also consistent with *written* state constitutional provisions providing protections similar to those provided by the Federal Second Amendment. I cannot agree with the majority that these laws are largely uninformative because the penalty for violating them was civil, rather than criminal. The Court has long recognized that the exercise of a constitutional right can be burdened by penalties far short of jail time. See, *e.g., Murdock v. Pennsylvania,* 319 U.S. 105 (1943) (invalidating $7 per week solicitation fee as applied to religious group); see also *Forsyth County v. Nationalist Movement,* 505 U.S. 123 (1992) ("A tax based on the content of speech does not become more constitutional because it is a small tax").

Regardless, why would the majority require a precise colonial regulatory analogue in order to save a modern gun regulation from constitutional challenge?
After all, insofar as we look to history to discover how we can constitutionally regulate a right to self-defense, we must look, not to what 18th-century
legislatures actually *did* enact, but to what they would have thought they *could*
enact. . . . The question should not be whether a modern restriction on a right to
self-defense *duplicates* a past one, but whether that restriction, when compared
with restrictions originally thought possible, enjoys a similarly strong justification. At a minimum that similarly strong justification is what the District's modern law, compared with Boston's colonial law, reveals.

Fourth, a contrary view, as embodied in today's decision, will have unfortunate consequences. The decision will encourage legal challenges to gun regulation throughout the Nation. Because it says little about the standards used to
evaluate regulatory decisions, it will leave the Nation without clear standards for
resolving those challenges. And litigation over the course of many years, or the
mere specter of such litigation, threatens to leave cities without effective protection against gun violence and accidents during that time.

As important, the majority's decision threatens severely to limit the ability of
more knowledgeable, democratically elected officials to deal with gun-related
problems. The majority says that it leaves the District "a variety of tools for
combating" such problems. It fails to list even one seemingly adequate replacement for the law it strikes down. I can understand how reasonable individuals
can disagree about the merits of strict gun control as a crime-control measure,
even in a totally urbanized area. But I cannot understand how one can take from
the elected branches of government the right to decide whether to insist upon a
handgun-free urban populace in a city now facing a serious crime problem and
which, in the future, could well face environmental or other emergencies that
threaten the breakdown of law and order.

V

The majority derides my approach as "judge-empowering." I take this criticism
seriously, but I do not think it accurate. As I have previously explained, this
is an approach that the Court has taken in other areas of constitutional law.
Application of such an approach, of course, requires judgment, but the very
nature of the approach—requiring careful identification of the relevant interests and evaluating the law's effect upon them—limits the judge's choices; and
the method's necessary transparency lays bare the judge's reasoning for all to
see and to criticize.

The majority's methodology is, in my view, substantially less transparent than
mine. At a minimum, I find it difficult to understand the reasoning that seems to
underlie certain conclusions that it reaches.

[I]n the majority's view, the Amendment also protects an interest in armed
personal self-defense, at least to some degree. But the majority does not tell
us precisely what that interest is. "Putting all of [the Second Amendment's]

textual elements together," the majority says, "we find that they guarantee the individual right to possess and carry weapons in case of confrontation." Then, three pages later, it says that "we do not read the Second Amendment to permit citizens to carry arms for *any sort* of confrontation." Yet, with one critical exception, it does not explain which confrontations count. It simply leaves that question unanswered.

The majority does, however, point to one type of confrontation that counts, for it describes the Amendment as "elevat[ing] above all other interests the right of law-abiding, responsible citizens to use arms in defense of hearth and home." What is its basis for finding that to be the core of the Second Amendment right? The only historical sources identified by the majority that even appear to touch upon that specific matter consist of an 1866 newspaper editorial discussing the Freedmen's Bureau Act, two quotations from that 1866 Act's legislative history, and a 1980 state court opinion saying that in colonial times the same were used to defend the home as to maintain the militia. How can citations such as these support the far-reaching proposition that the Second Amendment's primary concern is not its stated concern about the militia, but rather a right to keep loaded weapons at one's bedside to shoot intruders?

Nor is it at all clear to me how the majority decides *which* loaded "arms" a homeowner may keep. The majority says that that Amendment protects those weapons "typically possessed by law-abiding citizens for lawful purposes." This definition conveniently excludes machineguns, but permits handguns, which the majority describes as "the most popular weapon chosen by Americans for self-defense in the home." But what sense does this approach make? According to the majority's reasoning, if Congress and the States lift restrictions on the possession and use of machineguns, and people buy machineguns to protect their homes, the Court will have to reverse course and find that the Second Amendment *does,* in fact, protect the individual self-defense-related right to possess a machinegun. On the majority's reasoning, if tomorrow someone invents a particularly useful, highly dangerous self-defense weapon, Congress and the States had better ban it immediately, for once it becomes popular Congress will no longer possess the constitutional authority to do so. In essence, the majority determines what regulations are permissible by looking to see what existing regulations permit. There is no basis for believing that the Framers intended such circular reasoning.

I am similarly puzzled by the majority's list, in Part III of its opinion, of provisions that in its view would survive Second Amendment scrutiny. These consist of (1) "prohibitions on carrying concealed weapons"; (2) "prohibitions on the possession of firearms by felons"; (3) "prohibitions on the possession of firearms by . . . the mentally ill"; (4) "laws forbidding the carrying of firearms in sensitive places such as schools and government buildings"; and (5) government "conditions and qualifications" attached "to the commercial sale of arms." Why these? Is it that similar restrictions existed in the late 18th century? The majority fails to cite any colonial analogues. And even were it possible to find analogous colonial laws in respect to all these restrictions, why should these colonial laws count, while the Boston loaded-gun restriction (along with the other laws I have identified) apparently does not count?

At the same time the majority ignores a more important question: Given the purposes for which the Framers enacted the Second Amendment, how should it be applied to modern-day circumstances that they could not have anticipated? Assume, for argument's sake, that the Framers did intend the Amendment to offer a degree of self-defense protection. Does that mean that the Framers also intended to guarantee a right to possess a loaded gun near swimming pools, parks, and playgrounds? That they would not have cared about the children who might pick up a loaded gun on their parents' bedside table? That they (who certainly showed concern for the risk of fire) would have lacked concern for the risk of accidental deaths or suicides that readily accessible loaded handguns in urban areas might bring? Unless we believe that they intended future generations to ignore such matters, answering questions such as the questions in this case requires judgment—judicial judgment exercised within a framework for constitutional analysis that guides that judgment and which makes its exercise transparent. One cannot answer those questions by combining inconclusive historical research with judicial *ipse dixit*.

The argument about method, however, is by far the less important argument surrounding today's decision. Far more important are the unfortunate consequences that today's decision is likely to spawn. Not least of these, as I have said, is the fact that the decision threatens to throw into doubt the constitutionality of gun laws throughout the United States. I can find no sound legal basis for launching the courts on so formidable and potentially dangerous a mission. In my view, there simply is no untouchable constitutional right guaranteed by the Second Amendment to keep loaded handguns in the house in crime-ridden urban areas. . . .

Discussion

1. *Textualism and purposivism.* Note carefully Justice Scalia's methods for interpreting the Second Amendment. He delays discussing the so-called "purposive clause" of the Second Amendment until after parsing what he calls the "operative clause," which mentions the right to keep and bear arms. From the "operative clause" he derives an individual right to "possess and carry weapons in case of confrontation." Why does he proceed in this way?

Justice Scalia notes that the Second Amendment is equivalent to the statement that "Because a well regulated Militia is necessary to the security of a free State, the right of the people to keep and bear Arms shall not be infringed." He argues that "apart from [its] clarifying function, a prefatory clause does not limit or expand the scope of the operative clause." Why should this be? Suppose someone says, "Because I need someone to drive my parents around, you may use my car." Does this give permission to use the car other than as a chauffeur? Does it give permission to use the car if the parents move out of state or to a different country? Suppose the Constitution had said, "Freedom of discussion on public issues being necessary to a free state, Congress shall not abridge the right of free speech." Should this have affected what kinds of speech (e.g., music, painting, pornography, advertisements) are protected and unprotected?

With the Second Amendment, compare the Progress Clause of Article I, section 8, clause 8, which gives Congress the power "[t]o promote the progress of science and useful arts, by securing for limited times to authors and inventors the exclusive right to their respective writings and discoveries." The structure of the Progress Clause is somewhat different than the Second Amendment: the first clause offers a grant of power (to promote progress) that is limited by the second clause as to the means (granting exclusive rights for limited times). Conversely, the power to grant exclusive rights that appears in the second clause is glossed by the purpose (promoting progress) stated in the first clause.

2. *Dueling theories.* Justice Scalia argues that the Second Amendment was placed in the Constitution because of "the threat that the new Federal Government would destroy the citizens' militia by taking away their arms" and that the purpose of the citizen's militia, in turn, was "to oppose an oppressive military force if the constitutional order broke down." The common law right to keep and bear arms for self-defense and for hunting, Scalia argues, was codified in order to prevent such disarmament.

Justice Stevens, by contrast, argues that the common law right was not constitutionalized, at least at this point in history. Instead, the Second Amendment guaranteed "the right of the people of each of the several States to maintain a well-regulated militia" so as to prevent the Federal government from disarming state militias. Under Stevens' theory, what rights, if any, do individual Americans have under the Second Amendment? Presumably they have the right to the military use of weapons in state militias. But if the state no longer has a militia, or if the state excludes people from its organized militia, is there any remaining individual right? Under Stevens' account, do citizens have the right to form their own militias outside of state control?

In fact, Scalia argues that a major flaw with Stevens' theory is that it allows states (and the federal government) to disarm their citizens by closing down the militia or excluding most people from it. Does this mean that under Scalia's account, citizens have the right to form militias free from federal or state control or supervision? Such militias might be formed not only for mutual self-defense but also to ensure that federal and state law enforcement do not oppress the people or violate the Constitution as members of these militias understand it. Suppose the government considers such private armies (which we assume employ nothing other than weapons permitted to ordinary citizens) a danger to public safety. May it disband them as long as it allows citizens to retain ordinary weapons for self-defense? Cf. Presser v. Illinois, 116 U.S. 252 (1886) (upholding a law banning private militias, but holding that the Second Amendment did not apply to the states.). Suppose that the government proves that a group of citizens has formed a paramilitary organization designed to deter what the group regards as the potential for future government tyranny. May the government disarm those people? May it convict them of violating a ban on paramilitary organizations and then disarm them on the grounds that they are felons?

The history and the text of the Second Amendment focus on citizen militias because the Second Amendment was drafted in the context of a larger ideology of civic republicanism: citizens had duties to work together to promote the public good. Participating in citizen militias to resist or deter tyranny or invasion was one of the common duties of members of the community. See Sanford Levinson, The Embarrassing Second Amendment, 99 Yale L.J. 637 (1989). Thus, the right to keep and bear arms at the Founding was not a purely individualist or liberal right to be free from state interference, in the way we often think of rights today. Rather, it was a right that arose from a common political obligation and a common duty to fellow citizens and to the republic.

The need to preserve state militias to counteract federal tyranny, insurrection, and foreign invasion is a civic republican idea. So too is the preservation of an unorganized militia that could arise spontaneously to fight a tyrannical federal government, tyrannical state government, anti-republican insurrection, or foreign invasion. Citizens would band together, either organized by states, or spontaneously, to protect each other and the republic from invaders or tyrants.

3. *A vestigial right?* Scalia's argument is that in order to secure the militia to battle tyranny, the citizenry must have the sort of arms they would ordinarily use in self-defense of the home. In the 1790s, weapons commonly used in combat and weapons commonly used for self-defense overlapped considerably. They do no longer. As Scalia notes, a citizenry armed with handguns might be no match for today's heavy weaponry. Nevertheless, Scalia argues that the right to bear arms in defense of self and home endures even if it no longer effectively serves the original purpose for which it was codified in the Constitution — defending the people against tyranny. Why? Justice Scalia argues that originalism is consistent with responding to technological change, citing the First and Fourth Amendments as examples. Compare the effect of technological change on interpretations of federal power to regulate the economy. Industrialization, changes in transportation technology, economies of scale, and the growth of national markets eventually led courts to cut back on judicial restrictions on government power following the New Deal. What is the best response to technological change in this context?

4. *Which tyranny?* Scalia's historical account puts the best possible face on a tension inherent in the 1791 Constitution raised by the possibility of unorganized militias. On the one hand, the militia had the right to keep and bear arms to prevent tyranny, including a tyrannical federal government (or state government, in the case of state constitutions). On the other hand, the federal government had the obligation to put down insurrections and invasions (see the Guarantee Clause of Article IV), and it had the right to organize and take over state militias for this purpose. See the Militia Clauses, Article I, section 8, clauses 15 and 16.

This balance of powers did not decide which group — the "insurrectionists" or the "government" — was the problem and which was the solution.

The government might be tyrannical, or it might be a republican government defending against a mob or a putsch. The (unorganized) militia exercising its Second Amendment rights might be rising up against a tyrannical government, or it might be a force threatening republican government. *Heller* resolves this problem largely by ignoring it; it reads the Second Amendment as guaranteeing the right to bear arms for self-defense, but not the right to possess "dangerous" weapons.

Consider a civic republican reading of the ban on "dangerous" weapons. Civic republicanism requires cooperation and mutual support. Some weapons, such as nuclear bombs, tanks, or machine guns, don't require many people to cooperate to inflict enormous damage. Other weapons, such as swords and muskets, can inflict much less damage individually, and require people to band together to resist oppression. Under a civic republican reading, handguns and shotguns might be "republican" and are constitutionally protected while machine guns might be "anti-republican" and may be proscribed. Does *Heller* contemplate this distinction or a different one that is unrelated to civic republican ideology?

Does Scalia's reading of the individual right to keep and bear arms allow government to criminalize caches of arms that might someday be used to resist an oppressive government? *Heller* assumes that licensing requirements are constitutional. Do citizens have a constitutional right to stockpile as many weapons as they like, subject to obtaining a license for each one?

Suppose citizens stockpile weapons and engage in military exercises to resist government tyranny. Does *Heller* allow governments to prosecute these citizens for criminal conspiracy to commit insurrection or terrorism? What if the basis of the charge of conspiracy is that the citizens are stockpiling weapons, presumably, in order to allow them to resist future tyranny or invasion?

5. *The uses of history, originalism, and the living Constitution.* Both Justices Scalia and Stevens state their historical conclusions confidently, asserting that that the historical record is clear. As is often the case with attempts to recapture the past, however, the same facts can often be interpreted in more than one way, a point made abundantly clear by juxtaposing Scalia's and Stevens' equally self-assured claims about identical texts and events.

Justice Scalia's argument is that the Second Amendment codified the English common law right to use weapons for self-defense. There is some evidence for this position, but the historical record is mixed and can be read in several different ways. Different views about the nature of the right to keep and bear arms circulated during the Founding period, which is hardly surprising given that it was one of the most intellectually lively periods in American political thought. On the ambiguities of the historical record, see Mark V. Tushnet, Out of Range: Why the Constitution Can't End the Battle over Guns (New York: Oxford University Press, 2007); Saul Cornell, A Well-Regulated Militia: The Founding Fathers and the Origins of Gun Control in America (New York: Oxford University Press, 2006); Sanford Levinson, Guns and the Constitution, A Complex Relationship, 36 Reviews in American History, 1-14 (2008) (reviewing Tushnet and Cornell).

On the other hand, as Scalia notes, there is fairly strong evidence that during the 19th century people believed that the Second Amendment guaranteed a right to use arms in self-defense, and the evidence grows stronger as the century proceeds. As the casebook recounts (at p. 496) by the time of the Civil War, it was widely assumed that the common law right to keep and bear arms for self-defense was a fundamental constitutional right, whether it was protected by the Privileges and Immunities Clause of Article IV, the Second Amendment, or the Ninth Amendment.

Justice Scalia reads this history as evidence not of evolving views about basic rights, but as evidence of the common understandings of 1791. Scalia does this because his originalist theory of interpretation requires it. The danger, of course, is that his use of history is anachronistic. For the same reason, Scalia scoffs at "the proposition, unsupported by any evidence, that different people of the founding period had vastly different conceptions of the right to keep and bear arms. That simply does not comport with our longstanding view that the Bill of Rights codified venerable, widely understood liberties." But surely it is likely that people disagreed about the meaning of the right to bear arms in 1791 just as they disagree about basic rights today.

Does a sophisticated version of originalism require the degree of historical certainty and consensus that Scalia seems to assume? One potential problem is that if we assume that more than one view was circulating at the time, present day judges must pick one reading as more faithful than the others. Would doing this pose any problems for originalism's conception of the judicial role, or with the democratic legitimacy of judicial review?

A far more plausible reading of the history is that views about the purposes of the Amendment were in flux at the Founding and changed over the course of a century, and that by the time of Reconstruction, it was widely accepted that the right to self-defense was a constitutional liberty identified with the Second Amendment. Even if there was no consensus about whether the English common law right was constitutionalized in 1791, such a consensus had developed by Reconstruction. Hence the framers of the Fourteenth Amendment believed that the right to use arms in self-defense was one of the "Privileges or Immunities of Citizens of the United States" protected by the Fourteenth Amendment. (For example, see Senator Jacob Howard's Speech introducing the Fourteenth Amendment before the Senate in May 1866, reprinted in this supplement.)

Given this evidence, could a court read the text of the Second Amendment consistent with these 19th-century views, and particularly those widely held at the time of the Fourteenth Amendment? This would not be a necessary implication of the original meaning of the Second Amendment. Rather, it would be a constitutional *construction* of the original meaning that became commonplace in the 19th century. The original meaning of the text can easily bear this construction and, so the argument would go, we should accept it today, especially because it was assumed in the debates leading up to the ratification of the Fourteenth Amendment.

This reading of history, however, would require a "living Constitution" approach. It would maintain that a later generation's views on the scope of the Second Amendment can be accepted as part of the Constitution as long as those views are consistent with the original meaning of the words of the text. Why does the majority not adopt this model of interpretation? Equally important, why doesn't Justice Stevens' dissent?

What are the problems with accepting the 19th century's construction of the Second Amendment as the best interpretation? Does it commit us to accept 19th-century assumptions about the scope of other parts of the Bill of Rights, or, for that matter, the Fourteenth Amendment?

6. *Living Constitutionalism and the role of social movements.* Justice Stevens makes much of the fact that for the better part of a century, courts had assumed that the Second Amendment did not guarantee an individual right to use guns for self-defense. Indeed, this was the conventional wisdom for many years. In 1991, for example, retired Chief Justice Warren Burger, a conservative Republican, insisted that the individual rights view of the Second Amendment was "one of the greatest pieces of fraud—I repeat the word 'fraud'—on the American public by special interest groups that I have ever seen in my lifetime." Burger cast particular scorn on the efforts of the National Rifle Association (NRA) and other groups—which he pejoratively labeled "special interest groups"—to convince Americans otherwise. As we have seen elsewhere in this course, in the context of social movements like the women's movement and the gay rights movement, sustained political and social mobilization can persuade people to change their minds about what is "off the wall" and "on the wall" concerning legal and constitutional claims. For a history of how the work of social movements eventually led to the decision in *Heller*, see Reva B. Siegel, Dead or Alive: Originalism as Popular Constitutionalism in *Heller*, 122 Harv. L. Rev. 191, 201-246 (2008).

The modern movement for gun rights arose in reaction to increased political mobilization for stricter gun control laws, particularly after passage of the 1968 Crime Control Act, which Congress enacted following the assassinations of Martin Luther King and Robert F. Kennedy. Beginning in the 1970s, the NRA began national lobbying efforts to oppose gun control legislation, arguing that gun control laws violated Second Amendment rights and that the conventional wisdom about the Constitution was incorrect. The gun rights movement gained influence within the Republican Party, as gun rights became one of many interconnected issues in the culture wars. Movement conservatives who used originalism to attack liberal judicial decisions, also turned to originalism to defend Second Amendment rights. See, e.g., The Right to Keep and Bear Arms: Report of the Subcommittee on the Constitution of the Committee on the Judiciary 1 S. 97th Cong., 2d sess. (1982).

As conservatives gained increasing political influence during the last part of the twentieth century, the NRA's constitutional position gained increasing public support, and convinced members of a newer generation of conservative legal elites. In 1994, the Republicans took control of both Houses of Congress by making a key campaign issue of their opposition to recent gun control laws passed by a Democratic-controlled Congress. See Nicholas J. Johnson, A Second Amendment Moment: The Constitutional Politics of Gun Control, 71 Brook. L. Rev. 715 (2005). In May 2002, Attorney General John Ashcroft announced the Bush Justice Department's official position that the Second Amendment protected an individual right to use arms in self-defense.

As we have seen in *Brown v. Board of Education* and other cases, the Supreme Court tends to respond, in the long run, to the views of the dominant political coalition as well as to public opinion. The agendas of legal scholarship also tend to shift in response to political changes. An outpouring of new legal and historical scholarship began debating the individual rights interpretation in the 1990s and 2000s, and the Third Edition of Professor Laurence Tribe's Treatise, *American Constitutional Law*, published in 2000, argued — in contrast to the two previous editions — that the Second Amendment protected an individual right. See Laurence H. Tribe, American Constitutional Law §5-11, 901-02 n.221 (3d ed., Foundation Press 2000).

In this sense, the result in *Heller* was not entirely surprising. As in *Brown v. Board of Education*, the 1970s sex equality cases, and *Lawrence v. Texas*, the Supreme Court has kept its interpretation of the Constitution in line with changing public values. Another name for this phenomenon is living constitutionalism.

The irony of course, is that the arguments for modifying constitutional doctrine to reflect changed political realities were all phrased in the language of fidelity to original meaning. However, this makes perfect sense. The best way for social movements to persuade others that their views are correct is to show how they follow ineluctably from the nation's deepest commitments. Appeals to the framers and the Constitution's original meaning are one way, although not the only way, to do that. For example, opponents of affirmative action have not made arguments from the original meaning of the Fourteenth Amendment, but rather argued that colorblindness follows from the meaning of *Brown v. Board of Education* and the civil rights movement.

This account of *Heller* assumes a very different theory of the democratic legitimacy of judicial review than the one offered in Scalia's opinion. The implicit theory in *Heller* is that judges are simply bound by the original meaning and original understanding of the Constitution. That meaning is clear: It protects an individual right to use arms in self-defense. Therefore it is the duty of judges to enforce that meaning. But if we understand *Heller* as the result of a long process of mobilization seeking to change conventional wisdom, first among the general public and later among legal elites, we can offer a different account of the democratic legitimacy of judicial review. The American people today understand these rights as their rights, and the text can bear this construction.

The first theory views the judges' role as faithfully following an ancient law of the framers as they would have understood and applied it. It asserts (or at least must assert) that the text is clear and there can be no other reasonable construction. The second views the judges' role as articulating and applying vague or ambiguous texts in light of contemporary social values, securing American's present-day understanding of their basic rights. Why are the opinions in *Heller* written according to the first theory rather than the second?

7. *Judicial scrutiny under the Second Amendment.* Justice Breyer suggests that Second Amendment rights should be determined according to a balancing test, roughly akin to the intermediate scrutiny employed in the sex equality cases and in First Amendment cases involving regulations of time, place and manner. He notes that state courts with analogous constitutional provisions have, by and large, used a balancing or intermediate scrutiny approach. For a review of the state cases, see Adam Winkler, Scrutinizing the Second Amendment, 105 Mich. L. Rev. 683 (2007). The majority, although striking down parts of the D.C. ordinance, leaves open the question of the appropriate level of scrutiny for a future case. However it seems to reject Breyer's approach. Is this because it rejects the idea of applying intermediate scrutiny or merely Breyer's application of it?

Consider Breyer's argument that the empirical studies on gun control laws point in different directions; given this uncertainty, courts should defer to legislatures about the best way to balance home owners' rights and public safety. Compare Breyer's views with the Court's application of the "undue burden" test in abortion cases, in particular *Casey* and *Carhart II*. Could the majority respond that the D.C. ban on handguns is a complete ban of a commonly used weapon rather than merely a regulation of handgun use? Does the Second Amendment prohibit complete bans on any weapons that are currently in common use? Does it allow the government to prevent new weapons from becoming commonly used?

8. *What kind of self-defense?* Justice Scalia reads the Second Amendment to protect the common law right of self-defense. What precisely is this right? Does it protect only the right to keep firearms in the home for self-defense, or does it also include the right to keep them on one's person outside the home, for example, when one travels in dangerous neighborhoods? Does *Heller* protect the right to use weapons other than firearms for self-defense in the home? For example, are laws banning the possession of switchblades within the home constitutional under *Heller*? Does it protect the right to possess these weapons outside the home? See Moore v. Madigan, 702 F.3d 993 (7th Cir. 2012) (extending the logic of *Heller* outside the home and holding that Illinois statute that generally prohibits carrying of ready to use guns outside the home violated the Second Amendment); National Rifle Ass'n of America, Inc. v. McCraw, 719 F.3d 338 (5th Cir. 2013) (upholding Texas statute that prevented 18- to 20-year olds from carrying handguns in public).

Does *Heller* protect the right of self-defense per se, whether with or without a firearm? Does it mean, for example, that states must, as a constitutional matter, have a doctrine of self-defense in their criminal and tort laws? If there is a constitutional right of self-defense, is it limited only to situations where a person is directly attacked by another? For example, would the constitutional right of self-defense extend to the use of drugs and surgeries that patients reasonably believe are necessary for their survival? See Eugene Volokh, Medical Self-Defense, Prohibited Experimental Therapies, and Payment for Organs, 120 Harv.

L. Rev. 1813 (2007) (discussing possible rights of self-defense under the Due Process Clause); Abigail Alliance for Better Access to Developmental Drugs v. von Eschenbach, 495 F.3d 695 (D.C. Cir. 2007) (en banc), cert. denied, 552 U.S. 1159 (2008) (holding that terminally ill patients have no fundamental right under the Due Process Clause to obtain potentially live-saving medications still undergoing testing required by the Food and Drug Administration). Would the constitutional guarantee of self-defense protect the right of women to have abortions to save their lives? Compare the guarantee of abortions to save the mother's life in *Roe v. Wade*, casebook Chapter Eight, infra. Or does *Heller* merely hold that people have a right to keep weapons in their homes for purposes of self-defense where such weapons are of the sort commonly available and that might be used in a state militia, if the state had such a militia?

9. *Applying* Heller: *The two-step test.* Since *Heller*, many federal courts of appeals have adopted a "two-step" test for gun regulations.[1] First, as a threshold question, courts have asked whether the regulated conduct has historically fallen within the scope of the Second Amendment; or conversely, whether the conduct has historically been subject to regulation or prohibition. If so, then the Second Amendment does not apply at all.

The first step is motivated by several ideas. To begin with, in *Heller* itself, Justice Scalia asserted that only some kinds of weapons—those commonly used by law-abiding individuals for self-defense—were protected by the Second Amendment; the use of others was outside the amendment's scope. *Heller* also stated that "[n]othing in our opinion should be taken to cast doubt on longstanding prohibitions on the possession of firearms by felons and the mentally ill, or laws forbidding the carrying of firearms in sensitive places such as schools and government buildings, or laws imposing conditions and qualifications on the commercial sale of arms," and that this list of "presumptively lawful regulatory measures" was illustrative, not exhaustive. Justice Alito's opinion in McDonald v. City of Chicago (reprinted below) repeated *Heller*'s "assurances" about these exceptions. In addition, courts have drawn an analogy to the First Amendment, which has historically excluded categories like obscenity, fraud, and incitement from the class of protected speech.

Courts applying the first step generally engage in a historical inquiry: they ask whether regulations of the same kind as the one at issue were historically accepted or commonplace. Not surprisingly, there are often several ways to assess the history and its relationship to present-day regulations. Nevertheless, if the court concludes that regulations of the kind at issue were historically accepted, the Second Amendment does not apply at all.

---

1. See, e.g., NRA of Am. v. Bureau of Alcohol, 700 F.3d 185, 194 (5th Cir. 2012); United States v. Greeno, 679 F.3d 510 (6th Cir. 2012); Heller v. Dist. of Columbia, 670 F.3d 1244 (D.C. Cir. 2011) (*Heller II*); Ezell v. City of Chicago, 651 F.3d 684 (7th Cir. 2011); United States v. Chester, 628 F.3d 673 (4th Cir. 2010); United States v. Reese, 627 F.3d 792 (10th Cir. 2010); United States v. Marzzarella, 614 F.3d 85 (3d Cir. 2010).

Nevertheless, if the historical evidence is inconclusive or suggests that the regulated activity is not categorically unprotected, the courts then go on to the second part of the two-step test. They apply heightened scrutiny to the regulation, assessing the importance of the government's justifications and how well they are furthered by the regulation in question. Different circuits have adopted slightly different formulations of the test. See, e.g., NRA of America v. BATF, 700 F.3d 185, 205 (5th Cir. 2012) ("A law that burdens the core of the Second Amendment guarantee—for example, 'the right of law-abiding, responsible citizens to use arms in defense of hearth and home,' *Heller*—would trigger strict scrutiny, while a less severe law would be proportionately easier to justify. The latter, 'intermediate' standard of scrutiny requires the government to show a reasonable fit between the law and an important government objective.").

The two-step test requires courts to make a number of judgment calls, both about how broadly or narrowly to construe historical precedents, and about judicial scrutiny of government regulation. In theory, therefore, the test might lead to a fairly significant restriction on gun regulations. Nevertheless, the practical effect of the two-step test, at least in the first several years after *Heller*, is that relatively few gun regulations have been struck down. Why do you think this is so?

MCDONALD v. CITY OF CHICAGO
130 S. Ct. 3020 (2010)

Justice ALITO announced the judgment of the Court and delivered the opinion of the Court with respect to Parts I, II-A, II-B, II-D, III-A, and III-B, in which THE CHIEF JUSTICE, Justice SCALIA, Justice KENNEDY, and Justice THOMAS join, and an opinion with respect to Parts II-C, IV, and V, in which THE CHIEF JUSTICE, Justice SCALIA, and Justice KENNEDY join.

[Petitioners challenged city ordinances in Chicago and Oak Park that effectively banned handgun possession. Chicago's ordinance prohibits registration of most handguns and then provides that that "[n]o person shall . . . possess . . . any firearm unless such person is the holder of a valid registration certificate for such firearm." Chicago, Ill., Municipal Code §8-20-040(a) (2009). Oak Park makes it "unlawful for any person to possess . . . any firearm," a term that includes "pistols, revolvers, guns and small arms . . . commonly known as handguns." Oak Park, Ill., Municipal Code §§27-2-1 (2007), 27-1-1 (2009). Petitioners argued that that the Second Amendment right to keep and bear arms for the purpose of self-defense recognized in *Heller* applied to the states through the Fourteenth Amendment.]

II

A

Three years after the decision in the *Slaughter-House Cases,* the Court decided [*United States v.*] *Cruikshank,* [which held] that the right of bearing arms for a lawful purpose "is not a right granted by the Constitution" and is not "in any manner dependent upon that instrument for its existence." "The second amendment," the Court continued, "declares that it shall not be infringed; but this . . . means no more than that it shall not be infringed by Congress." Our later decisions in *Presser v. Illinois,* 116 U.S. 252, 265 (1886), and *Miller v. Texas,* 153 U.S. 535 (1894), reaffirmed that the Second Amendment applies only to the Federal Government. . . . Petitioners argue . . . that we should overrule those decisions and hold that the right to keep and bear arms is one of the "privileges or immunities of citizens of the United States." In petitioners' view, the Privileges or Immunities Clause protects all of the rights set out in the Bill of Rights, as well as some others, but petitioners are unable to identify the Clause's full scope. Nor is there any consensus on that question among the scholars who agree that the *Slaughter-House Cases'* interpretation is flawed.

We see no need to reconsider that interpretation here. For many decades, the question of the rights protected by the Fourteenth Amendment against state infringement has been analyzed under the Due Process Clause of that Amendment and not under the Privileges or Immunities Clause. We therefore decline to disturb the *Slaughter-House* holding.

At the same time, however, this Court's decisions in *Cruikshank, Presser,* and *Miller* do not preclude us from considering whether the Due Process Clause of the Fourteenth Amendment makes the Second Amendment right binding on the States. . . . Indeed, *Cruikshank* has not prevented us from holding that other rights that were at issue in that case are binding on the States through the Due Process Clause. In *Cruikshank,* the Court held that the general "right of the people peaceably to assemble for lawful purposes," which is protected by the First Amendment, applied only against the Federal Government and not against the States. Nonetheless, over 60 years later the Court held that the right of peaceful assembly was a "fundamental righ[t] . . . safeguarded by the due process clause of the Fourteenth Amendment." *De Jonge v. Oregon,* 299 U.S. 353, 364 (1937). . . .

D

In the late 19th century, the Court began to consider whether the Due Process Clause prohibits the States from infringing rights set out in the Bill of Rights. See *Hurtado v. California,* 110 U.S. 516 (1884) (due process does not require grand jury indictment); *Chicago, B. & Q.R. Co. v. Chicago,* 166 U.S. 226 (1897) (due process prohibits States from taking of private property for public use without just compensation). [During this period] the Court viewed the due process question as entirely separate from the question whether a right was a privilege or immunity of national citizenship. [It] explained that the only rights protected against state infringement by the Due Process Clause were those rights "of such a nature that they are included in the conception of due process of law." [*Twining v. New Jersey,* 211 U.S. 78, 99 (1908).] . . . The Court used different formulations in describing the boundaries of due process. For example, in *Twining,* the Court referred to "immutable principles of justice which inhere in the very idea of free government which no member of the Union may disregard." 211 U.S., at 102. In *Snyder v. Massachusetts,* 291 U.S. 97, 105 (1934), the Court spoke of rights that are "so rooted in the traditions and conscience of our people as to be ranked as fundamental." And in *Palko* [*v. Connecticut,* 302 U.S. 319 (1937)], the Court famously said that due process protects those rights that are "the very essence of a scheme of ordered liberty" and essential to "a fair and enlightened system of justice." [In] some cases decided during this era the Court "can be seen as having asked, when inquiring into whether some particular procedural safeguard was required of a State, if a civilized system could be imagined that would not accord the particular protection." [For example,] the Court found that due process did not provide a right against compelled incrimination in part because this right "has no place in the jurisprudence of civilized and free countries outside the domain of the common law." *Twining.*

Finally, even when a right set out in the Bill of Rights was held to fall within the conception of due process, the protection or remedies afforded against state infringement sometimes differed from the protection or remedies provided against abridgment by the Federal Government. To give one example, in *Betts* [*v. Brady,* 316 U.S. 455 (1942)] the Court held that, although the Sixth Amendment required the appointment of counsel in all federal criminal cases in which the defendant was unable to retain an attorney, the Due Process Clause required appointment of counsel in state criminal proceedings only where "want of counsel in [the] particular case . . . result[ed] in a conviction lacking in . . . fundamental fairness." Similarly, in *Wolf v. Colorado,* 338 U.S. 25 (1949), the Court held that the "core of the Fourth Amendment" was implicit in the concept of ordered liberty and thus "enforceable against the States through the Due Process Clause" but that the exclusionary rule, which applied in federal cases, did not apply to the States. . . .

Justice Black [argued] that §1 of the Fourteenth Amendment totally incorporated all of the provisions of the Bill of Rights [noting that] the chief congressional proponents of the Fourteenth Amendment espoused [this] view.

[T]he Court never has embraced Justice Black's "total incorporation" theory. [Nevertheless,] the Court eventually moved in that direction [through] a process of "selective incorporation," *i.e.,* the Court began to hold that the Due Process Clause fully incorporates particular rights contained in the first eight Amendments.

The decisions during this time abandoned three of the previously noted characteristics of the earlier period. The Court made it clear that the governing standard is not whether *any* "civilized system [can] be imagined that would not accord the particular protection." *Duncan v. Louisiana,* 391 U.S. 145, 149, n.14 (1968). Instead, the Court inquired whether a particular Bill of Rights guarantee is fundamental to *our* scheme of ordered liberty and system of justice. . . . The

Court eventually incorporated almost all of the provisions of the Bill of Rights. Only a handful of the Bill of Rights protections remain unincorporated.[a]

Finally, the Court abandoned "the notion that the Fourteenth Amendment applies to the States only a watered-down, subjective version of the individual guarantees of the Bill of Rights," stating that it would be "incongruous" to apply different standards "depending on whether the claim was asserted in a state or federal court." *Malloy v. Hogan,* 378 U.S. [1, 10-11 (1964).] Instead, the Court decisively held that incorporated Bill of Rights protections "are all to be enforced against the States under the Fourteenth Amendment according to the same standards that protect those personal rights against federal encroachment."[b]

III

[W]e must decide whether the right to keep and bear arms is fundamental to *our* scheme of ordered liberty, *Duncan,* or as we have said in a related context, whether this right is "deeply rooted in this Nation's history and tradition," *Washington v. Glucksberg,* 521 U.S. 702, 721 (1997).

A

Our decision in *Heller* points unmistakably to the answer. Self-defense is a basic right, recognized by many legal systems from ancient times to the present day, and in *Heller,* we held that individual self-defense is "the *central component*" of the Second Amendment right. Explaining that "the need for defense of self, family, and property is most acute" in the home, we found that this right

---

a. In addition to the right to keep and bear arms (and the Sixth Amendment right to a unanimous jury verdict), the only rights not fully incorporated are (1) the Third Amendment's protection against quartering of soldiers; (2) the Fifth Amendment's grand jury indictment requirement; (3) the Seventh Amendment right to a jury trial in civil cases; and (4) the Eighth Amendment's prohibition on excessive fines. We never have decided whether the Third Amendment or the Eighth Amendment's prohibition of excessive fines applies to the States through the Due Process Clause. Our governing decisions regarding the Grand Jury Clause of the Fifth Amendment and the Seventh Amendment's civil jury requirement long predate the era of selective incorporation.

b. There is one exception to this general rule. The Court has held that although the Sixth Amendment right to trial by jury requires a unanimous jury verdict in federal criminal trials, it does not require a unanimous jury verdict in state criminal trials. See *Apodaca v. Oregon,* 406 U.S. 404, (1972); see also *Johnson v. Louisiana,* 406 U.S. 356 (1972) (holding that the Due Process Clause does not require unanimous jury verdicts in state criminal trials). But that ruling was the result of an unusual division among the Justices, not an endorsement of the two-track approach to incorporation. In *Apodaca,* eight Justices agreed that the Sixth Amendment applies identically to both the Federal Government and the States. Nonetheless, among those eight, four Justices took the view that the Sixth Amendment does not require unanimous jury verdicts in either federal or state criminal trials, and four other Justices took the view that the Sixth Amendment requires unanimous jury verdicts in federal and state criminal trials. Justice Powell's concurrence in the judgment broke the tie, and he concluded that the Sixth Amendment requires juror unanimity in federal, but not state, cases. *Apodaca,* therefore, does not undermine the well-established rule that incorporated Bill of Rights protections apply identically to the States and the Federal Government.

applies to handguns because they are "the most preferred firearm in the nation to 'keep' and use for protection of one's home and family." . . . *Heller* makes it clear that this right is "deeply rooted in this Nation's history and tradition." *Glucksberg. Heller* explored the right's origins, noting that the 1689 English Bill of Rights explicitly protected a right to keep arms for self-defense, and that by 1765, Blackstone was able to assert that the right to keep and bear arms was "one of the fundamental rights of Englishmen."

Blackstone's assessment was shared by the American colonists. As we noted in *Heller,* King George III's attempt to disarm the colonists in the 1760's and 1770's "provoked polemical reactions by Americans invoking their rights as Englishmen to keep arms." The right to keep and bear arms was considered no less fundamental by those who drafted and ratified the Bill of Rights. "During the 1788 ratification debates, the fear that the federal government would disarm the people in order to impose rule through a standing army or select militia was pervasive in Antifederalist rhetoric." Federalists responded, not by arguing that the right was insufficiently important to warrant protection but by contending that the right was adequately protected by the Constitution's assignment of only limited powers to the Federal Government. Thus, Antifederalists and Federalists alike agreed that the right to bear arms was fundamental to the newly formed system of government. But those who were fearful that the new Federal Government would infringe traditional rights such as the right to keep and bear arms insisted on the adoption of the Bill of Rights as a condition for ratification of the Constitution. This is surely powerful evidence that the right was regarded as fundamental in the sense relevant here.

This understanding persisted in the years immediately following the ratification of the Bill of Rights. In addition to the four States that had adopted Second Amendment analogues before ratification, nine more States adopted state constitutional provisions protecting an individual right to keep and bear arms between 1789 and 1820. Founding-era legal commentators confirmed the importance of the right to early Americans. St. George Tucker, for example, described the right to keep and bear arms as "the true palladium of liberty" and explained that prohibitions on the right would place liberty "on the brink of destruction." 1 Blackstone's Commentaries, Editor's App. 300 (S. Tucker ed. 1803); see also W. Rawle, A View of the Constitution of the United States of America, 125-126 (2d ed. 1829) (reprint 2009); 3 J. Story, Commentaries on the Constitution of the United States §1890, p. 746 (1833) ("The right of the citizens to keep and bear arms has justly been considered, as the palladium of the liberties of a republic; since it offers a strong moral check against the usurpation and arbitrary power of rulers; and will generally, even if these are successful in the first instance, enable the people to resist and triumph over them").

B

By the 1850's, the perceived threat that had prompted the inclusion of the Second Amendment in the Bill of Rights — the fear that the National Government would disarm the universal militia—had largely faded as a popular concern, but the right to keep and bear arms was highly valued for purposes of self-defense. Abolitionist authors wrote in support of the right. And when attempts were made to disarm "Free-Soilers" in "Bloody Kansas," Senator Charles Sumner, who later played a leading role in the adoption of the Fourteenth Amendment, proclaimed that "[n]ever was [the rifle] more needed in just self-defense than now in Kansas." Indeed, the 1856 Republican Party Platform protested that in Kansas the constitutional rights of the people had been "fraudulently and violently taken from them" and the "right of the people to keep and bear arms" had been "infringed."[c]

After the Civil War, many of the over 180,000 African Americans who served in the Union Army returned to the States of the old Confederacy, where systematic efforts were made to disarm them and other blacks. The laws of some States formally prohibited African Americans from possessing firearms. . . . Throughout the South, armed parties, often consisting of ex-Confederate soldiers serving in the state militias, forcibly took firearms from newly freed slaves. In the first session of the 39th Congress, Senator Wilson told his colleagues: "In Mississippi rebel State forces, men who were in the rebel armies, are traversing the State, visiting the freedmen, disarming them, perpetrating murders and outrages upon them; and the same things are done in other sections of the country." The Report of the Joint Committee on Reconstruction—which was widely reprinted in the press and distributed by Members of the 39th Congress to their constituents shortly after Congress approved the Fourteenth Amendment—contained numerous examples of such abuses. . . . As Senator Wilson put it during the debate on a failed proposal to disband Southern militias: "There is one unbroken chain of testimony from all people that are loyal to this country, that the greatest outrages are perpetrated by armed men who go up and down the country searching houses, disarming people, committing outrages of every kind and description."

Union Army commanders took steps to secure the right of all citizens to keep and bear arms, but the 39th Congress concluded that legislative action was necessary. Its efforts to safeguard the right to keep and bear arms demonstrate that the right was still recognized to be fundamental.

The most explicit evidence of Congress' aim appears in §14 of the Freedmen's Bureau Act of 1866, which provided that "the right . . . to have full and equal benefit of all laws and proceedings concerning personal liberty, personal security, and the acquisition, enjoyment, and disposition of estate, real and personal, *including the constitutional right to bear arms,* shall be secured to and enjoyed by all the citizens . . . without respect to race or color, or previous condition of

---

c. Abolitionists and Republicans were not alone in believing that the right to keep and bear arms was a fundamental right. The 1864 Democratic Party Platform complained that the confiscation of firearms by Union troops occupying parts of the South constituted "the interference with and denial of the right of the people to bear arms in their defense."

slavery." 14 Stat. 176-177 (emphasis added). Section 14 thus explicitly guaranteed that "all the citizens," black and white, would have "the constitutional right to bear arms."

The Civil Rights Act of 1866, 14 Stat. 27, which was considered at the same time as the Freedmen's Bureau Act, similarly sought to protect the right of all citizens to keep and bear arms. Section 1 of the Civil Rights Act guaranteed the "full and equal benefit of all laws and proceedings for the security of person and property, as is enjoyed by white citizens." This language was virtually identical to language in §14 of the Freedmen's Bureau Act. . . . Representative Bingham believed that the Civil Rights Act protected the same rights as enumerated in the Freedmen's Bureau bill, which of course explicitly mentioned the right to keep and bear arms. The unavoidable conclusion is that the Civil Rights Act, like the Freedmen's Bureau Act, aimed to protect "the constitutional right to bear arms" and not simply to prohibit discrimination. . . .

Today, it is generally accepted that the Fourteenth Amendment was understood to provide a constitutional basis for protecting the rights set out in the Civil Rights Act of 1866. In debating the Fourteenth Amendment, the 39th Congress referred to the right to keep and bear arms as a fundamental right deserving of protection. Senator Samuel Pomeroy described three "indispensable" "safeguards of liberty under our form of Government." Cong. Globe, 39th Cong., 1st Sess. 1182. One of these, he said, was the right to keep and bear arms: "Every man . . . should have the right to bear arms for the defense of himself and family and his homestead. And if the cabin door of the freedman is broken open and the intruder enters for purposes as vile as were known to slavery, then should a well-loaded musket be in the hand of the occupant to send the polluted wretch to another world, where his wretchedness will forever remain complete." *Ibid.* Even those who thought the Fourteenth Amendment unnecessary believed that blacks, as citizens, "have equal right to protection, and to keep and bear arms for self-defense." *Id.*, at 1073 (Sen. James Nye).

. . . The right to keep and bear arms was also widely protected by state constitutions at the time when the Fourteenth Amendment was ratified. In 1868, 22 of the 37 States in the Union had state constitutional provisions explicitly protecting the right to keep and bear arms. . . . In sum, it is clear that the Framers and ratifiers of the Fourteenth Amendment counted the right to keep and bear arms among those fundamental rights necessary to our system of ordered liberty.

Despite all this evidence, municipal respondents contend that Congress, in the years immediately following the Civil War, merely sought to outlaw "discriminatory measures taken against freedmen, which it addressed by adopting a non-discrimination principle" and that even an outright ban on the possession of firearms was regarded as acceptable, "so long as it was not done in a discriminatory manner." They argue that Members of Congress overwhelmingly viewed §1 of the Fourteenth Amendment "as an antidiscrimination rule," and they cite statements to the effect that the section would outlaw discriminatory measures. This argument is implausible.

First, while §1 of the Fourteenth Amendment contains "an antidiscrimination rule," namely, the Equal Protection Clause, municipal respondents can hardly mean that §1 does no more than prohibit discrimination. If that were so, then the First Amendment, as applied to the States, would not prohibit nondiscriminatory abridgments of the rights to freedom of speech or freedom of religion; the Fourth Amendment, as applied to the States, would not prohibit all unreasonable searches and seizures but only discriminatory searches and seizures — and so on. We assume that this is not municipal respondents' view, so what they must mean is that the Second Amendment should be singled out for special — and specially unfavorable — treatment. We reject that suggestion.

Second, municipal respondents' argument ignores the clear terms of the Freedmen's Bureau Act of 1866 . . . §14 speaks of and protects "the constitutional right to bear arms," an unmistakable reference to the right protected by the Second Amendment. And it protects the "full and equal benefit" of this right in the States. It would have been nonsensical for Congress to guarantee the full and equal benefit of a constitutional right that does not exist.

Third, if the 39th Congress had outlawed only those laws that discriminate on the basis of race or previous condition of servitude, African Americans in the South would likely have remained vulnerable to attack by many of their worst abusers: the state militia and state peace officers. In the years immediately following the Civil War, a law banning the possession of guns by all private citizens would have been nondiscriminatory only in the formal sense. Any such law — like the Chicago and Oak Park ordinances challenged here — presumably would have permitted the possession of guns by those acting under the authority of the State and would thus have left firearms in the hands of the militia and local peace officers. And as the Report of the Joint Committee on Reconstruction revealed, those groups were widely involved in harassing blacks in the South.

Fourth, municipal respondents' purely antidiscrimination theory of the Fourteenth Amendment disregards the plight of whites in the South who opposed the Black Codes. If the 39th Congress and the ratifying public had simply prohibited racial discrimination with respect to the bearing of arms, opponents of the Black Codes would have been left without the means of self-defense — as had abolitionists in Kansas in the 1850's. . . .

IV

[M]unicipal respondents, in effect, ask us to treat the right recognized in *Heller* as a second-class right, subject to an entirely different body of rules than the other Bill of Rights guarantees that we have held to be incorporated into the Due Process Clause. . . . According to municipal respondents, if it is possible to imagine *any* civilized legal system that does not recognize a particular right, then the Due Process Clause does not make that right binding on the States. . . . Therefore, the municipal respondents continue, because such countries as England, Canada, Australia, Japan, Denmark, Finland, Luxembourg, and New Zealand either ban or severely limit handgun ownership, it must follow that no right to possess such weapons is protected by the Fourteenth Amendment.

This line of argument is, of course, inconsistent with the long-established standard we apply in incorporation cases. And the present-day implications of municipal respondents' argument are stunning. For example, many of the rights that our Bill of Rights provides for persons accused of criminal offenses are virtually unique to this country. If *our* understanding of the right to a jury trial, the right against self-incrimination, and the right to counsel were necessary attributes of *any* civilized country, it would follow that the United States is the only civilized Nation in the world.

Municipal respondents attempt to salvage their position by suggesting that their argument applies only to substantive as opposed to procedural rights. [But] several of the countries that municipal respondents recognize as civilized have established state churches. If we were to adopt municipal respondents' theory, all of this Court's Establishment Clause precedents involving actions taken by state and local governments would go by the boards.

Municipal respondents maintain that the Second Amendment differs from all of the other provisions of the Bill of Rights because it concerns the right to possess a deadly implement and thus has implications for public safety. And they note that there is intense disagreement on the question whether the private possession of guns in the home increases or decreases gun deaths and injuries.

The right to keep and bear arms, however, is not the only constitutional right that has controversial public safety implications. All of the constitutional provisions that impose restrictions on law enforcement and on the prosecution of crimes fall into the same category. Municipal respondents cite no case in which we have refrained from holding that a provision of the Bill of Rights is binding on the States on the ground that the right at issue has disputed public safety implications.

We likewise reject municipal respondents' argument that we should depart from our established incorporation methodology on the ground that making the Second Amendment binding on the States and their subdivisions is inconsistent with principles of federalism and will stifle experimentation. Municipal respondents point out — quite correctly — that conditions and problems differ from locality to locality and that citizens in different jurisdictions have divergent views on the issue of gun control. Municipal respondents therefore urge us to allow state and local governments to enact any gun control law that they deem to be reasonable, including a complete ban on the possession of handguns in the home for self-defense.

There is nothing new in the argument that, in order to respect federalism and allow useful state experimentation, a federal constitutional right should not be fully binding on the States. This argument was made repeatedly and eloquently by Members of this Court who rejected the concept of incorporation and urged retention of the two-track approach to incorporation. Throughout the era of "selective incorporation," Justice Harlan in particular, invoking the values of federalism and state experimentation, fought a determined rearguard action to preserve the two-track approach. Time and again, however, those pleas failed. Unless we turn back the clock or adopt a special incorporation test applicable only to the Second Amendment, municipal respondents' argument must be rejected. Under our precedents, if a Bill of Rights guarantee is fundamental from an American perspective, then, unless *stare decisis* counsels otherwise,[d] that guarantee is fully binding on the States and thus *limits* (but by no means eliminates) their ability to devise solutions to social problems that suit local needs and values.

Municipal respondents and their *amici* complain that incorporation of the Second Amendment right will lead to extensive and costly litigation, but this argument applies with even greater force to constitutional rights and remedies that have already been held to be binding on the States. Consider the exclusionary rule[, which] is said to result in "tens of thousands of contested suppression motions each year."

Municipal respondents assert that, although most state constitutions protect firearms rights, state courts have held that these rights are subject to "interest-balancing" and have sustained a variety of restrictions. In *Heller,* however, we expressly rejected the argument that the scope of the Second Amendment right should be determined by judicial interest balancing, and this Court decades ago abandoned "the notion that the Fourteenth Amendment applies to the States only a watered-down, subjective version of the individual guarantees of the Bill of Rights."

It is important to keep in mind that *Heller,* while striking down a law that prohibited the possession of handguns in the home, recognized that the right to keep and bear arms is not "a right to keep and carry any weapon whatsoever in any manner whatsoever and for whatever purpose." We made it clear in *Heller* that our holding did not cast doubt on such longstanding regulatory measures as "prohibitions on the possession of firearms by felons and the mentally ill," "laws forbidding the carrying of firearms in sensitive places such as schools and government buildings, or laws imposing conditions and qualifications on the commercial sale of arms." We repeat those assurances here. Despite municipal respondents' doomsday proclamations, incorporation does not imperil every law regulating firearms.

Municipal respondents argue, finally, that the right to keep and bear arms is unique among the rights set out in the first eight Amendments "because the reason for codifying the Second Amendment (to protect the militia) differs from the purpose (primarily, to use firearms to engage in self-defense) that is claimed to make the right implicit in the concept of ordered liberty." Municipal respondents

---

d. As noted above, cases that predate the era of selective incorporation held that the Grand Jury Clause of the Fifth Amendment and the Seventh Amendment's civil jury requirement do not apply to the States. See *Hurtado v. California,* 110 U.S. 516 (1884) (indictment); *Minneapolis & St. Louis R. Co. v. Bombolis,* 241 U.S. 211 (1916) (civil jury). As a result of *Hurtado,* most States do not require a grand jury indictment in all felony cases, and many have no grand juries. As a result of *Bombolis,* cases that would otherwise fall within the Seventh Amendment are now tried without a jury in state small claims courts.

suggest that the Second Amendment right differs from the rights heretofore incorporated because the latter were "valued for [their] own sake." But we have never previously suggested that incorporation of a right turns on whether it has intrinsic as opposed to instrumental value, and quite a few of the rights previously held to be incorporated—for example the right to counsel and the right to confront and subpoena witnesses—are clearly instrumental by any measure. Moreover, this contention repackages one of the chief arguments that we rejected in *Heller, i.e.,* that the scope of the Second Amendment right is defined by the immediate threat that led to the inclusion of that right in the Bill of Rights. In *Heller,* we recognized that the codification of this right was prompted by fear that the Federal Government would disarm and thus disable the militias, but we rejected the suggestion that the right was valued only as a means of preserving the militias. On the contrary, we stressed that the right was also valued because the possession of firearms was thought to be essential for self-defense. As we put it, self-defense was "the *central component* of the right itself."

V

Justice Stevens would "'ground the prohibitions against state action squarely on due process, without intermediate reliance on any of the first eight Amendments.'" . . . He would hold that "[t]he rights protected against state infringement by the Fourteenth Amendment's Due Process Clause need not be identical in shape or scope to the rights protected against Federal Government infringement by the various provisions of the Bill of Rights." . . . The relationship between the Bill of Rights' guarantees and the States must be governed by a single, neutral principle. It is far too late to exhume what Justice Brennan, writing for the Court 46 years ago, derided as "the notion that the Fourteenth Amendment applies to the States only a watered-down, subjective version of the individual guarantees of the Bill of Rights." . . .

Justice Breyer's conclusion that the Fourteenth Amendment does not incorporate the right to keep and bear arms appears to rest primarily on four factors: First, "there is no popular consensus" that the right is fundamental; second, the right does not protect minorities or persons neglected by those holding political power; third, incorporation of the Second Amendment right would "amount to a significant incursion on a traditional and important area of state concern, altering the constitutional relationship between the States and the Federal Government" and preventing local variations; and fourth, determining the scope of the Second Amendment right in cases involving state and local laws will force judges to answer difficult empirical questions regarding matters that are outside their area of expertise. . . .

First, we have never held that a provision of the Bill of Rights applies to the States only if there is a "popular consensus" that the right is fundamental, and we see no basis for such a rule. But in this case, as it turns out, there is evidence of such a consensus. An *amicus* brief submitted by 58 Members of the Senate and 251 Members of the House of Representatives urges us to hold that the right to keep and bear arms is fundamental. Another brief submitted by 38 States takes the same position.

Second, petitioners and many others who live in high-crime areas dispute the proposition that the Second Amendment right does not protect minorities and those lacking political clout. The plight of Chicagoans living in high-crime areas was recently highlighted when two Illinois legislators representing Chicago districts called on the Governor to deploy the Illinois National Guard to patrol the City's streets. The legislators noted that the number of Chicago homicide victims during the current year equaled the number of American soldiers killed during that same period in Afghanistan and Iraq and that 80% of the Chicago victims were black. *Amici* supporting incorporation of the right to keep and bear arms contend that the right is especially important for women and members of other groups that may be especially vulnerable to violent crime. If, as petitioners believe, their safety and the safety of other law-abiding members of the community would be enhanced by the possession of handguns in the home for self-defense, then the Second Amendment right protects the rights of minorities and other residents of high-crime areas whose needs are not being met by elected public officials.

Third, Justice Breyer is correct that incorporation of the Second Amendment right will to some extent limit the legislative freedom of the States, but this is always true when a Bill of Rights provision is incorporated. Incorporation always restricts experimentation and local variations, but that has not stopped the Court from incorporating virtually every other provision of the Bill of Rights. . . .

Finally, Justice Breyer is incorrect that incorporation will require judges to assess the costs and benefits of firearms restrictions and thus to make difficult empirical judgments in an area in which they lack expertise. As we have noted, while his opinion in *Heller* recommended an interest-balancing test, the Court specifically rejected that suggestion.

In *Heller,* we held that the Second Amendment protects the right to possess a handgun in the home for the purpose of self-defense. Unless considerations of *stare decisis* counsel otherwise, a provision of the Bill of Rights that protects a right that is fundamental from an American perspective applies equally to the Federal Government and the States. We therefore hold that the Due Process Clause of the Fourteenth Amendment incorporates the Second Amendment right recognized in *Heller.* The judgment of the Court of Appeals is reversed, and the case is remanded for further proceedings.

It is so ordered.

Justice SCALIA, concurring.

I join the Court's opinion. Despite my misgivings about Substantive Due Process as an original matter, I have acquiesced in the Court's incorporation of certain guarantees in the Bill of Rights "because it is both long established and narrowly limited." This case does not require me to reconsider that view, since straightforward application of settled doctrine suffices to decide it. . . .

Justice Stevens . . . urge[s] readoption of the theory of incorporation articulated in *Palko v. Connecticut,* [but] whether *Palko* requires only that "a fair and enlightened system of justice would be impossible without" the right sought to be incorporated, or requires in addition that the right be rooted in the "traditions and conscience of our people," many of the rights Justice Stevens thinks are incorporated could not past muster under either test: abortion (*Planned Parenthood of Southeastern Pa. v. Casey*); homosexual sodomy (*Lawrence v. Texas*); the right to have excluded from criminal trials evidence obtained in violation of the Fourth Amendment (*Mapp v. Ohio*); and the right to teach one's children foreign languages (*Meyer v. Nebraska*), among others.

Justice THOMAS, concurring in part and concurring in the judgment.

I agree with the Court that the Fourteenth Amendment makes the right to keep and bear arms set forth in the Second Amendment "fully applicable to the States." I write separately because I believe there is a more straightforward path to this conclusion, one that is more faithful to the Fourteenth Amendment's text and history. . . . [T]he right to keep and bear arms is a privilege of American citizenship that applies to the States through the Fourteenth Amendment's Privileges or Immunities Clause. . . .

While this Court has at times concluded that a right gains "fundamental" status only if it is essential to the American "scheme of ordered liberty" or "'deeply rooted in this Nation's history and tradition,'" the Court has just as often held that a right warrants Due Process Clause protection if it satisfies a far less measurable range of criteria, see *Lawrence v. Texas,* 539 U.S. 558, 562 (2003) (concluding that the Due Process Clause protects "liberty of the person both in its spatial and in its more transcendent dimensions"). Using the latter approach, the Court has determined that the Due Process Clause applies rights against the States that are not mentioned in the Constitution at all, even without seriously arguing that the Clause was originally understood to protect such rights. See, *e.g., Lochner v. New York,* 198 U.S. 45 (1905); *Roe v. Wade,* 410 U.S. 113 (1973); *Lawrence, supra.*

All of this is a legal fiction. The notion that a constitutional provision that guarantees only "process" before a person is deprived of life, liberty, or property could define the substance of those rights strains credulity for even the most casual user of words. Moreover, this fiction is a particularly dangerous one. The one theme that links the Court's substantive due process precedents together is their lack of a guiding principle to distinguish "fundamental" rights that warrant protection from nonfundamental rights that do not. Today's decision illustrates the point. Replaying a debate that has endured from the inception of the Court's substantive due process jurisprudence, the dissents laud the "flexibility" in this Court's substantive due process doctrine, while the plurality makes yet another effort to impose principled restraints on its exercise. But neither side argues that the meaning they attribute to the Due Process Clause was consistent with public understanding at the time of its ratification.

To be sure, the plurality's effort to cabin the exercise of judicial discretion under the Due Process Clause by focusing its inquiry on those rights deeply rooted in American history and tradition invites less opportunity for abuse than the alternatives. But any serious argument over the scope of the Due Process Clause must acknowledge that neither its text nor its history suggests that it protects the many substantive rights this Court's cases now claim it does.

I cannot accept a theory of constitutional interpretation that rests on such tenuous footing. This Court's substantive due process framework fails to account for both the text of the Fourteenth Amendment and the history that led to its adoption, filling that gap with a jurisprudence devoid of a guiding principle. I believe the original meaning of the Fourteenth Amendment offers a superior alternative, and that a return to that meaning would allow this Court to enforce the rights the Fourteenth Amendment is designed to protect with greater clarity and predictability than the substantive due process framework has so far managed.

I acknowledge the volume of precedents that have been built upon the substantive due process framework, and I further acknowledge the importance of *stare decisis* to the stability of our Nation's legal system. But *stare decisis* is only an "adjunct" of our duty as judges to decide by our best lights what the Constitution means. It is not "an inexorable command." *Lawrence*. Moreover, as judges, we interpret the Constitution one case or controversy at a time. The question presented in this case is not whether our entire Fourteenth Amendment jurisprudence must be preserved or revised, but only whether, and to what extent, a particular clause in the Constitution protects the particular right at issue here. With the inquiry appropriately narrowed, I believe this case presents an opportunity to reexamine, and begin the process of restoring, the meaning of the Fourteenth Amendment agreed upon by those who ratified it.

II

[T]he objective . . . is to discern what "ordinary citizens" at the time of ratification would have understood the Privileges or Immunities Clause to mean.

At the time of Reconstruction, the terms "privileges" and "immunities" had an established meaning as synonyms for "rights." The two words, standing alone or paired together, were used interchangeably with the words "rights," "liberties," and "freedoms," and had been since the time of Blackstone. . . . By the time of Reconstruction, it had long been established that both the States and the Federal Government existed to preserve their citizens' inalienable rights, and that these rights were considered "privileges" or "immunities" of citizenship. . . .

Section 1 protects the rights of citizens "of the United States" specifically. The evidence overwhelmingly demonstrates that the privileges and immunities of such citizens included individual rights enumerated in the Constitution, including the right to keep and bear arms.

Nineteenth-century treaties through which the United States acquired territory from other sovereigns routinely promised inhabitants of the newly acquired territories that they would enjoy all of the "rights," "privileges," and "immunities" of United States citizens. . . . Commentators of the time explained that the rights and immunities of "citizens of the United States" recognized in these treaties "undoubtedly mean[t] those privileges that are common to all citizens of this republic." It is therefore altogether unsurprising that several of these treaties identify liberties enumerated in the Constitution as privileges and immunities common to all United States citizens. . . .

Evidence from the political branches in the years leading to the Fourteenth Amendment's adoption demonstrates broad public understanding that the privileges and immunities of United States citizenship included rights set forth in the Constitution. . . . In 1868, President Andrew Johnson issued a proclamation granting amnesty to former Confederates, guaranteeing "to all and to every person who directly or indirectly participated in the late insurrection or rebellion, a full pardon and amnesty for the offence of treason . . . with restoration of *all rights, privileges, and immunities under the Constitution* and the laws which have been made in pursuance thereof." 15 Stat. 712. . . .

After the Civil War, Congress established the Joint Committee on Reconstruction to investigate circumstances in the Southern States and to determine whether, and on what conditions, those States should be readmitted to the Union. That Committee would ultimately recommend the adoption of the Fourteenth Amendment, justifying its recommendation by submitting a report to Congress that extensively catalogued the abuses of civil rights in the former slave States and argued that "adequate security for future peace and safety . . . can only be found in such changes of the organic law as shall determine the civil rights and privileges of all citizens in all parts of the republic." As the Court notes, the Committee's Report "was widely reprinted in the press and distributed by members of the 39th Congress to their constituents." In addition, newspaper coverage suggests that the wider public was aware of the Committee's work even before the Report was issued. . . .

Statements made by Members of Congress leading up to, and during, the debates on the Fourteenth Amendment point in the same direction. . . . When interpreting constitutional text, the goal is to discern the most likely public understanding of a particular provision at the time it was adopted. Statements by legislators can assist in this process to the extent they demonstrate the manner in which the public used or understood a particular word or phrase. They can further assist to the extent there is evidence that these statements were disseminated to the public. In other words, this evidence is useful not because it demonstrates what the draftsmen of the text may have been thinking, but only insofar as it illuminates what the public understood the words chosen by the draftsmen to mean.

[Justice Thomas discusses speeches by John Bingham, the primary drafter of the Fourteenth Amendment, and Jacob Howard, the Amendment's floor manager in the Senate, stating that the Privileges or Immunities Clause would enforce the Bill of Rights against the states.] As a whole, these well-circulated speeches indicate that §1 was understood to enforce constitutionally declared rights against the States, and they provide no suggestion that any language in the section other than the Privileges or Immunities Clause would accomplish that task. [T]he civil rights legislation adopted by the 39th Congress in 1866 further supports this view. . . . Both proponents and opponents of [the 1866 Civil Rights] Act described it as providing the "privileges" of citizenship to freedmen, and defined those privileges to include constitutional rights, such as the right to keep and bear arms. . . . Three months later, Congress passed the Freedmen's Bureau Act, which also entitled all citizens to the "full and equal benefit of all laws and proceedings concerning personal liberty" and "personal security." Act of July 16, 1866, ch. 200, §14, 14 Stat. 176. The Act stated expressly that the rights of personal liberty and security protected by the Act "includ[ed] the constitutional right to bear arms." . . .

Many statements by Members of Congress corroborate the view that the Privileges or Immunities Clause enforced constitutionally enumerated rights against the States. I am not aware of any statement that directly refutes that proposition. That said, the record of the debates—like most legislative history— is less than crystal clear. In particular, much ambiguity derives from the fact that at least several Members described §1 as protecting the privileges and immunities of citizens "in the several States," harkening back to Article IV, §2. These statements can be read to support the view that the Privileges or Immunities Clause protects some or all the fundamental rights of "citizens" described in *Corfield*. They can also be read to support the view that the Privileges or Immunities Clause, like Article IV, §2, prohibits only state discrimination with respect to those rights it covers, but does not deprive States of the power to deny those rights to all citizens equally. [Nevertheless,] it is significant that the most widely publicized statements by the legislators who voted on §1 . . . point unambiguously toward the conclusion that the Privileges or Immunities Clause enforces at least those fundamental rights enumerated in the Constitution against the States, including the Second Amendment right to keep and bear arms. . . . As the Court demonstrates, there can be no doubt that §1 was understood to enforce the Second Amendment against the States. In my view, this is because the right to keep and bear arms was understood to be a privilege of American citizenship guaranteed by the Privileges or Immunities Clause. . . .

III

[T]here was no reason [for the Court in *Slaughter-House*] to interpret the Privileges or Immunities Clause as putting the Court to the extreme choice of interpreting the "privileges and immunities" of federal citizenship to mean either all those rights listed in *Corfield* [v. *Coryell*], or almost no rights at all. The record is scant that the public understood the Clause to make the Federal Government "a perpetual censor upon all legislation of the States" as the *Slaughter-House* majority feared. For one thing, *Corfield* listed the "elective franchise" as one of the privileges and immunities of "citizens of the several states," yet Congress and the States still found it necessary to adopt the Fifteenth Amendment—which protects "[t]he right of citizens of the United States to vote"—two years after the Fourteenth Amendment's passage. If the Privileges or Immunities Clause were understood to protect every conceivable civil right from state abridgment, the Fifteenth Amendment would have been redundant.

The better view, in light of the States and Federal Government's shared history of recognizing certain inalienable rights in their citizens, is that the privileges and immunities of state and federal citizenship overlap. This is not to say that the privileges and immunities of state and federal citizenship are the same. At the time of the Fourteenth Amendment's ratification, States performed many more functions than the Federal Government, and it is unlikely that, simply by referring to "privileges or immunities," the Framers of §1 meant to transfer every right mentioned in *Corfield* to congressional oversight. . . . Because the privileges and immunities of American citizenship include rights enumerated in the Constitution, they overlap to at least some extent with the privileges and immunities traditionally recognized in citizens in the several States.

A separate question is whether the privileges and immunities of American citizenship include any rights besides those enumerated in the Constitution. The four dissenting Justices in *Slaughter-House* would have held that the Privileges or Immunities Clause protected the unenumerated right that the butchers in that case asserted. Because this case does not involve an unenumerated right, it is not necessary to resolve the question whether the Clause protects such rights, or whether the Court's judgment in *Slaughter-House* was correct.

Still, it is argued that the mere possibility that the Privileges or Immunities Clause may enforce unenumerated rights against the States creates "'special hazards'" that should prevent this Court from returning to the original meaning of the Clause. Ironically, the same objection applies to the Court's substantive due process jurisprudence, which illustrates the risks of granting judges broad discretion to recognize individual constitutional rights in the absence of textual or historical guideposts. But I see no reason to assume that such hazards apply to the Privileges or Immunities Clause. The mere fact that the Clause does not expressly list the rights it protects does not render it incapable of principled judicial application. The Constitution contains many provisions that require an examination of more than just constitutional text to determine whether a particular act is within Congress' power or is otherwise prohibited. See, *e.g.,* Art. I, §8, cl. 18 (Necessary and Proper Clause); Amdt. 8 (Cruel and Unusual Punishments Clause). When the inquiry focuses on what the ratifying era understood the Privileges or Immunities Clause to mean, interpreting it should be no more "hazardous" than interpreting these other constitutional provisions by using the same approach. To be sure, interpreting the Privileges or Immunities Clause may produce hard questions. But they will have the advantage of being questions the Constitution asks us to answer. I believe those questions are more worthy of this Court's attention—and far more likely to yield discernable answers—than the substantive due process questions the Court has for years created on its own, with neither textual nor historical support. . . .

. . . *Cruikshank* squarely held that the right to keep and bear arms was not a privilege of American citizenship, thereby overturning the convictions of militia members responsible for the brutal Colfax Massacre. *Cruikshank* is not a precedent entitled to any respect. . . . *Cruikshank*'s holding that blacks could look only to state governments for protection of their right to keep and bear arms enabled private forces, often with the assistance of local governments, to subjugate the newly freed slaves and their descendants through a wave of private violence designed to drive blacks from the voting booth and force them into peonage, an effective return to slavery. Without federal enforcement of the inalienable right to keep and bear arms, these militias and mobs were tragically successful in waging a campaign of terror against the very people the Fourteenth Amendment had just made citizens.

Organized terrorism . . . proliferated in the absence of federal enforcement of constitutional rights. Militias such as the Ku Klux Klan, the Knights of the White Camellia, the White Brotherhood, the Pale Faces, and the '76 Association spread terror among blacks and white Republicans by breaking up Republican meetings, threatening political leaders, and whipping black militiamen. These groups raped, murdered, lynched, and robbed as a means of intimidating, and instilling pervasive fear in, those whom they despised. . . . Klan tactics remained a constant presence in the lives of Southern blacks for decades. Between 1882 and 1968, there were at least 3,446 reported lynchings of blacks in the South. They were tortured and killed for a wide array of alleged crimes, without even the slightest hint of due process. . . . The use of firearms for self-defense was often the only way black citizens could protect themselves from mob violence. . . .

In my view, the record makes plain that the Framers of the Privileges or Immunities Clause and the ratifying-era public understood—just as the Framers of the Second Amendment did—that the right to keep and bear arms was essential to the preservation of liberty. The record makes equally plain that they deemed this right necessary to include in the minimum baseline of federal rights that the Privileges or Immunities Clause established in the wake of the War over slavery. There is nothing about *Cruikshank*'s contrary holding that warrants its retention. . . .

Justice STEVENS, dissenting.

[T]he question we should be answering in this case is whether the Constitution "guarantees individuals a fundamental right," enforceable against the States, "to possess a functional, personal firearm, including a handgun, within the home." That is a different—and more difficult—inquiry than asking if the Fourteenth Amendment "incorporates" the Second Amendment. The so-called incorporation question was squarely and, in my view, correctly resolved in the late 19th century. . . .

[Petitioners] marshal an impressive amount of historical evidence for their argument that the Court interpreted the Privileges or Immunities Clause too narrowly in the *Slaughter-House Cases*. But the original meaning of the Clause is not as clear as they suggest—and not nearly as clear as it would need to be to dislodge 137 years of precedent. The burden is severe for those who seek radical change in such an established body of constitutional doctrine. Moreover, the suggestion that invigorating the Privileges or Immunities Clause will reduce judicial discretion, strikes me as implausible, if not exactly backwards. "For the very reason that it has so long remained a clean slate, a revitalized Privileges or Immunities Clause holds special hazards for judges who are mindful that their proper task is not to write their personal views of appropriate public policy into the Constitution."

I further agree with the plurality that there are weighty arguments supporting petitioners' second submission, insofar as it concerns the possession of firearms for lawful self-defense in the home. But these arguments are less compelling than the plurality suggests; they are much less compelling when applied outside the home; and their validity does not depend on the Court's holding in *Heller*. For that holding sheds no light on the meaning of the Due Process Clause of the Fourteenth Amendment. Our decisions construing that Clause to render various procedural guarantees in the Bill of Rights enforceable against the States likewise tell us little about the meaning of the word "liberty" in the Clause or about the scope of its protection of nonprocedural rights. This is a substantive due process case. . . .

The rights protected against state infringement by the Fourteenth Amendment's Due Process Clause need not be identical in shape or scope to the rights protected against Federal Government infringement by the various provisions of the Bill of Rights. . . . Elementary considerations of constitutional text and structure suggest there may be legitimate reasons to hold state governments to different standards than the Federal Government in certain areas. . . . [W]e have never accepted a "total incorporation" theory of the Fourteenth Amendment. . . . We have, moreover, resisted a uniform approach to the Sixth Amendment's criminal jury guarantee, demanding 12-member panels and unanimous verdicts in federal trials, yet not in state trials. See *Apodaca v. Oregon*, 406 U.S. 404 (1972) (plurality opinion). . . . [T]he "incorporation" of a provision of the Bill of Rights into the Fourteenth Amendment does not, in itself, mean the provision must have precisely the same meaning in both contexts.

It is true, as well, that during the 1960's the Court decided a number of cases involving procedural rights in which it treated the Due Process Clause as if it transplanted language from the Bill of Rights into the Fourteenth Amendment. . . . "Jot-for-jot" incorporation was the norm in this expansionary era. Yet at least one subsequent opinion suggests that these precedents require perfect state/federal congruence only on matters "'at the core'" of the relevant constitutional guarantee. In my judgment, this line of cases is best understood as having concluded that, to ensure a criminal trial satisfies essential standards of fairness, some procedures should be the same in state and federal courts: The need for certainty and uniformity is more pressing, and the margin for error slimmer, when criminal justice is at issue. That principle has little relevance to the question whether a *non* procedural rule set forth in the Bill of Rights qualifies as an aspect of the liberty protected by the Fourteenth Amendment.

Notwithstanding some overheated dicta in *Malloy,* it is therefore an over-statement to say that the Court has "abandoned," a "two-track approach to incor-poration." The Court moved away from that approach in the area of criminal procedure. But the Second Amendment differs in fundamental respects from its neighboring provisions in the Bill of Rights, and if some 1960's opinions pur-ported to establish a general method of incorporation, that hardly binds us in this case. The Court has not hesitated to cut back on perceived Warren Court excesses in more areas than I can count.

I do not mean to deny that there can be significant practical, as well as esthetic, benefits from treating rights symmetrically with regard to the State and Federal Governments. Jot-for-jot incorporation of a provision may entail greater protec-tion of the right at issue and therefore greater freedom for those who hold it; jot-for-jot incorporation may also yield greater clarity about the contours of the legal rule. In a federalist system such as ours, however, this approach can carry sub-stantial costs. When a federal court insists that state and local authorities follow its dictates on a matter not critical to personal liberty or procedural justice, the latter may be prevented from engaging in the kind of beneficent "experimenta-tion in things social and economic" that ultimately redounds to the benefit of all Americans. *New State Ice Co. v. Liebmann,* 285 U.S. 262, 311 (1932) (Brandeis, J., dissenting). The costs of federal courts' imposing a uniform national standard may be especially high when the relevant regulatory interests vary significantly across localities, and when the ruling implicates the States' core police powers.

Furthermore, there is a real risk that, by demanding the provisions of the Bill of Rights apply identically to the States, federal courts will cause those provi-sions to "be watered down in the needless pursuit of uniformity." When one legal standard must prevail across dozens of jurisdictions with disparate needs and customs, courts will often settle on a relaxed standard. This watering-down risk is particularly acute when we move beyond the narrow realm of criminal procedure and into the relatively vast domain of substantive rights. So long as the requirements of fundamental fairness are always and everywhere respected, it is not clear that greater liberty results from the jot-for-jot application of a provision of the Bill of Rights to the States. Indeed, it is far from clear that pro-ponents of an individual right to keep and bear arms ought to celebrate today's decision. . . .

IV

The question in this case, then, is not whether the Second Amendment right to keep and bear arms (whatever that right's precise contours) applies to the States because the Amendment has been incorporated into the Fourteenth Amendment. It has not been. The question, rather, is whether the particular right asserted by petitioners applies to the States because of the Fourteenth Amendment itself, standing on its own bottom. . . . [T]he liberty interest petitioners have asserted is the "right to possess a functional, personal firearm, including a handgun, within the home." . . . Petitioners now frame the question that confronts us as "[w]hether the Second Amendment right to keep and bear arms is incorporated as against the States by the Fourteenth Amendment's Privileges or Immunities or Due Process Clauses." But it is our duty "to focus on the allegations in the complaint to determine how petitioner describes the constitutional right at stake," and the gravamen of this complaint is plainly an appeal to keep a handgun or other firearm of one's choosing in the home. . . . The majority opinion [in *Heller*] contained some dicta suggesting the possibility of a more expansive arms-bearing right, one that would travel with the individual to an extent into public places, as "in case of confrontation." But the *Heller* plaintiff sought only dispensation to keep an operable firearm in his home for lawful self-defense, and the Court's opinion was bookended by reminders that its holding was limited to that one issue. The distinction between the liberty right these petitioners have asserted and the Second Amendment right identified in *Heller* is therefore evanescent. . . .

In their briefs to this Court, several *amici* have sought to bolster petitioners' claim still further by invoking a right to individual self-defense. As petitioners note, the *Heller* majority discussed this subject extensively and remarked that "[t]he inherent right of self-defense has been central to the Second Amendment right." . . . But that is not the case before us. Petitioners have not asked that we establish a constitutional right to individual self-defense; neither their pleadings in the District Court nor their filings in this Court make any such request. Nor do petitioners contend that the city of Chicago—which, recall, allows its residents to keep most rifles and shotguns, and to keep them loaded—has unduly burdened any such right. What petitioners have asked is that we "incorporate" the Second Amendment and thereby establish a constitutional entitlement, enforceable against the States, to keep a handgun in the home. . . .

Of course, owning a handgun may be useful for practicing self-defense. But the right to take a certain type of action is analytically distinct from the right to acquire and utilize specific instrumentalities in furtherance of that action. And while some might favor handguns, it is not clear that they are a superior weapon for lawful self-defense, and nothing in petitioners' argument turns on that being the case. The notion that a right of self-defense *implies* an auxiliary right to own a certain type of firearm presupposes not only controversial judgments about the strength and scope of the (posited) self-defense right, but also controversial assumptions about the likely effects of making that type of firearm more broadly available. It is a very long way from the proposition that the Fourteenth Amendment protects a basic individual right of self-defense to the conclusion that a city may not ban handguns. . . .

V

While I agree with the Court that our substantive due process cases offer a principled basis for holding that petitioners have a constitutional right to possess a usable firearm in the home, I am ultimately persuaded that a better reading of our case law supports the city of Chicago. I would not foreclose the possibility that a particular plaintiff — say, an elderly widow who lives in a dangerous neighborhood and does not have the strength to operate a long gun — may have a cognizable liberty interest in possessing a handgun. But I cannot accept petitioners' broader submission. A number of factors, taken together, lead me to this conclusion.

First, firearms have a fundamentally ambivalent relationship to liberty. Just as they can help homeowners defend their families and property from intruders, they can help thugs and insurrectionists murder innocent victims. The threat that firearms will be misused is far from hypothetical, for gun crime has devastated many of our communities. *Amici* calculate that approximately one million Americans have been wounded or killed by gunfire in the last decade. Urban areas such as Chicago suffer disproportionately from this epidemic of violence. Handguns contribute disproportionately to it. Just as some homeowners may prefer handguns because of their small size, light weight, and ease of operation, some criminals will value them for the same reasons. In recent years, handguns were reportedly used in more than four-fifths of firearm murders and more than half of all murders nationwide.

Hence, in evaluating an asserted right to be free from particular gun-control regulations, liberty is on both sides of the equation. Guns may be useful for self-defense, as well as for hunting and sport, but they also have a unique potential to facilitate death and destruction and thereby to destabilize ordered liberty. *Your* interest in keeping and bearing a certain firearm may diminish *my* interest in being and feeling safe from armed violence. And while granting you the right to own a handgun might make you safer on any given day — assuming the handgun's marginal contribution to self-defense outweighs its marginal contribution to the risk of accident, suicide, and criminal mischief — it may make you and the community you live in less safe overall, owing to the increased number of handguns in circulation. It is at least reasonable for a democratically elected legislature to take such concerns into account in considering what sorts of regulations would best serve the public welfare.

The practical impact of various gun-control measures may be highly controversial, but this basic insight should not be. The idea that deadly weapons pose a distinctive threat to the social order — and that reasonable restrictions on their usage therefore impose an acceptable burden on one's personal liberty — is as old as the Republic. . . .

Limiting the federal constitutional right to keep and bear arms to the home complicates the analysis but does not dislodge this conclusion. Even though the Court has long afforded special solicitude for the privacy of the home, we have never understood that principle to "infring[e] upon" the authority of the States to proscribe certain inherently dangerous items, for "[i]n such cases, compelling reasons may exist for overriding the right of the individual to possess those materials." And, of course, guns that start out in the home may not stay in the home. Even if the government has a weaker basis for restricting domestic possession of firearms as compared to public carriage—and even if a blanket, statewide prohibition on domestic possession might therefore be unconstitutional—the line between the two is a porous one. A state or local legislature may determine that a prophylactic ban on an especially portable weapon is necessary to police that line.

Second, the right to possess a firearm of one's choosing is different in kind from the liberty interests we have recognized under the Due Process Clause. Despite the plethora of substantive due process cases that have been decided in the post-*Lochner* century, I have found none that holds, states, or even suggests that the term "liberty" encompasses either the common-law right of self-defense or a right to keep and bear arms. I do not doubt for a moment that many Americans feel deeply passionate about firearms, and see them as critical to their way of life as well as to their security. Nevertheless, it does not appear to be the case that the ability to own a handgun, or any particular type of firearm, is critical to leading a life of autonomy, dignity, or political equality: The marketplace offers many tools for self-defense, even if they are imperfect substitutes, and neither petitioners nor their *amici* make such a contention. Petitioners' claim is not the kind of substantive interest, accordingly, on which a uniform, judicially enforced national standard is presumptively appropriate. . . .

The liberty interest asserted by petitioners is also dissimilar from those we have recognized in its capacity to undermine the security of others. To be sure, some of the Bill of Rights' procedural guarantees may place "restrictions on law enforcement" that have "controversial public safety implications." But those implications are generally quite attenuated. A defendant's invocation of his right to remain silent, to confront a witness, or to exclude certain evidence cannot directly cause any threat. The defendant's liberty interest is constrained by (and is itself a constraint on) the adjudicatory process. The link between handgun ownership and public safety is much tighter. The handgun is itself a tool for crime; the handgun's bullets *are* the violence.

Similarly, it is undeniable that some may take profound offense at a remark made by the soapbox speaker, the practices of another religion, or a gay couple's choice to have intimate relations. But that offense is moral, psychological, or theological in nature; the actions taken by the rights-bearers do not actually threaten the physical safety of any other person. Firearms may be used to kill another person. If a legislature's response to dangerous weapons ends up impinging upon the liberty of any individuals in pursuit of the greater good, it invariably does so on the basis of more than the majority's "'own moral code,'" *Lawrence* (quoting *Casey*). While specific policies may of course be misguided, gun control is an area in which it "is quite wrong . . . to assume that regulation and liberty occupy mutually exclusive zones—that as one expands, the other must contract."

Third, the experience of other advanced democracies, including those that share our British heritage, undercuts the notion that an expansive right to keep and bear arms is intrinsic to ordered liberty. Many of these countries place restrictions on the possession, use, and carriage of firearms far more onerous than the restrictions found in this Nation. See Municipal Respondents' Brief 21-23 (discussing laws of England, Canada, Australia, Japan, Denmark, Finland, Luxembourg, and New Zealand). That the United States is an international outlier in the permissiveness of its approach to guns does not suggest that our laws are bad laws. It does suggest that this Court may not need to assume responsibility for making our laws still more permissive.

Admittedly, these other countries differ from ours in many relevant respects, including their problems with violent crime and the traditional role that firearms have played in their societies. But they are not so different from the United States that we ought to dismiss their experience entirely. The fact that our oldest allies have almost uniformly found it appropriate to regulate firearms extensively tends to weaken petitioners' submission that the right to possess a gun of one's choosing is fundamental to a life of liberty. While the "American perspective" must always be our focus, it is silly — indeed, arrogant — to think we have nothing to learn about liberty from the billions of people beyond our borders.

Fourth, the Second Amendment differs in kind from the Amendments that surround it, with the consequence that its inclusion in the Bill of Rights is not merely unhelpful but positively harmful to petitioners' claim. Generally, the inclusion of a liberty interest in the Bill of Rights points toward the conclusion that it is of fundamental significance and ought to be enforceable against the States. But the Second Amendment plays a peculiar role within the Bill, as announced by its peculiar opening clause. Even accepting the *Heller* Court's view that the Amendment protects an individual right to keep and bear arms disconnected from militia service, it remains undeniable that "the purpose for which the right was codified" was "to prevent elimination of the militia." It was the States, not private persons, on whose immediate behalf the Second Amendment was adopted. Notwithstanding the *Heller* Court's efforts to write the Second Amendment's preamble out of the Constitution, the Amendment still serves the structural function of protecting the States from encroachment by an overreaching Federal Government.

The Second Amendment, in other words, "is a federalism provision." It is directed at preserving the autonomy of the sovereign States, and its logic therefore "resists" incorporation by a federal court *against* the States. *Ibid.* No one suggests that the Tenth Amendment, which provides that powers not given to the Federal Government remain with "the States," applies to the States; such a reading would border on incoherent, given that the Tenth Amendment exists (in significant part) to safeguard the vitality of state governance. The Second Amendment is no different.

The Court is surely correct that Americans' conceptions of the Second Amendment right evolved over time in a more individualistic direction; that Members of the Reconstruction Congress were urgently concerned about the safety of the newly freed slaves; and that some Members believed that, following ratification of the Fourteenth Amendment, the Second Amendment would apply to the States. But it is a giant leap from these data points to the conclusion that the Fourteenth Amendment "incorporated" the Second Amendment as a matter of original meaning or postenactment interpretation. Consider, for example, that the text of the Fourteenth Amendment says nothing about the Second Amendment or firearms; that there is substantial evidence to suggest that, when the Reconstruction Congress enacted measures to ensure newly freed slaves and Union sympathizers in the South enjoyed the right to possess firearms, it was motivated by antidiscrimination and equality concerns rather than arms-bearing concerns *per se* that many contemporaneous courts and commentators did not understand the Fourteenth Amendment to have had an "incorporating" effect; and that the States heavily regulated the right to keep and bear arms both before and after the Amendment's passage. The Court's narrative largely elides these facts. The complications they raise show why even the most dogged historical inquiry into the "fundamentality" of the Second Amendment right (or any other) necessarily entails judicial judgment—and therefore judicial discretion—every step of the way.

I accept that the evolution in Americans' understanding of the Second Amendment may help shed light on the question whether a right to keep and bear arms is comprised within Fourteenth Amendment "liberty." But the reasons that motivated the Framers to protect the ability of militiamen to keep muskets available for military use when our Nation was in its infancy, or that motivated the Reconstruction Congress to extend full citizenship to the freedmen in the wake of the Civil War, have only a limited bearing on the question that confronts the homeowner in a crime-infested metropolis today. The many episodes of brutal violence against African-Americans that blight our Nation's history, do not suggest that every American must be allowed to own whatever type of firearm he or she desires—just that no group of Americans should be systematically and discriminatorily disarmed and left to the mercy of racial terrorists. And the fact that some Americans may have thought or hoped that the Fourteenth Amendment would nationalize the Second Amendment hardly suffices to justify the conclusion that it did.

Fifth, although it may be true that Americans' interest in firearm possession and state-law recognition of that interest are "deeply rooted" in some important senses, it is equally true that the States have a long and unbroken history of regulating firearms. The idea that States may place substantial restrictions on the right to keep and bear arms short of complete disarmament is, in fact, far more entrenched than the notion that the Federal Constitution protects any such right. Federalism is a far "older and more deeply rooted tradition than is a right to carry," or to own, "any particular kind of weapon."

From the early days of the Republic, through the Reconstruction era, to the present day, States and municipalities have placed extensive licensing requirements on firearm acquisition, restricted the public carriage of weapons, and banned altogether the possession of especially dangerous weapons, including handguns. After the 1860's just as before, the state courts almost uniformly upheld these measures: Apart from making clear that all regulations had to be constructed and applied in a nondiscriminatory manner, the Fourteenth Amendment hardly made a dent. And let us not forget that this Court did not recognize *any* non-militia-related interests under the Second Amendment until two Terms ago, in *Heller*. Petitioners do not dispute the city of Chicago's observation that "[n]o other substantive Bill of Rights protection has been regulated nearly as intrusively" as the right to keep and bear arms.

This history of intrusive regulation is not surprising given that the very text of the Second Amendment calls out for regulation, and the ability to respond to the social ills associated with dangerous weapons goes to the very core of the States' police powers. . . . Compared with today's ruling, most if not all of this Court's decisions requiring the States to comply with other provisions in the Bill of Rights did not exact nearly so heavy a toll in terms of state sovereignty.

Finally, even apart from the States' long history of firearms regulation and its location at the core of their police powers, this is a quintessential area in which federalism ought to be allowed to flourish without this Court's meddling. Whether or not we *can* assert a plausible constitutional basis for intervening, there are powerful reasons why we *should not* do so.

Across the Nation, States and localities vary significantly in the patterns and problems of gun violence they face, as well as in the traditions and cultures of lawful gun use they claim. The city of Chicago, for example, faces a pressing challenge in combating criminal street gangs. Most rural areas do not. The city of Chicago has a high population density, which increases the potential for a gunman to inflict mass terror and casualties. Most rural areas do not. The city of Chicago offers little in the way of hunting opportunities. Residents of rural communities are, one presumes, much more likely to stock the dinner table with game they have personally felled.

Given that relevant background conditions diverge so much across jurisdictions, the Court ought to pay particular heed to state and local legislatures' "right to experiment." So long as the regulatory measures they have chosen are not "arbitrary, capricious, or unreasonable," we should be allowing them to "try novel social and economic" policies. *Ibid.* It "is more in keeping . . . with our status as a court in a federal system," under these circumstances, "to avoid imposing a single solution . . . from the top down."

It is all the more unwise for this Court to limit experimentation in an area "where the best solution is far from clear." Few issues of public policy are subject to such intensive and rapidly developing empirical controversy as gun control. Chicago's handgun ban, in itself, has divided researchers. Of course, on some matters the Constitution requires that we ignore such pragmatic considerations. But the Constitution's text, history, and structure are not so clear on the matter before us — as evidenced by the groundbreaking nature of today's fractured decision — and this Court lacks both the technical capacity and the localized expertise to assess "the wisdom, need, and propriety" of most gun-control measures.

Nor will the Court's intervention bring any clarity to this enormously complex area of law. Quite to the contrary, today's decision invites an avalanche of litigation that could mire the federal courts in fine-grained determinations about which state and local regulations comport with the *Heller* right—the precise contours of which are far from pellucid—under a standard of review we have not even established. The plurality's "assuranc[e]" that "incorporation does not imperil every law regulating firearms," provides only modest comfort. For it is also an admission of just how many different types of regulations are potentially implicated by today's ruling, and of just how ad hoc the Court's initial attempt to draw distinctions among them was in *Heller*. The practical significance of the proposition that "the Second Amendment right is fully applicable to the States," remains to be worked out by this Court over many, many years.

Furthermore, and critically, the Court's imposition of a national standard is still more unwise because the elected branches have shown themselves to be perfectly capable of safeguarding the interest in keeping and bearing arms. The strength of a liberty claim must be assessed in connection with its status in the democratic process. And in this case, no one disputes "that opponents of [gun] control have considerable political power and do not seem to be at a systematic disadvantage in the democratic process," or that "the widespread commitment to an individual right to own guns . . . operates as a safeguard against excessive or unjustified gun control laws." Indeed, there is a good deal of evidence to suggest that, if anything, American lawmakers tend to *under* regulate guns, relative to the policy views expressed by majorities in opinion polls. If a particular State or locality has enacted some "improvident" gun-control measures, as petitioners believe Chicago has done, there is no apparent reason to infer that the mistake will not "eventually be rectified by the democratic process."

This is not a case, then, that involves a "special condition" that "may call for a correspondingly more searching judicial inquiry." *Carolene Products,* 304 U.S., at 153, n.4. Neither petitioners nor those most zealously committed to their views represent a group or a claim that is liable to receive unfair treatment at the hands of the majority. On the contrary, petitioners' views are supported by powerful participants in the legislative process. Petitioners have given us no reason to believe that the interest in keeping and bearing arms entails any special need for judicial lawmaking, or that federal judges are more qualified to craft appropriate rules than the people's elected representatives. Having failed to show why their asserted interest is intrinsic to the concept of ordered liberty or vulnerable to maltreatment in the political arena, they have failed to show why "the word liberty in the Fourteenth Amendment" should be "held to prevent the natural outcome of a dominant opinion" about how to deal with the problem of handgun violence in the city of Chicago. *Lochner,* 198 U.S., at 76 (Holmes, J., dissenting). . . .

Justice BREYER, with whom Justice GINSBURG and Justice SOTOMAYOR join, dissenting.

. . . I can find nothing in the Second Amendment's text, history, or underlying rationale that could warrant characterizing it as "fundamental" insofar as it seeks to protect the keeping and bearing of arms for private self-defense purposes. Nor can I find any justification for interpreting the Constitution as transferring ultimate regulatory authority over the private uses of firearms from democratically elected legislatures to courts or from the States to the Federal Government. I therefore conclude that the Fourteenth Amendment does not "incorporate" the Second Amendment's right "to keep and bear Arms." And I consequently dissent.

I

[T]he Court based its conclusions [in *Heller*] almost exclusively upon its reading of history. But the relevant history in *Heller* was far from clear: Four dissenting Justices disagreed with the majority's historical analysis. And subsequent scholarly writing reveals why disputed history provides treacherous ground on which to build decisions written by judges who are not expert at history.

Since *Heller*, historians, scholars, and judges have continued to express the view that the Court's historical account was flawed. . . . If history, and history alone, is what matters, why would the Court not now reconsider *Heller* in light of these more recently published historical views? At the least, where *Heller*'s historical foundations are so uncertain, why extend its applicability? . . . In my own view, the Court should not look to history alone but to other factors as well—above all, in cases where the history is so unclear that the experts themselves strongly disagree. It should, for example, consider the basic values that underlie a constitutional provision and their contemporary significance. And it should examine as well the relevant consequences and practical justifications that might, or might not, warrant removing an important question from the democratic decisionmaking process.

II

A

In my view, taking *Heller* as a given, the Fourteenth Amendment does not incorporate the Second Amendment right to keep and bear arms for purposes of private self-defense. Under this Court's precedents, to incorporate the private self-defense right the majority must show that the right is, *e.g.*, "fundamental to the American scheme of justice," *Duncan*. And this it fails to do. The majority here, like that in *Heller*, relies almost exclusively upon history to make the necessary showing. But to do so for incorporation purposes is both wrong and dangerous. [O]ur society has historically made mistakes—for example, when considering certain 18th- and 19th-century property rights to be fundamental. And in the incorporation context, as elsewhere, history often is unclear about the answers.

Accordingly, this Court, in considering an incorporation question, has never stated that the historical status of a right is the only relevant consideration. Rather, the Court has either explicitly or implicitly made clear in its opinions that the right in question has remained fundamental over time. . . . I thus think it proper, above all where history provides no clear answer, to look to other factors in considering whether a right is sufficiently "fundamental" to remove it from the political process in every State. I would include among those factors the nature of the right; any contemporary disagreement about whether the right is fundamental; the extent to which incorporation will further other, perhaps more basic, constitutional aims; and the extent to which incorporation will advance or hinder the Constitution's structural aims, including its division of powers among different governmental institutions (and the people as well). Is incorporation needed, for example, to further the Constitution's effort to ensure that the government treats each individual with equal respect? Will it help maintain the democratic form of government that the Constitution foresees? In a word, will incorporation prove consistent, or inconsistent, with the Constitution's efforts to create governmental institutions well suited to the carrying out of its constitutional promises? . . .

B

[I]t is difficult to see how a right that, as the majority concedes, has "largely faded as a popular concern" could possibly be so fundamental that it would warrant incorporation through the Fourteenth Amendment. Hence, the incorporation of the Second Amendment cannot be based on the militia-related aspect of what *Heller* found to be more extensive Second Amendment rights.

[A]s *Heller* concedes, the private self-defense right that the Court would incorporate has nothing to do with "the *reason*" the Framers "codified" the right to keep and bear arms "in a written Constitution." *Heller* immediately adds that the self-defense right was nonetheless "the *central component* of the right." In my view, this is the historical equivalent of a claim that water runs uphill. . . .

Further, there is no popular consensus that the private self-defense right described in *Heller* is fundamental. The plurality suggests that two *amici* briefs filed in the case show such a consensus, but, of course, numerous *amici* briefs have been filed opposing incorporation as well. Moreover, every State regulates firearms extensively, and public opinion is sharply divided on the appropriate level of regulation. Much of this disagreement rests upon empirical considerations. One side believes the right essential to protect the lives of those attacked in the home; the other side believes it essential to regulate the right in order to protect the lives of others attacked with guns. It seems unlikely that definitive evidence will develop one way or the other. And the appropriate level of firearm regulation has thus long been, and continues to be, a hotly contested matter of political debate. See, *e.g.,* Siegel, Dead or Alive: Originalism as Popular Constitutionalism in *Heller,* 122 Harv. L. Rev. 191, 201-246 (2008).

Moreover, there is no reason here to believe that incorporation of the private self-defense right will further any other or broader constitutional objective. We are aware of no argument that gun-control regulations target or are passed with the purpose of targeting "discrete and insular minorities." *Carolene Products Co., supra,* at 153, n.4. Nor will incorporation help to assure equal respect for individuals. Unlike the First Amendment's rights of free speech, free press, assembly, and petition, the private self-defense right does not comprise a necessary part of the democratic process that the Constitution seeks to establish. Unlike the First Amendment's religious protections, the Fourth Amendment's protection against unreasonable searches and seizures, the Fifth and Sixth Amendments' insistence upon fair criminal procedure, and the Eighth Amendment's protection against cruel and unusual punishments, the private self-defense right does not significantly seek to protect individuals who might otherwise suffer unfair or inhumane treatment at the hands of a majority. Unlike the protections offered by many of these same Amendments, it does not involve matters as to which judges possess a comparative expertise, by virtue of their close familiarity with the justice system and its operation. And, unlike the Fifth Amendment's insistence on just compensation, it does not involve a matter where a majority might unfairly seize for itself property belonging to a minority.

Finally, incorporation of the right *will* work a significant disruption in the constitutional allocation of decisionmaking authority, thereby interfering with the Constitution's ability to further its objectives.

First, on any reasonable accounting, the incorporation of the right recognized in *Heller* would amount to a significant incursion on a traditional and important area of state concern, altering the constitutional relationship between the States and the Federal Government. Private gun regulation is the quintessential exercise of a State's "police power"—*i.e.,* the power to "protec[t] . . . the lives, limbs, health, comfort, and quiet of all persons, and the protection of all property within the State," by enacting "all kinds of restraints and burdens" on both "persons and property." . . .

Second, determining the constitutionality of a particular state gun law requires finding answers to complex empirically based questions of a kind that legislatures are better able than courts to make. And it may require this kind of analysis in virtually every case. . . . With respect to other incorporated rights, this sort of inquiry is *sometimes* present. But here, this inquiry—calling for the fine tuning of protective rules—is likely to be part of a daily judicial diet. . . .

Perhaps the Court could lessen the difficulty of the mission it has created for itself by adopting a jurisprudential approach similar to the many state courts that administer a state constitutional right to bear arms. But the Court has not yet done so. Cf. *Heller* (rejecting an " 'interest-balancing' approach" similar to that employed by the States). Rather, the Court has haphazardly created a few simple rules, such as that it will not touch "prohibitions on the possession of firearms by felons and the mentally ill," "laws forbidding the carrying of firearms in sensitive places such as schools and government buildings," or "laws imposing conditions and qualifications on the commercial sale of arms." *Heller.* But why these rules and not others? Does the Court know that these regulations are justified by some special gun-related risk of death? In fact, the Court does not know. It has simply invented rules that sound sensible without being able to explain why or how Chicago's handgun ban is different.

The fact is that judges do not know the answers to the kinds of empirically based questions that will often determine the need for particular forms of gun regulation. Nor do they have readily available "tools" for finding and evaluating the technical material submitted by others. Judges cannot easily make empirically based predictions; they have no way to gather and evaluate the data required to see if such predictions are accurate; and the nature of litigation and concerns about *stare decisis* further make it difficult for judges to change course if predictions prove inaccurate. Nor can judges rely upon local community views and values when reaching judgments in circumstances where prediction is difficult because the basic facts are unclear or unknown.

Legislators are able to "amass the stuff of actual experience and cull conclusions from it." They are far better suited than judges to uncover facts and to understand their relevance. And legislators, unlike Article III judges, can be held democratically responsible for their empirically based and value-laden conclusions. We have thus repeatedly affirmed our preference for "legislative not judicial solutions" to this kind of problem, just as we have repeatedly affirmed the Constitution's preference for democratic solutions legislated by those whom the people elect. . . .

Third, the ability of States to reflect local preferences and conditions—both key virtues of federalism—here has particular importance. The incidence of gun ownership varies substantially as between crowded cities and uncongested rural communities, as well as among the different geographic regions of the country. Thus, approximately 60% of adults who live in the relatively sparsely populated Western States of Alaska, Montana, and Wyoming report that their household keeps a gun, while fewer than 15% of adults in the densely populated Eastern States of Rhode Island, New Jersey, and Massachusetts say the same.

The nature of gun violence also varies as between rural communities and cities. Urban centers face significantly greater levels of firearm crime and homicide, while rural communities have proportionately greater problems with non-homicide gun deaths, such as suicides and accidents. And idiosyncratic local factors can lead to two cities finding themselves in dramatically different circumstances: For example, in 2008, the murder rate was 40 times higher in New Orleans than it was in Lincoln, Nebraska. . . .

Given the empirical and local value-laden nature of the questions that lie at the heart of the issue, why, in a Nation whose Constitution foresees democratic decisionmaking, is it so *fundamental* a matter as to require taking that power from the people? What is it here that the people did not know? What is it that a judge knows better? . . .

I can find much in the historical record that shows that some Americans in some places at certain times thought it important to keep and bear arms for private self-defense. For instance, the reader will see that many States have constitutional provisions protecting gun possession. But, as far as I can tell, those provisions typically do no more than guarantee that a gun regulation will be a *reasonable* police power regulation. It is thus altogether unclear whether such provisions would prohibit cities such as Chicago from enacting laws, such as the law before us, banning handguns. . . . States and localities have consistently enacted firearms regulations, including regulations similar to those at issue here, throughout our Nation's history. Courts have repeatedly upheld such regulations. And it is, at the very least, possible, and perhaps likely, that incorporation will impose on every, or nearly every, State a different right to bear arms than they currently recognize — a right that threatens to destabilize settled state legal principles. . . .

Discussion

1. *Changing places.* The result in *McDonald* was widely expected following the 2008 decision in *Heller.* One remarkable feature of the opinion is how fairly standard arguments made in the past by conservative judges against incorporation and broad readings of the Bill of Rights have become the arguments of liberal judges and vice versa. Justice Stevens argues (as the second Justice Harlan did before him) that the provisions of the Bill of Rights need not apply fully to the states. Justices Stevens and Breyer make standard arguments for judicial restraint and emphasize the inability of judges to fully consider the consequences of new rights; both emphasize that courts should not attempt to intervene in difficult and contested social controversies, and both make standard arguments for respecting states' rights and for the ability of states to experiment with forms of regulation best attuned to local conditions. Justice Alito, on the other hand, emphasizes that constitutional rights must be respected whether or not they may make law enforcement more difficult or even put lives at risk. (Compare Justice Alito's willingness to sacrifice public safety to ensure constitutional liberty with the arguments of the conservative Justices in *Boumediene* a few years previously.) Justice Scalia, for his part, argues that *stare decisis* must trump originalist considerations.

2. *Deeply rooted in our nation's traditions.* While Justice Thomas' concurrence is strongly originalist, Justice Alito's plurality opinion offers an interesting mix of modalities. Justice Alito's approach is not strictly originalist, because he employs the Due Process Clause to incorporate the Second Amendment. On the other hand, he asks whether people in 1791 and 1868 considered the right to keep arms in the home for self-defense to be fundamental, which resembles an originalist inquiry into understandings at the time of the Founding and Reconstruction. But if the test is one of tradition, then Justice Alito should be concerned about a continuous regard for the right up to the present day. Why does he not focus more on respect for this right during the 20th century?

3. *The Civil Rights Act and the Freedman's Bureau Act.* Both Justice Alito and Justice Thomas emphasize congressional intent to protect individual rights to bear arms in self-defense in the Civil Rights Act of 1866 and the Freedman's Bureau Act of 1866. They argue that these acts protected not only equal rights but also substantive guarantees of liberty. The Civil Rights Act of 1866, reenacted as part of the 1870 Enforcement Act under Congress's powers to enforce the Fourteenth Amendment, currently appears at 42 U.S.C. §1981.

According to *McDonald* then, does §1981 already apply the right to bear arms against the states? If so, the constitutional holding of *McDonald* was unnecessary, because the Chicago ordinance (and any other state and local laws violating the right recognized in *Heller*) would be preempted by §1981. (Of course, the Court would still have to decide whether the Civil Rights Act of 1866 and the Enforcement Act of 1870 were constitutional exercises of Congress's powers under the Thirteenth and Fourteenth Amendments, respectively.)

Michael Kent Curtis points out that the intent of Congressional Republicans was not only to protect Second Amendment rights, but the individual rights guarantees of the Bill of Rights generally. See Michael Kent Curtis, No State Shall Abridge: The Fourteenth Amendment and the Bill of Rights 71-83, 104 (1986). If that is so, then §1981 already "incorporated" the Bill of Rights against the states in 1866, including portions that the Supreme Court has not yet incorporated. See Jack M. Balkin, "Supreme Court Holds That Congress Has Incorporated Entire Bill of Rights," Balkinization, July 2, 2010, at http://balkin. blogspot. com/2010/07/supreme-court-holds-that-congress-has.html.

4. *No privileges or immunities for you.* Justice Thomas is the only Justice willing to take seriously the original design of the Fourteenth Amendment. He argues that the Privileges or Immunities Clause was the primary vehicle for protecting substantive rights, not the Due Process Clause. The other eight Justices reject this idea, including Justice Scalia, the Court's other originalist judge. Why is this? One possibility is that the Justices do not know what would happen if the Court used the Privileges or Immunities Clause. Some Justices might fear that implied fundamental rights (like the rights recognized in *Lawrence* and *Casey*) would no longer be protected. Other Justices might fear, to the contrary, that moving to a clause that seems on its face to protect substantive rights would give judges greater discretion to protect new implied fundamental rights. Still other Justices might fear that reviving the Privileges or Immunities Clause would revive *Lochner*-style rights. And still others might fear that this would require incorporating the entire Bill of Rights, including the Seventh Amendment civil jury right and the Fifth Amendment right to grand jury indictments.

Given what you know about the path of doctrinal development in the United States Supreme Court in American history, how realistic are these fears? Is there any reason to think that a Justice who believes there is a right to abortion under the Due Process Clause would believe that such a right is not protected by the Privileges or Immunities Clause? Conversely, is there any reason to think that a Justice who does not think that abortion is a fundamental right under the Due Process Clause would conclude that it is protected as a privilege or immunity? Is there any reason to believe that a shift to the Privileges or Immunities Clause would cause a majority of the Justices (or even Justice Thomas) to reconsider *Lochner v. New York*? If constitutional protection of such rights came back into fashion, it is far more likely that it would be because of large-scale changes in American politics than because of a change in the relevant constitutional language.

Would a shift in focus to the Privileges or Immunities Clause require any significant changes in doctrine? One possibility concerns the rights of noncitizens. The Due Process Clause protects persons as well as citizens. Therefore the Court would have to use the Due Process and Equal Protection Clauses together to explain why non-citizens enjoy the same fundamental rights as citizens. However, this result is consistent with the views of the Reconstruction Era framers. See Akhil Amar, The Bill of Rights: Creation and Reconstruction 172-174 (1998). Another possibility is that the Court would be required to incorporate the remaining individual rights mentioned in the Bill of Rights, including the Third Amendment, the Eighth Amendment's ban on excessive fines, and the Fifth Amendment's guarantee of grand jury indictments. (Of course, as noted above, if the Court's construction of Congressional intent in §1981 is correct, that horse may already be out of the barn door.) It is unclear, however, whether the Seventh Amendment right to civil juries is such an individual right or is rather a structural *Erie*-like provision, requiring federal courts to provide litigants the same right to trial by jury they would receive in the state in which the federal court sits. See *id.* at 275-276.

5. *The effect of a national standard. McDonald* imposes a national standard on gun control measures. What effect will this have? Consider the following analysis:

> The big difference between applying a constitutional right only against the federal government and applying it against state and local governments is that there are many more state and local regulations of firearms than federal regulations, and these regulations occur in many different varieties. This increases the number of possible constitutional claims, and it also increases the opportunities for litigation. It does not, however, guarantee that Second Amendment rights will become too robust over time.
>
> We can guess what is likely to happen from the way that courts have protected other federal constitutional rights against states and local governments in the past. Federal judicial protection of fundamental rights tends to converge toward the preferences of the national political coalition, which includes executive branch and law enforcement officials. Federal courts tend to strike down mostly laws in outlier jurisdictions that are markedly different from the norm. That is what happened in the District of Columbia, and will likely happen in Chicago. More than 40 states already recognize an individual right to bear arms under their own constitutions. By and large, they have upheld most gun control laws under a loose standard of reasonableness. The federal courts will probably follow suit.
>
> Gun control advocates are concerned that a single federal rule for gun rights will leave urban areas defenseless. Ironically, however, a national standard that lumps cities and rural areas together is far more likely to produce moderation than radical change. That is because many more people live in metropolitan than in rural areas, and in the long run their preferences will shape the national political coalition.

Jack M. Balkin, "Creating a National Norm," New York Times, June 28, 2010, at http://roomfordebate.blogs.nytimes.com/2010/06/28/what-bolstering-gun-rights-will-mean/#jack. In a footnote in his dissenting opinion, Justice Stevens argues that following incorporation, "federal courts will face a profound pressure to reconcile [a single national] standard with the diverse interests of the States and their long history of regulating in this sensitive area. . . . [F]ederal courts will have little choice but to fix a highly flexible standard of review if they are to avoid leaving federalism and the separation of powers—not to mention gun policy—in shambles."

Do you agree? Another lesson of political science studies is that rights protections tend to expand if there are well-funded and continuous litigation campaigns assisted by other forms of grass-roots political organization. See generally Charles R. Epp, The Rights Revolution: Lawyers, Activists, and Supreme Courts in Comparative Perspective (1998). Why won't a sustained litigation campaign by conservative public interest organizations and by interest groups such as the National Rifle Association lead to increasingly stronger gun rights?

Chapter 5

Economic Regulation, Federalism, and Separation of Powers in the Modern Era

Insert the following before section 2 on p. 627:

UNITED STATES v. COMSTOCK, 560 U.S. 126 (2010): By a 7-2 vote, the Supreme Court upheld a federal civil commitment statute as within Congress's powers under the Necessary and Proper Clause without reaching any questions of its constitutionality under the Bill of Rights. 18 U.S.C. §4248 allows a district court to order the civil commitment of a mentally ill, sexually dangerous federal prisoner beyond the date he would otherwise be released. The statute authorizes the federal government to request civil commitment if neither the State of a prisoner's domicile nor the State in which the prisoner was tried will assume the responsibility for the prisoner's "custody, care, and treatment." §4248(d). The individual must (1) currently be "in the custody of the [Federal] Bureau of Prisons"; (2) have previously "engaged or attempted to engage in sexually violent conduct or child molestation"; (3) currently "suffer from a serious mental illness, abnormality, or disorder"; and (4) "as a result of" that mental illness, abnormality, or disorder be "sexually dangerous to others," in that "he would have serious difficulty in refraining from sexually violent conduct or child molestation if released." §§4247(a)(5)-(6).

Justice Breyer's majority opinion explained that "in determining whether the Necessary and Proper Clause grants Congress the legislative authority to enact a particular federal statute, we look to see whether the statute constitutes a means that is rationally related to the implementation of a constitutionally enumerated power. Sabri v. United States, 541 U.S. 600 (2004) (using term 'means-ends rationality' to describe the necessary relationship)."

"Neither Congress' power to criminalize conduct, nor its power to imprison individuals who engage in that conduct, nor its power to enact laws governing prisons and prisoners, is explicitly mentioned in the Constitution. But Congress nonetheless possesses broad authority to do each of those things" by the "authority granted by the Necessary and Proper Clause."

Justice Breyer pointed out that "Congress has long been involved in the delivery of mental health care to federal prisoners, and has long provided for their civil commitment." In the 1940s, for example, Congress amended its civil commitment regime to take account of mentally ill and mentally incompetent prisoners whose terms have expired, responding to concerns that long sentences of prisoners might sever their connection to any state so that no state would be willing to assume responsibility for them upon release. It was reasonable for Congress to extend its system to mentally ill sexually dangerous prisoners because "the Federal Government is the custodian of its prisoners" and "[a]s federal custodian, it has the constitutional power to act in order to protect nearby (and other) communities from the danger federal prisoners may pose." Section 4248 did not violate state sovereignty protected by the Tenth Amendment because "[t]he powers delegated to the United States by the Constitution include those specifically enumerated powers listed in Article I along with the implementation authority granted by the Necessary and Proper Clause. Virtually by definition, these powers are not powers that the Constitution reserved to the States."

Nor did §4248 "invade state sovereignty or otherwise improperly limit the scope of powers that remain with the States. . . . To the contrary, it requires *accommodation* of state interests: The Attorney General must inform the State in which the federal prisoner 'is domiciled or was tried' that he is detaining some-one with respect to whom those States may wish to assert their authority, and he must encourage those States to assume custody of the individual. He must also immediately 'release' that person 'to the appropriate official of' either State 'if such State will assume [such] responsibility.' And either State has the right, at any time, to assert its authority over the individual, which will prompt the indi-vidual's immediate transfer to State custody."

Finally, Justice Breyer rejected respondents' argument "that, when legislat-ing pursuant to the Necessary and Proper Clause, Congress' authority can be no more than one step removed from a specifically enumerated power. . . . [E]ven the dissent acknowledges that Congress has the implied power to criminalize any conduct that might interfere with the exercise of an enumerated power, and also the additional power to imprison people who violate those (inferentially authorized) laws, and the additional power to provide for the safe and reasonable management of those prisons, and the additional power to regulate the prisoners' behavior even after their release."

Justice Kennedy concurred in the judgment, arguing that the proper test is not the highly deferential minimum rationality test of Williamson v. Lee Optical. "Rather, under the Necessary and Proper Clause, application of a rational basis test should be at least as exacting as it has been in the Commerce Clause cases, if not more so." Commerce Clause precedents like United States v. Lopez, Justice Kennedy argued, "require a tangible link to commerce, not a mere conceivable rational relation, as in *Lee Optical*." They require "a demonstrated link in fact, based on empirical demonstration." Moreover, Justice Kennedy argued, "[i]t is of fundamental importance to consider whether essential attributes of state sov-ereignty are compromised by the assertion of federal power under the Necessary and Proper Clause; if so, that is a factor suggesting that the power is not one properly within the reach of federal power."

Justice Alito also concurred in the judgment, although stating "I am concerned about the breadth of the Court's language, and the ambiguity of the standard that the Court applies." Nevertheless, "[m]ost federal criminal statutes rest upon a congressional judgment that, in order to execute one or more of the powers conferred on Congress, it is necessary and proper to criminalize certain conduct, and in order to do that it is obviously necessary and proper to provide for the operation of a federal criminal justice system and a federal prison system. . . . Just as it is necessary and proper for Congress to provide for the apprehension of escaped federal prisoners, it is necessary and proper for Congress to provide for the civil commitment of dangerous federal prisoners who would otherwise escape civil commitment as a result of federal imprisonment."

"Some years ago, a distinguished study group created by the Judicial Conference of the United States found that, in a disturbing number of cases, no State was willing to assume the financial burden of providing for the civil commitment of federal prisoners who, if left at large after the completion of their sentences, would present a danger to any communities in which they chose to live or visit. These federal prisoners, having been held for years in a federal prison, often had few ties to any State; it was a matter of speculation where they would choose to go upon release; and accordingly no State was enthusiastic about volunteering to shoulder the burden of civil commitment. . . . This is not a case in which it is merely possible for a court to think of a rational basis on which Congress might have perceived an attenuated link between the powers underlying the federal criminal statutes and the challenged civil commitment provision. Here, there is a substantial link to Congress' constitutional powers."

Justice Thomas, joined by Justice Scalia, dissented: "[T]he power to care for the mentally ill and, where necessary, the power to protect the community from the dangerous tendencies of some mentally ill persons, are among the numerous powers that remain with the States. . . . Section 4248 closely resembles the involuntary civil-commitment laws that States have enacted under their *parens patriae* and general police powers. Indeed, it is clear, on the face of the Act and in the Government's arguments urging its constitutionality, that §4248 is aimed at protecting society from acts of sexual violence, not toward carrying into Execution any enumerated power or powers of the Federal Government."

"[P]rotecting society from violent sexual offenders is certainly an important end. . . . But the Constitution does not vest in Congress the authority to protect society from every bad act that might befall it. In my view, this should decide the question. Section 4248 runs afoul of our settled understanding of Congress' power under the Necessary and Proper Clause. Congress may act under that Clause only when its legislation 'carr[ies] into Execution one of the Federal Government's enumerated powers.' Section 4248 does not execute *any* enumerated power. Section 4248 is therefore unconstitutional. . . ."

"The absence of a constitutional delegation of general police power to Congress does not leave citizens vulnerable to the harms Congress seeks to regulate in §4248 because, as recent legislation indicates, the States have the capacity to address the threat that sexual offenders pose. . . . States plainly have the constitutional authority to take charge of a federal prisoner released within their jurisdiction. In addition, the assumption that a State knowingly would fail to exercise that authority is, in my view, implausible. . . . [N]either the Court nor the concurrences argue that a State has the power to refuse such a person domicile within its borders. Thus, they appear to assume that, in the absence of 18 U.S.C. §4248, a State would take no action when informed by the BOP [Bureau of Prisons] that a sexually dangerous federal prisoner was about to be released within its jurisdiction. In light of the plethora of state laws enacted in recent decades to protect communities from sex offenders, the likelihood of such an occurrence seems quite remote. But even in the event a State made such a decision, the Constitution assigns the responsibility for that decision, and its consequences, to the state government alone."

In a portion of the dissent not joined by Justice Scalia, Justice Thomas added: "The Necessary and Proper Clause does not provide Congress with authority to enact any law simply because it furthers *other laws* Congress has enacted in the exercise of its incidental authority; the Clause plainly requires a showing that every federal statute 'carr[ies] into Execution' one or more of the Federal Government's *enumerated* powers. . . . Federal laws that criminalize conduct that interferes with enumerated powers, establish prisons for those who engage in that conduct, and set rules for the care and treatment of prisoners awaiting trial or serving a criminal sentence satisfy this test because each helps to 'carr[y] into Execution' the enumerated powers that justify a criminal defendant's arrest or conviction. For example, Congress' enumerated power '[t]o establish Post Offices and post Roads,' Art. I, §8, cl. 7, would lack force or practical effect if Congress lacked the authority to enact criminal laws 'to punish those who steal letters from the post office, or rob the mail.' Similarly, that enumerated power would be compromised if there were no prisons to hold persons who violate those laws, or if those prisons were so poorly managed that prisoners could escape or demand their release on the grounds that the conditions of their confinement violate their constitutional rights, at least as we have defined them. Civil detention under §4248, on the other hand, lacks any such connection to an enumerated power."

Discussion

1. *Comstock* is based on a familiar justification for federal power: a collective action problem among the states, in this case what is sometimes called a NIMBY ("not in my back yard") problem. Once a known mentally ill sexual predator is released into a state's custody, the state is under enormous pressure to institute its own civil commitment proceedings, at which point the state will be stuck with the costs of taking care of the former prisoner, possibly indefinitely. Therefore no state has an incentive to ask for custody; each hopes that some other state will foot the bill. As Justice Alito puts it, "[t]he statute recognizes that, in many cases, no State will assume the heavy financial burden of civilly committing a dangerous federal prisoner who, as a result of lengthy federal incarceration, no longer has any substantial ties to any State." Most states would be happier if the federal

government simply solved this problem for them (using federal tax money), and that is why 29 states as amicus curiae argued for the constitutionality of the statute. Justices Thomas and Scalia counter that if the federal government simply releases a prisoner into some state's custody, that state will have ample incentives to assume responsibility. This solves the collective action problem a different way, by giving the federal government the power to choose which state will have to bear the costs of long term care and custody. Is this solution more or less respectful of state interests?

2. In its arguments before the Supreme Court, the government declined to base Congress's authority for the civil commitment scheme on the Commerce Clause, relying instead on the Necessary and Proper Clause. Why do you think the government made this choice? Was it correct to do so in light of *Lopez* and *Morrison*?

Consider possible theories under the commerce power: (1) The civil commitment system is "part of a broader regulatory scheme" under *Raich* that would be otherwise undermined; (2) the civil commitment scheme regulates the consumption and travel activities of former federal prisoners; (3) the civil commitment scheme is a reasonable means of preventing states from attempting to dump dangerous former prisoners on other states. Do you think the Court would accept any of these theories, or any other theories under the commerce power?

3. *Subsequent case, United States v. Kebodeaux.* In United States v. Kebodeaux, 133. S. Ct. 2496 (2013), the Supreme Court considered Congress's powers to apply the Sex Offender Registration and Notification Act (SORNA), which requires federal sex offenders to register in the States where they live, study, and work, to a discharged member of the Air Force who had previously been required to register as a sex offender under a predecessor statute, the Wetterling Act. The Court decided, 7-2, that SORNA was within Congress's powers under the Military Regulations Clause and the Necessary and Proper Clause.

Justice Breyer, writing for five Justices, noted that Congress did not apply SORNA to a person who had been "unconditionally released" and who lacked "any . . . special relationship with the federal government." Instead, Kebodeaux was "already subject to [constitutionally valid] federal registration requirements that were themselves a valid exercise of federal power under the Military Regulations Clause."

"Here, under the authority granted to it by the Military Regulation and Necessary and Proper Clauses, Congress could promulgate the Uniform Code of Military Justice. It could specify that the sex offense of which Kebodeaux was convicted was a military crime under that Code. It could punish that crime through imprisonment and by placing conditions upon Kebodeaux's release. And it could make the civil registration requirement at issue here a consequence of Kebodeaux's offense and conviction. This civil requirement, while not a specific condition of Kebodeaux's release, was in place at the time Kebodeaux committed his offense, and was a consequence of his violation of federal law."

Chief Justice Roberts concurred in the judgment, explaining that he disagreed with Justice Breyer's decision "to discuss the general public safety benefits of the registration requirement." To Chief Justice Roberts, this sounded too much like a suggestion that there is a "federal police power," which "does not exist."

Such a power could not be inferred from the Necessary and Proper Clause because it was not "proper." "Chief Justice Marshall was emphatic that no 'great substantive and independent power' can be 'implied as incidental to other powers, or used as a means of executing them.' [*McCulloch.*] . . . It is difficult to imagine a clearer example of such a 'great substantive and independent power' than the power to 'help protect the public . . . and alleviate public safety concerns'. . . . I find it implausible to suppose—and impossible to support—that the Framers intended to confer such authority by implication rather than by expression. A power of that magnitude vested in the Federal Government is not 'consist[ent] with the letter and spirit of the constitution,' *McCulloch*, and thus not a 'proper [means] for carrying into Execution' the enumerated powers of the Federal Government."

Consider Chief Justice Roberts's remarks about the Necessary and Proper Clause in the light of his opinion in *NFIB v. Sebelius*, infra. There Chief Justice Roberts argued that an individual mandate to purchase health insurance, even if "necessary," was not "proper" because it assumed a "great substantive and independent power" to compel people to enter into commercial transactions.

Justice Alito also concurred in the judgment. Justices Scalia and Thomas dissented.

Insert the following after section 2 on p. 629:

NATIONAL FEDERATION OF INDEPENDENT BUSINESS v. SEBELIUS
[The Health Care Case]
132 S. Ct. 1161 (2012)

[In March 2010, Congress enacted the Patient Protection and Affordable Care Act in order to increase the number of Americans covered by health insurance and decrease the cost of health care. Twenty-six states, several individuals, and the National Federation of Independent Business challenged two key provisions of the Act as unconstitutional, and argued that, because the Affordable Care Act lacked a severability clause, the entire Act should be declared unconstitutional.

The first provision is the individual mandate, which requires most Americans to maintain "minimum essential" health insurance coverage. 26 U.S.C. §5000A. Individuals are exempted if they have qualifying health insurance through their employer or otherwise, receive health care through Medicare or Medicaid, are below the poverty line, live outside the country, serve in the military, are dependents, or have a religious objection.

Beginning in 2014, those not exempted who have not purchased qualifying health insurance must make a "[s]hared responsibility payment" to the federal government. In 2016, for example, the payment will be 2.5 percent of an individual's household income, but no less than $695 and no more than the average yearly premium for insurance that covers 60 percent of the cost of ten specified services (for example, prescription drugs and hospitalization).

The Act provides that this "penalty" will be paid by the "taxpayer" to the Internal Revenue Service with "a taxpayer's return," and "shall be assessed and collected in the same manner" as tax penalties, such as the penalty for claiming too large an income tax refund. The Act, however, bars the IRS from using several of its normal enforcement tools, such as criminal prosecutions and levies. And some individuals who are subject to the mandate are nonetheless exempt from the penalty — for example, those with income below a certain threshold and members of Indian tribes.

The second challenged provision is the expansion of Medicaid. The preexisting Medicaid program offers federal funding to states to assist pregnant women, children, needy families, the blind, the elderly, and the disabled in obtaining medical care. The Affordable Care Act expands the scope of the Medicaid program and increases the number of individuals the states must cover. For example, the Act requires state programs to provide Medicaid coverage by 2014 to adults with incomes up to 133 percent of the federal poverty level. Many states before the Act cover adults with children only if their income is considerably lower, and do not cover childless adults at all. The Act increases federal funding to cover the states' costs in expanding Medicaid coverage. Until 2016 the federal government will cover 100 percent of the new costs, reducing gradually to 90 percent. (The percentages that the federal government covers under the existing Medicaid plan vary by state between 50 to 83 percent.) If a state does not comply with the Act's new coverage requirements, it may lose not only the federal funding for those requirements but also all of its federal Medicaid funds.]

Chief Justice ROBERTS announced the judgment of the Court and delivered the opinion of the Court with respect to Parts I, II, and III-C, an opinion with respect to Part IV, in which Justice BREYER and Justice KAGAN join, and an opinion with respect to Parts III-A, III-B, and III-D.

II

[The Tax Anti-Injunction Act provides that "no suit for the purpose of restraining the assessment or collection of any tax shall be maintained in any court by any person, whether or not such person is the person against whom such tax was assessed." 26 U.S.C. §7421(a). Because of the Anti-Injunction Act, taxes can ordinarily be challenged only after they are paid, by suing for a refund, which in this case would prevent courts from hearing challenges to the individual mandate until 2014. Chief Justice Roberts held that Congress did not intend for this provision to apply to the individual mandate, in part because Congress had designated the mandate as a "penalty" rather than as a "tax." Although some "penalties" are subject to the Anti-Injunction Act, Congress had not indicated that the mandate would be one of them. Therefore, the Anti-Injunction Act did not prevent proceeding to the merits.]

III

A

The Government's first argument is that the individual mandate is a valid exercise of Congress's power under the Commerce Clause and the Necessary and Proper Clause. According to the Government, the health care market is characterized by a significant cost-shifting problem. Everyone will eventually need health care at a time and to an extent they cannot predict, but if they do not have insurance, they often will not be able to pay for it. Because state and federal laws nonetheless require hospitals to provide a certain degree of care to individuals without regard to their ability to pay, hospitals end up receiving compensation for only a portion of the services they provide. To recoup the losses, hospitals pass on the cost to insurers through higher rates, and insurers, in turn, pass on the cost to policy holders in the form of higher premiums. Congress estimated that the cost of uncompensated care raises family health insurance premiums, on average, by over $1,000 per year.

In the Affordable Care Act, Congress addressed the problem of those who cannot obtain insurance coverage because of preexisting conditions or other health issues. It did so through the Act's "guaranteed-issue" and "community rating" provisions. These provisions together prohibit insurance companies from denying coverage to those with such conditions or charging unhealthy individuals higher premiums than healthy individuals.

The guaranteed-issue and community-rating reforms do not, however, address the issue of healthy individuals who choose not to purchase insurance to cover potential health care needs. In fact, the reforms sharply exacerbate that problem, by providing an incentive for individuals to delay purchasing health insurance until they become sick, relying on the promise of guaranteed and affordable coverage. The reforms also threaten to impose massive new costs on insurers, who are required to accept unhealthy individuals but prohibited from charging them rates necessary to pay for their coverage. This will lead insurers to significantly increase premiums on everyone.

The individual mandate was Congress's solution to these problems. By requiring that individuals purchase health insurance, the mandate prevents cost-shifting by those who would otherwise go without it. In addition, the mandate forces into the insurance risk pool more healthy individuals, whose premiums on average will be higher than their health care expenses. This allows insurers to subsidize the costs of covering the unhealthy individuals the reforms require them to accept. The Government claims that Congress has power under the Commerce and Necessary and Proper Clauses to enact this solution.

1

The Government contends that the individual mandate is within Congress's power because the failure to purchase insurance "has a substantial and deleterious effect on interstate commerce" by creating the cost-shifting problem. . . . We have recognized, for example, that "[t]he power of Congress over interstate commerce is not confined to the regulation of commerce among the states," but extends to activities that "have a substantial effect on interstate commerce." *United States v. Darby*. Congress's power, moreover, is not limited to regulation of an activity that by itself substantially affects interstate commerce, but also extends to activities that do so only when aggregated with similar activities of others. *Wickard.*

[C]ongress has never attempted to rely on that power to compel individuals not engaged in commerce to purchase an unwanted product.[a] Legislative novelty is not necessarily fatal; there is a first time for everything. But sometimes "the most telling indication of [a] severe constitutional problem . . . is the lack of historical precedent" for Congress's action. . . .

The Constitution grants Congress the power to "*regulate* Commerce." Art. I, §8, cl. 3 (emphasis added). The power to *regulate* commerce presupposes the existence of commercial activity to be regulated. If the power to "regulate" something included the power to create it, many of the provisions in the Constitution would be superfluous. For example, the Constitution gives Congress the power to "coin Money," in addition to the power to "regulate the Value thereof." *Id.,* cl. 5. And it gives Congress the power to "raise and support Armies" and to "provide and maintain a Navy," in addition to the power to "make Rules for the Government and Regulation of the land and naval Forces." *Id.,* cls. 12-14. If the power to regulate the armed forces or the value of money included the power to bring the subject of the regulation into existence, the specific grant of such powers would have been unnecessary. The language of the Constitution reflects the natural understanding that the power to regulate assumes there is already something to be regulated. See *Gibbons* ("[T]he enlightened patriots who framed our constitution, and the people who adopted it, must be understood to have employed words in their natural sense, and to have intended what they have said").[b]

Our precedent also reflects this understanding. As expansive as our cases construing the scope of the commerce power have been, they all have one thing in

a. The examples of other congressional mandates cited by Justice Ginsburg . . . are not to the contrary. Each of those mandates — to report for jury duty, to register for the draft, to purchase firearms in anticipation of militia service, to exchange gold currency for paper currency, and to file a tax return — are based on constitutional provisions other than the Commerce Clause. See Art. I, §8, cl. 9 (to "constitute Tribunals inferior to the supreme Court"); *id.,* cl. 12 (to "raise and support Armies"); *id.,* cl. 16 (to "provide for organizing, arming, and disciplining, the Militia"); *id.,* cl. 5 (to "coin Money"); *id.,* cl. 1 (to "lay and collect Taxes").

b. Justice Ginsburg suggests that "at the time the Constitution was framed, to 'regulate' meant, among other things, to require action," [relying] on a dictionary in which "[t]o order; to command" was the fifth-alternative definition of "to direct," which was itself the second-alternative definition of "to regulate." (citing S. Johnson, Dictionary of the English Language (4th ed. 1773) (reprinted 1978)). It is unlikely that the Framers had such an obscure meaning in mind when they used the word "regulate." Far more commonly, "[t]o regulate" meant "[t]o adjust by rule or method," which presupposes something to adjust. 2 Johnson, *supra;* see also *Gibbons* (defining the commerce power as the power "to prescribe the rule by which commerce is to be governed").

common: They uniformly describe the power as reaching "activity." It is nearly impossible to avoid the word when quoting them. See, *e.g., Lopez* ("Where economic activity substantially affects interstate commerce, legislation regulating that activity will be sustained"); *Perez* ("Where the *class of activities* is regulated and that *class* is within the reach of federal power, the courts have no power to excise, as trivial, individual instances of the class" (emphasis in original; internal quotation marks omitted)); *Wickard* ("[E]ven if appellee's activity be local and though it may not be regarded as commerce, it may still, whatever its nature, be reached by Congress if it exerts a substantial economic effect on interstate commerce"); *NLRB v. Jones & Laughlin Steel Corp.* ("Although activities may be intrastate in character when separately considered, if they have such a close and substantial relation to interstate commerce that their control is essential or appropriate to protect that commerce from burdens and obstructions, Congress cannot be denied the power to exercise that control").

The individual mandate, however, does not regulate existing commercial activity. It instead compels individuals to *become* active in commerce by purchasing a product, on the ground that their failure to do so affects interstate commerce. Construing the Commerce Clause to permit Congress to regulate individuals precisely *because* they are doing nothing would open a new and potentially vast domain to congressional authority. Every day individuals do not do an infinite number of things. In some cases they decide not to do something; in others they simply fail to do it. Allowing Congress to justify federal regulation by pointing to the effect of inaction on commerce would bring countless decisions an individual could *potentially* make within the scope of federal regulation, and — under the Government's theory — empower Congress to make those decisions for him.

Applying the Government's logic to the familiar case of *Wickard v. Filburn* shows how far that logic would carry us from the notion of a government of limited powers. . . . Under *Wickard* it is within Congress's power to regulate the market for wheat by supporting its price. But price can be supported by increasing demand as well as by decreasing supply. The aggregated decisions of some consumers not to purchase wheat have a substantial effect on the price of wheat, just as decisions not to purchase health insurance have on the price of insurance. Congress can therefore command that those not buying wheat do so, just as it argues here that it may command that those not buying health insurance do so. The farmer in *Wickard* was at least actively engaged in the production of wheat, and the Government could regulate that activity because of its effect on commerce. The Government's theory here would effectively override that limitation, by establishing that individuals may be regulated under the Commerce Clause whenever enough of them are not doing something the Government would have them do.

Indeed, the Government's logic would justify a mandatory purchase to solve almost any problem. To consider a different example in the health care market, many Americans do not eat a balanced diet. That group makes up a larger percentage of the total population than those without health insurance. The failure of that group to have a healthy diet increases health care costs, to a greater extent than the failure of the uninsured to purchase insurance. Those increased costs are borne in part by other Americans who must pay more, just as the uninsured shift costs to the insured. Congress addressed the insurance problem by ordering everyone to buy insurance. Under the Government's theory, Congress could address the diet problem by ordering everyone to buy vegetables.

People, for reasons of their own, often fail to do things that would be good for them or good for society. Those failures—joined with the similar failures of others—can readily have a substantial effect on interstate commerce. Under the Government's logic, that authorizes Congress to use its commerce power to compel citizens to act as the Government would have them act.

That is not the country the Framers of our Constitution envisioned. James Madison explained that the Commerce Clause was "an addition which few oppose and from which no apprehensions are entertained." The Federalist No. 45. While Congress's authority under the Commerce Clause has of course expanded with the growth of the national economy, our cases have "always recognized that the power to regulate commerce, though broad indeed, has limits." *Maryland v. Wirtz*. The Government's theory would erode those limits, permitting Congress to reach beyond the natural extent of its authority, "everywhere extending the sphere of its activity and drawing all power into its impetuous vortex." The Federalist No. 48 (J. Madison). Congress already enjoys vast power to regulate much of what we do. Accepting the Government's theory would give Congress the same license to regulate what we do not do, fundamentally changing the relation between the citizen and the Federal Government.[c]

To an economist, perhaps, there is no difference between activity and inactivity; both have measurable economic effects on commerce. But the distinction between doing something and doing nothing would not have been lost on the Framers, who were "practical statesmen," not metaphysical philosophers. . . . The Framers gave Congress the power to *regulate* commerce, not to *compel* it, and for over 200 years both our decisions and Congress's actions have reflected this understanding. There is no reason to depart from that understanding now.

The Government sees things differently. It argues that because sickness and injury are unpredictable but unavoidable, "the uninsured as a class are active in the market for health care, which they regularly seek and obtain." The individual mandate "merely regulates how individuals finance and pay for that active participation—requiring that they do so through insurance, rather than through attempted self-insurance with the back-stop of shifting costs to others."

---

c. In an attempt to recast the individual mandate as a regulation of commercial activity, Justice Ginsburg suggests that "[a]n individual who opts not to purchase insurance from a private insurer can be seen as actively selecting another form of insurance: self-insurance." But "self-insurance" is, in this context, nothing more than a description of the failure to purchase insurance. Individuals are no more "activ[e] in the self-insurance market" when they fail to purchase insurance, than they are active in the "rest" market when doing nothing.

[T]he phrase "active in the market for health care" . . . has no constitutional significance. An individual who bought a car two years ago and may buy another in the future is not "active in the car market" in any pertinent sense. The phrase "active in the market" cannot obscure the fact that most of those regulated by the individual mandate are not currently engaged in any commercial activity involving health care, and that fact is fatal to the Government's effort to "regulate the uninsured as a class." Our precedents recognize Congress's power to regulate "class[es] of *activities*," *Gonzales v. Raich* (emphasis added), not classes of *individuals,* apart from any activity in which they are engaged.

The individual mandate's regulation of the uninsured as a class is, in fact, particularly divorced from any link to existing commercial activity. The mandate primarily affects healthy, often young adults who are less likely to need significant health care and have other priorities for spending their money. It is precisely because these individuals, as an actuarial class, incur relatively low health care costs that the mandate helps counter the effect of forcing insurance companies to cover others who impose greater costs than their premiums are allowed to reflect. If the individual mandate is targeted at a class, it is a class whose commercial inactivity rather than activity is its defining feature.

The Government, however, claims that this does not matter. The Government regards it as sufficient to trigger Congress's authority that almost all those who are uninsured will, at some unknown point in the future, engage in a health care transaction. Asserting that "[t]here is no temporal limitation in the Commerce Clause," the Government argues that because "[e]veryone subject to this regulation is in or will be in the health care market," they can be "regulated in advance."

The proposition that Congress may dictate the conduct of an individual today because of prophesied future activity finds no support in our precedent. We have said that Congress can anticipate the *effects* on commerce of an economic activity. But we have never permitted Congress to anticipate that activity itself in order to regulate individuals not currently engaged in commerce. Each one of our cases . . . involved preexisting economic activity. See, *e.g., Wickard* (producing wheat); *Raich* (growing marijuana).

Everyone will likely participate in the markets for food, clothing, transportation, shelter, or energy; that does not authorize Congress to direct them to purchase particular products in those or other markets today. The Commerce Clause is not a general license to regulate an individual from cradle to grave, simply because he will predictably engage in particular transactions. Any police power to regulate individuals as such, as opposed to their activities, remains vested in the States.

The Government argues that the individual mandate can be sustained as a sort of exception to this rule, because health insurance is a unique product. According to the Government, upholding the individual mandate would not justify mandatory purchases of items such as cars or broccoli because, as the Government puts it, "[h]ealth insurance is not purchased for its own sake like a car or broccoli; it is a means of financing healthcare consumption and covering universal risks." But cars and broccoli are no more purchased for their "own sake" than health insurance. They are purchased to cover the need for transportation and food.

The Government says that health insurance and health care financing are "inherently integrated." But that does not mean the compelled purchase of the first is properly regarded as a regulation of the second. No matter how "inherently integrated" health insurance and health care consumption may be, they are not the same thing: They involve different transactions, entered into at different times, with different providers. And for most of those targeted by the mandate, significant health care needs will be years, or even decades, away. The proximity and degree of connection between the mandate and the subsequent commercial activity is too lacking to justify an exception of the sort urged by the Government. The individual mandate forces individuals into commerce precisely because they elected to refrain from commercial activity. Such a law cannot be sustained under a clause authorizing Congress to "regulate Commerce."

2

The Government next contends that Congress has the power under the Necessary and Proper Clause to enact the individual mandate because the mandate is an "integral part of a comprehensive scheme of economic regulation" — the guaranteed-issue and community-rating insurance reforms. Under this argument, it is not necessary to consider the effect that an individual's inactivity may have on interstate commerce; it is enough that Congress regulate commercial activity in a way that requires regulation of inactivity to be effective.

The power to "make all Laws which shall be necessary and proper for carrying into Execution" the powers enumerated in the Constitution, Art. I, §8, cl. 18, vests Congress with authority to enact provisions "incidental to the [enumerated] power, and conducive to its beneficial exercise," *McCulloch*. Although the Clause gives Congress authority to "legislate on that vast mass of incidental powers which must be involved in the constitution," it does not license the exercise of any "great substantive and independent power[s]" beyond those specifically enumerated. Instead, the Clause is " 'merely a declaration, for the removal of all uncertainty, that the means of carrying into execution those [powers] otherwise granted are included in the grant.' "

As our jurisprudence under the Necessary and Proper Clause has developed, we have been very deferential to Congress's determination that a regulation is "necessary." We have thus upheld laws that are " 'convenient, or useful' or 'conducive' to the authority's 'beneficial exercise.' " *Comstock*. But we have also carried out our responsibility to declare unconstitutional those laws that undermine the structure of government established by the Constitution. Such laws, which are not "consist[ent] with the letter and spirit of the constitution," *McCulloch*, are not "*proper* [means] for carrying into Execution" Congress's enumerated powers. Rather, they are, "in the words of The Federalist, 'merely acts of usurpation' which 'deserve to be treated as such.' "

Applying these principles, the individual mandate cannot be sustained under the Necessary and Proper Clause as an essential component of the insurance reforms. Each of our prior cases upholding laws under that Clause involved exercises of authority derivative of, and in service to, a granted power. For example, we have upheld provisions permitting continued confinement of those *already in federal custody* when they could not be safely released, *Comstock*; criminalizing bribes involving organizations *receiving federal funds, Sabri v. United States,* 541 U.S. 600 (2004); and tolling state statutes of limitations while cases are *pending in federal court, Jinks v. Richland County,* 538 U.S. 456 (2003). The individual mandate, by contrast, vests Congress with the extraordinary ability to create the necessary predicate to the exercise of an enumerated power.

This is in no way an authority that is "narrow in scope," or "incidental" to the exercise of the commerce power. Rather, such a conception of the Necessary and Proper Clause would work a substantial expansion of federal authority. No longer would Congress be limited to regulating under the Commerce Clause those who by some preexisting activity bring themselves within the sphere of federal regulation. Instead, Congress could reach beyond the natural limit of its authority and draw within its regulatory scope those who otherwise would be outside of it. Even if the individual mandate is "necessary" to the Act's insurance reforms, such an expansion of federal power is not a "proper" means for making those reforms effective.

[I]n [*Gonzales v.*] *Raich,* we considered "comprehensive legislation to regulate the interstate market" in marijuana. Certain individuals sought an exemption from that regulation on the ground that they engaged in only intrastate possession and consumption. We denied any exemption, on the ground that marijuana is a fungible commodity, so that any marijuana could be readily diverted into the interstate market. Congress's attempt to regulate the interstate market for marijuana would therefore have been substantially undercut if it could not also regulate intrastate possession and consumption. Accordingly, we recognized that "Congress was acting well within its authority" under the Necessary and Proper Clause even though its "regulation ensnare[d] some purely intrastate activity." *Raich* thus did not involve the exercise of any "great substantive and independent power," *McCulloch,* of the sort at issue here. Instead, it concerned only the constitutionality of "individual *applications* of a concededly valid statutory scheme." *Raich* (emphasis added).

Just as the individual mandate cannot be sustained as a law regulating the substantial effects of the failure to purchase health insurance, neither can it be upheld as a "necessary and proper" component of the insurance reforms. The commerce power thus does not authorize the mandate. Accord, *post,* at 4-16 (joint opinion of Scalia, Kennedy, Thomas, and Alito, JJ., dissenting).

B

That is not the end of the matter. Because the Commerce Clause does not support the individual mandate, it is necessary to turn to the Government's second argument: that the mandate may be upheld as within Congress's enumerated power to "lay and collect Taxes." Art. I, §8, cl. 1.

The Government's tax power argument asks us to view the statute differently than we did in considering its commerce power theory. In making its Commerce Clause argument, the Government defended the mandate as a regulation requiring individuals to purchase health insurance. The Government does not claim that the taxing power allows Congress to issue such a command. Instead, the Government asks us to read the mandate not as ordering individuals to buy insurance, but rather as imposing a tax on those who do not buy that product.

The text of a statute can sometimes have more than one possible meaning. To take a familiar example, a law that reads "no vehicles in the park" might, or might not, ban bicycles in the park. And it is well established that if a statute has two possible meanings, one of which violates the Constitution, courts should adopt the meaning that does not do so. Justice Story said that 180 years ago: "No court ought, unless the terms of an act rendered it unavoidable, to give a construction to it which should involve a violation, however unintentional, of the constitution." Justice Holmes made the same point a century later: "[T]he rule is settled that as between two possible interpretations of a statute, by one of which it would be unconstitutional and by the other valid, our plain duty is to adopt that which will save the Act."

The most straightforward reading of the mandate is that it commands individuals to purchase insurance. After all, it states that individuals "shall" maintain health insurance. 26 U.S.C. §5000A(a). Congress thought it could enact such a command under the Commerce Clause, and the Government primarily defended the law on that basis. But, for the reasons explained above, the Commerce Clause does not give Congress that power. Under our precedent, it is therefore necessary to ask whether the Government's alternative reading of the statute — that it only imposes a tax on those without insurance — is a reasonable one.

Under the mandate, if an individual does not maintain health insurance, the only consequence is that he must make an additional payment to the IRS when he pays his taxes. See §5000A(b). That, according to the Government, means the mandate can be regarded as establishing a condition — not owning health insurance — that triggers a tax — the required payment to the IRS. Under that theory, the mandate is not a legal command to buy insurance. Rather, it makes going without insurance just another thing the Government taxes, like buying gasoline or earning income. And if the mandate is in effect just a tax hike on certain taxpayers who do not have health insurance, it may be within Congress's constitutional power to tax.

The question is not whether that is the most natural interpretation of the mandate, but only whether it is a "fairly possible" one. As we have explained, "every reasonable construction must be resorted to, in order to save a statute from unconstitutionality." The Government asks us to interpret the mandate as imposing a tax, if it would otherwise violate the Constitution. Granting the Act the full measure of deference owed to federal statutes, it can be so read, for the reasons set forth below.

C

The exaction the Affordable Care Act imposes on those without health insurance looks like a tax in many respects. The "[s]hared responsibility payment," as the statute entitles it, is paid into the Treasury by "taxpayer[s]" when they file their tax returns. 26 U.S.C. §5000A(b). It does not apply to individuals who do not pay federal income taxes because their household income is less than the filing threshold in the Internal Revenue Code. For taxpayers who do owe the payment, its amount is determined by such familiar factors as taxable income, number of dependents, and joint filing status. The requirement to pay is found in the Internal Revenue Code and enforced by the IRS, which — as we previously explained — must assess and collect it "in the same manner as taxes." This process yields the essential feature of any tax: it produces at least some revenue for the Government. *United States v. Kahriger,* 345 U.S. 22 (1953). Indeed, the payment is expected to raise about $4 billion per year by 2017.

It is of course true that the Act describes the payment as a "penalty," not a "tax." But while that label is fatal to the application of the Anti-Injunction Act, it does not determine whether the payment may be viewed as an exercise of Congress's taxing power. It is up to Congress whether to apply the Anti-Injunction Act to any particular statute, so it makes sense to be guided by Congress's choice of label on that question. That choice does not, however, control whether an exaction is within Congress's constitutional power to tax.

Our precedent reflects this: In 1922, we decided two challenges to the "Child Labor Tax" on the same day. In the first, we held that a suit to enjoin collection of the so-called tax was barred by the Anti-Injunction Act. [*Bailey v.*] *George,* 259 U.S. 16 (1922). Congress knew that suits to obstruct taxes had to await payment under the Anti-Injunction Act; Congress called the child labor tax a tax; Congress therefore intended the Anti-Injunction Act to apply. In the second case, however, we held that the same exaction, although labeled a tax, was not in fact authorized by Congress's taxing power. [*Bailey v.*] *Drexel Furniture,* 259 U.S., at 38 (1922). That constitutional question was not controlled by Congress's choice of label.

We have similarly held that exactions not labeled taxes nonetheless were authorized by Congress's power to tax. In the *License Tax Cases,* for example, we held that federal licenses to sell liquor and lottery tickets — for which the licensee had to pay a fee — could be sustained as exercises of the taxing power. And in *New York v. United States* we upheld as a tax a "surcharge" on out-of-state nuclear waste shipments, a portion of which was paid to the Federal Treasury. We thus ask whether the shared responsibility payment falls within Congress's taxing power, "[d]isregarding the designation of the exaction, and viewing its substance and application." *United States v. Constantine,* 296 U.S. 287 (1935); cf. *Quill Corp. v. North Dakota,* 504 U.S. 298 (1992) ("[M]agic words or labels" should not "disable an otherwise constitutional levy" (internal quotation marks omitted)); *Nelson v. Sears, Roebuck & Co.,* 312 U.S. 359 (1941) ("In passing on the constitutionality of a tax law, we are concerned only with its practical operation, not its definition or the precise form of descriptive words which may be applied to it" (internal quotation marks omitted)); *United States v. Sotelo,* 436 U.S. 268 (1978) ("That the funds due are referred to as a 'penalty' . . . does not alter their essential character as taxes").

Our cases confirm this functional approach. For example, in *Drexel Furniture,* we focused on three practical characteristics of the so-called tax on employing child laborers that convinced us the "tax" was actually a penalty. First, the tax imposed an exceedingly heavy burden — 10 percent of a company's net income — on those who employed children, no matter how small their infraction. Second, it imposed that exaction only on those who knowingly employed underage laborers. Such scienter requirements are typical of punitive statutes, because Congress often wishes to punish only those who intentionally break the law. Third, this "tax" was enforced in part by the Department of Labor, an agency responsible for punishing violations of labor laws, not collecting revenue. 259 U.S., at 36-37; see also, *e.g.,* [*Department of Revenue of Mont. v.*] *Kurth Ranch,* [511 U.S. 767 (1994)] (considering, *inter alia,* the amount of the exaction, and the fact that it was imposed for violation of a separate criminal law); *Constantine* (same).

The same analysis here suggests that the shared responsibility payment may for constitutional purposes be considered a tax, not a penalty: First, for most Americans the amount due will be far less than the price of insurance, and, by statute, it can never be more.[d] It may often be a reasonable financial decision to make the payment rather than purchase insurance, unlike the "prohibitory" financial punishment in *Drexel Furniture.* Second, the individual mandate contains no scienter requirement. Third, the payment is collected solely by the IRS through the normal means of taxation — except that the Service is *not* allowed to use those means most suggestive of a punitive sanction, such as criminal prosecution. The reasons the Court in *Drexel Furniture* held that what was called a "tax" there was a penalty support the conclusion that what is called a "penalty" here may be viewed as a tax.[e]

None of this is to say that the payment is not intended to affect individual conduct. Although the payment will raise considerable revenue, it is plainly designed

---

d. In 2016, for example, individuals making $35,000 a year are expected to owe the IRS about $60 for any month in which they do not have health insurance. Someone with an annual income of $100,000 a year would likely owe about $200. The price of a qualifying insurance policy is projected to be around $400 per month.

e. We do not suggest that any exaction lacking a scienter requirement and enforced by the IRS is within the taxing power. Congress could not, for example, expand its authority to impose criminal fines by creating strict liability offenses enforced by the IRS rather than the FBI. But the fact that the exaction here is paid like a tax, to the agency that collects taxes — rather than, for example, exacted by Department of Labor inspectors after ferreting out willful malfeasance — suggests that this exaction may be viewed as a tax.

to expand health insurance coverage. But taxes that seek to influence conduct are nothing new. Some of our earliest federal taxes sought to deter the purchase of imported manufactured goods in order to foster the growth of domestic industry. Today, federal and state taxes can compose more than half the retail price of cigarettes, not just to raise more money, but to encourage people to quit smoking. And we have upheld such obviously regulatory measures as taxes on selling marijuana and sawed-off shotguns. Indeed, "[e]very tax is in some measure regulatory. To some extent it interposes an economic impediment to the activity taxed as compared with others not taxed." *Sonzinsky* [*v. United States,* 300 U.S. 506 (1937).] That §5000A seeks to shape decisions about whether to buy health insurance does not mean that it cannot be a valid exercise of the taxing power.

In distinguishing penalties from taxes, this Court has explained that "if the concept of penalty means anything, it means punishment for an unlawful act or omission." *United States v. Reorganized CF & I Fabricators of Utah, Inc.,* 518 U.S. 213 (1996); see also *United States v. La Franca,* 282 U.S. 568 (1931) ("[A] penalty, as the word is here used, is an exaction imposed by statute as punishment for an unlawful act"). While the individual mandate clearly aims to induce the purchase of health insurance, it need not be read to declare that failing to do so is unlawful. Neither the Act nor any other law attaches negative legal consequences to not buying health insurance, beyond requiring a payment to the IRS. The Government agrees with that reading, confirming that if someone chooses to pay rather than obtain health insurance, they have fully complied with the law.

Indeed, it is estimated [by the Congressional Budget Office] that four million people each year will choose to pay the IRS rather than buy insurance. We would expect Congress to be troubled by that prospect if such conduct were unlawful. That Congress apparently regards such extensive failure to comply with the mandate as tolerable suggests that Congress did not think it was creating four million outlaws. It suggests instead that the shared responsibility payment merely imposes a tax citizens may lawfully choose to pay in lieu of buying health insurance.

The plaintiffs contend that Congress's choice of language — stating that individuals "shall" obtain insurance or pay a "penalty" — requires reading §5000A as punishing unlawful conduct, even if that interpretation would render the law unconstitutional. We have rejected a similar argument before. In *New York v. United States* we examined a statute providing that "'[e]ach State shall be responsible for providing . . . for the disposal of . . . low-level radioactive waste.'" A State that shipped its waste to another State was exposed to surcharges by the receiving State, a portion of which would be paid over to the Federal Government. And a State that did not adhere to the statutory scheme faced "[p]enalties for failure to comply," including increases in the surcharge. New York urged us to read the statute as a federal command that the state legislature enact legislation to dispose of its waste, which would have violated the Constitution. To avoid that outcome, we interpreted the statute to impose only "a series of incentives" for the State to take responsibility for its waste. We then sustained the charge paid to the Federal Government as an exercise of the taxing power. We see no insurmountable obstacle to a similar approach here.

The joint dissenters argue that we cannot uphold §5000A as a tax because Congress did not "frame" it as such. In effect, they contend that even if the Constitution permits Congress to do exactly what we interpret this statute to do, the law must be struck down because Congress used the wrong labels. An example may help illustrate why labels should not control here. Suppose Congress enacted a statute providing that every taxpayer who owns a house without energy efficient windows must pay $50 to the IRS. The amount due is adjusted based on factors such as taxable income and joint filing status, and is paid along with the taxpayer's income tax return. Those whose income is below the filing threshold need not pay. The required payment is not called a "tax," a "penalty," or anything else. No one would doubt that this law imposed a tax, and was within Congress's power to tax. That conclusion should not change simply because Congress used the word "penalty" to describe the payment. . . .

Our precedent demonstrates that Congress had the power to impose the exaction in §5000A under the taxing power, and that §5000A need not be read to do more than impose a tax. That is sufficient to sustain it. The "question of the constitutionality of action taken by Congress does not depend on recitals of the power which it undertakes to exercise." *Woods v. Cloyd W. Miller Co.,* 333 U.S. 138 (1948).

Even if the taxing power enables Congress to impose a tax on not obtaining health insurance, any tax must still comply with other requirements in the Constitution. Plaintiffs argue that the shared responsibility payment does not do so, citing Article I, §9, clause 4. That clause provides: "No Capitation, or other direct, Tax shall be laid, unless in Proportion to the Census or Enumeration herein before directed to be taken." This requirement means that any "direct Tax" must be apportioned so that each State pays in proportion to its population. According to the plaintiffs, if the individual mandate imposes a tax, it is a direct tax, and it is unconstitutional because Congress made no effort to apportion it among the States.

Even when the Direct Tax Clause was written it was unclear what else, other than a capitation (also known as a "head tax" or a "poll tax"), might be a direct tax. See *Springer v. United States,* 102 U.S. 586 (1881). Soon after the framing, Congress passed a tax on ownership of carriages, over James Madison's objection that it was an unapportioned direct tax. This Court upheld the tax, in part reasoning that apportioning such a tax would make little sense, because it would have required taxing carriage owners at dramatically different rates depending on how many carriages were in their home State. See *Hylton v. United States,* 3 Dall. 171 (1796) (opinion of Chase, J.). The Court was unanimous, and those Justices who wrote opinions either directly asserted or strongly suggested that only two forms of taxation were direct: capitations and land taxes. See *id.,* at 175; *id.,* at 177 (opinion of Paterson, J.); *id.,* at 183 (opinion of Iredell, J.).

That narrow view of what a direct tax might be persisted for a century. In 1880, for example, we explained that "*direct taxes,* within the meaning of the Constitution, are only capitation taxes, as expressed in that instrument, and taxes on real estate." *Springer.* In 1895, we expanded our interpretation to include taxes on personal property and income from personal property, in the course of striking down aspects of the federal income tax. *Pollock v. Farmers' Loan & Trust Co.,* 158 U.S. 601 (1895). That result was overturned by the Sixteenth Amendment, although we continued to consider taxes on personal property to be direct taxes. See *Eisner v. Macomber,* 252 U.S. 189 (1920).

A tax on going without health insurance does not fall within any recognized category of direct tax. It is not a capitation. Capitations are taxes paid by every person, "without regard to property, profession, or *any other circumstance.*" *Hylton, supra,* at 175 (opinion of Chase, J.) (emphasis altered). The whole point of the shared responsibility payment is that it is triggered by specific circumstances—earning a certain amount of income but not obtaining health insurance. The payment is also plainly not a tax on the ownership of land or personal property. The shared responsibility payment is thus not a direct tax that must be apportioned among the several States.

There may, however, be a more fundamental objection to a tax on those who lack health insurance. Even if only a tax, the payment under §5000A(b) remains a burden that the Federal Government imposes for an omission, not an act. If it is troubling to interpret the Commerce Clause as authorizing Congress to regulate those who abstain from commerce, perhaps it should be similarly troubling to permit Congress to impose a tax for not doing something.

Three considerations allay this concern. First, and most importantly, it is abundantly clear the Constitution does not guarantee that individuals may avoid taxation through inactivity. A capitation, after all, is a tax that everyone must pay simply for existing, and capitations are expressly contemplated by the Constitution. The Court today holds that our Constitution protects us from federal regulation under the Commerce Clause so long as we abstain from the regulated activity. But from its creation, the Constitution has made no such promise with respect to taxes. See Letter from Benjamin Franklin to M. Le Roy (Nov. 13, 1789) ("Our new Constitution is now established . . . but in this world nothing can be said to be certain, except death and taxes").

Whether the mandate can be upheld under the Commerce Clause is a question about the scope of federal authority. Its answer depends on whether Congress can exercise what all acknowledge to be the novel course of directing individuals to purchase insurance. Congress's use of the Taxing Clause to encourage buying something is, by contrast, not new. Tax incentives already promote, for example, purchasing homes and professional educations. Sustaining the mandate as a tax depends only on whether Congress *has* properly exercised its taxing power to encourage purchasing health insurance, not whether it *can*. Upholding the individual mandate under the Taxing Clause thus does not recognize any new federal power. It determines that Congress has used an existing one.

Second, Congress's ability to use its taxing power to influence conduct is not without limits. A few of our cases policed these limits aggressively, invalidating punitive exactions obviously designed to regulate behavior otherwise regarded at the time as beyond federal authority. See, *e.g., United States v. Butler,* 297 U.S. 1 (1936); [*Bailey v.*] *Drexel Furniture.* More often and more recently we have declined to closely examine the regulatory motive or effect of revenue-raising measures. See *Kahriger* (collecting cases). We have nonetheless maintained that "'there comes a time in the extension of the penalizing features of the so-called tax when it loses its character as such and becomes a mere penalty with the characteristics of regulation and punishment.'" *Kurth Ranch* (quoting *Drexel Furniture*).

We have already explained that the shared responsibility payment's practical characteristics pass muster as a tax under our narrowest interpretations of the taxing power. Because the tax at hand is within even those strict limits, we need not here decide the precise point at which an exaction becomes so punitive that the taxing power does not authorize it. It remains true, however, that the "'power to tax is not the power to destroy while this Court sits.'" *Oklahoma Tax Comm'n v. Texas Co.,* 336 U.S. 342 (1949) (quoting *Panhandle Oil Co. v. Mississippi ex rel. Knox,* 277 U.S. 218 (1928) (Holmes, J., dissenting)).

Third, although the breadth of Congress's power to tax is greater than its power to regulate commerce, the taxing power does not give Congress the same degree of control over individual behavior. Once we recognize that Congress may regulate a particular decision under the Commerce Clause, the Federal Government can bring its full weight to bear. Congress may simply command individuals to do as it directs. An individual who disobeys may be subjected to criminal sanctions. Those sanctions can include not only fines and imprisonment, but all the attendant consequences of being branded a criminal: deprivation of otherwise protected civil rights, such as the right to bear arms or vote in elections; loss of employment opportunities; social stigma; and severe disabilities in other controversies, such as custody or immigration disputes.

By contrast, Congress's authority under the taxing power is limited to requiring an individual to pay money into the Federal Treasury, no more. If a tax is properly paid, the Government has no power to compel or punish individuals subject to it. We do not make light of the severe burden that taxation—especially taxation motivated by a regulatory purpose—can impose. But imposition of a tax nonetheless leaves an individual with a lawful choice to do or not do a certain act, so long as he is willing to pay a tax levied on that choice.[f]

---

f. Of course, individuals do not have a lawful choice not to pay a tax due, and may sometimes face prosecution for failing to do so (although not for declining to make the shared responsibility payment, see 26 U.S.C. §5000A(g)(2)). But that does not show that the tax restricts the lawful choice whether to undertake or forgo the activity on which the tax is predicated. Those subject to the individual mandate may lawfully forgo health insurance and pay higher taxes, or buy health insurance and pay lower taxes. The only thing they may not lawfully do is not buy health insurance and not pay the resulting tax.

The Affordable Care Act's requirement that certain individuals pay a financial penalty for not obtaining health insurance may reasonably be characterized as a tax. Because the Constitution permits such a tax, it is not our role to forbid it, or to pass upon its wisdom or fairness.

D

Justice Ginsburg questions the necessity of rejecting the Government's commerce power argument, given that §5000A can be upheld under the taxing power. But the statute reads more naturally as a command to buy insurance than as a tax, and I would uphold it as a command if the Constitution allowed it. It is only because the Commerce Clause does not authorize such a command that it is necessary to reach the taxing power question. And it is only because we have a duty to construe a statute to save it, if fairly possible, that §5000A can be interpreted as a tax. Without deciding the Commerce Clause question, I would find no basis to adopt such a saving construction.

The Federal Government does not have the power to order people to buy health insurance. Section 5000A would therefore be unconstitutional if read as a command. The Federal Government does have the power to impose a tax on those without health insurance. Section 5000A is therefore constitutional, because it can reasonably be read as a tax.

IV

A

The States also contend that the Medicaid expansion exceeds Congress's authority under the Spending Clause. They claim that Congress is coercing the States to adopt the changes it wants by threatening to withhold all of a State's Medicaid grants, unless the State accepts the new expanded funding and complies with the conditions that come with it. This, they argue, violates the basic principle that the "Federal Government may not compel the States to enact or administer a federal regulatory program."

There is no doubt that the Act dramatically increases state obligations under Medicaid. The current Medicaid program requires States to cover only certain discrete categories of needy individuals—pregnant women, children, needy families, the blind, the elderly, and the disabled. There is no mandatory coverage for most childless adults, and the States typically do not offer any such coverage. The States also enjoy considerable flexibility with respect to the coverage levels for parents of needy families. On average States cover only those unemployed parents who make less than 37 percent of the federal poverty level, and only those employed parents who make less than 63 percent of the poverty line.

The Medicaid provisions of the Affordable Care Act, in contrast, require States to expand their Medicaid programs by 2014 to cover *all* individuals under the age of 65 with incomes below 133 percent of the federal poverty line. The Act also establishes a new "[e]ssential health benefits" package, which States must provide to all new Medicaid recipients — a level sufficient to satisfy a recipient's obligations under the individual mandate. The Affordable Care Act provides that the Federal Government will pay 100 percent of the costs of covering these newly eligible individuals through 2016. In the following years, the federal payment level gradually decreases, to a minimum of 90 percent. In light of the expansion in coverage mandated by the Act, the Federal Government estimates that its Medicaid spending will increase by approximately $100 billion per year, nearly 40 percent above current levels.

The Spending Clause grants Congress the power "to pay the Debts and provide for the . . . general Welfare of the United States." U.S. Const., Art. I, §8, cl. 1. We have long recognized that Congress may use this power to grant federal funds to the States, and may condition such a grant upon the States' "taking certain actions that Congress could not require them to take." Such measures "encourage a State to regulate in a particular way, [and] influenc[e] a State's policy choices." *New York*. The conditions imposed by Congress ensure that the funds are used by the States to "provide for the . . . general Welfare" in the manner Congress intended.

At the same time, our cases have recognized limits on Congress's power under the Spending Clause to secure state compliance with federal objectives. "We have repeatedly characterized . . . Spending Clause legislation as 'much in the nature of a *contract*.'" *Barnes v. Gorman,* 536 U.S. 181 (2002) (quoting *Pennhurst State School and Hospital v. Halderman,* 451 U.S. 1 (1981)). The legitimacy of Congress's exercise of the spending power "thus rests on whether the State voluntarily and knowingly accepts the terms of the 'contract.'" *Pennhurst*. Respecting this limitation is critical to ensuring that Spending Clause legislation does not undermine the status of the States as independent sovereigns in our federal system. That system "rests on what might at first seem a counterintuitive insight, that 'freedom is enhanced by the creation of two governments, not one.'" For this reason, "the Constitution has never been understood to confer upon Congress the ability to require the States to govern according to Congress' instructions." *New York*. Otherwise the two-government system established by the Framers would give way to a system that vests power in one central government, and individual liberty would suffer.

That insight has led this Court to strike down federal legislation that commandeers a State's legislative or administrative apparatus for federal purposes. See, *e.g., Printz*; *New York*. It has also led us to scrutinize Spending Clause legislation to ensure that Congress is not using financial inducements to exert a "power akin to undue influence." *Steward Machine Co. v. Davis,* 301 U.S. 548 (1937). Congress may use its spending power to create incentives for States to act in accordance with federal policies. But when "pressure turns into compulsion," *ibid.,* the legislation runs contrary to our system of federalism. "[T]he Constitution simply does not give Congress the authority to require the States to regulate." *New York*. That is true whether Congress directly commands a State to regulate or indirectly coerces a State to adopt a federal regulatory system as its own.

Permitting the Federal Government to force the States to implement a federal program would threaten the political accountability key to our federal system. "[W]here the Federal Government directs the States to regulate, it may be state officials who will bear the brunt of public disapproval, while the federal officials who devised the regulatory program may remain insulated from the electoral ramifications of their decision." [*New York.*] Spending Clause programs do not pose this danger when a State has a legitimate choice whether to accept the federal conditions in exchange for federal funds. In such a situation, state officials can fairly be held politically accountable for choosing to accept or refuse the federal offer. But when the State has no choice, the Federal Government can achieve its objectives without accountability, just as in *New York* and *Printz*. Indeed, this danger is heightened when Congress acts under the Spending Clause, because Congress can use that power to implement federal policy it could not impose directly under its enumerated powers.

We addressed such concerns in *Steward Machine*. That case involved a federal tax on employers that was abated if the businesses paid into a state unemployment plan that met certain federally specified conditions. An employer sued, alleging that the tax was impermissibly "driv[ing] the state legislatures under the whip of economic pressure into the enactment of unemployment compensation laws at the bidding of the central government." We acknowledged the danger that the Federal Government might employ its taxing power to exert a "power akin to undue influence" upon the States. But we observed that Congress adopted the challenged tax and abatement program to channel money to the States that would otherwise have gone into the Federal Treasury for use in providing national unemployment services. Congress was willing to direct businesses to instead pay the money into state programs only on the condition that the money be used for the same purposes. Predicating tax abatement on a State's adoption of a particular type of unemployment legislation was therefore a means to "safeguard [the Federal Government's] own treasury." We held that "[i]n such circumstances, if in no others, inducement or persuasion does not go beyond the bounds of power."

In rejecting the argument that the federal law was a "weapon[ ] of coercion, destroying or impairing the autonomy of the states," the Court noted that there was no reason to suppose that the State in that case acted other than through "her unfettered will." Indeed, the State itself did "not offer a suggestion that in passing the unemployment law she was affected by duress."

As our decision in *Steward Machine* confirms, Congress may attach appropriate conditions to federal taxing and spending programs to preserve its control over the use of federal funds. In the typical case we look to the States to defend their prerogatives by adopting "the simple expedient of not yielding" to federal blandishments when they do not want to embrace the federal policies as their own. The States are separate and independent sovereigns. Sometimes they have to act like it.

The States, however, argue that the Medicaid expansion is far from the typical case. They object that Congress has "crossed the line distinguishing encouragement from coercion," *New York*, in the way it has structured the funding: Instead of simply refusing to grant the new funds to States that will not accept the new conditions, Congress has also threatened to withhold those States' existing Medicaid funds. The States claim that this threat serves no purpose other than to force unwilling States to sign up for the dramatic expansion in health care coverage effected by the Act.

Given the nature of the threat and the programs at issue here, we must agree. We have upheld Congress's authority to condition the receipt of funds on the States' complying with restrictions on the use of those funds, because that is the means by which Congress ensures that the funds are spent according to its view of the "general Welfare." Conditions that do not here govern the use of the funds, however, cannot be justified on that basis. When, for example, such conditions take the form of threats to terminate other significant independent grants, the conditions are properly viewed as a means of pressuring the States to accept policy changes.

In *South Dakota v. Dole,* we considered a challenge to a federal law that threatened to withhold five percent of a State's federal highway funds if the State did not raise its drinking age to 21. The Court found that the condition was "directly related to one of the main purposes for which highway funds are expended—safe interstate travel." At the same time, the condition was not a restriction on how the highway funds—set aside for specific highway improvement and maintenance efforts—were to be used.

We accordingly asked whether "the financial inducement offered by Congress" was "so coercive as to pass the point at which 'pressure turns into compulsion.'" By "financial inducement" the Court meant the threat of losing five percent of highway funds; no new money was offered to the States to raise their drinking ages. We found that the inducement was not impermissibly coercive, because Congress was offering only "relatively mild encouragement to the States." We observed that "all South Dakota would lose if she adheres to her chosen course as to a suitable minimum drinking age is 5%" of her highway funds. In fact, the federal funds at stake constituted less than half of one percent of South Dakota's budget at the time. In consequence, "we conclude[d] that [the] encouragement to state action [was] a valid use of the spending power." Whether to accept the drinking age change "remain[ed] the prerogative of the States not merely in theory but in fact."

In this case, the financial "inducement" Congress has chosen is much more than "relatively mild encouragement"—it is a gun to the head. Section 1396c of the Medicaid Act provides that if a State's Medicaid plan does not comply with the Act's requirements, the Secretary of Health and Human Services may declare that "further payments will not be made to the State." 42 U.S.C. § 1396c. A State that opts out of the Affordable Care Act's expansion in health care coverage thus stands to lose not merely "a relatively small percentage" of its existing Medicaid funding, but *all* of it. Medicaid spending accounts for over 20 percent of the average State's total budget, with federal funds covering 50 to 83 percent of those costs. The Federal Government estimates that it will pay out approximately

$3.3 trillion between 2010 and 2019 in order to cover the costs of *pre*expansion Medicaid. In addition, the States have developed intricate statutory and administrative regimes over the course of many decades to implement their objectives under existing Medicaid. It is easy to see how the *Dole* Court could conclude that the threatened loss of less than half of one percent of South Dakota's budget left that State with a "prerogative" to reject Congress's desired policy, "not merely in theory but in fact." The threatened loss of over 10 percent of a State's overall budget, in contrast, is economic dragooning that leaves the States with no real option but to acquiesce in the Medicaid expansion.[g]

Justice Ginsburg claims that *Dole* is distinguishable because here "Congress has not threatened to withhold funds earmarked for any other program." But that begs the question: The States contend that the expansion is in reality a new program and that Congress is forcing them to accept it by threatening the funds for the existing Medicaid program. We cannot agree that existing Medicaid and the expansion dictated by the Affordable Care Act are all one program simply because "Congress styled" them as such. If the expansion is not properly viewed as a modification of the existing Medicaid program, Congress's decision to so title it is irrelevant.[h]

Here, the Government claims that the Medicaid expansion is properly viewed merely as a modification of the existing program because the States agreed that Congress could change the terms of Medicaid when they signed on in the first place. The Government observes that the Social Security Act, which includes the original Medicaid provisions, contains a clause expressly reserving "[t]he right to alter, amend, or repeal any provision" of that statute. 42 U.S.C. §1304. So it does. But "if Congress intends to impose a condition on the grant of federal moneys, it must do so unambiguously." *Pennhurst*. A State confronted with statutory language reserving the right to "alter" or "amend" the pertinent provisions of the Social Security Act might reasonably assume that Congress was entitled to make adjustments to the Medicaid program as it developed. Congress has in fact done so, sometimes conditioning only the new funding, other times both old and new.

---

g. Justice Ginsburg observes that state Medicaid spending will increase by only 0.8 percent after the expansion. That not only ignores increased state administrative expenses, but also assumes that the Federal Government will continue to fund the expansion at the current statutorily specified levels. It is not unheard of, however, for the Federal Government to increase requirements in such a manner as to impose unfunded mandates on the States. More importantly, the size of the new financial burden imposed on a State is irrelevant in analyzing whether the State has been coerced into accepting that burden. "Your money or your life" is a coercive proposition, whether you have a single dollar in your pocket or $500.

h. Nor, of course, can the number of pages the amendment occupies, or the extent to which the change preserves and works within the existing program, be dispositive. Take, for example, the following hypothetical amendment: "All of a State's citizens are now eligible for Medicaid." That change would take up a single line and would not alter any "operational aspect[ ] of the program" beyond the eligibility requirements. Yet it could hardly be argued that such an amendment was a permissible modification of Medicaid, rather than an attempt to foist an entirely new health care system upon the States.

The Medicaid expansion, however, accomplishes a shift in kind, not merely degree. The original program was designed to cover medical services for four particular categories of the needy: the disabled, the blind, the elderly, and needy families with dependent children. Previous amendments to Medicaid eligibility merely altered and expanded the boundaries of these categories. Under the Affordable Care Act, Medicaid is transformed into a program to meet the health care needs of the entire nonelderly population with income below 133 percent of the poverty level. It is no longer a program to care for the neediest among us, but rather an element of a comprehensive national plan to provide universal health insurance coverage.[i]

Indeed, the manner in which the expansion is structured indicates that while Congress may have styled the expansion a mere alteration of existing Medicaid, it recognized it was enlisting the States in a new health care program. Congress created a separate funding provision to cover the costs of providing services to any person made newly eligible by the expansion. While Congress pays 50 to 83 percent of the costs of covering individuals currently enrolled in Medicaid, once the expansion is fully implemented Congress will pay 90 percent of the costs for newly eligible persons. The conditions on use of the different funds are also distinct. Congress mandated that newly eligible persons receive a level of coverage that is less comprehensive than the traditional Medicaid benefit package.

As we have explained, "[t]hough Congress' power to legislate under the spending power is broad, it does not include surprising participating States with postacceptance or 'retroactive' conditions." *Pennhurst*. A State could hardly anticipate that Congress's reservation of the right to "alter" or "amend" the Medicaid program included the power to transform it so dramatically.

Justice Ginsburg claims that in fact this expansion is no different from the previous changes to Medicaid, such that "a State would be hard put to complain that it lacked fair notice." But the prior change she discusses — presumably the most dramatic alteration she could find — does not come close to working the transformation the expansion accomplishes. She highlights an amendment requiring States to cover pregnant women and increasing the number of eligible children. But this modification can hardly be described as a major change in a program that — from its inception — provided health care for "families with dependent children." Previous Medicaid amendments simply do not fall into the same category as the one at stake here.

---

i. Justice Ginsburg suggests that the States can have no objection to the Medicaid expansion, because "Congress could have repealed Medicaid [and,] [t]hereafter, . . . could have enacted Medicaid II, a new program combining the pre-2010 coverage with the expanded coverage required by the ACA." But it would certainly not be that easy. Practical constraints would plainly inhibit, if not preclude, the Federal Government from repealing the existing program and putting every feature of Medicaid on the table for political reconsideration. Such a massive undertaking would hardly be "ritualistic." The same is true of Justice Ginsburg's suggestion that Congress could establish Medicaid as an exclusively federal program.

The Court in *Steward Machine* did not attempt to "fix the outermost line" where persuasion gives way to coercion. The Court found it "[e]nough for present purposes that wherever the line may be, this statute is within it." We have no need to fix a line either. It is enough for today that wherever that line may be, this statute is surely beyond it. Congress may not simply "conscript state [agencies] into the national bureaucratic army," and that is what it is attempting to do with the Medicaid expansion.

B

Nothing in our opinion precludes Congress from offering funds under the Affordable Care Act to expand the availability of health care, and requiring that States accepting such funds comply with the conditions on their use. What Congress is not free to do is to penalize States that choose not to participate in that new program by taking away their existing Medicaid funding. Section 1396c gives the Secretary of Health and Human Services the authority to do just that. It allows her to withhold *all* "further [Medicaid] payments . . . to the State" if she determines that the State is out of compliance with any Medicaid requirement, including those contained in the expansion. In light of the Court's holding, the Secretary cannot apply §1396c to withdraw existing Medicaid funds for failure to comply with the requirements set out in the expansion.

That fully remedies the constitutional violation we have identified. The chapter of the United States Code that contains §1396c includes a severability clause confirming that we need go no further. That clause specifies that "[i]f any provision of this chapter, or the application thereof to any person or circumstance, is held invalid, the remainder of the chapter, and the application of such provision to other persons or circumstances shall not be affected thereby." Today's holding does not affect the continued application of §1396c to the existing Medicaid program. Nor does it affect the Secretary's ability to withdraw funds provided under the Affordable Care Act if a State that has chosen to participate in the expansion fails to comply with the requirements of that Act.

This is not to say, as the joint dissent suggests, that we are "rewriting the Medicaid Expansion." Instead, we determine, first, that §1396c is unconstitutional when applied to withdraw existing Medicaid funds from States that decline to comply with the expansion. We then follow Congress's explicit textual instruction to leave unaffected "the remainder of the chapter, and the application of [the challenged] provision to other persons or circumstances." When we invalidate an application of a statute because that application is unconstitutional, we are not "rewriting" the statute; we are merely enforcing the Constitution.

The question remains whether today's holding affects other provisions of the Affordable Care Act. In considering that question, "[w]e seek to determine what Congress would have intended in light of the Court's constitutional holding." Our "touchstone for any decision about remedy is legislative intent, for a court cannot use its remedial powers to circumvent the intent of the legislature." The question here is whether Congress would have wanted the rest of the Act to stand, had it known that States would have a genuine choice whether to participate in the new Medicaid expansion. Unless it is "evident" that the answer is no, we must leave the rest of the Act intact.

We are confident that Congress would have wanted to preserve the rest of the Act. It is fair to say that Congress assumed that every State would participate in the Medicaid expansion, given that States had no real choice but to do so. The States contend that Congress enacted the rest of the Act with such full participation in mind; they point out that Congress made Medicaid a means for satisfying the mandate, and enacted no other plan for providing coverage to many low-income individuals. According to the States, this means that the entire Act must fall.

We disagree. The Court today limits the financial pressure the Secretary may apply to induce States to accept the terms of the Medicaid expansion. As a practical matter, that means States may now choose to reject the expansion; that is the whole point. But that does not mean all or even any will. Some States may indeed decline to participate, either because they are unsure they will be able to afford their share of the new funding obligations, or because they are unwilling to commit the administrative resources necessary to support the expansion. Other States, however, may voluntarily sign up, finding the idea of expanding Medicaid coverage attractive, particularly given the level of federal funding the Act offers at the outset.

We have no way of knowing how many States will accept the terms of the expansion, but we do not believe Congress would have wanted the whole Act to fall, simply because some may choose not to participate. The other reforms Congress enacted, after all, will remain "fully operative as a law," and will still function in a way "consistent with Congress' basic objectives in enacting the statute[.]" Confident that Congress would not have intended anything different, we conclude that the rest of the Act need not fall in light of our constitutional holding.

* * *

The Affordable Care Act is constitutional in part and unconstitutional in part. The individual mandate cannot be upheld as an exercise of Congress's power under the Commerce Clause. That Clause authorizes Congress to regulate interstate commerce, not to order individuals to engage in it. In this case, however, it is reasonable to construe what Congress has done as increasing taxes on those who have a certain amount of income, but choose to go without health insurance. Such legislation is within Congress's power to tax.

As for the Medicaid expansion, that portion of the Affordable Care Act violates the Constitution by threatening existing Medicaid funding. Congress has no authority to order the States to regulate according to its instructions. Congress may offer the States grants and require the States to comply with accompanying conditions, but the States must have a genuine choice whether to accept the offer. The States are given no such choice in this case: They must either accept a basic change in the nature of Medicaid, or risk losing all Medicaid funding. The remedy for that constitutional violation is to preclude the Federal Government from imposing such a sanction. That remedy does not require striking down other portions of the Affordable Care Act.

The Framers created a Federal Government of limited powers, and assigned to this Court the duty of enforcing those limits. The Court does so today. But the Court does not express any opinion on the wisdom of the Affordable Care Act. Under the Constitution, that judgment is reserved to the people.

The judgment of the Court of Appeals for the Eleventh Circuit is affirmed in part and reversed in part.

It is so ordered.

Justice GINSBURG, with whom Justice SOTOMAYOR joins, and with whom Justice BREYER and Justice KAGAN join as to Parts I, II, III, and IV, concurring in part, concurring in the judgment in part, and dissenting in part.

I agree with The Chief Justice that the Anti-Injunction Act does not bar the Court's consideration of this case, and that the minimum coverage provision is a proper exercise of Congress' taxing power. I therefore join Parts I, II, and III-C of The Chief Justice's opinion. Unlike The Chief Justice, however, I would hold, alternatively, that the Commerce Clause authorizes Congress to enact the minimum coverage provision. I would also hold that the Spending Clause permits the Medicaid expansion exactly as Congress enacted it.

I

. . .

A

In enacting the Patient Protection and Affordable Care Act (ACA), Congress comprehensively reformed the national market for health-care products and services. By any measure, that market is immense. Collectively, Americans spent $2.5 trillion on health care in 2009, accounting for 17.6% of our Nation's economy. Within the next decade, it is anticipated, spending on health care will nearly double.

The health-care market's size is not its only distinctive feature. Unlike the market for almost any other product or service, the market for medical care is one in which all individuals inevitably participate. Virtually every person residing in the United States, sooner or later, will visit a doctor or other healthcare professional. See Dept. of Health and Human Services, National Center for Health Statistics, Summary Health Statistics for U.S. Adults: National Health Interview Survey 2009 (Dec. 2010) (Over 99.5% of adults above 65 have visited a health-care professional.). Most people will do so repeatedly. See *id.* (In 2009 alone, 64% of adults made two or more visits to a doctor's office.).

When individuals make those visits, they face another reality of the current market for medical care: its high cost. In 2010, on average, an individual in the United States incurred over $7,000 in health-care expenses. Over a lifetime, costs mount to hundreds of thousands of dollars. When a person requires non-routine care, the cost will generally exceed what he or she can afford to pay. A single hospital stay, for instance, typically costs upwards of $10,000. Treatments for many serious, though not uncommon, conditions similarly cost a substantial sum.

Although every U.S. domiciliary will incur significant medical expenses during his or her lifetime, the time when care will be needed is often unpredictable. An accident, a heart attack, or a cancer diagnosis commonly occurs without warning. Inescapably, we are all at peril of needing medical care without a moment's notice.

To manage the risks associated with medical care — its high cost, its unpredictability, and its inevitability — most people in the United States obtain health insurance. Many (approximately 170 million in 2009) are insured by private insurance companies. Others, including those over 65 and certain poor and disabled persons, rely on government-funded insurance programs, notably Medicare and Medicaid. Combined, private health insurers and State and Federal Governments finance almost 85% of the medical care administered to U.S. residents.

Not all U.S. residents, however, have health insurance. In 2009, approximately 50 million people were uninsured, either by choice or, more likely, because they could not afford private insurance and did not qualify for government aid. As a group, uninsured individuals annually consume more than $100 billion in health-care services, nearly 5% of the Nation's total. Over 60% of those without insurance visit a doctor's office or emergency room in a given year.

B

The large number of individuals without health insurance, Congress found, heavily burdens the national health-care market. As just noted, the cost of emergency care or treatment for a serious illness generally exceeds what an individual can afford to pay on her own. Unlike markets for most products, however, the inability to pay for care does not mean that an uninsured individual will receive no care. Federal and state law, as well as professional obligations and embedded social norms, require hospitals and physicians to provide care when it is most needed, regardless of the patient's ability to pay.

As a consequence, medical-care providers deliver significant amounts of care to the uninsured for which the providers receive no payment. In 2008, for example, hospitals, physicians, and other health-care professionals received no compensation for $43 billion worth of the $116 billion in care they administered to those without insurance.

Health-care providers do not absorb these bad debts. Instead, they raise their prices, passing along the cost of uncompensated care to those who do pay reliably: the government and private insurance companies. In response, private insurers increase their premiums, shifting the cost of the elevated bills from providers onto those who carry insurance. The net result: Those with health insurance subsidize the medical care of those without it. As economists would describe what happens, the uninsured "free ride" on those who pay for health insurance.

The size of this subsidy is considerable. Congress found that the cost-shifting just described "increases family [insurance] premiums by on average over $1,000 a year." Higher premiums, in turn, render health insurance less affordable, forcing more people to go without insurance and leading to further costshifting.

And it is hardly just the currently sick or injured among the uninsured who prompt elevation of the price of health care and health insurance. Insurance companies and health-care providers know that some percentage of healthy, uninsured people will suffer sickness or injury each year and will receive medical care despite their inability to pay. In anticipation of this uncompensated care, health-care companies raise their prices, and insurers their premiums. In other words, because any uninsured person may need medical care at any moment and because health-care companies must account for that risk, every uninsured person impacts the market price of medical care and medical insurance.

The failure of individuals to acquire insurance has other deleterious effects on the health-care market. Because those without insurance generally lack access to preventative care, they do not receive treatment for conditions—like hypertension and diabetes—that can be successfully and affordably treated if diagnosed early on. When sickness finally drives the uninsured to seek care, once treatable conditions have escalated into grave health problems, requiring more costly and extensive intervention. The extra time and resources providers spend serving the uninsured lessens the providers' ability to care for those who do have insurance.

C

States cannot resolve the problem of the uninsured on their own. Like Social Security benefits, a universal health-care system, if adopted by an individual State, would be "bait to the needy and dependent elsewhere, encouraging them to migrate and seek a haven of repose." *Helvering v. Davis*. An influx of unhealthy individuals into a State with universal health care would result in increased spending on medical services. To cover the increased costs, a State would have to raise taxes, and private health-insurance companies would have to increase premiums. Higher taxes and increased insurance costs would, in turn, encourage businesses and healthy individuals to leave the State.

States that undertake health-care reforms on their own thus risk "placing themselves in a position of economic disadvantage as compared with neighbors or competitors." *Davis*. See also Brief for Health Care for All, Inc., et al. as *Amici Curiae* in No. 11-398, p. 4 ("[O]ut-of-state residents continue to seek and receive millions of dollars in uncompensated care in Massachusetts hospitals, limiting the State's efforts to improve its health care system through the elimination of uncompensated care."). Facing that risk, individual States are unlikely to take the initiative in addressing the problem of the uninsured, even though solving that problem is in all States' best interests. Congress' intervention was needed to overcome this collective action impasse.

D

Aware that a national solution was required, Congress could have taken over the health-insurance market by establishing a tax-and-spend federal program like Social Security. Such a program, commonly referred to as a single-payer system (where the sole payer is the Federal Government), would have left little, if any, room for private enterprise or the States. Instead of going this route, Congress enacted the ACA, a solution that retains a robust role for private insurers and state governments. To make its chosen approach work, however, Congress had to use some new tools, including a requirement that most individuals obtain private health insurance coverage. . . .

The minimum coverage provision serves a further purpose vital to Congress' plan to reduce the number of uninsured. Congress knew that encouraging individuals to purchase insurance would not suffice to solve the problem, because most of the uninsured are not uninsured by choice. Of particular concern to Congress were people who, though desperately in need of insurance, often cannot acquire it: persons who suffer from preexisting medical conditions.

Before the ACA's enactment, private insurance companies took an applicant's medical history into account when setting insurance rates or deciding whether to insure an individual. Because individuals with preexisting medical conditions cost insurance companies significantly more than those without such conditions, insurers routinely refused to insure these individuals, charged them substantially higher premiums, or offered only limited coverage that did not include the preexisting illness.

To ensure that individuals with medical histories have access to affordable insurance, Congress devised a three-part solution. First, Congress imposed a "guaranteed issue" requirement, which bars insurers from denying coverage to any person on account of that person's medical condition or history. Second, Congress required insurers to use "community rating" to price their insurance policies. See §300gg. Community rating, in effect, bars insurance companies from charging higher premiums to those with preexisting conditions.

But these two provisions, Congress comprehended, could not work effectively unless individuals were given a powerful incentive to obtain insurance.

In the 1990's, several States—including New York, New Jersey, Washington, Kentucky, Maine, New Hampshire, and Vermont—enacted guaranteed-issue and community-rating laws without requiring universal acquisition of insurance coverage. The results were disastrous. "All seven states suffered from skyrocketing insurance premium costs, reductions in individuals with coverage, and reductions in insurance products and providers." Brief for American Association of People with Disabilities et al. as *Amici Curiae* in No. 11-398, p. 9 (hereinafter AAPD Brief). See also Brief for Governor of Washington Christine Gregoire as *Amicus Curiae* in No. 11-398, pp. 11-14 (describing the "death spiral" in the insurance market Washington experienced when the State passed a law requiring coverage for preexisting conditions).

Congress comprehended that guaranteed-issue and community-rating laws alone will not work. When insurance companies are required to insure the sick at affordable prices, individuals can wait until they become ill to buy insurance. Pretty soon, those in need of immediate medical care—*i.e.,* those who cost insurers the most—become the insurance companies' main customers. This "adverse selection" problem leaves insurers with two choices: They can either raise premiums dramatically to cover their ever-increasing costs or they can exit the market. In the seven States that tried guaranteed-issue and community-rating requirements without a minimum coverage provision, that is precisely what insurance companies did. See, *e.g.,* AAPD Brief 10 ("[In Maine,] [m]any insurance providers doubled their premiums in just three years or less."); *id.,* at 12 ("Like New York, Vermont saw substantial increases in premiums after its . . . insurance reform measures took effect in 1993."); Hall, An Evaluation of New York's Reform Law, 25 J. Health Pol. Pol'y & L. 71, 91-92 (2000) (Guaranteed-issue and community-rating laws resulted in a "dramatic exodus of indemnity insurers from New York's individual [insurance] market."); Brief for Barry Friedman et al. as *Amici Curiae* in No. 11-398, p. 17 ("In Kentucky, all but two insurers (one State-run) abandoned the State.").

Massachusetts, Congress was told, cracked the adverse selection problem. By requiring most residents to obtain insurance, the Commonwealth ensured that insurers would not be left with only the sick as customers. As a result, federal lawmakers observed, Massachusetts succeeded where other States had failed. In coupling the minimum coverage provision with guaranteed-issue and community-rating prescriptions, Congress followed Massachusetts' lead. . . .

II

A

The Commerce Clause, it is widely acknowledged, "was the Framers' response to the central problem that gave rise to the Constitution itself." Under the Articles of Confederation, the Constitution's precursor, the regulation of commerce was left to the States. This scheme proved unworkable, because the individual States, understandably focused on their own economic interests, often failed to take actions critical to the success of the Nation as a whole.

What was needed was a "national Government . . . armed with a positive & compleat authority in all cases where uniform measures are necessary." See Letter from James Madison to Edmund Randolph (Apr. 8, 1787), in 9 Papers of James Madison 368, 370 (R. Rutland ed. 1975). See also Letter from George Washington to James Madison (Nov. 30, 1785), in 8 *id.,* at 428, 429 ("We are either a United people, or we are not. If the former, let us, in all matters of general concern act as a nation, which ha[s] national objects to promote, and a national character to support."). The Framers' solution was the Commerce Clause, which, as they perceived it, granted Congress the authority to enact economic legislation "in all Cases for the general Interests of the Union, and also in those Cases to which the States are separately incompetent." 2 Records of the Federal Convention of 1787, pp. 131-132, 8 (M. Farrand rev.1966).

The Framers understood that the "general Interests of the Union" would change over time, in ways they could not anticipate. Accordingly, they recognized that the Constitution was of necessity a "great outlin[e]," not a detailed blueprint, see *McCulloch v. Maryland*, and that its provisions included broad concepts, to be "explained by the context or by the facts of the case," Letter from James Madison to N.P. Trist (Dec. 1831), in 9 Writings of James Madison 471, 475 (G. Hunt ed. 1910). . . .

B

[W]e owe a large measure of respect to Congress when it frames and enacts economic and social legislation. . . . When appraising such legislation, we ask only (1) whether Congress had a "rational basis" for concluding that the regulated activity substantially affects interstate commerce, and (2) whether there is a "reasonable connection between the regulatory means selected and the asserted ends." In answering these questions, we presume the statute under review is constitutional and may strike it down only on a "plain showing" that Congress acted irrationally.

C

Straightforward application of these principles would require the Court to hold that the minimum coverage provision is proper Commerce Clause legislation. Beyond dispute, Congress had a rational basis for concluding that the uninsured, as a class, substantially affect interstate commerce. Those without insurance consume billions of dollars of health-care products and services each year. Those goods are produced, sold, and delivered largely by national and regional companies who routinely transact business across state lines. The uninsured also cross state lines to receive care. Some have medical emergencies while away from home. Others, when sick, go to a neighboring State that provides better care for those who have not prepaid for care.

Not only do those without insurance consume a large amount of health care each year; critically, as earlier explained, their inability to pay for a significant portion of that consumption drives up market prices, foists costs on other consumers, and reduces market efficiency and stability. Given these far-reaching effects on interstate commerce, the decision to forgo insurance is hardly inconsequential or equivalent to "doing nothing," . . . ; it is, instead, an economic decision Congress has the authority to address under the Commerce Clause. See also *Wickard* ("It is well established by decisions of this Court that the power to regulate commerce includes the power to regulate the prices at which commodities in that commerce are dealt in and *practices affecting such prices*." (emphasis added)).

The minimum coverage provision, furthermore, bears a "reasonable connection" to Congress' goal of protecting the health-care market from the disruption caused by individuals who fail to obtain insurance. By requiring those who do not carry insurance to pay a toll, the minimum coverage provision gives individuals a strong incentive to insure. This incentive, Congress had good reason to believe, would reduce the number of uninsured and, correspondingly, mitigate the adverse impact the uninsured have on the national health-care market.

Congress also acted reasonably in requiring uninsured individuals, whether sick or healthy, either to obtain insurance or to pay the specified penalty. As earlier observed, because every person is at risk of needing care at any moment, all those who lack insurance, regardless of their current health status, adversely affect the price of health care and health insurance. Moreover, an insurance-purchase requirement limited to those in need of immediate care simply could not work. Insurance companies would either charge these individuals prohibitively expensive premiums, or, if community-rating regulations were in place, close up shop.

"[W]here we find that the legislators . . . have a rational basis for finding a chosen regulatory scheme necessary to the protection of commerce, our investigation is at an end." Congress' enactment of the minimum coverage provision, which addresses a specific interstate problem in a practical, experience-informed manner, easily meets this criterion.

D

Rather than evaluating the constitutionality of the minimum coverage provision in the manner established by our precedents, The Chief Justice relies on a newly minted constitutional doctrine. The commerce power does not, The Chief Justice announces, permit Congress to "compe[l] individuals to become active in commerce by purchasing a product."

1

a

[E]veryone will, at some point, consume health-care products and services. See *supra,* at 3. Thus, if The Chief Justice is correct that an insurance-purchase requirement can be applied only to those who "actively" consume health care, the minimum coverage provision fits the bill.

The Chief Justice does not dispute that all U.S. residents participate in the market for health services over the course of their lives. But, The Chief Justice insists, the uninsured cannot be considered active in the market for health care, because "[t]he proximity and degree of connection between the [uninsured today] and [their] subsequent commercial activity is too lacking."

This argument has multiple flaws. First, more than 60% of those without insurance visit a hospital or doctor's office each year. Nearly 90% will within five years. An uninsured's consumption of health care is thus quite proximate: It is virtually certain to occur in the next five years and more likely than not to occur this year.

Equally evident, Congress has no way of separating those uninsured individuals who will need emergency medical care today (surely their consumption of medical care is sufficiently imminent) from those who will not need medical services for years to come. No one knows when an emergency will occur, yet emergencies involving the uninsured arise daily. To capture individuals who unexpectedly will obtain medical care in the very near future, then, Congress needed to include individuals who will not go to a doctor anytime soon. Congress, our decisions instruct, has authority to cast its net that wide.

Second, it is Congress' role, not the Court's, to delineate the boundaries of the market the Legislature seeks to regulate. The Chief Justice defines the health-care market as including only those transactions that will occur either in the next instant or within some (unspecified) proximity to the next instant. But Congress could reasonably have viewed the market from a long-term perspective, encompassing all transactions virtually certain to occur over the next decade, not just those occurring here and now.

Third, contrary to The Chief Justice's contention, our precedent does indeed support "[t]he proposition that Congress may dictate the conduct of an individual today because of prophesied future activity." In *Wickard,* the Court upheld a penalty the Federal Government imposed on a farmer who grew more wheat than he was permitted to grow under the Agricultural Adjustment Act of 1938 (AAA). He could not be penalized, the farmer argued, as he was growing the wheat for home consumption, not for sale on the open market. The Court rejected this argument. Wheat intended for home consumption, the Court noted, "overhangs the market, and if induced by rising prices, tends to flow into the market and check price increases [intended by the AAA]."

Similar reasoning supported the Court's judgment in *Raich,* which upheld Congress' authority to regulate marijuana grown for personal use. Homegrown marijuana substantially affects the interstate market for marijuana, we observed, for "the high demand in the interstate market will [likely] draw such marijuana into that market."

Our decisions thus acknowledge Congress' authority, under the Commerce Clause, to direct the conduct of an individual today (the farmer in *Wickard,* stopped from growing excess wheat; the plaintiff in *Raich,* ordered to cease cultivating marijuana) because of a prophesied future transaction (the eventual sale of that wheat or marijuana in the interstate market). Congress' actions are even more rational in this case, where the future activity (the consumption of medical care) is certain to occur, the sole uncertainty being the time the activity will take place.

Maintaining that the uninsured are not active in the health-care market, The Chief Justice draws an analogy to the car market. An individual "is not 'active in the car market,'" The Chief Justice observes, simply because he or she may someday buy a car. The analogy is inapt. The inevitable yet unpredictable need for medical care and the guarantee that emergency care will be provided when required are conditions nonexistent in other markets. That is so of the market for cars, and of the market for broccoli as well. Although an individual *might* buy a car or a crown of broccoli one day, there is no certainty she will ever do so. And if she eventually wants a car or has a craving for broccoli, she will be obliged to pay at the counter before receiving the vehicle or nourishment. She will get no free ride or food, at the expense of another consumer forced to pay an inflated price. Upholding the minimum coverage provision on the ground that all are participants or will be participants in the health-care market would therefore carry no implication that Congress may justify under the Commerce Clause a mandate to buy other products and services.

Nor is it accurate to say that the minimum coverage provision "compel[s] individuals . . . to purchase an unwanted product," or "suite of products." If unwanted today, medical service secured by insurance may be desperately needed tomorrow. Virtually everyone, I reiterate, consumes health care at some point in his or her life. Health insurance is a means of paying for this care, nothing more. In requiring individuals to obtain insurance, Congress is therefore not mandating the purchase of a discrete, unwanted product. Rather, Congress is merely defining the terms on which individuals pay for an interstate good they consume: Persons subject to the mandate must now pay for medical care in advance (instead of at the point of service) and through insurance (instead of out of pocket). Establishing payment terms for goods in or affecting interstate commerce is quintessential economic regulation well within Congress' domain.

The Chief Justice also calls the minimum coverage provision an illegitimate effort to make young, healthy individuals subsidize insurance premiums paid by the less hale and hardy. This complaint, too, is spurious. Under the current health-care system, healthy persons who lack insurance receive a benefit for which they do not pay: They are assured that, if they need it, emergency medical care will be available, although they cannot afford it. Those who have insurance bear the cost of this guarantee. By requiring the healthy uninsured to obtain insurance or pay a penalty structured as a tax, the minimum coverage provision ends the free ride these individuals currently enjoy.

In the fullness of time, moreover, today's young and healthy will become society's old and infirm. Viewed over a lifespan, the costs and benefits even out: The young who pay more than their fair share currently will pay less than their fair share when they become senior citizens. And even if, as undoubtedly will be the case, some individuals, over their lifespans, will pay more for health insurance than they receive in health services, they have little to complain about, for that is how insurance works. Every insured person receives protection against a catastrophic loss, even though only a subset of the covered class will ultimately need that protection.

b

[A]rticle I, §8, of the Constitution grants Congress the power "[t]o regulate Commerce . . . among the several States." Nothing in this language implies that Congress' commerce power is limited to regulating those actively engaged in commercial transactions. Indeed, as the D.C. Circuit observed, "[a]t the time the Constitution was [framed], to 'regulate' meant," among other things, "to require action." See *Seven-Sky v. Holder,* 661 F.3d 1, 16 (2011).

Arguing to the contrary, The Chief Justice notes that "the Constitution gives Congress the power to 'coin Money,' in addition to the power to 'regulate the Value thereof,' " and similarly "gives Congress the power to 'raise and support Armies' and to 'provide and maintain a Navy,' in addition to the power to 'make Rules for the Government and Regulation of the land and naval Forces.' " In separating the power to regulate from the power to bring the subject of the regulation into existence, The Chief Justice asserts, "[t]he language of the Constitution reflects the natural understanding that the power to regulate assumes there is already something to be regulated."

This argument is difficult to fathom. Requiring individuals to obtain insurance unquestionably regulates the interstate health-insurance and health-care markets, both of them in existence well before the enactment of the ACA. See *Wickard,* 317 U.S., at 128 ("The stimulation of commerce is a use of the regulatory function quite as definitely as prohibitions or restrictions thereon."). Thus, the "something to be regulated" was surely there when Congress created the minimum coverage provision.[a]

Nor does our case law toe the activity versus inactivity line. In *Wickard,* for example, we upheld the penalty imposed on a farmer who grew too much wheat, even though the regulation had the effect of compelling farmers to purchase wheat in the open market. "[F]orcing some farmers into the market to buy what they could provide for themselves" was, the Court held, a valid means of regulating commerce. In another context, this Court similarly upheld Congress' authority under the commerce power to compel an "inactive" landholder to submit to an unwanted sale. See *Monongahela Nav. Co. v. United States,* 148 U.S. 312 (1893) ("[U]pon *the [great] power to regulate commerce*[,]" Congress has the authority to mandate the sale of real property to the Government, where the sale is essential to the improvement of a navigable waterway (emphasis added)); *Cherokee Nation v. Southern Kansas R. Co.,* 135 U.S. 641 (1890) (similar reliance on the commerce power regarding mandated sale of private property for railroad construction).

[T]his Court's former endeavors to impose categorical limits on the commerce power have not fared well. In several pre-New Deal cases, the Court attempted to cabin Congress' Commerce Clause authority by distinguishing "commerce" from activity once conceived to be noncommercial, notably, "production," "mining,"

---

a. The Chief Justice's reliance on the quoted passages of the Constitution . . . is also dubious on other grounds. The power to "regulate the Value" of the national currency presumably includes the power to increase the currency's worth—*i.e.,* to create value where none previously existed. And if the power to "[r]egulat[e] . . . the land and naval Forces" presupposes "there is already [in existence] something to be regulated," *i.e.,* an Army and a Navy, does Congress lack authority to create an Air Force?

and "manufacturing." See, *e.g., United States v. E.C. Knight Co.,* 156 U.S. 1 (1895) ("Commerce succeeds to manufacture, and is not a part of it."); *Carter v. Carter Coal Co.,* 298 U.S. 238 (1936) ("Mining brings the subject matter of commerce into existence. Commerce disposes of it."). The Court also sought to distinguish activities having a "direct" effect on interstate commerce, and for that reason, subject to federal regulation, from those having only an "indirect" effect, and therefore not amenable to federal control. See, *e.g., A.L.A. Schechter Poultry Corp. v. United States,* 295 U.S. 495 (1935) ("[T]he distinction between direct and indirect effects of intrastate transactions upon interstate commerce must be recognized as a fundamental one.").

These line-drawing exercises were untenable, and the Court long ago abandoned them. "[Q]uestions of the power of Congress [under the Commerce Clause]," we held in *Wickard,* "are not to be decided by reference to any formula which would give controlling force to nomenclature such as 'production' and 'indirect' and foreclose consideration of the actual effects of the activity in question upon interstate commerce." Failing to learn from this history, The Chief Justice plows ahead with his formalistic distinction between those who are "active in commerce," and those who are not.

It is not hard to show the difficulty courts (and Congress) would encounter in distinguishing statutes that regulate "activity" from those that regulate "inactivity." As Judge Easterbrook noted, "it is possible to restate most actions as corresponding inactions with the same effect." *Archie v. Racine,* 847 F.2d 1211, 1213 (C.A.7 1988) (en banc). Take this case as an example. An individual who opts not to purchase insurance from a private insurer can be seen as actively selecting another form of insurance: self-insurance. The minimum coverage provision could therefore be described as regulating activists in the self-insurance market.[b] *Wickard* is another example. Did the statute there at issue target activity (the growing of too much wheat) or inactivity (the farmer's failure to purchase wheat in the marketplace)? If anything, the Court's analysis suggested the latter.

At bottom, The Chief Justice's and the joint dissenters' "view that an individual cannot be subject to Commerce Clause regulation absent voluntary, affirmative acts that enter him or her into, or affect, the interstate market expresses a concern for individual liberty that [is] more redolent of Due Process Clause arguments." Plaintiffs have abandoned any argument pinned to substantive due process, however, and now concede that the provisions here at issue do not offend the Due Process Clause.

[The concern that without the activity/inactivity distinction] the commerce power would otherwise know no limits . . . is unfounded.

First, The Chief Justice could certainly uphold the individual mandate without giving Congress *carte blanche* to enact any and all purchase mandates. As

---

b. The Chief Justice's characterization of individuals who choose not to purchase private insurance as "doing nothing[]" is similarly questionable. A person who self-insures opts against prepayment for a product the person will in time consume. When aggregated, exercise of that option has a substantial impact on the healthcare market.

several times noted, the unique attributes of the healthcare market render everyone active in that market and give rise to a significant freeriding problem that does not occur in other markets. . . .

Congress would remain unable to regulate noneconomic conduct that has only an attenuated effect on interstate commerce and is traditionally left to state law. See *Lopez*; *Morrison*. . . . [But] [a]n individual's decision to self-insure . . . is an economic act with the requisite connection to interstate commerce. Other choices individuals make are unlikely to fit the same or similar description. . . . The Chief Justice cites a Government mandate to purchase green vegetables. One could call this concern "the broccoli horrible." Congress, The Chief Justice posits, might adopt such a mandate, reasoning that an individual's failure to eat a healthy diet, like the failure to purchase health insurance, imposes costs on others.

Consider the chain of inferences the Court would have to accept to conclude that a vegetable-purchase mandate was likely to have a substantial effect on the healthcare costs borne by lithe Americans. The Court would have to believe that individuals forced to buy vegetables would then eat them (instead of throwing or giving them away), would prepare the vegetables in a healthy way (steamed or raw, not deepfried), would cut back on unhealthy foods, and would not allow other factors (such as lack of exercise or little sleep) to trump the improved diet.[c] Such "pil[ing of] inference upon inference" is just what the Court refused to do in *Lopez* and *Morrison*.

Other provisions of the Constitution also check congressional overreaching. A mandate to purchase a particular product would be unconstitutional if, for example, the edict impermissibly abridged the freedom of speech, interfered with the free exercise of religion, or infringed on a liberty interest protected by the Due Process Clause.

Supplementing these legal restraints is a formidable check on congressional power: the democratic process. As the controversy surrounding the passage of the Affordable Care Act attests, purchase mandates are likely to engender political resistance. This prospect is borne out by the behavior of state legislators. Despite their possession of unquestioned authority to impose mandates, state governments have rarely done so.

When contemplated in its extreme, almost any power looks dangerous. The commerce power, hypothetically, would enable Congress to prohibit the purchase and home production of all meat, fish, and dairy goods, effectively compelling Americans to eat only vegetables. Yet no one would offer the "hypothetical and unreal possibilit[y][]" of a vegetarian state as a credible reason to deny Congress

---

c. The failure to purchase vegetables in The Chief Justice's hypothetical, then, is *not* what leads to higher healthcare costs for others; rather, it is the failure of individuals to maintain a healthy diet, and the resulting obesity, that creates the costshifting problem. Requiring individuals to purchase vegetables is thus several steps removed from solving the problem. The failure to obtain health insurance, by contrast, is the *immediate cause* of the costshifting Congress sought to address through the ACA. Requiring individuals to obtain insurance attacks the source of the problem directly, in a single step.

the authority ever to ban the possession and sale of goods. The Chief Justice accepts just such specious logic when he cites the broccoli horrible as a reason to deny Congress the power to pass the individual mandate. Cf. R. Bork, The Tempting of America 169 (1990) ("Judges and lawyers live on the slippery slope of analogies; they are not supposed to ski it to the bottom."). . . .

III

A

[T]he Necessary and Proper Clause "empowers Congress to enact laws in effectuation of its [commerce] powe[r] that are not within its authority to enact in isolation." *Raich,* 545 U.S., at 39 (Scalia, J., concurring in judgment). Hence, "[a] complex regulatory program . . . can survive a Commerce Clause challenge without a showing that every single facet of the program is independently and directly related to a valid congressional goal." "It is enough that the challenged provisions are an integral part of the regulatory program and that the regulatory scheme when considered as a whole satisfies this test." See also *Raich,* 545 U.S., at 24-25 (A challenged statutory provision fits within Congress' commerce authority if it is an "essential par[t] of a larger regulation of economic activity," such that, in the absence of the provision, "the regulatory scheme could be undercut." (quoting *Lopez,* 514 U.S., at 561)); *Raich,* 545 U.S., at 37 (Scalia, J., concurring in judgment) ("Congress may regulate even noneconomic local activity if that regulation is a necessary part of a more general regulation of interstate commerce. The relevant question is simply whether the means chosen are 'reasonably adapted' to the attainment of a legitimate end under the commerce power."). . . .

Congress knew . . . that simply barring insurance companies from relying on an applicant's medical history would not work in practice. Without the individual mandate, Congress learned, guaranteed-issue and community-rating requirements would trigger an adverse-selection death-spiral in the health-insurance market: Insurance premiums would skyrocket, the number of uninsured would increase, and insurance companies would exit the market. When complemented by an insurance mandate, on the other hand, guaranteed issue and community rating would work as intended, increasing access to insurance and reducing uncompensated care. The minimum coverage provision is thus an "essential par[t] of a larger regulation of economic activity"; without the provision, "the regulatory scheme [w]ould be undercut." *Raich.* Put differently, the minimum coverage provision, together with the guaranteed-issue and community-rating requirements, is "'reasonably adapted' to the attainment of a legitimate end under the commerce power": the elimination of pricing and sales practices that take an applicant's medical history into account.

B

[The Chief Justice contends that] [a] mandate to purchase health insurance is not "proper" legislation, . . . because the command "undermine[s] the structure of government established by the Constitution." [relying on *Printz* and *New York v. United States*]. The statutes at issue in both cases, however, compelled *state officials* to act on the Federal Government's behalf. . . . The minimum coverage provision, in contrast, acts "directly upon individuals, without employing the States as intermediaries." The provision is thus entirely consistent with the Constitution's design. See *Printz,* 521 U.S., at 920 ("[T]he Framers explicitly chose a Constitution that confers upon Congress the power to regulate individuals, not States."). . . .

The Chief Justice [does not] pause to explain *why* the power to direct either the purchase of health insurance or, alternatively, the payment of a penalty collectible as a tax is more far-reaching than other implied powers this Court has found meet under the Necessary and Proper Clause. These powers include the power to enact criminal laws; the power to imprison, including civil imprisonment, see, *e.g., Comstock*; and the power to create a national bank, see *McCulloch*.[d]

[H]ow is a judge to decide, when ruling on the constitutionality of a federal statute, whether Congress employed an "independent power," or merely a "derivative" one, [w]hether the power used is "substantive," or just "incidental"? The instruction The Chief Justice, in effect, provides lower courts: You will know it when you see it.

It is more than exaggeration to suggest that the minimum coverage provision improperly intrudes on "essential attributes of state sovereignty." First, the Affordable Care Act does not operate "in [an] are[a] such as criminal law enforcement or education where States historically have been sovereign." *Lopez.* As evidenced by Medicare, Medicaid, the Employee Retirement Income Security Act of 1974 (ERISA), and the Health Insurance Portability and Accountability Act of 1996 (HIPAA), the Federal Government plays a lead role in the healthcare sector, both as a direct payer and as a regulator.

Second, and perhaps most important, the minimum coverage provision, along with other provisions of the ACA, addresses the very sort of interstate problem that made the commerce power essential in our federal system. The crisis created by the large number of U.S. residents who lack health insurance is one of national dimension that States are "separately incompetent" to handle. See also Maryland Brief 15-26 (describing "the impediments to effective state policymaking that flow from the interconnectedness of each state's healthcare economy" and emphasizing that "state-level reforms cannot fully address the problems associated with uncompensated care"). Far from trampling on States' sovereignty, the ACA attempts a federal solution for the very reason that the States, acting separately, cannot meet the need. Notably, the ACA serves the

---

d. Indeed, Congress regularly and uncontroversially requires individuals who are "doing nothing," to take action. Examples include federal requirements to report for jury duty; to register for selective service; to purchase firearms and gear in anticipation of service in the Militia ([as it did in the] Uniform Militia Act of 1792); to turn gold currency over to the Federal Government in exchange for paper currency; and to file a tax return.

general welfare of the people of the United States while retaining a prominent role for the States.[e]

. . .

V

[T]he spending power conferred by the Constitution, the Court has never doubted, permits Congress to define the contours of programs financed with federal funds. And to expand coverage, Congress could have recalled the existing legislation, and replaced it with a new law making Medicaid as embracive of the poor as Congress chose.

The question posed by the 2010 Medicaid expansion, then, is essentially this: To cover a notably larger population, must Congress take the repeal/reenact route, or may it achieve the same result by amending existing law? The answer should be that Congress may expand by amendment the classes of needy persons entitled to Medicaid benefits. A ritualistic requirement that Congress repeal and reenact spending legislation in order to enlarge the population served by a federally funded program would advance no constitutional principle and would scarcely serve the interests of federalism. To the contrary, such a requirement would rigidify Congress' efforts to empower States by partnering with them in the implementation of federal programs.

Medicaid is a prototypical example of federal-state cooperation in serving the Nation's general welfare. Rather than authorizing a federal agency to administer a uniform national healthcare system for the poor, Congress offered States the opportunity to tailor Medicaid grants to their particular needs, so long as they remain within bounds set by federal law. In shaping Medicaid, Congress did not endeavor to fix permanently the terms participating states must meet; instead, Congress reserved the "right to alter, amend, or repeal" any provision of the Medicaid Act. States, for their part, agreed to amend their own Medicaid plans consistent with changes from time to time made in the federal law. And from 1965 to the present, States have regularly conformed to Congress' alterations of the Medicaid Act.

The Chief Justice'[s argument] that the 2010 expansion is unduly coercive . . . rests on three premises, each of them essential to his theory. First, the Medicaid expansion is . . . a new grant program, not an addition to the Medicaid program existing before the ACA's enactment. Congress . . . has threatened States with the loss of funds from an old program in an effort to get them to adopt a new one.

---

e. [T]he joint dissenters contend that the minimum coverage provision is not necessary and proper because it was not the "only . . . way" Congress could have made the guaranteed-issue and community-rating reforms work. . . . [E]ven assuming there were "practicable" alternatives to the minimum coverage provision, "we long ago rejected the view that the Necessary and Proper Clause demands that an Act of Congress be '*absolutely* necessary' to the exercise of an enumerated power." Rather, the statutory provision at issue need only be "conducive" and "[reasonably] adapted" to the goal Congress seeks to achieve.

Second, the expansion was unforeseeable by the States when they first signed on to Medicaid. Third, the threatened loss of funding is so large that the States have no real choice but to participate in the Medicaid expansion. The Chief Justice therefore—*for the first time ever*—finds an exercise of Congress' spending power unconstitutionally coercive.

Medicaid, as amended by the ACA, however, is not two spending programs; it is a single program with a constant aim—to enable poor persons to receive basic health care when they need it. Given past expansions, plus express statutory warning that Congress may change the requirements participating States must meet, there can be no tenable claim that the ACA fails for lack of notice. Moreover, States have no entitlement to receive any Medicaid funds; they enjoy only the opportunity to accept funds on Congress' terms. Future Congresses are not bound by their predecessors' dispositions; they have authority to spend federal revenue as they see fit. The Federal Government, therefore, is not, as The Chief Justice charges, threatening States with the loss of "existing" funds from one spending program in order to induce them to opt into another program. Congress is simply requiring States to do what States have long been required to do to receive Medicaid funding: comply with the conditions Congress prescribes for participation.

A majority of the Court, however, buys the argument that prospective withholding of funds formerly available exceeds Congress' spending power. Given that holding, I entirely agree with The Chief Justice as to the appropriate remedy. It is to bar the withholding found impermissible—not, as the joint dissenters would have it, to scrap the expansion altogether. The dissenters' view that the ACA must fall in its entirety is a radical departure from the Court's normal course. When a constitutional infirmity mars a statute, the Court ordinarily removes the infirmity. It undertakes a salvage operation; it does not demolish the legislation. See, *e.g., Brockett v. Spokane Arcades, Inc.,* 472 U.S. 491 (1985) (Court's normal course is to declare a statute invalid "to the extent that it reaches too far, but otherwise [to leave the statute] intact"). That course is plainly in order where, as in this case, Congress has expressly instructed courts to leave untouched every provision not found invalid. See 42 U.S.C. §1303. Because The Chief Justice finds the withholding—not the granting—of federal funds incompatible with the Spending Clause, Congress' extension of Medicaid remains available to any State that affirms its willingness to participate.

A

[S]ince 1965, Congress has amended the Medicaid program on more than 50 occasions, sometimes quite sizably. Most relevant here, between 1988 and 1990, Congress required participating States to include among their beneficiaries pregnant women with family incomes up to 133% of the federal poverty level, children up to age 6 at the same income levels, and children ages 6 to 18 with family incomes up to 100% of the poverty level. These amendments added millions to the Medicaid-eligible population.

Between 1966 and 1990, annual federal Medicaid spending grew from $631.6 million to $42.6 billion; state spending rose to $31 billion over the same period. And between 1990 and 2010, federal spending increased to $269.5 billion. Enlargement of the population and services covered by Medicaid, in short, has been the trend.

Compared to past alterations, the ACA is notable for the extent to which the Federal Government will pick up the tab. Medicaid's 2010 expansion is financed largely by federal outlays. In 2014, federal funds will cover 100% of the costs for newly eligible beneficiaries; that rate will gradually decrease before settling at 90% in 2020. By comparison, federal contributions toward the care of beneficiaries eligible pre-ACA range from 50% to 83%, and averaged 57% between 2005 and 2008.

Nor will the expansion exorbitantly increase state Medicaid spending. The Congressional Budget Office (CBO) projects that States will spend 0.8% more than they would have, absent the ACA.[f] . . .

[T]he alternative to conditional federal spending, it bears emphasis, is not state autonomy but state marginalization. In 1965, Congress elected to nationalize health coverage for seniors through Medicare. It could similarly have established Medicaid as an exclusively federal program. Instead, Congress gave the States the opportunity to partner in the program's administration and development. Absent from the nationalized model, of course, is the state-level policy discretion and experimentation that is Medicaid's hallmark; undoubtedly the interests of federalism are better served when States retain a meaningful role in the implementation of a program of such importance. See Caminker, State Sovereignty and Subordinacy, 95 Colum. L. Rev. 1001, 1002-1003 (1995) (cooperative federalism can preserve "a significant role for state discretion in achieving specified federal goals, where the alternative is complete federal preemption of any state regulatory role"); Rose-Ackerman, Cooperative Federalism and Co-optation, 92 Yale L.J. 1344, 1346 (1983) ("If the federal government begins to take full responsibility for social welfare spending and preempts the states, the result is likely to be weaker . . . state governments.").[g] . . .

B

[T]here are federalism-based limits on the use of Congress' conditional spending power. In the leading decision in this area, *South Dakota v. Dole,* the Court

---

f. Even the study on which the plaintiffs rely, see Brief for Petitioners 10, concludes that "[w]hile most states will experience some increase in spending, this is quite small relative to the federal matching payments and low relative to the costs of uncompensated care that [the states] would bear if the[re] were no health reform." Thus there can be no objection to the ACA's expansion of Medicaid as an "unfunded mandate." Quite the contrary, the program is impressively well funded.

g. The Chief Justice and the joint dissenters perceive in cooperative federalism a "threa[t]" to "political accountability." By that, they mean voter confusion: Citizens upset by unpopular government action, they posit, may ascribe to state officials blame more appropriately laid at Congress' door. But no such confusion is apparent in this case: Medicaid's status as a federally funded, state-administered program is hardly hidden from view.

identified four criteria. The conditions placed on federal grants to States must (a) promote the "general welfare," (b) "unambiguously" inform States what is demanded of them, (c) be germane "to the federal interest in particular national projects or programs," and (d) not "induce the States to engage in activities that would themselves be unconstitutional."

The Court in *Dole* mentioned, but did not adopt, a further limitation, one hypothetically raised a half-century earlier: In "some circumstances," Congress might be prohibited from offering a "financial inducement . . . so coercive as to pass the point at which 'pressure turns into compulsion.'" (quoting *Steward Machine Co. v. Davis*). Prior to today's decision, however, the Court has never ruled that the terms of any grant crossed the indistinct line between temptation and coercion. . . . The small percentage of highway-construction funds South Dakota stood to lose by adhering to 19 as the age of eligibility to purchase 3.2% beer, however, was not enough to qualify as coercion, the Court concluded.

This case does not present the concerns that led the Court in *Dole* even to consider the prospect of coercion. In *Dole,* the condition—set 21 as the minimum drinking age—did not tell the States how to use funds Congress provided for highway construction. Further, in view of the Twenty-First Amendment, it was an open question whether Congress could directly impose a national minimum drinking age.

The ACA, in contrast, relates solely to the federally funded Medicaid program; if States choose not to comply, Congress has not threatened to withhold funds earmarked for any other program. Nor does the ACA use Medicaid funding to induce States to take action Congress itself could not undertake. The Federal Government undoubtedly could operate its own health-care program for poor persons, just as it operates Medicare for seniors' health care.

That is what makes this such a simple case, and the Court's decision so unsettling. Congress, aiming to assist the needy, has appropriated federal money to subsidize state health-insurance programs that meet federal standards. The principal standard the ACA sets is that the state program cover adults earning no more than 133% of the federal poverty line. Enforcing that prescription ensures that federal funds will be spent on health care for the poor in furtherance of Congress' present perception of the general welfare.

C

1

. . . The Chief Justice calls the ACA new, but in truth, it simply reaches more of America's poor than Congress originally covered.

Medicaid was created to enable States to provide medical assistance to "needy persons." By bringing health care within the reach of a larger population of Americans unable to afford it, the Medicaid expansion is an extension of that basic aim.

The Medicaid Act contains hundreds of provisions governing operation of the program. . . . The Medicaid expansion leaves unchanged the vast majority of these provisions; it adds beneficiaries to the existing program and specifies the rate at which States will be reimbursed for services provided to the added beneficiaries. The ACA does not describe operational aspects of the program for these newly eligible persons; for that information, one must read the existing Medicaid Act.

Congress styled and clearly viewed the Medicaid expansion as an amendment to the Medicaid Act, not as a "new" health-care program. . . .

Endeavoring to show that Congress created a new program, The Chief Justice cites three aspects of the expansion. First, he asserts that, in covering those earning no more than 133% of the federal poverty line, the Medicaid expansion, unlike pre-ACA Medicaid, does not "care for the neediest among us." What makes that so? Single adults earning no more than $14,856 per year — 133% of the current federal poverty level — surely rank among the Nation's poor.

Second, according to The Chief Justice, "Congress mandated that newly eligible persons receive a level of coverage that is less comprehensive than the traditional Medicaid benefit package." That less comprehensive benefit package, however, is not an innovation introduced by the ACA; since 2006, States have been free to use it for many of their Medicaid beneficiaries. The level of benefits offered therefore does not set apart post-ACA Medicaid recipients from all those entitled to benefits pre-ACA.

Third, The Chief Justice correctly notes that the reimbursement rate for participating States is different regarding individuals who became Medicaid-eligible through the ACA. *Ibid.* But the rate differs only in its generosity to participating States. Under pre-ACA Medicaid, the Federal Government pays up to 83% of the costs of coverage for current enrollees. Even if one agreed that a change of as little as 7 percentage points carries constitutional significance, is it not passing strange to suggest that the purported incursion on state sovereignty might have been averted, or at least mitigated, had Congress offered States *less* money to carry out the same obligations?

Consider also that Congress could have repealed Medicaid. Thereafter, Congress could have enacted Medicaid II, a new program combining the pre-2010 coverage with the expanded coverage required by the ACA. By what right does a court stop Congress from building up without first tearing down?

2

The Chief Justice finds the Medicaid expansion vulnerable because it took participating States by surprise. [He relies on] *Pennhurst*[, which] instructs that "if Congress intends to impose a condition on the grant of federal moneys, it must do so unambiguously." That requirement is met in this case. Section 2001 does not take effect until 2014. The ACA makes perfectly clear what will be required of States that accept Medicaid funding after that date: They must extend eligibility to adults with incomes no more than 133% of the federal poverty line.

The Chief Justice appears to find in *Pennhurst* a requirement that, when spending legislation is first passed, or when States first enlist in the federal program, Congress must provide clear notice of conditions it might later impose. If I understand his point correctly, it was incumbent on Congress, in 1965, to warn the States clearly of the size and shape potential changes to Medicaid might take. And absent such notice, sizable changes could not be made mandatory. Our decisions do not support such a requirement.[h]

In *Bennett v. New Jersey,* 470 U.S. 632 (1985), . . . we rejected the Secretary [of Education]'s attempt to recover funds based on the States' alleged violation of a rule that did not exist when the State accepted and spent the funds. . . . [But] [w]hen amendment of an existing grant program has no such retroactive effect, however, we have upheld Congress' instruction. . . . *Pennhurst*'s rule demands that conditions on federal funds be unambiguously clear at the time a State receives and uses the money — not at the time, perhaps years earlier, when Congress passed the law establishing the program.

In any event, from the start, the Medicaid Act put States on notice that the program could be changed: "The right to alter, amend, or repeal any provision of [Medicaid]," the statute has read since 1965, "is hereby reserved to the Congress." The "effect of these few simple words" has long been settled. See *National Railroad Passenger Corporation v. Atchison, T. & S.F.R. Co.,* 470 U.S. 451 (1985) (citing *Sinking Fund Cases,* 99 U.S. 700, 720, 25 L. Ed. 496 (1879)). By reserving the right to "alter, amend, [or] repeal" a spending program, Congress "has given special notice of its intention to retain . . . full and complete power to make such alterations and amendments . . . as come within the just scope of legislative power." . . .

The Chief Justice insists that the most recent expansion, in contrast to its predecessors, "accomplishes a shift in kind, not merely degree." But why was Medicaid altered only in degree, not in kind, when Congress required States to cover millions of children and pregnant women? In short, given § 1304, this Court's construction of §1304's language in [previous decisions], and the enlargement of Medicaid in the years since 1965, a State would be hard put to complain that it lacked fair notice when, in 2010, Congress altered Medicaid to embrace a larger portion of the Nation's poor.

3

The Chief Justice sees no need to "fix the outermost line," *Steward Machine,* "where persuasion gives way to coercion[.]" Neither do the joint dissenters. Notably, the decision on which they rely, *Steward Machine,* found the statute at issue inside the line, "wherever the line may be."

---

h. The Chief Justice observes that "Spending Clause legislation [i]s much in the nature of a *contract.*" But the Court previously has recognized that "[u]nlike normal contractual undertakings, federal grant programs originate in and remain governed by statutory provisions expressing the judgment of Congress concerning desirable public policy." *Bennett v. Kentucky Dept. of Ed.,* 470 U.S. 656 (1985).

When future Spending Clause challenges arrive, as they likely will in the wake of today's decision, how will litigants and judges assess whether "a State has a legitimate choice whether to accept the federal conditions in exchange for federal funds"? Are courts to measure the number of dollars the Federal Government might withhold for noncompliance? The portion of the State's budget at stake? And which State's — or States' — budget is determinative: the lead plaintiff, all challenging States (26 in this case, many with quite different fiscal situations), or some national median? Does it matter that Florida, unlike most States, imposes no state income tax, and therefore might be able to replace foregone federal funds with new state revenue?[i] Or that the coercion state officials in fact fear is punishment at the ballot box for turning down a politically popular federal grant?

The coercion inquiry, therefore, appears to involve political judgments that defy judicial calculation. See *Baker v. Carr,* 369 U.S. 186 (1962). Even commentators sympathetic to robust enforcement of *Dole*'s limitations . . . have concluded that conceptions of "impermissible coercion" premised on States' perceived inability to decline federal funds "are just too amorphous to be judicially administrable."

At bottom, my colleagues' position is that the States' reliance on federal funds limits Congress' authority to alter its spending programs. This gets things backwards: Congress, not the States, is tasked with spending federal money in service of the general welfare. And each successive Congress is empowered to appropriate funds as it sees fit. When the 110th Congress reached a conclusion about Medicaid funds that differed from its predecessors' view, it abridged no State's right to "existing," or "pre-existing," funds. For, in fact, there are no such funds. There is only money States *anticipate* receiving from future Congresses.

D

[T]he Court does not strike down any provision of the ACA. It prohibits only the "application" of the Secretary's authority to withhold Medicaid funds from States that decline to conform their Medicaid plans to the ACA's requirements. Thus the ACA's authorization of funds to finance the expansion remains intact,

---

i. Federal taxation of a State's citizens, according to the joint dissenters, may diminish a State's ability to raise new revenue. This, in turn, could limit a State's capacity to replace a federal program with an "equivalent" state-funded analog. But it cannot be true that "the amount of the federal taxes extracted from the taxpayers of a State to pay for the program in question is relevant in determining whether there is impermissible coercion." When the United States Government taxes United States citizens, it taxes them "in their individual capacities" as "the people of America" — not as residents of a particular State. . . . A State therefore has no claim on the money its residents pay in federal taxes, and federal "spending programs need not help people in all states in the same measure." In 2004, for example, New Jersey received 55 cents in federal spending for every dollar its residents paid to the Federal Government in taxes, while Mississippi received $1.77 per tax dollar paid. Thus no constitutional problem was created when Arizona declined for 16 years to participate in Medicaid, even though its residents' tax dollars financed Medicaid programs in every other State.

and the Secretary's authority to withhold funds for reasons other than noncompliance with the expansion remains unaffected. . . . The Chief Justice is undoubtedly right to conclude that Congress may offer States funds "to expand the availability of health care, and requir[e] that States accepting such funds comply with the conditions on their use." I therefore concur in the judgment with respect to Part IV-B of The Chief Justice's opinion. . . .

Justice SCALIA, Justice KENNEDY, Justice THOMAS, and Justice ALITO, dissenting.

[T]here are structural limits upon federal power—upon what it can prescribe with respect to private conduct, and upon what it can impose upon the sovereign States. Whatever may be the conceptual limits upon the Commerce Clause and upon the power to tax and spend, they cannot be such as will enable the Federal Government to regulate all private conduct and to compel the States to function as administrators of federal programs.

[T]he Act before us here exceeds federal power both in mandating the purchase of health insurance and in denying nonconsenting States all Medicaid funding. These parts of the Act are central to its design and operation, and all the Act's other provisions would not have been enacted without them. In our view it must follow that the entire statute is inoperative.

I

The Individual Mandate

Article I, §8, of the Constitution gives Congress the power to "regulate Commerce . . . among the several States." The Individual Mandate in the Act commands that every "applicable individual shall for each month beginning after 2013 ensure that the individual, and any dependent of the individual who is an applicable individual, is covered under minimum essential coverage." 26 U.S.C. §5000A(a) (2006 ed., Supp. IV). If this provision "regulates" anything, it is the *failure* to maintain minimum essential coverage. One might argue that it regulates that failure by requiring it to be accompanied by payment of a penalty. But that failure—that abstention from commerce—is not "Commerce." To be sure, *purchasing* insurance *is* "Commerce"; but one does not regulate commerce that does not exist by compelling its existence.

In *Gibbons v. Ogden*, Chief Justice Marshall wrote that the power to regulate commerce is the power "to prescribe the rule by which commerce is to be governed." That understanding is consistent with the original meaning of "regulate" at the time of the Constitution's ratification, when "to regulate" meant "[t]o adjust by rule, method or established mode," 2 N. Webster, An American Dictionary of the English Language (1828); "[t]o adjust by rule or method," 2 S. Johnson, A Dictionary of the English Language (7th ed. 1785); "[t]o adjust, to direct according to rule," 2 J. Ash, New and Complete Dictionary of the English Language (1775); "to put in order, set to rights, govern or keep in order," T. Dyche & W. Pardon, A New General English Dictionary (16th ed. 1777). It can mean to direct the manner of something but not to direct that something come into being. There is no instance in which this Court or Congress (or anyone else, to our knowledge) has used "regulate" in that peculiar fashion. If the word bore that meaning, Congress' authority "[t]o make Rules for the Government and Regulation of the land and naval Forces," U.S. Const., Art. I, §8, cl. 14, would have made superfluous the later provision for authority "[t]o raise and support Armies," *id.,* §8, cl. 12, and "[t]o provide and maintain a Navy," *id.,* §8, cl. 13.

We do not doubt that the buying and selling of health insurance contracts is commerce generally subject to federal regulation. But when Congress provides that (nearly) all citizens must buy an insurance contract, it goes beyond "adjust[ing] by rule or method," or "direct[ing] according to rule," it directs the creation of commerce.

A

[T]he Government presents the Individual Mandate as a unique feature of a complicated regulatory scheme governing many parties with countervailing incentives that must be carefully balanced. [The problem of adverse selection] is not a dilemma unique to regulation of the health-insurance industry. Government regulation typically imposes costs on the regulated industry — especially regulation that prohibits economic behavior in which most market participants are already engaging, such as "piecing out" the market by selling the product to different classes of people at different prices (in the present context, providing much lower insurance rates to young and healthy buyers). And many industries so regulated face the reality that, without an artificial increase in demand, they cannot continue on. When Congress is regulating these industries directly, it enjoys the broad power to enact "'all appropriate legislation'" to "'protec[t]'" and "'advanc[e]'" commerce, *NLRB v. Jones & Laughlin Steel Corp.* Thus, Congress might protect the imperiled industry by prohibiting low-cost competition, or by according it preferential tax treatment, or even by granting it a direct subsidy.

Here, however, Congress has impressed into service third parties, healthy individuals who could be but are not customers of the relevant industry, to offset the undesirable consequences of the regulation. Congress' desire to force these individuals to purchase insurance is motivated by the fact that they are further removed from the market than unhealthy individuals with pre-existing conditions, because they are less likely to need extensive care in the near future. If Congress can reach out and command even those furthest removed from an interstate market to participate in the market, then the Commerce Clause becomes a font of unlimited power, or in Hamilton's words, "the hideous monster whose devouring jaws . . . spare neither sex nor age, nor high nor low, nor sacred nor profane." The Federalist No. 33, p. 202 (C. Rossiter ed. 1961). . . .

Raich is no precedent for what Congress has done here. That case's prohibition of growing (cf. *Wickard*), and of possession (cf. innumerable federal statutes) did not represent the expansion of the federal power to direct into a broad new field. The mandating of economic activity does, and since it is a field so limitless that it converts the Commerce Clause into a general authority to direct the economy, that mandating is not "consist[ent] with the letter and spirit of the constitution." *McCulloch v. Maryland.*

Moreover, . . . [t]he Court's opinion in *Raich* pointed out that the growing and possession prohibitions were the only practicable way of enabling the prohibition of interstate traffic in marijuana to be effectively enforced. [But] [t]here are many ways other than this unprecedented Individual Mandate by which the regulatory scheme's goals of reducing insurance premiums and ensuring the profitability of insurers could be achieved. For instance, those who did not purchase insurance could be subjected to a surcharge when they do enter the health insurance system. Or they could be denied a full income tax credit given to those who do purchase the insurance.

The Government was invited, at oral argument, to suggest what federal controls over private conduct (other than those explicitly prohibited by the Bill of Rights or other constitutional controls) could *not* be justified as necessary and proper for the carrying out of a general regulatory scheme. It was unable to name any. As we said at the outset, whereas the precise scope of the Commerce Clause and the Necessary and Proper Clause is uncertain, the proposition that the Federal Government cannot do everything is a fundamental precept. Section 5000A is defeated by that proposition.

B

The Government [also argues that the mandate] directs the manner in which individuals purchase health care services and related goods (directing that they be purchased through insurance) and is therefore a straightforward exercise of the commerce power.

The primary problem with this argument is that §5000A does not apply only to persons who purchase all, or most, or even any, of the health care services or goods that the mandated insurance covers. Indeed, the main objection many have to the Mandate is that they have no intention of purchasing most or even any of such goods or services and thus no need to buy insurance for those purchases. The Government responds that the health-care market involves "essentially universal participation[.]" [This is] not true. It is true enough that everyone consumes "health care," if the term is taken to include the purchase of a bottle of aspirin. But the health care "market" that is the object of the Individual Mandate not only includes but principally consists of goods and services that the young people primarily affected by the Mandate *do not purchase*. They are quite simply not participants in that market, and cannot be made so (and thereby subjected to regulation) by the simple device of defining participants to include all those who will, later in their lifetime, probably purchase the goods or services covered by the mandated insurance. Such a definition of market participants is unprecedented, and were it to be a premise for the exercise of national power, it would have no principled limits.

[T]he Government [argues] that Congress . . . has purported to regulate "economic and financial decision[s] to forego [*sic*] health insurance coverage and [to] attempt to self-insure," since those decisions have "a substantial and deleterious effect on interstate commerce[.]" But . . . the decision to forgo participation in an interstate market is not itself commercial activity (or indeed any activity at all) within Congress' power to regulate. It is true that, at the end of the day, it is inevitable that each American will affect commerce and become a part of it, even if not by choice. But if every person comes within the Commerce Clause power of Congress to regulate by the simple reason that he will one day engage in commerce, the idea of a limited Government power is at an end. . . .

[Both] *Wickard v. Filburn* [and] *Perez v. United States* . . . involved commercial *activity*. To go beyond that, and to say that the failure to grow wheat or the refusal to make loans affects commerce, so that growing and lending can be federally compelled, is to extend federal power to virtually everything. All of us consume food, and when we do so the Federal Government can prescribe what its quality must be and even how much we must pay. But the mere fact that we all consume food and are thus, sooner or later, participants in the "market" for food, does not empower the Government to say when and what we will buy. That is essentially what this Act seeks to do with respect to the purchase of health care. It exceeds federal power.

C

[I]t is true enough that Congress needs only a "'rational basis' for concluding that the *regulated activity* substantially affects interstate commerce[.]" But it must be *activity* affecting commerce that is regulated, and not merely the failure to engage in commerce. And one is not now purchasing the health care covered by the insurance mandate simply because one is likely to be purchasing it in the future. Our test's premise of regulated activity is not invented out of whole cloth, but rests upon the Constitution's requirement that it be commerce which is regulated. If all inactivity affecting commerce is commerce, commerce is everything. Ultimately [Justice Ginsburg's] dissent is driven to saying that there is really no difference between action and inaction, a proposition that has never recommended itself, neither to the law nor to common sense. To say, for example, that the inaction here consists of activity in "the self-insurance market[]" seems to us wordplay. By parity of reasoning the failure to buy a car can be called participation in the nonprivate-car-transportation market. Commerce becomes everything.

[T]he individual mandate threatens our constitutional order . . . because it gives such an expansive meaning to the Commerce Clause that *all* private conduct (including failure to act) becomes subject to federal control, effectively destroying the Constitution's division of governmental powers. Thus the dissent, on the theories proposed for the validity of the Mandate, would alter the accepted constitutional relation between the individual and the National Government. The dissent protests that the Necessary and Proper Clause has been held to include "the power to enact criminal laws, . . . the power to imprison, . . .

and the power to create a national bank[.]" Is not the power to compel purchase of health insurance much lesser? No, not if (unlike those other dispositions) its application rests upon a theory that everything is within federal control simply because it exists.

The dissent's exposition of the wonderful things the Federal Government has achieved through exercise of its assigned powers, such as "the provision of old-age and survivors' benefits" in the Social Security Act, is quite beside the point. The issue here is whether the federal government can impose the Individual Mandate through the Commerce Clause. And the relevant history is not that Congress has achieved wide and wonderful results through the proper exercise of its assigned powers in the past, but that it has never before used the Commerce Clause to compel entry into commerce. The dissent treats the Constitution as though it is an enumeration of those problems that the Federal Government can address — among which, it finds, is "the Nation's course in the economic and social welfare realm," and more specifically "the problem of the uninsured." The Constitution is not that. It enumerates not federally soluble *problems,* but federally available *powers.* The Federal Government can address whatever problems it wants but can bring to their solution only those powers that the Constitution confers, among which is the power to regulate commerce. None of our cases say anything else. Article I contains no whatever-it-takes-to-solve-a-national-problem power.

The dissent dismisses the conclusion that the power to compel entry into the health-insurance market would include the power to compel entry into the new-car or broccoli markets. The latter purchasers, it says, "will be obliged to pay at the counter before receiving the vehicle or nourishment," whereas those refusing to purchase health-insurance will ultimately get treated anyway, at others' expense. "[T]he unique attributes of the health-care market . . . give rise to a significant free-riding problem that does not occur in other markets." And "a vegetable-purchase mandate" (or a car-purchase mandate) is not "likely to have a substantial effect on the health-care costs" borne by other Americans. Those differences make a very good argument by the dissent's own lights, since they show that the failure to purchase health insurance, unlike the failure to purchase cars or broccoli, creates a national, social-welfare problem that is (in the dissent's view) included among the unenumerated "problems" that the Constitution authorizes the Federal Government to solve. But those differences do not show that the failure to enter the health-insurance market, unlike the failure to buy cars and broccoli, is an *activity* that Congress can "regulate." (Of course one day the failure of some of the public to purchase American cars may endanger the existence of domestic automobile manufacturers; or the failure of some to eat broccoli may be found to deprive them of a newly discovered cancer-fighting chemical which only that food contains, producing health-care costs that are a burden on the rest of us — in which case, under the theory of Justice Ginsburg's dissent, moving against those inactivities will also come within the Federal Government's unenumerated problem-solving powers.)

II

The Taxing Power

[T]he Government contends, however, as expressed in the caption to Part II of its brief, that "THE MINIMUM COVERAGE PROVISION IS INDEPENDENTLY AUTHORIZED BY CONGRESS'S TAXING POWER." [This] suggests the existence of a creature never hitherto seen in the United States Reports: A penalty for constitutional purposes that is *also* a tax for constitutional purposes. In all our cases the two are mutually exclusive. The provision challenged under the Constitution is either a penalty or else a tax. Of course in many cases what was a regulatory mandate enforced by a penalty *could have been* imposed as a tax upon permissible action; or what was imposed as a tax upon permissible action *could have been* a regulatory mandate enforced by a penalty. But we know of no case, and the Government cites none, in which the imposition was, for constitutional purposes, both. The issue is not whether Congress had the *power* to frame the minimum-coverage provision as a tax, but whether it *did* so.[a]

In answering that question we must, if "fairly possible," construe the provision to be a tax rather than a mandate-with-penalty, since that would render it constitutional rather than unconstitutional (*ut res magis valeat quam pereat*). But we cannot rewrite the statute to be what it is not. [T]here is simply no way, "without doing violence to the fair meaning of the words used," to escape what Congress enacted: a mandate that individuals maintain minimum essential coverage, enforced by a penalty.

Our cases establish a clear line between a tax and a penalty: "'[A] tax is an enforced contribution to provide for the support of government; a penalty . . . is an exaction imposed by statute as punishment for an unlawful act.'" In a few cases, this Court has held that a "tax" imposed upon private conduct was so onerous as to be in effect a penalty. But we have never held—*never*—that a penalty imposed for violation of the law was so trivial as to be in effect a tax. We have never held that *any* exaction imposed for violation of the law is an exercise of Congress' taxing power—even when the statute *calls* it a tax, much less when (as here) the statute repeatedly calls it a penalty. When an act "adopt[s] the criteria of wrongdoing" and then imposes a monetary penalty as the "principal consequence on those who transgress its standard," it creates a regulatory penalty, not a tax. *Child Labor Tax Case* [Bailey v. Drexel Furniture Co.], 259 U.S. 20 (1922).

So the question is, quite simply, whether the exaction here is imposed for violation of the law. It unquestionably is. The minimum-coverage provision is found in 26 U.S.C. §5000A, entitled "*Requirement* to maintain minimum essential coverage." (Emphasis added.) It commands that every "applicable individual *shall* . . . ensure that the individual . . . is covered under minimum essential coverage." *Ibid.* (emphasis added). And the immediately following provision states

---

a. No one seriously contends that any of Congress' other enumerated powers gives it the authority to enact §5000A *as a regulation*. [Relocated footnote—Eds.]

that, "[i]f . . . an applicable individual . . . fails to meet the *requirement* of subsection (a) . . . there is hereby imposed . . . a *penalty.*" §5000A(b) (emphasis added). And several of Congress' legislative "findings" with regard to §5000A confirm that it sets forth a legal requirement and constitutes the assertion of regulatory power, not mere taxing power. See 42 U.S.C. §18091(2)(A) ("The requirement regulates activity . . ."); §18091(2)(C) ("The requirement . . . will add millions of new consumers to the health insurance market . . ."); §18091(2)(D) ("The requirement achieves near-universal coverage"); §18091(2)(H) ("The requirement is an essential part of this larger regulation of economic activity, and the absence of the requirement would undercut Federal regulation of the health insurance market"); §18091(3) ("[T]he Supreme Court of the United States ruled that insurance is interstate commerce subject to Federal regulation"). . . .

Quite separately, the fact that Congress (in its own words) "imposed . . . a penalty," 26 U.S.C. §5000A(b)(1), for failure to buy insurance is alone sufficient to render that failure unlawful. It is one of the canons of interpretation that a statute that penalizes an act makes it unlawful. . . .

We never have classified as a tax an exaction imposed for violation of the law, and so too, we never have classified as a tax an exaction described in the legislation itself as a penalty. To be sure, we have sometimes treated as a tax a statutory exaction (imposed for something other than a violation of law) which bore an agnostic label that does not entail the significant constitutional consequences of a penalty — such as "license" or "surcharge[.]" But we have never — *never* — treated as a tax an exaction which faces up to the critical difference between a tax and a penalty, and explicitly denominates the exaction a "penalty." Eighteen times in §5000A itself and elsewhere throughout the Act, Congress called the exaction in §5000A(b) a "penalty."

That §5000A imposes not a simple tax but a mandate to which a penalty is attached is demonstrated by the fact that some are exempt from the tax who are not exempt from the mandate — a distinction that would make no sense if the mandate were not a mandate. Section 5000A(d) exempts three classes of people from the definition of "applicable individual" subject to the minimum coverage requirement: Those with religious objections or who participate in a "health care sharing ministry," those who are "not lawfully present" in the United States, and those who are incarcerated. Section 5000A(e) then creates a separate set of exemptions, excusing from liability for the penalty certain individuals who are subject to the minimum coverage requirement: Those who cannot afford coverage, who earn too little income to require filing a tax return, who are members of an Indian tribe, who experience only short gaps in coverage, and who, in the judgment of the Secretary of Health and Human Services, "have suffered a hardship with respect to the capability to obtain coverage[.]" If §5000A were a tax, these two classes of exemption would make no sense; there being no requirement, *all* the exemptions would attach to the penalty (renamed tax) alone.

In the face of all these indications of a regulatory requirement accompanied by a penalty, the Solicitor General assures us that "neither the Treasury Department nor the Department of Health and Human Services interprets Section 5000A as imposing a legal obligation," and that "[i]f [those subject to the Act] pay the tax penalty, they're in compliance with the law[.]" These self-serving litigating positions are entitled to no weight. What counts is what the statute says, and that is entirely clear. . . .

Against the mountain of evidence that the minimum coverage requirement is what the statute calls it — a requirement — and that the penalty for its violation is what the statute calls it — a penalty — the Government brings forward the flimsiest of indications to the contrary. It notes that "[t]he minimum coverage provision amends the Internal Revenue Code to provide that a non-exempted individual . . . will owe a monetary penalty, in addition to the income tax itself," and that "[t]he [Internal Revenue Service (IRS)] will assess and collect the penalty in the same manner as assessable penalties under the Internal Revenue Code." The manner of collection could perhaps suggest a tax if IRS penalty-collection were unheard-of or rare. It is not. In *Reorganized CF & I Fabricators of Utah, Inc.,* 518 U.S. 213, we held that an exaction not only *enforced* by the Commissioner of Internal Revenue but even *called* a "tax" was in fact a penalty. "[I]f the concept of penalty means anything," we said, "it means punishment for an unlawful act or omission." Moreover, while the penalty is assessed and collected by the IRS, §5000A is administered both by that agency and by the Department of Health and Human Services (and also the Secretary of Veteran Affairs), which is responsible for defining its substantive scope — a feature that would be quite extraordinary for taxes.

The Government points out that "[t]he amount of the penalty will be calculated as a percentage of household income for federal income tax purposes, subject to a floor and [a] ca[p]," and that individuals who earn so little money that they "are not required to file income tax returns for the taxable year are not subject to the penalty" (though they are, as we discussed earlier, subject to the mandate). But varying a penalty according to ability to pay is an utterly familiar practice.

The last of the feeble arguments in favor of petitioners that we will address is the contention that what this statute repeatedly calls a penalty is in fact a tax because it contains no scienter requirement. The *presence* of such a requirement suggests a penalty — though one can imagine a tax imposed only on willful action; but the *absence* of such a requirement does not suggest a tax. Penalties for absolute-liability offenses are commonplace. And where a statute is silent as to scienter, we traditionally presume a *mens rea* requirement if the statute imposes a "severe penalty." Since we have an entire jurisprudence addressing when it is that a scienter requirement should be inferred from a penalty, it is quite illogical to suggest that a penalty is not a penalty for want of an express scienter requirement.

And the nail in the coffin is that the mandate and penalty are located in Title I of the Act, its operative core, rather than where a tax would be found — in Title IX, containing the Act's "Revenue Provisions." In sum, "the terms of [the] act rende[r] it unavoidable[]" that Congress imposed a regulatory penalty, not a tax.

For all these reasons, to say that the Individual Mandate merely imposes a tax is not to interpret the statute but to rewrite it. Judicial tax-writing is particularly troubling. Taxes have never been popular, see, *e.g.,* Stamp Act of 1765, and in part for that reason, the Constitution requires tax increases to originate in the House of Representatives. See Art. I, §7, cl. 1. That is to say, they must originate in the legislative body most accountable to the people, where legislators must weigh the need for the tax against the terrible price they might pay at their next election, which is never more than two years off. The Federalist No. 58 "defend[ed] the decision to give the origination power to the House on the ground that the Chamber that is more accountable to the people should have the primary role in raising revenue." We have no doubt that Congress knew precisely what it was doing when it rejected [the House] version of this legislation that imposed a tax instead of a requirement-with-penalty. Imposing a tax through judicial legislation inverts the constitutional scheme, and places the power to tax in the branch of government least accountable to the citizenry.

Finally, we must observe that rewriting §5000A as a tax in order to sustain its constitutionality would force us to confront a difficult constitutional question: whether this is a direct tax that must be apportioned among the States according to their population. Art. I, §9, cl. 4. Perhaps it is not (we have no need to address the point); but the meaning of the Direct Tax Clause is famously unclear, and its application here is a question of first impression that deserves more thoughtful consideration than the lick-and-a-promise accorded by the Government and its supporters. . . . One would expect this Court to demand more than fly-by-night briefing and argument before deciding a difficult constitutional question of first impression.

. . .

IV

The Medicaid Expansion

[I]n light of the ACA's goal of near-universal coverage, petitioners argue, if Congress had thought that anything less than 100% state participation was a realistic possibility, Congress would have provided a backup scheme. But no such scheme is to be found anywhere in the more than 900 pages of the Act. This shows, they maintain, that Congress was certain that the ACA's Medicaid offer was one that no State could refuse. [T]he Government contends that any congressional assumption about uniform state participation was based on the simple fact that the offer of federal funds associated with the expanded coverage is such a generous gift that no State would want to turn it down. . . .

C

This practice of attaching conditions to federal funds greatly increases federal power. "[O]bjectives not thought to be within Article I's enumerated legislative fields, may nevertheless be attained through the use of the spending power and the conditional grant of federal funds." *Dole.*

This formidable power, if not checked in any way, would present a grave threat to the system of federalism created by our Constitution. . . . When federal legislation gives the States a real choice whether to accept or decline a federal aid package, the federal-state relationship is in the nature of a contractual relationship. And just as a contract is voidable if coerced, "[t]he legitimacy of Congress' power to legislate under the spending power . . . rests on whether the State *voluntarily* and knowingly accepts the terms of the 'contract.' " If a federal spending program coerces participation the States have not "exercise[d] their choice" — let alone made an "informed choice."

Coercing States to accept conditions risks the destruction of the "unique role of the States in our system." "[T]he Constitution has never been understood to confer upon Congress the ability to require the States to govern according to Congress' instructions." *New York*. Congress may not "simply commandeer the legislative processes of the States by directly compelling them to enact and enforce a federal regulatory program." Congress effectively engages in this impermissible compulsion when state participation in a federal spending program is coerced, so that the States' choice whether to enact or administer a federal regulatory program is rendered illusory.

Where all Congress has done is to "encourag[e] state regulation rather than compe[l] it, state governments remain responsive to the local electorate's preferences; state officials remain accountable to the people. [But] where the Federal Government compels States to regulate, the accountability of both state and federal officials is diminished." *New York*.

Amici who support the Government argue that forcing state employees to implement a federal program is more respectful of federalism than using federal workers to implement that program. They note that Congress, instead of expanding Medicaid, could have established an entirely federal program to provide coverage for the same group of people. By choosing to structure Medicaid as a cooperative federal-state program, they contend, Congress allows for more state control.

This argument reflects a view of federalism that our cases have rejected — and with good reason. When Congress compels the States to do its bidding, it blurs the lines of political accountability. If the Federal Government makes a controversial decision while acting on its own, "it is the Federal Government that makes the decision in full view of the public, and it will be federal officials that suffer the consequences if the decision turns out to be detrimental or unpopular." *New York*. But when the Federal Government compels the States to take unpopular actions, "it may be state officials who will bear the brunt of public disapproval, while the federal officials who devised the regulatory program may remain insulated from the electoral ramifications of their decision." For this reason, federal officeholders may view this "departur[e] from the federal structure to be in their personal interests . . . as a means of shifting responsibility for the eventual decision." *New York*. And even state officials may favor such a "departure from the constitutional plan," since uncertainty concerning responsibility may also permit them to escape accountability. If a program is popular, state officials may claim credit; if it is unpopular, they may protest that they were merely responding to a federal directive.

. . .

D

[I]f States really have no choice other than to accept the package, the offer is coercive, and the conditions cannot be sustained under the spending power. And as our decision in *South Dakota v. Dole* makes clear, theoretical voluntariness is not enough. . . .

The Federal Government suggests that it is sufficient if States are "free, *as a matter of law,* to turn down" federal funds. According to the Federal Government, neither the amount of the offered federal funds nor the amount of the federal taxes extracted from the taxpayers of a State to pay for the program in question is relevant in determining whether there is impermissible coercion.

This argument ignores reality. When a heavy federal tax is levied to support a federal program that offers large grants to the States, States may, as a practical matter, be unable to refuse to participate in the federal program and to substitute a state alternative. Even if a State believes that the federal program is ineffective and inefficient, withdrawal would likely force the State to impose a huge tax increase on its residents, and this new state tax would come on top of the federal taxes already paid by residents to support subsidies to participating States.[b]

Acceptance of the Federal Government's interpretation of the anticoercion rule would permit Congress to dictate policy in areas traditionally governed primarily at the state or local level. Suppose, for example, that Congress enacted legislation offering each State a grant equal to the State's entire annual expenditures for primary and secondary education. Suppose also that this funding came with conditions governing such things as school curriculum, the hiring and tenure of teachers, the drawing of school districts, the length and hours of the school day, the school calendar, a dress code for students, and rules for student discipline. *As a matter of law,* a State could turn down that offer, but if it did so, its residents would not only be required to pay the federal taxes needed to support this expensive new program, but they would also be forced to pay an equivalent amount in state taxes. And if the State gave in to the federal law, the State and its subdivisions would surrender their traditional authority in the field of education. Asked at oral argument whether such a law would be allowed under the spending power, the Solicitor General responded that it would.

---

b. Justice Ginsburg argues that "[a] State . . . has no claim on the money its residents pay in federal taxes." This is true as a formal matter. "When the United States Government taxes United States citizens, it taxes them 'in their individual capacities' as 'the people of America' — not as residents of a particular State." But unless Justice Ginsburg thinks that there is no limit to the amount of money that can be squeezed out of taxpayers, heavy federal taxation diminishes the practical ability of States to collect their own taxes.

E

Whether federal spending legislation crosses the line from enticement to coercion is often difficult to determine, and courts should not conclude that legislation is unconstitutional on this ground unless the coercive nature of an offer is unmistakably clear. In this case, however, there can be no doubt. In structuring the ACA, Congress unambiguously signaled its belief that every State would have no real choice but to go along with the Medicaid Expansion. If the anticoercion rule does not apply in this case, then there is no such rule.

1

[M]edicaid has long been the largest federal program of grants to the States. In 2010, the Federal Government directed more than $552 billion in federal funds to the States. *This amount equals nearly 22% of all state expenditures combined.*

The Court of Appeals concluded that the States failed to establish coercion in this case in part because the "states have the power to tax and raise revenue, and therefore can create and fund programs of their own if they do not like Congress's terms." But the sheer size of this federal spending program in relation to state expenditures means that a State would be very hard pressed to compensate for the loss of federal funds by cutting other spending or raising additional revenue. Arizona, for example, commits 12% of its state expenditures to Medicaid, and relies on the Federal Government to provide the rest: $5.6 billion, equaling roughly one-third of Arizona's annual state expenditures of $17 billion. Therefore, if Arizona lost federal Medicaid funding, the State would have to commit an additional 33% of all its state expenditures to fund an equivalent state program along the lines of pre-expansion Medicaid. This means that the State would have to allocate 45% of its annual expenditures for that one purpose.

The States are far less reliant on federal funding for any other program. After Medicaid, the next biggest federal funding item is aid to support elementary and secondary education, which amounts to 12.8% of total federal outlays to the States, and equals only 6.6% of all state expenditures combined.

A State forced out of the Medicaid program would face burdens in addition to the loss of federal Medicaid funding. For example, a nonparticipating State might be found to be ineligible for other major federal funding sources, such as Temporary Assistance for Needy Families (TANF), which is premised on the expectation that States will participate in Medicaid. And withdrawal or expulsion from the Medicaid program would not relieve a State's hospitals of their obligation under federal law to provide care for patients who are unable to pay for medical services. The Emergency Medical Treatment and Active Labor Act requires hospitals that receive any federal funding to provide stabilization care for indigent patients but does not offer federal funding to assist facilities in carrying out its mandate. Many of these patients are now covered by Medicaid.

If providers could not look to the Medicaid program to pay for this care, they would find it exceedingly difficult to comply with federal law unless they were given substantial state support.

For these reasons, the offer that the ACA makes to the States—go along with a dramatic expansion of Medicaid or potentially lose all federal Medicaid funding—is quite unlike anything that we have seen in a prior spending-power case. In *South Dakota v. Dole,* the total amount that the States would have lost if every single State had refused to comply with the 21-year-old drinking age was approximately $614.7 million—or about 0.19% of all state expenditures combined. South Dakota stood to lose, at most, funding that amounted to less than 1% of its annual state expenditures. Under the ACA, by contrast, the Federal Government has threatened to withhold 42.3% of all federal outlays to the states, or approximately $233 billion. South Dakota stands to lose federal funding equaling 28.9% of its annual state expenditures. Withholding $614.7 million, equaling only 0.19% of all state expenditures combined, is aptly characterized as "relatively mild encouragement," but threatening to withhold $233 billion, equaling 21.86% of all state expenditures combined, is a different matter.

2

[I]n crafting the ACA, Congress clearly expressed its informed view that no State could possibly refuse the offer that the ACA extends.

The stated goal of the ACA is near-universal health care coverage. . . . [F]or low-income individuals who are simply not able to obtain insurance, Congress expanded Medicaid, transforming it from a program covering only members of a limited list of vulnerable groups into a program that provides at least the requisite minimum level of coverage for the poor. This design was intended to provide at least a specified minimum level of coverage for all Americans, but the achievement of that goal obviously depends on participation by every single State. If any State—not to mention all of the 26 States that brought this suit—chose to decline the federal offer, there would be a gaping hole in the ACA's coverage.

It is true that some persons who are eligible for Medicaid coverage under the ACA may be able to secure private insurance, either through their employers or by obtaining subsidized insurance through an exchange. But the new federal subsidies are not available to those whose income is below the federal poverty level, and the ACA provides no means, other than Medicaid, for these individuals to obtain coverage and comply with the Mandate. The Government counters that these people will not have to pay the penalty, but that argument misses the point: Without Medicaid, these individuals will not have coverage and the ACA's goal of near-universal coverage will be severely frustrated.

If Congress had thought that States might actually refuse to go along with the expansion of Medicaid, Congress would surely have devised a backup scheme so that the most vulnerable groups in our society, those previously eligible for Medicaid, would not be left out in the cold. But nowhere in the over 900-page Act is such a scheme to be found. By contrast, because Congress thought that some States might decline federal funding for the operation of a "health benefit exchange," Congress provided a backup scheme; if a State declines to participate in the operation of an exchange, the Federal Government will step in and operate an exchange in that State. Likewise, knowing that States would not necessarily provide affordable health insurance for aliens lawfully present in the United States—because Medicaid does not require States to provide such coverage—Congress extended the availability of the new federal insurance subsidies to all aliens. Congress did not make these subsidies available for citizens with incomes below the poverty level because Congress obviously assumed that they would be covered by Medicaid. . . .

The Federal Government does not dispute the inference that Congress anticipated 100% state participation, but it argues that this assumption was based on the fact that ACA's offer was an "exceedingly generous" gift. . . . [But] [i]f that offer is "exceedingly generous," as the Federal Government maintains, why have more than half the States brought this lawsuit, contending that the offer is coercive? And why did Congress find it necessary to threaten that any State refusing to accept this "exceedingly generous" gift would risk losing all Medicaid funds? Congress could have made just the *new* funding provided under the ACA contingent on acceptance of the terms of the Medicaid Expansion. Congress took such an approach in some earlier amendments to Medicaid, separating new coverage requirements and funding from the rest of the program so that only new funding was conditioned on new eligibility extensions. See, *e.g.*, Social Security Amendments of 1972, 86 Stat. 1465.

Congress' decision to do otherwise here reflects its understanding that the ACA offer is not an "exceedingly generous" gift that no State in its right mind would decline. Instead, acceptance of the offer will impose very substantial costs on participating States. It is true that the Federal Government will bear most of the initial costs associated with the Medicaid Expansion, first paying 100% of the costs of covering newly eligible individuals between 2014 and 2016. But that is just part of the picture. Participating States will be forced to shoulder substantial costs as well, because after 2019 the Federal Government will cover only 90% of the costs associated with the Expansion, with state spending projected to increase by at least $20 billion by 2020 as a consequence. After 2019, state spending is expected to increase at a faster rate; the CBO estimates new state spending at $60 billion through 2021. And these costs may increase in the future because of the very real possibility that the Federal Government will change funding terms and reduce the percentage of funds it will cover. This would leave the States to bear an increasingly large percentage of the bill. Finally, after 2015, the States will have to pick up the tab for 50% of all administrative costs associated with implementing the new program, costs that could approach $12 billion between fiscal years 2014 and 2020.

In sum, it is perfectly clear from the goal and structure of the ACA that the offer of the Medicaid Expansion was one that Congress understood no State could refuse. The Medicaid Expansion therefore exceeds Congress' spending power and cannot be implemented.

F

Seven Members of the Court agree that the Medicaid Expansion, as enacted by Congress, is unconstitutional. Because the Medicaid Expansion is unconstitutional, the question of remedy arises. The most natural remedy would be to invalidate the Medicaid Expansion. However, the Government proposes—in two cursory sentences at the very end of its brief—preserving the Expansion. Under its proposal, States would receive the additional Medicaid funds if they expand eligibility, but States would keep their preexisting Medicaid funds if they do not expand eligibility. We cannot accept the Government's suggestion.

[T]he ACA depends on States' having no choice, because its Mandate requires low-income individuals to obtain insurance many of them can afford only through the Medicaid Expansion. Furthermore, a State's withdrawal might subject everyone in the State to much higher insurance premiums. That is because the Medicaid Expansion will no longer offset the cost to the insurance industry imposed by the ACA's insurance regulations and taxes. . . . To make the Medicaid Expansion optional despite the ACA's structure and design "'would be to make a new law, not to enforce an old one. This is no part of our duty.'"

Worse, the Government's proposed remedy introduces a new dynamic: States must choose between expanding Medicaid or paying huge tax sums to the federal fisc for the sole benefit of expanding Medicaid in other States. If this divisive dynamic between and among States can be introduced at all, it should be by conscious congressional choice, not by Court-invented interpretation. We do not doubt that States are capable of making decisions when put in a tight spot. We do doubt the authority of this Court to put them there.

The Government cites a severability clause codified with Medicaid . . . [b]ut that clause tells us only that other provisions in Chapter 7 should not be invalidated if §1396c, the authorization for the cut-off of all Medicaid funds, is unconstitutional. It does not tell us that §1396c can be judicially revised, to say what it does not say. . . . The Court today opts for permitting the cut-off of only incremental Medicaid funding, but it might just as well have permitted, say, the cut-off of funds that represent no more than x percent of the State's budget. The Court severs nothing, but simply revises §1396c to read as the Court would desire.

We should not accept the Government's invitation to attempt to solve a constitutional problem by rewriting the Medicaid Expansion so as to allow States that reject it to retain their pre-existing Medicaid funds. Worse, the Government's remedy, now adopted by the Court, takes the ACA and this Nation in a new direction and charts a course for federalism that the Court, not the Congress, has chosen; but under the Constitution, that power and authority do not rest with this Court.

V

Severability

[T]he two pillars of the [Affordable Care] Act are the Individual Mandate and the expansion of coverage under Medicaid. In our view, both these central provisions of the Act . . . are invalid. It follows . . . that all other provisions of the Act must fall as well.

[A]n automatic or too cursory severance of statutory provisions risks "rewrit[ing] a statute and giv[ing] it an effect altogether different from that sought by the measure viewed as a whole." The Judiciary, if it orders uncritical severance, then assumes the legislative function; for it imposes on the Nation, by the Court's decree, its own new statutory regime, consisting of policies, risks, and duties that Congress did not enact. That can be a more extreme exercise of the judicial power than striking the whole statute and allowing Congress to address the conditions that pertained when the statute was considered at the outset.

The Court has applied a two-part guide as the framework for severability analysis. The test has been deemed "well established." First, if the Court holds a statutory provision unconstitutional, it then determines whether the now truncated statute will operate in the manner Congress intended. If not, the remaining provisions must be invalidated. . . . Second, even if the remaining provisions can operate as Congress designed them to operate, the Court must determine if Congress would have enacted them standing alone and without the unconstitutional portion. If Congress would not, those provisions, too, must be invalidated. . . .

Major provisions of the Affordable Care Act—*i.e.,* the insurance regulations and taxes, the reductions in federal reimbursements to hospitals and other Medicare spending reductions, the exchanges and their federal subsidies, and the employer responsibility assessment—cannot remain once the Individual Mandate and Medicaid Expansion are invalid. That result follows from the undoubted inability of the other major provisions to operate as Congress intended without the Individual Mandate and Medicaid Expansion. . . . Without the Individual Mandate and Medicaid Expansion, the Affordable Care Act's insurance regulations and insurance taxes impose risks on insurance companies and their customers that this Court cannot measure. Those risks would undermine Congress' scheme of "shared responsibility." . . . Higher costs may mean higher premiums for consumers, despite the Act's goal of "lower[ing] health insurance premiums." Higher costs also could threaten the survival of health-insurance companies, despite the Act's goal of "effective health insurance markets."

The actual cost of the regulations and taxes may be more or less than predicted. What is known, however, is that severing other provisions from the Individual Mandate and Medicaid Expansion necessarily would impose significant risks and real uncertainties on insurance companies, their customers, all other major actors in the system, and the government treasury. And what also is known is this: Unnecessary risks and avoidable uncertainties are hostile to economic progress and fiscal stability and thus to the safety and welfare of the Nation and the Nation's freedom. If those risks and uncertainties are to be imposed, it must not be by the Judiciary.

[T]he Affordable Care Act reduces payments by the Federal Government to hospitals by more than $200 billion over 10 years [because] [n]ear-universal coverage will reduce uncompensated care, which will increase hospitals' revenues, which will offset the government's reductions in Medicare and Medicaid reimbursements to hospitals. Responsibility will be shared, as burdens and benefits balance each other. This is typical of the whole dynamic of the Act.

Invalidating the key mechanisms for expanding insurance coverage, such as community rating and the Medicaid Expansion, without invalidating the reductions in Medicare and Medicaid, distorts the ACA's design of "shared responsibility." Some hospitals may be forced to raise the cost of care in order to offset the reductions in reimbursements, which could raise the cost of insurance premiums, in contravention of the Act's goal of "lower[ing] health insurance premiums." Other hospitals, particularly safety-net hospitals that serve a large number of uninsured patients, may be forced to shut down. Like the effect of preserving the insurance regulations and taxes, the precise degree of risk to hospitals is unknowable. It is not the proper role of the Court, by severing part of a statute and allowing the rest to stand, to impose unknowable risks that Congress could neither measure nor predict. And Congress could not have intended that result in any event.

[Second,] Congress chose to offset new federal expenditures with budget cuts and tax increases. . . . If the Medicare and Medicaid reductions would no longer be needed to offset the costs of the Medicaid Expansion, the reductions would no longer operate in the manner Congress intended. They would lose their justification and foundation. In addition, to preserve them would be "to eliminate a significant *quid pro quo* of the legislative compromise" and create a statute Congress did not enact. It is no secret that cutting Medicare is unpopular; and it is most improbable Congress would have done so without at least the assurance that it would render the ACA deficit-neutral. . . .

The ACA requires each State to establish a health-insurance "exchange." Each exchange is a one-stop marketplace for individuals and small businesses to compare community-rated health insurance and purchase the policy of their choice. The exchanges cannot operate in the manner Congress intended if the Individual Mandate, Medicaid Expansion, and insurance regulations cannot remain in force.

The Act's design is to allocate billions of federal dollars to subsidize individuals' purchases on the exchanges. . . . Without the community-rating insurance regulation, however, the average federal subsidy could be much higher; for community rating greatly lowers the enormous premiums unhealthy individuals would otherwise pay. Federal subsidies would make up much of the difference.

The result would be an unintended boon to insurance companies, an unintended harm to the federal fisc, and a corresponding breakdown of the "shared responsibility" between the industry and the federal budget that Congress intended. Thus, the federal subsidies must be invalidated.

In the absence of federal subsidies to purchasers, insurance companies will have little incentive to sell insurance on the exchanges. . . . Without the federal subsidies, individuals would lose the main incentive to purchase insurance inside the exchanges, and some insurers may be unwilling to offer insurance inside of exchanges. With fewer buyers and even fewer sellers, the exchanges would not operate as Congress intended and may not operate at all.

[In addition,] Congress designed the exchanges so the shopper can compare benefits and prices. But the comparison cannot be made in the way Congress designed if the prices depend on the shopper's pre-existing health conditions. The prices would vary from person to person. So without community rating — which prohibits insurers from basing the price of insurance on pre-existing conditions — the exchanges cannot operate in the manner Congress intended.

[T]he employer responsibility assessment provides an incentive for employers with at least 50 employees to provide their employees with health insurance options that meet minimum criteria. Unlike the Individual Mandate, the employer-responsibility assessment does not require employers to provide an insurance option. Instead, it requires them to make a payment to the Federal Government if they do not offer insurance to employees and if insurance is bought on an exchange by an employee who qualifies for the exchange's federal subsidies.

For two reasons, the employer-responsibility assessment must be invalidated. First, the ACA makes a direct link between the employer-responsibility assessment and the exchanges. The financial assessment against employers occurs only under certain conditions. One of them is the purchase of insurance by an employee on an exchange. With no exchanges, there are no purchases on the exchanges; and with no purchases on the exchanges, there is nothing to trigger the employer-responsibility assessment.

Second, after the invalidation of burdens on individuals (the Individual Mandate), insurers (the insurance regulations and taxes), States (the Medicaid Expansion), the Federal Government (the federal subsidies for exchanges and for the Medicaid Expansion), and hospitals (the reductions in reimbursements), the preservation of the employer-responsibility assessment would upset the ACA's design of "shared responsibility." It would leave employers as the only parties bearing any significant responsibility. That was not the congressional intent.

[T]he ACA is over 900 pages long. Its regulations include requirements ranging from a break time and secluded place at work for nursing mothers, to displays of nutritional content at chain restaurants. The Act raises billions of dollars in taxes and fees, including exactions imposed on high-income taxpayers, and tanning booths. It spends government money on, among other things, the study of how to spend less government money. And it includes a number of provisions that provide benefits to the State of a particular legislator. For example, §10323 . . . extends Medicare coverage to individuals exposed to asbestos from a mine in Libby, Montana. Another provision, §2006, increases Medicaid payments only in Louisiana.

Such provisions validate the Senate Majority Leader's statement, "'I don't know if there is a senator that doesn't have something in this bill that was important to them. . . . [And] if they don't have something in it important to them, then it doesn't speak well of them. That's what this legislation is all about: It's the art of compromise.'" Often, a minor provision will be the price paid for support of a major provision. So, if the major provision were unconstitutional, Congress would not have passed the minor one.

Without the ACA's major provisions, many of these minor provisions will not operate in the manner Congress intended. . . . Some provisions, such as requiring chain restaurants to display nutritional content, appear likely to operate as Congress intended, but they fail the second test for severability. There is no reason to believe that Congress would have enacted them independently. The Court has not previously had occasion to consider severability in the context of an omnibus enactment like the ACA, which includes not only many provisions that are ancillary to its central provisions but also many that are entirely unrelated—hitched on because it was a quick way to get them passed despite opposition, or because their proponents could exact their enactment as the *quid pro quo* for their needed support. When we are confronted with such a so-called "Christmas tree," a law to which many nongermane ornaments have been attached, we think the proper rule must be that when the tree no longer exists the ornaments are superfluous. We have no reliable basis for knowing which pieces of the Act would have passed on their own. It is certain that many of them would not have, and it is not a proper function of this Court to guess which. . . .

This Court must not impose risks unintended by Congress or produce legislation Congress may have lacked the support to enact. For those reasons, the unconstitutionality of both the Individual Mandate and the Medicaid Expansion requires the invalidation of the Affordable Care Act's other provisions.

* * *

The Court today decides to save a statute Congress did not write. It rules that what the statute declares to be a requirement with a penalty is instead an option subject to a tax. And it changes the intentionally coercive sanction of a total cutoff of Medicaid funds to a supposedly noncoercive cut-off of only the incremental funds that the Act makes available.

The Court regards its strained statutory interpretation as judicial modesty. It is not. It amounts instead to a vast judicial overreaching. It creates a debilitated, inoperable version of health-care regulation that Congress did not enact and the public does not expect. It makes enactment of sensible health-care regulation more difficult, since Congress cannot start afresh but must take as its point of departure a jumble of now senseless provisions, provisions that certain interests favored under the Court's new design will struggle to retain. And it leaves the public and the States to expend vast sums of money on requirements that may or may not survive the necessary congressional revision.

The Court's disposition, invented and atextual as it is, does not even have the merit of avoiding constitutional difficulties. It creates them. The holding that the Individual Mandate is a tax raises a difficult constitutional question (what is a direct tax?) that the Court resolves with inadequate deliberation. And the judgment on the Medicaid Expansion issue ushers in new federalism concerns and places an unaccustomed strain upon the Union. Those States that decline the

Medicaid Expansion must subsidize, by the federal tax dollars taken from their citizens, vast grants to the States that accept the Medicaid Expansion. If that destabilizing political dynamic, so antagonistic to a harmonious Union, is to be introduced at all, it should be by Congress, not by the Judiciary.

The values that should have determined our course today are caution, minimalism, and the understanding that the Federal Government is one of limited powers. But the Court's ruling undermines those values at every turn. In the name of restraint, it overreaches. In the name of constitutional avoidance, it creates new constitutional questions. In the name of cooperative federalism, it undermines state sovereignty.

The Constitution, though it dates from the founding of the Republic, has powerful meaning and vital relevance to our own times. The constitutional protections that this case involves are protections of structure. Structural protections — notably, the restraints imposed by federalism and separation of powers — are less romantic and have less obvious a connection to personal freedom than the provisions of the Bill of Rights or the Civil War Amendments. Hence they tend to be undervalued or even forgotten by our citizens. It should be the responsibility of the Court to teach otherwise, to remind our people that the Framers considered structural protections of freedom the most important ones, for which reason they alone were embodied in the original Constitution and not left to later amendment. The fragmentation of power produced by the structure of our Government is central to liberty, and when we destroy it, we place liberty at peril. Today's decision should have vindicated, should have taught, this truth; instead, our judgment today has disregarded it.

For the reasons here stated, we would find the Act invalid in its entirety. We respectfully dissent.

Justice THOMAS, dissenting.

I dissent for the reasons stated in our joint opinion, but I write separately to say a word about the Commerce Clause. The joint dissent and The Chief Justice correctly apply our precedents to conclude that the Individual Mandate is beyond the power granted to Congress under the Commerce Clause and the Necessary and Proper Clause. Under those precedents, Congress may regulate "economic activity [that] substantially affects interstate commerce." I adhere to my view that "the very notion of a 'substantial effects' test under the Commerce Clause is inconsistent with the original understanding of Congress' powers and with this Court's early Commerce Clause cases." As I have explained, the Court's continued use of that test "has encouraged the Federal Government to persist in its view that the Commerce Clause has virtually no limits." The Government's unprecedented claim in this suit that it may regulate not only economic activity but also *inactivity* that substantially affects interstate commerce is a case in point.

Discussion

1. *The* Health Care Case *and the Constitution outside the courts*. The *Health Care Case* offers an excellent example of how constitutional ideas in politics

eventually influence judicial decisions. The debate over the Affordable Care Act in 2009 and 2010 was extremely contentious, with opponents arguing that the Act would involve a government takeover of health care, and former vice presidential candidate Sarah Palin (among others) darkly warning about "death panels" hidden in the Act. The individual mandate had originally been a Republican idea, developed at the Heritage Foundation as a conservative alternative to the Clinton health care proposal in the 1990s. However, after President Obama and the Democrats made it a key element of their proposal, Congressional Republicans began to oppose it, first on policy grounds, and later, on constitutional grounds. The Act passed along party lines in March 2010. Several lawsuits were quickly filed around the country, targeting the individual mandate and the Medicaid extension. The hope was that if either or both of these elements were struck down, the courts might invalidate the entire Act.

When the litigation began, most constitutional scholars, relying on existing precedents, believed that the odds that either provision would be held unconstitutional were fairly small. Nevertheless, the rise of the Tea Party and the Republican landslide of 2010 gave hope to mandate opponents. The unconstitutionality of the mandate became virtually the official position of the Republican Party, which put its considerable resources behind promoting constitutional arguments against the mandate, not only in the courts but also in the public sphere. As a result, constitutional arguments against the mandate quickly moved from "off the wall" to "on the wall," and, by the conclusion of the oral arguments at the Supreme Court in March 2012, many observers expected that the individual mandate would be held unconstitutional. For a discussion of the role of different actors in altering public understandings of the challenge, see Jack M. Balkin, From Off the Wall to On the Wall: How the Mandate Challenge Went Mainstream, Atlantic, June 4, 2012, at *http://www.theatlantic.com/national/archive/2012/06/from-off-the-wall-to-on-thewall-how-the-mandate-challenge-went-mainstream/258040/.*

What do these events tell us about the relationship between political change and constitutional change? Can you think of other examples in the cases we have studied in which powerful political mobilizations changed the plausibility of constitutional arguments? What are the similarities to and differences from the health care litigation?

2. *The Commerce Clause and individual liberty.* Mandate opponents argued that it was unprecedented for the government to force individuals to purchase goods and services from private parties. If the mandate was upheld, Congress could force individuals to do all sorts of things, thus undermining personal liberty, and working a fundamental change in the relationship between the federal government and its citizens. See Randy E. Barnett, Commandeering the People: Why the Individual Health Insurance Mandate Is Unconstitutional, 5 N.Y.U. J.L. & Liberty 581 (2010). Although the arguments against the mandate technically concerned the limits to Congress's commerce power (and the Necessary and Proper Clause), they sounded in notions of individual liberty, including, in particular, economic liberty.

In the post–New Deal era, mandate opponents were unlikely to argue for protecting freedom of contract as a matter of substantive due process. (And nothing in Chief Justice Roberts's opinion or the joint dissent would prevent *states* from imposing mandates identical to the ACA's.) Nevertheless, the idea of protecting economic liberty through limitations on federal power has a long history in debates in American constitutional law. Can you think of examples?

3. *The* Health Care Case *and the future of constitutional development.* One remarkable feature of the *Health Care Case* is that the Supreme Court gave its blessing to the most important change to the social contract since the Great Society in the 1960s. Yet, at the same time, five Justices argued for a more limited understanding of the Commerce Clause and the Necessary and Proper Clause, while seven Justices argued—for the first time since the New Deal—for significant limits on the spending power.

Which result turns out to be more important in the long run—the change in the role of government or the change in constitutional doctrine—will likely depend on who wins the next several presidential elections and thus gets to appoint most of the federal judiciary. A Republican-dominated judiciary will likely expand on the decision's innovations, while a Democrat-dominated judiciary may read them quite narrowly. In the meantime, the doctrinal puzzles created by the *Health Care Case* will keep lawyers busy for many years to come.

4. *The constitutional avoidance canon.* Was Roberts's Commerce Clause argument necessary to his tax power holding? If it was not, then presumably the discussion is merely dicta. At issue is the constitutional avoidance canon, which counsels that courts should avoid interpreting statutes in ways that render them unconstitutional if reasonably possible. What theory of judicial review justifies this canon?

Roberts argued that "[t]he most straightforward reading of the mandate is that it commands individuals to purchase insurance" because it imposes a "requirement" and says that the relevant individuals "shall" purchase insurance. Therefore, he argued that he had to consider the Commerce Clause/Necessary and Proper Clause issues before he could reach the taxing power argument, which was only a "fairly possible" reading. Do you agree? Does the answer depend on whether the tax interpretation is also a natural or obvious reading?

Here is the text of Section 5000A as it currently appears in the U.S. Code:

USC Title 26—Internal Revenue Code

Subtitle D: Miscellaneous Excise Taxes

CHAPTER 48—MAINTENANCE OF MINIMUM ESSENTIAL COVERAGE
§5000A. Requirement to maintain minimum essential coverage
   (a)   Requirement to maintain minimum essential coverage
An applicable individual shall for each month beginning after 2013 ensure that the individual, and any dependent of the individual who is an applicable individual, is covered under minimum essential coverage for such month.
   (b)   Shared responsibility payment

(1)   In general

If a taxpayer who is an applicable individual, or an applicable individual for whom the taxpayer is liable under paragraph (3), fails to meet the requirement of subsection (a) for 1 or more months, then, except as provided in subsection (e), there is hereby imposed on the taxpayer a penalty with respect to such failures in the amount determined under subsection (c).

(2)   Inclusion with return

Any penalty imposed by this section with respect to any month shall be included with a taxpayer's return under chapter 1 for the taxable year which includes such month.

(3)   Payment of penalty

If an individual with respect to whom a penalty is imposed by this section for any month—

(A)   is a dependent (as defined in section 152) of another taxpayer for the other taxpayer's taxable year including such month, such other taxpayer shall be liable for such penalty, or

(B)   files a joint return for the taxable year including such month, such individual and the spouse of such individual shall be jointly liable for such penalty.

(c)   Amount of penalty

(1)   In general

The amount of the penalty imposed by this section on any taxpayer for any taxable year with respect to failures described in subsection (b)(1) shall be equal to the lesser of—

(A)   the sum of the monthly penalty amounts determined under paragraph (2) for months in the taxable year during which 1 or more such failures occurred, or

(B)   an amount equal to the national average premium for qualified health plans which have a bronze level of coverage, provide coverage for the applicable family size involved, and are offered through Exchanges for plan years beginning in the calendar year with or within which the taxable year ends.

Subsection (d) defines "applicable individual . . . as an individual other than an individual described in paragraph[s] (2), (3), or (4)"—which refer to people with religious objections, people operating "health care sharing ministries," aliens (lawfully or unlawfully present), and incarcerated persons. In addition, subsection (e) states that "[n]o penalty shall be imposed under subsection (a) with respect to . . . (1) Individuals who cannot afford coverage[;] (2) Taxpayers with income below [the income tax] filing threshold[;] (3) Members of Indian tribes; (4) [Persons who have] short coverage gaps [in insurance; and] (5) [Cases of] [h]ardship."

5. *The taxing power.* What are the limits of the taxing power after the *Health Care Case*? Roberts points to four features that distinguish a lawful tax from an unlawful penalty: First, "for most Americans the amount due will be far less than the price of insurance, and, by statute, it can never be more." This means "that [i]t may often be a reasonable financial decision to make the payment rather than purchase insurance, unlike the 'prohibitory' financial punishment in *Drexel Furniture*." Second, the tax was not structured like a criminal penalty—for example, it did not have a scienter requirement. Third, the tax was administered

and collected by the IRS like other taxes. Fourth, failure to purchase insurance was not treated as an unlawful act, and there were no adverse consequences other than having to pay the tax. Which of these criteria is the most important?

Note that the upshot of Roberts's argument is that a constitutional tax creates *incentives* rather than *mandates* for behavior; that is, it always preserves the option to pay the tax, which is not so high that it effectively compels or coerces compliance with the government's preferred regulatory outcome. For a discussion of the constitutional limits on the tax power, see Robert D. Cooter & Neil Siegel, Not the Power to Destroy: An Effects Theory of the Tax Power, 98 Virginia Law Review 1195 (2012).

Roberts could also have added a fifth criterion: the tax did not burden a fundamental right. Thus, a tax on people who refuse to attend church weekly would violate the Free Exercise Clause (and the Establishment Clause); a tax on people who refuse to eat broccoli might violate the Due Process Clause. Are all taxes that affect the exercise of fundamental rights unconstitutional? The federal income tax sometimes taxes married couples filing jointly more than two people filing separately. Is this constitutional?

6. *Using taxes rather than mandates.* The effect of Roberts's argument is that if Congress wishes to impose mandates on people who are not already engaged in an activity that could be regulated by the Commerce Clause, it must use the taxing power instead, always giving people the option to pay the tax. Are there structural reasons to prefer taxes to mandates in these circumstances? Does the doctrine promote federalism? Regardless of whether it promotes federalism, does it promote individual liberty?

7. *Holding or dicta?* What parts of Roberts's opinion constitute the holding of the Court? Parts III-A and III-B (which no other Justices join) purport to hold that Congress may not enact the individual mandate under the Commerce Clause, even assisted by the Necessary and Proper Clause, and Part IV (joined only by Breyer and Kagan) holds that the Medicaid extension goes beyond Congress's spending power. (Justice Ginsburg and Justice Sotomayor join only the remedy.)

In *Marks v. United States,* 430 U.S. 188, 193 (1977), the Court explained its test for determining the holding of a case when there is no majority opinion on a particular issue: "When a fragmented Court decides a case and no single rationale explaining the result enjoys the assent of five Justices, the holding of the Court may be viewed as that position taken by those Members who concurred in the judgments on the narrowest grounds."

The problem here is that the Justices who agree with Roberts on limiting the Commerce Clause and the Necessary and Proper Clause do not concur in the judgment; they dissent. The joint dissenters make arguments similar to and even more restrictive than Roberts' arguments, but they do not agree with the judgment of the Court and they do not join either Part III or Part IV of Roberts's opinion. Instead, they merely criticize his holding on the tax power, and the remedy with respect to the Medicaid extension.

Are Roberts's positions on these issues binding law? Note, interestingly, that Part III-C of his opinion, joined by five Justices, notes in passing that "[t]he Court today holds that our Constitution protects us from federal regulation under the Commerce Clause so long as we abstain from the regulated activity." Part IV-B, joined only by Roberts, Breyer, and Kagan, states that "[i]n light of the Court's holding, the Secretary cannot apply §1396c to withdraw existing Medicaid funds for failure to comply with the requirements set out in the expansion."

Even if you believe that Roberts's arguments (other than the tax power holding) are either dicta or a plurality opinion, do you expect that lower federal courts will treat them as law, given that lower courts know that five Justices now support doctrines that limit federal powers? How *should* lower courts interpret these opinions?

8. *The activity/inactivity distinction.* Both Roberts and the joint dissent argue that Congress can regulate activities under the Commerce Clause (and Necessary and Proper Clause), but not inactivity. If Congress could regulate inactivity, they argue, there would be no limit to the federal government's powers. However, such limits already exist, for example, in *Lopez* and *Morrison*. Is the activity/inactivity distinction necessary to preserve the rule of *Lopez* and *Morrison* or the principle that the federal government is one of limited and enumerated powers? Why? Does the distinction promote federalism, individual freedom, or both?

The activity/inactivity distinction is related to the act/omission distinction. Lawyers are sometimes able to manipulate this distinction by expanding or contracting the relevant time frame or by redescribing events in different ways. See Mark Kelman, Interpretive Construction in the Substantive Criminal Law, 33 Stan. L. Rev. 591 (1981); Jack M. Balkin, The Rhetoric of Responsibility, 76 Va. L. Rev. 197 (1990).

Is the activity/inactivity distinction subject to manipulation in the same way? For example, people may be active or inactive in commerce depending on how broadly we describe the market in which they participate (health care, health insurance, purchase of over-the-counter remedies, etc.) and depending on how broadly we consider the relevant time frame (day, month, year, decade, lifetime). Another example: at the time Title II of the Civil Rights Act was passed in 1964, the proprietor of the Heart of Atlanta Motel was not serving black people — and the law required him to do so. However, the owner was operating a hotel that served white people. In *Wickard v. Filburn*, Justice Jackson described Filburn's conduct both as activity and inactivity: "The effect of the statute before us is to restrict the amount which may be produced for market and the extent, as well, to which one may forestall resort to the market by producing to meet his own needs." That is, the problem that Congress sought to address was that Filburn was failing to purchase wheat in the market. Mark Tushnet, The "Activity-Inactivity" Distinction, Balkinization, Dec. 13, 2010, at http://balkin. blogspot. com/2010/12/activity-inactivity-distinction.html.

Are there administrable ways for courts to fix the relevant description of events, the relevant market, and the relevant time frame in order to decide how to apply the activity/inactivity distinction? Can judges just rely on "common sense"? In her opinion in the *Health Care Case*, Justice Ginsburg argued that it was obvious that almost everyone was engaged in the health care market, or soon would be; therefore requiring the purchase of health insurance was simply a way of regulating how people pay for commercial transactions in which they will inevitably engage. The joint dissent argued that this description of the situation was too broad—because it would suggest that since everyone is in the food market, or soon will be, they can be required to purchase broccoli—and that the relevant market was the market for health insurance. Is there a correct answer to this question?

9. *Workarounds*. Assuming that the activity/inactivity distinction is now part of Commerce Clause doctrine, could Congress get around the distinction by requiring that everyone who purchases more than $500 of health care related products or services in a calendar year must henceforth be subject to an insurance mandate or pay a $500 yearly penalty? Could Congress require that everyone who buys more than $500 worth of food in a given year must henceforth purchase $500 of broccoli each year or be subject to a $500 penalty?

Could Congress require purchase of health insurance if a person has ever been previously covered by health insurance? Has ever visited an emergency room and received subsidized treatment? Has ever crossed state lines in order to receive medical care? Has ever received medical care in more than one state? (Would such requirements be constitutional if applied retroactively? What if they were only applied prospectively?)

10. *Necessary but not proper?* Chief Justice Roberts and the joint dissent argue that the mandate was not necessary and proper to make the guaranteed issue and community ratings rules effective. Roberts claimed that even if the mandate was "necessary," it was not "proper." He argued that the mandate would "undermine the structure of government established by the Constitution" and was "not consist[ent] with the letter and spirit of the constitution." It would involve a "great substantive and independent power," and work "a substantial expansion of federal authority." How should judges apply these ideas in future cases? Did the vast expansion of Commerce Clause authority in *Darby* and *Wickard* (already) violate this test? Note that Roberts assumes that the statute challenged in *Wickard* is "proper." If so, is Roberts's argument just another way of saying that Congress cannot reach inactivity through the Necessary and Proper Clause if it cannot reach it through the Commerce Clause? To what extent is this consistent with the logic of *McCulloch*? With logic of *Comstock*?

The joint dissent reached the same conclusion a little differently. It argued that the mandate is not necessary and proper for two reasons. First, *Raich* involved a situation of true necessity, whereas in this case there were other ways to achieve the goals of the ACA other than using a mandate. (Is this consistent with *McCulloch*?) Second, the joint dissent argued that mandates greatly expand federal power into new fields. If mandates are necessary and proper to realize the statute's goals, there are no limits to federal power, and that cannot be proper. Again, does this assume that *Lopez* and *Morrison* would become effectively irrelevant?

Is it clear that there is no limiting principle that would allow the mandate but not give the federal government unlimited regulatory power? For example, what if the Court had held that only mandates to exchange money for goods or services — that is, to engage in commerce — were permitted under the Commerce Clause and Necessary and Proper Clause, but no other mandates? (Thus, a mandate to eat broccoli or to exercise once a day would not fall within the commerce power, even when assisted by the Necessary and Proper Clause). Is *this* distinction significantly less administrable than the activity/inactivity distinction?

11. *The spending power.* Note carefully the differences between Chief Justice Roberts's account of the spending power (joined by Justices Breyer and Kagan) and that of the joint dissent.

The joint dissent argues that because the size of the threatened withdrawal of federal funding is so great, the Medicaid expansion is an offer the states cannot refuse, and therefore it is coercive. This might suggest that the federal government may not impose new conditions on (and thus threaten to withdraw funding from) *any* program that has become a sufficiently large percentage of a state's budget. Does the joint dissent's test allow the federal government to abolish existing programs that constitute a significant proportion of a state's budget?

The joint dissenters also argue that if the federal government offers the states participation in a sufficiently large social welfare program, states may not be able to refuse and so the offer is coercive. First, the federal tax dollars paid by a state's citizens that the state forgoes will be given to the poor in other states. Second, the state will have to raise additional state taxes to provide comparable services. Does this mean that it was unconstitutional for Congress to offer the states Medicaid in the first place? Does it mean that there is a limit on how much money the federal government can offer to the states with conditions attached?

Roberts's argument is different. He distinguishes between two situations. In the first, Congress places conditions on funds it gives to states for a particular program. For example, Congress gives highway funds to states in exchange for states' promise that the roads will be built with certain types of materials, and will have certain types of safety signs. These conditions, Roberts argues, are perfectly appropriate because they help ensure that Congress's distribution of money serves the general welfare, as required by the text of the General Welfare Clause.

The second situation is when Congress asks states to do something or else it will withdraw funds from an *unrelated* or *independent* program. Imagine, for example, that Congress requires states to spend highway funds on extra roadway signs; but if a state refuses, Congress will withdraw not only its highway funding but also all of its educational grants to the state. In this situation, Roberts argues, we must inquire into whether there is undue coercion.

In *South Dakota v. Dole*, for example, federal highway funding was made conditional on raising a state's drinking age. *Dole* held that the condition had to be — and was — germane to the purposes for which the funds were offered, in this case, highway safety. Nevertheless, Roberts pointed out, the condition did not concern how states should use the highway funds themselves.

In this sort of situation, when "conditions take the form of threats to terminate other significant independent grants," Roberts argues, courts must inquire whether the bargain is unduly coercive. In *Dole*, the amount of money that the state would lose was very small: about 5 percent of South Dakota's highway funds, and less than half of 1 percent of South Dakota's budget. Therefore, the Court concluded that the bargain was not coercive. In the case of the Medicaid extension, by contrast, "Medicaid spending accounts for over 20 percent of the average State's total budget, with federal funds covering 50 to 83 percent of those costs." Therefore, Roberts concludes, this bargain, which threatens to withdraw at least 10 percent of a state's budget, is coercive. (Note in particular Roberts's statement that although one half of 1 percent would not be coercive, 10 percent would be "dragooning").

There is an obvious rejoinder: in this case, Congress is not threatening to terminate *another* program. Its conditions are all conditions on states' use of Medicaid funds. The ACA simply expands Medicaid, and all the federal government has done is add new conditions. That is permissible because Congress had reserved the right to add new conditions to Medicaid by statute, and the states agreed to that bargain.

Roberts responds that if the changes to an existing program are sufficiently drastic, they are changes in kind rather than degree, and the resulting program is a "new" and independent program. In essence, Roberts says, Congress is threatening to withdraw funding from Old Medicaid if the states do not agree to participate in New Medicaid. It is true that Congress reserved the right to add new conditions to Medicaid in its original agreement with the states. However, "[a] State could hardly anticipate that Congress's reservation of the right to 'alter' or 'amend' the Medicaid program included the power to transform it so dramatically." Because there is no fair warning, courts should treat the new conditions as part of a new program separate from Old Medicaid. Therefore, we must ask whether the amount that Congress threatens to withdraw from the older program is so great as to be coercive.

How would this test apply to other federal statutes, for example, federal civil rights laws? Title IX of the Education Amendments of 1972 and Title VI of the Civil Rights Act of 1964 impose conditions on federal grants of funds to states and local governments and require nondiscrimination on the basis of sex, race, and other categories. The Civil Rights Restoration Act of 1988, 42 U.S.C. §2000d4a, states that state agencies, school districts, and municipalities that receive federal funds must comply with these laws in all areas of their operations, not merely in the particular program or activity that has received federal funding. If Congress amended its civil rights laws to prohibit sexual orientation discrimination in entities that receive federal funds, could states refuse to accept the new conditions on the grounds that Congress had created a "new" program? On the grounds that they had become dependent on federal funding for many decades and could not realistically refuse any new conditions?

12. *More workarounds.* How easy will it be for Congress to work around Roberts's new test? For example, could Congress simply abolish Medicaid and create a new program in its place and invite the states to participate? Could Congress stipulate that a state may participate in Medicaid for only a year at a time and then must reapply each year to a new program in order to receive funding?

Congress can, if it wishes, simply convert Medicaid into a fully federal program like Medicare. But then it would have to increase the number of federal employees in order to administer the program. Are there good reasons for the federal government to ask states to administer federal-state cooperative programs like Medicaid? How does Roberts's new test affect the federal government's incentives?

BOND v. UNITED STATES, 134 S. Ct. 2077 (2014): In 1997, the United States ratified the international Convention on the Prohibition of the Development, Production, Stockpiling, and Use of Chemical Weapons and on Their Destruction. The treaty is not self-executing, and in order to implement it, Congress enacted the Chemical Weapons Convention Implementation Act of 1998. The statute forbids any person knowingly to "possess[ ] or use . . . any chemical weapon," defined as "[a] toxic chemical" not used for "[a]ny peaceful purpose related to an industrial, agricultural, research, medical, or pharmaceutical activity or other activity."

Petitioner Bond discovered that her husband had an affair with her best friend, Myrlinda Haynes. Seeking revenge, she spread two toxic chemicals on Haynes's car, mailbox, and door knob, hoping that Haynes would develop an uncomfortable rash. Haynes suffered a minor chemical burn that she treated by rinsing with water; otherwise Bond's attempt at revenge was entirely unsuccessful. Federal prosecutors charged Bond with violating the Implementation Act, and Bond challenged the Act on the grounds that the Act was beyond Congress's powers.

Chief Justice Roberts, writing for six Justices, held that it was unnecessary to reach the constitutional question. Invoking the clear statement rule of Gregory v. Ashcroft and United States v. Bass, 404 U.S. 336 (1971), the Court held that the Implementation Act did not reach Bond's conduct: "[I]t is appropriate to refer to basic principles of federalism embodied in the Constitution to resolve ambiguity in a federal statute. In this case, the ambiguity derives from the improbably broad reach of the [term] 'chemical weapon' . . . ; the deeply serious consequences of adopting such a boundless reading; and the lack of any apparent need to do so in light of the context from which the statute arose—a treaty about chemical warfare and terrorism. [W]e can insist on a clear indication that Congress meant to reach purely local crimes, before interpreting the statute's expansive language in a way that intrudes on the police power of the States." Roberts explained that "the chemicals in this case are not of the sort that an ordinary person would associate with instruments of chemical warfare." Accordingly, the Act should not be "transform[ed] . . . from one whose core concerns are acts of war, assassination, and terrorism into a massive federal anti-poisoning regime that reaches the simplest of assaults."

Justice Scalia, joined by Justice Thomas, concurred in the judgment. He argued that the Court should reach the constitutional question and limit Congress's powers. He denied that the Necessary and Proper Clause gives Congress the power "to enact laws for carrying into execution 'Treaties,' even treaties that do not execute themselves, such as the Chemical Weapons Convention." The Necessary and Proper Clause, Scalia, explained, gives Congress the power "[t]o make all Laws which shall be necessary and proper for carrying into Execution the foregoing Powers and all other Powers vested by this Constitution in the Government of the United States, or in any Department or Officer thereof." But the Treaty Power of Article II only gives the President and the Senate the power "to make Treaties," not to enforce them: "a power to help the President *make* treaties is not a power to *implement* treaties already made."

Justice Thomas, joined by Justices Scalia and Alito, also concurred in the judgment. He argued that "the Treaty Power can be used to arrange intercourse with other nations, but not to regulate purely domestic affairs. . . . [T]he Treaty Power is limited to matters of international intercourse. Even if a treaty may reach some local matters, it still *must* relate to intercourse with other nations." Thomas argued that the Court's central precedent construing the Treaty Power, *Missouri v. Holland* (see Chapter 4, Section IV.D, The Treaty Power, pp. 456-460) was correct on its facts, although he disagreed with its broad statement of congressional power. "[T]he treaty at issue addressed migratory birds that were 'only transitorily within the State and ha[d] no permanent habitat therein.'" . . . As such, the birds were naturally a matter of international intercourse because they were creatures in international transit. Thomas added, "I acknowledge that the distinction between matters of international intercourse and matters of purely domestic regulation may not be obvious in all cases. But this Court has long recognized that the Treaty Power is limited, and hypothetical difficulties in line-drawing are no reason to ignore a constitutional limit on federal power. . . ."

Justice Alito also concurred in the judgment: "I believe that the treaty power is limited to agreements that address matters of legitimate international concern. . . . [T]he heart of the Convention clearly represents a valid exercise of the treaty power. But insofar as the Convention may be read to obligate the United States to enact domestic legislation criminalizing conduct of the sort at issue in this case, which typically is the sort of conduct regulated by the States, the Convention exceeds the scope of the treaty power."

Discussion

1. *An unclear statement?* The *Bond* litigation, which encompassed many years, and two separate Supreme Court decisions, was organized as a full-throated attack on *Missouri v. Holland*'s statement that "[i]f the treaty is valid there can be no dispute about the validity of the statute under Article 1, Section 8, as a

necessary and proper means to execute the powers of the Government." The concern of *Holland*'s critics is that this might allow an end-run around constitutional limits on federal power. The majority chose not to address that question. Instead, its clear statement rule allows federal courts to impose federalism limitations on legislation that implements treaties through statutory construction.

If a majority of the Justices were unwilling to impose limits on the Treaty Power in this case, it is hard to think of a situation in which the current Court would be tempted. Nevertheless, Justice Thomas lays a marker for future litigation, perhaps hoping that new appointments will change the Court's mind.

Note that one irony of the Court's clear statement rule is that the actual scope of the Implementation Act has now become less clear. Future litigation will have to determine whether a particular chemical is "of the sort that an ordinary person would associate with instruments of chemical warfare" or whether a toxic chemical is used in ways related to "war, assassination, and terrorism." The Court notes later in the opinion that dumping chemicals in a city's water supply might be prohibited by the statute even if the chemicals are not the sort used in chemical warfare. Does terrorism have to be motivated by purely political goals? Should the statute reach a case in which a person poisons the city's water supply because his girlfriend had recently broken up with him?

2. *"Purely domestic affairs."* Justice Thomas argues that the Treaty Power should be limited to questions of international concern or "international intercourse," but should not reach matters of purely domestic concern. The problem is making sense of this distinction in the modern world. Today countries are interested in reaching agreements on a wide variety of questions ranging from human rights to the environment, public health, terrorism, and kidnapping. That is because many seemingly "domestic" concerns have spillover effects internationally, and vice versa.

Both Justice Scalia and Justice Thomas are concerned about the expanding scope of treaties, which, in Scalia's words, have "sought to regulate states' treatment of their own citizens, or even 'the activities of individuals and private entities.'" One important reason for this is the growth of international human rights discourse. Human rights claims often seek to regulate the way that nation states treat their own citizens or people living within their borders. The litigation in *Bond* occurred against the background of a larger political debate over whether international law in general, and human rights treaties in particular, unduly interfere with American sovereignty. Note that while a federalism objection seeks to limit federal power, an objection based on sovereignty is an assertion of national power. How are the two concerns connected?

American foreign policy has long been concerned with the treatment and well-being of people in other countries for economic, diplomatic, and security reasons, as well as for "purely" humanitarian reasons. Human rights problems often become economic, military, and strategic problems, and vice versa. If America is concerned with how other countries treat people living within their borders, why should other countries not be equally interested in how Americans treat people living within the United States? Justice Thomas "acknowledge[s] that the distinction between matters of international intercourse and matters of purely domestic regulation may not be obvious in all cases." Can you think of a plausible way to draw this line?

3. *What is the scope of the Treaty Power?* A central purpose of the new national government created by the 1787 Constitution was to enable the national government to deal effectively with foreign affairs. That meant that the federal government had to have the power to make credible commitments to foreign powers in order to promote the interests of the Union as a whole. If the federal government "wrote checks that could not be cashed," other countries would be less likely to deal with it cooperatively and peacefully. This basic structural insight suggests that (with a few exceptions to be noted presently) as long as another country is genuinely interested in bargaining over a particular subject matter, it is a proper concern of the Treaty Power.

It follows that sham treaties would not be constitutional. Imagine that the United States agrees with the government of Kuwait that each country will ban the possession of guns near schools, that Kuwait has no other interest in the question, and that the federal government wants to get around the *Lopez* decision. Such a sham treaty would not be within the Treaty Power. (The question remains, of course, how one would prove that such a treaty was a sham.)

Note that this analysis derives the scope of the power to make and implement treaties from the structural need to solve collective action problems in a federal union of states. The basic principle is that federal powers arise from federal problems. But even federal powers that solve such collective action problems are limited in two ways. First, the federal government is always limited by individual rights protections in the Bill of Rights and other parts of the Constitution. See Reid v. Covert, 357 U.S. 1 (1957) (plurality opinion). If so, treaties can't bargain away constitutional rights any more than Congress can rescind these rights through the Commerce Clause. Second, to the extent that states as states enjoy certain intergovernmental immunities (see the discussion of New York v. United States), those immunities would also seem to limit treaties just as they limit the other powers of Congress. So (for example) the United States could not agree to a treaty that required a state to move its capital to a port city to make trade with another nation easier. See Coyle v. Oklahoma, 221 U.S. 559 (1911).

In the Virginia Ratifying Convention, James Madison suggested a further limit on the Treaty Power: "I do not conceive that power is given to the President and Senate to dismember the empire, or to alienate any great, essential right." 3 Elliot 514 (June 18, 1788). Read literally, that would mean that the United States could never give up any portion of its territory through a treaty. That would make little sense given the historical practice of nations; in fact, the United States has settled disputes with other countries (most notably Great Britain) by surrendering claims to disputed territories or by adjusting boundaries. In fact, to settle a war, the United States would presumably be permitted to give up the entire state of Alaska to Russia, although it would not have the power to agree to move Alaska's capital from Juneau to Anchorage!

4. *The Treaty Power and the foreign and Indian commerce power.* Quite apart from the Treaty Power, it is worth noting that among its enumerated powers, Congress already has the power "[t]o regulate commerce [that is, intercourse and exchanges] with foreign nations, . . . and with the Indian tribes." A statute genuinely designed to facilitate relations or exchanges with a foreign nation (or an Indian tribe) is already within Congress's enumerated powers even in the absence of a foreign treaty. See Akhil Amar, America's Constitution: A Biography 107 & n. 17 (2005); Jack M. Balkin, Living Originalism 155-159 (2011).

5. *Necessary and proper to make but not to execute treaties?* Is Justice Scalia's distinction between the power to make and the power to execute treaties plausible? Does the constitutional text require it? Note that the President's ability to make treaties with other countries in the future may be affected by whether the United States can make credible commitments to execute and enforce its treaties. What is Scalia's best response to this argument? There is also a certain degree of tension between Scalia's argument and *McCulloch*: Chief Justice Marshall argued that implied powers inevitably accompany the enumerated powers. Why isn't the power to enforce or execute treaties an implied power that naturally accompanies the power to make treaties?

6. *The power to implement treaties.* Justice Alito concedes that the Chemical Weapons Convention is a legitimate subject of treaty making. At that point, why doesn't the logic of *McCulloch* and *Gonzales v. Raich* come into play? In Commerce Clause jurisprudence, Congress has the power to reach purely local activities if it believes that doing so is necessary to effectuate a larger interstate regulatory scheme. Why doesn't it follow, then, that Congress has the power to reach domestic activities as part of a larger international regulatory scheme? At the same time, just as in the Commerce Clause area, the Court's new clear statement rule in *Bond* allows the federal judiciary to interpret statutes sympathetically and narrowly to avoid unnecessary interference in local concerns.

Insert the following before Section III on p. 649:

COLEMAN v. COURT OF APPEALS OF MARYLAND, 132 S. Ct. 1327 (2012): 29 U.S.C. §2612(a)(1), part of the Family and Medical Leave Act, entitles an employee to take up to 12 workweeks of unpaid leave per year for the employee's own serious health condition when the condition interferes with the employee's ability to perform at work. Justice Kennedy, in a plurality opinion joined by Chief Justice Roberts, Justice Alito, and Justice Thomas, held that the logic of Nevada Department of Human Resources v. Hibbs, 538 U.S. 721 (2003), did not apply to the FMLA's "self-care provisions." Therefore, Congress lacked the power under section 5 of the Fourteenth Amendment to abrogate the states' immunity from damage lawsuits when state employers unlawfully refused to grant self-care leaves to their employees: "Without widespread evidence of sex discrimination or sex stereotyping in the administration of sick leave, it is apparent that the congressional purpose in enacting the self-care provision is unrelated to these supposed wrongs. The legislative history of the self-care provision reveals a concern for the economic burdens on the employee and the employee's family resulting from illness-related job loss and a concern for discrimination on the basis of illness, not sex." Justice Thomas concurred, adding that he believed *Hibbs* was wrongly decided. Justice Scalia concurred in the judgment, arguing that the Court should abandon its "congruence and proportionality" test: "I would limit Congress's §5 power to the regulation of conduct that *itself* violates the Fourteenth Amendment. Failing to grant state employees leave for the purpose of self-care — or any other purpose, for that matter — does not come close."

Justice Ginsburg, joined by Justice Breyer, Justice Sotomayor, and Justice Kagan, dissented. Justice Ginsburg argued that the FMLA was designed, among other things, to prevent discrimination against pregnant women. Accordingly, Justice Ginsburg would overrule *Geduldig v. Aiello* and hold that discrimination against pregnant women is a form of sex discrimination. "The self-care provision responds to . . . evidence [of discrimination against pregnant women] by requiring employers to allow leave for "ongoing pregnancy, miscarriages, . . . the need for prenatal care, childbirth, and recovery from childbirth." Justice Ginsburg quoted congressional reports explaining that it was better to require employers to provide self-care leave for *both* men and women — instead of providing leave only following pregnancy or due to pregnancy-related illness — because this would remove employers' incentives to discriminate against pregnant women and women of child-bearing age. Because a guarantee of self-care leave for both men and women alleviated employer incentives toward pregnancy discrimination, and because it was without pay and therefore not too burdensome to employers, Justice Ginsburg concluded that it was congruent and proportional to Congress's evidence of pregnancy discrimination in employment.

Even if pregnancy discrimination did not count as sex discrimination, Ginsburg argued, Congress understood that "[r]equiring States to provide gender-neutral parental and family-care leave alone [without self-care leave] . . . would promote precisely the type of workplace discrimination Congress sought to reduce. The 'pervasive sex-role stereotype that caring for family members is women's work,' [Congress believed], led employers to regard required parental and family-care leave as a woman's benefit" that few men would use. "Congress therefore had good reason to conclude that the self-care provision — which men no doubt would use — would counter employers' impressions that the FMLA would otherwise install female leave. Providing for self-care would thus reduce employers' corresponding incentive to discriminate against women in hiring and promotion."

SHELBY COUNTY, ALABAMA v. HOLDER
133. S. Ct. 2612 (2013)

[Section 5 of the Voting Rights Act of 1965 requires that covered jurisdictions — which are listed in section 4(b) of the Act — must preclear any changes to their voting systems with the Department of Justice (or with a three judge district court in Washington) to ensure that they do not "ha[ve] the purpose nor . . . the effect of denying or abridging the right to vote on account of race or color." 42 U.S.C. §1973c(a). Jurisdictions listed in section 4(b)'s coverage formula were originally determined by a test of those states that had used a forbidden test or device in November 1964, and had less than 50 percent voter registration or turnout in the 1964 Presidential election. Today covered jurisdictions include most of the South, Arizona, and Alaska, along with various counties and townships throughout the United States.

Congress reauthorized the Act for five years in 1970, for seven years in 1975, and for 25 years in 1982. The coverage formula, based on the use of voting-eligibility tests and the rate of registration and turnout among all voters, remained the same, but the measurements were based on 1968 and eventually 1972 levels. In 2006, Congress extended the Voting Rights Act for 25 more years. Once again it maintained the existing coverage formula, keeping 1972 as the baseline date for measuring which jurisdictions would be subject to preclearance requirements.

In 2009, the Supreme Court considered a challenge to the constitutionality of section 5 of the Voting Rights Act from a Texas municipal utility district. In *Northwest Austin Municipal Util. Dist. No. One v. Holder*, 557 U.S. 193 (2009), the Court stated that "[t]he Act's preclearance requirements and its coverage formula raise serious constitutional questions under either [the] test" of *City of Boerne v. Flores* or *South Carolina v. Katzenbach*, but avoided the constitutional question by interpreting the statute to exclude the district from the Act's coverage.

Shelby County, as a political subdivision of Alabama, is a covered jurisdiction under section 4(b). It brought a new challenge to the VRA, arguing that section 4(b), the VRA's coverage formula, and section 5, the preclearance requirement, are facially unconstitutional and asked for a permanent injunction against their enforcement.]

Chief Justice ROBERTS delivered the opinion of the Court.

. . .

II

In *Northwest Austin,* we stated that "the Act imposes current burdens and must be justified by current needs." And we concluded that "a departure from the fundamental principle of equal sovereignty requires a showing that a statute's disparate geographic coverage is sufficiently related to the problem that it targets." These basic principles guide our review of the question before us.

A

[T]he Federal Government does not . . . have a general right to review and veto state enactments before they go into effect. A proposal to grant such authority to "negative" state laws was considered at the Constitutional Convention, but rejected in favor of allowing state laws to take effect, subject to later challenge under the Supremacy Clause.

Outside the strictures of the Supremacy Clause, States retain broad autonomy in structuring their governments and pursuing legislative objectives. Indeed, the Constitution provides that all powers not specifically granted to the Federal Government are reserved to the States or citizens. Amdt. 10. This "allocation of powers in our federal system preserves the integrity, dignity, and residual sovereignty of the States." But the federal balance "is not just an end in itself: Rather, federalism secures to citizens the liberties that derive from the diffusion of sovereign power."

More specifically, " 'the Framers of the Constitution intended the States to keep for themselves, as provided in the Tenth Amendment, the power to regulate elections.' " *Gregory v. Ashcroft,* 501 U.S. 452 (1991). Of course, the Federal Government retains significant control over federal elections. For instance, the Constitution authorizes Congress to establish the time and manner for electing Senators and Representatives. Art. I, §4, cl. 1. But States have "broad powers to determine the conditions under which the right of suffrage may be exercised." And "[e]ach State has the power to prescribe the qualifications of its officers and the manner in which they shall be chosen." *Boyd v. Nebraska ex rel. Thayer,* 143 U.S. 135 (1892). . . .

Not only do States retain sovereignty under the Constitution, there is also a "fundamental principle of *equal* sovereignty" among the States. *Northwest Austin.* Over a hundred years ago, this Court explained that our Nation "was and is a union of States, equal in power, dignity and authority." *Coyle v. Smith,* 221 U.S. 559 (1911). Indeed, "the constitutional equality of the States is essential to the harmonious operation of the scheme upon which the Republic was organized." *Coyle* concerned the admission of new States, and *Katzenbach* rejected the notion that the principle operated as a *bar* on differential treatment outside that context. At the same time, as we made clear in *Northwest Austin,* the fundamental principle of equal sovereignty remains highly pertinent in assessing subsequent disparate treatment of States.

The Voting Rights Act sharply departs from these basic principles. It suspends "*all* changes to state election law — however innocuous — until they have been precleared by federal authorities in Washington, D.C." States must beseech the Federal Government for permission to implement laws that they would otherwise have the right to enact and execute on their own, subject of course to any injunction in a §2 action. The Attorney General has 60 days to object to a preclearance request, longer if he requests more information. If a State seeks preclearance from a three-judge court, the process can take years.

And despite the tradition of equal sovereignty, the Act applies to only nine States (and several additional counties). While one State waits months or years and expends funds to implement a validly enacted law, its neighbor can typically put the same law into effect immediately, through the normal legislative process. Even if a noncovered jurisdiction is sued, there are important differences between those proceedings and preclearance proceedings; the preclearance proceeding "not only switches the burden of proof to the supplicant jurisdiction, but also applies substantive standards quite different from those governing the rest of the nation."

All this explains why, when we first upheld the Act in 1966, we described it as "stringent" and "potent." *Katzenbach*. We recognized that it "may have been an uncommon exercise of congressional power," but concluded that "legislative measures not otherwise appropriate" could be justified by "exceptional conditions." We have since noted that the Act "authorizes federal intrusion into sensitive areas of state and local policymaking," and represents an "extraordinary departure from the traditional course of relations between the States and the Federal Government." As we reiterated in *Northwest Austin,* the Act constitutes "extraordinary legislation otherwise unfamiliar to our federal system."

B

In 1966, we found these departures from the basic features of our system of government justified. The "blight of racial discrimination in voting" had "infected the electoral process in parts of our country for nearly a century." *Katzenbach*. Several States had enacted a variety of requirements and tests "specifically designed to prevent" African-Americans from voting. Case-by-case litigation had proved inadequate to prevent such racial discrimination in voting, in part because States "merely switched to discriminatory devices not covered by the federal decrees," "enacted difficult new tests," or simply "defied and evaded court orders." Shortly before enactment of the Voting Rights Act, only 19.4 percent of African-Americans of voting age were registered to vote in Alabama, only 31.8 percent in Louisiana, and only 6.4 percent in Mississippi. Those figures were roughly 50 percentage points or more below the figures for whites.

In short, we concluded that "[u]nder the compulsion of these unique circumstances, Congress responded in a permissibly decisive manner." We also noted then and have emphasized since that this extraordinary legislation was intended to be temporary, set to expire after five years.

At the time, the coverage formula—the means of linking the exercise of the unprecedented authority with the problem that warranted it—made sense. We found that "Congress chose to limit its attention to the geographic areas where immediate action seemed necessary." The areas where Congress found "evidence of actual voting discrimination" shared two characteristics: "the use of tests and devices for voter registration, and a voting rate in the 1964 presidential election at least 12 points below the national average." We explained that "[t]ests and devices are relevant to voting discrimination because of their long history as a tool for perpetrating the evil; a low voting rate is pertinent for the obvious reason that widespread disenfranchisement must inevitably affect the number of actual voters." We therefore concluded that "the coverage formula [was] rational in both practice and theory." It accurately reflected those jurisdictions uniquely characterized by voting discrimination "on a pervasive scale," linking coverage to the devices used to effectuate discrimination and to the resulting disenfranchisement. The formula ensured that the "stringent remedies [were] aimed at areas where voting discrimination ha[d] been most flagrant."

C

Nearly 50 years later, things have changed dramatically. Shelby County contends that the preclearance requirement, even without regard to its disparate coverage, is now unconstitutional. Its arguments have a good deal of force. In the covered jurisdictions, "[v]oter turnout and registration rates now approach parity. Blatantly discriminatory evasions of federal decrees are rare. And minority candidates hold office at unprecedented levels." The tests and devices that blocked access to the ballot have been forbidden nationwide for over 40 years.

Those conclusions are not ours alone. Congress said the same when it reauthorized the Act in 2006, writing that "[s]ignificant progress has been made in eliminating first generation barriers experienced by minority voters, including increased numbers of registered minority voters, minority voter turnout, and minority representation in Congress, State legislatures, and local elected offices." §2(b)(1), 120 Stat. 577. The House Report elaborated that "the number of African-Americans who are registered and who turn out to cast ballots has increased significantly over the last 40 years, particularly since 1982," and noted that "[i]n some circumstances, minorities register to vote and cast ballots at levels that surpass those of white voters." That Report also explained that there have been "significant increases in the number of African-Americans serving in elected offices"; more specifically, there has been approximately a 1,000 percent increase since 1965 in the number of African-American elected officials in the six States originally covered by the Voting Rights Act.

The following chart, compiled from the Senate and House Reports, compares voter registration numbers from 1965 to those from 2004 in the six originally covered States. These are the numbers that were before Congress when it reauthorized the Act in 2006:

	1965			2004		
	White	Black	Gap	White	Black	Gap
Alabama	62.9	19.3	49.9	73.8	72.9	0.9
Georgia	62.[6]	27.4	35.2	63.5	64.2	−0.7
Louisiana	80.5	31.6	48.9	75.1	71.1	4.0
Mississippi	69.9	6.7	63.2	72.3	76.1	−3.8
South Carolina	75.7	37.3	38.4	74.4	71.1	3.3
Virginia	61.1	38.3	22.8	68.2	57.4	10.8

[C]ensus Bureau data from the most recent election indicate that African-American voter turnout exceeded white voter turnout in five of the six States originally covered by §5, with a gap in the sixth State of less than one half of one percent. The preclearance statistics are also illuminating. In the first decade after enactment of §5, the Attorney General objected to 14.2 percent of proposed voting changes. In the last decade before reenactment, the Attorney General objected to a mere 0.16 percent.

There is no doubt that these improvements are in large part *because of* the Voting Rights Act. The Act has proved immensely successful at redressing racial discrimination and integrating the voting process. During the "Freedom Summer" of 1964, in Philadelphia, Mississippi, three men were murdered while working in the area to register African-American voters. On "Bloody Sunday" in 1965, in Selma, Alabama, police beat and used tear gas against hundreds marching in support of African-American enfranchisement. Today both of those towns are governed by African-American mayors. Problems remain in these States and others, but there is no denying that, due to the Voting Rights Act, our Nation has made great strides.

Yet the Act has not eased the restrictions in §5 or narrowed the scope of the coverage formula in §4(b) along the way. Those extraordinary and unprecedented features were reauthorized—as if nothing had changed. In fact, the Act's unusual remedies have grown even stronger. When Congress reauthorized the Act in 2006, it did so for another 25 years on top of the previous 40—a far cry from the initial five-year period. Congress also expanded the prohibitions in §5. We had previously interpreted §5 to prohibit only those redistricting plans that would have the purpose or effect of worsening the position of minority groups. In 2006, Congress amended §5 to prohibit laws that could have favored such groups but did not do so because of a discriminatory purpose, see 42 U.S.C. §1973c(c), even though we had stated that such broadening of §5 coverage would "exacerbate the substantial federalism costs that the preclearance procedure already exacts, perhaps to the extent of raising concerns about §5's constitutionality," *Reno v. Bossier Parish School Bd.*, 528 U.S. 320 (2000) (*Bossier II*). In addition, Congress expanded §5 to prohibit any voting law "that has the purpose of or will have the effect of diminishing the ability of any citizens of the United States," on account of race, color, or language minority status, "to elect their preferred candidates of choice." §1973c(b). In light of those two amendments, the bar that covered jurisdictions must clear has been raised even as the conditions justifying that requirement have dramatically improved.

We have also previously highlighted the concern that "the preclearance requirements in one State [might] be unconstitutional in another." *Northwest Austin.* See *Georgia v. Ashcroft*, 539 U.S., at 491 (Kennedy, J., concurring) ("considerations of race that would doom a redistricting plan under the Fourteenth Amendment or §2 [of the Voting Rights Act] seem to be what save it under §5"). Nothing has happened since to alleviate this troubling concern about the current application of §5.

Respondents do not deny that there have been improvements on the ground, but argue that much of this can be attributed to the deterrent effect of §5, which dissuades covered jurisdictions from engaging in discrimination that they would resume should §5 be struck down. Under this theory, however, §5 would be effectively immune from scrutiny; no matter how "clean" the record of covered jurisdictions, the argument could always be made that it was deterrence that accounted for the good behavior.

The provisions of §5 apply only to those jurisdictions singled out by §4. We now consider whether that coverage formula is constitutional in light of current conditions.

III

A

When upholding the constitutionality of the coverage formula in 1966, we concluded that it was "rational in both practice and theory." *Katzenbach.* The formula looked to cause (discriminatory tests) and effect (low voter registration and turnout), and tailored the remedy (preclearance) to those jurisdictions exhibiting both.

By 2009, however, we concluded that the "coverage formula raise[d] serious constitutional questions." *Northwest Austin.* As we explained, a statute's "current burdens" must be justified by "current needs," and any "disparate geographic coverage" must be "sufficiently related to the problem that it targets." The coverage formula met that test in 1965, but no longer does so.

Coverage today is based on decades-old data and eradicated practices. The formula captures States by reference to literacy tests and low voter registration and turnout in the 1960s and early 1970s. But such tests have been banned nationwide for over 40 years. And voter registration and turnout numbers in the covered States have risen dramatically in the years since. Racial disparity in those numbers was compelling evidence justifying the preclearance remedy and the coverage formula. There is no longer such a disparity.

In 1965, the States could be divided into two groups: those with a recent history of voting tests and low voter registration and turnout, and those without those characteristics. Congress based its coverage formula on that distinction. Today the Nation is no longer divided along those lines, yet the Voting Rights Act continues to treat it as if it were.

B

The Government's defense of the formula is limited. First, the Government contends that the formula is "reverse-engineered": Congress identified the jurisdictions to be covered and *then* came up with criteria to describe them. Under that reasoning, there need not be any logical relationship between the criteria in the formula and the reason for coverage; all that is necessary is that the formula happen to capture the jurisdictions Congress wanted to single out.

The Government suggests that *Katzenbach* sanctioned such an approach, but the analysis in *Katzenbach* was quite different. *Katzenbach* reasoned that the coverage formula was rational because the "formula . . . was relevant to the problem": "Tests and devices are relevant to voting discrimination because of their long history as a tool for perpetrating the evil; a low voting rate is pertinent for the obvious reason that widespread disenfranchisement must inevitably affect the number of actual voters."

Here, by contrast, the Government's reverse engineering argument does not even attempt to demonstrate the continued relevance of the formula to the problem it targets. And in the context of a decision as significant as this one — subjecting a disfavored subset of States to "extraordinary legislation otherwise unfamiliar to our federal system" — that failure to establish even relevance is fatal.

The Government falls back to the argument that because the formula was relevant in 1965, its continued use is permissible so long as any discrimination remains in the States Congress identified back then — regardless of how that discrimination compares to discrimination in States unburdened by coverage. This argument does not look to "current political conditions," but instead relies on a comparison between the States in 1965. That comparison reflected the different histories of the North and South. It was in the South that slavery was upheld by law until uprooted by the Civil War, that the reign of Jim Crow denied African-Americans the most basic freedoms, and that state and local governments worked tirelessly to disenfranchise citizens on the basis of race. The Court invoked that history — rightly so — in sustaining the disparate coverage of the Voting Rights Act in 1966. See *Katzenbach* ("The constitutional propriety of the Voting Rights Act of 1965 must be judged with reference to the historical experience which it reflects.").

But history did not end in 1965. By the time the Act was reauthorized in 2006, there had been 40 more years of it. In assessing the "current need[ ]" for a preclearance system that treats States differently from one another today, that history cannot be ignored. During that time, largely because of the Voting Rights Act, voting tests were abolished, disparities in voter registration and turnout due to race were erased, and African-Americans attained political office in record numbers. And yet the coverage formula that Congress reauthorized in 2006 ignores these developments, keeping the focus on decades-old data relevant to decades-old problems, rather than current data reflecting current needs.

The Fifteenth Amendment commands that the right to vote shall not be denied or abridged on account of race or color, and it gives Congress the power to enforce that command. The Amendment is not designed to punish for the past; its purpose is to ensure a better future. To serve that purpose, Congress — if it is to divide the States — must identify those jurisdictions to be singled out on a basis that makes sense in light of current conditions. It cannot rely simply on the past. We made that clear in *Northwest Austin,* and we make it clear again today.

C

In defending the coverage formula, the Government, the intervenors, and the dissent also rely heavily on data from the record that they claim justify disparate coverage. Congress compiled thousands of pages of evidence before reauthorizing the Voting Rights Act. The court below and the parties have debated what that record shows—they have gone back and forth about whether to compare covered to noncovered jurisdictions as blocks, how to disaggregate the data State by State, how to weigh §2 cases as evidence of ongoing discrimination, and whether to consider evidence not before Congress, among other issues. Regardless of how to look at the record, however, no one can fairly say that it shows anything approaching the "pervasive," "flagrant," "widespread," and "rampant" discrimination that faced Congress in 1965, and that clearly distinguished the covered jurisdictions from the rest of the Nation at that time.

But a more fundamental problem remains: Congress did not use the record it compiled to shape a coverage formula grounded in current conditions. It instead reenacted a formula based on 40-year-old facts having no logical relation to the present day. The dissent relies on "second-generation barriers," which are not impediments to the casting of ballots, but rather electoral arrangements that affect the weight of minority votes. That does not cure the problem. Viewing the preclearance requirements as targeting such efforts simply highlights the irrationality of continued reliance on the §4 coverage formula, which is based on voting tests and access to the ballot, not vote dilution. We cannot pretend that we are reviewing an updated statute, or try our hand at updating the statute ourselves, based on the new record compiled by Congress. Contrary to the dissent's contention, we are not ignoring the record; we are simply recognizing that it played no role in shaping the statutory formula before us today.

The dissent also turns to the record to argue that, in light of voting discrimination in Shelby County, the county cannot complain about the provisions that subject it to preclearance. But that is like saying that a driver pulled over pursuant to a policy of stopping all redheads cannot complain about that policy, if it turns out his license has expired. Shelby County's claim is that the coverage formula here is unconstitutional in all its applications, because of how it selects the jurisdictions subjected to preclearance. The county was selected based on that formula, and may challenge it in court.

D

The dissent proceeds from a flawed premise. It quotes the famous sentence from *McCulloch v. Maryland*: "Let the end be legitimate, let it be within the scope of the constitution, and *all means which are appropriate, which are plainly adapted to that end,* which are not prohibited, but consist with the letter and spirit of the constitution, are constitutional." But this case is about a part of the sentence that the dissent does not emphasize—the part that asks whether a legislative means is "consist[ent] with the letter and spirit of the constitution." The dissent states that "[i]t cannot tenably be maintained" that this is an issue with regard to the Voting Rights Act, but four years ago, in an opinion joined by two of today's dissenters, the Court expressly stated that "[t]he Act's preclearance requirement and its coverage formula raise serious constitutional questions."

Northwest Austin. The dissent does not explain how those "serious constitutional questions" became untenable in four short years.

The dissent treats the Act as if it were just like any other piece of legislation, but this Court has made clear from the beginning that the Voting Rights Act is far from ordinary. At the risk of repetition, *Katzenbach* indicated that the Act was "uncommon" and "not otherwise appropriate," but was justified by "exceptional" and "unique" conditions. Multiple decisions since have reaffirmed the Act's "extraordinary" nature. Yet the dissent goes so far as to suggest instead that the preclearance requirement and disparate treatment of the States should be upheld into the future "unless there [is] no or almost no evidence of unconstitutional action by States."

In other ways as well, the dissent analyzes the question presented as if our decision in *Northwest Austin* never happened. For example, the dissent refuses to consider the principle of equal sovereignty, despite *Northwest Austin*'s emphasis on its significance. *Northwest Austin* also emphasized the "dramatic" progress since 1965, but the dissent describes current levels of discrimination as "flagrant," "widespread," and "pervasive." Despite the fact that *Northwest Austin* requires an Act's "disparate geographic coverage" to be "sufficiently related" to its targeted problems, the dissent maintains that an Act's limited coverage actually eases Congress's burdens, and suggests that a fortuitous relationship should suffice. Although *Northwest Austin* stated definitively that "current burdens" must be justified by "current needs," the dissent argues that the coverage formula can be justified by history, and that the required showing can be weaker on reenactment than when the law was first passed.

There is no valid reason to insulate the coverage formula from review merely because it was previously enacted 40 years ago. If Congress had started from scratch in 2006, it plainly could not have enacted the present coverage formula. It would have been irrational for Congress to distinguish between States in such a fundamental way based on 40-year-old data, when today's statistics tell an entirely different story. And it would have been irrational to base coverage on the use of voting tests 40 years ago, when such tests have been illegal since that time. But that is exactly what Congress has done.

* * *

Striking down an Act of Congress "is the gravest and most delicate duty that this Court is called on to perform." We do not do so lightly. That is why, in 2009, we took care to avoid ruling on the constitutionality of the Voting Rights Act when asked to do so, and instead resolved the case then before us on statutory grounds. But in issuing that decision, we expressed our broader concerns about the constitutionality of the Act. Congress could have updated the coverage formula at that time, but did not do so. Its failure to act leaves us today with no choice but to declare §4(b) unconstitutional. The formula in that section can no longer be used as a basis for subjecting jurisdictions to preclearance.

Our decision in no way affects the permanent, nationwide ban on racial discrimination in voting found in §2. We issue no holding on §5 itself, only on the coverage formula. Congress may draft another formula based on current conditions. Such a formula is an initial prerequisite to a determination that exceptional conditions still exist justifying such an "extraordinary departure from the traditional course of relations between the States and the Federal Government." Our country has changed, and while any racial discrimination in voting is too much, Congress must ensure that the legislation it passes to remedy that problem speaks to current conditions.

The judgment of the Court of Appeals is reversed.

It is so ordered.

Justice THOMAS, concurring.

I join the Court's opinion in full but write separately to explain that I would find §5 of the Voting Rights Act unconstitutional as well. The Court's opinion sets forth the reasons. . . .

Today, our Nation has changed. "[T]he conditions that originally justified [§5] no longer characterize voting in the covered jurisdictions." As the Court explains: " '[V]oter turnout and registration rates now approach parity. Blatantly discriminatory evasions of federal decrees are rare. And minority candidates hold office at unprecedented levels.' "

In spite of these improvements, however, Congress *increased* the already significant burdens of §5. Following its reenactment in 2006, the Voting Rights Act was amended to "prohibit more conduct than before." "Section 5 now forbids voting changes with 'any discriminatory purpose' as well as voting changes that diminish the ability of citizens, on account of race, color, or language minority status, 'to elect their preferred candidates of choice.' " While the pre-2006 version of the Act went well beyond protection guaranteed under the Constitution, it now goes even further.

It is, thus, quite fitting that the Court repeatedly points out that this legislation is "extraordinary" and "unprecedented" and recognizes the significant constitutional problems created by Congress' decision to raise "the bar that covered jurisdictions must clear," even as "the conditions justifying that requirement have dramatically improved." However one aggregates the data compiled by Congress, it cannot justify the considerable burdens created by §5. As the Court aptly notes: "[N]o one can fairly say that [the record] shows anything approaching the 'pervasive,' 'flagrant,' 'widespread,' and 'rampant' discrimination that faced Congress in 1965, and that clearly distinguished the covered jurisdictions from the rest of the Nation at that time." Indeed, circumstances in the covered jurisdictions can no longer be characterized as "exceptional" or "unique." "The extensive pattern of discrimination that led the Court to previously uphold §5 as enforcing the Fifteenth Amendment no longer exists." Section 5 is, thus, unconstitutional.

While the Court claims to "issue no holding on §5 itself," its own opinion compellingly demonstrates that Congress has failed to justify " 'current burdens' " with a record demonstrating " 'current needs.' " By leaving the inevitable conclusion unstated, the Court needlessly prolongs the demise of that provision. For the reasons stated in the Court's opinion, I would find §5 unconstitutional.

Justice GINSBURG, with whom Justice BREYER, Justice SOTOMAYOR, and Justice KAGAN join, dissenting.

In the Court's view, the very success of §5 of the Voting Rights Act demands its dormancy. Congress was of another mind. Recognizing that large progress has been made, Congress determined, based on a voluminous record, that the scourge of discrimination was not yet extirpated. The question this case presents is who decides whether, as currently operative, §5 remains justifiable, this Court, or a Congress charged with the obligation to enforce the post-Civil War Amendments "by appropriate legislation." [The Court purports to declare unconstitutional only the coverage formula set out in §4(b). But without that formula, §5 is immobilized.] [Relocated footnote — EDS.]

With overwhelming support in both Houses, Congress concluded that, for two prime reasons, §5 should continue in force, unabated. First, continuance would facilitate completion of the impressive gains thus far made; and second, continuance would guard against backsliding. Those assessments were well within Congress' province to make and should elicit this Court's unstinting approbation.

I

[The Court acknowledges that] "voting discrimination still exists; no one doubts that." But the Court today terminates the remedy that proved to be best suited to block that discrimination. The Voting Rights Act of 1965 (VRA) has worked to combat voting discrimination where other remedies had been tried and failed. Particularly effective is the VRA's requirement of federal preclearance for all changes to voting laws in the regions of the country with the most aggravated records of rank discrimination against minority voting rights.

A century after the Fourteenth and Fifteenth Amendments guaranteed citizens the right to vote free of discrimination on the basis of race, the "blight of racial discrimination in voting" continued to "infec[t] the electoral process in parts of our country." Early attempts to cope with this vile infection resembled battling the Hydra. Whenever one form of voting discrimination was identified and prohibited, others sprang up in its place. This Court repeatedly encountered the remarkable "variety and persistence" of laws disenfranchising minority citizens. To take just one example, the Court, in 1927, held unconstitutional a Texas law barring black voters from participating in primary elections, *Nixon v. Herndon* 273 U.S. 536; in 1944, the Court struck down a "reenacted" and slightly altered version of the same law, *Smith v. Allwright,* 321 U.S. 649; and in 1953, the Court once again confronted an attempt by Texas to "circumven[t]" the Fifteenth Amendment by adopting yet another variant of the all-white primary, *Terry v. Adams,* 345 U.S. 461.

During this era, the Court recognized that discrimination against minority voters was a quintessentially political problem requiring a political solution. As Justice Holmes explained: If "the great mass of the white population intends to keep the blacks from voting," "relief from [that] great political wrong, if done, as alleged, by the people of a State and the State itself, must be given by them or by the legislative and political department of the government of the United States." *Giles v. Harris,* 189 U.S. 475 (1903).

Congress learned from experience that laws targeting particular electoral practices or enabling case-by-case litigation were inadequate to the task. In the Civil Rights Acts of 1957, 1960, and 1964, Congress authorized and then expanded the power of "the Attorney General to seek injunctions against public and private interference with the right to vote on racial grounds." But circumstances reduced the ameliorative potential of these legislative Acts:

"Voting suits are unusually onerous to prepare, sometimes requiring as many as 6,000 man-hours spent combing through registration records in preparation for trial. Litigation has been exceedingly slow, in part because of the ample opportunities for delay afforded voting officials and others involved in the proceedings. Even when favorable decisions have finally been obtained, some of the States affected have merely switched to discriminatory devices not covered by the federal decrees or have enacted difficult new tests designed to prolong the existing disparity between white and Negro registration. Alternatively, certain local officials have defied and evaded court orders or have simply closed their registration offices to freeze the voting rolls." *Katzenbach.*

Patently, a new approach was needed.

Answering that need, the Voting Rights Act became one of the most consequential, efficacious, and amply justified exercises of federal legislative power in our Nation's history. Requiring federal preclearance of changes in voting laws in the covered jurisdictions—those States and localities where opposition to the Constitution's commands were most virulent—the VRA provided a fit solution for minority voters as well as for States. Under the preclearance regime established by §5 of the VRA, covered jurisdictions must submit proposed changes in voting laws or procedures to the Department of Justice (DOJ), which has 60 days to respond to the changes. 79 Stat. 439, codified at 42 U.S.C. §1973c(a). A change will be approved unless DOJ finds it has "the purpose [or] . . . the effect of denying or abridging the right to vote on account of race or color." In the alternative, the covered jurisdiction may seek approval by a three-judge District Court in the District of Columbia.

After a century's failure to fulfill the promise of the Fourteenth and Fifteenth Amendments, passage of the VRA finally led to signal improvement on this front. "The Justice Department estimated that in the five years after [the VRA's] passage, almost as many blacks registered [to vote] in Alabama, Mississippi, Georgia, Louisiana, North Carolina, and South Carolina as in the entire century before 1965." Davidson, The Voting Rights Act: A Brief History, in Controversies in Minority Voting 7, 21 (B. Grofman & C. Davidson eds. 1992).

And in assessing the overall effects of the VRA in 2006, Congress found that "[s]ignificant progress has been made in eliminating first generation barriers experienced by minority voters, including increased numbers of registered minority voters, minority voter turnout, and minority representation in Congress, State legislatures, and local elected offices. This progress is the direct result of the Voting Rights Act of 1965." Fannie Lou Hamer, Rosa Parks, and Coretta Scott King Voting Rights Act Reauthorization and Amendments Act of 2006 (hereinafter 2006 Reauthorization), §2(b)(1), 120 Stat. 577. On that matter of cause and effects there can be no genuine doubt.

Although the VRA wrought dramatic changes in the realization of minority voting rights, the Act, to date, surely has not eliminated all vestiges of discrimination against the exercise of the franchise by minority citizens. Jurisdictions covered by the preclearance requirement continued to submit, in large numbers, proposed changes to voting laws that the Attorney General declined to approve, auguring that barriers to minority voting would quickly resurface were the preclearance remedy eliminated. Congress also found that as "registration and voting of minority citizens increas[ed], other measures may be resorted to which would dilute increasing minority voting strength." Efforts to reduce the impact of minority votes, in contrast to direct attempts to block access to the ballot, are aptly described as "second-generation barriers" to minority voting.

Second-generation barriers come in various forms. One of the blockages is racial gerrymandering, the redrawing of legislative districts in an "effort to segregate the races for purposes of voting." Another is adoption of a system of at-large voting in lieu of district-by-district voting in a city with a sizable black minority. By switching to at-large voting, the overall majority could control the election of each city council member, effectively eliminating the potency of the minority's votes. A similar effect could be achieved if the city engaged in discriminatory annexation by incorporating majority-white areas into city limits, thereby decreasing the effect of VRA-occasioned increases in black voting. Whatever the device employed, this Court has long recognized that vote dilution, when adopted with a discriminatory purpose, cuts down the right to vote as certainly as denial of access to the ballot. See also H.R. Rep. No. 109-478, p. 6 (2006) (although "[d]iscrimination today is more subtle than the visible methods used in 1965," "the effect and results are the same, namely a diminishing of the minority community's ability to fully participate in the electoral process and to elect their preferred candidates").

In response to evidence of these substituted barriers, Congress reauthorized the VRA for five years in 1970, for seven years in 1975, and for 25 years in 1982. Each time, this Court upheld the reauthorization as a valid exercise of congressional power. As the 1982 reauthorization approached its 2007 expiration date, Congress again considered whether the VRA's preclearance mechanism remained an appropriate response to the problem of voting discrimination in covered jurisdictions.

Congress did not take this task lightly. Quite the opposite. The 109th Congress that took responsibility for the renewal started early and conscientiously. In

October 2005, the House began extensive hearings, which continued into November and resumed in March 2006. In April 2006, the Senate followed suit, with hearings of its own. In May 2006, the bills that became the VRA's reauthorization were introduced in both Houses. The House held further hearings of considerable length, as did the Senate, which continued to hold hearings into June and July. In mid-July, the House considered and rejected four amendments, then passed the reauthorization by a vote of 390 yeas to 33 nays. 152 Cong. Rec. H5207 (July 13, 2006). The bill was read and debated in the Senate, where it passed by a vote of 98 to 0. 152 Cong. Rec. S8012 (July 20, 2006). President Bush signed it a week later, on July 27, 2006, recognizing the need for "further work . . . in the fight against injustice," and calling the reauthorization "an example of our continued commitment to a united America where every person is valued and treated with dignity and respect."

In the long course of the legislative process, Congress "amassed a sizable record." *Northwest Austin* (describing the "extensive record" supporting Congress' determination that "serious and widespread intentional discrimination persisted in covered jurisdictions"). The House and Senate Judiciary Committees held 21 hearings, heard from scores of witnesses, received a number of investigative reports and other written documentation of continuing discrimination in covered jurisdictions. In all, the legislative record Congress compiled filled more than 15,000 pages. The compilation presents countless "examples of flagrant racial discrimination" since the last reauthorization; Congress also brought to light systematic evidence that "intentional racial discrimination in voting remains so serious and widespread in covered jurisdictions that section 5 preclearance is still needed."

After considering the full legislative record, Congress made the following findings: The VRA has directly caused significant progress in eliminating first-generation barriers to ballot access, leading to a marked increase in minority voter registration and turnout and the number of minority elected officials. 2006 Reauthorization §2(b)(1). But despite this progress, "second generation barriers constructed to prevent minority voters from fully participating in the electoral process" continued to exist, as well as racially polarized voting in the covered jurisdictions, which increased the political vulnerability of racial and language minorities in those jurisdictions. §§2(b)(2)-(3). Extensive "[e]vidence of continued discrimination," Congress concluded, "clearly show[ed] the continued need for Federal oversight" in covered jurisdictions. §§2(b)(4)-(5). The overall record demonstrated to the federal lawmakers that, "without the continuation of the Voting Rights Act of 1965 protections, racial and language minority citizens will be deprived of the opportunity to exercise their right to vote, or will have their votes diluted, undermining the significant gains made by minorities in the last 40 years." §2(b)(9).

Based on these findings, Congress reauthorized preclearance for another 25 years, while also undertaking to reconsider the extension after 15 years to ensure that the provision was still necessary and effective. 42 U.S.C. §1973b(a)(7), (8)

(2006 ed., Supp. V). The question before the Court is whether Congress had the authority under the Constitution to act as it did.

II

In answering this question, the Court does not write on a clean slate. It is well established that Congress' judgment regarding exercise of its power to enforce the Fourteenth and Fifteenth Amendments warrants substantial deference. The VRA addresses the combination of race discrimination and the right to vote, which is "preservative of all rights." When confronting the most constitutionally invidious form of discrimination, and the most fundamental right in our democratic system, Congress' power to act is at its height.

The basis for this deference is firmly rooted in both constitutional text and precedent. The Fifteenth Amendment, which targets precisely and only racial discrimination in voting rights, states that, in this domain, "Congress shall have power to enforce this article by appropriate legislation."[a] In choosing this language, the Amendment's framers invoked Chief Justice Marshall's formulation of the scope of Congress' powers under the Necessary and Proper Clause: "Let the end be legitimate, let it be within the scope of the constitution, and *all means which are appropriate, which are plainly adapted to that end,* which are not prohibited, but consist with the letter and spirit of the constitution, are constitutional." *McCulloch v. Maryland* (emphasis added).

It cannot tenably be maintained that the VRA, an Act of Congress adopted to shield the right to vote from racial discrimination, is inconsistent with the letter or spirit of the Fifteenth Amendment, or any provision of the Constitution read in light of the Civil War Amendments. Nowhere in today's opinion, or in *Northwest Austin,* is there clear recognition of the transformative effect the Fifteenth Amendment aimed to achieve. Notably, "the Founders' first successful amendment told Congress that it could 'make no law' over a certain domain"; in contrast, the Civil War Amendments used "language [that] authorized transformative new federal statutes to uproot all vestiges of unfreedom and inequality" and provided "sweeping enforcement powers . . . to enact 'appropriate' legislation targeting state abuses."

The stated purpose of the Civil War Amendments was to arm Congress with the power and authority to protect all persons within the Nation from violations

---

a. The Constitution uses the words "right to vote" in five separate places: the Fourteenth, Fifteenth, Nineteenth, Twenty-Fourth, and Twenty-Sixth Amendments. Each of these Amendments contains the same broad empowerment of Congress to enact "appropriate legislation" to enforce the protected right. The implication is unmistakable: Under our constitutional structure, Congress holds the lead rein in making the right to vote equally real for all U.S. citizens. These Amendments are in line with the special role assigned to Congress in protecting the integrity of the democratic process in federal elections. U.S. Const., Art. I, §4 ("[T]he Congress may at any time by Law make or alter" regulations concerning the "Times, Places and Manner of holding Elections for Senators and Representatives."); *Arizona v. Inter Tribal Council of Ariz., Inc.*

of their rights by the States. In exercising that power, then, Congress may use "all means which are appropriate, which are plainly adapted" to the constitutional ends declared by these Amendments. *McCulloch.* So when Congress acts to enforce the right to vote free from racial discrimination, we ask not whether Congress has chosen the means most wise, but whether Congress has rationally selected means appropriate to a legitimate end. "It is not for us to review the congressional resolution of [the need for its chosen remedy]. It is enough that we be able to perceive a basis upon which the Congress might resolve the conflict as it did." *Katzenbach v. Morgan.*

Until today, in considering the constitutionality of the VRA, the Court has accorded Congress the full measure of respect its judgments in this domain should garner. *South Carolina v. Katzenbach* supplies the standard of review: "As against the reserved powers of the States, Congress may use any rational means to effectuate the constitutional prohibition of racial discrimination in voting." Faced with subsequent reauthorizations of the VRA, the Court has reaffirmed this standard. *E.g., City of Rome.* Today's Court does not purport to alter settled precedent establishing that the dispositive question is whether Congress has employed "rational means."

For three reasons, legislation *re*-authorizing an existing statute is especially likely to satisfy the minimal requirements of the rational-basis test. First, when reauthorization is at issue, Congress has already assembled a legislative record justifying the initial legislation. Congress is entitled to consider that preexisting record as well as the record before it at the time of the vote on reauthorization. This is especially true where, as here, the Court has repeatedly affirmed the statute's constitutionality and Congress has adhered to the very model the Court has upheld.

Second, the very fact that reauthorization is necessary arises because Congress has built a temporal limitation into the Act. It has pledged to review, after a span of years (first 15, then 25) and in light of contemporary evidence, the continued need for the VRA.

Third, a reviewing court should expect the record supporting reauthorization to be less stark than the record originally made. Demand for a record of violations equivalent to the one earlier made would expose Congress to a catch-22. If the statute was working, there would be less evidence of discrimination, so opponents might argue that Congress should not be allowed to renew the statute. In contrast, if the statute was not working, there would be plenty of evidence of discrimination, but scant reason to renew a failed regulatory regime.

This is not to suggest that congressional power in this area is limitless. It is this Court's responsibility to ensure that Congress has used appropriate means. The question meet for judicial review is whether the chosen means are "adapted to carry out the objects the amendments have in view." *Ex parte Virginia,* 100 U.S. 339 (1880). The Court's role, then, is not to substitute its judgment for that of Congress, but to determine whether the legislative record sufficed to show that "Congress could rationally have determined that [its chosen] provisions were appropriate methods." *City of Rome.*

In summary, the Constitution vests broad power in Congress to protect the right to vote, and in particular to combat racial discrimination in voting. This Court has repeatedly reaffirmed Congress' prerogative to use any rational means in exercise of its power in this area. And both precedent and logic dictate that the rational-means test should be easier to satisfy, and the burden on the statute's challenger should be higher, when what is at issue is the reauthorization of a remedy that the Court has previously affirmed, and that Congress found, from contemporary evidence, to be working to advance the legislature's legitimate objective.

III

The 2006 reauthorization of the Voting Rights Act fully satisfies the standard stated in *McCulloch*: Congress may choose any means "appropriate" and "plainly adapted to" a legitimate constitutional end. As we shall see, it is implausible to suggest otherwise.

A

I begin with the evidence on which Congress based its decision to continue the preclearance remedy. The surest way to evaluate whether that remedy remains in order is to see if preclearance is still effectively preventing discriminatory changes to voting laws. On that score, the record before Congress [in 2006] was huge. In fact, Congress found there were *more* DOJ objections between 1982 and 2004 (626) than there were between 1965 and the 1982 reauthorization (490).

All told, between 1982 and 2006, DOJ objections blocked over 700 voting changes based on a determination that the changes were discriminatory. Congress found that the majority of DOJ objections included findings of discriminatory intent, and that the changes blocked by preclearance were "calculated decisions to keep minority voters from fully participating in the political process." On top of that, over the same time period the DOJ and private plaintiffs succeeded in more than 100 actions to enforce the §5 preclearance requirements.

In addition to blocking proposed voting changes through preclearance, DOJ may request more information from a jurisdiction proposing a change. In turn, the jurisdiction may modify or withdraw the proposed change. The number of such modifications or withdrawals provides an indication of how many discriminatory proposals are deterred without need for formal objection. Congress received evidence that more than 800 proposed changes were altered or withdrawn since the last reauthorization in 1982.[b] Congress also received empirical

b. This number includes only changes actually proposed. Congress also received evidence that many covered jurisdictions engaged in an "informal consultation process" with DOJ before formally submitting a proposal, so that the deterrent effect of preclearance was far broader than the formal submissions alone suggest. All agree that an unsupported assertion about "deterrence" would not be sufficient to justify keeping a remedy in place in perpetuity. But it was certainly reasonable for Congress to consider the testimony of witnesses who had worked with officials in covered jurisdictions and observed a real-world deterrent effect.

studies finding that DOJ's requests for more information had a significant effect on the degree to which covered jurisdictions "compl[ied] with their obligatio[n]" to protect minority voting rights.

Congress also received evidence that litigation under §2 of the VRA was an inadequate substitute for preclearance in the covered jurisdictions. Litigation occurs only after the fact, when the illegal voting scheme has already been put in place and individuals have been elected pursuant to it, thereby gaining the advantages of incumbency. An illegal scheme might be in place for several election cycles before a §2 plaintiff can gather sufficient evidence to challenge it. And litigation places a heavy financial burden on minority voters. Congress also received evidence that preclearance lessened the litigation burden on covered jurisdictions themselves, because the preclearance process is far less costly than defending against a §2 claim, and clearance by DOJ substantially reduces the likelihood that a §2 claim will be mounted.

The number of discriminatory changes blocked or deterred by the preclearance requirement suggests that the state of voting rights in the covered jurisdictions would have been significantly different absent this remedy. Surveying the type of changes stopped by the preclearance procedure conveys a sense of the extent to which §5 continues to protect minority voting rights. Set out below are characteristic examples of changes blocked in the years leading up to the 2006 reauthorization:

- In 1995, Mississippi sought to reenact a dual voter registration system, "which was initially enacted in 1892 to disenfranchise Black voters," and for that reason, was struck down by a federal court in 1987.
- Following the 2000 census, the City of Albany, Georgia, proposed a redistricting plan that DOJ found to be "designed with the purpose to limit and retrogress the increased black voting strength . . . in the city as a whole."
- In 2001, the mayor and all-white five-member Board of Aldermen of Kilmichael, Mississippi, abruptly canceled the town's election after "an unprecedented number" of African-American candidates announced they were running for office. DOJ required an election, and the town elected its first black mayor and three black aldermen.
- In 2006, this Court found that Texas' attempt to redraw a congressional district to reduce the strength of Latino voters bore "the mark of intentional discrimination that could give rise to an equal protection violation," and ordered the district redrawn in compliance with the VRA. *League of United Latin American Citizens v. Perry,* 548 U.S. 399 (2006). In response, Texas sought to undermine this Court's order by curtailing early voting in the district, but was blocked by an action to enforce the §5 preclearance requirement.
- In 2003, after African-Americans won a majority of the seats on the school board for the first time in history, Charleston County, South Carolina, proposed an at-large voting mechanism for the board. The proposal, made without consulting any of the African-American members of the school

board, was found to be an "'exact replica'" of an earlier voting scheme that, a federal court had determined, violated the VRA. DOJ invoked §5 to block the proposal.

- In 1993, the City of Millen, Georgia, proposed to delay the election in a majority-black district by two years, leaving that district without representation on the city council while the neighboring majority-white district would have three representatives. DOJ blocked the proposal. The county then sought to move a polling place from a predominantly black neighborhood in the city to an inaccessible location in a predominantly white neighborhood outside city limits.

- In 2004, Waller County, Texas, threatened to prosecute two black students after they announced their intention to run for office. The county then attempted to reduce the availability of early voting in that election at polling places near a historically black university.

- In 1990, Dallas County, Alabama, whose county seat is the City of Selma, sought to purge its voter rolls of many black voters. DOJ rejected the purge as discriminatory, noting that it would have disqualified many citizens from voting "simply because they failed to pick up or return a voter update form, when there was no valid requirement that they do so."

These examples, and scores more like them, fill the pages of the legislative record. The evidence was indeed sufficient to support Congress' conclusion that "racial discrimination in voting in covered jurisdictions [remained] serious and pervasive."[c]

Congress further received evidence indicating that formal requests of the kind set out above represented only the tip of the iceberg. There was what one commentator described as an "avalanche of case studies of voting rights violations in the covered jurisdictions," ranging from "outright intimidation and violence against minority voters" to "more subtle forms of voting rights deprivations." This evidence gave Congress ever more reason to conclude that the time had not yet come for relaxed vigilance against the scourge of race discrimination in voting.

True, conditions in the South have impressively improved since passage of the Voting Rights Act. Congress noted this improvement and found that the VRA was the driving force behind it. But Congress also found that voting discrimination

---

c. For an illustration postdating the 2006 reauthorization, see *South Carolina v. United States,* 898 F. Supp. 2d 30 (D.C. 2012), which involved a South Carolina voter-identification law enacted in 2011. Concerned that the law would burden minority voters, DOJ brought a §5 enforcement action to block the law's implementation. In the course of the litigation, South Carolina officials agreed to binding interpretations that made it "far easier than some might have expected or feared" for South Carolina citizens to vote. A three-judge panel precleared the law after adopting both interpretations as an express "condition of preclearance." Two of the judges commented that the case demonstrated "the continuing utility of Section 5 of the Voting Rights Act in deterring problematic, and hence encouraging non-discriminatory, changes in state and local voting laws."

had evolved into subtler second-generation barriers, and that eliminating pre-clearance would risk loss of the gains that had been made. Concerns of this order, the Court previously found, gave Congress adequate cause to reauthorize the VRA. *City of Rome* (congressional reauthorization of the preclearance require-ment was justified based on "the number and nature of objections interposed by the Attorney General" since the prior reauthorization; extension was "necessary to preserve the limited and fragile achievements of the Act and to promote fur-ther amelioration of voting discrimination") (internal quotation marks omitted). Facing such evidence then, the Court expressly rejected the argument that dis-parities in voter turnout and number of elected officials were the only metrics capable of justifying reauthorization of the VRA.

B

I turn next to the evidence on which Congress based its decision to reautho-rize the coverage formula in §4(b). Because Congress did not alter the cover-age formula, the same jurisdictions previously subject to preclearance continue to be covered by this remedy. The evidence just described, of preclearance's continuing efficacy in blocking constitutional violations in the covered jurisdic-tions, itself grounded Congress' conclusion that the remedy should be retained for those jurisdictions.

There is no question, moreover, that the covered jurisdictions have a unique history of problems with racial discrimination in voting. Consideration of this long history, still in living memory, was altogether appropriate. The Court criti-cizes Congress for failing to recognize that "history did not end in 1965." But the Court ignores that "what's past is prologue." W. Shakespeare, The Tempest, act 2, sc. 1. And "[t]hose who cannot remember the past are condemned to repeat it." 1 G. Santayana, The Life of Reason 284 (1905). Congress was especially mind-ful of the need to reinforce the gains already made and to prevent backsliding.

Of particular importance, even after 40 years and thousands of discriminatory changes blocked by preclearance, conditions in the covered jurisdictions demon-strated that the formula was still justified by "current needs." *Northwest Austin.*

Congress learned of these conditions through a report, known as the Katz study, that looked at §2 suits between 1982 and 2004. Because the private right of action authorized by §2 of the VRA applies nationwide, a comparison of §2 lawsuits in covered and noncovered jurisdictions provides an appropriate yard-stick for measuring differences between covered and noncovered jurisdictions. If differences in the risk of voting discrimination between covered and noncov-ered jurisdictions had disappeared, one would expect that the rate of successful §2 lawsuits would be roughly the same in both areas.[d] The study's findings,

---

d. Because preclearance occurs only in covered jurisdictions and can be expected to stop the most obviously objectionable measures, one would expect a *lower* rate of successful §2 lawsuits in those jurisdictions if the risk of voting discrimination there were the same as elsewhere in the country.

however, indicated that racial discrimination in voting remains "concentrated in the jurisdictions singled out for preclearance." *Northwest Austin.*

Although covered jurisdictions account for less than 25 percent of the country's population, the Katz study revealed that they accounted for 56 percent of successful §2 litigation since 1982. Controlling for population, there were nearly *four* times as many successful §2 cases in covered jurisdictions as there were in noncovered jurisdictions. The Katz study further found that §2 lawsuits are more likely to succeed when they are filed in covered jurisdictions than in noncovered jurisdictions. From these findings—ignored by the Court—Congress reasonably concluded that the coverage formula continues to identify the jurisdictions of greatest concern.

The evidence before Congress, furthermore, indicated that voting in the covered jurisdictions was more racially polarized than elsewhere in the country. While racially polarized voting alone does not signal a constitutional violation, it is a factor that increases the vulnerability of racial minorities to discriminatory changes in voting law. The reason is twofold. First, racial polarization means that racial minorities are at risk of being systematically outvoted and having their interests underrepresented in legislatures. Second, "when political preferences fall along racial lines, the natural inclinations of incumbents and ruling parties to entrench themselves have predictable racial effects. Under circumstances of severe racial polarization, efforts to gain political advantage translate into race-specific disadvantages."

In other words, a governing political coalition has an incentive to prevent changes in the existing balance of voting power. When voting is racially polarized, efforts by the ruling party to pursue that incentive "will inevitably discriminate against a racial group." Just as buildings in California have a greater need to be earthquake-proofed, places where there is greater racial polarization in voting have a greater need for prophylactic measures to prevent purposeful race discrimination. This point was understood by Congress and is well recognized in the academic literature. See 2006 Reauthorization §2(b)(3), 120 Stat. 577 ("The continued evidence of racially polarized voting in each of the jurisdictions covered by the [preclearance requirement] demonstrates that racial and language minorities remain politically vulnerable").

The case for retaining a coverage formula that met needs on the ground was therefore solid. Congress might have been charged with rigidity had it afforded covered jurisdictions no way out or ignored jurisdictions that needed superintendence. Congress, however, responded to this concern. Critical components of the congressional design are the statutory provisions allowing jurisdictions to "bail out" of preclearance, and for court-ordered "bail ins." The VRA permits a jurisdiction to bail out by showing that it has complied with the Act for ten years, and has engaged in efforts to eliminate intimidation and harassment of voters. 42 U.S.C. §1973b(a) (2006 ed. and Supp. V). It also authorizes a court to subject a noncovered jurisdiction to federal preclearance upon finding that violations of the Fourteenth and Fifteenth Amendments have occurred there. §1973a(c) (2006 ed.).

Congress was satisfied that the VRA's bailout mechanism provided an effective means of adjusting the VRA's coverage over time. Nearly 200 jurisdictions have successfully bailed out of the preclearance requirement, and DOJ has consented to every bailout application filed by an eligible jurisdiction since the current bailout procedure became effective in 1984. The bail-in mechanism has also worked. Several jurisdictions have been subject to federal preclearance by court orders, including the States of New Mexico and Arkansas.

This experience exposes the inaccuracy of the Court's portrayal of the Act as static, unchanged since 1965. Congress designed the VRA to be a dynamic statute, capable of adjusting to changing conditions. True, many covered jurisdictions have not been able to bail out due to recent acts of noncompliance with the VRA, but that truth reinforces the congressional judgment that these jurisdictions were rightfully subject to preclearance, and ought to remain under that regime.

IV

Congress approached the 2006 reauthorization of the VRA with great care and seriousness. The same cannot be said of the Court's opinion today. The Court makes no genuine attempt to engage with the massive legislative record that Congress assembled. Instead, it relies on increases in voter registration and turnout as if that were the whole story. Without even identifying a standard of review, the Court dismissively brushes off arguments based on "data from the record," and declines to enter the "debat[e about] what [the] record shows." One would expect more from an opinion striking at the heart of the Nation's signal piece of civil-rights legislation.

I note the most disturbing lapses. First, by what right, given its usual restraint, does the Court even address Shelby County's facial challenge to the VRA? Second, the Court veers away from controlling precedent regarding the "equal sovereignty" doctrine without even acknowledging that it is doing so. Third, hardly showing the respect ordinarily paid when Congress acts to implement the Civil War Amendments, and as just stressed, the Court does not even deign to grapple with the legislative record.

A

Shelby County launched a purely facial challenge to the VRA's 2006 reauthorization. "A facial challenge to a legislative Act," the Court has other times said, "is, of course, the most difficult challenge to mount successfully, since the challenger must establish that no set of circumstances exists under which the Act would be valid." *United States v. Salerno,* 481 U.S. 739 (1987). . . . "Embedded in the traditional rules governing constitutional adjudication is the principle that a person to whom a statute may constitutionally be applied will not be heard to challenge that statute on the ground that it may conceivably be applied uncon-stitutionally to others, in other situations not before the Court." Yet the Court's opinion in this case contains not a word explaining why Congress lacks the power to subject to preclearance the particular plaintiff that initiated this law-suit—Shelby County, Alabama. The reason for the Court's silence is apparent, for as applied to Shelby County, the VRA's preclearance requirement is hardly contestable.

Alabama is home to Selma, site of the "Bloody Sunday" beatings of civil-rights demonstrators that served as the catalyst for the VRA's enactment. Following those events, Martin Luther King, Jr., led a march from Selma to Montgomery, Alabama's capital, where he called for passage of the VRA. If the Act passed, he foresaw, progress could be made even in Alabama, but there had to be a steadfast national commitment to see the task through to completion. In King's words, "the arc of the moral universe is long, but it bends toward justice."

History has proved King right. Although circumstances in Alabama have changed, serious concerns remain. Between 1982 and 2005, Alabama had one of the highest rates of successful §2 suits, second only to its VRA-covered neighbor Mississippi. In other words, even while subject to the restraining effect of §5, Alabama was found to have "deni[ed] or abridge[d]" voting rights "on account of race or color" more frequently than nearly all other States in the Union. . . . Alabama's sorry history of §2 violations alone provides sufficient justification for Congress' determination in 2006 that the State should remain subject to §5's preclearance requirement.[e]

A few examples suffice to demonstrate that, at least in Alabama, the "current burdens" imposed by §5's preclearance requirement are "justified by current needs." In the interim between the VRA's 1982 and 2006 reauthorizations, this Court twice confronted purposeful racial discrimination in Alabama. . . . [And] [i]n 1986, a Federal District Judge concluded that the at-large election systems in several Alabama counties violated §2. *Dillard v. Crenshaw Cty.*, 640 F. Supp. 1347 (M.D. Ala. 1986). Summarizing its findings, the court stated that "[f]rom the late 1800's through the present, [Alabama] has consistently erected barriers to keep black persons from full and equal participation in the social, economic, and political life of the state."

The *Dillard* litigation ultimately expanded to include 183 cities, counties, and school boards employing discriminatory at-large election systems. One of

---

e. This lawsuit was filed by Shelby County, a political subdivision of Alabama, rather than by the State itself. Nevertheless, it is appropriate to judge Shelby County's constitutional challenge in light of instances of discrimination statewide because Shelby County is subject to §5's preclearance requirement by virtue of *Alabama's* designation as a covered jurisdiction under §4(b) of the VRA. In any event, Shelby County's recent record of employing an at-large electoral system tainted by intentional racial discrimination is by itself sufficient to justify subjecting the county to §5's pre-clearance mandate.

those defendants was Shelby County, which eventually signed a consent decree to resolve the claims against it.

Although the *Dillard* litigation resulted in overhauls of numerous electoral systems tainted by racial discrimination, concerns about backsliding persist. In 2008, for example, the city of Calera, located in Shelby County, requested preclearance of a redistricting plan that "would have eliminated the city's sole majority-black district, which had been created pursuant to the consent decree in *Dillard*." Although DOJ objected to the plan, Calera forged ahead with elections based on the unprecleared voting changes, resulting in the defeat of the incumbent African-American councilman who represented the former majority-black district. The city's defiance required DOJ to bring a §5 enforcement action that ultimately yielded appropriate redress, including restoration of the majority-black district.

A recent FBI investigation provides a further window into the persistence of racial discrimination in state politics. See *United States v. McGregor,* 824 F. Supp. 2d 1339 (M.D. Ala. 2011). Recording devices worn by state legislators cooperating with the FBI's investigation captured conversations between members of the state legislature and their political allies. The recorded conversations are shocking. Members of the state Senate derisively refer to African-Americans as "Aborigines" and talk openly of their aim to quash a particular gambling-related referendum because the referendum, if placed on the ballot, might increase African-American voter turnout. *Id.,* at 1345-1346 (internal quotation marks omitted). See also *id.,* at 1345 (legislators and their allies expressed concern that if the referendum were placed on the ballot, " '[e]very black, every illiterate' would be 'bused [to the polls] on HUD financed buses' "). These conversations occurred not in the 1870's, or even in the 1960's, they took place in 2010. The District Judge presiding over the criminal trial at which the recorded conversations were introduced commented that the "recordings represent compelling evidence that political exclusion through racism remains a real and enduring problem" in Alabama. Racist sentiments, the judge observed, "remain regrettably entrenched in the high echelons of state government."

These recent episodes forcefully demonstrate that §5's preclearance requirement is constitutional as applied to Alabama and its political subdivisions. And under our case law, that conclusion should suffice to resolve this case. . . . This Court has consistently rejected constitutional challenges to legislation enacted pursuant to Congress' enforcement powers under the Civil War Amendments upon finding that the legislation was constitutional as applied to the particular set of circumstances before the Court.[f]

---

f. The Court does not contest that Alabama's history of racial discrimination provides a sufficient basis for Congress to require Alabama and its political subdivisions to preclear electoral changes. Nevertheless, the Court asserts that Shelby County may prevail on its facial challenge to §4's coverage formula because it is subject to §5's preclearance requirement by virtue of that formula. This misses the reality that Congress decided to subject Alabama to preclearance based on evidence of continuing constitutional violations in that State.

The VRA's exceptionally broad severability provision makes it particularly inappropriate for the Court to allow Shelby County to mount a facial challenge to §§4(b) and 5 of the VRA, even though application of those provisions to the county falls well within the bounds of Congress' legislative authority. The severability provision states: "If any provision of [this Act] or the application thereof to any person or circumstances is held invalid, the remainder of [the Act] and the application of the provision to other persons not similarly situated or to other circumstances shall not be affected thereby." 42 U.S.C. §1973p.

In other words, even if the VRA could not constitutionally be applied to certain States — e.g., Arizona and Alaska — §1973p calls for those unconstitutional applications to be severed, leaving the Act in place for jurisdictions as to which its application does not transgress constitutional limits.

Nevertheless, the Court suggests that limiting the jurisdictional scope of the VRA in an appropriate case would be "to try our hand at updating the statute." Just last Term, however, the Court rejected this very argument when addressing a materially identical severability provision, explaining that such a provision is "Congress' explicit textual instruction to leave unaffected the remainder of [the Act]" if any particular "application is unconstitutional." *National Federation of Independent Business v. Sebelius.* . . . Leaping to resolve Shelby County's facial challenge without considering whether application of the VRA to Shelby County is constitutional, or even addressing the VRA's severability provision, the Court's opinion can hardly be described as an exemplar of restrained and moderate decisionmaking. Quite the opposite. Hubris is a fit word for today's demolition of the VRA.

B

The Court stops any application of §5 by holding that §4(b)'s coverage formula is unconstitutional. It pins this result, in large measure, to "the fundamental principle of equal sovereignty." In *Katzenbach,* however, the Court held, in no uncertain terms, that the principle *"applies only to the terms upon which States are admitted to the Union,* and not to the remedies for local evils which have subsequently appeared." (emphasis added).

Katzenbach, the Court acknowledges, "rejected the notion that the [equal sovereignty] principle operate[s] as a bar on differential treatment outside [the] context [of the admission of new States]." (emphasis omitted). But the Court clouds that once clear understanding by citing dictum from *Northwest Austin* to convey that the principle of equal sovereignty "remains highly pertinent in assessing subsequent disparate treatment of States." If the Court is suggesting that dictum in *Northwest Austin* silently overruled *Katzenbach*'s limitation of the equal sovereignty doctrine to "the admission of new States," the suggestion is untenable. *Northwest Austin* cited *Katzenbach*'s holding in the course of *declining to decide* whether the VRA was constitutional or even what standard of review applied to the question. In today's decision, the Court ratchets up what was pure dictum in *Northwest Austin,* attributing breadth to the equal sovereignty principle in flat contradiction of *Katzenbach*. The Court does so with nary an explanation of why it finds *Katzenbach* wrong, let alone any discussion of whether *stare decisis* nonetheless counsels adherence to *Katzenbach*'s ruling on the limited "significance" of the equal sovereignty principle.

Today's unprecedented extension of the equal sovereignty principle outside its proper domain — the admission of new States — is capable of much mischief. Federal statutes that treat States disparately are hardly novelties. See, *e.g.,* 28 U.S.C. §3704 (no State may operate or permit a sports-related gambling scheme, unless that State conducted such a scheme "at any time during the period beginning January 1, 1976, and ending August 31, 1990"); 26 U.S.C. §142(*l*) (EPA required to locate green building project in a State meeting specified population criteria); 42 U.S.C. §3796bb (at least 50 percent of rural drug enforcement assistance funding must be allocated to States with "a population density of fifty-two or fewer persons per square mile or a State in which the largest county has fewer than one hundred and fifty thousand people, based on the decennial census of 1990 through fiscal year 1997"); §§13925, 13971 (similar population criteria for funding to combat rural domestic violence); §10136 (specifying rules applicable to Nevada's Yucca Mountain nuclear waste site, and providing that "[n]o State, other than the State of Nevada, may receive financial assistance under this subsection after December 22, 1987"). Do such provisions remain safe given the Court's expansion of equal sovereignty's sway?

Of gravest concern, Congress relied on our pathmarking *Katzenbach* decision in each reauthorization of the VRA. It had every reason to believe that the Act's limited geographical scope would weigh in favor of, not against, the Act's constitutionality. See, *e.g., United States v. Morrison,* 529 U.S. 598 (2000) (confining preclearance regime to States with a record of discrimination bolstered the VRA's constitutionality). Congress could hardly have foreseen that the VRA's limited geographic reach would render the Act constitutionally suspect.

In the Court's conception, it appears, defenders of the VRA could not prevail upon showing what the record overwhelmingly bears out, *i.e.,* that there is a need for continuing the preclearance regime in covered States. In addition, the defenders would have to disprove the existence of a comparable need elsewhere. I am aware of no precedent for imposing such a double burden on defenders of legislation.

C

The Court has time and again declined to upset legislation of this genre unless there was no or almost no evidence of unconstitutional action by States. See, *e.g., City of Boerne v. Flores,* 521 U.S. 507 (1997). No such claim can be made about the congressional record for the 2006 VRA reauthorization. Given a record replete with examples of denial or abridgment of a paramount federal right, the Court should have left the matter where it belongs: in Congress' bailiwick.

Instead, the Court strikes §4(b)'s coverage provision because, in its view, the provision is not based on "current conditions." It discounts, however, that one such condition was the preclearance remedy in place in the covered jurisdictions, a remedy Congress designed both to catch discrimination before it causes harm, and to guard against return to old ways. Volumes of evidence supported Congress' determination that the prospect of retrogression was real. Throwing out preclearance when it has worked and is continuing to work to stop discriminatory changes is like throwing away your umbrella in a rainstorm because you are not getting wet.

But, the Court insists, the coverage formula is no good; it is based on "decades-old data and eradicated practices." Even if the legislative record shows, as engaging with it would reveal, that the formula accurately identifies the jurisdictions with the worst conditions of voting discrimination, that is of no moment, as the Court sees it. Congress, the Court decrees, must "star[t] from scratch." I do not see why that should be so.

Congress' chore was different in 1965 than it was in 2006. In 1965, there were a "small number of States . . . which in most instances were familiar to Congress by name," on which Congress fixed its attention. *Katzenbach.* In drafting the coverage formula, "Congress began work with reliable evidence of actual voting discrimination in a great majority of the States" it sought to target. "The formula [Congress] eventually evolved to describe these areas" also captured a few States that had not been the subject of congressional factfinding. Nevertheless, the Court upheld the formula in its entirety, finding it fair "to infer a significant danger of the evil" in all places the formula covered.

The situation Congress faced in 2006, when it took up *re*-authorization of the coverage formula, was not the same. By then, the formula had been in effect for many years, and *all* of the jurisdictions covered by it were "familiar to Congress by name." The question before Congress: Was there still a sufficient basis to support continued application of the preclearance remedy in each of those already-identified places? There was at that point no chance that the formula might inadvertently sweep in new areas that were not the subject of congressional findings. And Congress could determine from the record whether the jurisdictions captured by the coverage formula still belonged under the preclearance regime. If they did, there was no need to alter the formula. That is why the Court, in addressing prior reauthorizations of the VRA, did not question the continuing "relevance" of the formula.

Consider once again the components of the record before Congress in 2006. The coverage provision identified a known list of places with an undisputed history of serious problems with racial discrimination in voting. Recent evidence relating to Alabama and its counties was there for all to see. Multiple Supreme Court decisions had upheld the coverage provision, most recently in 1999. There was extensive evidence that, due to the preclearance mechanism, conditions in the covered jurisdictions had notably improved. And there was evidence that preclearance was still having a substantial real-world effect, having stopped hundreds of discriminatory voting changes in the covered jurisdictions since the last reauthorization. In addition, there was evidence that racial polarization in voting was higher in covered jurisdictions than elsewhere, increasing the vulnerability of minority citizens in those jurisdictions. And countless witnesses, reports, and case studies documented continuing problems with voting discrimination in those jurisdictions. In light of this record, Congress had more than a reasonable basis to conclude that the existing coverage formula was not out of sync with conditions on the ground in covered areas. And certainly Shelby County was no candidate for release through the mechanism Congress provided.

The Court holds §4(b) invalid on the ground that it is "irrational to base coverage on the use of voting tests 40 years ago, when such tests have been illegal since that time." But the Court disregards what Congress set about to do in enacting the VRA. That extraordinary legislation scarcely stopped at the particular tests and devices that happened to exist in 1965. The grand aim of the Act is to secure to all in our polity equal citizenship stature, a voice in our democracy undiluted by race. As the record for the 2006 reauthorization makes abundantly clear, second-generation barriers to minority voting rights have emerged in the covered jurisdictions as attempted *substitutes* for the first-generation barriers that originally triggered preclearance in those jurisdictions.

The sad irony of today's decision lies in its utter failure to grasp why the VRA has proven effective. The Court appears to believe that the VRA's success in eliminating the specific devices extant in 1965 means that preclearance is no longer needed. With that belief, and the argument derived from it, history repeats itself. The same assumption—that the problem could be solved when particular methods of voting discrimination are identified and eliminated—was indulged and proved wrong repeatedly prior to the VRA's enactment. Unlike prior statutes, which singled out particular tests or devices, the VRA is grounded in Congress' recognition of the "variety and persistence" of measures designed to impair minority voting rights. *Katzenbach*. In truth, the evolution of voting discrimination into more subtle second-generation barriers is powerful evidence that a remedy as effective as preclearance remains vital to protect minority voting rights and prevent backsliding.

Beyond question, the VRA is no ordinary legislation. It is extraordinary because Congress embarked on a mission long delayed and of extraordinary importance: to realize the purpose and promise of the Fifteenth Amendment. For a half century, a concerted effort has been made to end racial discrimination in voting. Thanks to the Voting Rights Act, progress once the subject of a dream has been achieved and continues to be made.

The record supporting the 2006 reauthorization of the VRA is also extraordinary. It was described by the Chairman of the House Judiciary Committee as "one of the most extensive considerations of any piece of legislation that the United States Congress has dealt with in the 27 1/2 years" he had served in the House. 152 Cong. Rec. H5143 (July 13, 2006) (statement of Rep. Sensenbrenner). After exhaustive evidence-gathering and deliberative process, Congress reauthorized the VRA, including the coverage provision, with overwhelming bipartisan support. It was the judgment of Congress that "40 years has not been a sufficient amount of time to eliminate the vestiges of discrimination following nearly 100 years of disregard for the dictates of the 15th amendment and to ensure that the right of all citizens to vote is protected as guaranteed by the Constitution." 2006 Reauthorization §2(b)(7), 120 Stat. 577. That determination of the body empowered to enforce the Civil War Amendments "by appropriate legislation" merits this Court's utmost respect. In my judgment, the Court errs egregiously by overriding Congress' decision.

* * *

For the reasons stated, I would affirm the judgment of the Court of Appeals.

Discussion

1. *A new doctrine?* Shelby County promised to resolve the question whether the "congruence and proportionality" standard of *Boerne* would also apply to the Voting Rights Act, or whether the Court would retain the test of reasonableness in *McCulloch* used in the civil rights era cases of *South Carolina v. Katzenbach, Katzenbach v. Morgan,* and *Oregon v. Mitchell.*

Shelby County ducks that question completely. Instead, it creates a new doctrine of equal sovereignty: "a departure from the fundamental principle of equal sovereignty requires a showing that a statute's disparate geographic coverage is sufficiently related to the problem that it targets." Because "the Act imposes current burdens" it "must be justified by current needs."

As Justice Ginsburg points out, the equal sovereignty doctrine was mostly concerned with questions of state admission, and even in this context it was honored in the breach as much as the observance. It had never been applied to Fourteenth Amendment section 5 or Fifteenth Amendment section 2 legislation in the past; and *South Carolina v. Katzenbach* said the principle was not germane. The idea of "equal sovereignty" was offered as dicta in *Northwest Austin*, joined by eight Justices. In the hands of Chief Justice Roberts, however, it has now been elevated into a powerful new doctrine by five Justices in *Shelby County.*

2. *Equal sovereignty versus the Reconstruction paradigm.* One reason why the doctrine of equal sovereignty seems puzzling in this context concerns the history of Reconstruction itself. Congress, then acting under the authority of the Guarantee Clause, divided southern states into military districts, supervised them as wards of the Union, and restored them to full status only after they had given blacks the right to vote and ratified the Fourteenth Amendment. The paradigm case that led to the Reconstruction Amendments involved treating states differently based on the history of how they had treated blacks. See Akhil Reed Amar, The Lawfulness of Section 5 — and Thus of Section 5, 126 Harv. L. Rev. Forum 109, 110 (2013) ("In short, any serious constitutional analysis of the special preclearance system of the Voting Rights Act must come to grips with the special preclearance system that generated the Fourteenth Amendment itself in the 1860s."). Are the two situations distinguishable? Could Congress have passed the VRA under the Guarantee Clause today? If so, do you believe the Supreme Court would have used the equal sovereignty principle to limit Congress's powers under that clause as well?

3. *Equal sovereignty as heightened scrutiny?* What level of scrutiny is implicit in the new "equal sovereignty" doctrine? It seems to be clearly more than *McCulloch* and *Katzenbach*, which used tests either of reasonableness or rationality.

In fact, the new test seems to be even more stringent than the congruence and proportionality test of *Boerne* itself. *Boerne* itself went out of its way not to disturb the civil rights era cases. Later cases like *Hibbs* and *Tennessee v. Lane* suggested that Congress is on strongest ground when it attempts to support constitutional guarantees against suspect classifications or violations of fundamental rights that the Court has already recognized. This is especially so when Congress makes detailed findings of fact of previous violations of constitutional rights.

The VRA concerned *both* suspect classifications (race, ethnicity, and nationality) and fundamental rights (the right to vote). It also featured an ample record of voting rights violations and factual findings. All this, however, turned out to be insufficient under the new doctrine of "equal sovereignty."

4. *The Court's treatment of Congressional findings of fact.* Justice Ginsburg spends considerable time walking us through Congress's findings of bad behavior by covered jurisdictions and she emphasizes Congress's thoroughness and conscientiousness in compiling the record. Chief Justice Roberts, by contrast, says far less about the record other than emphasizing the fact that black registrations in covered jurisdictions are now at parity with non-covered jurisdictions. Justice Ginsburg notes that Congress believed that it needed to address second-generation denials of voting rights; Chief Justice Roberts regards these as an inadequate justification for maintaining the current coverage formula. How respectful is the majority of Congressional judgments? How respectful should it be?

Is the problem the size of the congressional record or simply the length of years the coverage formula has been in effect without substantial change? Assuming that Congress was determined to maintain the current coverage formula, is there any record that the majority would have accepted?

5. *The reach of the equal sovereignty doctrine.* How far does the new "equal sovereignty" doctrine extend? Justice Ginsburg's dissent points out a number of federal programs that treat states differently. Also consider the interaction of the "equal sovereignty" principle with the General Welfare Clause: many social welfare programs, including, for example, Medicaid reimbursements, vary by state. Different states get very different amounts of funding in various federal programs, largely as a result of logrolling and the political strength of small-state Senators. Does the new doctrine reach these programs?

Another possibility is that the "equal sovereignty" doctrine was created in order to resolve this particular case—to strike down section 4 of the Voting Rights Act—and that it will rarely be invoked again outside of the civil rights context. In that case, it is merely an artifact of the Court's inability to cobble together five votes for an interpretation of the *Boerne* standard.

6. *Half-measures versus the whole ball of wax.* Note that Justice Thomas argues that if the majority is really serious about the "equal sovereignty"

principle, it should strike down section 5 as well as section 4, because there is no justification for courts requiring only some states to preclear their changes in voting practices. Is Thomas right? Note that the case was primarily litigated about the constitutionality of section 5; the final opinion, however, focuses on section 4 and emphasizes that it leaves section 5 still standing. Why do you think there were only five votes to strike down section 4 but not section 5?

7. *The VRA as a "racial entitlement."* The majority appeared to be suspicious of Congress's decision to maintain the old coverage formula. At oral argument, Justice Scalia was particularly suspicious of the fact that the VRA was reauthorized for 25 years by overwhelming margins.

> [T]his last enactment, not a single vote in the Senate against it. And the House is pretty much the same. Now, I don't think that's attributable to the fact that it is so much clearer now that we need this. I think it is . . . very likely attributable, to a . . . perpetuation of racial entitlement. . . . Whenever a society adopts racial entitlements, it is very difficult to get out of them through the normal political processes.
>
> I don't think there is anything to be gained by any Senator to vote against continuation of this act. And I am fairly confident it will be reenacted in perpetuity unless — unless a court can say it does not comport with the Constitution. You have to show, when you are treating different States differently, that there's a good reason for it.
>
> [I]t's a concern that this is not the kind of a question you can leave to Congress. There are certain districts in the House that are black districts by law just about now. And even the Virginia Senators, they have no interest in voting against this. The State government is not their government, and they are going to lose — they are going to lose votes if they do not reenact the Voting Rights Act. Even the name of it is wonderful: The Voting Rights Act. Who is going to vote against that in the future?

Shelby County v. Holder, Oral Arg. Trans. 47-48.

What does Justice Scalia mean by "racial entitlement" in this context?

Putting aside the language of "racial entitlement," isn't Justice Scalia right that it was very difficult for most politicians to vote against the extension of the Voting Rights Act, one of the crown jewels of the civil rights movement? Once the Court strikes down the coverage formula, however, it changes the status quo and political expectations. It now becomes easier for Congressmen and Senators to resist passing a new version of the VRA on the grounds that the Court has declared parts of the old version unconstitutional. Which way should this cut? Is the Court's attempt to shake up political understandings a good thing or a bad thing?

8. *Changing the coverage formula is hard to do.* One reason why Congress has maintained basically the same coverage formula for decades is that it was quite difficult for Congress to agree on a new one. Many legislators did not want their states added to the covered jurisdictions, and some were opposed to the idea of preclearance in general. Most of the new jurisdictions that would be added were Republican strongholds, which raised partisan hackles.

The *Boerne* test, which most legislators thought would apply to any constitutional challenge of the 2006 re-extension, created additional problems. Congress had to guess how the courts would apply *Boerne* to a law like the Voting Rights Act, which was prophylactic, had already been in operation for years, and applied only to certain parts of the country. How could Congress show congruence and proportionality in a law that is already in place? What record of discrimination would be sufficient? The difficulty was that virtually any theory one might come up with could be employed by a critic to prove the opposite conclusion.

For example, one might think evidence of voting rights violations in covered jurisdictions would be helpful in showing why the Act was congruent and proportional. On the other hand, if the Act was working well, there might be relatively few voting rights violations in the covered jurisdictions. That evidence, in turn, could mean either that the Act was necessary or that it was superfluous. And if the voting rights violations continued, that might suggest that the law wasn't working very well.

Moreover, one had to take into account the fact that the law reached only some parts of the country. Again, Congress didn't know what the courts would end up requiring under *Boerne*. Courts might require a showing that covered jurisdictions were more likely to violate voting rights than non-covered jurisdictions. But if there wasn't a significant discrepancy, or non-covered jurisdictions actually had more voting rights violations, it might mean either that the Act was working well (because it prevented violations in covered jurisdictions), or that it was unnecessary. As a result, Professor Nathaniel Persily explains:

> Supporters of reauthorization decided that the safest course of action was to stick with the coverage formula that the Supreme Court had previously upheld. Despite the recognized need to extend coverage to the newest generation of voting rights violators, constitutional and political constraints prevented any alteration of the statute's geographic reach. . . . [A]ny change in the coverage formula [created] an additional gamble on the ability of Congress to predict what types of evidence the Court would find important. . . . [Therefore] [t]he new Act [did not try] to capture all of the worst voting rights violators, but rather an effort to capture some of them and to preserve historic gains where they had been made. [S]upporters of the Act sought to develop an evidentiary record for the principal purpose of explaining why the covered jurisdictions should remain covered, rather than justifying the coverage of certain jurisdictions but not others.

Nathaniel Persily, The Promise and Pitfalls of the New Voting Rights Act, 117 Yale L.J. 174, 193-195 (2007).

Political incentives also help explain why the Voting Rights Act's reauthorizations have been for increasingly longer periods. A twenty-five-year reauthorization, unlike the original five-year reauthorization in 1965, allows politicians to kick the can down the road and not have to take up very messy questions. Twenty-five years is longer than the careers of most national politicians and covers two to three reapportionment cycles. In addition, many politicians have adjusted to the status quo, just as they did to the reapportionment doctrines that began with *Reynolds v. Sims*. Many politicians may conclude that it is better to live with the current coverage formula than risk a new status quo that might undermine their interests.

Finally, the Voting Rights Act creates cross-cutting alliances between the two major political parties. The Act gives incentives for Republicans to pack as many Democratic leaning voters as possible into districts virtually guaranteed to elect minority representatives. This allows Republicans to create a relatively larger number of districts dominated by conservative, white, and rural voters who are likely to elect Republicans to office. The status quo thus appeals to some conservative Republicans who would otherwise oppose elements of the Act, as well as to Democrats who want to maximize minority representation, especially in the South.

9. *Remedies after* Shelby County. Many political observers are skeptical that the current Congress, which is ideologically polarized, can come up with a new coverage formula. The House of Representatives, controlled by the Republican Party, is a considerable ideological distance from the Democrats who control the Senate. In addition, the Senate filibuster rules, which now require 60 votes on any seriously contested legislation, may make compromise difficult.

If the VRA actually serves the status quo, won't politicians of both parties have an interest in coming up with something that approximates it? On the other hand, once the status quo is dissolved, the effect of doing nothing changes, and so too does the calculus of interests. Collective action problems may result in inertia, even if the previous system was somewhat more desirable for many politicians.

Note, however, that lawsuits under section 2 of the Voting Rights Act are still available to protect minority voting rights, although they are expensive and time-consuming and lack the advantages that made preclearance such an effective remedy. In addition, section 3(c) of the Voting Rights Act allows a court in a successful voting rights lawsuit involving a non-covered jurisdiction to impose preclearance requirements on that jurisdiction for a specified period of time. Section 3(c) thus allows voting rights litigation to temporarily create a new set of covered jurisdictions. Under *Shelby County*'s new doctrine of equal sovereignty, is section 3(c) constitutional because it involves a court order premised on a previous violation of law as opposed to Congressional findings of voting rights violations under section 5?

10. *The Elections Clause*. Another possible source of congressional power to protect voting rights is the Elections Clause of Article I, §4, cl. 1: "The Times, Places and Manner of holding Elections for Senators and Representatives, shall be prescribed in each State by the Legislature thereof; but the Congress may at any time by Law make or alter such Regulations, except as to the places of chusing Senators." Although the Elections Clause does not concern election of state officers, states normally hold elections for both state and federal offices on the same day so in practice federal regulations will set the norm.

In Arizona v. Intertribal Council of Arizona, 133 S. Ct. 2247 (2013), the Supreme Court held, 7-2, that Arizona's requirement that voters seeking to register provide documentary evidence of citizenship was preempted by the National Voter Registration Act of 1993. The NVRA prescribes a federal registration form that requires that a registrant aver that he or she is a citizen, but does not require documentary evidence of citizenship.

Justice Scalia's majority opinion explained that under the Elections Clause Congress had plenary power to displace state law with respect to how federal elections would be conducted, but it did not give Congress the power to impose different voter qualifications than the states: "[T]he Elections Clause empowers Congress to regulate *how* federal elections are held, but not *who* may vote in them." This statement is inconsistent with the judgment of *Oregon v. Mitchell*, which held that Congress could, by statute, give 18-year olds the right to vote in federal elections. Justice Scalia explained, however, that although a majority of Justices agreed that Congress could pass such a law, four relied on Congress's powers under section 5 of the Fourteenth Amendment, and only Justice Black relied on the Elections Clause.

Could Congress have passed—or could it reenact—section 4 of the Voting Rights Act under the Elections Clause? Note that under the Elections Clause, Congress could not require preclearance of changes in voting rules affecting only state and local government offices—and a very large number of preclearance issues concern elections for state and local officials. In addition, Congress could not require preclearance of changes in voter eligibility rules, only changes in the way that states proved eligibility to register or vote, the kinds of voting machines used, the number and location of polling places, the hours and days available for polling, and so on. For example, Congress could probably not require preclearance of voting rules that disenfranchise felons, but it might be able to regulate how states purge voter rolls of suspected felons and non-citizens.

In *Intertribal Council of Arizona,* Justice Scalia stated that Congress's power over the "Times, Places and Manner" of congressional elections "is paramount, and may be exercised at any time, and to any extent which it deems expedient; and so far as it is exercised, and no farther, the regulations effected supersede those of the State which are inconsistent therewith." (quoting Ex parte Siebold, 100 U.S. 371, 392 (1880)). How would *Shelby County*'s new "equal sovereignty" principle interact with this test?

Insert before section C on p. 795:

FREE ENTERPRISE FUND v. PUBLIC COMPANY ACCOUNTING OVERSIGHT BOARD, 561 U.S. 477 (2010): [Congress created the Public Company Accounting Oversight Board (PCAOB), as part of a series of accounting reforms in the Sarbanes-Oxley Act of 2002, which responded to corporate scandals in the early 2000s. The Board is modeled on private self-regulatory organizations in the securities industry — such as the New York Stock Exchange — that investigate and discipline their own members subject to Commission oversight. The PCAOB, however, is a Government-created entity with expansive powers to govern an entire industry. Every accounting firm that audits public companies under the securities laws must register with the Board, pay it an annual fee, and comply with its rules and oversight. The Board may inspect registered firms, initiate formal investigations, and issue severe sanctions in its disciplinary proceedings.

The Board inspected petitioner Beckstead and Watts, an accounting firm, released a report critical of its auditing procedures, and began a formal investigation. The firm and petitioner Free Enterprise Fund, a nonprofit trade organization of to which Beckstead and Watts belonged, sued the Board and its members, arguing that the Board was unconstitutional because, among other things, the President could not remove members of the Board directly.

The Board is composed of five members appointed by the Securities and Exchange Commission. While the SEC has oversight of the Board, it cannot remove Board members at will, but only "for good cause shown," and in accordance with specified procedures. For purposes of the litigation the parties agreed that the Board is part of the Government for constitutional purposes, that its members are "Officers of the United States," and that the SEC Commissioners cannot be removed by the President except for "inefficiency, neglect of duty, or malfeasance in office." *Humphrey's Executor v. United States*.]

ROBERTS, C.J.:

[W]e have previously upheld limited restrictions on the President's removal power. In those cases, however, only one level of protected tenure separated the President from an officer exercising executive power. It was the President — or a subordinate he could remove at will — who decided whether the officer's conduct merited removal under the good-cause standard.

The Act before us does something quite different. It not only protects Board members from removal except for good cause, but withdraws from the President any decision on whether that good cause exists. That decision is vested instead in other tenured officers — the Commissioners — none of whom is subject to the President's direct control. The result is a Board that is not accountable to the President, and a President who is not responsible for the Board.

[A] second level of tenure protection changes the nature of the President's review. Now the Commission cannot remove a Board member at will. The President therefore cannot hold the Commission fully accountable for the Board's conduct, to the same extent that he may hold the Commission accountable for everything else that it does. The Commissioners are not responsible for the Board's actions. They are only responsible for their own determination of whether the Act's rigorous good-cause standard is met. And even if the President disagrees with their determination, he is powerless to intervene — unless that determination is so unreasonable as to constitute "inefficiency, neglect of duty, or malfeasance in office."

[N]either the President, nor anyone directly responsible to him, nor even an officer whose conduct he may review only for good cause, has full control over the Board. The President is stripped of the power our precedents have preserved, and his ability to execute the laws — by holding his subordinates accountable for their conduct — is impaired.

That arrangement is contrary to Article II's vesting of the executive power in the President. Without the ability to oversee the Board, or to attribute the Board's failings to those whom he can oversee, the President is no longer the judge of the Board's conduct. He is not the one who decides whether Board members are abusing their offices or neglecting their duties. He can neither ensure that the laws are faithfully executed, nor be held responsible for a Board member's breach of faith. This violates the basic principle that the President "cannot delegate ultimate responsibility or the active obligation to supervise that goes with it," because Article II "makes a single President responsible for the actions of the Executive Branch."

[I]f Congress can shelter the bureaucracy behind two layers of good-cause tenure, why not a third? . . . The officers of such an agency — safely encased within a Matryoshka doll of tenure protections — would be immune from Presidential oversight, even as they exercised power in the people's name.

Perhaps an individual President might find advantages in tying his own hands. But the separation of powers does not depend on the views of individual Presidents. The President can always choose to restrain himself in his dealings with subordinates. He cannot, however, choose to bind his successors by diminishing their powers, nor can he escape responsibility for his choices by pretending that they are not his own.

The diffusion of power carries with it a diffusion of accountability. The people do not vote for the "Officers of the United States." Art. II, §2, cl. 2. They instead look to the President to guide the "assistants or deputies . . . subject to his superintendence." The Federalist No. 72, p. 487 (J. Cooke ed. 1961) (A. Hamilton). Without a clear and effective chain of command, the public cannot "determine on whom the blame or the punishment of a pernicious measure, or series of pernicious measures ought really to fall." Id., No. 70, at 476 (same). . . . By granting the Board executive power without the Executive's oversight, this Act subverts the President's ability to ensure that the laws are faithfully executed — as well as the public's ability to pass judgment on his efforts. The Act's restrictions are incompatible with the Constitution's separation of powers. . . . [Moreover,] multilevel protection . . . "provides a blueprint for extensive expansion of the legislative power." . . . Congress has plenary control over the salary, duties, and even existence of executive offices. Only Presidential oversight can counter its influence. That is why the Constitution vests certain powers in the President that "the Legislature has no right to diminish or modify." 1 Annals of Cong., at 463 (J. Madison). . . .

[M]any civil servants within independent agencies would not qualify as "Officers of the United States," who [like members of the Board] "exercis[e] significant authority pursuant to the laws of the United States." . . . We do not decide the status of other Government employees, nor do we decide whether "lesser functionaries subordinate to officers of the United States" must be subject to the same sort of control as those who exercise "significant authority pursuant to the laws." . . . Nothing in our opinion . . . should be read to cast doubt on the use of what is colloquially known as the civil service system within independent agencies.

[F]or similar reasons, our holding also does not address that subset of independent agency employees who serve as administrative law judges. Whether administrative law judges are necessarily "Officers of the United States" is disputed. And unlike members of the Board, many administrative law judges of course perform adjudicative rather than enforcement or policymaking functions, or possess purely recommendatory powers. [Relocated footnote—EDS.]

[Nor does] today's opinion . . . increase the President's authority to remove military officers. Without expressing any view whatever on the scope of that authority, it is enough to note that we see little analogy between our Nation's armed services and the Public Company Accounting Oversight Board. Military officers are broadly subject to Presidential control through the chain of command and through the President's powers as Commander in Chief. The President and his subordinates may also convene boards of inquiry or courts-martial to hear claims of misconduct or poor performance by those officers. Here, by contrast, the President has no authority to initiate a Board member's removal for cause. . . .

[The majority held that the for-cause provisions were severable and did not affect the constitutionality of the rest of the Sarbanes-Oxley Act. It also rejected other challenges to the act. It held that the Securities and Exchange Commission is a "Department" under the meaning of the Appointments Clause, that the members of the Commission collectively constitute the head of the department for purposes of the Constitution, and that the members of the PCAOB are inferior officers whose appointment Congress may permissibly vest in a "Hea[d] of Departmen[t]" under Article II, Section 2, Clause 2.]

BREYER, J., dissenting, joined by STEVENS, J., GINSBURG, J., and SOTOMAYOR, J.:

[T]he restriction [at issue] directly limits, not the President's power, but the power of an already independent agency. . . . According to the Court, the President "is powerless to intervene" if he has determined that the Board members' "conduct merit[s] removal" because "[t]hat decision is vested instead in other tenured officers—the Commissioners—none of whom is subject to the President's direct control." But so long as the President is legitimately foreclosed from removing the Commissioners except for cause (as the majority assumes), nullifying the Commission's power to remove Board members only for cause will not resolve the problem the Court has identified: The President will still be "powerless to intervene" by removing the Board members if the Commission reasonably decides not to do so.

In other words, the Court fails to show why two layers of "for cause" protection—Layer One insulating the Commissioners from the President, and Layer Two insulating the Board from the Commissioners—impose any more serious limitation upon the President's powers than one layer. Consider the four scenarios that might arise:

1. The President and the Commission both want to keep a Board member in office. Neither layer is relevant.

2. The President and the Commission both want to dismiss a Board member. Layer Two stops them both from doing so without cause. The President's ability to remove the Commission (Layer One) is irrelevant, for he and the Commission are in agreement.

3. The President wants to dismiss a Board member, but the Commission wants to keep the member. Layer One allows the Commission to make that determination notwithstanding the President's contrary view. Layer Two is irrelevant because the Commission does not seek to remove the Board member.

4. The President wants to keep a Board member, but the Commission wants to dismiss the Board member. Here, Layer Two helps the President, for it hinders the Commission's ability to dismiss a Board member whom the President wants to keep in place.

Thus, the majority's decision to eliminate only Layer Two accomplishes virtually nothing. [What really matters is] the real-world nature of the President's relationship with the Commission. If the President confronts a Commission that seeks to resist his policy preferences—a distinct possibility when, as here, a Commission's membership must reflect both political parties,—the restriction on the Commission's ability to remove a Board member is either irrelevant (as in scenario 3) or may actually help the President (as in scenario 4). And if the President faces a Commission that seeks to implement his policy preferences, Layer One is irrelevant, for the President and Commission see eye to eye.

[T]he Court creates two alternative scenarios. In the first, the Commission and the President both want to remove a Board member, but have varying judgments as to whether they have good "cause" to do so—i.e., the President and the Commission both conclude that a Board member should be removed, but disagree as to whether that conclusion (which they have both reached) is reasonable. In the second, the President wants to remove a Board member and the Commission disagrees; [but instead tells the President that its hands are tied by the "for-cause" provisions.]

Both of these circumstances seem unusual. I do not know if they have ever occurred. But I do not deny their logical possibility. I simply doubt their importance. And the fact that, with respect to the President's power, the double layer of for-cause removal sometimes might help, sometimes might hurt, leads me to conclude that its overall effect is at most indeterminate. . . .

[Perhaps more important,] the statute provides the Commission with full authority and virtually comprehensive control over all of the Board's functions.

[I]f the President's control over the Commission is sufficient [for purposes of the Constitution], and the Commission's control over the Board is virtually absolute, then, as a practical matter, the President's control over the Board should prove sufficient as well.

[C]ongress and the President had good reason for enacting the challenged "for cause" provision. First and foremost, the Board adjudicates cases. This Court has long recognized the appropriateness of using "for cause" provisions to protect the personal independence of those who even only sometimes engage in adjudicatory functions. Indeed, as early as 1789 James Madison stated that "there may be strong reasons why an" executive "officer" such as the Comptroller of the United States "should not hold his office at the pleasure of the Executive branch" if one of his "principal dut[ies]" "partakes strongly of the judicial character." 1 Annals of Congress 611-612. . . .

Moreover, . . . the Accounting Board members supervise, and are themselves, technical professional experts. This Court has recognized that the "difficulties involved in the preparation of" sound auditing reports require the application of "scientific accounting principles." And this Court has recognized the constitutional legitimacy of a justification that rests agency independence upon the need for technical expertise. See *Humphrey's Executor*. [H]ere, the justification for insulating the "technical experts" on the Board from fear of losing their jobs due to political influence is particularly strong [because] the Accounting Board was created in response to "a series of celebrated accounting debacles." And historically, this regulatory subject matter — financial regulation — has been thought to exhibit a particular need for independence. . . .

[B]y . . . providing the Board with a revenue stream independent of the congressional appropriations process, [Congress] helped insulate the Board from congressional, as well as other, political influences. . . . [I]n a world in which we count on the Federal Government to regulate matters as complex as, say, nuclear-power production, the Court's assertion that we should simply learn to get by "without being" regulated "by experts" is, at best, unrealistic — at worst, dangerously so.

[Our] "separation-of-powers jurisprudence generally focuses on the danger of one branch's *aggrandizing its power* at the expense of another branch." . . . Congress here has "drawn" no power to itself to remove the Board members. It has instead sought to *limit* its own power, by, for example, providing the Accounting Board with a revenue stream independent of the congressional appropriations process. . . .

[E]ven if I assume that the majority categorically excludes the competitive service from the scope of its new rule, the exclusion would be insufficient . . . because the Court's "double for-cause" rule applies to appointees who are "inferior officer[s]." And who are they? Courts and scholars have struggled for more than a century to define the constitutional term "inferior officers," without much success. . . . The problem is not simply that the term "inferior officer" is indefinite but also that efforts to define it inevitably conclude that the term's sweep is unusually broad. Consider the Court's definitions: Inferior officers are, *inter alia*, (1) those charged with "the administration and enforcement of the public law;" (2) those granted "significant authority;" (3) those with "responsibility for conducting civil litigation in the courts of the United States;" and (4) those "who can be said to hold an office," that has been created either by "regulations" or by "statute." . . .

I see no way to avoid sweeping hundreds, perhaps thousands of high level government officials within the scope of the Court's holding, putting their job security and their administrative actions and decisions constitutionally at risk. To make even a conservative estimate, one would have to begin by listing federal departments, offices, bureaus and other agencies whose heads are by statute removable only "for cause." I have found 48 such agencies, Then it would be necessary to identify the senior officials in those agencies (just below the top) who themselves are removable only "for cause." I have identified 573 such high-ranking officials. They include most of the leadership of the Nuclear Regulatory Commission (including that agency's executive director as well as the directors of its Office of Nuclear Reactor Regulation and Office of Enforcement), virtually all of the leadership of the Social Security Administration, the executive directors of the Federal Energy Regulatory Commission and the Federal Trade Commission, as well as the general counsels of the Chemical Safety Board, the Federal Mine Safety and Health Review Commission, and the National Mediation Board.

[T]he potential list of those whom today's decision affects is yet larger [because] administrative law judges (ALJs) "are all executive officers." And ALJs are each removable "only for good cause established and determined by the Merit Systems Protection Board," But the members of the Merit Systems Protection Board are themselves protected from removal by the President absent good cause.

My research reflects that the Federal Government relies on 1,584 ALJs to adjudicate administrative matters in over 25 agencies. These ALJs adjudicate Social Security benefits, employment disputes, and other matters highly important to individuals. Does every losing party before an ALJ now have grounds to appeal on the basis that the decision entered against him is unconstitutional?

And what about the military? Commissioned military officers "are 'inferior officers.'" There are over 210,000 active-duty commissioned officers currently serving in the armed forces. And such officers can generally be so removed only by *other* commissioned officers, who themselves enjoy the same career protections.

The majority might simply say that the military is different. But it will have to explain *how* it is different. It is difficult to see why the Constitution would provide a President who is the military's "commander-in-chief," Art. II, §2, cl. 1, with *less* authority to remove "inferior" military "officers" than to remove comparable civil officials.

The majority sees "no reason . . . to address whether" any of "these positions," "or any others," might be deemed unconstitutional under its new rule, preferring instead to leave these matters for a future case. But what is to happen in the meantime? Is the work of all these various officials to be put on hold while the courts of appeals determine whether today's ruling applies to them? Will

Congress have to act to remove the "for cause" provisions? Can the President then restore them via executive order? And, still, what about the military? A clearer line would help avoid these practical difficulties.

The majority asserts that its opinion will not affect the Government's ability to function while these many questions are litigated in the lower courts because the Court's holding concerns only "the conditions under which th[e]se officers might some day be removed." But this case was not brought by federal officials challenging their potential removal. It was brought by private individuals who were *subject to regulation* "*'here-and-now'*" and who "object to the" very "existence" of the regulators themselves. And those private individuals have prevailed. Thus, any person similarly regulated by a federal official who is potentially subject to the Court's amorphous new rule will be able to bring an "implied private right of action directly under the Constitution" "seeking . . . a declaratory judgment that" the official's actions are "unconstitutional and an injunction preventing the" official "from exercising [his] powers." Such a plaintiff need not even first exhaust his administrative remedies.

Nor is it clear that courts will always be able to cure such a constitutional defect merely by severing an offending removal provision. . . . [C]ourts called upon to resolve the many questions the majority's opinion raises [may have to] determine that the only available remedy to certain double for-cause problems is to invalidate entire agencies.

Thus, notwithstanding the majority's assertions to the contrary, the potential consequences of today's holding are worrying. The upshot, I believe, is a legal dilemma. To interpret the Court's decision as applicable only in a few circumstances will make the rule less harmful but arbitrary. To interpret the rule more broadly will make the rule more rational, but destructive.

Discussion

1. *Taking a good thing too far?* Justice Breyer tries to show that the Court's principle of decision does not realistically engage with the way that the federal government is actually structured, putting at risk large swaths of the administrative state and basic military structure. What would be your prediction as to whether the Court will use *Free Enterprise Fund* to drastically reshape the federal government? What principle limits the scope of the decision in a way that would not also legitimate the for-cause provisions struck down in this case?

2. *The "unitary executive" and presidential control of the Administration.* Behind debates over the principle of a "unitary executive" is the sprawling character of the executive branch and the fact that many persons within it are practically beyond the control of the President and the advisers closest to him. Will the Court's new rule outlawing double (or triple) good-cause provisions significantly assist the President's control over the executive branch? The Court also emphasizes the importance of political accountability. Will the new rule actually make the President and the actions of the executive branch more accountable to the public? Is increased presidential control over every facet of the executive

branch the best way to make Presidents accountable to the public and ensure that Presidents are faithful to the law? Justice Breyer emphasizes that where expertise is important or where executive branch officials engage in adjudication, it may be better to isolate them from the President's political ambitions. Consider in this light the debate over the independence of the Office of Legal Counsel during the Bush Administration and the debate over the so-called "Torture Memos" discussed in the casebook at pp. 878-881.

NATIONAL LABOR RELATIONS BOARD v. NOEL CANNING, 134 S. Ct. 2550 (2014): The National Labor Relations Board consists of five members, appointed by the President. The Board requires a quorum of three members in order to make its decisions. See 29 U.S.C. §153(b).

By 2008, the terms of three of the five members had expired and President George W. Bush and the Senate were unable to agree on new appointments. As a result, the Board had only two active members. The two-member Board continued to issue opinions and orders, which the Supreme Court declared illegal in New Process Steel, L.P. v. NLRB, 560 U.S. 674, 687-688 (2010) (holding that in the absence of a lawfully appointed quorum, the Board cannot exercise its powers). President Barack Obama nominated three new members to the Board to fill the expired terms, but Senate Republicans filibustered the appointments.

Ordinarily the President must obtain "the Advice and Consent of the Senate" before appointing an "Office[r] of the United States." U.S. Const., Art. II, §2, cl. 2. However, there is an exception for "recess appointments." The Constitution gives the President the power "to fill up all Vacancies that may happen during the Recess of the Senate, by granting Commissions which shall expire at the End of their next Session." Art. II, §2, cl. 3.

To enable the Board to continue operations, President Obama made two recess appointments to the NLRB in March 2010. These appointments expired at the end of 2011, at which point the NLRB once again lacked a quorum to do business.

To prevent Obama from making any new recess appointments to the NLRB, the House of Representatives, which was now controlled by Republicans as a result of the 2010 elections, refused to adjourn and refused to allow the Senate to adjourn. According to Art. I, §5, cl. 4, "Neither House, during the Session of Congress, shall, without the Consent of the other, adjourn for more than three days." As a result, from December 17, 2011 to January 20, 2012, the Senate held a series of *pro forma* meetings on Tuesdays and Fridays at which no business was conducted. (Sundays do not count as legislative days.) During this period, the second session of the 112th Congress officially began on January 3, 2012.

In response, President Obama argued that despite the *pro forma* meetings, the Senate was actually in recess. He appointed three people he had previously nominated to the NLRB through recess appointments on January 4, 2012, the day after the second session of the Senate officially began, although the Senate did not resume its ordinary business until January 20, 2012.

On February 8, 2012, the Board found that Noel Canning, a Pepsi-Cola distributor, had engaged in an unfair labor practice in violation of the National Labor Relations Act because it had unlawfully refused to execute a collective bargaining agreement with a labor union. On appeal, Noel Canning argued that the Board's orders were void because the new Board members were not legally appointed and therefore the Board lacked a quorum to do business.

1a. *Inter-session and intra-session recesses.* Noel Canning argued that "the Recess of the Senate" applied only to "inter-session" recesses that occur between the formal sessions of the House and Senate. These end when the House or Senate passes a resolution adjourning *"sine die,"* i.e., without specifying a date to return (in which case Congress reconvenes when the next formal session is scheduled to begin). Both the Senate and House also take other breaks in the middle of formal sessions. The Senate or House takes an "intra-session" recess by passing a resolution stating that it will adjourn to a fixed date. Noel Canning argued that "the Recess of the Senate" did not include these "intra-session" breaks. Because President Obama made his appointments on January 4, after the second session began, his appointments did not fall within the scope of the Recess Appointments Clause.

Justice Breyer, writing for five Justices, disagreed. "[T]he word 'the' frequently (but not always) indicates 'a particular thing.' But the word can also refer 'to a term used generically or universally.' The Constitution, for example, directs the Senate to choose a President *pro tempore* 'in *the* Absence of the Vice-President.' Art. I, §3, cl. 5 (emphasis added). And the Federalist Papers refer to the chief magistrate of an ancient Achaean league who 'administered the government in *the* recess of the Senate.' The Federalist No. 18, at 113 (J. Madison) (emphasis added). . . . The constitutional text is thus ambiguous. And we believe the Clause's purpose demands the broader interpretation. The Clause gives the President authority to make appointments during 'the recess of the Senate' so that the President can ensure the continued functioning of the Federal Government when the Senate is away. The Senate is equally away during both an inter-session and an intra-session recess."

Justice Breyer then turned to historical practice, which, he claimed, "offers strong support for the broad interpretation." Congress generally took no intra-session breaks before the Civil War. But "[i]n 1867 and 1868, Congress for the first time took substantial, nonholiday intra-session breaks, and President Andrew Johnson made dozens of recess appointments. . . . In all, between the founding and the Great Depression, Congress took substantial intra-session breaks (other than holiday breaks) in four years: 1867, 1868, 1921, and 1929. And in each of those years the President made intra-session recess appointments."

Moreover, "[s]ince 1929, and particularly since the end of World War II, Congress has shortened its inter-session breaks as it has taken longer and more frequent intra-session breaks; Presidents have correspondingly made more intra-session recess appointments. Indeed, if we include military appointments, Presidents have made thousands of intra-session recess appointments."

The Senate, Justice Breyer, explained, has acquiesced in this practice: "Since Presidents began making intra-session recess appointments, individual Senators have taken differing views about the proper definition of 'the recess.' But neither the Senate considered as a body nor its committees, despite opportunities to express opposition to the practice of intra-session recess appointments, has done so."

1b. *How long an intra-session recess is sufficient?* Justice Breyer next turned to the question of "how long a recess must be in order to fall within the Clause. Is a break of a week, or a day, or an hour too short to count as a recess'? The Clause itself does not say." The Court "agree[d] with the Solicitor General that a 3-day recess would be too short. . . . The Adjournments Clause reflects the fact that a 3-day break is not a significant interruption of legislative business. . . . A Senate recess that is so short that it does not require the consent of the House is not long enough to trigger the President's recess-appointment power." At the same time, "we have not found a single example of a recess appointment made during an intra-session recess that was shorter than 10 days. . . . There are a few historical examples of recess appointments made during inter-session recesses shorter than 10 days [but we regard these few scattered examples as anomalies." The Court therefore concluded that "in light of historical practice, . . . a recess of more than 3 days but less than 10 days is presumptively too short to fall within the Clause," while leaving open "the possibility that some very unusual circumstance—a national catastrophe, for instance, that renders the Senate unavailable but calls for an urgent response—could demand the exercise of the recess-appointment power during a shorter break."

2. *Which vacancies can the President fill with a recess appointment?* Noel Canning's second argument was that the phrase "vacancies that may happen during the recess of the Senate," Art. II, §2, cl. 3, applies only to vacancies that first *occurred* when the Senate was in recess. Because the NLRB vacancies began while the Senate was in session, President Obama could not later use a recess appointment to fill them when the Senate was in recess. Justice Breyer rejected this argument as well; he explained that the phrase also applies "to vacancies that initially occur before a recess and continue to exist during the recess." Justice Breyer "concede[d] that the most natural meaning of 'happens'" to a modern ear "is that the vacancy 'happens' when it initially occurs." But, he argued, the phrase is ambiguous. Thomas Jefferson once wrote that the Clause is "certainly susceptible of [two] constructions." It "may mean 'vacancies that may happen to be' or 'may happen to fall'" during a recess.

Breyer noted particularly Attorney General William Wirt's advice to President Monroe in 1823. Wirt explained that the broader interpretation is "most accordant with" the Constitution's "reason and spirit" and that a narrower interpretation would frustrate the purpose of the Clause: "Put the case of a vacancy occurring in an office, held in a distant part of the country, on the last day of the Senate's session. Before the vacancy is made known to the President, the Senate rises. The office may be an important one; the vacancy may paralyze a whole line of action in some essential branch of our internal police; the public interests may imperiously demand that it shall be immediately filled. But the vacancy happened to occur during the session of the Senate; and if the President's power is to be limited to such vacancies only as happen to occur during the recess of the Senate, the vacancy in the case put must continue, however ruinous the consequences may be to the public." 1 Op. Atty. Gen. 631, 632 (1823).

Once again Breyer looked to historical practice to confirm his interpretation: "The tradition of applying the Clause to pre-recess vacancies dates at least to President James Madison. . . . Nearly every subsequent Attorney General to consider the question throughout the Nation's history has thought the same. Indeed, as early as 1862, Attorney General Bates advised President Lincoln that his power to fill pre-recess vacancies was 'settled . . . as far . . . as a constitutional question can be settled,' and a century later Acting Attorney General Walsh gave President Eisenhower the same advice 'without any doubt.' . . . [W]e have enough information to believe that the Presidents since Madison have made many recess appointments filling vacancies that initially occurred prior to a recess, [and] [n]o one disputes that every President since James Buchanan has made recess appointments to pre-existing vacancies. [Given the data available to us,] we think it is a fair inference that a large proportion of the recess appointments in the history of the Nation have filled pre-existing vacancies."

To be sure, Breyer explained, "there was some sporadic disagreement [in the Senate] with the broad interpretation. [In] 1863 the Senate Judiciary Committee disagreed with the broad interpretation." The Senate also passed the Pay Act, which provided that "no money shall be paid . . . as a salary, to any person appointed during the recess of the Senate, to fill a vacancy . . . which . . . existed while the Senate was in session." But by 1905 "the Senate [had] subsequently abandoned its hostility," and "in 1940 Congress amended the Pay Act to authorize salary payments (with some exceptions) [in cases] where . . . a vacancy . . . did not initially occur during a recess but happened to exist during that recess. By paying salaries to this kind of recess appointee, the 1940 Senate (and later Senates) in effect supported the President's interpretation of the Clause." Given a consistent interpretation by the executive branch since Madison's presidency, and the fact that "[t]he Senate as a body has not countered this practice for nearly three-quarters of a century, perhaps longer, . . . we are reluctant to upset this traditional practice where doing so would seriously shrink the authority that Presidents have believed existed and have exercised for so long."

3. *Can the President disregard the* pro forma *sessions as a sham?* Noel Canning's third argument was that the Senate was not in recess because of the *pro forma* sessions, while the Solicitor General argued that they were a sham and that the President could disregard them because the Senate conducted no business until January 20.

This time the Court agreed with Noel Canning: "We hold that, for purposes of the Recess Appointments Clause, the Senate is in session when it says it is, provided that, under its own rules, it retains the capacity to transact Senate business." Justice Breyer noted that the Constitution explicitly empowers the Senate to "determine the Rules of its Proceedings." Art. I, §5, cl. 2, and that the Court's precedents have given the Senate broad authority to decide how and when to conduct its business, citing Marshall Field & Co. v. Clark, 143 U.S. 649 (1892); United States v. Ballin, 144 U.S. 1 (1892). The Court nevertheless cautioned that "deference to the Senate cannot be absolute. When the Senate is without the *capacity* to act, under its own rules, it is not in session even if it so declares." But in this case, "the Senate *has* enacted legislation during *pro forma* sessions even when it has said that no business will be transacted. Indeed, the Senate passed a bill by unanimous consent [extending cuts in the payroll tax] during the second *pro forma* session after its December 17 adjournment. And that bill quickly became law. Pub. L. 112-78, 125 Stat. 1280."

Justice Scalia, joined by Chief Justice Roberts and by Justices Thomas and Alito, concurred in the judgment. Justice Scalia agreed with Noel Canning that the President can only make recess appointments during an inter-session recess, and then only when the vacancy occurred while the Senate was between sessions. He argued that the "plain meaning" of the text was unambiguous. He also read historical practice quite differently than Justice Breyer, arguing that there was no consensus on the part of executive branch officials or acquiescence by the Senate. Finally, he argued that even if these had existed, the Court should not defer to intra-branch conventions in the face of the text's plain meaning.

> The Constitution's core, government-structuring provisions are no less critical to preserving liberty than are the later adopted provisions of the Bill of Rights. . . . Those structural provisions reflect the founding generation's deep conviction that "checks and balances were the foundation of a structure of government that would protect liberty." [Our] decisions all rest on the bedrock principle that "the constitutional structure of our Government" is designed first and foremost not to look after the interests of the respective branches, but to "protec[t] individual liberty."
>
> [T]his Court does not defer to the other branches' resolution of . . . controversies [about the Constitution's government-structuring provisions]; . . . our role is in no way "lessened" because it might be said that "the two political branches are adjusting their own powers between themselves." Since the separation of powers exists for the protection of individual liberty, its vitality "does not depend" on "whether 'the encroached-upon branch approves the encroachment.'" Rather, policing the "enduring structure" of constitutional government when the political branches fail to do so is "one of the most vital functions of this Court." . . . [A] self-aggrandizing practice adopted by one branch well after the founding, often challenged, and never before blessed by this Court—in other words, the sort of practice on which the majority relies in this case—does not relieve us of our duty to interpret the Constitution in light of its text, structure, and original understanding.

Discussion

1. *The political context. Noel Canning* arises in the context of recent political struggles between the President and Congress that, in turn, reflect increasing political polarization and dysfunction in Washington. As the country's politics

polarized at the close of the twentieth century, an unwritten norm emerged that all significant action in the Senate required 60 votes. This allowed Senators of the party opposite the President to block many executive appointments that previously would not have been filibustered.

Perhaps unsurprisingly, increasing polarization has led to increasing use of recess appointments. Modern practice allowed Presidents to make intra-session appointments when the Senate was adjourned for a significant period of time. When the Democrats regained control of the Senate in 2007, they sought to prevent President George W. Bush from using recess appointments to appoint figures they considered objectionable by conducting *pro forma* sessions when most members of Congress were not in town. Although President Bush's legal advisors did not regard the strategy as constitutionally effective, he did not challenge it during the remainder of his presidency.

Once Barack Obama became President, Republicans engaged in a selective strategy of frustrating his appointments to key agencies, including the NLRB and the new Consumer Financial Protection Bureau created as part of the Dodd-Frank financial services reforms. Republicans used holds and filibusters to prevent appointments while the Senate was in session. This left the possibility of recess appointments, and Obama made one such appointment to the NLRB during a recess in July 2009 after the Republicans had filibustered the nomination. Although the Republicans did not control the Senate, after the 2010 elections, they did control the House. House Republicans refused to consent to an adjournment in order to keep the Senate in session and prevent President Obama from making recess appointments.

Unlike President Bush, President Obama decided to test the legality of the Senate's new practices. If he did not act, the NLRB would soon lack enough members to constitute a quorum, which would effectively disable it. Republicans, who often opposed the Board's enforcement of labor regulations, did not regard this as a major disadvantage. Republicans also served notice that they would not confirm anyone to head the Consumer Financial Protection Bureau, regardless of qualifications, unless the President agreed to turn the Bureau into a multimember commission and make other changes to Dodd-Frank. Dodd-Frank only allows the CFPB to exercise some of its powers once an agency head is successfully appointed. By preventing an appointment, Republicans would, in effect, cripple the agency and limit its ability to engage in enforcement and rulemaking. These political maneuvers set the stage for the legal battle in *Noel Canning*.

In July 2013, Senate Democrats threatened to alter the Senate's filibuster rules for executive nominations by simple majority vote—the "nuclear option." (Senate Republicans had threatened a similar strategy in 2005 when the Democrats had filibustered several George W. Bush circuit court appointments.) In response, Senate Republicans agreed to allow confirmation of several nominees, including to the NLRB and the Consumer Financial Protection Bureau. Then on November 21, 2013, the Senate voted 52-48 to eliminate the use of the filibuster against all executive branch nominees and judicial nominees other than to the Supreme Court. On the constitutional issues, see Akhil Reed Amar, America's Unwritten Constitution: The Precedents and Principles We Live By 356-369 (2012). As noted below, the change in Senate rules greatly lessens the need for Presidents to turn to recess appointments, at least when the President's party controls the Senate.

2. *Separation of powers or separation of parties?* Although *Noel Canning* was litigated as a case about separation of powers between the executive and legislative branches, the more important constitutional check in today's world is that of party. After all, if both the House and Senate had been controlled by Democrats, there would have been no constitutional conflict with President Obama.

One effect of *Noel Canning* is that the Court has legitimated the current strategy of using *pro forma* Senate sessions to prevent recess appointments. Hence if the party opposing the President controls the Senate, it can effectively prevent all recess appointments by refusing to adjourn.

It might also seem that if the opposition party controls the House, the House can prevent recess appointments — as it did in this case — by refusing to adjourn, thus forcing the Senate to engage in *pro forma* sessions. That may not be the end of the story, however. In 2012, Senate Majority Leader Harry Reid, a Democrat, went along with House Speaker John Boehner's gambit to keep both chambers open over the holidays. But suppose that the Senate Majority Leader informs the President by letter, signed by all of the members of the majority party, that the *pro forma* sessions demanded by the House are actually a sham and that no business will be conducted? Justice Breyer's opinion argues that the Court should defer to the Senate's own judgment about its operations. What result? (Is it clear that a third party like Noel Canning would have standing to assert a constitutional claim if the Senate maintains that it is in recess? Would the House have standing? See Raines v. Byrd, 521 U.S. 811 (1997).)[1]

There is an additional wild card: Art. II, §3 states that "in Case of Disagreement between [the Houses], with Respect to the Time of Adjournment, [the President] may adjourn them to such Time as he shall think proper." Could the President, holding such a letter from the Majority Leader, announce that the two Houses are in disagreement, adjourn Congress temporarily, and make a series of recess appointments? Would this be consistent with the purposes of the advice and consent requirements of Art. II, §2, cl. 2? Would the question of disagreement between the Houses, or of the President's powers to adjourn Congress, be justiciable?

Although quite interesting, many of these questions may never arise in practice for a simple reason. Once the Senate changed its filibuster rules for appointments, the House's leverage was greatly reduced. A disciplined Senate of the

---

1. For a more detailed discussion, see Akhil Reed Amar and Timothy Noah, How to Resolve the Recess Appointment Crisis: An Elegant Legal Solution, The New Republic, Jan. 6, 2012, at http://www.newrepublic.com/article/politics/99285/how-resolve-the-recess-appointment-crisis-elegant-legal-solution.

same party as the President will normally make it unnecessary for the President to resort to recess appointments in most cases. The ordinary process of advice and consent will be available to make all the appointments the President needs when the Senate is in session. (Obviously the President will have trouble appointing people that even Senators in the President's *own* party oppose.)

If the President's party controls the Senate, and supports the President's nominees, then the only way to prevent presidential appointments is if the opposition party in the Senate is willing to bring the business of the Senate to a halt through means other than filibusters. And that may lead the Senate majority to change the rules once again.

3. *The role of subsequent practice.* Note that Justice Breyer's opinion turns to the history of subsequent practice because he asserts that the text is ambiguous. Indeed, one of the great themes of his opinion is that " '[l]ong settled and established practice is a consideration of great weight in a proper interpretation of constitutional provisions' regulating the relationship between Congress and the President. . . . [T]his Court has treated practice as an important interpretive factor even when the nature or longevity of that practice is subject to dispute, and even when that practice began after the founding era."

Justice Scalia strongly disagrees that the text is at all ambiguous. If the majority and dissent disagree, does that mean that the text really is ambiguous? If the text *is* unambiguous, do you believe that subsequent practice can legitimately change the text's practical meaning? (Note that one's conclusions about ambiguity are not made in the abstract. They may be affected by one's views about the purpose of the provision, its relationship to other parts of the Constitution, the legitimacy of subsequent practice, and so on. See the discussion in note 6, infra.)

4. *Evolving constitutional norms or adverse possession?* Justice Breyer views the relevant history as evolving toward a settled set of conventions concerning when Presidents may use the recess appointments power. Justice Scalia, by contrast, argues that there are no settled conventions; there is only an executive power grab that members of the Senate have protested from time to time, both in public statements and in legislation like the 1863 Pay Act. He points out that the Senate, because it is a multimember body, has a much harder time protesting presidential usurpation, and making its objections stick. Therefore courts should be especially alert to the possibility of presidential overreaching.

Because inter-branch conventions often arise out of the push and pull of everyday politics, how do we tell which account of the history is correct? Is this just a form of "winner's history" or is there a more or less apolitical or objective way to decide the question?

Justice Scalia also argues that even if a settled convention had developed, it cannot change the meaning of the Constitution. An earlier Congress cannot constitutionally give away the power of future Congresses. Note that the Office of Legal Counsel generally takes the same view of executive power—an earlier President cannot bind all future Presidents by surrendering executive power. Recall Acting Solicitor General Walter Dellinger's memo on presidential authority to decline to execute unconstitutional statutes in Chapter 1, in which he points out that "there is no constitutional analogue to the principles of waiver and estoppel." Yet even if both branches deny that previous waivers or adjustments bind their successors, shifts in inter-branch relations nevertheless do develop over time. What is the best explanation of this? Should we say that inter-branch conventions continue to exist for so long as both sides find them convenient? If so, why should judges enforce those conventions?

Finally, Justice Scalia points out that the Court did not defer to settled conventions in INS v. Chadha, even though Congress had placed legislative vetoes in provisions for half a century. Yet there are important differences between the practices of recess appointments and of the legislative veto. The practice of recess appointments begins in James Madison's presidency, not in the middle of the 20th century. In addition, while every President from Woodrow Wilson forward disputed the constitutionality of legislative veto until the Supreme Court held it unconstitutional, the Senate eventually acquiesced to recess appointments.

5. *The interpretive status of inter-branch conventions.* Even if the history unambiguously demonstrates settled practice, why *should* subsequent practice between Congress and the President settle constitutional meaning, either between the branches themselves, or in judicial constructions of the Constitution? To what extent are the reasons similar to or different from the reason why judges attempt to respect prior judicial precedents? Following precedent is sometimes justified on grounds of (1) rule of law values—treating like cases alike and avoiding the appearance of political decisionmaking; (2) the fact that the public and other branches of government rely on precedents as stable law; and (3) judicial humility in the face of a reasonable judgment by past actors. Which of these reasons apply to inter-branch conventions?

Note that there is a difference between Congress and the President accepting a course of conduct as a practical matter and judges writing that course of conduct into constitutional doctrine. Conventions may change over time, but judicial doctrine fixes them into place at a particular moment in time. To avoid that result, courts could treat inter-branch conventions as nonjusticiable, but that is hard to do when private parties' interests—like those of Noel Canning and the labor union—are at stake.

6. *William Wirt's argument—purposivism versus plain meaning.* Note carefully Attorney General Wirt's argument—which Justice Breyer quotes—for why Presidents must be able to make recess appointments even if the vacancy originally occurs while the Senate is in session. Wirt's view is that you cannot understand whether a constitutional provision is ambiguous until you understand its purposes and how it works in conjunction with other features of the constitutional system. Breyer, adopting Wirt's purposive approach to interpretation, rejects a "plain meaning" reading of the text in favor of a pragmatic reading.

Note that Wirt's concern is not simply one of presidential convenience. If an executive branch position is important, and a replacement is urgent, the President could, in theory, call the Senate back into session to consider a new appointment. See Art. II, §3. But the Senators may not *want* to have to travel back to Washington for a special session to consider a single appointment. In some cases, allowing the President to make recess appointments may serve the Senate's interests as well as the President's.

7. *Using framework statutes to prevent gaming the system.* Justice Breyer points out that under Wirt's reading, Presidents might be able to game the system by waiting until the Senate leaves town to make recess appointments. But these appointments will be temporary, and if the appointee wants eventual confirmation, Presidents have incentives not to anger the Senators by tricking them. That is why many if not most recess appointments have been relatively noncontroversial. (Breyer gives several examples in his opinion: "President Franklin Roosevelt . . . commissioned Dwight Eisenhower as a permanent Major General during an intra-session recess; President Truman made Dean Acheson Under Secretary of State; and President George H.W. Bush reappointed Alan Greenspan as Chairman of the Federal Reserve Board.")

Moreover, Congress can pass legislation to encourage good faith presidential behavior. The 1940 Pay Act—still on the books—is a useful example of how this might be done. If a vacancy arises less than 30 days before the end of a session, the President may make a recess appointment and the appointee will be compensated as usual. But if the appointment is made more than 30 days before the end of the session, the appointee will receive no pay until the Senate confirms, at which point pay will be awarded retroactively.

Note the logic behind such a framework statute: the Senate designs the rules so that the President's use of recess appointments furthers the Senate's own interests. In the last 30 days of a session, the Senate may not want its agenda sidetracked by presidential appointments. (Similarly, Senators may not want to be called back for a special session when they are back home meeting their constituents and raising money.) The Pay Act allows the President to make short-term appointments in these cases. But if a vacancy occurs earlier, the rules are different. Recess appointees should not expect to be paid if the President appoints someone particularly unpalatable or controversial.

8. *Separation of powers and liberty.* While Justice Breyer emphasizes that courts should construe the Constitution so that government can function, Justice Scalia argues that the point of separation of powers is to hinder government efficiency in certain ways in the interests of liberty. What kind of liberty is Scalia concerned with? Sometimes it is obvious how separation of powers promotes liberty: allowing the same actor to be prosecutor, judge, and jury would be quite dangerous. But what is the liberty interest that is protected by a narrow reading of the Recess Appointments Clause?

In *Noel Canning* itself, the effect of banning recess appointments would be to prevent the National Labor Relations Board from enforcing the country's labor laws. This certainly furthers the liberty of Noel Canning, which refused to execute a collective bargaining agreement and was charged with an unfair labor practice by the Board. But it also might undermine the practical liberty of the union and its members, who rely on collective bargaining rights to protect themselves. Similarly, until the Senate rules were changed in November 2013, Republicans refused to allow any appointments to the Consumer Financial Protection Bureau, in part because they thought that the Bureau was a bad idea. Moreover, they believed that without a change in its organization, the Bureau would likely adopt consumer protection regulations that they thought were unfair to banks and other financial institutions. Such regulations might impinge on the liberty of some actors in society. But they might also provide valuable rights to others, for example, citizens who are harmed by predatory lending practices.

Under this account, limits on presidential appointments protect the sort of liberty that is realized through government *inaction* or *non-enforcement* of the laws. They do not protect the kinds of liberty — or security — that depend on government action or enforcement of the laws. (Compare the arguments connecting federalism to liberty.)

What about the appointment of judges? Is liberty enhanced when there are not enough judges to vindicate the constitutional rights of individuals? Note, however, that there is a different concern about allowing recess appointments for federal judges. If federal judges — who would ordinarily enjoy life tenure — are appointed for a one-year term, they are effectively on "probation" and they may be tempted to decide cases to increase their chances of Senate confirmation. While it might be a good idea for recess appointees in the *executive branch* to work harmoniously with Senators so as to ensure later confirmation, we should expect more independence from federal *judges*.

9. *Separation of powers and government integrity.* The example of judges suggests a different rationale for how checks and balances might protect liberty. The point is not ensuring liberty through government *inaction* but rather liberty through government *integrity*. Without checks on the President's appointment powers, Presidents may appoint cronies and corrupt people to office. These people may turn out to be incompetent or dishonest. Sometimes they will do nothing when they should act, but other times they will act badly or stupidly, or based on improper motives. The argument for checks and balances to preserve government integrity protects all kinds of liberties, not simply those that might follow from government inaction.

Why might Congressional Republicans believe that President Obama should not be trusted to have a free hand in his appointments to the NLRB? To the IRS? To the CIA? Should Senators be allowed to refuse to confirm *anyone* to a certain office, regardless of their honesty and qualifications?

Insert after note 1 on p. 836:

1a. *Why didn't Truman use the Taft-Hartley Act?* Note that instead of seizing the steel mills, President Truman could have sought an injunction to stop a labor strike, a course of action available to him under the 1947 Taft-Hartley Act. See Maeva Marcus, Truman and the Steel Seizure Case: The Limits of Presidential Power 77-78 (1994).

Nevertheless, Truman rejected the use of Taft-Hartley to resolve the crisis for several reasons. First, Truman had long been a supporter of (and supported by) organized labor; the Taft-Hartley Act was strongly opposed by labor and in fact had been passed over Truman's veto. Second, Truman believed that seeking a labor injunction was unfair to workers because it would freeze their wages in place and give management little incentive to bargain, thus in effect taking management's side over labor's. Third, Truman argued that the Taft-Hartley procedure did not allow an immediate injunction, and that invoking it would only delay the ultimate resolution of the dispute between labor and management. See Harry S Truman, Special Message to the Congress on the Steel Strike, June 10th, 1952, The American Presidency Project, at http://www. presidency.ucsb.edu/ws/index.php?pid=14152.

As Neal Devins and Louis Fisher explain, "[a]gainst this backdrop, Truman had a hard time convincing the nation that the steel seizure represented a national emergency instead of a labor dispute. . . . *Time* magazine accused Truman of acting 'primarily as a politician, not as a President. . . . Politician Harry Truman was obviously operating on the axiom of political arithmetic that there are more votes in Big Labor than in Big Steel.' And the *Nation* argued that 'a just settlement of a labor dispute' is not enough to excuse the president's 'arbitrary exercise of executive power.'" Neal Devins & Louis Fisher, The Steel Seizure Case: One of a Kind?, 19 Const. Comm. 63, 67 (2002) (citing Marcus at 89-90).

In addition, by this point in his Presidency Truman was a very unpopular President, in large part due to the deeply unpopular Korean War, which Truman had used to justify the seizure in the first place. Truman had sent troops into Korea without a formal declaration of war. Although the public initially supported his action, Truman took much of the blame as the war dragged on. Devins and Fisher speculate that "[h]ad the nation supported Truman and his war, there would have been no public outcry following the seizure and, consequently, the courts would not have been pressured to check a runaway president. For example, had Truman seized the steel mills in 1950 (when the public stood behind his Korean initiative), the Supreme Court might well have looked for a way to avoid ruling against the president." *Id.* at 74. Do you agree?

Insert after note 11 on p. 841 and omit note 9 on pp. 838-839:

Note: The Power to Wage War

Congress has not formally declared war on an enemy since 1941. Yet the United States has been involved in recurrent military hostilities since the end of World War II, including the Korean, Vietnamese, Iraqi, and Serbian conflicts. Although in none of these did Congress invoke its Article I power "to declare war," it has often purported to approve military action; consider, for example, the 1964 Gulf of Tonkin Resolution authorizing the President to engage in retaliation for alleged attacks on American military forces in Vietnam, which served as the legal underpinning for the subsequent buildup of American forces. In addition, there have been numerous "minor" military actions, in areas of the world ranging from Lebanon to the Dominican Republic and Grenada. There has been recurrent debate about the constitutional legitimacy of these military actions.

1. *The constitutional issues.* Consider three positions. One position is that Presidents can use military force at their complete discretion whenever they like. The Declare War Clause is irrelevant to this decision; it means only that Congress has power to declare that war exists for purposes of international law. (In addition, under the General Welfare Clause, Congress also has the power to appropriate or refuse to appropriate funds for military actions.)

A second view would maintain that "declare war" in Article I, section 8 means "make war" or "engage in war" and hence whenever the President uses military force he must obtain congressional consent. This position must make an exception for serious emergencies but would otherwise restrict most presidential uses of armed forces abroad. In addition, Congress could give the President continuing advance authorization for emergencies; an example of such a statute is the early Militia Acts discussed in the *Prize Cases.*

A third position is closer to actual practice since World War II. It holds that the President, even without prior Congressional authorization, has discretion to use military force in furtherance of American interests in at least two situations: The first are comparatively "minor" actions of brief duration and involving limited military intervention. The second are emergency situations where important American interests are at stake and there is no time for Congress to deliberate and approve military action in advance. In other cases, Congress must offer some kind of authorization of military force, which may or may not also include a formal declaration of war. Under this third reading, some (but not all) military actions constitute "war" within the meaning of the Declare War Clause and therefore require Congressional authorization, even if they do not require a formal declaration of war for purposes of international law and no such declaration ever occurs.

This textual argument creates its own difficulties. The Constitution also uses the term "war" in Article I, section 10, which provides that "No state shall, without the consent of Congress, . . . engage in a war, unless actually invaded, or in such imminent danger as will not admit of delay." Does this mean that the President must obtain Congressional approval in all cases in which a state would have to obtain Congressional approval to engage in "war"?

The answer is almost certainly no. Quite apart from the differences between "declare war" and "engage in a war," there are important structural differences between these two provisions. Article I, section 10 is designed to prevent the states, as much as possible, from interfering with (and causing problems for) a single national foreign policy. By contrast, the President generally takes the lead in shaping American foreign policy, and strategic use of military force may be an important element in conducting an effective foreign policy. Thus, the balance of powers between the President and Congress is designed to ensure *democratic accountability* for significant military interventions rather than to prevent meddlesome states from creating foreign policy crises. Hence, the question of "war" for purposes of Article I, section 10, concerns state interventions that might interfere with a unitary U.S. foreign and military policy, while the question of "war" for purposes of the Declare War Clause concerns those interventions that, for reasons of democratic accountability, both President and Congress should have to commit to.

The debates on these questions in the Philadelphia convention are particularly sparse. The original text gave Congress the power to "make war." The following discussion ensued on August 17th. (spellings as in the original):

"To make war"

Mr Pinkney opposed the vesting this power in the Legislature. Its proceedings were too slow. It wd. meet but once a year. The Hs. of Reps. would be too numerous for such deliberations. The Senate would be the best depositary, being more acquainted with foreign affairs, and most capable of proper resolutions. If the States are equally represented in Senate, so as to give no advantage to large States, the power will notwithstanding be safe, as the small have their all at stake in such cases as well as the large States. It would be singular for one authority to make war, and another peace.

Mr Butler. The Objections agst the Legislature lie in a great degree agst the Senate. He was for vesting the power in the President, who will have all the requisite qualities, and will not make war but when the Nation will support it.

Mr. Madison and Mr Gerry moved to insert "declare," striking out "make" war; leaving to the Executive the power to repel sudden attacks.

Mr Sharman thought it stood very well. The Executive shd. be able to repel and not to commence war. "Make" better than "declare" the latter narrowing the power too much.

Mr Gerry never expected to hear in a republic a motion to empower the Executive alone to declare war.

Mr. Elseworth. there is a material difference between the cases of making war, and making peace. It shd. be more easy to get out of war, than into it. War also is a simple and overt declaration. peace attended with intricate & secret negociations.

Mr. Mason was agst giving the power of war to the Executive, because not safely to be trusted with it; or to the Senate, because not so constructed as to be entitled to it. He was for clogging rather than facilitating war; but for facilitating peace. He preferred "declare" to "make".

On the Motion to insert declare — in place of Make, it was agreed to.

2. *The statutory issues: the War Powers Resolution.* In the aftermath of the Vietnam War, Congress passed, over President Nixon's veto, the War Powers Resolution of 1973. Its central purpose was to increase Congress's role in decisionmaking regarding the commitment of American troops. Section 4(a) of the WPR requires the President to submit a report to Congress within 48 hours of the introduction of American troops, in the absence of a declaration of war,

(1) into hostilities or into situations where imminent involvement in hostilities is clearly indicated by the circumstances;

(2) into the territory, airspace or waters of a foreign nation, while equipped for combat, except for deployments which relate solely to supply, replacement, repair, or training of such forces; or

(3) in numbers which substantially enlarge United States Armed Forces equipped for combat already located in a foreign country.

Submission of such a report triggers a 60-day decisionmaking period. Section 5(b) provides that at the end of that period, "the President shall terminate any use of United States Armed forces" reported on "unless the Congress (1) has declared war or has enacted a specific authorization for such use of United States Armed Forces, (2) has extended by law such sixty-day period, or (3) is physically unable to meet as a result of an armed attack upon the United States." This 60-day period can also be extended by 30 additional days should the President notify Congress "that unavoidable military necessity respecting the safety of United States Armed Forces requires the continued use of such armed forces in the course of bringing about a prompt removal of such forces."

Section 5(c) provides that, notwithstanding these requirements, whenever "United States Armed Forces are engaged in hostilities outside the territory of the United States, its possessions and territories without a declaration of war or specific statutory authorization, such forces shall be removed by the President if the Congress so directs by concurrent resolution."

The War Powers Act has been the topic of major constitutional debate, in large measure because of the specific process chosen for invocation of congressional power. Under section 5(c), the President is given no opportunity to veto a concurrent resolution directing immediate withdrawal. Every President since Nixon has argued that this aspect of the Act is unconstitutional. Congress has not yet attempted to use the War Powers Act to limit presidential action. Dramatic examples of the practical irrelevance of the Act involved President Reagan's and Bush's commitments of American military forces to the Persian Gulf. Congressional majorities self-consciously avoided invoking the Act, over the heated protest of several legislators. Imagine that Congress, over the President's veto, passed a law directing the removal of American troops from a particular theater of involvement. Would the statute be constitutional?

Although most Administrations have taken the position that Congress may not end presidential involvement through a joint resolution that is not subject to a presidential veto, this constitutional objection does not apply to the rest of the War Powers Resolution. For example, the Obama Administration, relying on a 1980 Office of Legal Counsel opinion, has assumed that the 60-day requirement of the War Powers Act in section 5(b) is constitutional. See *Presidential Power to Use the Armed Forces Abroad Without Statutory Authorization*, 4A Op. O.L.C. 185, 196 (1980).

How would you analyze the 60-day requirement under *Youngstown*? Note that the President might well argue that section 5(b), like the early Militia Acts, should be construed as a standing authorization for the President to take military action for up to 60 days. Moreover, as discussed below, even if section 5(b) is constitutional, Congress has fairly limited ways to enforce the 60-day limit, as discussed below.

3. *So what?* Even if a military intervention goes beyond presidential power or violates the War Powers Resolution, it is not clear that these issues can be challenged in court. In Raines v. Byrd, 521 U.S. 811 (1997), the Supreme Court held that Congressmen and Senators did not have standing as legislators to challenge the constitutionality of a line-item-veto bill. In Campbell v. Clinton, 203 F.3d 19, 21 (D.C. Cir. 2000), cert. denied, 531 U.S. 815 (2000), which relied on *Raines v. Byrd*, the D.C. Circuit rejected the standing of congressmen to challenge President Clinton's intervention in Kosovo. (Note that, even if one gets past the standing question, one must also show that the constitutional and statutory questions are not political questions. Assuming that the constitutional question involves a political question, why would the application of a statute like the War Powers Resolution be non-justiciable?)

4. *Political remedies and collective action problems.* Even if members of Congress lack standing to challenge a President's decision to use military force, that does not mean that there is no constitutional or legal remedy. As the Court noted in *Raines*, the most likely remedy comes from the political process. Congress can attempt to pass legislation over the President's veto requiring that the President end the intervention. Congress can refuse to appropriate funding for the intervention and it can refuse to allow existing funds to be used for the intervention. And, of course, if all else fails, Congress can threaten to impeach the President or threaten to hold up other legislation that the President wants passed.

It may not even be necessary for Congress to pass new legislation to have an effect. Pressure exercised through resolutions by one House or a joint resolution by both Houses may strongly signal to presidents that the country is not behind them or, that they are in violation of the law, and that they should end the intervention quickly. Congress can also use public debates and hearings to shape public opinion against an intervention, although usually not as effectively as the President can.

Nevertheless, political remedies face political obstacles. Congress as a whole has incentives to sit on its hands and wait to see whether a military mission is successful or not. That is because Congress as a whole is composed of individual Congressmen and Senators, who have various incentives to avoid responsibility. Congressmen and Senators, especially those who may consider running for president someday, do not want to guess wrong about military operations. If a candidate takes a strong stand against a military action that goes well, this will be used against the candidate later. Conversely, as Hillary Clinton discovered in the 2008 presidential campaign, supporting a war that later becomes unpopular can undermine a candidate's political support.

As a result of these pressures, Congress may adopt a position of what we might call belligerent acquiescence: While individual members denounce the

Administration, measures designed either to approve or to hinder a presidential intervention are difficult to pass.

A further complicating factor is that in military interventions the United States often works in concert with international organizations like the North Atlantic Treaty Organization (NATO). The United States has sometimes turned to its allies in NATO, for example, when it is unlikely that the United Nations will take effective action or action that is consistent with U.S. interests.

Quite apart from Congress's tendencies toward inertia, Congress has incentives not to undermine such international organizations because their effectiveness serves the long-term interests of the United States. Thus, if Congress believes that defunding a particular intervention would destroy NATO's future credibility, or the credibility of the United States within NATO, it may do nothing.

These considerations help explain why Congress decided to create the decisional structure of the War Powers Resolution. If Congress does nothing, the President must end an intervention after 60 days. Does this shifting of the default rule better serve American interests?

Since the passage of the War Powers Act, Congress has authorized major operations in the Gulf and Iraq wars. Other military operations since 1973 have, for the most part, either been relatively brief (so that they fall within the 60-day period) or relatively inconsequential. The most interesting contrary example before the 2011 Libya intervention (discussed infra) was President Clinton's decision to bomb Kosovo in 1999. The Kosovo intervention was also performed in conjunction with NATO, and it was also justified largely on humanitarian grounds. Ultimately, the Clinton Administration argued that Congress had retroactively authorized the intervention because of a subsequent appropriations measure. The Kosovo example shows why Congress is in a difficult situation; if Congress funds an ongoing mission to maintain the credibility of the United States or NATO, or to avoid a military disaster, the President may use this as evidence of implicit congressional approval.

Note, however, that many members of Congress might want to have it both ways. They might want to assert that the President has gone beyond the 60-day limit and is acting illegally but they might not want to force the President to end an intervention that has already begun. As a result, Congress does nothing, or, as in the Kosovo case, provides appropriations. Does this mean that the 60-day clock is a bad idea? Would another model make more sense?

5. *Humanitarian intervention: the Libya intervention.* In mid-February 2011 a popular uprising began against the autocratic government of Colonel Muammar Qaddafi of Libya, which led to a civil war. The Libyan government was reported to have bombed and strafed protesters and deliberately targeted civilians. On March 12, the Arab League called for a no-fly zone in Libya, and on March 17, the United Nations Security Council adopted Resolution 1973, which imposed a no-fly zone and called for the use of military force to protect civilians. In response, on March 19, the United States along with its NATO allies launched airstrikes against Libyan targets to enforce Resolution 1973. President Obama provided a report to Congress on March 21, stating that no ground troops would be deployed.

Sometime around April 4, NATO took over leadership in maintaining the no-fly zone in Libya, and the United States adopted a supporting role. According to the Obama Administration, the United States provided surveillance and refueling for allied warplanes. The United States continued to fire missiles from unmanned drones; it also engaged in a relatively small percentage of manned air missions (approximately 10 percent) in proportion to the manned air missions by NATO forces.

Treating the March 21, 2011 report as the starting date of the introduction of American forces into hostilities, the War Power Resolution's 60-day clock would have run out on May 20, 2011, and the 30-day extension to withdraw forces would have run out around June 18. The intervention continued, however, and as noted below, the Obama Administration took the position that the clock was tolled when it handed leadership off to NATO.

Fighting in Libya ended in October 2011 following the death of Muammar Qaddafi. Congress debated but ultimately never authorized the Libya operation. In June 2011, the House of Representatives passed two resolutions. The first protested the operation and stated that "[t]he President shall not deploy, establish, or maintain the presence of units and members of the United States Armed Forces on the ground in Libya unless the purpose of the presence is to rescue a member of the Armed Forces from imminent danger." The second, added to an appropriations bill funding military construction and the Department of Veterans Affairs, stated that none of the money in the bill could be spent "in contravention of the War Powers Act." The Senate never passed a similar resolution, and Congressional interest in the controversy lapsed following the end of the operation.

On June 15, the Obama Administration provided an explanation to Congress. It argued that the President had constitutional authority to begin the Libya operation without Congressional approval "[g]iven the important U.S. interests served by U.S. military operations in Libya and the limited nature, scope and duration of the anticipated actions."[7] President Obama was not responding to an attack on American soil, to threats of danger to Americans living abroad, to threats to American property, or to an attack on American allies. Instead, the President intervened in Libya in order to avoid a humanitarian disaster. By imposing a no-fly zone, NATO sought to limit Qaddafi's forces and weaken his military power so that he could not threaten or harm innocent civilians.

At a press conference on March 18, President Obama argued that the intervention promoted important American interests:

Now, here is why this matters to us. Left unchecked, we have every reason to believe that Qaddafi would commit atrocities against his people. Many thousands could die. A humanitarian crisis would ensue. The entire region could be

---

7. "United States Activities in Libya," June 15, 2011, at http://www.foreignpolicy. com/files/fp_uploaded_documents/110615_United_States_Activities_in_Libya_-_6_15_11.pdf.

destabilized, endangering many of our allies and partners. The calls of the Libyan people for help would go unanswered. The democratic values that we stand for would be overrun. Moreover, the words of the international community would be rendered hollow.

Remarks by the President on the Situation in Libya (Mar. 18, 2011), at http://www.whitehouse.gov/the-press-office/2011/03/18/remarks-president-situation-libya.

Are these interests sufficient to justify presidential military intervention without Congressional authorization? When the President uses force for humanitarian reasons rather than to protect American citizens, troops, or material interests, is there a greater reason to require Congressional authorization, either before or immediately after the intervention begins? In an April 2011 OLC opinion, the Administration also argued that supporting the United Nations Security Council's "credibility and effectiveness" was another national interest. Is this sufficient justification under the circumstances? Couldn't the President almost always justify humanitarian intervention on these grounds if the Administration is working in concert with NATO or other international organizations?

6. *The Libya intervention: technological change and the Constitution.* Consider how changes in the technology of warfare might alter the constitutional and statutory issues discussed above. America's use of air power and drone technology in the Libya intervention limited potential American casualties. Accordingly, the Obama Administration, in an OLC opinion, argued that the Libya intervention was not a "war" that required congressional authorization because the operation was limited in three ways. First, the operation was limited to airpower, and did not use ground troops. Airpower limits the number and degree of casualties that can be inflicted on American soldiers; compared to airpower, the use of ground troops makes withdrawal difficult and hence tends to restrict Congress's options once the operation begins. Second, the Administration argued that the use of airpower was connected to the limited goals of the Libya intervention: enforcing the no-fly zone and preventing humanitarian disaster; it did not involve conquest of territory. Third, the Administration argued that the bombing would not prepare the way for a later ground invasion, which reduced the risk that the intervention would result in a sustained commitment.[8]

What do you make of these arguments? Why does the fact that America uses a technology that (mostly) shields troops from harm mean that "war" is not occurring and that Congress need not approve the action? Does this mean that presidents can use any amount of long-range missiles, unmanned drones, and various forms of military robotics without engaging in "war"? Even if American troops face no immediate threat of reprisal, does this mean that no reprisals will be forthcoming, especially in the form of terrorist attacks and other forms of asymmetrical warfare?

8. Authority to Use Military Force in Libya, April 1, 2011, at http://www.justice.gov/olc/2011/authority-military-usein-libya.pdf.

Indeed, one might worry that the development of long-distance technologies that are likely to risk harm only to people who are not Americans might mean that ordinary democratic processes are no longer sufficient to check presidential ambitions or presidential adventurism. Because Americans will not return home in body bags, the President will feel freer to employ these technologies and intervene militarily in other parts of the world. Could this change in technology create some of the same problems that originally led the framers to require consultation with Congress before the country goes to war?

The Administration also argued that the Libya operation was in full compliance with the War Powers Resolution because the 60-day clock stopped in early April, when American forces took what was largely a supporting role to NATO operations. In terms of the language of section 4(a)(1) of the WPR, the Obama Administration argued that "United States Armed Forces" were no longer "introduced . . . into hostilities or into situations where imminent involvement in hostilities is clearly indicated by the circumstances."

Testifying before Congress, State Department Legal Advisor Harold Koh argued that "the operative term 'hostilities,' is an ambiguous standard" which must be developed case by case through inter-branch dialogue in light of changing circumstances that the drafters could not have foreseen. However, as a general matter, "the Executive Branch understands the term 'to mean a situation in which units of the U.S. armed forces are actively engaged in exchanges of fire with opposing units of hostile forces.' "[9] Following the handoff to NATO, U.S. military activities did not "involve active exchanges of fire with hostile forces," and members of the U.S. military were not "involved in significant armed confrontations or sustained confrontations of any kind with hostile forces. . . . American strikes have been confined, on an as-needed basis, to the suppression of enemy air defenses to enforce the no-fly zone, and to limited strikes by Predator unmanned aerial vehicles against discrete targets in support of the civilian protection mission; since the handoff to NATO, the total number of U.S. munitions dropped has been a tiny fraction of the number dropped in Kosovo."

Why does the switch to unmanned drones increase the chances that "hostilities" have ended? One possible reason is that "hostilities" require more or less continuous exchanges of fire between combatants. As long as unmanned drones are doing most of the killing, and American troops are not being fired at, or only being attacked intermittently, there are no hostilities. The use of drones, moreover, means that American involvement can be ended easily, unlike the use of ground troops.

This statutory argument, however, recapitulates the constitutional issues discussed above: the fact that an aggressor is not vulnerable does not mean that there are no hostilities occurring. Such a reading would give presidents incentives

---

9. Testimony by Legal Adviser Harold Hongju Koh, U.S. Department of State, on Libya and War Powers Before the Senate Foreign Relations Committee June 28, 2011, at http:// foreign.senate.gov/ imo/media/doc/Koh_Testimony.pdf.

to use remote-control weapons and make increased investments in missiles, unmanned drones, and robotics in order to get around the 60-day limitation.

The War Powers Resolution was drafted in light of the experience of the Vietnam War: a large commitment of ground troops that was difficult to extricate once operations had begun. Yet military technology and military strategy have changed in the interim. How should we interpret the War Powers Resolution in interventions that primarily involve long-distance warfare like drones or robotics? Consider the possibility that the War Powers Resolution, designed for Vietnam-style conflicts, is technologically outmoded and must be redrafted to take into account these changed realities.

Consider, for example, the problem of cyberattacks, where belligerents seek to use the Internet to destroy infrastructural capacities, or in the alternative, seek to exploit computers (and the resources these computers control) in other countries. Do cyberattacks count as "hostilities" under the WPR? How should the WPR be redrafted to account for them?

Substitute the following for the discussion notes following *Hamdi* and section 3 on Military Tribunals, pp. 864-878:

Discussion

1. *The aftermath of* Hamdi. Following the decision in *Hamdi,* the government decided not to give Hamdi a hearing to determine his status. Instead, it announced that it believed that Hamdi no longer posed a threat to the United States or had any intelligence value, and released Hamdi to Saudi Arabia in October 2004, after holding him without charges for almost three years. In return Hamdi agreed to renounce terrorism, surrender his U.S. citizenship, and not to visit Afghanistan, Iraq, Israel, Pakistan, or Syria. Finally, he agreed not to sue the United States over his captivity.[10] What reasons might the government have had to continue to hold Hamdi and litigate its right to detain him indefinitely even if it believed that Hamdi had no intelligence value and did not constitute a threat?

2. *Construing the scope of Congressional authorization.* Where deviations from normal legal procedures are justified on grounds of war and national security, the Court is more likely to defer to the President when it believes that Congress approves; conversely, it is more likely to seek to check the President only when he acts unilaterally or in the face of Congressional disapproval.[11]

---

10. USA Today, Hamdi Returns to Saudi Arabia, *http://www.usatoday.com/news/world/2004-10-11-hamdi_x.htm?POE=NEWISVA* (last visited Nov. 8, 2005); Findlaw, Yaser Esam Hamdi v. Donald Rumsfeld: Settlement Agreement, *http://news.findlaw.com/hdocs/docs/hamdi/91704stlagrmnt.html* (last visited Nov. 8, 2005).

11. See Samuel Issacharoff and Richard Pildes, Between Civil Libertarianism and Executive Unilateralism: An Institutional Process Approach to Rights During Wartime, in The Constitution in Wartime: Beyond Alarmism and Complacency 161-197 (Mark Tushnet ed., 2005), for a more developed version of this argument, with abundant historical examples.

This means that courts often play their most significant role in determining the existence and scope of Congressional approval. By finding or refusing to find such approval, or by construing the scope of Congressional approval broadly or narrowly, courts can limit and channel presidential ambitions without directly denying the existence of executive power.

Thus, in *Hamdi,* Justice O'Connor avoids deciding whether the President may detain enemy combatants on his own authority as Commander-in-Chief; instead she argues that Congress has approved some detentions and then construes that approval narrowly. The plurality's narrow definition of "enemy combatant" limits the political and legal legitimacy of the President's actions if he seeks to detain people on the basis of a broader definition. Of course, the President can always go to Congress to seek a broader authorization. But if he does so, he will be acting many years after the September 11 attacks, when passions have cooled and Congress may provide greater oversight. Thus, by construing the terms of consent between the two branches and then deferring to that constructed agreement, the Court creates a space of power for itself.

Do you agree with the plurality's assertion that the language of the AUMF is sufficiently clear to authorize the President to detain enemy combatants, under the laws of war, for the purposes of incapacitation? Should a clearer statement be required where detention of citizens is at stake?

According to Justice Scalia, the President may only detain citizens as enemy combatants if Congress suspends the writ of habeas corpus. Otherwise the government must use the normal resources of the criminal justice system. None of the Justices believed that the AUMF suspended the writ. Why? If the AUMF is not clear enough to suspend the writ of habeas corpus, why does it provide a sufficiently clear authorization to detain citizens as enemy combatants, especially if this will also deny citizens Bill of Rights protections?

Justice Souter argues that the President cannot avail himself of the right to detain persons under the laws of war because the Administration has not complied with the laws of war, in particular the Geneva Conventions, which require that signatory nations hold hearings to determine whether detainees are prisoners of war. Couldn't the President respond that whether or not his interpretation of particular elements of the laws of war is mistaken, he still has the authority to detain enemy combatants under the laws of war?

3. *Who is an enemy combatant?* The *Hamdi* plurality defines the term "enemy combatant" narrowly to include "an individual who . . . was part of or supporting forces hostile to the United States or coalition partners in Afghanistan and who engaged in an armed conflict against the United States there" (internal quotation marks omitted). May the President hold citizen detainees who do not fit this definition?

Consider for example, the example of Jose Padilla, a U.S. citizen who had converted to Islam and taken the name Abdullah al Muhajir. Padilla was arrested at O'Hare Airport on May 8, 2002, after returning from Pakistan. He was detained under a material witness warrant issued by a federal district court in New York. On June 9, 2002, he was declared an enemy combatant and placed in a military brig in South Carolina for three and a half years. Originally, the Justice Department claimed that Padilla was an al Qaeda operative who was planning to explode a "dirty bomb" — a conventional bomb that would spread radioactive material — in an American city. Two years later, the Justice Department stated that it believed that Padilla was planning to leak natural gas into apartment buildings and blow them up.

The *Hamdi* plurality suggests that capture on the battlefield in a foreign country is an important factor in its decision. It distinguishes *Ex parte Milligan* on the grounds that "Milligan was not a prisoner of war, but a resident of Indiana arrested while at home there. . . . Had Milligan been captured while he was assisting Confederate soldiers by carrying a rifle against Union troops on a Confederate battlefield, the holding of the Court might well have been different." How does the plurality's reasoning apply to the War on Terror, in which operatives and spies may not be apprehended on anything remotely resembling a "battlefield"?

In Rumsfeld v. Padilla, 542 U.S. 426 (2004), the Supreme Court held, 5-4, without reaching the merits, that Padilla should have filed his habeas petition in the District Court for the Southern District of South Carolina, rather than in New York, where he had originally been detained as a material witness. Justice Stevens, joined by Justices Souter, Ginsburg, and Breyer, dissented, arguing that the federal court in New York had jurisdiction to hear Padilla's claims and that his detention was illegal. Ultimately, the Bush Administration decided to avoid a Supreme Court opinion on the President's ability to detain Padilla as an enemy combatant, and it moved Padilla to the criminal justice system in January 2006. A federal jury convicted him of conspiracy to murder persons overseas and of providing material support to terrorists overseas. He was never indicted or convicted for the acts for which he was originally detained.

4. Hamdi *and the NDAA.* In December 2011, Congress passed and President Obama signed into law the National Defense Authorization Act for Fiscal Year 2012 (NDAA). Section 1021 gives Congressional authorization for indefinite military detention "pending disposition under the laws of war." It provides:

> (a) IN GENERAL. — Congress affirms that the authority of the President to use all necessary and appropriate force pursuant to the Authorization for Use of Military Force . . . includes the authority for the Armed Forces of the United States to detain covered persons (as defined in subsection (b)) pending disposition under the law of war.
>
> (b) COVERED PERSONS. — A covered person under this section is any person as follows:
>
> (1) A person who planned, authorized, committed, or aided the terrorist attacks that occurred on September 11, 2001, or harbored those responsible for those attacks.
>
> (2) A person who was a part of or substantially supported al-Qaeda, the Taliban, or associated forces that are engaged in hostilities against the

United States or its coalition partners, including any person who has committed a belligerent act or has directly supported such hostilities in aid of such enemy forces.

(c) DISPOSITION UNDER LAW OF WAR.—The disposition of a person under the law of war as described in subsection (a) may include the following:

(1) Detention under the law of war without trial until the end of the hostilities authorized by the Authorization for Use of Military Force.

(2) Trial under chapter 47A of title 10, United States Code (as amended by the Military Commissions Act of 2009).

(3) Transfer for trial by an alternative court or competent tribunal having lawful jurisdiction.

(4) Transfer to the custody or control of the person's country of origin, any other foreign country, or any other foreign entity.

(d) CONSTRUCTION.—Nothing in this section is intended to limit or expand the authority of the President or the scope of the Authorization for Use of Military Force.

(e) AUTHORITIES.—Nothing in this section shall be construed to affect existing law or authorities relating to the detention of United States citizens, lawful resident aliens of the United States, or any other persons who are captured or arrested in the United States.

How does the NDAA affect the Court's analysis in *Hamdi*? On the one hand, the NDAA seems to offer a much broader definition of who may be detained than the Court employed in *Hamdi*. Presumably, this should affect the *Youngstown* analysis and the Court's construction of the AUMF.

On the other hand, by stating that it does not purport to alter the President's existing authority, the NDAA is artfully drafted to leave many questions unclear. Does the NDAA authorize indefinite detention of persons away from a battlefield? Does it authorize indefinite detention of persons like Jose Padilla, apprehended inside the United States? Does it distinguish between the detention of citizens and aliens?

Another open question is the meaning of "substantial suppor[t]" in (b)(2). Under the broadest reading, the President would have the power to detain indefinitely persons who have no hostile intent toward the United States but who in some way supported an organization engaged in hostilities with one of America's coalition partners, whether or not the United States is in any way involved. (Imagine, for example, a person who gives advice or charitable contributions, or makes speeches on behalf of such an organization.) A narrower reading would interpret substantial support by analogy to traditional armed conflicts. It would be limited to persons whose actions on behalf of the enemy would justify detention according to the laws of war.

Section 1022(a) of the NDAA creates a statutory presumption in favor of indefinite military detention for persons suspected of terrorism, as opposed to criminal arrest and prosecution. It requires that the President place in military custody "pending disposition under the laws of war" all persons whom the President determines are part of al Qaeda or associated forces, and who "have participated in the course of planning or carrying out an attack or attempted attack against the United States or its coalition partners." Section (a)(4) allows a waiver of this requirement "if the President submits to Congress a certification in writing that such a waiver is in the national security interests of the United States." Section 1022(b)(1) exempts citizens from the requirement of military custody; section 1022(b)(2) exempts "lawful resident aliens" who are detained "on the basis of conduct taking place within the United States, except to the extent permitted by the Constitution of the United States."

5. *Detention for purposes of interrogation.* The *Hamdi* plurality argues that the President is justified in detaining citizens according to the laws of war in order to prevent the captured person from returning to the battlefield. What if the purpose of detention is not incapacitation but to facilitate interrogation?

The government's admitted purpose in holding Jose Padilla, for example, was primarily to obtain information from him. In fact, the government initially opposed allowing Padilla to meet with an attorney because it "could set back by months the government's efforts to bring psychological pressure to bear upon Padilla in an effort to interrogate him, and could compromise the government's interrogation techniques." Padilla ex rel. Newman v. Rumsfeld, 243 F. Supp. 2d 42, 46 (S.D.N.Y. 2003). According to a January 9, 2003 declaration of Vice Admiral Lowell E. Jacoby, Director of the Defense Intelligence Agency, successful interrogation "is largely dependent upon creating an atmosphere of dependency and trust between the subject and the interrogator." It may take "months, or even years," to "obtain valuable intelligence from a subject." "Any insertion of counsel into the subject-interrogator relationship, for example — even if only for a limited duration or for a specific purpose — can undo months of work and may permanently shut down the interrogation process." *Id.* at 50.

If someone like Padilla is held primarily for the purposes of interrogation, is his detention authorized under the AUMF? The plurality says that "indefinite detention for the purpose of interrogation is not authorized." What about detention for five years? Could the government insist that a citizen's detention is justified for purposes of both interrogation and incapacitation?

6. *Indefinite detention.* The *Hamdi* plurality holds that Hamdi may only be detained "for the duration of the relevant conflict," in this case the war in Afghanistan. What about a citizen, like Padilla, who is accused of being an al Qaeda operative? The War on Terror has no definite endpoint. If the purpose for detention is incapacitation, does this mean that someone like Padilla could, in theory, be held for the rest of his life? Given that the purpose of attacking Afghanistan was to eliminate al Qaeda, why can't the government insist that Hamdi is part of the War on Terror as well?

7. *The unitary executive and judicial review.* Justice Thomas's dissent assumes that "Congress . . . has a substantial and essential role in both foreign affairs and national security. But it is crucial to recognize that *judicial* interference in

these domains destroys the purpose of vesting primary responsibility in a unitary Executive" (emphasis in original). Thomas argues that the courts lack the necessary expertise to determine whether citizens like Hamdi are enemy combatants. If so, then is the President's decision that a citizen is an enemy combatant effectively unreviewable? Does Thomas's logic apply equally to citizens apprehended in the United States? Would Thomas's position permit indefinite detention of citizens for purposes of interrogation, without rights to a hearing or a right to counsel?

8. *Guantanamo Bay and the detention of non-citizens.* Following the September 11, 2001 attacks, the United States arrested persons from many different countries suspected of fighting on behalf of the Taliban in Afghanistan, working for al Qaeda, or working for various other terrorist organizations. Many of these persons were detained at the U.S. Naval Base in Guantanamo Bay, Cuba. The United States occupies Guantanamo Bay under a lease and treaty recognizing Cuba's ultimate sovereignty, but which gives the United States complete jurisdiction and control for so long as it does not abandon the leased areas. Other detainees, including those believed to be top members of al Qaeda, have been placed in secret locations around the world operated by the CIA. The Administration's acknowledged purpose for placing detainees at Guantanamo Bay and in other undisclosed locations was to avoid falling under the supervision of American courts. The detainees have been interrogated but most have not been charged with any crime.

Over the years the Bush and Obama Administrations sought to release detainees to their home countries. As of June 2013, approximately 166 detainees still remain in Guantanamo. A 2010 report by an Obama Administration task force of lawyers, military officers, and intelligence agents identified 48 Guantanamo prisoners as too dangerous to release. (Two of these have since died in prison, making the number of indefinite detainees 46.) The task force report said these prisoners "could not be tried, either because there was no evidence linking them to specific attacks or because evidence against them was tainted by coercion or abuse." Jane Sutton, "Guantanamo Indefinite Detainees List Released by Obama Administration," Reuters (Huffington Post), June 17, 2013, at http://www.huffingtonpost.com/2013/06/17/guantanamo-indefinite-detainees-list_n_3456256.html.

In Rasul v. Bush, 542 U.S. 466 (2004), the Supreme Court, in a 5-4 decision written by Justice Stevens, held that the Guantanamo detainees had the right to bring habeas petitions to challenge the legality of their detention. *Rasul* was premised on an interpretation of the scope of the federal habeas statute. In response, Congress passed sections 1005(e) and (h) of the Detainee Treatment Act of 2005 (also known as the Graham-Levin amendment), which withdrew habeas jurisdiction for petitions filed by aliens detained "by the Department of Defense at Guantanamo Bay, Cuba" and "any other action against the United States or its agents relating to any aspect of the detention" of aliens there. In Hamdan v. Rumsfeld, discussed infra, the Supreme Court evaded these jurisdictional limitations by holding that they did not apply retroactively to cases already on appeal.

3.   Military Tribunals

On November 13, 2001, President Bush issued an executive order authorizing the creation of military tribunals to try persons suspected of terrorist activities arising out of the September 11 attacks on the United States. Detention, Treatment, and Trial of Certain Non-Citizens in the War Against Terrorism, 66 Fed. Reg. 57,833 (Nov. 13, 2001). A person was subject to detention and to trial by a military tribunal if the President determined that there was reason to believe that the individual is or was a member of the al Qaeda terrorist organization, "has engaged in, aided or abetted, or conspired to commit, acts of international terrorism, or acts in preparation therefore, that have caused, threaten to cause, or have as their aim to cause, injury to or adverse effects on the United States, its citizens, national security, foreign policy, or economy," or has harbored such a person. The order provided for conviction and sentencing upon a two-thirds vote of the members of the commission present at the time of voting. (Subsequent Department of Defense regulations issued in March 2002 made clear that a unanimous verdict would be required for a death sentence but not for noncapital offenses.) Review of the decision rested solely in the President or in military officials that he or the Secretary of Defense designated. The Order stated that defendants "shall not be privileged to seek any remedy or maintain any proceeding, directly or indirectly, or to have any such remedy or proceeding sought on the individual's behalf, in (i) any court of the United States, or any State thereof, (ii) any court of any foreign nation, or (iii) any international tribunal."

Traditional rules of criminal procedure and evidence that apply in ordinary criminal courts were relaxed and evidence that would ordinarily be excluded from a criminal trial (or a military court-martial) could be admitted as long as it would "have probative value to a reasonable person." There was no requirement of grand jury presentment or indictment. Finally, the military tribunals could be held in secret. The presiding officer could exclude the accused and defense counsel from parts of the proceedings and the accused did not have the right to examine all of the evidence against him.

In Hamdan v. Rumsfeld, 548 U.S. 557 (2006), the Supreme Court held 5-3 that the system of military commissions was illegal, and violated the Uniform Code of Military Justice (UCMJ) and the Geneva Conventions. Justice Stevens's majority opinion analyzed the legality of the commissions in terms of Congressional authorization. It was unnecessary to decide whether the President could create military commissions without Congressional approval, because Congress had approved the creation of military commissions in Article 21 of the UCMJ. Given Congress's previous action in passing the UCMJ, the Court would treat Congress's authorization as the basis of the President's power. In a footnote, Justice Stevens explained: "Whether or not the President has independent power, absent congressional authorization, to convene military commissions, he may not disregard limitations that Congress has, in proper exercise of its own war powers, placed on his powers. See Youngstown Sheet & Tube Co. v. Sawyer, 343 U.S. 579, 637 (1952) (Jackson, J., concurring). The Government does not argue otherwise."

Justice Stevens argued that "there is nothing in the text or legislative history of the AUMF even hinting that Congress intended to expand or alter the authorization set forth in Article 21 of the UCMJ. . . . Together, the UCMJ, the AUMF, and the [2005 Detainee Treatment Act] at most acknowledge a general Presidential authority to convene military commissions in circumstances where justified under the 'Constitution and laws,' including the law of war." For this reason, Justice Stevens, concluded, the military commission convened to try Hamdan was illegal because its procedures differed from—and were less protective than—those authorized under the UCMJ and Common Article 3 of the Geneva Conventions.

"Article 36 [of the UCMJ] places two restrictions on the President's power to promulgate rules of procedure for courts-martial and military commissions alike. First, no procedural rule he adopts may be 'contrary to or inconsistent with' the UCMJ—however practical it may seem. Second, the rules adopted must be 'uniform insofar as practicable.' That is, the rules applied to military commissions must be the same as those applied to courts-martial unless such uniformity proves impracticable." Justice Stevens argued that "[n]othing in the record before us demonstrates that it would be impracticable to apply court-martial rules in this case. [T]he only reason offered in support of that determination is the danger posed by international terrorism. Without for one moment underestimating that danger, it is not evident to us why it should require, in the case of Hamdan's trial, any variance from the rules that govern courts-martial."

"Common Article 3 [of the Geneva Conventions] . . . requires that Hamdan be tried by a 'regularly constituted court affording all the judicial guarantees which are recognized as indispensable by civilized peoples.' . . . [and] [t]he regular military courts in our system are the courts-martial established by congressional statutes."

Justice Alito, joined by Justice Scalia and Justice Thomas (in part), dissented. Chief Justice Roberts, who had participated on the D.C. Circuit panel below before he was confirmed to the Supreme Court, did not participate.

Hamdan is another example of how judicial construction of Congressional authorization shapes the constitutional powers of the President; although the decision is nominally statutory, it has strongly constitutional overtones. *Hamdan* required a new congressional authorization (as interpreted by the Court) in order to create a new set of military commissions that differed from the requirements of the UCMJ and the Geneva Conventions (as the Court interpreted them). It did not prevent special military commissions for Guantanamo detainees, but by striking down the existing commissions it required Congress to publicly state (1) that it no longer wanted to abide by the principle of uniformity announced in the

UCMJ, (2) that it no longer would require that military commissions abide by the laws of war as the Court had interpreted them, or, (3) that Congress no longer considered the Geneva Conventions binding on the United States. (The third possibility was politically infeasible.)

In response to *Hamdan*, Congress passed the Military Commissions Act of 2006. The MCA established a new set of military commissions with special rules of evidence and procedure less protective than those in the UMCJ for the purpose of trying "alien unlawful enemy combatants." Responding to the Court's holding that the previous commissions violated the Geneva Conventions, the MCA declared that the new commissions complied with the Geneva Conventions, and prohibited defendants before such commissions from "invok[ing] the Geneva Conventions as a source of rights." It also stated that "no person may invoke the Geneva Conventions as a source of legal rights in habeas corpus or civil actions against the United States, current or former officers, employees, agents, military personnel, in any U.S. or state court." Several of the MCA's evidentiary and procedural provisions were subsequently modified in the Military Commissions Act of 2009.

What constitutional values are served by requiring Congress (and the President) to make such choices publicly? Given the result, was the Court's intervention an exercise in futility? An act of legitimation? What are the costs of courts intervening in this way?

4.   *Habeas Corpus for the Guantanamo Detainees*

As noted above, Congress responded to *Hamdi* with the Detainee Treatment Act of 2005 in order to prevent Guantanamo detainees from raising habeas challenges in the federal courts. The Court was only able to hear *Hamdan* because the majority interpreted the Detainee Treatment Act to permit a limited set of habeas appeals. Section 7 of the Military Commissions Act of 2006 responded to that interpretation, shutting the door the Court had opened. Section 7(a) of the MCA eliminated habeas corpus jurisdiction to hear habeas petitions by aliens that the President had designated as enemy combatants.

Article I, section 9, clause 2, provides that: "The Privilege of the Writ of Habeas Corpus shall not be suspended, unless when in Cases of Rebellion or Invasion the public Safety may require it." The Bush Administration, argued that the Suspension Clause was not violated. Habeas did not extend to the Guantanamo detainees, or, if it did, that the Administration and Congress had provided an effective alternative to habeas.

Following *Hamdi*, the Secretary of Defense set up Combatant Status Review Tribunals to review claims that detainees were being held unlawfully. Under the Detainee Treatment Act of 2005, detainees could appeal these determinations of their status as enemy combatants only to the D.C. Circuit, which was limited to whether the status determination was consistent with the "standards and procedures" set forth by the Secretary of Defense, and whether those standards and procedures were "consistent with the Constitution and laws of the United States." Similarly, the MCA provided that the D.C. Circuit had exclusive jurisdiction to hear appeals from the new military tribunals, limited to "matters of law" and to whether the decision was consistent with "the standards and practices" in the MCA, and, "to the extent applicable, the Constitution and laws of the United States."

In Boumediene v. Bush, 553 U.S. 723 (2008), the Court, in a 5-4 decision, held that the Suspension Clause applied to detainees held at Guantanamo Bay, that Congress had not declared that it was suspending the writ of habeas corpus, and that section 7 of the MCA was an inadequate substitute for habeas corpus and therefore illegal.

Justice Kennedy explained: "[T]he Government says the Suspension Clause affords petitioners no rights because the United States does not claim sovereignty over the place of detention. [We] do not question the Government's position that Cuba, not the United States, maintains sovereignty, in the legal and technical sense of the term, over Guantanamo Bay. [But] it is not altogether uncommon for a territory to be under the de jure sovereignty of one nation, while under the plenary control, or practical sovereignty, of another. . . ."

"The Government's formal sovereignty-based test raises troubling separation-of-powers concerns as well. . . . The United States has maintained complete and uninterrupted control of the bay for over 100 years. . . . Yet the Government's view is that the Constitution [has] had no effect there, at least as to noncitizens, because the United States disclaimed sovereignty in the formal sense of the term. The necessary implication of the argument is that by surrendering formal sovereignty over any unincorporated territory to a third party, while at the same time entering into a lease that grants total control over the territory back to the United States, it would be possible for the political branches to govern without legal constraint."

"Our basic charter cannot be contracted away like this. . . . [T]o hold the political branches have the power to switch the Constitution on or off at will . . . would permit a striking anomaly in our tripartite system of government, leading to a regime in which Congress and the President, not this Court, say 'what the law is.' Marbury v. Madison, 1 Cranch 137 (1803)."

"These concerns have particular bearing upon the Suspension Clause question in the cases now before us, for the writ of habeas corpus is itself an indispensable mechanism for monitoring the separation of powers. The test for determining the scope of this provision must not be subject to manipulation by those whose power it is designed to restrain. . . ."

"We hold that Art. I, §9, cl. 2, of the Constitution has full effect at Guantanamo Bay. If the privilege of habeas corpus is to be denied to the detainees now before us, Congress must act in accordance with the requirements of the Suspension Clause. The MCA does not purport to be a formal suspension of the writ; and the Government, in its submissions to us, has not argued that it is. Petitioners, therefore, are entitled to the privilege of habeas corpus to challenge the legality of their detention. . . ."

"Petitioners identify what they see as myriad deficiencies in the CSRTs. The most relevant for our purposes are the constraints upon the detainee's ability to rebut the factual basis for the Government's assertion that he is an enemy combatant. [T]he detainee has limited means to find or present evidence to challenge the Government's case against him. He does not have the assistance of counsel and may not be aware of the most critical allegations that the Government relied upon to order his detention. See App. to Pet. for Cert. in No. 06-1196, at 156, F(8) (noting that the detainee can access only the 'unclassified portion of the Government Information.'). The detainee can confront witnesses that testify during the CSRT proceedings. But given that there are in effect no limits on the admission of hearsay evidence — the only requirement is that the tribunal deem the evidence 'relevant and helpful,' — the detainee's opportunity to question witnesses is likely to be more theoretical than real. . . ."

"[A]lthough we make no judgment as to whether the CSRTs, as currently constituted, satisfy due process standards, we agree with petitioners that, even when all the parties involved in this process act with diligence and in good faith, there is considerable risk of error in the tribunal's findings of fact. . . . And given that the consequence of error may be detention of persons for the duration of hostilities that may last a generation or more, this is a risk too significant to ignore."

"For the writ of habeas corpus, or its substitute, to function as an effective and proper remedy in this context, the court that conducts the habeas proceeding must have the means to correct errors that occurred during the CSRT proceedings. This includes some authority to assess the sufficiency of the Government's evidence against the detainee. It also must have the authority to admit and consider relevant exculpatory evidence that was not introduced during the earlier proceeding. . . ."

Chief Justice Roberts dissented, joined by Justices Scalia, Thomas, and Alito: "This statutory scheme provides the combatants held at Guantanamo greater procedural protections than have ever been afforded alleged enemy detainees — whether citizens or aliens — in our national history. So who has won? Not the detainees. The Court's analysis leaves them with only the prospect of further litigation to determine the content of their new habeas right, followed by further litigation to resolve their particular cases, followed by further litigation before the D.C. Circuit — where they could have started had they invoked the DTA procedure."

Justice Scalia also wrote a dissenting opinion, joined by Chief Justice Roberts, Justice Thomas, and Justice Alito: "Today, for the first time in our Nation's history, the Court confers a constitutional right to habeas corpus on alien enemies detained abroad by our military forces in the course of an ongoing war. . . . The game of bait-and-switch that today's opinion plays upon the Nation's Commander in Chief will make the war harder on us. It will almost certainly cause more Americans to be killed."

Discussion

1. *A tug of war. Boumediene* is the third in a series of cases (along with *Rasul v. Bush* and *Hamdan*) involving the Court's jurisdiction to hear appeals from the Guantanamo detainees, restricting what the President could do and inviting the President and Congress to respond if they liked. Congress and the President have done so repeatedly. In response to *Rasul*, Congress passed the Detainee Treatment Act of 2005 to keep the federal courts from hearing habeas petitions from Guantanamo detainees. In response, in *Hamdan* the Court construed the DTA to allow it to hear habeas petitions in the cases before it and then held that the President's military commissions were illegal. Then, in response to *Hamdan*, the President and Congress passed the Military Commissions Act of 2006, reinstating the commissions. Section 7 of the MCA once again sought to eliminate habeas and federal question jurisdiction for the Guantanamo detainees. In *Boumediene*, the Court struck down section 7, making clear that the Suspension Clause applies to detainees held at Guantanamo Bay. In theory, the President and Congress could respond once again by officially suspending the writ of habeas corpus, but it is very unlikely that they will so do.

In one sense, the sequence of cases from *Hamdi v. Rumsfeld* to *Rasul* to *Hamdan* to *Boumediene* is remarkable: They are among a very small number of decisions in which the Supreme Court rejects a claim made by the President in wartime, *Youngstown* being the most obvious example.

In *Youngstown*, the Court believed that Congress had not gone along with the President's decision to seize the steel mills. Hence, it treated the case as falling into "box three" of Justice Jackson's theory, where the President's power was at its lowest ebb. Similarly, in *Hamdi* and *Hamdan*, the Court construed Congress as giving its authority (under the AUMF and the UCMJ) for some presidential actions but not for others. And in *Rasul* and *Hamdan*, it artfully read jurisdictional provisions to give it permission to hear the cases before it.

In *Boumediene*, by contrast, the President and Congress explicitly agreed to strip jurisdiction in habeas cases. Why then isn't this a case in "box one" of *Youngstown* where the full war powers of the national government are being asserted, and why didn't the Court defer?

One answer might be the political situation in the country: an unpopular war in Iraq coupled with continuing reports of torture and abuse at Guantanamo Bay, Abu Ghraib, Bagram, and the CIA "black sites." *Youngstown* was decided in 1952 when President Truman was weakened by the Korean War and had lost much of his popularity. Given President Bush's record-setting levels of unpopularity, and the fact that the Democrats took control of Congress following the 2006 elections (after the passage of the Military Commissions Act), the Court risked very little by refusing to defer to the President. Is it particularly inappropriate for courts to intervene in matters of war when presidents are politically weakened; or on the contrary, is it only when presidents are weakened politically that courts feel able to insist that presidents abide by constitutional guarantees?

A second possible reason why the Court intervened in *Boumediene* is that the majority no longer believed that the separation of powers between Congress and the White House acted as a realistic check on the President, especially when one party controlled the political branches. As Justice Jackson explained in *Youngstown*: "[The] rise of the party system has made a significant extraconstitutional supplement to real executive power. No appraisal of his necessities is realistic which overlooks that he heads a political system as well as a legal system. Party loyalties and interests, sometimes more binding than law, extend his effective control into branches of government other than his own and he often may win, as a political leader, what he cannot command under the Constitution." In this context, note that members of Congress might have been unwilling to cross a President of their own party but perfectly happy to let the courts take the political heat. Senator Arlen Specter, head of the Senate Judiciary Committee, denounced the Military Commissions Act for unconstitutionally suspending habeas corpus but voted for it anyway, presumably hoping that the courts would strike it down. See Charles Babington and Jonathan Weisman, "Senate Approves Detainee Bill Backed by Bush: Constitutional Challenges Predicted," Washington Post, September 29, 2006 at A01, available at http://www.washingtonpost.com/wp-dyn/content/article/2006/09/28/AR2006092800824.html (quoting Specter as supporting the bill because "the court will clean it up"). Does this mean that courts *should* be less deferential to national security laws passed under periods of one-party rule?

A third possible explanation of *Boumediene* was that the MCA was not simply a dispute about the relative powers of Congress vis-à-vis the President, but involved an attempt to strip the Court of its own jurisdiction. Hence the Court was far more likely to be protective of its own turf and far more willing to push back at the President. This, however, begs the question of what the Court's power should have been. According to Justice Scalia and the dissenters, the Court had no authority to hear the cases in the first place, so it lost nothing by the passage of section 7.

2. *You've come a long way, baby.* Justice Kennedy, without a trace of irony, cites to *Marbury v. Madison* as a justification for the Court's jurisdiction to hear these cases and subject the actions of the political branches to the rule of law. In *Marbury*, the Supreme Court went out of its way to hold that it did not have jurisdiction to hear Marbury's case in order to avoid provoking a confrontation with a Republican President and Congress. (And in *Stuart v. Laird*, decided a week later, the Court meekly refused to stand up to the Republicans' elimination of circuit judgeships despite the Constitution's guarantee of life tenure.) Clearly, the Court feels it is more powerful today than it was in Jefferson's time. Is it fair to say that *Boumediene* could only have occurred in a world after *Cooper v. Aaron* and *Bush v. Gore*?

3. *Could Congress respond by suspending the writ?* In theory, at least, Congress and the President could respond by repassing section 7 of the MCA with a clear statement that they intended to suspend the writ of habeas corpus under Article I, section 9. However, as noted above, it is very unlikely that the current Congress would do this.

Suspensions under the habeas corpus clause are permitted only if the United States is currently in a state of rebellion or invasion, and the public safety requires suspension. Is this test satisfied under current conditions? Note that section 7 of the MCA is permanent legislation that is not limited to a temporary state of emergency — it has no sunset provision, and it applies to detainees captured and held anywhere in the world.

One argument for the constitutionality of a suspension would be that the judgment whether these tests have been satisfied and a state of emergency exists rests solely with Congress and is a political question that cannot be reviewed by the courts. So if Congress declares that the United States is under an emergency of indefinite or even permanent duration, the Court should defer to its decision. Does this prove too much?

Note: After Boumediene

Following its decisions in *Hamdi*, *Hamdan*, and *Boumediene*, the Supreme Court has largely delegated the task of developing the law of executive detention to the District of Columbia Circuit Court of Appeals. In a series of decisions following *Boumediene*, the D.C. Circuit has interpreted the Supreme Court's decisions mostly in favor of executive power and against the claims of detainees.

1. *The reach of* Boumediene. In Maqaleh v. Gates, 605 F.3d 84 (D.C. Cir. 2010), the D.C. Circuit held that *Boumediene*'s reading of the Suspension Clause was premised on the special conditions at Guantanamo Bay, Cuba: "The United States has maintained its total control of Guantanamo Bay for over a century, even in the face of a hostile government maintaining *de jure* sovereignty over the property." In addition, there were relatively few practical obstacles to allowing habeas proceedings there. These considerations did not apply to non-citizens detained in the Afghan theater of war at Bagram Air Field. The United States operates Bagram through a lease with the Afghan government and it does not enjoy *de facto* sovereignty there. In addition, practical obstacles existed at Bagram because it was in a theater of war, and "all of the attributes of a facility exposed to the vagaries of war are present." Therefore, the court held, "the jurisdiction of the courts to afford the right to habeas relief and the protection of the Suspension Clause does not extend to aliens held in Executive detention in the Bagram detention facility in the Afghan theater of war."

2. *The power to detain.* In *Hamdi*, the Supreme Court used the laws of war to limit the scope of the President's power to detain enemy combatants. In Al-Bihani v. Obama, 590 F.3d 866 (D.C. Cir. 2010), cert. denied, 131 S. Ct. 1814 (2011), however, Judge Janice Rodgers Brown's opinion argued that reference to the laws of war was not constitutionally required: "[W]hile the international laws of war are helpful to courts when identifying the general set of war powers to which the AUMF speaks, their lack of controlling legal force and firm definition render their use both inapposite and inadvisable when courts seek to determine the limits of the President's war powers." *Id.* at 871. Looking instead to

the Military Commissions Act of 2006, Judge Brown held that the President may detain persons "who are part of forces associated with Al Qaeda or the Taliban or those who purposefully and materially support such forces in hostilities against U.S. Coalition partners." Read most expansively, this formula would allow the President to detain indefinitely anyone that he believed had violated the material support provisions of federal criminal law, a very broad category that might include people who gave charitable contributions or legal advice to an organization associated with al Qaeda or the Taliban. See Holder v. Humanitarian Law Project, 130 S. Ct. 2705 (2010). Indeed, the position taken by the panel was much broader than the Obama Administration had asked for. The D.C. Circuit ultimately denied rehearing en banc on the grounds that "the panel's discussion of [the role of international law in interpreting the President's powers under the AUMF] is not necessary to the disposition of the merits." Al-Bihani v. Obama, 619 F.3d 1 (D.C. Cir. 2010) (mem.).

3. *The burden of proof and procedural protections in habeas proceedings.* In *Al-Bihani*, the D.C. Circuit also held that a preponderance of the evidence standard, while not constitutionally required, is appropriate in habeas cases challenging executive detention, and that hearsay evidence is generally admissible. 590 F.3d at 877-879. Later decisions confirmed these rules and held that district courts should not "weigh each piece of evidence in isolation, but consider all of the evidence taken as a whole." Awad v. Obama, 608 F.3d 1, 6-7 (D.C. Cir. 2010), cert. denied, 131 S. Ct. 1814 (2011). See also Al-Adahi v. Obama, 613 F.3d 1102, 1105 (D.C. Cir. 2010), cert. denied, 131 S. Ct. 1001 (2011) (accepting preponderance of the evidence standard *arguendo*, but expressing doubts that a preponderance of the evidence is constitutionally required to justify detention and implicitly criticizing the government for failing to argue for a lesser standard).

Concurring in Esmail v. Obama, 639 F.3d 1075 (D.C. Cir. 2011), Judge Silberman reflected on "the unusual incentives and disincentives that bear on judges on the D.C. Circuit courts — particularly the Court of Appeals — charged with deciding these detainee habeas cases." He criticized the Supreme Court and argued that his colleagues should always err on the side of denying habeas petitions brought by Guantanamo inmates:

> In the typical criminal case, a good judge will vote to overturn a conviction if the prosecutor lacked sufficient evidence, even when the judge is virtually certain that the defendant committed the crime. That can mean that a thoroughly bad person is released onto our streets, but I need not explain why our criminal justice system treats that risk as one we all believe, or should believe, is justified.
>
> When we are dealing with detainees, candor obliges me to admit that one can not help but be conscious of the infinitely greater downside risk to our country, and its people, of an order releasing a detainee who is likely to return to terrorism. . . . That means that there are powerful reasons for the government to rely on our opinion in *Al-Adahi v. Obama*, 613 F.3d 1102 (D.C. Cir. 2010), which persuasively explains that in a habeas corpus proceeding the preponderance of evidence standard that the government assumes binds it, is unnecessary — and moreover, unrealistic. *Id.*

at 1104-05. I doubt any of my colleagues will vote to grant a petition if he or she believes that it is somewhat likely that the petitioner is an al Qaeda adherent or an active supporter. Unless, of course, the Supreme Court were to adopt the preponderance of the evidence standard (which it is unlikely to do—taking a case might obligate it to assume direct responsibility for the consequences of *Boumediene v. Bush*). But I, like my colleagues, certainly would release a petitioner against whom the government could not muster even "some evidence."

Of course, if it turns out that regardless of our decisions the executive branch does not release winning petitioners because no other country will accept them and they will not be released into the United States, see *Kiyemba v. Obama*, 605 F.3d 1046, 1048 (D.C. Cir. 2010); *Kiyemba v. Obama*, 561 F.3d 509, 516 (D.C. Cir. 2009), then the whole process leads to virtual advisory opinions. It becomes a charade prompted by the Supreme Court's defiant—if only theoretical—assertion of judicial supremacy, see *Boumediene*, sustained by posturing on the part of the Justice Department, and providing litigation exercise for the detainee bar.

Note that in *Hamdi* the Supreme Court rejected the view that the executive could detain merely on the basis of "some evidence" when it was offered by the Bush Administration. See 542 U.S. at 537 (plurality opinion).

Discussion

1. What do you make of Judge Silberman's remarkably candid opinion? Given that the D.C. Circuit has been given the responsibility for developing the law of executive detention, do its members have good reason to read the Supreme Court's decisions as narrowly as possible in favor of the executive and, in some cases, even beyond what the executive itself asks for?

2. On one reading, the cases from *Hamdi* through *Boumediene* have defended rule of law values against an overreaching executive in a time of national emergency, although they have not necessarily done very much in the way of protecting civil liberties. On another reading, these cases have been an unwarranted and meddlesome interference with the President's attempt to secure the safety of the nation in a rapidly changing political and military context. And on still another reading, these cases have neither been a victory for the rule of law or a significant interference with the President's ability to innovate. Rather, the effect of these cases has been to legitimate the construction of a new system of preventative detention outside the criminal process in which persons suspected of terrorism or material assistance to terrorism can be maintained indefinitely with little chance that federal courts will ever release them. Which reading strikes you as most plausible?

5. Targeted Killings

In his dissent in *Hamdi*, Justice Thomas noted that instead of detaining a person on the battlefield, the President could simply order an unmanned drone to execute them. In fact, the Obama Administration has increasingly employed drone attacks to target persons it believes are al Qaeda operatives, including American citizens. Does the Constitution limit the President's ability to order such attacks?

In answering this question, first consider the question of presidential power under *Youngstown* and *Hamdi*. Does the AUMF authorize targeted killings according to its terms, or impliedly because such attacks are consistent with the laws of war? Next, consider whether targeted killings are consistent with the Bill of Rights. *Hamdi* interprets the Fifth Amendment to require due process when citizens suspected of being terrorists are detained. What does due process mean in the context of targeted killings using drones?

Consider the case of Anwar al-Awlaki, an American citizen born in New Mexico, who was placed on the Obama Administration's secret "kill list" and was eventually killed by a drone operated by the CIA in Yemen in September 2011. American officials speaking without attribution argued that a drone attack on al-Awlaki was appropriate because he was an influential cleric who became a leader of Al-Qaeda in the Arabian Peninsula, and he was suspected of instructing Umar Farouk Abdulmutallab, the so-called Underwear Bomber, to blow up a plane flying over Detroit in 2009, as well as inspiring other homegrown American terrorists.[12] al-Awlaki, however, was never changed with a crime, and these allegations were never proved in court. Another drone strike in October 2011 killed a group of people including al-Awlaki's 16-year old son, Abdulrahman al-Awlaki, who was born in Colorado.

Because the drone program had been run by the CIA, the Obama Administration did not officially acknowledge the existence of the program, or the authorization of strikes against American citizens, despite the fact that the events were widely reported in the press. However, on May 23, 2013, President Obama acknowledged the program in a speech before the National Defense University in Washington, D.C.

The same day, the Administration produced a memo explaining its policies on the use of lethal force against persons it believes to be terrorists or in league with terrorist organizations:[13]

> The policy of the United States is not to use lethal force when it is feasible to capture a terrorist suspect. . . . Lethal force will not be proposed or pursued as punishment or as a substitute for prosecuting a terrorist suspect in a civilian court or a military commission. Lethal force will be used only to prevent or stop attacks against U.S. persons, and even then, only when capture is not feasible and no other reasonable alternatives exist to address the threat effectively. In particular, lethal

---

12. Carrie Johnson, *Holder Spells Out Why Drones Target U.S. Citizens*, *NPR*, March 6, 2012, at http://www.npr.org/2012/03/06/148000630/holder-gives-rationale-for-drone-strikes-on-citizens.

13. U.S. Policy Standards and Procedures for the Use of Force in Counterterrorism Operations Outside the United States and Areas of Active Hostilities, May 23, 2013) at http://www.whitehouse.gov/sites/default/files/uploads/2013.05.23_fact_sheet_on_ppg.pdf.

force will be used outside areas of active hostilities only when the following pre-conditions are met:

First, there must be a legal basis for using lethal force, whether it is against a senior operational leader of a terrorist organization or the forces that organization is using or intends to use to conduct terrorist attacks.

Second, the United States will use lethal force only against a target that poses a continuing, imminent threat to U.S. persons. It is simply not the case that all terrorists pose a continuing, imminent threat to U.S. persons; if a terrorist does not pose such a threat, the United States will not use lethal force.

Third, the following criteria must be met before lethal action may be taken:

1) Near certainty that the terrorist target is present;
2) Near certainty that non-combatants will not be injured or killed;
3) An assessment that capture is not feasible at the time of the operation;
4) An assessment that the relevant governmental authorities in the country where action is contemplated cannot or will not effectively address the threat to U.S. persons; and
5) An assessment that no other reasonable alternatives exist to effectively address the threat to U.S. persons.

Finally, whenever the United States uses force in foreign territories, international legal principles, including respect for sovereignty and the law of armed conflict, impose important constraints on the ability of the United States to act unilaterally — and on the way in which the United States can use force. The United States respects national sovereignty and international law.

Central to the Obama Administration's argument is that there must be "a continuing, imminent threat to U.S. persons." However, a DOJ White Paper leaked to the press in February 2013 suggested that the Administration defines "imminence" in a special way:

[T]he condition that an operational leader present an "imminent" threat of violent attack against the United States does not require the United States to have clear evidence that a specific attack on U.S. persons and interests will take place in the immediate future. . . . The threat posed by al-Qa'ida and its associated forces demands a broader concept of imminence in judging when a person continually planning terror attacks presents an imminent threat. . . . [I]mminence must incorporate considerations of the relevant window of opportunity, the possibility of reducing collateral damage to civilians, and the likelihood of heading off future disastrous attacks on Americans. . . . [A] high level official could conclude, for example, that an individual poses an "imminent threat" of violent attack against the United States where he is an operational leader of al-Qa'ida or an associated force and is personally and continually involved in planning terrorist attacks against the United States. Moreover, where the al-Qa'ida member in question has recently been involved in activities posing an imminent threat of violent attack against the United States, and there is no evidence that he has renounced or abandoned such activities, that member's involvement in al-Qa'ida's continuing terrorist campaign against the United States would support the conclusion that the member poses an imminent threat.

Department of Justice White Paper, "Lawfulness of Lethal Operation Directed Against a U.S. Citizen Who is a Senior Operational Leader of Al-Qaida or An Associated Force," pp. 7-8, at http://msnbcmedia.msn.com/i/msnbc/sections/news/020413_DOJ_White_Paper.pdf. In a May 23, 2013 letter from Attorney General Holder to Senate Judiciary Chairman Senator Patrick Leahy, the Attorney General explained that Anwar al-Awlaki posed an imminent threat because of his past plots against the United States and because "information that remains classified to protect sensitive sources and methods evidences al-Aulaqi's involvement in the planning of numerous other plots against U.S. and Western interests and makes clear he was continuing to plot attacks when he was killed."[14]

When the concept of imminence is understood in this way, do you believe that the Administration's criteria are consistent with the Fifth Amendment's Due Process Clause? Should the President be required to seek permission from a court akin to a warrant before the President may order a targeted killing? Such proceedings would likely have to be held ex parte and in secret. Is this the sort of activity that is appropriate for judicial oversight?

Another model of analysis argues that a judicial hearing is not necessary because the correct analogy is to the police shooting a fleeing criminal suspect whom the police reasonably believe poses a danger to others. No hearings are involved in such cases; the police officer simply acts based on his or her best judgment in order to protect the public safety. This analogy views the Fifth Amendment as irrelevant, and instead looks to the Fourth Amendment, which protects the security of the person against unreasonable searches and seizures. (The shooting is a "seizure" of the suspect's person.)

In Tennessee v. Garner, 471 U.S. 1 (1985), the Court considered the constitutional limits on the use of deadly force against a suspect fleeing from the police. The Court conceptualized the question as whether there was a "seizure" of a person under the Fourth Amendment, and if so, whether the seizure was reasonable under the circumstances. The Court held that "[t]he use of deadly force to prevent the escape of all felony suspects, whatever the circumstances, is constitutionally unreasonable. It is not better that all felony suspects die than that they escape. Where the suspect poses no immediate threat to the officer and no threat to others, the harm resulting from failing to apprehend him does not justify the use of deadly force to do so. . . . [But] [w]here the officer has probable cause to believe that the suspect poses a threat of serious physical harm, either to the officer or to others, it is not constitutionally unreasonable to prevent escape by using deadly force." How would you apply *Garner* to targeted killings? What role does imminent harm play in the determination?

---

14. See also Letter from Attorney General Holder to Senator Patrick Leahy, May 22, 2013, at p. 3, at http://www.justice.gov/slideshow/AG-letter-5-22-13.pdf.

Chapter 6

The Burdens of History: The Constitutional Treatment of Race

Insert the following after discussion note 2 on p. 950:

PARENTS INVOLVED IN COMMUNITY SCHOOLS v. SEATTLE
SCHOOL DISTRICT NO. 1
551 U.S. 701 (2007)

Chief Justice ROBERTS announced the judgment of the Court, and delivered the opinion of the Court with respect to Parts I, II, III-A, and III-C, and an opinion with respect to Parts III-B and IV, in which Justices SCALIA, THOMAS, and ALITO join.

[The Seattle School District No. 1 and Jefferson County Public Schools in Louisville voluntarily adopted plans to promote racial diversity. Seattle has never been subject to court-ordered desegregation for operating segregated schools, but adopted its plan to correct for the effects of racially identifiable housing patterns on school assignments.

Seattle allocated slots in oversubscribed high schools by using tiebreakers. The first selects for students who have a sibling enrolled at the chosen school. The second selects for students whose race will help balance the oversubscribed school. Approximately 41 percent of enrolled students in the district's public schools are white; 59 percent are nonwhite. If an oversubscribed school is not within 10 percentage points of the district's overall white/nonwhite racial balance, the tiebreaker selects for the student who would bring the school closer into balance. The third tiebreaker selects for students who are closest in geographic proximity to the oversubscribed school.

The Louisville school district had been subject to a court-ordered desegregation decree since 1975. It was dissolved in 2000 when the district was declared unitary, having eliminated "[t]o the greatest extent practicable" the vestiges of its prior policy of segregation.

In 2001, after the decree was dissolved, Jefferson County adopted its voluntary student assignment plan. Schools that are not magnet schools must maintain a minimum black enrollment of 15 percent, and a maximum black enrollment of 50 percent. Approximately 34 percent of the district's 97,000 students are black; most of the remaining 66 percent are white.

Parents of kindergartners, first-graders, and students new to the district may select first and second choices among schools within their geographical area for initial assignment. Students are assigned based on available space, but once a school has reached less than 15 percent or more than 50 percent black, it will take only students who will keep the racial balance within these guidelines. Students initially assigned may also transfer to other schools in the district, subject to availability of space and the same requirements of racial balance. Petitioner Crystal Meredith, who sought to transfer her son Joshua for kindergarten from a school ten miles away to one a mile away was refused because she was told it would adversely impact the racial balance of the school to which he had been assigned.]

. . .

III.

A

It is well established that when the government distributes burdens or benefits on the basis of individual racial classifications, that action is reviewed under strict scrutiny. In order to satisfy this searching standard of review, the school districts must demonstrate that the use of individual racial classifications in the assignment plans here under review is "narrowly tailored" to achieve a "compelling" government interest.

[O]ur prior cases, in evaluating the use of racial classifications in the school context, have recognized two interests that qualify as compelling. The first is the compelling interest of remedying the effects of past intentional discrimination. Yet the Seattle public schools have not shown that they were ever segregated by law, and were not subject to court-ordered desegregation decrees. The Jefferson County public schools were previously segregated by law [but] [i]n 2000, the District Court that entered that decree dissolved it, finding that Jefferson County had "eliminated the vestiges associated with the former policy of segregation and its pernicious effects," and thus had achieved "unitary" status. . . . We have emphasized that the harm being remedied by mandatory desegregation plans is the harm that is traceable to segregation, and that "the Constitution is not violated by racial imbalance in the schools, without more." *Milliken v. Bradley.* Once Jefferson County achieved unitary status, it had remedied the constitutional wrong that allowed race-based assignments. Any continued use of race must be justified on some other basis.[a]

---

a. The districts point to dicta in a prior opinion in which the Court suggested that, while not constitutionally mandated, it would be constitutionally permissible for a school district to seek racially balanced schools as a matter of "educational policy." See Swann v. Charlotte-Mecklenburg Bd. of Ed., 402 U.S. 1, 16 (1971). . . . *Swann*, evaluating a school district engaged in court-ordered desegregation, had no occasion to consider whether a district's voluntary adoption of race-based assignments in the absence of a finding of prior *de jure* segregation was constitutionally permissible, an issue that was again expressly reserved in Washington v. Seattle School Dist. No. 1, 458 U.S. 457, 472, n.15 (1982). . . .

The second government interest we have recognized as compelling for purposes of strict scrutiny is the interest in diversity in higher education upheld in *Grutter* [v. Bollinger, 539 U.S. 306, 326 (2003)]. . . . The diversity interest was not focused on race alone but encompassed "all factors that may contribute to student body diversity." [including] "admittees who have lived or traveled widely abroad, are fluent in several languages, have overcome personal adversity and family hardship, have exceptional records of extensive community service, and have had successful careers in other fields." [*Grutter* quoted] Justice Powell's opinion in Regents of the University of California v. Bakke, 438 U.S. 265 (1978), noting that "it is not an interest in simple ethnic diversity, in which a specified percentage of the student body is in effect guaranteed to be members of selected ethnic groups, that can justify the use of race." Instead, what was upheld in *Grutter* was consideration of "a far broader array of qualifications and characteristics of which racial or ethnic origin is but a single though important element." . . . [T]he admissions program at issue [in *Grutter*] focused on each applicant as an individual, and not simply as a member of a particular racial group. The classification of applicants by race upheld in *Grutter* was only as part of a "highly individualized, holistic review." As the Court explained, "[t]he importance of this individualized consideration in the context of a race-conscious admissions program is paramount." The point of the narrow tailoring analysis in which the *Grutter* Court engaged was to ensure that the use of racial classifications was indeed part of a broader assessment of diversity, and not simply an effort to achieve racial balance, which the Court explained would be "patently unconstitutional."

In the present cases, by contrast, race is not considered as part of a broader effort to achieve "exposure to widely diverse people, cultures, ideas, and viewpoints"; race, for some students, is determinative standing alone. The districts argue that other factors, such as student preferences, affect assignment decisions under their plans, but under each plan when race comes into play, it is decisive by itself. It is not simply one factor weighed with others in reaching a decision, as in *Grutter*; it is *the* factor. Like the University of Michigan undergraduate plan struck down in *Gratz* [v. Bollinger], the plans here "do not provide for a meaningful individualized review of applicants" but instead rely on racial classifications in a "nonindividualized, mechanical" way.

Even when it comes to race, the plans here employ only a limited notion of diversity, viewing race exclusively in white/nonwhite terms in Seattle and black/"other" terms in Jefferson County.[b] The Seattle "Board Statement Reaffirming Diversity Rationale" speaks of the "inherent educational value" in "[p]roviding

---

b. The way Seattle classifies its students bears this out. Upon enrolling their child with the district, parents are required to identify their child as a member of a particular racial group. If a parent identifies more than one race on the form, "[t]he application will not be accepted and, if necessary, the enrollment service person taking the application will indicate one box."

students the opportunity to attend schools with diverse student enrollment." But under the Seattle plan, a school with 50 percent Asian-American students and 50 percent white students but no African-American, Native American, or Latino students would qualify as balanced, while a school with 30 percent Asian-American, 25 percent African-American, 25 percent Latino, and 20 percent white students would not. It is hard to understand how a plan that could allow these results can be viewed as being concerned with achieving enrollment that is " 'broadly diverse,' " *Grutter*.

. . . In upholding the admissions plan in *Grutter*, [moreover] . . . this Court relied upon considerations unique to institutions of higher education, noting that in light of "the expansive freedoms of speech and thought associated with the university environment, universities occupy a special niche in our constitutional tradition." . . . The present cases are not governed by *Grutter*.

B

Perhaps recognizing that reliance on *Grutter* cannot sustain their plans, both school districts assert additional interests. . . . Seattle contends that its use of race helps to reduce racial concentration in schools and to ensure that racially concentrated housing patterns do not prevent nonwhite students from having access to the most desirable schools. Jefferson County has articulated a similar goal, phrasing its interest in terms of educating its students "in a racially integrated environment." Each school district argues that educational and broader socialization benefits flow from a racially diverse learning environment, and each contends that because the diversity they seek is racial diversity — not the broader diversity at issue in *Grutter* — it makes sense to promote that interest directly by relying on race alone.

The parties and their *amici* dispute whether racial diversity in schools in fact has a marked impact on test scores and other objective yardsticks or achieves intangible socialization benefits. The debate is not one we need to resolve, however, because it is clear that the racial classifications employed by the districts are not narrowly tailored to the goal of achieving the educational and social benefits asserted to flow from racial diversity. In design and operation, the plans are directed only to racial balance, pure and simple, an objective this Court has repeatedly condemned as illegitimate.

The plans are tied to each district's specific racial demographics, rather than to any pedagogic concept of the level of diversity needed to obtain the asserted educational benefits. In Seattle, the district seeks white enrollment of between 31 and 51 percent (within 10 percent of "the district white average" of 41 percent), and nonwhite enrollment of between 49 and 69 percent (within 10 percent of "the district minority average" of 59 percent). In Jefferson County, by contrast, the district seeks black enrollment of no less than 15 or more than 50 percent, a range designed to be "equally above and below Black student enrollment systemwide," based on the objective of achieving at "all schools . . . an African-American enrollment equivalent to the average district wide African-American enrollment" of 34 percent. In Seattle, then, the benefits of racial diversity require enrollment of at least 31 percent white students; in Jefferson County, at least 50 percent. There must be at least 15 percent nonwhite students under Jefferson County's plan; in Seattle, more than three times that figure. This comparison makes clear that the racial demographics in each district—whatever they happen to be—drive the required "diversity" numbers. The plans here are not tailored to achieving a degree of diversity necessary to realize the asserted educational benefits; instead the plans are tailored, in the words of Seattle's Manager of Enrollment Planning, Technical Support, and Demographics, to "the goal established by the school board of attaining a level of diversity within the schools that approximates the district's overall demographics."

The districts offer no evidence that the level of racial diversity necessary to achieve the asserted educational benefits happens to coincide with the racial demographics of the respective school districts—or rather the white/nonwhite or black/ "other" balance of the districts, since that is the only diversity addressed by the plans. . . .

Jefferson County's expert referred to the importance of having "at least 20 percent" minority group representation for the group "to be visible enough to make a difference," and noted that "small isolated minority groups in a school are not likely to have a strong effect on the overall school." The Jefferson County plan, however, is based on a goal of replicating at each school "an African-American enrollment equivalent to the average district-wide African American enrollment." Joshua McDonald's requested transfer was denied because his race was listed as "other" rather than black, and allowing the transfer would have had an adverse effect on the racial guideline compliance of Young Elementary, the school he sought to leave. At the time, however, Young Elementary was 46.8 percent black. The transfer might have had an adverse effect on the effort to approach district-wide racial proportionality at Young, but it had nothing to do with preventing either the black or "other" group from becoming "small" or "isolated" at Young.

. . .

In *Grutter*, the number of minority students the school sought to admit was an undefined "meaningful number" necessary to achieve a genuinely diverse student body. [T]he majority concluded that the law school did not count back from its applicant pool to arrive at the "meaningful number" it regarded as necessary to diversify its student body. Here the racial balance the districts seek is a defined range set solely by reference to the demographics of the respective school districts.

This working backward to achieve a particular type of racial balance, rather than working forward from some demonstration of the level of diversity that provides the purported benefits, is a fatal flaw under our existing precedent. We have many times over reaffirmed that "[r]acial balance is not to be achieved for its own sake." *Grutter* itself reiterated that "outright racial balancing" is "patently unconstitutional."

Accepting racial balancing as a compelling state interest would justify the imposition of racial proportionality throughout American society, contrary to our repeated recognition that "[a]t the heart of the Constitution's guarantee of equal protection lies the simple command that the Government must treat citizens as individuals, not as simply components of a racial, religious, sexual or national class." Miller v. Johnson, 515 U.S. 900, 911 (1995). Allowing racial balancing as a compelling end in itself would "effectively assur[e] that race will always be relevant in American life, and that the 'ultimate goal' of 'eliminating entirely from governmental decisionmaking such irrelevant factors as a human being's race' will never be achieved." Croson. An interest "linked to nothing other than proportional representation of various races . . . would support indefinite use of racial classifications, employed first to obtain the appropriate mixture of racial views and then to ensure that the [program] continues to reflect that mixture."

The validity of our concern that racial balancing has "no logical stopping point," Croson, is demonstrated here by the degree to which the districts tie their racial guidelines to their demographics. As the districts' demographics shift, so too will their definition of racial diversity.

[I]n Seattle the plans are defended as necessary to address the consequences of racially identifiable housing patterns. The sweep of the mandate claimed by the district is contrary to our rulings that remedying past societal discrimination does not justify race-conscious government action. See, e.g., Shaw v. Hunt, 517 U.S. 899, 909-910 (1996) ("[A]n effort to alleviate the effects of societal discrimination is not a compelling interest"); Croson.

The principle that racial balancing is not permitted is one of substance, not semantics. Racial balancing is not transformed from "patently unconstitutional" to a compelling state interest simply by relabeling it "racial diversity." While the school districts use various verbal formulations to describe the interest they seek to promote—racial diversity, avoidance of racial isolation, racial integration—they offer no definition of the interest that suggests it differs from racial balance.

Jefferson County phrases its interest as "racial integration," but integration certainly does not require the sort of racial proportionality reflected in its plan. Even in the context of mandatory desegregation, we have stressed that racial proportionality is not required, see Milliken, 433 U.S., at 280, n.14 ("[A desegregation] order contemplating the substantive constitutional right [to a] particular degree of racial balance or mixing is . . . infirm as a matter of law" (internal quotation marks omitted)); Swann v. Charlotte-Mecklenburg Bd. of Ed., 402 U.S. 1, 24 (1971) ("The constitutional command to desegregate schools does not mean that every school in every community must always reflect the racial composition of the school system as a whole"), and here Jefferson County has already been found to have eliminated the vestiges of its prior segregated school system.

The en banc Ninth Circuit declared that "when a racially diverse school system is the goal (or racial concentration or isolation is the problem), there is no more effective means than a consideration of race to achieve the solution."

For the foregoing reasons, this conclusory argument cannot sustain the plans. However closely related race-based assignments may be to achieving racial balance, that itself cannot be the goal, whether labeled "racial diversity" or anything else. To the extent the objective is sufficient diversity so that students see fellow students as individuals rather than solely as members of a racial group, using means that treat students solely as members of a racial group is fundamentally at cross-purposes with that end.

C

The districts assert, as they must, that the way in which they have employed individual racial classifications is necessary to achieve their stated ends. The minimal effect these classifications have on student assignments, however, suggests that other means would be effective. Seattle's racial tiebreaker results, in the end, only in shifting a small number of students between schools. . . . Similarly, Jefferson County's use of racial classifications has only a minimal effect on the assignment of students. . . . While we do not suggest that *greater* use of race would be preferable, the minimal impact of the districts' racial classifications on school enrollment casts doubt on the necessity of using racial classifications. . . .

The districts have also failed to show that they considered methods other than explicit racial classifications to achieve their stated goals. Narrow tailoring requires "serious, good faith consideration of workable race-neutral alternatives," *Grutter*, and yet in Seattle several alternative assignment plans — many of which would not have used express racial classifications — were rejected with little or no consideration. Jefferson County has failed to present any evidence that it considered alternatives, even though the district already claims that its goals are achieved primarily through means other than the racial classifications.

IV.

. . . Justice Breyer seeks to justify the plans at issue under our precedents recognizing the compelling interest in remedying past intentional discrimination. . . . The distinction between segregation by state action and racial imbalance caused by other factors has been central to our jurisprudence in this area for generations. The dissent elides this distinction between *de jure* and *de facto* segregation, casually intimates that Seattle's school attendance patterns reflect illegal segregation, and fails to credit the judicial determination — under the most rigorous standard — that Jefferson County had eliminated the vestiges of prior segregation. The dissent thus alters in fundamental ways not only the facts presented here but the established law. . . . The present cases are before us, however, because the Seattle school district was never segregated by law, and the Jefferson County district has been found to be unitary, having eliminated the vestiges of its prior dual status. . . . The dissent's persistent refusal to accept this distinction — its insistence on viewing the racial classifications here as . . . "devised to overcome a history of segregated public schools," explains its inability to understand why the remedial justification for racial classifications cannot decide these cases.

Justice Breyer's dissent next relies heavily on dicta from Swann v. Charlotte Mecklenburg Bd. of Ed. [W]hen *Swann* was decided, this Court had not yet confirmed that strict scrutiny applies to racial classifications like those before us. [Moreover,] *Swann* addresses only a possible state objective; it says nothing of the permissible *means*—race conscious or otherwise—that a school district might employ to achieve that objective. The reason for this omission is clear enough, since the case did not involve any voluntary means adopted by a school district. The dissent's characterization of *Swann* as recognizing that "the Equal Protection Clause permits local school boards to use race-conscious criteria to achieve positive race-related goals" is—at best—a dubious inference. . . .

Justice Breyer's dissent also . . . overreads *Grutter* . . . in suggesting that it renders pure racial balancing a constitutionally compelling interest; *Grutter* itself recognized that using race simply to achieve racial balance would be "patently unconstitutional." . . . We simply do not understand how Justice Breyer can maintain that classifying every schoolchild as black or white, and using that classification as a determinative factor in assigning children to achieve pure racial balance, can be regarded as "less burdensome, and hence more narrowly tailored" than the consideration of race in *Grutter*, when the Court in *Grutter* stated that "[t]he importance of . . . individualized consideration" in the program was "paramount," and consideration of race was one factor in a "highly individualized, holistic review." . . .

. . . Justice Breyer's dissent candidly dismisses the significance of this Court's repeated *holdings* that all racial classifications must be reviewed under strict scrutiny, arguing that a different standard of review should be applied because the districts use race for beneficent rather than malicious purposes. . . . Justice Breyer . . . relies on the good intentions and motives of the school districts, stating that he has found "no case that . . . repudiated this constitutional asymmetry between that which seeks to *exclude* and that which seeks to *include* members of minority races." We have found many. Our cases clearly reject the argument that motives affect the strict scrutiny analysis. See *Johnson* [v. California]; *Adarand*; *Croson.*

This argument that different rules should govern racial classifications designed to include rather than exclude is not new; it has been repeatedly pressed in the past, and has been repeatedly rejected.

. . .

Justice Breyer also suggests that other means for achieving greater racial diversity in schools are necessarily unconstitutional if the racial classifications at issue in these cases cannot survive strict scrutiny. These other means—e.g., where to construct new schools, how to allocate resources among schools, and which academic offerings to provide to attract students to certain schools— implicate different considerations than the explicit racial classifications at issue in these cases, and we express no opinion on their validity—not even in dicta. Rather, we employ the familiar and well-established analytic approach of strict scrutiny to evaluate the plans at issue today, an approach that in no way warrants the dissent's cataclysmic concerns. Under that approach, the school districts have not carried their burden of showing that the ends they seek justify the particular extreme means they have chosen—classifying individual students on the basis of their race and discriminating among them on that basis.

. . .

If the need for the racial classifications embraced by the school districts is unclear, even on the districts' own terms, the costs are undeniable. "[D]istinctions between citizens solely because of their ancestry are by their very nature odious to a free people whose institutions are founded upon the doctrine of equality." *Adarand.* Government action dividing us by race is inherently suspect because such classifications promote "notions of racial inferiority and lead to a politics of racial hostility," *Croson,* "reinforce the belief, held by too many for too much of our history, that individuals should be judged by the color of their skin," Shaw v. Reno, 509 U.S. 630, 657 (1993), and "endorse race-based reasoning and the conception of a Nation divided into racial blocs, thus contributing to an escalation of racial hostility and conflict." As the Court explained in Rice v. Cayetano, 528 U.S. 495, 517 (2000), "[o]ne of the principal reasons race is treated as a forbidden classification is that it demeans the dignity and worth of a person to be judged by ancestry instead of by his or her own merit and essential qualities."

All this is true enough in the contexts in which these statements were made—government contracting, voting districts, allocation of broadcast licenses, and electing state officers—but when it comes to using race to assign children to schools, history will be heard. In Brown v. Board of Education, 347 U.S. 483 (1954) (*Brown I*), we held that segregation deprived black children of equal educational opportunities regardless of whether school facilities and other tangible factors were equal, because government classification and separation on grounds of race themselves denoted inferiority. It was not the inequality of the facilities but the fact of legally separating children on the basis of race on which the Court relied to find a constitutional violation in 1954. See *id.,* at 494 (" 'The impact [of segregation] is greater when it has the sanction of the law' "). The next Term, we accordingly stated that "full compliance" with *Brown I* required school districts "to achieve a system of determining admission to the public schools *on a nonracial basis.*" *Brown II* (emphasis added).

The parties and their *amici* debate which side is more faithful to the heritage of *Brown,* but the position of the plaintiffs in *Brown* was spelled out in their brief and could not have been clearer: "[T]he Fourteenth Amendment prevents states from according differential treatment to American children on the basis of their color or race." What do the racial classifications at issue here do, if not accord differential treatment on the basis of race? As counsel who appeared before this Court for the plaintiffs in *Brown* put it: "We have one fundamental contention which we will seek to develop in the course of this argument, and that contention is that no State has any authority under the equal-protection clause of the Fourteenth Amendment to use race as a factor in affording educational opportunities among its citizens." There is no ambiguity in that statement. And it was that position that prevailed in this Court, which emphasized in its remedial opinion that what was "[a]t stake is the personal interest of the plaintiffs in admission to public schools as soon as practicable *on a nondiscriminatory basis*," and what was required was "determining admission to the public schools *on a nonracial basis*." *Brown II* (emphasis added). What do the racial classifications do in these cases, if not determine admission to a public school on a racial basis? Before *Brown*, schoolchildren were told where they could and could not go to school based on the color of their skin. The school districts in these cases have not carried the heavy burden of demonstrating that we should allow this once again — even for very different reasons. For schools that never segregated on the basis of race, such as Seattle, or that have removed the vestiges of past segregation, such as Jefferson County, the way "to achieve a system of determining admission to the public schools on a nonracial basis," *Brown II*, is to stop assigning students on a racial basis. The way to stop discrimination on the basis of race is to stop discriminating on the basis of race. . . .

Justice THOMAS, concurring.

Today, the Court holds that state entities may not experiment with race-based means to achieve ends they deem socially desirable. I wholly concur in The Chief Justice's opinion. I write separately to address several of the contentions in Justice Breyer's dissent. . . . Contrary to the dissent's arguments, resegregation is not occurring in Seattle or Louisville; these school boards have no present interest in remedying past segregation; and these race-based student assignment programs do not serve any compelling state interest. Accordingly, the plans are unconstitutional. Disfavoring a color-blind interpretation of the Constitution, the dissent would give school boards a free hand to make decisions on the basis of race-an approach reminiscent of that advocated by the segregationists in *Brown v. Board of Education*. This approach is just as wrong today as it was a half-century ago. The Constitution and our cases require us to be much more demanding before permitting local school boards to make decisions based on race.

I.

[R]acial imbalance is not segregation, and the mere incantation of terms like resegregation and remediation cannot make up the difference. [I]n the context of public schooling, segregation is the deliberate operation of a school system to "carry out a governmental policy to separate pupils in schools solely on the basis of race." *Swann*. . . . Racial imbalance is the failure of a school district's individual schools to match or approximate the demographic makeup of the student population at large. Racial imbalance is not segregation.[a] Although presently observed racial imbalance might result from past *de jure* segregation, racial imbalance can also result from any number of innocent private decisions, including voluntary housing choices. Because racial imbalance is not inevitably linked to unconstitutional segregation, it is not unconstitutional in and of itself.

Although there is arguably a danger of racial imbalance in schools in Seattle and Louisville, there is no danger of resegregation. No one contends that Seattle has established or that Louisville has reestablished a dual school system that separates students on the basis of race. The statistics cited [by Justice Breyer] are not to the contrary. At most, those statistics show a national trend toward classroom racial imbalance. However, racial imbalance without intentional state action to separate the races does not amount to segregation. To raise the specter of resegregation to defend these programs is to ignore the meaning of the word and the nature of the cases before us.[b]

Just as the school districts lack an interest in preventing resegregation, they also have no present interest in remedying past segregation. The Constitution generally prohibits government race-based decisionmaking, but this Court has authorized the use of race-based measures for remedial purposes in two narrowly defined circumstances. First, in schools that were formerly segregated by law, race-based measures are sometimes constitutionally compelled to remedy prior school segregation. Second, in *Croson*, the Court appeared willing to authorize a government unit to remedy past discrimination for which it was responsible. [T]hese plans do not fall within either existing category of permissible race-based remediation.

The Constitution does not permit race-based government decisionmaking simply because a school district claims a remedial purpose and proceeds in good faith with arguably pure motives. Rather, race-based government decisionmaking is categorically prohibited unless narrowly tailored to serve a compelling interest. This exacting scrutiny "has proven automatically fatal" in most cases. And appropriately so. "The Constitution abhors classifications based on race,

---

a. The dissent refers repeatedly and reverently to "'integration.'" However, outside of the context of remediation for past *de jure* segregation, "integration" is simply racial balancing. Therefore, the school districts' attempts to further "integrate" are properly thought of as little more than attempts to achieve a particular racial balance.

b. The dissent's assertion that these plans are necessary for the school districts to maintain their "hard-won gains" reveals its conflation of segregation and racial imbalance. For the dissent's purposes, the relevant hard-won gains are the present racial compositions in the individual schools in Seattle and Louisville. However, the actual hard-won gain in these cases is the elimination of the vestiges of the system of state-enforced racial separation that once existed in Louisville. To equate the achievement of a certain statistical mix in several schools with the elimination of the system of systematic *de jure* segregation trivializes the latter accomplishment. Nothing but an interest in classroom aesthetics and a hypersensitivity to elite sensibilities justifies the school districts' racial balancing programs. But "the principle of inherent equality that underlies and infuses our Constitution" required the disestablishment of *de jure* segregation. Assessed in any objective manner, there is no comparison between the two.

not only because those classifications can harm favored races or are based on illegitimate motives, but also because every time the government places citizens on racial registers and makes race relevant to the provision of burdens or benefits, it demeans us all." Therefore, as a general rule, all race based government decisionmaking—regardless of context—is unconstitutional.

This Court has carved out a narrow exception to that general rule for cases in which a school district has a "history of maintaining two sets of schools in a single school system deliberately operated to carry out a governmental policy to separate pupils in schools solely on the basis of race." In such cases, race-based remedial measures are sometimes required.[c] But without a history of state enforced racial separation, a school district has no affirmative legal obligation to take race-based remedial measures to eliminate segregation and its vestiges.

Neither of the programs before us today is compelled as a remedial measure, and no one makes such a claim. Seattle has no history of *de jure* segregation; therefore, the Constitution did not require Seattle's plan. Although Louisville once operated a segregated school system and was subject to a Federal District Court's desegregation decree, that decree was dissolved in 2000. Since then, no race-based remedial measures have been required in Louisville. Thus, the race based student-assignment plan at issue here, which was instituted the year after the dissolution of the desegregation decree, was not even arguably required by the Constitution.

Aside from constitutionally compelled remediation in schools, this Court has permitted government units to remedy prior racial discrimination only in narrow circumstances. [N]either school board asserts that its race-based actions were taken to remedy prior discrimination. Seattle provides three forward-looking—as opposed to remedial—justifications for its race-based assignment plan. Louisville asserts several similar forward-looking interests, and at oral argument, counsel for Louisville disavowed any claim that Louisville's argument "depend[ed] in any way on the prior de jure segregation,"

Furthermore, for a government unit to remedy past discrimination for which it was responsible, the Court has required it to demonstrate "a 'strong basis in evidence for its conclusion that remedial action was necessary.'" *Croson*. Establishing a "strong basis in evidence" requires proper findings regarding the extent of the government unit's past racial discrimination. The findings should "define the scope of any injury [and] the necessary remedy," and must be more than "inherently unmeasurable claims of past wrongs." Assertions of general

---

c. [T]he remedies this Court authorized lower courts to compel in early desegregation cases like *Green* and *Swann* were exceptional. Sustained resistance to *Brown* prompted the Court to authorize extraordinary race-conscious remedial measures (like compelled racial mixing) to turn the Constitution's dictate to desegregate into reality. Even if these measures were appropriate as remedies in the face of widespread resistance to *Brown*'s mandate, they are not forever insulated from constitutional scrutiny. Rather, "such powers should have been temporary and used only to overcome the widespread resistance to the dictates of the Constitution."

societal discrimination are plainly insufficient. Neither school district has made any such specific findings. For Seattle, the dissent attempts to make up for this failing by adverting to allegations made in past complaints filed against the Seattle school district. However, allegations in complaints cannot substitute for specific findings of prior discrimination—even when those allegations lead to settlements with complaining parties. As for Louisville, its slate was cleared by the District Court's 2000 dissolution decree, which effectively declared that there were no longer any effects of *de jure* discrimination in need of remediation.[d] . . .

[T]he dissent conflates the concepts of segregation and racial imbalance. [F]or at least two reasons, however, it is wrong to place the remediation of segregation on the same plane as the remediation of racial imbalance. First, as demonstrated above, the two concepts are distinct. Although racial imbalance can result from *de jure* segregation, it does not necessarily, and the further we get from the era of state-sponsored racial separation, the less likely it is that racial imbalance has a traceable connection to any prior segregation.

Second, a school cannot "remedy" racial imbalance in the same way that it can remedy segregation. Remediation of past *de jure* segregation is a one-time process involving the redress of a discrete legal injury inflicted by an identified entity. At some point, the discrete injury will be remedied, and the school district will be declared unitary. Unlike *de jure* segregation, there is no ultimate remedy for racial imbalance. Individual schools will fall in and out of balance in the natural course, and the appropriate balance itself will shift with a school district's changing demographics. Thus, racial balancing will have to take place on an indefinite basis—a continuous process with no identifiable culpable party and no discernable end point. In part for those reasons, the Court has never permitted outright racial balancing solely for the purpose of achieving a particular racial balance.

II.

Lacking a cognizable interest in remediation, neither of these plans can survive strict scrutiny because neither plan serves a genuinely compelling state interest. The dissent avoids reaching that conclusion by unquestioningly accepting the assertions of selected social scientists while completely ignoring the fact that those assertions are the subject of fervent debate. Ultimately, the dissent's

---

d. Contrary to the dissent's argument, the Louisville school district's interest in remedying its past *de jure* segregation did vanish the day the District Court found that Louisville had eliminated the vestiges of its historic *de jure* segregation. If there were further remediation to be done, the District Court could not logically have reached the conclusion that Louisville "ha[d] eliminated the vestiges associated with the former policy of segregation and its pernicious effects." Because Louisville could use race-based measures only as a remedy for past *de jure* segregation, it is not "incoherent," to say that race-based decisionmaking was allowed to Louisville one day—while it was still remedying—and forbidden to it the next—when remediation was finished. That seemingly odd turnaround is merely a result of the fact that the remediation of *de jure* segregation is a jealously guarded exception to the Equal Protection Clause's general rule against government race-based decisionmaking.

entire analysis is corrupted by the considerations that lead it initially to question whether strict scrutiny should apply at all. What emerges is a version of "strict scrutiny" that combines hollow assurances of harmlessness with reflexive acceptance of conventional wisdom. When it comes to government race-based decisionmaking, the Constitution demands more.

A

[W]e have made it unusually clear that strict scrutiny applies to *every* racial classification. *Adarand*; *Grutter*; Johnson v. California. There are good reasons not to apply a lesser standard to these cases. The constitutional problems with government race-based decisionmaking are not diminished in the slightest by the presence or absence of an intent to oppress any race or by the real or asserted well-meaning motives for the race-based decisionmaking. *Adarand*. Purportedly benign race-based decisionmaking suffers the same constitutional infirmity as invidious race-based decisionmaking. *Id.,* at 240 (Thomas, J., concurring in part and concurring in judgment) ("As far as the Constitution is concerned, it is irrelevant whether a government's racial classifications are drawn by those who wish to oppress a race or by those who have a sincere desire to help those thought to be disadvantaged").

Even supposing it mattered to the constitutional analysis, the race-based student assignment programs before us are not as benign as the dissent believes. As these programs demonstrate, every time the government uses racial criteria to "bring the races together," someone gets excluded, and the person excluded suffers an injury solely because of his or her race. The petitioner in the Louisville case received a letter from the school board informing her that her *kindergartener* would not be allowed to attend the school of petitioner's choosing because of the child's race. Doubtless, hundreds of letters like this went out from both school boards every year these race-based assignment plans were in operation. This type of exclusion, solely on the basis of race, is precisely the sort of government action that pits the races against one another, exacerbates racial tension, and "provoke[s] resentment among those who believe that they have been wronged by the government's use of race." . . .

B

[A]ccording to the dissent, integration involves "an interest in setting right the consequences of prior conditions of segregation." For the reasons explained above, the records in these cases do not demonstrate that either school board's plan is supported by an interest in remedying past discrimination.

Moreover, the school boards have no interest in remedying the sundry consequences of prior segregation unrelated to schooling, such as "housing patterns, employment practices, economic conditions, and social attitudes." General claims that past school segregation affected such varied societal trends are "too amorphous a basis for imposing a racially classified remedy," because "[i]t is sheer speculation" how decades-past segregation in the school system might have affected these trends. Consequently, school boards seeking to remedy those societal problems with race-based measures in schools today would have no way to gauge the proper scope of the remedy. Indeed, remedial measures geared toward such broad and unrelated societal ills have " 'no logical stopping point,' " and threaten to become "ageless in their reach into the past, and timeless in their ability to affect the future," *Wygant*. . . .

Next, the dissent argues that the interest in integration has an educational element. The dissent asserts that racially balanced schools improve educational outcomes for black children. In support, the dissent unquestioningly cites certain social science research to support propositions that are hotly disputed among social scientists. In reality, it is far from apparent that coerced racial mixing has any educational benefits, much less that integration is necessary to black achievement.

Scholars have differing opinions as to whether educational benefits arise from racial balancing. Some have concluded that black students receive genuine educational benefits. Others have been more circumspect. And some have concluded that there are no demonstrable educational benefits. The *amicus* briefs in the cases before us mirror this divergence of opinion.

[A]dd to the inconclusive social science the fact of black achievement in "racially isolated" environments. . . . Even after *Brown*, some schools with predominantly black enrollments have achieved outstanding educational results. There is also evidence that black students attending historically black colleges achieve better academic results than those attending predominantly white colleges.

The Seattle school board itself must believe that racial mixing is not necessary to black achievement. Seattle operates a K-8 "African-American Academy," which has a "nonwhite" enrollment of 99%. That school was founded in 1990 as part of the school board's effort to "increase academic achievement." According to the school's most recent annual report, "[a]cademic excellence" is its "primary goal." This racially imbalanced environment has reportedly produced test scores "higher across all grade levels in reading, writing and math." Contrary to what the dissent would have predicted, the children in Seattle's African-American Academy have shown gains when placed in a "highly segregated" environment.

Given this tenuous relationship between forced racial mixing and improved educational results for black children, the dissent cannot plausibly maintain that an educational element supports the integration interest, let alone makes it compelling. See *Jenkins*, 515 U.S., at 121-122 (Thomas, J., concurring) ("[T]here is no reason to think that black students cannot learn as well when surrounded by members of their own race as when they are in an integrated environment").

Perhaps recognizing as much, the dissent argues that the social science evidence is "strong enough to permit a democratically elected school board reasonably to determine that this interest is a compelling one." This assertion is inexplicable. It is not up to the school boards—the very government entities whose race-based practices we must strictly scrutinize—to determine what interests qualify as compelling under the Fourteenth Amendment to the United States Constitution. Rather, this Court must assess independently the nature of the interest asserted and the evidence to support it in order to determine whether it qualifies as compelling under our precedents. In making such a determination, we have deferred to state authorities only once, see *Grutter*, and that deference was prompted by factors uniquely relevant to higher education. The dissent's proposed test—whether sufficient social science evidence supports a government unit's conclusion that the interest it asserts is compelling—calls to mind the rational-basis standard of review the dissent purports not to apply. Furthermore, it would leave our equal-protection jurisprudence at the mercy of elected government officials evaluating the evanescent views of a handful of social scientists. To adopt the dissent's deferential approach would be to abdicate our constitutional responsibilities.[e]

Finally, the dissent asserts a "democratic element" to the integration interest. It defines the "democratic element" as "an interest in producing an educational environment that reflects the 'pluralistic society' in which our children will live." Environmental reflection, though, is just another way to say racial balancing. And "[p]referring members of any one group for no reason other than race or ethnic origin is discrimination for its own sake." *Bakke* (opinion of Powell, J.). . . .

[T]he dissent argues that the racial balancing in these plans is not an end in itself but is instead intended to "teac[h] children to engage in the kind of cooperation among Americans of all races that is necessary to make a land of three hundred million people one Nation." These "generic lessons in socialization and good citizenship" are too sweeping to qualify as compelling interests. And they are not "uniquely relevant" to schools or "uniquely 'teachable' in a formal educational setting." Therefore, if governments may constitutionally use racial balancing to achieve these aspirational ends in schools, they may use racial balancing to achieve similar goals at every level—from state-sponsored 4-H clubs, to the state civil service.

---

e. The dissent accuses me of "feel[ing] confident that, to end invidious discrimination, one must end *all* governmental use of race-conscious criteria" and chastises me for not deferring to democratically elected majorities. Regardless of what Justice Breyer's goals might be, this Court does not sit to "create a society that includes all Americans" or to solve the problems of "troubled inner-city schooling." We are not social engineers. The United States Constitution dictates that local governments cannot make decisions on the basis of race. Consequently, regardless of the perceived negative effects of racial imbalance, I will not defer to legislative majorities where the Constitution forbids it.

It should escape no one that behind Justice Breyer's veil of judicial modesty hides an inflated role for the Federal Judiciary. The dissent's approach confers on judges the power to say what sorts of discrimination are benign and which are invidious. Having made that determination (based on no objective measure that I can detect), a judge following the dissent's approach will set the level of scrutiny to achieve the desired result. Only then must the judge defer to a democratic majority. In my view, to defer to one's preferred result is not to defer at all.

Moreover, the democratic interest has no durational limit, contrary to *Grutter*'s command. In other words, it will always be important for students to learn cooperation among the races. If this interest justifies race-conscious measures today, then logically it will justify race-conscious measures forever. Thus, the democratic interest, limitless in scope and "timeless in [its] ability to affect the future," cannot justify government race-based decisionmaking.

[T]he dissent points to data that indicate that "black and white students in desegregated schools are less racially prejudiced than those in segregated schools." By the dissent's account, improvements in racial attitudes depend upon the increased contact between black and white students thought to occur in more racially balanced schools. There is no guarantee, however, that students of different races in the same school will actually spend time with one another. Schools frequently group students by academic ability as an aid to efficient instruction, but such groupings often result in classrooms with high concentrations of one race or another. In addition to classroom separation, students of different races within the same school may separate themselves socially. Therefore, even supposing interracial contact leads directly to improvements in racial attitudes and race relations, a program that assigns students of different races to the same schools might not capture those benefits. Simply putting students together under the same roof does not necessarily mean that the students will learn together or even interact.

Furthermore, it is unclear whether increased interracial contact improves racial attitudes and relations. One researcher has stated that "the reviews of desegregation and intergroup relations were unable to come to any conclusion about what the probable effects of desegregation were . . . [;] virtually all of the reviewers determined that few, if any, firm conclusions about the impact of desegregation on intergroup relations could be drawn." Some studies have even found that a deterioration in racial attitudes seems to result from racial mixing in schools. Therefore, it is not nearly as apparent as the dissent suggests that increased interracial exposure automatically leads to improved racial attitudes or race relations. . . .

[T]he school boards cannot plausibly maintain that their plans further a compelling interest. As I explained in *Grutter*, only "those measures the State must take to provide a bulwark against anarchy . . . or to prevent violence" and "a government's effort to remedy past discrimination for which it is responsible" constitute compelling interests. Neither of the parties has argued—nor could they—that race-based student assignment is necessary to provide a bulwark against anarchy or to prevent violence. And as I explained above, the school districts have no remedial interest in pursuing these programs. Accordingly, the school boards cannot satisfy strict scrutiny. These plans are unconstitutional.

III.

Most of the dissent's criticisms of today's result can be traced to its rejection of the color-blind Constitution. The dissent attempts to marginalize the notion of a color-blind Constitution by consigning it to me and Members of today's plurality.[f] But I am quite comfortable in the company I keep. My view of the Constitution is Justice Harlan's view in *Plessy*: "Our Constitution is color blind, and neither knows nor tolerates classes among citizens." Plessy v. Ferguson (dissenting opinion). And my view was the rallying cry for the lawyers who litigated *Brown*. See, e.g., Brief for Appellants in Brown v. Board of Education, O.T. 1953, Nos. 1, 2, and 4 p. 65 ("That the Constitution is color blind is our dedicated belief"); Brief for Appellants in Brown v. Board of Education, O.T. 1952, No. 1, p. 5 ("The Fourteenth Amendment precludes a state from imposing distinctions or classifications based upon race and color alone").

The dissent appears to pin its interpretation of the Equal Protection Clause to current societal practice and expectations, deference to local officials, likely practical consequences, and reliance on previous statements from this and other courts. Such a view was ascendant in this Court's jurisprudence for several decades. It first appeared in *Plessy*, where the Court asked whether a state law providing for segregated railway cars was "a reasonable regulation." The Court deferred to local authorities in making its determination, noting that in inquiring into reasonableness "there must necessarily be a large discretion on the part of the legislature." The Court likewise paid heed to societal practices, local expectations, and practical consequences by looking to "the established usages, customs and traditions of the people, and with a view to the promotion of their comfort, and the preservation of the public peace and good order." Guided by these principles, the Court concluded: "[W]e cannot say that a law which authorizes or even requires the separation of the two races in public conveyances is unreasonable, or more obnoxious to the Fourteenth Amendment than the acts of Congress requiring separate schools for colored children in the District of Columbia."

The segregationists in *Brown* embraced the arguments the Court endorsed in *Plessy*. Though *Brown* decisively rejected those arguments, today's dissent replicates them to a distressing extent. Thus, the dissent argues that "[e]ach plan embodies the results of local experience and community consultation." Similarly, the segregationists made repeated appeals to societal practice and expectation. The dissent argues that "weight [must be given] to a local school board's knowledge, expertise, and concerns," and with equal vigor, the segregationists argued for deference to local authorities. The dissent argues that today's decision "threatens to substitute for present calm a disruptive round of race-related litigation," and claims that today's decision "risks serious harm to the law and for the Nation." The segregationists also relied upon the likely practical consequences of ending the state-imposed system of racial separation. And

---

f. [I] have no quarrel with the proposition that the Fourteenth Amendment sought to bring former slaves into American society as full members. [But] the color-blind Constitution does not bar the government from taking measures to remedy past state-sponsored discrimination-indeed, it requires that such measures be taken in certain circumstances. Race-based government measures during the 1860's and 1870's to remedy *state-enforced slavery* were therefore not inconsistent with the color-blind Constitution.

foreshadowing today's dissent, the segregationists most heavily relied upon judicial precedent.

The similarities between the dissent's arguments and the segregationists' arguments do not stop there. Like the dissent, the segregationists repeatedly cautioned the Court to consider practicalities and not to embrace too theoretical a view of the Fourteenth Amendment. And just as the dissent argues that the need for these programs will lessen over time, the segregationists claimed that reliance on segregation was lessening and might eventually end.

What was wrong in 1954 cannot be right today.[g] Whatever else the Court's rejection of the segregationists' arguments in *Brown* might have established, it certainly made clear that state and local governments cannot take from the Constitution a right to make decisions on the basis of race by adverse possession. The fact that state and local governments had been discriminating on the basis of race for a long time was irrelevant to the *Brown* Court. The fact that racial discrimination was preferable to the relevant communities was irrelevant to the *Brown* Court. And the fact that the state and local governments had relied on statements in this Court's opinions was irrelevant to the *Brown* Court. The same principles guide today's decision. None of the considerations trumpeted by the dissent is relevant to the constitutionality of the school boards' race based plans because no contextual detail—or collection of contextual details, can "provide refuge from the principle that under our Constitution, the government may not make distinctions on the basis of race."

In place of the color-blind Constitution, the dissent would permit measures to keep the races together and proscribe measures to keep the races apart.[h] Although no such distinction is apparent in the Fourteenth Amendment, the dissent would constitutionalize today's faddish social theories that embrace that distinction. The Constitution is not that malleable. Even if current social theories favor classroom racial engineering as necessary to "solve the problems at hand," the Constitution enshrines principles independent of social theories. See *Plessy*, 163 U.S., at 559 (Harlan, J., dissenting) ("The white race deems itself to be the dominant race in this country. And so it is, in prestige, in achievements, in education, in wealth and in power. So, I doubt not, it will continue to be for all time. . . . But in view of the Constitution, in the eye of the law, there is in this country no

---

g. It is no answer to say that these cases can be distinguished from *Brown* because *Brown* involved invidious racial classifications whereas the racial classifications here are benign. How does one tell when a racial classification is invidious? The segregationists in *Brown* argued that their racial classifications were benign, not invidious. It is the height of arrogance for Members of this Court to assert blindly that their motives are better than others.

h. The dissent does not face the complicated questions attending its proposed standard. For example, where does the dissent's principle stop? Can the government force racial mixing against the will of those being mixed? Can the government force black families to relocate to white neighborhoods in the name if bringing the races together? What about historically black colleges, which have "established traditions and programs that might disproportionately appeal to one race or another"? The dissent does not and cannot answer these questions because the contours of the distinction it propounds rest entirely in the eye of the beholder.

superior, dominant, ruling class of citizens. . . . Our Constitution is color-blind, and neither knows nor tolerates classes among citizens"). Indeed, if our history has taught us anything, it has taught us to beware of elites bearing racial theories.[i] More recently, the school district sent a delegation of high school students to a "White Privilege Conference." See Equity and Race Relations White Privilege Conference, https://www.seattleschools.org/area/equityandrace/white-privilegeconference.xml. One conference participant described "white privilege" as "an invisible package of unearned assets which I can count on cashing in each day, but about which I was meant to remain oblivious. White Privilege is like an invisible weightless knapsack of special provisions, maps, passports, code-books, visas, clothes, tools, and blank checks." See White Privilege Conference, Questions and Answers, http://www. uccs.edu/ wpc/faqs.htm; see generally Westneat, School Districts Obsessed with Race, Seattle Times, Apr. 1, 2007, p. B1 (describing racial issues in Seattle schools). See, e.g., Dred Scott v. Sandford, 19 How. 393, 407 (1857) ("[T]hey [members of the 'negro African race'] had no rights which the white man was bound to respect"). Can we really be sure that the racial theories that motivated *Dred Scott* and *Plessy* are a relic of the past or that future theories will be nothing but beneficent and progressive? That is a gamble I am unwilling to take, and it is one the Constitution does not allow.

Justice KENNEDY, concurring in part and concurring in the judgment.

[I] join Parts III-A and III-C for reasons provided below. My views do not allow me to join the balance of the opinion by The Chief Justice, which seems to me to be inconsistent in both its approach and its implications with the history, meaning, and reach of the Equal Protection Clause. Justice Breyer's dissenting opinion, on the other hand, rests on what in my respectful submission is a misuse and mistaken interpretation of our precedents. This leads it to advance propositions that, in my view, are both erroneous and in fundamental conflict with basic equal protection principles. As a consequence, this separate opinion is necessary to set forth my conclusions in the two cases before the Court.

---

i. Justice Breyer's good intentions, which I do not doubt, have the shelf life of Justice Breyer's tenure. Unlike the dissenters, I am unwilling to delegate my constitutional responsibilities to local school boards and allow them to experiment with race-based decisionmaking on the assumption that their intentions will forever remain as good as Justice Breyer's. See The Federalist No. 51, p. 349 (J. Cooke ed. 1961) ("If men were angels, no government would be necessary"). Indeed, the racial theories endorsed by the Seattle school board should cause the dissenters to question whether local school boards should be entrusted with the power to make decisions on the basis of race. The Seattle school district's Website formerly contained the following definition of "cultural racism": "Those aspects of society that overtly and covertly attribute value and normality to white people and whiteness, and devalue, stereotype, and label people of color as 'other,' different, less than, or render them invisible. Examples of these norms include defining white skin tones as nude or flesh colored, having a future time orientation, emphasizing individualism as opposed to a more collective ideology, defining one form of English as standard. . . ." After the site was removed, the district offered the comforting clarification that the site was not intended "'to hold onto unsuccessful concepts such as melting pot or color-blind mentality.'"

I.

[T]he dissent finds that the school districts have identified a compelling interest in increasing diversity, including for the purpose of avoiding racial isolation. The plurality, by contrast, does not acknowledge that the school districts have identified a compelling interest here. For this reason, among others, I do not join Parts III-B and IV. Diversity, depending on its meaning and definition, is a compelling educational goal a school district may pursue.

[T]he inquiry into less restrictive alternatives demanded by the narrow tailoring analysis requires in many cases a thorough understanding of how a plan works. The government bears the burden of justifying its use of individual racial classifications. As part of that burden it must establish, in detail, how decisions based on an individual student's race are made in a challenged governmental program. The Jefferson County Board of Education fails to meet this threshold mandate. . . . Jefferson County in its briefing has explained how and when it employs these classifications only in terms so broad and imprecise that they cannot withstand strict scrutiny. While it acknowledges that racial classifications are used to make certain assignment decisions, it fails to make clear, for example, who makes the decisions; what if any oversight is employed; the precise circumstances in which an assignment decision will or will not be made on the basis of race; or how it is determined which of two similarly situated children will be subjected to a given race-based decision.

[J]efferson County fails to make clear to this Court—even in the limited respects implicated by Joshua's initial assignment and transfer denial—whether in fact it relies on racial classifications in a manner narrowly tailored to the interest in question, rather than in the far-reaching, inconsistent, and ad hoc manner that a less forgiving reading of the record would suggest. When a court subjects governmental action to strict scrutiny, it cannot construe ambiguities in favor of the State.

As for the Seattle case, the school district has gone further in describing the methods and criteria used to determine assignment decisions on the basis of individual racial classifications. The district, nevertheless, has failed to make an adequate showing in at least one respect. It has failed to explain why, in a district composed of a diversity of races, with fewer than half of the students classified as "white," it has employed the crude racial categories of "white" and "non-white" as the basis for its assignment decisions.

The district has identified its purposes as follows: "(1) to promote the educational benefits of diverse school enrollments; (2) to reduce the potentially harmful effects of racial isolation by allowing students the opportunity to opt out of racially isolated schools; and (3) to make sure that racially segregated housing patterns did not prevent non-white students from having equitable access to the most popular over-subscribed schools." Yet the school district does not explain how, in the context of its diverse student population, a blunt distinction between "white" and "non-white" furthers these goals. As the Court explains, "a school with 50 percent Asian-American students and 50 percent white students but no African-American, Native-American, or Latino students would qualify as balanced, while a school with 30 percent Asian-American, 25 percent African-American, 25 percent Latino, and 20 percent white students would not." Far from being narrowly tailored to its purposes, this system threatens to defeat its own ends, and the school district has provided no convincing explanation for its design. Other problems are evident in Seattle's system, but there is no need to address them now. As the district fails to account for the classification system it has chosen, despite what appears to be its ill fit, Seattle has not shown its plan to be narrowly tailored to achieve its own ends; and thus it fails to pass strict scrutiny.

II.

[P]arts of the opinion by The Chief Justice imply an all-too-unyielding insistence that race cannot be a factor in instances when, in my view, it may be taken into account. The plurality opinion is too dismissive of the legitimate interest government has in ensuring all people have equal opportunity regardless of their race. The plurality's postulate that "[t]he way to stop discrimination on the basis of race is to stop discriminating on the basis of race," is not sufficient to decide these cases. Fifty years of experience since Brown v. Board of Education, should teach us that the problem before us defies so easy a solution. School districts can seek to reach *Brown*'s objective of equal educational opportunity. The plurality opinion is at least open to the interpretation that the Constitution requires school districts to ignore the problem of *de facto* resegregation in schooling. I cannot endorse that conclusion. To the extent the plurality opinion suggests the Constitution mandates that state and local school authorities must accept the status quo of racial isolation in schools, it is, in my view, profoundly mistaken.

The statement by Justice Harlan that "[o]ur Constitution is color-blind" was most certainly justified in the context of his dissent in Plessy v. Ferguson, 163 U.S. 537, 559 (1896). [A]s an aspiration, Justice Harlan's axiom must command our assent. In the real world, it is regrettable to say, it cannot be a universal constitutional principle.

In the administration of public schools by the state and local authorities it is permissible to consider the racial makeup of schools and to adopt general policies to encourage a diverse student body, one aspect of which is its racial composition. If school authorities are concerned that the student-body compositions of certain schools interfere with the objective of offering an equal educational opportunity to all of their students, they are free to devise race conscious measures to address the problem in a general way and without treating each student in different fashion solely on the basis of a systematic, individual typing by race.

School boards may pursue the goal of bringing together students of diverse backgrounds and races through other means, including strategic site selection of new schools; drawing attendance zones with general recognition of the demographics of neighborhoods; allocating resources for special programs; recruiting students and faculty in a targeted fashion; and tracking enrollments, performance, and other statistics by race. These mechanisms are race conscious but do not lead to different treatment based on a classification that tells each student he or she is to be defined by race, so it is unlikely any of them would demand strict scrutiny to be found permissible. Executive and legislative branches, which for generations now have considered these types of policies and procedures, should be permitted to employ them with candor and with confidence that a constitutional violation does not occur whenever a decisionmaker considers the impact a given approach might have on students of different races. Assigning to each student a personal designation according to a crude system of individual racial classifications is quite a different matter; and the legal analysis changes accordingly.

Each respondent has asserted that its assignment of individual students by race is permissible because there is no other way to avoid racial isolation in the school districts. Yet, as explained, each has failed to provide the support necessary for that proposition. And individual racial classifications employed in this manner may be considered legitimate only if they are a last resort to achieve a compelling interest.

In the cases before us it is noteworthy that the number of students whose assignment depends on express racial classifications is limited. I join Part III-C of the Court's opinion because I agree that in the context of these plans, the small number of assignments affected suggests that the schools could have achieved their stated ends through different means. These include the facially race-neutral means set forth above or, if necessary, a more nuanced, individual evaluation of school needs and student characteristics that might include race as a component. The latter approach would be informed by *Grutter*, though of course the criteria relevant to student placement would differ based on the age of the students, the needs of the parents, and the role of the schools.

III.

The dissent rests on the assumptions that these sweeping race-based classifications of persons are permitted by existing precedents; that its confident endorsement of race categories for each child in a large segment of the community presents no danger to individual freedom in other, prospective realms of governmental regulation; and that the racial classifications used here cause no hurt or anger of the type the Constitution prevents. Each of these premises is, in my respectful view, incorrect. [I]n his critique of that analysis, I am in many respects in agreement with The Chief Justice. The conclusions he has set forth in Part III-A of the Court's opinion are correct, in my view, because the compelling interests implicated in the cases before us are distinct from the interests the Court has recognized in remedying the effects of past intentional discrimination and in increasing diversity in higher education. As the Court notes, we recognized the compelling nature of the interest in remedying past intentional discrimination in Freeman v. Pitts, 503 U.S. 467, 494 (1992), and of the interest in diversity in higher education in *Grutter*. At the same time, these compelling interests, in my view, do help inform the present inquiry. And to the extent the plurality opinion can be interpreted to foreclose consideration of these interests, I disagree with that reasoning.

[T]he general conclusions upon which [the dissent] relies have no principled limit and would result in the broad acceptance of governmental racial classifications in areas far afield from schooling. The dissent's permissive strict scrutiny (which bears more than a passing resemblance to rational-basis review) could invite widespread governmental deployment of racial classifications. There is every reason to think that, if the dissent's rationale were accepted, Congress, assuming an otherwise proper exercise of its spending authority or commerce power, could mandate either the Seattle or the Jefferson County plans nation-wide. There seems to be no principled rule, moreover, to limit the dissent's ratio-nale to the context of public schools. The dissent emphasizes local control, the unique history of school desegregation, and the fact that these plans make less use of race than prior plans, but these factors seem more rhetorical than integral to the analytical structure of the opinion.

[T]o say, [as the dissent does], that we must ratify the racial classifications here at issue based on the majority opinions in *Gratz* and *Grutter* is, with all respect, simply baffling.

Gratz involved a system where race was not the entire classification. The procedures in *Gratz* placed much less reliance on race than do the plans at issue here. The issue in *Gratz* arose, moreover, in the context of college admissions where students had other choices and precedent supported the proposition that First Amendment interests give universities particular latitude in defining diver-sity. Even so the race factor was found to be invalid.

[In] *Grutter* . . . the Court sustained a system that, it found, was flexible enough to take into account "all pertinent elements of diversity," and considered race as only one factor among many, *id.*, at 340. Seattle's plan, by contrast, relies upon a mechanical formula that has denied hundreds of students their preferred schools on the basis of three rigid criteria: placement of siblings, distance from schools, and race. If those students were considered for a whole range of their talents and school needs with race as just one consideration, *Grutter* would have some application. That, though, is not the case. . . .

B

To uphold these programs the Court is asked to brush aside two concepts of central importance for determining the validity of laws and decrees designed to alleviate the hurt and adverse consequences resulting from race discrimination. The first is the difference between *de jure* and *de facto* segregation; the second, the presumptive invalidity of a State's use of racial classifications to differentiate its treatment of individuals.

[T]o remedy the wrong [of segregation], school districts that had been segre-gated by law had no choice, whether under court supervision or pursuant to vol-untary desegregation efforts, but to resort to extraordinary measures including individual student and teacher assignment to schools based on race. . . . Our cases recognized a fundamental difference between those school districts that had engaged in *de jure* segregation and those whose segregation was the result of other factors. School districts that had engaged in *de jure* segregation had an affirmative constitutional duty to desegregate; those that were *de facto* segregated did not. The distinctions between *de jure* and *de facto* segregation extended to the remedies available to governmental units in addition to the courts. For example, in Wygant v. Jackson Bd. of Ed., 476 U.S. 267, 274 (1986), the plurality noted: "This Court never has held that societal discrimination alone is sufficient to justify a racial classification. Rather, the Court has insisted upon some showing of prior discrimination by the governmental unit involved before allowing limited use of racial classifications in order to remedy such discrimination." The Court's decision in *Croson* reinforced the difference between the remedies available to redress *de facto* and *de jure* discrimination [by rejecting the] "claim that past societal discrimination alone can serve as the basis for rigid racial preferences." . . .

From the standpoint of the victim, it is true, an injury stemming from racial prejudice can hurt as much when the demeaning treatment based on race identity stems from bias masked deep within the social order as when it is imposed by law. The distinction between government and private action, furthermore, can be amorphous both as a historical matter and as a matter of present-day finding of fact. Laws arise from a culture and vice versa. Neither can assign to the other all responsibility for persisting injustices.

Yet, like so many other legal categories that can overlap in some instances, the constitutional distinction between *de jure* and *de facto* segregation has been thought to be an important one. It must be conceded its primary function in school cases was to delimit the powers of the Judiciary in the fashioning of remedies. See, e.g., *Milliken*. The distinction ought not to be altogether disregarded, however, when we come to that most sensitive of all racial issues, an attempt by the government to treat whole classes of persons differently based on the government's systematic classification of each individual by race. There, too, the distinction serves as a limit on the exercise of a power that reaches to the very verge of constitutional authority. Reduction of an individual to an assigned racial identity for differential treatment is among the most pernicious actions our government can undertake. The allocation of governmental burdens and benefits, contentious under any circumstances, is even more divisive when allocations are made on the basis of individual racial classifications. See, e.g., *Bakke*; *Adarand*.

Notwithstanding these concerns, allocation of benefits and burdens through individual racial classifications was found sometimes permissible in the context of remedies for *de jure* wrong. Where there has been *de jure* segregation, there is a cognizable legal wrong, and the courts and legislatures have broad power to remedy it. The remedy, though, was limited in time and limited to the wrong. The Court has allowed school districts to remedy their prior *de jure* segregation by classifying individual students based on their race. The limitation of this power to instances where there has been *de jure* segregation serves to confine the nature, extent, and duration of governmental reliance on individual racial classifications.

The cases here were argued upon the assumption, and come to us on the premise, that the discrimination in question did not result from *de jure* actions. And when *de facto* discrimination is at issue our tradition has been that the remedial rules are different. The State must seek alternatives to the classification and differential treatment of individuals by race, at least absent some extraordinary showing not present here.

C

[One might object:] If it is legitimate for school authorities to work to avoid racial isolation in their schools, must they do so only by indirection and general policies? Does the Constitution mandate this inefficient result? Why may the authorities not recognize the problem in candid fashion and solve it altogether through resort to direct assignments based on student racial classifications? . . .

The argument ignores the dangers presented by individual classifications, dangers that are not as pressing when the same ends are achieved by more indirect means. When the government classifies an individual by race, it must first define what it means to be of a race. Who exactly is white and who is nonwhite? To be forced to live under a state-mandated racial label is inconsistent with the dignity of individuals in our society. And it is a label that an individual is powerless to change. Governmental classifications that command people to march in different directions based on racial typologies can cause a new divisiveness. The practice can lead to corrosive discourse, where race serves not as an element of our diverse heritage but instead as a bargaining chip in the political process. On the other hand race-conscious measures that do not rely on differential treatment based on individual classifications present these problems to a lesser degree.

The idea that if race is the problem, race is the instrument with which to solve it cannot be accepted as an analytical leap forward. And if this is a frustrating duality of the Equal Protection Clause it simply reflects the duality of our history and our attempts to promote freedom in a world that sometimes seems set against it. Under our Constitution the individual, child or adult, can find his own identity, can define her own persona, without state intervention that classifies on the basis of his race or the color of her skin.

. . .

This Nation has a moral and ethical obligation to fulfill its historic commitment to creating an integrated society that ensures equal opportunity for all of its children. A compelling interest exists in avoiding racial isolation, an interest that a school district, in its discretion and expertise, may choose to pursue. Likewise, a district may consider it a compelling interest to achieve a diverse student population. Race may be one component of that diversity, but other demographic factors, plus special talents and needs, should also be considered. What the government is not permitted to do, absent a showing of necessity not made here, is to classify every student on the basis of race and to assign each of them to schools based on that classification. Crude measures of this sort threaten to reduce children to racial chits valued and traded according to one school's supply and another's demand.

[A] sense of stigma may already become the fate of those separated out by circumstances beyond their immediate control. But . . . [e]ven so, measures other than differential treatment based on racial typing of individuals first must be exhausted.

The decision today should not prevent school districts from continuing the important work of bringing together students of different racial, ethnic, and economic backgrounds. Due to a variety of factors—some influenced by government, some not—neighborhoods in our communities do not reflect the diversity of our Nation as a whole. Those entrusted with directing our public schools can bring to bear the creativity of experts, parents, administrators, and other concerned citizens to find a way to achieve the compelling interests they face without resorting to widespread governmental allocation of benefits and burdens on the basis of racial classifications.

With this explanation I concur in the judgment of the Court.

Justice STEVENS, dissenting.

. . . There is a cruel irony in The Chief Justice's reliance on our decision in Brown v. Board of Education. The first sentence in the concluding paragraph of his opinion states: "Before *Brown,* schoolchildren were told where they could and could not go to school based on the color of their skin." . . . The Chief Justice fails to note that it was only black schoolchildren who were so ordered; indeed, the history books do not tell stories of white children struggling to attend black schools. In this and other ways, The Chief Justice rewrites the history of one of this Court's most important decisions.

. . .

The Court's misuse of the three-tiered approach to Equal Protection analysis merely reconfirms my own view that there is only one such Clause in the Constitution. If we look at cases decided during the interim between *Brown* and *Adarand,* we can see how a rigid adherence to tiers of scrutiny obscures *Brown*'s clear message. Perhaps the best example is provided by our approval of the decision of the Supreme Judicial Court of Massachusetts in 1967 upholding a state statute mandating racial integration in that State's school system. See School Comm. of Boston v. Board of Education, 352 Mass. 693, 227 N.E.2d 729. Rejecting arguments comparable to those that the plurality accepts today, that court noted: "It would be the height of irony if the racial imbalance act, enacted as it was with the laudable purpose of achieving equal educational opportunities, should, by prescribing school pupil allocations based on race, founder on unsuspected shoals in the Fourteenth Amendment." . . . Our ruling on the merits [on appeal] simply stated that the appeal was "dismissed for want of a substantial federal question." School Comm. of Boston v. Board of Education, 389 U.S.

572 (1968) (per curiam). That decision not only expressed our appraisal of the merits of the appeal, but it constitutes a precedent that the Court overrules today. The subsequent statements by the unanimous Court in Swann v. Charlotte-Mecklenburg Bd. of Ed., 402 U.S. 1, 16 (1971), by then Justice Rehnquist in chambers in Bustop, Inc. v. Los Angeles Bd. of Ed., 439 U.S. 1380, 1383 (1978), and by the host of state court decisions cited by Justice Breyer, were fully consistent with that disposition. Unlike today's decision, they were also entirely loyal to *Brown.*

The Court has changed significantly since it decided *School Comm. of Boston* in 1968. It was then more faithful to *Brown* and more respectful of our precedent than it is today. It is my firm conviction that no Member of the Court that I joined in 1975 would have agreed with today's decision.

Justice BREYER, with whom Justice STEVENS, Justice SOUTER, and Justice GINSBURG join, dissenting.

[I]n dozens of . . . cases [following *Brown*], this Court told school districts previously segregated by law what they must do at a minimum to comply with *Brown*'s constitutional holding. The measures required by those cases often included race-conscious practices, such as mandatory busing and race based restrictions on voluntary transfers.

Beyond those minimum requirements, the Court left much of the determination of how to achieve integration to the judgment of local communities. . . . As a result, different districts—some acting under court decree, some acting in order to avoid threatened lawsuits, some seeking to comply with federal administrative orders, some acting purely voluntarily, some acting after federal courts had dissolved earlier orders—adopted, modified, and experimented with hosts of different kinds of plans, including race-conscious plans, all with a similar objective: greater racial integration of public schools. The techniques that different districts have employed range "from voluntary transfer programs to mandatory reassignment." . . .

Overall these efforts brought about considerable racial integration. More recently, however, progress has stalled. Between 1968 and 1980, the number of black children attending a school where minority children constituted more than half of the school fell from 77% to 63% in the Nation (from 81% to 57% in the South) but then reversed direction by the year 2000, rising from 63% to 72% in the Nation (from 57% to 69% in the South). Similarly, between 1968 and 1980, the number of black children attending schools that were more than 90% minority fell from 64% to 33% in the Nation (from 78% to 23% in the South), but that too reversed direction, rising by the year 2000 from 33% to 37% in the Nation (from 23% to 31% in the South). As of 2002, almost 2.4 million students, or over 5% of all public school enrollment, attended schools with a white population of less than 1%. Of these, 2.3 million were black and Latino students, and only 72,000 were white. Today, more than one in six black children attend a school that is 99-100% minority. In light of the evident risk of a return to school systems that are in fact (though not in law) resegregated, many school districts have felt a need to maintain or to extend their integration efforts.

The upshot is that myriad school districts operating in myriad circumstances have devised myriad plans, often with race-conscious elements, all for the sake of eradicating earlier school segregation, bringing about integration, or preventing retrogression. Seattle and Louisville are two such districts, and the histories of their present plans set forth typical school integration stories.

[T]he distinction between *de jure* segregation (caused by school systems) and *de facto* segregation (caused, e.g., by housing patterns or generalized societal discrimination) is meaningless in the present context, thereby dooming the plurality's endeavor to find support for its views in that distinction. [R]ealworld efforts to substitute racially diverse for racially segregated schools (however caused) are complex, to the point where the Constitution cannot plausibly be interpreted to rule out categorically all local efforts to use means that are "conscious" of the race of individuals.

In both Seattle and Louisville, the local school districts began with schools that were highly segregated in fact. In both cities plaintiffs filed lawsuits claiming unconstitutional segregation. In Louisville, a federal district court found that school segregation reflected pre-*Brown* state laws separating the races. In Seattle, the plaintiffs alleged that school segregation unconstitutionally reflected not only generalized societal discrimination and residential housing patterns, but also *school board policies and actions* that had helped to create, maintain, and aggravate racial segregation. In Louisville, a federal court entered a remedial decree. In Seattle, the parties settled after the school district pledged to undertake a desegregation plan. In both cities, the school boards adopted plans designed to achieve integration by bringing about more racially diverse schools. In each city the school board modified its plan several times in light of, for example, hostility to busing, the threat of resegregation, and the desirability of introducing greater student choice. And in each city, the school boards' plans have evolved over time in ways that progressively *diminish* the plans' use of explicit race-conscious criteria.

[Justice Breyer offers a detailed history of desegregation efforts in both cities. He points out that complaints about Seattle's segregated schools began as early as 1956, pointing to segregative housing practices and school board policies that exacerbated racial segregation. The NAACP filed its first lawsuit against the Seattle School Board in 1969, leading to a plan that required race-based transfers and mandatory busing. The NAACP filed a complaint with the Office of Civil Rights (OCR) of the Department of Health, Education and Welfare in 1977, which led to a formal settlement agreement, the "Seattle Plan," which also used busing to prevent racial imbalance in the schools. To prevent the plan from taking effect, Washington State voters passed an initiative that required students to be assigned to the schools closest to their homes. The U.S. Supreme Court struck the referendum down in Washington v. Seattle School Dist. No. 1, 458 U.S. 457 (1982). By 1988, many white families had left the district, and many Asian families had moved in. Seattle moved to a school-choice plan with race-based constraints. In 1996, the school board adopted the present plan, which deemphasized racial criteria and increased the likelihood that a student would receive an assignment to his first or second choice high school.

In 1956, Louisville created a geography-based student assignment policy in response to *Brown*, but by 1972 the school district remained heavily segregated. Civil rights groups brought suit in 1972, leading to a federal court order requiring desegregation, redrawing school attendance zones, closing 12 schools, and busing groups of students. The district court removed the case from its active docket in 1978; by 1984, several schools had fallen out of compliance with the order's target racial percentages due to changing demographics. The school board created a new plan. By 1991, the board tried a new strategy that emphasized student choice, devised in consultation with parents and the local community. In 1996, the board further revised its plan after further consultations with the community. The district court dissolved the 1975 order in 2000; and the board continued its 1996 plan.]

Both [Louisville and Seattle] faced problems that reflected initial periods of severe racial segregation, followed by such remedial efforts as busing, followed by evidence of resegregation, followed by a need to end busing and encourage the return of, e.g., suburban students through increased student choice. When formulating the plans under review, both districts drew upon their considerable experience with earlier plans, having revised their policies periodically in light of that experience. Both districts rethought their methods over time and explored a wide range of other means, including nonrace-conscious policies. Both districts also considered elaborate studies and consulted widely within their communities.

Both districts sought greater racial integration for educational and democratic, as well as for remedial, reasons. Both sought to achieve these objectives while preserving their commitment to other educational goals, e.g., districtwide commitment to high-quality public schools, increased pupil assignment to neighborhood schools, diminished use of busing, greater student choice, reduced risk of white flight, and so forth. Consequently, the present plans expand student choice; they limit the burdens (including busing) that earlier plans had imposed upon students and their families; and they use race-conscious criteria in limited and gradually diminishing ways. In particular, they use race-conscious criteria only to mark the outer bounds of broad population-related ranges.

The histories also make clear the futility of looking simply to whether earlier school segregation was *de jure* or *de facto* in order to draw firm lines separating the constitutionally permissible from the constitutionally forbidden use of "race-conscious" criteria. . . .

No one here disputes that Louisville's segregation was *de jure*. But what about Seattle's? Was it *de facto*? *De jure*? A mixture? Opinions differed. Or is it that a prior federal court had not adjudicated the matter? Does that make a difference? Is Seattle free on remand to say that its schools were *de jure* segregated, just as in 1956 a memo for the School Board admitted? . . .

A court finding of *de jure* segregation cannot be the crucial variable. After all, a number of school districts in the South that the Government or private plaintiffs challenged as segregated *by law* voluntarily desegregated their schools *without a court order*—just as Seattle did. . . . Moreover, Louisville's history makes clear that a community under a court order to desegregate might submit a race-conscious remedial plan *before* the court dissolved the order, but with every intention of following that plan even *after* dissolution. How could such a plan be lawful the day before dissolution but then become unlawful the very next day? On what legal ground can the majority rest its contrary view?

Are courts really to treat as merely *de facto* segregated those school districts that avoided a federal order by voluntarily complying with *Brown*'s requirements? This Court has previously done just the opposite, permitting a race conscious remedy without any kind of court decree. Because the Constitution emphatically does not forbid the use of race-conscious measures by districts in the South that voluntarily desegregated their schools, on what basis does the plurality claim that the law forbids Seattle to do the same?

The histories also indicate the complexity of the tasks and the practical difficulties that local school boards face when they seek to achieve greater racial integration. The boards work in communities where demographic patterns change, where they must meet traditional learning goals, where they must attract and retain effective teachers, where they should (and will) take account of parents' views and maintain *their* commitment to public school education, where they must adapt to court intervention, where they must encourage voluntary student and parent action—where they will find that their own good faith, their knowledge, and their understanding of local circumstances are always necessary but often insufficient to solve the problems at hand. . . .

II.

. . .

A longstanding and unbroken line of legal authority tells us that the Equal Protection Clause permits local school boards to use race-conscious criteria to achieve positive race-related goals, even when the Constitution does not compel it [In] *Swann* [v. Charlotte-Mecklenburg Bd. of Ed., 402 U.S. 1, 16 (1971)] Chief Justice Burger, on behalf of a unanimous Court in a case of exceptional importance, wrote:

> School authorities are traditionally charged with broad power to formulate and implement educational policy and might well conclude, for example, that in order to prepare students to live in a pluralistic society each school should have a prescribed ratio of Negro to white students reflecting the proportion for the district as a whole. To do this as an educational policy is within the broad discretionary powers of school authorities.

[I]n North Carolina Bd. of Ed. v. Swann, 402 U.S. 43, 45 (1971), this Court, citing *Swann,* restated the point. "[S]chool authorities," the Court said, "have wide discretion in formulating school policy, and . . . as a matter of educational policy school authorities may well conclude that some kind of racial balance in the schools is desirable quite apart from any constitutional requirements." Then-Justice Rehnquist echoed this view in Bustop, Inc. v. Los Angeles Bd. of Ed., 439 U.S. 1380, 1383 (1978) (opinion in chambers), making clear that he too believed that *Swann*'s statement reflected settled law: "While I have the gravest doubts that [a state supreme court] was *required* by the United States Constitution to take the [desegregation] action that it has taken in this case, I have very little doubt that it was *permitted* by that Constitution to take such action." (Emphasis in original.)

These statements nowhere suggest that this freedom is limited to school districts where court-ordered desegregation measures are also in effect. Indeed, in McDaniel v. Barresi, 402 U.S. 39 (1971), a case decided the same day as *Swann*, a group of parents challenged a race-conscious student assignment plan that the Clarke County School Board had *voluntarily* adopted as a remedy without a court order (though under federal agency pressure—pressure Seattle also encountered). . . . This Court upheld the plan, rejecting the parents' argument that "a person may not be *included* or *excluded* solely because he is a Negro or because he is white."

Federal authorities had claimed—as the NAACP and the OCR did in Seattle—that Clarke County schools were segregated in law, not just in fact. The plurality's claim that Seattle was "never segregated by law" is simply not accurate. The plurality could validly claim that *no court* ever found that Seattle schools were segregated in law. But that is also true of the Clarke County schools in *McDaniel*. Unless we believe that the Constitution enforces one legal standard for the South and another for the North, this Court should grant Seattle the permission it granted Clarke County, Georgia.

This Court has also held that school districts may be required by federal statute to undertake race-conscious desegregation efforts even when there is no likelihood that *de jure* segregation can be shown. In Board of Ed. of City School Dist. of New York v. Harris, 444 U.S. 130, 148-149 (1979), the Court concluded that a federal statute required school districts receiving certain federal funds to remedy faculty segregation, even though in this Court's view the racial disparities in the affected schools were purely *de facto* and would not have been actionable under the Equal Protection Clause. Not even the dissenters thought the race-conscious remedial program posed a *constitutional* problem.

Lower state and federal courts had considered the matter settled and uncontroversial even before this Court decided *Swann*. . . . *Swann* was not a sharp or unexpected departure from prior rulings; it reflected a consensus that had already emerged among state and lower federal courts. . . . Numerous state and federal courts explicitly relied upon *Swann*'s guidance for decades to follow. . . . [The] principle [in *Swann*] has been accepted by every branch of government and is rooted in the history of the Equal Protection Clause itself. Thus, Congress has enacted numerous race-conscious statutes that illustrate that principle or rely upon its validity. See, e.g., 20 U.S.C. §6311(b)(2)(C)(v) (No Child Left Behind

Act); §1067 *et seq.* (authorizing aid to minority institutions). In fact, without being exhaustive, I have counted 51 federal statutes that use racial classifications. I have counted well over 100 state statutes that similarly employ racial classifications. Presidential administrations for the past half-century have used and supported various race-conscious measures. And during the same time, hundreds of local school districts have adopted student assignment plans that use race-conscious criteria.

That *Swann*'s legal statement should find such broad acceptance is not surprising. For *Swann* is predicated upon a well-established legal view of the Fourteenth Amendment. That view understands the basic objective of those who wrote the Equal Protection Clause as forbidding practices that lead to racial exclusion. The Amendment sought to bring into American society as full members those whom the Nation had previously held in slavery.

There is reason to believe that those who drafted an Amendment with this basic purpose in mind would have understood the legal and practical difference between the use of race-conscious criteria in defiance of that purpose, namely to keep the races apart, and the use of race-conscious criteria to further that purpose, namely to bring the races together. Although the Constitution almost always forbids the former, it is significantly more lenient in respect to the latter.

Sometimes Members of this Court have disagreed about the degree of leniency that the Clause affords to programs designed to include. But I can find no case in which this Court has followed Justice Thomas' "colorblind" approach. And I have found no case that otherwise repudiated this constitutional asymmetry between that which seeks to *exclude* and that which seeks to *include* members of minority races.

[T]he constitutional principle enunciated in *Swann,* reiterated in subsequent cases, and relied upon over many years, provides, and has widely been thought to provide, authoritative legal guidance. And if the plurality now chooses to reject that principle, it cannot adequately justify its retreat simply by affixing the label "dicta" to reasoning with which it disagrees. Rather, it must explain to the courts and to the Nation *why* it would abandon guidance set forth many years before, guidance that countless others have built upon over time, and which the law has continuously embodied.

[N]o case — not *Adarand, Gratz, Grutter,* or any other — has ever held that the test of "strict scrutiny" means that all racial classifications — no matter whether they seek to include or exclude — must in practice be treated the same. . . . [In] *Adarand,* [t]he Court made clear that "[s]trict scrutiny does not trea[t] dissimilar race-based decisions as though they were equally objectionable." It added that the fact that a law "treats [a person] unequally because of his or her race . . . says nothing about the ultimate validity of any particular law." And the Court, . . . sought to "*dispel the notion* that strict scrutiny" is as likely to condemn *inclusive* uses of "race-conscious" criteria as it is to invalidate *exclusionary* uses. That is, it is *not* in all circumstances "'strict in theory, but fatal in fact.'" . . . The Court's holding in *Grutter* demonstrates that the Court meant what it said, for the Court upheld an elite law school's race conscious admissions program.

The upshot is that the cases to which the plurality refers, though all applying strict scrutiny, do not treat exclusive and inclusive uses the same. Rather, they apply the strict scrutiny test in a manner that is "fatal in fact" only to racial classifications that harmfully *exclude*; they apply the test in a manner that is *not* fatal in fact to racial classifications that seek to *include*. . . .

Governmental use of race-based criteria can arise in the context of, for example, census forms, research expenditures for diseases, assignments of police officers patrolling predominantly minority-race neighborhoods, efforts to desegregate racially segregated schools, policies that favor minorities when distributing goods or services in short supply, actions that create majority minority electoral districts, peremptory strikes that remove potential jurors on the basis of race, and others. Given the significant differences among these contexts, it would be surprising if the law required an identically strict legal test for evaluating the constitutionality of race-based criteria as to each of them.

Here, the context is one in which school districts seek to advance or to maintain racial integration in primary and secondary schools. It is a context, as *Swann* makes clear, where history has required special administrative remedies. And it is a context in which the school boards' plans simply set race-conscious limits at the outer boundaries of a broad range.

This context is *not* a context that involves the use of race to decide who will receive goods or services that are normally distributed on the basis of merit and which are in short supply. It is not one in which race-conscious limits stigmatize or exclude; the limits at issue do not pit the races against each other or otherwise significantly exacerbate racial tensions. They do not impose burdens unfairly upon members of one race alone but instead seek benefits for members of all races alike. The context here is one of racial limits that seek, not to keep the races apart, but to bring them together.

[T]he districts' plans reflect efforts to overcome a history of segregation, embody the results of broad experience and community consultation, seek to expand student choice while reducing the need for mandatory busing, and use race-conscious criteria in highly limited ways that diminish the use of race compared to preceding integration efforts. They do not seek to award a scarce commodity on the basis of merit, for they are not magnet schools; rather, by design and in practice, they offer substantially equivalent academic programs and electives. Although some parents or children prefer some schools over others, school popularity has varied significantly over the years. . . .

I believe that the law requires application here of a standard of review that is not "strict" in the traditional sense of that word, . . . Nonetheless, in light of *Grutter* and other precedents, . . . I shall apply the version of strict scrutiny that those cases embody. . . .

III.

[T]he principal interest advanced in these cases [is] an interest in promoting or preserving greater racial "integration" of public schools. By this term, I mean the school districts' interest in eliminating school-by-school racial isolation and increasing the degree to which racial mixture characterizes each of the district's schools and each individual student's public school experience.

[This] interest . . . possesses three essential elements. First, there is a historical and remedial element: an interest in setting right the consequences of prior conditions of segregation. . . . It is an interest in continuing to combat the remnants of segregation caused in whole or in part by these school-related policies, which have often affected not only schools, but also housing patterns, employment practices, economic conditions, and social attitudes. It is an interest in maintaining hard-won gains. And it has its roots in preventing what gradually may become the *de facto* resegregation of America's public schools.

Second, there is an educational element: an interest in overcoming the adverse educational effects produced by and associated with highly segregated schools. Studies suggest that children taken from those schools and placed in integrated settings often show positive academic gains. Other studies reach different conclusions. But the evidence supporting an educational interest in racially integrated schools is well established and strong enough to permit a democratically elected school board reasonably to determine that this interest is a compelling one.

Research suggests, for example, that black children from segregated educational environments significantly increase their achievement levels once they are placed in a more integrated setting. Indeed in Louisville itself the achievement gap between black and white elementary school students grew substantially smaller (by seven percentage points) after the integration plan was implemented in 1975. Conversely, to take another example, evidence from a district in Norfolk, Virginia, shows that resegregated schools led to a decline in the achievement test scores of children of all races.

One commentator, reviewing dozens of studies of the educational benefits of desegregated schooling, found that the studies have provided "remarkably consistent" results, showing that: (1) black students' educational achievement is improved in integrated schools as compared to racially isolated schools, (2) black students' educational achievement is improved in integrated classes, and (3) the earlier that black students are removed from racial isolation, the better their educational outcomes. Multiple studies also indicate that black alumni of integrated schools are more likely to move into occupations traditionally closed to African-Americans, and to earn more money in those fields.

Third, there is a democratic element: an interest in producing an educational environment that reflects the "pluralistic society" in which our children will live. It is an interest in helping our children learn to work and play together with children of different racial backgrounds. It is an interest in teaching children to engage in the kind of cooperation among Americans of all races that is necessary to make a land of three hundred million people one Nation.

Again, data support this insight. There are again studies that offer contrary conclusions. Again, however, the evidence supporting a democratic interest in racially integrated schools is firmly established and sufficiently strong to permit a school board to determine, as this Court has itself often found, that this interest is compelling.

For example, one study documented that "black and white students in deseg-regated schools are less racially prejudiced than those in segregated schools," and that "interracial contact in desegregated schools leads to an increase in inter-racial sociability and friendship." Other studies have found that both black and white students who attend integrated schools are more likely to work in deseg-regated companies after graduation than students who attended racially iso-lated schools. Further research has shown that the desegregation of schools can help bring adult communities together by reducing segregated housing. Cities that have implemented successful school desegregation plans have witnessed increased interracial contact and neighborhoods that tend to become less racially segregated. These effects not only reinforce the prior gains of integrated primary and secondary education; they also foresee a time when there is less need to use race-conscious criteria.

. . . In light of this Court's conclusions in *Grutter,* the "compelling" nature of these interests in the context of primary and secondary public education follows here *a fortiori.* . . . Hence, I am not surprised that Justice Kennedy finds that, "a district may consider it a compelling interest to achieve a diverse student popu-lation," including a *racially* diverse population.

The compelling interest at issue here, then, includes an effort to eradicate the remnants, not of general "societal discrimination," but of primary and secondary school segregation; it includes an effort to create school environments that pro-vide better educational opportunities for all children; it includes an effort to help create citizens better prepared to know, to understand, and to work with people of all races and backgrounds, thereby furthering the kind of democratic govern-ment our Constitution foresees. If an educational interest that combines these three elements is not "compelling," what is?

[H]ow do the educational and civic interests differ in kind from those that underlie and justify the racial "diversity" that the law school sought in *Grutter,* where this Court found a compelling interest? The plurality tries to draw a dis-tinction by reference to the well-established conceptual difference between *de jure* segregation ("segregation by state action") and *de facto* segregation ("racial imbalance caused by other factors"). But that distinction concerns what the Constitution *requires* school boards to do, not what it *permits* them to do.

The opinions cited by the plurality to justify its reliance upon the *de jure/de facto* distinction only address what remedial measures a school district may be constitutionally *required* to undertake. As to what is *permitted*, nothing in our equal protection law suggests that a State may right only those wrongs that it committed. No case of this Court has ever relied upon the *de jure/de facto* dis-tinction in order to limit what a school district is voluntarily allowed to do. . . .

Nor does any precedent indicate, as the plurality suggests with respect to Louisville, that remedial interests vanish the day after a federal court declares that a district is "unitary." Of course, Louisville adopted those portions of the plan at issue here *before* a court declared Louisville "unitary." Moreover, in *Freeman*, this Court pointed out that in "one sense of the term, vestiges of past segregation by state decree do remain in our society and in our schools. Past wrongs to the black race, wrongs committed by the State and in its name, are a stubborn fact of history. And stubborn facts of history linger and persist." I do not understand why this Court's cases, which rest the significance of a "unitary" finding in part upon the wisdom and desirability of returning schools to local control, should deprive those local officials of legal *permission* to use means they once found necessary to combat persisting injustices.

For his part, Justice Thomas faults my citation of various studies supporting the view that school districts can find compelling educational and civic interests in integrating their public schools. He is entitled of course to his own opinion as to which studies he finds convincing. . . . [But] [i]f we are to insist upon unanimity in the social science literature before finding a compelling interest, we might never find one. I believe only that the Constitution allows democratically elected school boards to make up their own minds as to how best to include people of all races in one America.

. . .

I next ask whether the plans before us are "narrowly tailored" to achieve these "compelling" objectives. . . . Several factors, taken together, . . . lead me to conclude that the boards' use of race-conscious criteria in these plans passes even the strictest "tailoring" test.

First, the race-conscious criteria at issue only help set the outer bounds of *broad* ranges. They constitute but one part of plans that depend primarily upon other, nonracial elements. To use race in this way is not to set a forbidden "quota."

In fact, the defining feature of both plans is greater emphasis upon student choice. In Seattle, for example, in more than 80% of all cases, that choice alone determines which high schools Seattle's ninth graders will attend. After ninth grade, students can decide voluntarily to transfer to a preferred district high school (without any consideration of race-conscious criteria). *Choice*, therefore, is the "predominant factor" in these plans. *Race* is not.

Indeed, the race-conscious ranges at issue in these cases often have no effect, either because the particular school is not oversubscribed in the year in question, or because the racial makeup of the school falls within the broad range, or because the student is a transfer applicant or has a sibling at the school. In these respects, the broad ranges are less like a quota and more like the kinds of "useful starting points" that this Court has consistently found permissible, even when they set boundaries upon voluntary transfers, and even when they are based upon a community's general population.

Second, broad-range limits on voluntary school choice plans are less burdensome, and hence more narrowly tailored, than other race-conscious restrictions this Court has previously approved. See, e.g., *Swann*. Indeed, the plans before us are *more narrowly tailored* than the race-conscious admission plans that this Court approved in *Grutter*. Here, race becomes a factor only in a fraction of students' non-merit-based assignments — not in large numbers of students' merit-based applications. Moreover, the effect of applying race conscious criteria here affects potentially disadvantaged students *less severely,* not more severely, than the criteria at issue in *Grutter*. Disappointed students are not rejected from a State's flagship graduate program; they simply attend a different one of the district's many public schools, which in aspiration and in fact are substantially equal. And, in Seattle, the disadvantaged student loses at most one year at the high school of his choice. . . .

Third, the manner in which the school boards developed these plans itself reflects "narrow tailoring." Each plan was devised to overcome a history of segregated public schools. Each plan embodies the results of local experience and community consultation. Each plan is the product of a process that has sought to enhance student choice, while diminishing the need for mandatory busing. And each plan's use of race-conscious elements is *diminished* compared to the use of race in preceding integration plans.

The school boards' widespread consultation, their experimentation with numerous other plans, indeed, the 40-year history [of their attempts at desegregation], make clear that plans that are less explicitly race-based are unlikely to achieve the board's "compelling" objectives. The history of each school system reveals highly segregated schools, followed by remedial plans that involved forced busing, followed by efforts to attract or retain students through the use of plans that abandoned busing and replaced it with greater student choice. Both cities once tried to achieve more integrated schools by relying solely upon measures such as redrawn district boundaries, new school building construction, and unrestricted voluntary transfers. In neither city did these prior attempts prove sufficient to achieve the city's integration goals.

Moreover, giving some degree of weight to a local school board's knowledge, expertise, and concerns in these particular matters is not inconsistent with rigorous judicial scrutiny. It simply recognizes that judges are not well suited to act as school administrators. Indeed, in the context of school desegregation, this Court has repeatedly stressed the importance of acknowledging that local school boards better understand their own communities and have a better knowledge of what in practice will best meet the educational needs of their pupils. . . .

Having looked at dozens of *amicus* briefs, public reports, news stories, and the records in many of this Court's prior cases, which together span 50 years of desegregation history in school districts across the Nation, I have discovered many examples of districts that sought integration through explicitly race conscious methods, including mandatory busing. Yet, I have found *no* example or model that would permit this Court to say to Seattle and to Louisville: "Here is an instance of a desegregation plan that is likely to achieve your objectives and also makes less use of race-conscious criteria than your plans." And, if the plurality cannot suggest such a model — and it cannot — then it seeks to impose a "narrow tailoring" requirement that in practice would never be met.

[T]he plurality also points to the school districts' use of numerical goals based upon the racial breakdown of the general school population, and it faults the districts for failing to prove that *no other set of numbers will work*. The plurality refers to no case in support of its demand. Nor is it likely to find such a case. After all, this Court has in many cases explicitly permitted districts to use target ratios based upon the district's underlying population. See, e.g., *Swann*; *North Carolina Bd. of Ed; Montgomery County Bd. of Ed.* The reason is obvious: In Seattle, where the overall student population is 41% white, permitting 85% white enrollment at a single school would make it much more likely that other schools would have very few white students, whereas in Jefferson County, with a 60% white enrollment, one school with 85% white students would be less likely to skew enrollments elsewhere.

Moreover, there is research-based evidence supporting, for example, that a ratio no greater than 50% minority—which is Louisville's starting point, and as close as feasible to Seattle's starting point—is helpful in limiting the risk of "white flight." . . . What other numbers are the boards to use as a "starting point"?

[N]or could the school districts have accomplished their desired aims (e.g., avoiding forced busing, countering white flight, maintaining racial diversity) by other means. Nothing in the extensive history of desegregation efforts over the past 50 years gives the districts, or this Court, any reason to believe that another method is possible to accomplish these goals.

[Justice Kennedy asks:] Why does Seattle's plan group Asian-Americans, Hispanic-Americans, Native-Americans, and African-Americans together, treating all as similar minorities? The majority suggests that Seattle's classification system could permit a school to be labeled "diverse" with a 50% Asian American and 50% white student body, and no African-American students, Hispanic students, or students of other ethnicity.

The 50/50 hypothetical has no support in the record here; it is conjured from the imagination. In fact, Seattle apparently began to treat these different minority groups alike in response to the federal Emergency School Aid Act's requirement that it do so. Moreover, maintaining this federally mandated system of classification makes sense insofar as Seattle's experience indicates that the relevant circumstances in respect to each of these different minority groups are roughly similar, e.g., in terms of residential patterns, and call for roughly similar responses. This is confirmed by the fact that Seattle has been able to achieve a desirable degree of diversity without the *greater* emphasis on race that drawing fine lines among minority groups would require. . . . [T]he plurality cannot object that the constitutional defect is the individualized use of race and simultaneously object that not enough account of individuals' race has been taken.

[T]he Court seeks to distinguish *Grutter* from these cases by claiming that *Grutter* arose in " 'the context of higher education.' " But . . . I do not believe the Constitution could possibly find "compelling" the provision of a racially diverse education for a 23-year-old law student but not for a 13-year-old high school pupil. [Nor is it relevant] that these school districts did not examine the merits of applications "individual[ly]." The context here does not involve admission by merit; a child's academic, artistic, and athletic "merits" are not at all relevant to the child's placement. These are not affirmative action plans, and hence "individualized scrutiny" is simply beside the point. . . .

IV.

. . .

No one claims that (the relevant portion of) Louisville's plan was unlawful in 1996 when Louisville adopted it. To the contrary, there is every reason to believe that it represented part of an effort to implement the 1978 desegregation order. But if the plan was lawful when it was first adopted and if it was lawful the day before the District Court dissolved its order, how can the plurality now suggest that it became *unlawful* the following day? Is it conceivable that the Constitution, implemented through a court desegregation order, could permit (perhaps *require*) the district to make use of a race-conscious plan the day before the order was dissolved and then *forbid* the district to use the identical plan the day after? The Equal Protection Clause is not incoherent. And federal courts would rightly hesitate to find unitary status if the consequences of the ruling were so dramatically disruptive.

[T]he original Seattle Plan [was] a *more heavily race-conscious predecessor* of the very plan now before us. In *Seattle School Dist. No. 1*, this Court struck down a state referendum that effectively barred implementation of Seattle's desegregation plan and "burden[ed] all future attempts to integrate Washington schools in districts throughout the State." Because the referendum would have prohibited the adoption of a school-integration plan that involved mandatory busing, and because it would have imposed a special burden on school integration plans (plans that sought to integrate previously segregated schools), the Court found it unconstitutional. . . . It is difficult to believe that the Court that held unconstitutional a referendum that would have interfered with the implementation of this plan thought that the integration plan it sought to preserve was itself an *unconstitutional* plan. And if *Seattle School Dist. No. 1* is premised upon the constitutionality of the original Seattle Plan, it is equally premised upon the constitutionality of the present plan, for the present plan *is* the Seattle Plan, modified only insofar as it places even *less* emphasis on race-conscious elements than its predecessors.

It is even more difficult to accept the plurality's contrary view, namely that the underlying plan was unconstitutional. If that is so, then *all* of Seattle's earlier (even more race-conscious) plans must also have been unconstitutional. That necessary implication of the plurality's position strikes the 13th chime of the clock. How could the plurality adopt a constitutional standard that would hold unconstitutional large numbers of race-conscious integration plans adopted by numerous school boards over the past 50 years while remaining true to this Court's desegregation precedent?

V.

[C]onsider the effect of the plurality's views on the parties before us and on similar school districts throughout the Nation. Will Louisville and all similar school districts have to return to systems like Louisville's initial 1956 plan, which did not consider race at all? That initial 1956 plan proved ineffective. . . . The districts' past and current plans are not unique. They resemble other plans, promulgated by hundreds of local school boards, which have attempted a variety of desegregation methods that have evolved over time in light of experience. . . . A majority of these desegregation techniques explicitly considered a student's race. Transfer plans, for example, allowed students to shift from a school in which they were in the racial majority to a school in which they would be in a racial minority. Some districts, such as Richmond, California, and Buffalo, New York, permitted only "one-way" transfers, in which only black students attending predominantly black schools were permitted to transfer to designated receiver schools.

[A]t a minimum, the plurality's views would threaten a surge of race-based litigation. Hundreds of state and federal statutes and regulations use racial classifications for educational or other purposes. In many such instances, the contentious force of legal challenges to these classifications, meritorious or not, would displace earlier calm.

[D]e facto resegregation is on the rise. It is reasonable to conclude that such resegregation can create serious educational, social, and civic problems. Given the conditions in which school boards work to set policy, they may need all of the means presently at their disposal to combat those problems. Yet the plurality would deprive them of at least one tool that some districts now consider vital — the limited use of broad race-conscious student population ranges.

I use the words "may need" here deliberately. The plurality, or at least those who follow Justice Thomas' " 'color-blind' " approach, may feel confident that, to end invidious discrimination, one must end all governmental use of race conscious criteria including those with inclusive objectives. By way of contrast, I do not claim to know how best to stop harmful discrimination; how best to create a society that includes all Americans; how best to overcome our serious problems of increasing de facto segregation, troubled inner city schooling, and poverty correlated with race. But, as a judge, I do know that the Constitution does not authorize judges to dictate solutions to these problems. Rather, the Constitution creates a democratic political system through which the people themselves must together find answers. And it is for them to debate how best to educate the Nation's children and how best to administer America's schools to achieve that aim. The Court should leave them to their work. And it is for them to decide, to quote the plurality's slogan, whether the best "way to stop discrimination on the basis of race is to stop discriminating on the basis of race." That is why the Equal Protection Clause outlaws invidious discrimination, but does not similarly forbid all use of race-conscious criteria. . . .

VI.

[T]he plurality cites in support those who argued in *Brown* against segregation, and Justice Thomas likens the approach that I have taken to that of segregation's defenders. But segregation policies did not simply tell schoolchildren "where they could and could not go to school based on the color of their skin"; they perpetuated a caste system rooted in the institutions of slavery and 80 years of legalized subordination. The lesson of history is not that efforts to continue racial segregation are constitutionally indistinguishable from efforts to achieve racial integration. Indeed, it is a cruel distortion of history to compare Topeka, Kansas, in the 1950's to Louisville and Seattle in the modern day — to equate the plight of Linda Brown (who was ordered to attend a Jim Crow school) to the circumstances of Joshua McDonald (whose request to transfer to a school closer to home was initially declined). This is not to deny that there is a cost in applying "a state-mandated racial label." But that cost does not approach, in degree or in kind, the terrible harms of slavery, the resulting caste system, and 80 years of legal racial segregation.

[N]ot everyone welcomed this Court's decision in *Brown*. Three years after that decision was handed down, the Governor of Arkansas ordered state militia to block the doors of a white schoolhouse so that black children could not enter. The President of the United States dispatched the 101st Airborne Division to Little Rock, Arkansas, and federal troops were needed to enforce a desegregation decree. See Cooper v. Aaron, 358 U.S. 1 (1958). Today, almost 50 years later, attitudes toward race in this Nation have changed dramatically. Many parents, white and black alike, want their children to attend schools with children of different races. Indeed, the very school districts that once spurned integration now strive for it. The long history of their efforts reveals the complexities and difficulties they have faced. And in light of those challenges, they have asked us not to take from their hands the instruments they have used to rid their schools of racial segregation, instruments that they believe are needed to overcome the problems of cities divided by race and poverty. The plurality would decline their modest request.

The plurality is wrong to do so. The last half-century has witnessed great strides toward racial equality, but we have not yet realized the promise of *Brown*. To invalidate the plans under review is to threaten the promise of *Brown*. The plurality's position, I fear, would break that promise. This is a decision that the Court and the Nation will come to regret.

Discussion

1. *Fighting over the legacy of* Brown. All the Justices claim to be faithful to the memory and the principles of *Brown v. Board of Education*. But they have very different ideas of what *Brown* meant. The plurality argues that *Brown* stood for color blindness in student assignment policies and strict scrutiny for racial classifications by the state. The dissent argues that *Brown* stood for the principles of racial integration and antisubordination.

Justice Thomas tries to show that the arguments of the dissenters are the same as those of the defenders of segregation and massive resistance. On the other hand, Justice Thomas's own arguments have much in common with segregationist critics of *Brown*. Thomas is deeply skeptical of elite and social science arguments that integration is good for children — or that racial isolation is bad. He finds little advantage to racial mixing, assumes that different races will self segregate socially, and suggests that predominantly black schools may be better for blacks.

During the 1960s and 1970s proponents of racial integration often looked to federal courts to enforce *Brown* against recalcitrant state school boards; their opponents sought to promote states' rights, localism, and deference to the expertise of local school boards. In *Parents Involved*, the plurality wants federal courts to carefully supervise school districts so that they do not violate the Equal Protection Clause in their quest for racial integration, which the plurality refers to as "racial balancing." Conversely, the dissent, which supports the school boards' attempts at integration, wants to defer to their expertise and knowledge of local conditions. During the 1960s and 1970s, opponents of student assignment policies accused federal courts of judicial activism, elitism, and "social engineering" when they second-guessed local school boards in the name of the Constitution. In *Parents Involved*, Justice Thomas accuses the Seattle and Louisville school boards of elitism and social engineering in pursuing racial integration and insists that federal courts must stop them in the name of the Constitution.

2. De jure *and* de facto. Behind the wrangling over the meaning of *Swann* and over the *de facto/de jure* distinction is the political context of early attempts at desegregation. After *Brown*, federal courts faced the task of desegregating the nation's schools, and often encountered a hostile reception from local school boards. Federal courts could not enjoin every school board in the country, and they could not long succeed against school boards determined to resist them. Any realistic attempt at integration required substantial compliance and cooperation by local school boards. As a result, courts encouraged voluntary plans for integration, as *Swann* itself suggests. This meant that the *de jure/de facto* distinction became relevant only if a school district actually went to court and contested its duty to integrate.

The political context of the 1960s and 1970s meant that courts would look favorably on school boards that chose to integrate without a court order as well as school boards that worked with courts to produce integration plans and maintained them over time without court supervision. Similarly, courts might want to declare districts unitary and turn over the task of desegregation to school districts that they believed had acted in good faith and were willing to take the political heat for integration. Thus, declaring a district unitary did not necessarily mean that desegregation plans were no longer needed; rather it assumed that they would continue under the supervision and adjustment of the local school board as opposed to a federal court. Moreover, in the 1990s, in cases like Board of Education of Oklahoma City v. Dowell and Freeman v. Pitts (see casebook at pp. 943-944), a more conservative Supreme Court strongly signaled to the lower courts that they should end federal court supervision and declare districts unitary as soon as possible. In Freeman v. Pitts, the Court held that federal courts could declare districts unitary even before full compliance had occurred, as long as school districts had made "a good faith commitment to the entirety of a desegregation plan."

The plurality opinion does not focus on this history. It regards school districts that voluntarily desegregated without court order as never having any constitutional obligation to desegregate. And it regards school districts that federal courts declared unitary as being legally pristine — in the same position as districts that were never segregated. As a result, it treats race-conscious plans by districts in Seattle and Louisville not as attempts to continue and adjust remedial plans but as illegal attempts at racial balancing.

3. *Desegregation, not integration.* Following *Brown*, critics who wanted to limit the force of the opinion argued that it required only desegregation, not integration. Section III-B of the plurality opinion (which Justice Kennedy does not join) suggests that "racial balancing" is not a compelling interest. Is racial integration a legitimate interest for the plurality? How does the plurality explain the difference between racial balancing and racial integration? One theory would be that a school is racially integrated if it has been declared unitary, as in the case of Louisville, or, as in the case of Seattle, has never been found to engage in unlawful segregation. If so, would this mean that any attempts to change the racial demographics of schools that are not required by court order are illegitimate racial balancing?

4. *Justice Kennedy's concurrence.* Because his vote is necessary to make a majority, Justice Kennedy's limiting concurrence will no doubt be the focus of much future litigation. Like Justice Powell's *Bakke* opinion, it may determine what *Parents Involved* actually means in practice.

Two points about Kennedy's approach are worth noting at the outset. First, contrary to the plurality, Justice Kennedy argues that increasing diversity and avoiding racial isolation can be compelling state interests. Second, Kennedy argues that school districts may take race-conscious measures to combat *de facto* resegregation and bring students of different backgrounds together.

Kennedy primarily objects to student assignment policies that use the race of an individual student as the controlling factor in determining where that individual student goes to school. Thus, Kennedy distinguishes between two kinds of race-conscious policies. The first considers the race of an individual student in deciding where the student goes to school. Any such policy, Kennedy argues, is subject to strict scrutiny.

To survive strict scrutiny, the school district must show that other policies that do not assign individual students to schools based on their race will not be as effective. Kennedy believes that the minimal effects of race-based assignment policies in this case show that they were unnecessary and therefore not narrowly tailored. Does this mean that if race-based assignment policies produced far more significant effects than the alternatives that they would be narrowly tailored? Kennedy also objects to the use of a binary white/nonwhite divide in racial assignment policies. Does this mean that if school districts used more racial categories their plans would be narrowly tailored?

Kennedy also suggests that student assignment policies that use the race of individual students to determine where the student will be placed must involve, at a minimum, multifactor individualized considerations roughly akin to the sort approved in *Grutter*. We might call this the *Grutter*-ization of school assignment policies.

Requiring multifactor individualized considerations of individual students would convert student assignment policies into something more like individual applications to colleges. Individualized considerations would be costly and thus far less likely to be employed by large school districts. Note that Kennedy also objected to the Louisville plan because the criteria it used were not sufficiently transparent. Ironically, *Grutter* is premised on the notion that decisions using multifactor individualized considerations will be less transparent and therefore less overtly based on race.

A second type of race-conscious policy does not assign individual students to schools on the basis of their race. Rather, it uses facially race-neutral criteria for race-conscious reasons. Examples would be decisions about where to place new schools, where to draw attendance zones, and student assignment criteria based on poverty and socioeconomic status. Kennedy suggests that "it is unlikely that any of [these policies] would demand strict scrutiny to be found permissible." Does that mean that narrow tailoring requirements would not apply? Would rational basis apply?

Note that Chief Justice Roberts's plurality opinion specifically avoids stating its views about the constitutionality of such race-conscious policies. However, if the avowed purpose of these policies is to assign percentages of students to different schools because of their race, why aren't these policies subject to strict scrutiny under *Washington v. Davis*? Kennedy's approach seems to view benign race-conscious *purpose* that uses race-neutral *means* as outside of strict scrutiny. Given the plurality's views about motive in Part IV, can the Justices in the plurality adopt the same approach?

Insert the following on p. 1035 after discussion note 4:

RICCI v. DESTEFANO, 557 U.S. 557 (2009): Title VII of the 1964 Civil Rights Act makes it unlawful for an employer "to discriminate against any individual with respect to his compensation, terms, conditions, or privileges of employment, because of such individual's race, color, religion, sex, or national origin." 42 U.S.C. §2000e-2(a)(1). It prohibits both disparate treatment discrimination and disparate impact discrimination.

Disparate treatment discrimination occurs when an employer has treated a particular person less favorably than others because of a protected trait. A

disparate-treatment plaintiff must establish that the defendant had a discriminatory intent or motive for taking a job-related action. Disparate impact discrimination occurs when an employer uses a particular employment practice that
causes a disparate impact on the basis of race, color, religion, sex, or national
origin. 42 U.S.C. §2000e-2(k)(1)(A)(i). The employer may defend by demonstrating that the practice is job related for the position in question and consistent
with business necessity. If the employer meets that burden, a plaintiff may still
succeed by showing that the employer refuses to adopt an available alternative
employment practice that has less disparate impact and serves the employer's
legitimate needs. §§2000e-2(k)(1)(A)(ii) and (C).

The City of New Haven, Connecticut used a combination of written and oral
tests to identify firefighters for promotion to vacant lieutenant and captain positions. Under these tests, white candidates significantly outperformed minority
candidates. Under the rules for filling vacancies, only white candidates would
be immediately promoted to lieutenant; of the nine candidates who would be
immediately promoted to captain, seven where white and two were Hispanic. No
African-American candidates would be immediately promoted to either position.
A rancorous public debate ensued, with different groups arguing about whether
the tests were fair or biased. Those claiming bias argued that the tests had a
discriminatory impact on racial minorities and threatened a disparate impact
lawsuit if the City made promotions based on the tests. Those claiming the tests
were fair and neutral threatened a disparate treatment lawsuit if the City, relying
on the statistical racial disparity, ignored the test results and denied promotions
to the candidates who had performed well.

The City ultimately threw out the examination results. Seventeen white firefighters and one Hispanic firefighter who passed the exams sued the City on a
disparate treatment theory, arguing that throwing out the test results treated them
less favorably than other employees because of race. They also alleged a violation of the Equal Protection Clause. The City argued in defense that if it had certified the test results, it could have faced Title VII liability for adopting a practice
that had a disparate impact on minority firefighters. The District Court granted
summary judgment for the defendants, and the Second Circuit affirmed.

The Supreme Court reversed, in an opinion by Justice Kennedy. "The City's
actions would violate the disparate-treatment prohibition of Title VII absent some
valid defense. All the evidence demonstrates that the City chose not to certify
the examination results because of the statistical disparity based on race—*i.e.,*
how minority candidates had performed when compared to white candidates. . . .
Whatever the City's ultimate aim—however well intentioned or benevolent it
might have seemed—the City made its employment decision because of race.
The City rejected the test results solely because the higher scoring candidates
were white."

The Court then considered when "the purpose to avoid disparate-impact liability excuses what otherwise would be prohibited disparate-treatment discrimination." The Court rejected the petitioner's argument "that an employer in fact

must be in violation of the disparate-impact provision before it can use compliance as a defense in a disparate-treatment suit." Justice Kennedy argued that Congress intended to encourage voluntary compliance with desegregation of workplaces. "Forbidding employers to act unless they know, with certainty, that a practice violates the disparate-impact provision would bring compliance efforts to a near standstill. Even in the limited situations when this restricted standard could be met, employers likely would hesitate before taking voluntary action for fear of later being proven wrong in the course of litigation and then held to account for disparate treatment." Justice Kennedy also rejected the respondents' argument "that an employer's good-faith belief that its actions are necessary to comply with Title VII's disparate-impact provision should be enough" to avoid liability for disparate treatment. Such a test "would encourage race-based action at the slightest hint of disparate impact" and "would amount to a de facto quota system, in which a focus on statistics . . . could put undue pressure on employers to adopt inappropriate prophylactic measures. Even worse, an employer could discard test results (or other employment practices) with the intent of obtaining the employer's preferred racial balance."

Borrowing from the Court's affirmative action cases construing the Equal Protection Clause, Justice Kennedy argued that in Title VII cases, before an employer can engage in intentional discrimination to avoid or remedy an unintentional disparate impact, the employer must "demonstrate a strong basis in evidence that, had it not taken the action, it would have been liable under the disparate-impact statute." The Court held that the City of New Haven could not meet that standard, and therefore violated Title VII. It therefore did not reach the question whether New Haven's actions also violated the Equal Protection Clause, or "whether a legitimate fear of disparate impact is ever sufficient to justify discriminatory treatment under the Constitution."

Justice Ginsberg, joined by Justices Stevens, Souter, and Breyer, dissented. She disagreed with the majority's assumption that "[w]hen an employer changes an employment practice in an effort to comply with Title VII's disparate-impact provision . . . it acts 'because of race.'" Justice Ginsburg argued that "Title VII's disparate-treatment and disparate-impact proscriptions must be read as complementary" rather than in conflict, as the majority did, because Title VII's purpose is to encourage voluntary compliance to desegregate workplaces. "[E]mployers who reject . . . criteria [that operate to the disadvantage of minorities] due to reasonable doubts about their reliability can hardly be held to have engaged in discrimination 'because of' race. . . . I would therefore hold that an employer who jettisons a selection device when its disproportionate racial impact becomes apparent does not violate Title VII's disparate-treatment bar automatically or at all, subject to this key condition: The employer must have good cause to believe the device would not withstand examination for business necessity."

Justice Ginsburg pointed to New Haven's choice of a 60/40 ratio for written and oral parts of the examination as particularly vulnerable to criticism. The weighting toward written questions was not necessary to effective job performance, because "the oral component, more so than the written component, addressed the sort of 'real-life scenarios' fire officers encounter on the job." In addition, many municipalities prefer assessment tests that simulate actual work conditions.

Even so, the majority's new "strong basis in evidence" standard, she argued, would make efforts at voluntary compliance more difficult, would encourage "costly disparate treatment litigation," and was tantamount to a demand that the employer establish that it has violated the law.

Justice Alito, concurring, agreed with the majority's "strong basis in evidence" test and also agreed that New Haven could not meet that standard. He argued that no matter which test was used, summary judgment for the city was inappropriate if "professed concern about disparate-impact litigation was simply a pretext" for intentional racial discrimination. Justice Alito argued that there was evidence that "the City's real reason was illegitimate, namely, the desire to placate a politically important racial constituency," in this case African-Americans, who were essential to the mayor's political viability.

Justice Ginsburg responded: "The real issue . . . is not whether the mayor and his staff were politically motivated; it is whether their attempt to score political points was legitimate (i.e., nondiscriminatory). Were they seeking to exclude white firefighters from promotion (unlikely, as a fair test would undoubtedly result in the addition of white firefighters to the officer ranks), or did they realize, at least belatedly, that their tests could be toppled in a disparate-impact suit? In the latter case, there is no disparate-treatment violation. Justice Alito, I recognize, would disagree."

Justice Scalia, concurring, argued that the case raised the larger issue of whether disparate impact liability was constitutional in the first place. The present case asked "[w]hether . . . Title VII's disparate-treatment provisions forbid 'remedial' race-based actions when a disparate-impact violation would *not* otherwise result." But the real problem, Justice Scalia explained, is that Title VII "not only permits but affirmatively *requires* [race based] actions when a disparate-impact violation *would* otherwise result."

"But if the Federal Government is prohibited from discriminating on the basis of race, then surely it is also prohibited from enacting laws mandating that third parties—e.g., employers, whether private, State, or municipal-discriminate on the basis of race. As the facts of these cases illustrate, Title VII's disparate-impact provisions place a racial thumb on the scales, often requiring employers to evaluate the racial outcomes of their policies, and to make decisions based on (because of) those racial outcomes. That type of racial decisionmaking is, as the Court explains, discriminatory. See Personnel Administrator of Mass. v. Feeney, 442 U.S. 256 (1979)."

"To be sure, the disparate-impact laws do not mandate imposition of quotas, but it is not clear why that should provide a safe harbor. Would a private employer not be guilty of unlawful discrimination if he refrained from establishing a racial hiring quota but intentionally designed his hiring practices to achieve the same end? Surely he would. Intentional discrimination is still occurring, just one step up the chain. Government compulsion of such design would therefore seemingly violate equal protection principles. Nor would it matter that Title VII requires consideration of race on a wholesale, rather than retail, level. . . . And of course the purportedly benign motive for the disparate-impact provisions cannot save the statute. See Adarand Constructors, Inc. v. Pena, 515 U.S. 200 (1995)."

"It might be possible to defend the law by framing it as simply an evidentiary tool used to identify genuine, intentional discrimination — to "smoke out," as it were, disparate treatment. . . . But arguably the disparate-impact provisions sweep too broadly to be fairly characterized in such a fashion — since they fail to provide an affirmative defense for good-faith (i.e., nonracially motivated) conduct, or perhaps even for good faith plus hiring standards that are entirely reasonable. . . . It is one thing to free plaintiffs from proving an employer's illicit intent, but quite another to preclude the employer from proving that its motives were pure and its actions reasonable."

"The Court's resolution of these cases makes it unnecessary to resolve these matters today. But the war between disparate impact and equal protection will be waged sooner or later, and it behooves us to begin thinking about how — and on what terms — to make peace between them."

Discussion

Although *Ricci* is specifically decided on non-constitutional grounds, the Justices clearly have constitutional issues in mind. These concern what is a racial classification and what is an improper discriminatory purpose.

1. *When is a decision "because of" or "based on" race?* Allied to the debate over intention is the question of what we mean by a decision "based on" race. The majority in *Ricci* assumes that New Haven's decision to change the employment test was "based on" race because the City was concerned that using the test might result in its hiring no African-American officers. At other points in its opinion, however, the majority suggests that the City violated the law, not because it was concerned with the potential exclusionary impact of the test, but because it publicly adopted the test and then publicly invalidated the test for race-related reasons, changing course in ways that invited reliance and stimulated racial resentments.

If government decisionmakers recognize that one of several possible methods of meeting the government needs will have a foreseeable adverse impact on minorities and, consequently, decide to meet the government's needs in some other way, is that change of course an unlawful decision "because of" race? Consider Justice Kennedy's concurring opinion in *Parents Involved*:

> School boards may pursue the goal of bringing together students of diverse backgrounds and races through other means, including strategic site selection of new schools; drawing attendance zones with general recognition of the demographics of neighborhoods; allocating resources for special programs; recruiting students and faculty in a targeted fashion; and tracking enrollments, performance, and other statistics by race. These mechanisms are race conscious but do not lead to

different treatment based on a classification that tells each student he or she is to be defined by race, so it is unlikely any of them would demand strict scrutiny to be found permissible. See Bush v. Vera, 517 U.S. 952, 958 (1996) (plurality opinion) ("Strict scrutiny does not apply merely because redistricting is performed with consciousness of race. . . . Electoral district lines are 'facially race neutral' so a more searching inquiry is necessary before strict scrutiny can be found applicable in redistricting cases than in cases of 'classifications based explicitly on race'" (quoting *Adarand*)). Executive and legislative branches, which for generations now have considered these types of policies and procedures, should be permitted to employ them with candor and with confidence that a constitutional violation does not occur whenever a decisionmaker considers the impact a given approach might have on students of different races. Assigning to each student a personal designation according to a crude system of individual racial classifications is quite a different matter; and the legal analysis changes accordingly.

Parents Involved, 551 U.S. at 789 (Kennedy, J., concurring).

Is the choice or invalidation of the employment test in *Ricci* more like the strategic site selection of a new school—or instead more like the consideration of the race of individual applicants for school admission that the Court rejected in *Parents Involved*? If the City may consider how changing the site of a school will affect its likely racial composition, why may it not consider how changing an employment test will affect the likely racial composition of the pool from which it may select officers for its fire department? (Suppose, for example, that the City learns from various experts that a test that emphasizes oral presentations and assessments of on-the-job-skills will likely result in improved achievement by minority applicants.) May it consider this information before selecting an employment test? If it may, why not after? Is the problem then that the City should have thought of this before it administered the test, and now it looks bad for it to change the rules after the test has been given? Put another way, is the motive or mental state of the decisionmaker crucial, or is the crucial factor the perceptions—and likely resentment—of the public? Is there any principled basis on which appearance could or should matter in deciding whether a policy decision is impermissibly race-based?

2. *What is discriminatory purpose?* In the 1970s and 1980s, in cases such as *Washington v. Davis*, the Court developed doctrines that allowed government policies with a disparate racial impact on racial minorities—even if entirely known or foreseeable—unless plaintiffs could show intentional discrimination. To prove intentional discrimination, plaintiffs would have to show government animus toward the group suffering disparate impact. As the Court put it in *Personnel Administrator v. Feeney*, "the decisionmaker [must have] selected or reaffirmed a particular course of action at least in part 'because of,' not merely 'in spite of,' its adverse effects upon an identifiable group."

In *Ricci*, however, and in disparate impact situations more generally, an employer's decision to take steps to prevent disparate impact on minorities primarily burdens whites. Justice Scalia assumes that deliberately choosing employment practices to prevent disparate impact on minorities would violate *Feeney*.

Is this correct? Why isn't the employer's decision "in spite of" the effects on whites? Perhaps more to the point, since the state action in this case is the federal government's, why isn't the federal government's purpose the integration of workforces rather than a desire to harm members of the white majority?

Suppose one applied Scalia's interpretation of *Washington v. Davis* and *Feeney* to previous constitutional challenges of legislation that had disparate impacts on African-Americans, Latinos, and women. Would the cases come out differently?

Perhaps Scalia's argument is that disparate impact is constitutionally troublesome because it requires employers to consider the racial effects of their actions. If so, why wouldn't this concern make unconstitutional any federal policies that encourage voluntary compliance with workplace integration? Note that Scalia's argument in *Ricci* recapitulates in the employment context the debate between the Justices in *Parents Involved* about whether voluntary attempts to integrate schools are a forbidden form of racial balancing.

Note also the issue of symmetry between deliberate integration and segregation implicit in Scalia's argument: Scalia assumes that federal attempts to get employers to integrate workforces (through threats of disparate impact liability) are just as constitutionally objectionable as federal efforts to encourage the maintenance of segregated workforces because both "requir[e] employers to evaluate the racial outcomes of their policies, and to make decisions based on (because of) those racial outcomes." Should the Constitution treat these two purposes differently?

Justice Alito's concurrence focuses on the statutory question of forbidden purpose in Title VII. He assumes that scrapping the firefighter's test to please a powerful African-American constituency is an illegitimate form of racial discrimination. But if so, does this mean that making political decisions with predictable disparate impacts on minorities in order to please white voters also makes a decision illegitimate?

Suppose that a state decides to offer admission to any person who graduates in the top ten percent of their high school class to the state university, regardless of their test scores or cumulative grade point average, with the purpose of increasing minority enrollments. Suppose also that the state adopts this policy in order to please minority voters while simultaneously avoiding political opposition by white parents who are opposed to race-based affirmative action. Assuming that the state has limited slots available, the foreseeable effect is that fewer whites will be admitted to the university. Is this a racially motivated decision under *Feeney*?

Replace Hunter v. Erickson on p. 1067 with the following:

Note: The Rise and Fall of the Political Process Doctrine

During the Second Reconstruction, states sometimes reacted to increasing minority political power by changing political decisionmaking rules to make it more difficult to pass civil rights laws. In response, the Supreme Court developed the "political process" doctrine.

HUNTER v. ERICKSON, 393 U.S. 385 (1969): [The Akron City Council passed a fair housing ordinance to prevent housing discrimination. The ordinance was then suspended by an amendment to the Akron City Charter, section 137, which imposed special barriers to civil rights laws. City Council ordinances regulating the sale and leasing of real property "on the basis of race, color, religion, national origin or ancestry" would become effective only if approved by a majority of the electors voting at a general or special election. (The amendment also specified that the requirement would apply to existing ordinances.) By contrast, most other ordinances became effective 30 days after passage, subject to repeal by referendum initiated by 10 percent of the voters.

The Court, by a 6-3 majority, held that section 137 violated the Equal Protection Clause.]

WHITE, J.: [This case involves] an explicitly racial classification treating racial housing matters differently from other racial and housing matters. . . .

Only laws to end housing discrimination based on "race, color, religion, national origin or ancestry" must run 137's gantlet. It is true that the section draws no distinctions among racial and religious groups. Negroes and whites, Jews and Catholics are all subject to the same requirements if there is housing discrimination against them which they wish to end. But 137 nevertheless disadvantages those who would benefit from laws barring racial, religious, or ancestral discriminations as against those who would bar other discriminations or who would otherwise regulate the real estate market in their favor. The automatic referendum system does not reach housing discrimination on sexual or political grounds, or against those with children or dogs, nor does it affect tenants seeking more heat or better maintenance from landlords, nor those seeking rent control, urban renewal, public housing, or new building codes.

Moreover, although the law on its face treats Negro and white, Jew and gentile in an identical manner, the reality is that the law's impact falls on the minority. The majority needs no protection against discrimination and if it did, a referendum might be bothersome but no more than that. . . . [T]he State may no more disadvantage any particular group by making it more difficult to enact legislation in its behalf than it may dilute any person's vote or give any group a smaller representation than another of comparable size. We hold that 137 discriminates against minorities, and constitutes a real, substantial, and invidious denial of the equal protection of the laws.

HARLAN, J., joined by STEWART, J., concurring. . . .

Akron has adopted the referendum system because its citizens believe that whenever an action of the City Council raises the emotional opposition of *any* significant group in the community, the people should have a right to decide the matter directly. Statutes of this type, which are grounded upon general democratic principle, do not violate the Equal Protection Clause simply because they occasionally operate to disadvantage Negro political interests. If a governmental institution is to be fair, one group cannot always be expected to win. If the Council's fair housing legislation were defeated at a referendum, Negroes would undoubtedly lose an important political battle, but they would not thereby be denied equal protection. . . .

In the case before us, however, the city of Akron has not attempted to allocate governmental power on the basis of any general principle. Here we have a provision that has the clear purpose of making it more difficult for certain racial and religious minorities to achieve legislation that is in their interest. Since the charter amendment is discriminatory on its face, Akron must "bear a far heavier burden of justification" than is required in the normal case. McLaughlin v. Florida, 379 U.S. 184, 194 (1964). And Akron has failed to sustain this burden. . . .

[A dissenting opinion by Justice Black is omitted.]

Hunter, which characterized the referendum as "an explicitly racial classification," was decided before *Washington v. Davis* and *Personnel Director v. Feeney.* (Note Justice White's statement that "although the law on its face treats Negro and white, Jew and gentile in an identical manner, the reality is that the law's impact falls on the minority.") The Court reinterpreted *Hunter* as a case about the political process in two post-*Feeney* cases decided the same day in 1982. The emergence of a "political process doctrine" reflected judicial concern that, as the federal courts reduced oversight of democratic decisionmaking about race, that minorities not be left exposed by unfair modifications to the political process.

WASHINGTON v. SEATTLE SCHOOL DISTRICT NO. 1, 458 U.S. 457 (1982): [In 1978, after the implementation of a mandatory busing plan to reduce de facto school desegregation, 66 percent of the voters of the State of Washington approved Initiative 350, which provided that "no school board . . . shall directly or indirectly require any student to attend a school other than the school which is geographically nearest or next nearest the student's place of residence. . . . " The initiative then set out a number of broad exceptions to this requirement. For example, students could be assigned beyond their neighborhood school if they "require[d] special education, care or guidance," or if "there are health or safety hazards, either natural or man made, or physical barriers or obstacles . . . between [a] student's place of residence and the nearest or next nearest school," or if "the school nearest or next nearest to [a student's] place of residence is unfit or inadequate because of overcrowding, unsafe conditions or lack of physical facilities." The practical effect was to allow busing except for desegregative purposes. Several school districts that had noncomplying desegregation plans challenged Initiative 350 under the Equal Protection Clause. The Court held that Initiative 350 violated the Equal Protection Clause.]

BLACKMUN, J:

[T]he political majority may generally restructure the political process to place obstacles in the path of everyone seeking to secure the benefits of governmental action. But a different analysis is required when the State allocates governmental power nonneutrally, by explicitly using *racial* nature of a decision to determine the decisionmaking process. [D]espite its facial neutrality there is little doubt that the initiative was effectively drawn for racial purposes. . . . Proponents of the initiative candidly "represented that there would be no loss of school district flexibility other than in busing for desegregation purposes." . . . Initiative 350 in fact allows school districts to bus their students "for most, if not all," of the non-integrative purposes required by their educational policies.

[I]t undoubtedly is true . . . that the proponents of mandatory integration cannot be classified by race: Negroes and whites may be counted among both the supporters and the opponents of Initiative 350. And it should be equally clear that white as well as Negro children benefit from exposure to "ethnic and racial diversity in the classroom." But neither of these factors serves to distinguish *Hunter*, for we may fairly assume that members of the racial majority both favored and benefited from Akron's fair housing ordinance. For present purposes, it is enough that minorities may consider busing for integration to be "legislation that is in their interest." Hunter v. Erickson, 393 U.S., at 395 (Harlan, J., concurring). Given the racial focus of Initiative 350, this suffices to trigger application of the *Hunter* doctrine.

[T]he practical effect of Initiative 350 is to work a reallocation of power of the kind condemned in *Hunter.* The initiative removes the authority to address a racial problem — and only a racial problem — from the existing decisionmaking body, in such a way as to burden minority interests. Those favoring the elimination of de facto school segregation now must seek relief from the state legislature, or from the statewide electorate. Yet authority over all other student assignment decisions, as well as over most other areas of educational policy, remains vested in the local school board. . . . As in *Hunter*, then, the community's political mechanisms are modified to place effective decisionmaking authority over a racial issue at a different level of government.

[In response to the argument that *Hunter* was really a disparate impact case that had been overruled by Washington v. Davis, Justice Blackmun explained:] While decisions such as Washington v. Davis . . . considered classifications facially unrelated to race, the charter amendment at issue in *Hunter* dealt in explicitly racial terms with legislation designed to benefit minorities "as minorities," not legislation intended to benefit some larger group of underprivileged citizens among whom minorities were disproportionately represented. This does not mean, of course, that every attempt to address a racial issue gives rise to an impermissible racial classification. But when the political process or the decisionmaking mechanism used to *address* racially conscious legislation — and only such legislation — is singled out for peculiar and disadvantageous treatment, the governmental action plainly "rests on 'distinctions based on race.'"

And when the State's allocation of power places unusual burdens on the ability of racial groups to enact legislation specifically designed to overcome the "special condition" of prejudice, the governmental action seriously "curtail[s] the operation of those political processes ordinarily to be relied upon to protect minorities." United States v. Carolene Products Co., 304 U.S. 144, 152-153, n.4 (1938). In a most direct sense, this implicates the judiciary's special role in safeguarding the interests of those groups that are "relegated to such a position of political powerlessness as to command extraordinary protection from the majoritarian political process."

POWELL, J., dissenting, joined by BURGER, C.J., and REHNQUIST and O'CONNOR, JJ.:

I dissent from the Court's unprecedented intrusion into the structure of a state government. The School Districts in this case were under no federal constitutional obligation to adopt mandatory busing programs [because there had been no finding of de jure segregation.] The State of Washington, the governmental body ultimately responsible for the provision of public education, has determined that certain mandatory busing programs are detrimental to the education of its children. . . .

This is certainly not a case where a State—in moving to change a locally adopted policy—has established a racially discriminatory requirement. Initiative 350 does not impede enforcement of the Fourteenth Amendment. If a Washington school district should be found to have established a segregated school system, Initiative 350 will place no barrier in the way of a remedial busing order. Nor does Initiative 350 authorize or approve segregation in any form or degree. It is neutral on its face, and racially neutral as public policy. Children of all races benefit from neighborhood schooling, just as children of all races benefit from exposure to " 'ethnic and racial diversity in the classroom.' "

Finally, Initiative 350 places no "special burdens on racial minorities within the governmental process," *Hunter*, such that interference with the State's distribution of authority is justified. Initiative 350 is simply a reflection of the State's political process at work. It does not alter that process in any respect. It does not require, for example, that all matters dealing with race—or with integration in the schools—must henceforth be submitted to a referendum of the people. The State has done no more than precisely what the Court has said that it should do: It has "resolved through the political process" the "desirability and efficacy of [mandatory] school desegregation" where there has been no unlawful segregation. . . .

The political process in Washington, as in other States, permits persons who are dissatisfied at a local level to appeal to the state legislature or the people of the State for redress. It permits the people of a State to pre-empt local policies, and to formulate new programs and regulations. Such a process is inherent in the continued sovereignty of the States. This is our system. Any time a State chooses to address a major issue some persons or groups may be disadvantaged. In a democratic system there are winners and losers. But there is no inherent unfairness in this and certainly no constitutional violation. . . .

Nothing in *Hunter* supports the Court's extraordinary invasion into the State's distribution of authority. Even could it be assumed that Initiative 350 imposed a burden on racial minorities, it simply does not place unique political obstacles in the way of racial minorities. In this case, unlike in *Hunter*, the political system has *not* been redrawn or altered. The authority of the State over the public school system, acting through Initiative or the legislature, is plenary. Thus, the State's political system is not altered when it adopts for the first time a policy, concededly within the area of its authority, for the regulation of local school districts. And certainly racial minorities are not uniquely or comparatively burdened by the State's adoption of a policy that would be lawful if adopted by any School District in the State.

In Crawford v. Los Angeles Board of Education, 458 U.S. 527 (1982), decided the same day, the Court, with only Justice Marshall dissenting, upheld a California proposition, passed by referendum, that barred state courts from using busing as a remedy for school segregation that was illegal under state, but not federal, law. (The California Constitution had been interpreted to prohibit de facto segregation.) Justice Blackmun, joined by Justice Brennan, concurred in order to explain that "State courts do not create the rights they enforce; those rights originate elsewhere—in the state legislature, in the State's political subdivisions, or in the state constitution itself. When one of those rights is repealed, and therefore is rendered unenforceable by the courts, that action can hardly be said to restructure the State's decisionmaking mechanism. While the California electorate may have made it more difficult to achieve desegregation when it enacted Proposition I, [it] did so not by working a structural change in the political *process* so much as by simply repealing the right to invoke a judicial busing remedy."

Thirty-two years later, the Roberts Court revisited the political process doctrine in the context of a state referendum passed to eliminate affirmative action policies.

SCHUETTE v. COALITION TO DEFEND AFFIRMATIVE ACTION (BAMN), 134 S. Ct. 1623 (2014): [Michigan's voters passed an amendment to the Michigan Constitution, codified as section 26, which provided that "(1) The University of Michigan, Michigan State University, Wayne State University, and any other public college or university, community college, or school district shall not discriminate against, or grant preferential treatment to, any individual or group on the basis of race, sex, color, ethnicity, or national origin in the operation of public employment, public education, or public contracting" and "(2) The state [defined to include all cities, subdivisions, and instrumentalities of the state] shall not discriminate against, or grant preferential treatment to, any individual or group on the basis of race, sex, color, ethnicity, or national origin in the operation of public employment, public education, or public contracting."

The Court, in a plurality opinion by Justice Kennedy, upheld the amendment. Justice Kagan did not participate.]

KENNEDY, J., joined by ROBERTS, C.J., and ALITO, J.:

[T]his case is not about . . . the constitutionality, or the merits, of race-conscious admissions policies in higher education . . . but [about] whether, and in what manner, voters in the States may choose to prohibit the consideration of racial preferences in governmental decisions, in particular with respect to school admissions. . . .

[Justice Kennedy distinguished *Hunter* and *Seattle* on the ground that they involved laws designed to harm racial minorities:]

In [Reitman v. Mulkey, 387 U.S. 369 (1967)], voters amended the California Constitution to prohibit any state legislative interference with an owner's prerogative to decline to sell or rent residential property on any basis. . . . The Court agreed with the California Supreme Court that the amendment operated to insinuate the State into the decision to discriminate by encouraging that practice. The . . . "immediate design and intent" of the amendment was to "establis[h] a purported constitutional right to privately discriminate." . . . [T]he amendment "expressly authorized and constitutionalized the private right to discriminate" [and] [t]he effect of the state constitutional amendment was to "significantly encourage and involve the State in private racial discriminations."

Central to the Court's reasoning in *Hunter* [v. *Erickson*] was that the charter amendment was enacted in circumstances where widespread racial discrimination in the sale and rental of housing led to segregated housing, forcing many to live in "'unhealthful, unsafe, unsanitary and overcrowded conditions.'" . . . Akron attempted to characterize the charter amendment "simply as a public decision to move slowly in the delicate area of race relations" and as a means "to allow the people of Akron to participate" in the decision. The Court rejected Akron's flawed "justifications for its discrimination," justifications that by their own terms had the effect of acknowledging the targeted nature of the charter amendment. The Court noted, furthermore, that the charter amendment was unnecessary as a general means of public control over the city council; for the people of Akron already were empowered to overturn ordinances by referendum. The Court found that the city charter amendment, by singling out antidiscrimination ordinances, "places special burden on racial minorities within the governmental process," thus becoming as impermissible as any other government action taken with the invidious intent to injure a racial minority.

[Although] Justice Harlan['s] concurrence . . . argued the city charter amendment "has the clear purpose of making it more difficult for certain racial and religious minorities to achieve legislation that is in their interest[,]" . . . *Hunter* rests on the unremarkable principle that the State may not alter the procedures of government to target racial minorities. The facts in *Hunter* established that invidious discrimination would be the necessary result of the procedural restructuring. Thus, in *Mulkey* and *Hunter*, there was a demonstrated injury on the basis of race that, by reasons of state encouragement or participation, became more aggravated.

[Likewise,] *Seattle* is best understood as a case in which the state action in question (the bar on busing enacted by the State's voters) had the serious risk, if not purpose, of causing specific injuries on account of race, just as had been the case in *Mulkey* and *Hunter*. [T]here had been no judicial finding of *de jure* segregation with respect to Seattle's school district, [and such a finding would be required today to authorize the school board's busing plan, see Parents Involved in Community Schools v. Seattle School Dist. No. 1, 551 U.S. 701 (2007)]. Justice Breyer . . . observe[d] in dissent [in *Parents Involved*] that one permissible reading of the record was that the [Seattle] school board had maintained policies to perpetuate racial segregation in the schools. [Nevertheless,] we must understand *Seattle* as *Seattle* understood itself, as a case in which neither the State nor the United States "challenge[d] the propriety of race-conscious student assignments for the purpose of achieving integration, even absent a finding of prior *de jure* segregation." [T]he legitimacy and constitutionality of . . . busing for desegregation . . . was [then] assumed. *Seattle* involved a state initiative that "was carefully tailored to interfere only with desegregative busing." The *Seattle* Court . . . found that the State's disapproval of the school board's busing remedy was an aggravation of the very racial injury in which the State itself was complicit.

The broad language used in *Seattle,* however, went well beyond the analysis needed to resolve the case. The Court there seized upon the statement in Justice Harlan's concurrence in *Hunter* that the procedural change in that case had "the clear purpose of making it more difficult for certain racial and religious minorities to achieve legislation that is in their interest." . . . The *Seattle* Court . . . used [that] language . . . to establish a new and far-reaching rationale. *Seattle* stated that where a government policy "inures primarily to the benefit of the minority" and "minorities . . . consider" the policy to be " 'in their interest,' " then any state action that "place[s] effective decisionmaking authority over" that policy "at a different level of government" must be reviewed under strict scrutiny. [Thus], any state action with a "racial focus" that makes it "more difficult for certain racial minorities than for other groups" to "achieve legislation that is in their interest" is subject to strict scrutiny. [T]hat reading [of *Seattle*] must be rejected.

[T]o the extent *Seattle* is read to require the Court to determine and declare which political policies serve the "interest" of a group defined in racial terms, that rationale was unnecessary to the decision in *Seattle*; it has no support in precedent; and it raises serious constitutional concerns. . . . In cautioning against "impermissible racial stereotypes," this Court has rejected the assumption that "members of the same racial group—regardless of their age, education, economic status, or the community in which they live—think alike, share the same political interests, and will prefer the same candidates at the polls." *Shaw v. Reno,* 509 U.S. 630 (1993). It cannot be entertained as a serious proposition that all individuals of the same race think alike. . . . And if it were deemed necessary to probe how some races define their own interest in political matters, still another beginning point would be to define individuals according to race. But in a society in which those lines are becoming more blurred, the attempt to define race-based categories also raises serious questions of its own. Government action that classifies individuals on the basis of race is inherently suspect and carries the danger of perpetuating the very racial divisions the polity seeks to transcend. Were courts to embark upon this venture not only would it be undertaken with no clear legal standards or accepted sources to guide judicial decision but also it would result in, or at least impose a high risk of, inquiries and categories dependent upon demeaning stereotypes, classifications of questionable constitutionality on their own terms.

[T]he court would next be required to determine the policy realms in which certain groups — groups defined by race — have a political interest. That undertaking, again without guidance from any accepted legal standards, would risk, in turn, the creation of incentives for those who support or oppose certain policies to cast the debate in terms of racial advantage or disadvantage. [R]acial antagonisms and conflict [could] tend to arise in the context of judicial decisions as courts undertook to announce what particular issues of public policy should be classified as advantageous to some group defined by race. . . . In a nation in which governmental policies are wide ranging, those who seek to limit voter participation might be tempted, were this Court to adopt the *Seattle* formulation, to urge that a group they choose to define by race or racial stereotypes are advantaged or disadvantaged by any number of laws or decisions. Tax policy, housing subsidies, wage regulations, and even the naming of public schools, highways, and monuments are just a few examples of what could become a list of subjects that some organizations could insist should be beyond the power of voters to decide, or beyond the power of a legislature to decide when enacting limits on the power of local authorities or other governmental entities to address certain subjects. Racial division would be validated, not discouraged . . . .

[One might argue] that objections to the larger consequences of the *Seattle* formulation need not be confronted in this case, for here race was an undoubted subject of the ballot issue. But a number of problems raised by *Seattle*, such as racial definitions, still apply. And this principal flaw in the ruling of the Court of Appeals does remain: Here there was no infliction of a specific injury of the kind at issue in *Mulkey* and *Hunter* and in the history of the Seattle schools. Here there is no precedent for extending these cases to restrict the right of Michigan voters to determine that race-based preferences granted by Michigan governmental entities should be ended. [And the *Seattle* formulation] of necessity calls into question other long-settled rulings on similar state policies [that have ended racial preferences in public contracting and education, and] in essence would announce a finding that the past 15 years of state public debate on this issue have been improper. . . .

[The] question [in this case] is not how to address or prevent injury caused on account of race but whether voters may determine whether a policy of race-based preferences should be continued.

By approving Proposal 2 and thereby adding §26 to their State Constitution, the Michigan voters exercised their privilege to enact laws as a basic exercise of their democratic power. . . . Michigan voters used the initiative system to bypass public officials who were deemed not responsive to the concerns of a majority of the voters with respect to a policy of granting race-based preferences that raises difficult and delicate issues.

The freedom secured by the Constitution consists, in one of its essential dimensions, of the right of the individual not to be injured by the unlawful exercise of governmental power. . . . Yet freedom does not stop with individual rights. Our constitutional system embraces, too, the right of citizens to debate so they can learn and decide and then, through the political process, act in concert to try to shape the course of their own times and the course of a nation that must strive always to make freedom ever greater and more secure. Here Michigan voters acted in concert and statewide to seek consensus and adopt a policy on a difficult subject against a historical background of race in America that has been a source of tragedy and persisting injustice. That history demands that we continue to learn, to listen, and to remain open to new approaches if we are to aspire always to a constitutional order in which all persons are treated with fairness and equal dignity. Were the Court to rule that the question addressed by Michigan voters is too sensitive or complex to be within the grasp of the electorate; or that the policies at issue remain too delicate to be resolved save by university officials or faculties, acting at some remove from immediate public scrutiny and control; or that these matters are so arcane that the electorate's power must be limited because the people cannot prudently exercise that power even after a full debate, that holding would be an unprecedented restriction on the exercise of a fundamental right held not just by one person but by all in common. It is the right to speak and debate and learn and then, as a matter of political will, to act through a lawful electoral process.

The respondents in this case insist that a difficult question of public policy must be taken from the reach of the voters, and thus removed from the realm of public discussion, dialogue, and debate in an election campaign. Quite in addition to the serious First Amendment implications of that position with respect to any particular election, it is inconsistent with the underlying premises of a responsible, functioning democracy. One of those premises is that a democracy has the capacity — and the duty — to learn from its past mistakes; to discover and confront persisting biases; and by respectful, rationale deliberation to rise above those flaws and injustices. That process is impeded, not advanced, by court decrees based on the proposition that the public cannot have the requisite repose to discuss certain issues. It is demeaning to the democratic process to presume that the voters are not capable of deciding an issue of this sensitivity on decent and rational grounds. The process of public discourse and political debate should not be foreclosed even if there is a risk that during a public campaign there will be those, on both sides, who seek to use racial division and discord to their own political advantage. An informed public can, and must, rise above this. The idea of democracy is that it can, and must, mature. Freedom embraces the right, indeed the duty, to engage in a rational, civic discourse in order to determine how best to form a consensus to shape the destiny of the Nation and its people. These First Amendment dynamics would be disserved if this Court were to say that the question here at issue is beyond the capacity of the voters to debate and then to determine.

These precepts are not inconsistent with the well-established principle that when hurt or injury is inflicted on racial minorities by the encouragement or command of laws or other state action, the Constitution requires redress by the courts. [T]hose were the circumstances that the Court found present in *Mulkey, Hunter,* and *Seattle.* But those circumstances are not present here.

[In] *Mulkey, Hunter,* and *Seattle . . .* the political restriction in question was designed to be used, or was likely to be used, to encourage infliction of injury by reason of race. What is at stake here is not whether injury will be inflicted but whether government can be instructed not to follow a course that entails, first, the definition of racial categories and, second, the grant of favored status to persons in some racial categories and not others.

[A concurring opinion by Chief Justice Roberts is omitted.]

SCALIA, J., joined by THOMAS, J., concurring in the judgment:
Patently atextual, unadministrable, and contrary to our traditional equal-protection jurisprudence, *Hunter* and *Seattle* should be overruled.

[T]he problems with the political-process doctrine begin with its triggering prong, which assigns to a court the task of determining whether a law that reallocates policymaking authority concerns a "racial issue." *Seattle . . .* suggests that an issue is racial if adopting one position on the question would "at bottom inur[e] primarily to the benefit of the minority, and is designed for that purpose." It is irrelevant that, as in *Hunter* and *Seattle,* both the racial minority and the racial majority benefit from the policy in question, and members of both groups favor it. Judges should instead focus their guesswork on their own juridical sense of what is primarily for the benefit of minorities. On second thought, maybe judges need only ask this question: Is it possible "that minorities may consider" the policy in question to be "in their interest"? If so, you can be sure that you are dealing with a "racial issue."

No good can come of such random judicial musing. [I]t involves judges in the dirty business of dividing the Nation "into racial blocs." That task is as difficult as it is unappealing. (Does a half-Latino, half-American Indian have Latino interests, American-Indian interests, both, half of both?) What is worse, the exercise promotes the noxious fiction that, knowing only a person's color or ethnicity, we can be sure that he has a predetermined set of policy "interests," thus "reinforc[ing] the perception that members of the same racial group—regardless of their age, education, economic status, or the community in which they live—think alike, [and] share the same political interests." Whether done by a judge or a school board, such "racial stereotyping [is] at odds with equal protection mandates." . . . More fundamentally, it misreads the Equal Protection Clause to protect "particular group[s]," a construction that we have tirelessly repudiated in a "long line of cases understanding equal protection as a personal right." . . .

Seattle insists that only those political-process alterations that burden racial *minorities* deny equal protection. [Yet] [i]n the years since *Seattle*, we have repeatedly rejected "a reading of the guarantee of equal protection under which the level of scrutiny varies according to the ability of different groups to defend their interests in the representative process." *Richmond v. J.A. Croson Co.*, 488 U.S. 469 (1989). Meant to obliterate rather than endorse the practice of racial classifications, the Fourteenth Amendment's guarantees "obtai[n] with equal force regardless of 'the race of those burdened or benefitted.'" . . .

The dissent trots out the old saw, derived from dictum in a footnote, that legislation motivated by "'prejudice against discrete and insular minorities'" merits "'more exacting judicial scrutiny.'" (quoting *United States v. Carolene Products*, 304 U.S. 144, 152-153, n.4). I say derived from that dictum (expressed by the four-Justice majority of a seven-Justice Court) because the dictum itself merely said "*[n]or need we enquire* . . . whether prejudice against discrete and insular minorities may be a special condition," *id.*, at 153, n.4 (emphasis added). The dissent does not argue, of course, that such "prejudice" produced §26. Nor does it explain why certain racial minorities in Michigan qualify as "'insular,'" meaning that "other groups will not form coalitions with them — and, critically, not because of lack of common interests but because of 'prejudice.'" Nor does it even make the case that a group's "discreteness" and "insularity" are political *liabilities* rather than political *strengths* — a serious question that alone demonstrates the prudence of the *Carolene Products* dictumizers in leaving the "enquir[y]" for another day. As for the question whether "legislation which restricts those political processes which can ordinarily be expected to bring about repeal of undesirable legislation . . . is to be subjected to more exacting judicial scrutiny," the *Carolene Products* Court found it "unnecessary to consider [that] now." 304 U.S., at 152, n.4. If the dissent thinks that worth considering today, it should explain why the election of a university's governing board is a "political process which can ordinarily be expected to bring about repeal of undesirable legislation," but Michigan voters' ability to amend their Constitution is not. It seems to me quite the opposite. . . . But the more important point is that we should not design our jurisprudence to conform to dictum in a footnote in a four-Justice opinion.

Moving from the appalling to the absurd, I turn now to the second part of the *Hunter-Seattle* analysis[, which] directs a court to determine whether the challenged act "place[s] effective decisionmaking authority over [the] racial issue at a different level of government." . . . [Yet] in another line of cases, we have emphasized the near-limitless sovereignty of each State to design its governing structure as it sees fit. Generally, "a State is afforded wide leeway when experimenting with the appropriate allocation of state legislative power" and may create "political subdivisions such as cities and counties . . . 'as convenient agencies for exercising such of the governmental powers of the state as may be entrusted to them.'" *Holt Civic Club v. Tuscaloosa,* 439 U.S. 60, 71 (1978). Accordingly, States have "absolute discretion" to determine the "number, nature and duration of the powers conferred upon [municipal] corporations and the territory over which they shall be exercised." *Holt Civic Club, supra,* at 71. So it would seem to go without saying that a State may give certain powers to cities, later assign the same powers to counties, and even reclaim them for itself.

Taken to the limits of its logic, *Hunter-Seattle* is the gaping exception that nearly swallows the rule of structural state sovereignty. . . . *Seattle*'s logic would create affirmative-action safe havens wherever subordinate officials in public universities (1) traditionally have enjoyed "effective decisionmaking authority" over admissions policy but (2) have not yet used that authority to prohibit race-conscious admissions decisions. The mere existence of a subordinate's discretion over the matter would work a kind of reverse pre-emption. It is "a strange notion—alien to our system—that local governmental bodies can forever pre-empt the ability of a State—the sovereign power—to address a matter of compelling concern to the State." But that is precisely what the political-process doctrine contemplates.

. . .

I part ways with *Hunter, Seattle,* and (I think) the plurality for an additional reason: Each endorses a version of the proposition that a facially neutral law may deny equal protection solely because it has a disparate racial impact. Few equal-protection theories have been so squarely and soundly rejected. "An unwavering line of cases from this Court holds that a violation of the Equal Protection Clause requires state action motivated by discriminatory intent," *Hernandez v. New York,* 500 U.S. 352, 372-373 (1991) (O'Connor, J., concurring in judgment), and that "official action will not be held unconstitutional solely because it results in a racially disproportionate impact," *Arlington Heights.* . . . [T]he plurality opinion leaves ajar an effects-test escape hatch modeled after *Hunter* and *Seattle,* suggesting that state action denies equal protection when it "ha[s] the *serious risk,* if not purpose, of causing specific injuries on account of race," or is either "designed to be used, or . . . *likely to be used,* to encourage infliction of injury by reason of race." Since these formulations enable a determination of an equal-protection violation where there is no discriminatory intent, they are inconsistent with the long *Washington v. Davis* line of cases.

Respondents argue that we need not bother with the discriminatory-purpose test, since §26 may be struck more straightforwardly as a racial "classification." Admitting (as they must) that §26 does not on its face "distribut[e] burdens or benefits on the basis of individual racial classifications," *Parents Involved,* respondents rely on *Seattle*'s statement that "when the political process or the decisionmaking mechanism used to address racially conscious legislation—and only such legislation—is singled out for peculiar and disadvantageous treatment," then that "singling out" is a racial classification. But this is just the political-process theory bedecked in different doctrinal dress. A law that "neither says nor implies that persons are to be treated differently on account of their race" is not a racial classification. That is particularly true of statutes mandating equal treatment. "[A] law that prohibits the State from classifying individuals by race . . . *a fortiori* does not classify individuals by race."

Thus, the question in this case, as in every case in which neutral state action is said to deny equal protection on account of race, is whether the action reflects a racially discriminatory purpose. *Seattle* stresses that "singling out the political processes affecting racial issues for uniquely disadvantageous treatment inevitably raises dangers of impermissible motivation." True enough, but that motivation must be proved. And respondents do not have a prayer of proving it here. . . . In my view, any law expressly requiring state actors to afford all persons equal protection of the laws (such as Initiative 350 in *Seattle*, though not the charter amendment in *Hunter*) does not—*cannot*—deny "to any person . . . equal protection of the laws," U.S. Const., Amdt. 14, §1, regardless of whatever evidence of seemingly foul purposes plaintiffs may cook up in the trial court.

* * *

As Justice Harlan observed over a century ago, "[o]ur Constitution is colorblind, and neither knows nor tolerates classes among citizens." *Plessy v. Ferguson* (dissenting opinion). The people of Michigan wish the same for their governing charter. It would be shameful for us to stand in their way.

BREYER, J., concurring in the judgment:

I agree with the plurality that the amendment is consistent with the Federal Equal Protection Clause. But I believe this for different reasons.

First, [this case considers a ban on affirmative action justified on grounds of increasing diversity]; we do not address the amendment insofar as it forbids the use of race-conscious admissions programs designed to remedy past exclusionary racial discrimination or the direct effects of that discrimination. Application of the amendment in that context would present different questions which may demand different answers.

Second, . . . I continue to believe that the Constitution permits, though it does not require, the use of the kind of [diversity-seeking] race-conscious programs that are now barred by the Michigan Constitution. . . . The Constitution allows local, state, and national communities to adopt narrowly tailored race-conscious programs designed to bring about greater inclusion and diversity. But the Constitution foresees the ballot box, not the courts, as the normal instrument for resolving differences and debates about the merits of these programs. . . .

Third, [unlike] *Hunter* and *Seattle*, [t]his case . . . does not involve a reordering of the *political* process; it does not in fact involve the movement of decisionmaking from one political level to another. Rather, here, Michigan law delegated broad policymaking authority to elected university boards, but those boards delegated admissions-related decisionmaking authority to unelected university faculty members and administrators. Although the boards unquestionably retained the *power* to set policy regarding race-conscious admissions, in *fact* faculty members and administrators set the race-conscious admissions policies in question. (It is often true that elected bodies — including, for example, school boards, city councils, and state legislatures — have the power to enact policies, but in fact delegate that power to administrators.) Although at limited times the university boards were advised of the content of their race-conscious admissions policies, to my knowledge no board voted to accept or reject any of those policies. Thus, unelected faculty members and administrators, not voters or their elected representatives, adopted the race-conscious admissions programs affected by Michigan's constitutional amendment. The amendment took decisionmaking authority away from these unelected actors and placed it in the hands of the voters.

[T]he doctrine set forth in *Hunter* and *Seattle* does not easily fit this case. In those cases minorities had participated in the political process and they had won. The majority's subsequent reordering of the political process repealed the minority's successes and made it more difficult for the minority to succeed in the future. The majority thereby diminished the minority's ability to participate meaningfully in the electoral process. But one cannot as easily characterize the movement of the decisionmaking mechanism at issue here — from an administrative process to an electoral process — as diminishing the minority's ability to participate meaningfully in the *political* process. There is no prior electoral process in which the minority participated. [T]o extend the holding of *Hunter* and *Seattle* to reach situations in which decisionmaking authority is moved from an administrative body to a political one would pose significant difficulties. The administrative process encompasses vast numbers of decisionmakers answering numerous policy questions in hosts of different fields. Administrative bodies modify programs in detail, and decisionmaking authority within the administrative process frequently moves around — due to amendments to statutes, new administrative rules, and evolving agency practice. It is thus particularly difficult in this context for judges to determine when a change in the locus of decisionmaking authority places a comparative structural burden on a racial minority. And to apply *Hunter* and *Seattle* to the administrative process would, by tending to hinder change, risk discouraging experimentation, interfering with efforts to see when and how race-conscious policies work.

Finally, the principle that underlies *Hunter* and *Seattle* runs up against a competing principle, discussed above. This competing principle favors decisionmaking though the democratic process. Just as this principle strongly supports the right of the people, or their elected representatives, to adopt race-conscious policies for reasons of inclusion, so must it give them the right to vote not to do so.

SOTOMAYOR, J., joined by GINSBURG, J., dissenting:
[A] fundamental strand of our equal protection jurisprudence focuses on process, securing to all citizens the right to participate meaningfully and equally in

self-government. That right is the bedrock of our democracy, for it preserves all other rights.

Yet to know the history of our Nation is to understand its long and lamentable record of stymieing the right of racial minorities to participate in the political process. At first, the majority acted with an open, invidious purpose. Notwithstanding the command of the Fifteenth Amendment, certain States shut racial minorities out of the political process altogether by withholding the right to vote. This Court intervened to preserve that right. The majority tried again, replacing outright bans on voting with literacy tests, good character requirements, poll taxes, and gerrymandering. The Court was not fooled; it invalidated those measures, too. The majority persisted. This time, although it allowed the minority access to the political process, the majority changed the ground rules of the process so as to make it more difficult for the minority, and the minority alone, to obtain policies designed to foster racial integration. Although these political restructurings may not have been discriminatory in purpose, the Court reaffirmed the right of minority members of our society to participate meaningfully and equally in the political process.

This case involves this last chapter of discrimination: A majority of the Michigan electorate changed the basic rules of the political process in that State in a manner that uniquely disadvantaged racial minorities. Prior to the enactment of the constitutional initiative at issue here, all of the admissions policies of Michigan's public colleges and universities — including race-sensitive admissions policies — were in the hands of each institution's governing board. The members of those boards are nominated by political parties and elected by the citizenry in statewide elections. After over a century of being shut out of Michigan's institutions of higher education, racial minorities in Michigan had succeeded in persuading the elected board representatives to adopt admissions policies that took into account the benefits of racial diversity. And this Court twice blessed such efforts — first in *Regents of Univ. of Cal. v. Bakke*, 438 U.S. 265 (1978), and again in *Grutter v. Bollinger*, 539 U.S. 306 (2003), a case that itself concerned a Michigan admissions policy.

In the wake of *Grutter*, some voters in Michigan set out to eliminate the use of race-sensitive admissions policies. Those voters were of course free to pursue this end in any number of ways. For example, they could have persuaded existing board members to change their minds through individual or grassroots lobbying efforts, or through general public awareness campaigns. Or they could have mobilized efforts to vote uncooperative board members out of office, replacing them with members who would share their desire to abolish race-sensitive admissions policies. When this Court holds that the Constitution permits a particular policy, nothing prevents a majority of a State's voters from choosing not to adopt that policy. Our system of government encourages — and indeed, depends on — that type of democratic action.

But instead, the majority of Michigan voters changed the rules in the middle of the game, reconfiguring the existing political process in Michigan in a manner that burdened racial minorities. They did so in the 2006 election by amending the Michigan Constitution to enact Art. I, §26, which provides in relevant part that Michigan's public universities "shall not discriminate against, or grant preferential treatment to, any individual or group on the basis of race, sex, color, ethnicity, or national origin in the operation of public employment, public education, or public contracting."

As a result of §26, there are now two very different processes through which a Michigan citizen is permitted to influence the admissions policies of the State's universities: one for persons interested in race-sensitive admissions policies and one for everyone else. A citizen who is a University of Michigan alumnus, for instance, can advocate for an admissions policy that considers an applicant's legacy status by meeting individually with members of the Board of Regents to convince them of her views, by joining with other legacy parents to lobby the Board, or by voting for and supporting Board candidates who share her position. The same options are available to a citizen who wants the Board to adopt admissions policies that consider athleticism, geography, area of study, and so on. The one and only policy a Michigan citizen may not seek through this long-established process is a race-sensitive admissions policy that considers race in an individualized manner when it is clear that race-neutral alternatives are not adequate to achieve diversity. For that policy alone, the citizens of Michigan must undertake the daunting task of amending the State Constitution.

. . .

[In response to the Civil Rights Revolution of the 1960s and 1970s,] [m]any States tried to suppress the political voice of racial minorities . . . by reconfiguring the manner in which they filled vacancies in local offices, often transferring authority from the electorate (where minority citizens had a voice at the local level) to the States' executive branch (where minorities wielded little if any influence). . . . It was in this historical context that the Court intervened in *Hunter v. Erickson*, 393 U.S. 385 (1969), and *Washington v. Seattle School Dist. No. 1*, 458 U.S. 457 (1982). Together, *Hunter* and *Seattle* recognized a fundamental strand of this Court's equal protection jurisprudence: the political-process doctrine.

. . .

Hunter and *Seattle* vindicated a principle that is as elementary to our equal protection jurisprudence as it is essential: The majority may not suppress the minority's right to participate on equal terms in the political process. Under this doctrine, governmental action deprives minority groups of equal protection when it (1) has a racial focus, targeting a policy or program that "inures primarily to the benefit of the minority," *Seattle*; and (2) alters the political process in a manner that uniquely burdens racial minorities' ability to achieve their goals through that process. A faithful application of the doctrine resoundingly resolves this case in respondents' favor.

Section 26 has a "racial focus." *Seattle*. That is clear from its text, which prohibits Michigan's public colleges and universities from "grant[ing] preferential treatment to any individual or group on the basis of race." Mich. Const.,

Art. I, §26. Like desegregation of public schools, race-sensitive admissions policies "inur[e] primarily to the benefit of the minority," as they are designed to increase minorities' access to institutions of higher education.

The racial-focus prong has never required a policy to benefit *only* a minority group . . . [but only] asks whether a policy "benefits *primarily* a racial minority." [Relocated footnote — Eds.]

Petitioner argues that race-sensitive admissions policies cannot "inur[e] primarily to the benefit of the minority," *ibid.*, as the Court has upheld such policies only insofar as they further "the educational benefits that flow from a diverse student body," *Grutter*. But there is no conflict between this Court's pronouncement in *Grutter* and the common-sense reality that race-sensitive admissions policies benefit minorities. Rather, race-sensitive admissions policies further a compelling state interest in achieving a diverse student body precisely because they increase minority enrollment, which necessarily benefits minority groups. In other words, constitutionally permissible race-sensitive admissions policies can both serve the compelling interest of obtaining the educational benefits that flow from a diverse student body, and inure to the benefit of racial minorities. There is nothing mutually exclusive about the two. Cf. *Seattle* (concluding that the desegregation plan had a racial focus even though "white as well as Negro children benefit from exposure to 'ethnic and racial diversity in the classroom'").

It is worth emphasizing, moreover, that §26 is relevant only to admissions policies that have survived strict scrutiny under *Grutter*; other policies, under this Court's rulings, would be forbidden with or without §26. A *Grutter*-compliant admissions policy must use race flexibly, not maintain a quota; must be limited in time; and must be employed only after "serious, good faith consideration of workable race-neutral alternatives." The policies banned by §26 meet all these requirements and thus already constitute the least restrictive ways to advance Michigan's compelling interest in diversity in higher education.

[In addition,] Section 26 restructures the political process in Michigan in a manner that places unique burdens on racial minorities. It establishes a distinct and more burdensome political process for the enactment of admissions plans that consider racial diversity.

Long before the enactment of §26, the Michigan Constitution granted plenary authority over all matters relating to Michigan's public universities, including admissions criteria, to each university's eight-member governing board. The boards have the "power to enact ordinances, by-laws and regulations for the government of the university." They are " 'constitutional corporation[s] of independent authority, which, within the scope of [their] functions, [are] co-ordinate with and equal to . . . the legislature.' "

The boards are indisputably a part of the political process in Michigan. Each political party nominates two candidates for membership to each board, and board members are elected to 8-year terms in the general statewide election. Prior to §26, board candidates frequently included their views on race-sensitive admissions in their campaigns. For example, in 2005, one candidate pledged to "work to end so-called 'Affirmative-Action,' a racist, degrading system."

Before the enactment of §26, Michigan's political structure permitted both supporters and opponents of race-sensitive admissions policies to vote for their candidates of choice and to lobby the elected and politically accountable boards. Section 26 reconfigured that structure. After §26, the boards retain plenary authority over all admissions criteria *except* for race-sensitive admissions policies. To change admissions policies on this one issue, a Michigan citizen must instead amend the Michigan Constitution. That is no small task. To place a proposed constitutional amendment on the ballot requires either the support of two-thirds of both Houses of the Michigan Legislature or a vast number of signatures from Michigan voters — 10 percent of the total number of votes cast in the preceding gubernatorial election. See Mich. Const., Art. XII, §§1, 2. Since more than 3.2 million votes were cast in the 2010 election for Governor, more than 320,000 signatures are currently needed to win a ballot spot. Moreover, "[t]o account for invalid and duplicative signatures, initiative sponsors 'need to obtain substantially more than the actual required number of signatures, typically by a 25% to 50% margin.'"

And the costs of qualifying an amendment are significant. . . . In 2008, for instance, over $800 million was spent nationally on state-level initiative and referendum campaigns, nearly $300 million more than was spent in the 2006 cycle. "In several states, more money [is] spent on ballot initiative campaigns than for all other races for political office combined."

Michigan's Constitution has only rarely been amended through the initiative process. Between 1914 and 2000, voters have placed only 60 statewide initiatives on the Michigan ballot, of which only 20 have passed. Minority groups face an especially uphill battle. "[O]n issues dealing with racial and ethnic matters, studies show that racial and ethnic minorities do end up more on the losing side of the popular vote." In fact, "[i]t is difficult to find even a single statewide initiative in any State in which voters approved policies that explicitly favor racial or ethnic minority groups."

This is the onerous task that §26 forces a Michigan citizen to complete in order to change the admissions policies of Michigan's public colleges and universities with respect to racial sensitivity. While substantially less grueling paths remain open to those advocating for any other admissions policies, a constitutional amendment is the only avenue by which race-sensitive admissions policies may be obtained. The effect of §26 is that a white graduate of a public Michigan university who wishes to pass his historical privilege on to his children may freely lobby the board of that university in favor of an expanded legacy admissions policy, whereas a black Michigander who was denied the opportunity to attend that very university cannot lobby the board in favor of a policy that might give his children a chance that he never had and that they might never have absent that policy.

Such reordering of the political process contravenes *Hunter* and *Seattle*. Where, as here, the majority alters the political process to the detriment of a racial minority, the governmental action is subject to strict scrutiny. Michigan does not assert that §26 satisfies a compelling state interest. That should settle the matter.

. . .

[A]ccording to the plurality, the *Hunter* and *Seattle* Courts were not concerned with efforts to reconfigure the political process to the detriment of racial minorities; rather, those cases invalidated governmental actions merely because they reflected an invidious purpose to discriminate. This is not a tenable reading of those cases. . . . It is impossible to assess whether the housing amendment in *Hunter* was motivated by discriminatory purpose, for the opinion does not discuss the question of intent. What is obvious, however, is that the possibility of invidious discrimination played no role in the Court's reasoning. We ordinarily understand our precedents to mean what they actually say, not what we later think they could or should have said. The *Hunter* Court was clear about why it invalidated the Akron charter amendment: It was impermissible as a restructuring of the political process, not as an action motivated by discriminatory intent. See 393 U.S., at 391 (striking down the Akron charter amendment because it "places a special burden on racial minorities within the governmental process").

Similarly, the plurality disregards what *Seattle* actually says and instead opines that "the political restriction in question was designed to be used, or was likely to be used, to encourage infliction of injury by reason of race." Here, the plurality derives its conclusion not from *Seattle* itself, but from evidence unearthed more than a quarter-century later in *Parents Involved in Community Schools v. Seattle School Dist. No. 1*, 551 U.S. 701 (2007).

The plurality relies on Justice Breyer's dissent in *Parents Involved* to conclude that "one permissible reading of the record was that the school board had maintained policies to perpetuate racial segregation in the schools." Remarkably, some Members of today's plurality criticized Justice Breyer's reading of the record in *Parents Involved* itself. [Relocated footnote — EDS.] [I]t follows, according to the plurality, that Seattle's desegregation plan was constitutionally required, so that the initiative halting the plan was an instance of invidious discrimination aimed at inflicting a racial injury.

Again, the plurality might prefer that the *Seattle* Court had said that, but it plainly did not. Not once did the Court suggest the presence of *de jure* segregation in Seattle. Quite the opposite: The opinion explicitly suggested the desegregation plan was adopted to remedy *de facto* rather than *de jure* segregation. The Court, moreover, assumed that no "constitutional violation" through *de jure* segregation had occurred. And it unmistakably rested its decision on *Hunter*, holding Seattle's initiative invalid because it "use[d] the racial nature of an issue to define the governmental decisionmaking structure, and thus impose[d] substantial and unique burdens on racial minorities."

It is nothing short of baffling, then, for the plurality to insist — in the face of clear language in *Hunter* and *Seattle* saying otherwise — that those cases were about nothing more than the intentional and invidious infliction of a racial injury. . . . After the plurality's revision of *Hunter* and *Seattle*, it is unclear what is left [of the political process doctrine]. . . . On this point, and this point only, I agree with Justice Scalia that the plurality has rewritten those precedents beyond recognition.

Justice Breyer concludes that *Hunter* and *Seattle* do not apply [because] Section 26 . . . did not move the relevant decisionmaking authority from one political level to another; rather, it removed that authority from "unelected actors and placed it in the hands of the voters." [But] it is undeniable that prior to §26, board candidates often pledged to end or carry on the use of race-sensitive admissions policies at Michigan's public universities. . . . Indeed, the issue of race-sensitive admissions policies often dominated board elections. . . . [A] careful examination of the boards and their governing structure reveals that they remain actively involved in setting admissions policies and procedures. . . . Although the elected and politically accountable boards may well entrust university officials with certain day-to-day admissions responsibilities, they often weigh in on admissions policies themselves and, at all times, they retain complete supervisory authority over university officials and over all admissions decisions.

There is no question, then, that the elected boards in Michigan had the power to eliminate or adopt race-sensitive admissions policies prior to §26. There is also no question that §26 worked an impermissible reordering of the political process; it removed that power from the elected boards and placed it instead at a higher level of the political process in Michigan. This case is no different from *Hunter* and *Seattle* in that respect. Just as in *Hunter* and *Seattle*, minorities in Michigan "participated in the political process and won." And just as in *Hunter* and *Seattle*, "the majority's subsequent reordering of the political process repealed the minority's successes and made it more difficult for the minority to succeed in the future," thereby "diminish[ing] the minority's ability to participate meaningfully in the electoral process." There is therefore no need to consider "extend[ing] the holding of *Hunter* and *Seattle* to reach situations in which decisionmaking authority is moved from an administrative body to a political one." Such a scenario is not before us.

. . .

The political-process doctrine not only resolves this case as a matter of *stare decisis*; it is correct as a matter of first principles. . . . We often think of equal protection as a guarantee that the government will apply the law in an equal fashion — that it will not intentionally discriminate against minority groups. But equal protection of the laws means more than that; it also secures the right of all citizens to participate meaningfully and equally in the process through which laws are created. . . . The minority plainly does not have a right to prevail over majority groups in any given political contest. But the minority does have a right to play by the same rules as the majority. It is this right that *Hunter* and *Seattle* so boldly vindicated.

[T]his Court focused on the vital importance of safeguarding minority groups' access to the political process in *United States v. Carolene Products Co.*, 304 U.S. 144 (1938). . . . The values identified in *Carolene Products* lie at the heart of the political-process doctrine. Indeed, *Seattle* explicitly relied on *Carolene Products*. See 458 U.S., at 486 ("[W]hen the State's allocation of power places unusual burdens on the ability of racial groups to enact legislation specifically designed to overcome the 'special condition' of prejudice, the governmental action seriously 'curtail[s] the operation of those political processes ordinarily to be relied upon to protect minorities'" (quoting *Carolene Products*, 304 U.S., at 153, n.4)). These values are central tenets of our equal protection jurisprudence.

Our cases recognize at least three features of the right to meaningful participation in the political process. Two of them, thankfully, are uncontroversial. First, every eligible citizen has a right to vote. This, woefully, has not always been the case. But it is a right no one would take issue with today. Second, the majority may not make it more difficult for the minority to exercise the right to vote. This, too, is widely accepted. After all, the Court has invalidated grandfather clauses, good character requirements, poll taxes, and gerrymandering provisions. The third feature, the one the plurality dismantles today, is that a majority may not reconfigure the existing political process in a manner that creates a two-tiered system of political change, subjecting laws designed to protect or benefit discrete and insular minorities to a more burdensome political process than all other laws. This is the political-process doctrine of *Hunter* and *Seattle*.

[C]ontrary to today's decision, protecting the right to meaningful participation in the political process must mean more than simply removing barriers to participation. It must mean vigilantly policing the political process to ensure that the majority does not use other methods to prevent minority groups from partaking in that process on equal footing. Why? For the same reason we guard the right of every citizen to vote. If "[e]fforts to reduce the impact of minority votes, in contrast to direct attempts to block access to the ballot," were "'second-generation barriers'" to minority voting, *Shelby County v. Holder* (Ginsburg, J., dissenting), efforts to reconfigure the political process in ways that uniquely disadvantage minority groups who have already long been disadvantaged are third-generation barriers. For as the Court recognized in *Seattle*, "minorities are no less powerless with the vote than without it when a racial criterion is used to assign governmental power in such a way as to exclude particular racial groups 'from effective participation in the political proces[s].'"

To accept the first two features of the right to meaningful participation in the political process, while renouncing the third, paves the way for the majority to do what it has done time and again throughout our Nation's history: afford the minority the opportunity to participate, yet manipulate the ground rules so as to ensure the minority's defeat. This is entirely at odds with our idea of equality under the law.

[N]othing prevents a majority of citizens from pursuing or obtaining its preferred outcome in a political contest. Here, for instance, I agree with the plurality that Michiganders who were unhappy with *Grutter* were free to pursue an end to race-sensitive admissions policies in their State. They were free to elect governing boards that opposed race-sensitive admissions policies or, through public discourse and dialogue, to lobby the existing boards toward that end. They were also free to remove from the boards the authority to make any decisions with respect to admissions policies, as opposed to only decisions concerning race-sensitive admissions policies. But what the majority could not do, consistent with the Constitution, is change the ground rules of the political process in a manner that makes it more difficult for racial minorities alone to achieve their goals. In doing so, the majority effectively rigs the contest to guarantee a particular outcome. That is the very wrong the political-process doctrine seeks to remedy. The doctrine "hews to the unremarkable notion that when two competitors are running a race, one may not require the other to run twice as far or to scale obstacles not present in the first runner's course."

. . .

My colleagues also attack the first prong of the [political process] doctrine as "rais[ing] serious constitutional concerns," *ante*, at 11 (plurality opinion), and being "unadministrable," *ante*, at 7 (Scalia, J., concurring in judgment). Justice Scalia wonders whether judges are equipped to weigh in on what constitutes a "racial issue." The plurality, too, thinks courts would be "with no clear legal standards or accepted sources to guide judicial decision." Yet as Justice Scalia recognizes, *Hunter* and *Seattle* provide a standard: Does the public policy at issue "inur[e] primarily to the benefit of the minority, and [was it] designed for that purpose"? Surely this is the kind of factual inquiry that judges are capable of making. Justice Scalia, for instance, accepts the standard announced in *Washington v. Davis*, which requires judges to determine whether discrimination is intentional or whether it merely has a discriminatory effect. Such an inquiry is at least as difficult for judges as the one called for by *Hunter* and *Seattle*. In any event, it is clear that the constitutional amendment in this case has a racial focus; it is facially race-based and, by operation of law, disadvantages only minorities.

"No good can come" from these inquiries, Justice Scalia responds, because they divide the Nation along racial lines and perpetuate racial stereotypes. The plurality shares that view; it tells us that we must not assume all individuals of the same race think alike. The same could have been said about desegregation: Not all members of a racial minority in *Seattle* necessarily regarded the integration of public schools as good policy. Yet the *Seattle* Court had little difficulty saying that school integration as a general matter "inure[d] . . . to the benefit of" the minority.

My colleagues are of the view that we should leave race out of the picture entirely and let the voters sort it out. See *ante* (plurality opinion) ("Racial division would be validated, not discouraged, were the *Seattle* formulation . . . to remain in force"). We have seen this reasoning before. See *Parents Involved* ("The way to stop discrimination on the basis of race is to stop discriminating on the basis of race"). It is a sentiment out of touch with reality, one not required by our Constitution, and one that has properly been rejected as "not sufficient" to resolve cases of this nature.

Race matters. Race matters in part because of the long history of racial minorities' being denied access to the political process. And although we have made great strides, "voting discrimination still exists; no one doubts that." *Shelby County*.

Race also matters because of persistent racial inequality in society—inequality that cannot be ignored and that has produced stark socioeconomic disparities. See *Gratz* [*v. Bollinger*], 539 U.S. [244], 298-300 [(2003)] (Ginsburg, J., dissenting) (cataloging the many ways in which "the effects of centuries of law-sanctioned inequality remain painfully evident in our communities and schools," in areas like employment, poverty, access to health care, housing, consumer transactions, and education); *Adarand* [*Constructors, Inc. v. Pena,*] 515 U.S. 200, 273 (1995) (Ginsburg, J., dissenting) (recognizing that the "lingering effects" of discrimination, "reflective of a system of racial caste only recently ended, are evident in our workplaces, markets, and neighborhoods").

And race matters for reasons that really are only skin deep, that cannot be discussed any other way, and that cannot be wished away. Race matters to a young man's view of society when he spends his teenage years watching others tense up as he passes, no matter the neighborhood where he grew up. Race matters to a young woman's sense of self when she states her hometown, and then is pressed, "No, where are you *really* from?", regardless of how many generations her family has been in the country. Race matters to a young person addressed by a stranger in a foreign language, which he does not understand because only English was spoken at home. Race matters because of the slights, the snickers, the silent judgments that reinforce that most crippling of thoughts: "I do not belong here."

In my colleagues' view, examining the racial impact of legislation only perpetuates racial discrimination. This refusal to accept the stark reality that race matters is regrettable. The way to stop discrimination on the basis of race is to speak openly and candidly on the subject of race, and to apply the Constitution with eyes open to the unfortunate effects of centuries of racial discrimination. As members of the judiciary tasked with intervening to carry out the guarantee of equal protection, we ought not sit back and wish away, rather than confront, the racial inequality that exists in our society. It is this view that works harm, by perpetuating the facile notion that what makes race matter is acknowledging the simple truth that race *does* matter.

Discussion

1. Both Justices Scalia and Sotomayor agree that after the plurality decision, there is very little left of the political process doctrine of *Hunter* and *Seattle*. While Justice Scalia would simply finish the job, Justice Sotomayor seeks to resuscitate the doctrine. Why do you believe the plurality does not overturn *Hunter* and *Seattle* directly?

2. Is Michigan's section 26 a "racial classification," or rather, as Justice Scalia argues, a prohibition on racial classifications and therefore presumptively constitutional? Is this obvious from its language, or does the answer require inferences from background context? What values are implicit in deciding this question?

3. The *Schuette* plurality argues that the decisions in *Hunter* and *Seattle* were not based on changes to the political decisionmaking process that burdened racial

minorities' ability to gain victories in the democratic process. Rather, "*Seattle* is best understood as a case in which the state action in question (the bar on busing enacted by the State's voters) had the serious risk, if not purpose, of causing specific injuries on account of race, just as had been the case in *Mulkey* and *Hunter*." What, precisely, is the nature of these "specific injuries"? Can one articulate them without offering some version of the political process theory—i.e., that majorities sought to make it more difficult for minorities to win political victories?

4. *Animus.* The plurality might also be arguing that the passage of referenda in *Hunter* or *Seattle* turned in part on racial animus: Kennedy notes that "the bar on busing enacted by the State's voters [in *Seattle*] had the serious risk, if not purpose, of causing specific injuries on account of race, just as had been the case in *Mulkey* and *Hunter*." "Those cases were ones in which the political restriction in question was designed to be used, or was likely to be used, to encourage infliction of injury by reason of race." Similarly, he says that *Mulkey*, *Hunter*, and *Seattle* involved cases in which "hurt or injury [was] inflicted on racial minorities by the encouragement or command of laws or other state action . . . . But those circumstances are not present here."

How does the Court know what the purposes of the voters were in *Mulkey*, *Hunter*, and *Seattle*? How does it know that the same could not be true of Michigan's voters in passing section 26? Is Justice Kennedy's point that one cannot assume that opponents of affirmative action have racial animus, because it is arguable that affirmative action programs, even when constitutional, give minorities special rights rather than guarantee equal rights? (Note that in *Seattle* the referendum at issue banned voluntary desegregation efforts that were not required by the federal Constitution; in fact, today these same policies would be treated like affirmative action policies, and subjected to strict scrutiny. How does Kennedy deal with this problem?)

Justice Scalia argues that it is impossible as a matter of law for those seeking to ban affirmative action to act with unconstitutional racial animus: "In my view, any law expressly requiring state actors to afford all persons equal protection of the laws (such as Initiative 350 in Seattle, though not the charter amendment in *Hunter*) does not—cannot—deny 'to any person . . . equal protection of the laws,' U.S. Const., Amdt. 14, §1, regardless of whatever evidence of seemingly foul purposes plaintiffs may cook up in the trial court."

5. *Romer v. Schuette.* Compare Justice Kennedy's argument in *Schuette* with his 1996 opinion in Romer v. Evans, discussed in Chapter 8. Colorado's Amendment 2 stripped gays, lesbians, and bisexuals of all legal protections against discrimination based on sexual orientation that had previously existed in various localities. See Susannah W. Pollvogt, Thought Experiment: What If Kennedy Had Approached Romer v. Evans the Way He Approached Schuette v. BAMN?, http://papers.ssrn.com/sol3/papers.cfm?abstract_id=2436616.

At the time *Romer* was decided, government discrimination against gays and lesbians was subject to ordinary rational basis scrutiny, and indeed, in 1986 the Court had held that gays and lesbians could even be imprisoned for engaging in same-sex sexual activity. Nevertheless, five members of the Court, in an opinion by Justice Kennedy, reasoned that "laws of the kind now before us raise the inevitable inference that the disadvantage imposed is born of animosity toward the class of persons affected." Why does Justice Kennedy not draw the same inference about section 26 in *Schuette*? Conversely, why doesn't Amendment 2 reflect the same learning process through democratic deliberation by Colorado's voters that the Court extolled and sought to protect in *Schuette*? As Justice Kennedy points out in *Schuette*, "a democracy has the capacity — and the duty — to learn from its past mistakes; to discover and confront persisting biases; and by respectful, rational deliberation to rise above those flaws and injustices. That process is impeded, not advanced, by court decrees based on the proposition that the public cannot have the requisite repose to discuss certain issues. It is demeaning to the democratic process to presume that the voters are not capable of deciding an issue of this sensitivity on decent and rational grounds." In received doctrine, at least, racial decisionmaking is treated as likely to be more invidious than decisionmaking based on sexual orientation.

Justice Kennedy's two opinions suggest that judges can tell the difference between situations involving democratic deliberation about sensitive issues and attempts to inflict harm on minorities. But if so, what criteria should judges use?

6. *"Demeaning stereotypes" about group interests.* Both the plurality and Justice Scalia argue that it is demeaning to minorities to assume that members of minority groups will support certain kinds of laws because they believe that these laws are likely to be in their interest. The reason is that not all members of a group think alike on all issues. To give only one prominent example, Justice Thomas has been a forthright opponent of affirmative action programs. The argument, however, may prove too much. The African-American community was not universally behind the NAACP's attempt to overturn Plessy v. Ferguson in the context of elementary and secondary public education. Black schoolteachers in segregated schools, for example, worried that desegregation would reduce their job opportunities. And it is certainly possible that at least some members of minority groups have been concerned about the adverse consequences of almost every important civil rights reform. (Consider, for example, the dissensus within the gay and lesbian community about the wisdom of seeking the right to same-sex marriage.) Does the political process doctrine of *Hunter* and *Seattle* require unanimity of views among members of minority groups? What kinds of judgments does it require?

Note that the Court's contemporary affirmative action jurisprudence assumes that racial classifications can hurt members of dis-preferred groups — for example, whites. Do such claims also involve inappropriate stereotyping about the beliefs and attitudes of whites?

Does Justice Kennedy's interpretation of *Hunter* and *Seattle* engage in demeaning assumptions about the beliefs of white voters? For example, doesn't his argument assume that white voters as a group thought that certain laws were not in their interests because these laws might unfairly benefit members of minority groups? Under the intent standard of *Davis* and *Feeney*, is it possible for courts to avoid attributing to political actors assessments about group interest?

7. Carolene Products *and democracy protection.* Justice Sotomayor argues that courts have a special obligation to safeguard minority rights in the democratic process through the Equal Protection Clause, an approach that dates back to Justice Stone's opinion in *Carolene Products.* As she announces at the beginning of her dissent: "We are fortunate to live in a democratic society. But without checks, democratically approved legislation can oppress minority groups. For that reason, our Constitution places limits on what a majority of the people may do. . . . [A] fundamental strand of our equal protection jurisprudence focuses on process, securing to all citizens the right to participate meaningfully and equally in self-government. That right is the bedrock of our democracy, for it preserves all other rights." Justice Scalia rejects this view of the judicial role, stating that "we should not design our jurisprudence to conform to dictum in a footnote in a four-Justice opinion."

The dispute between Justice Sotomayor and Justice Kennedy is whether or not section 26 is an example of a well-functioning democratic process in which voters deliberate about the public good or an attempt to rig the political system at the expense of minority groups. What judgments and values are implicit in deciding this question?

The dispute between Justice Sotomayor and Justice Scalia, on the other hand, turns on the types of democratic dysfunction that courts should police. Justice Sotomayor, reasoning in the tradition of *Carolene Products* — as elaborated by John Hart Ely and generations of American legal scholars — believes courts should guard against the majority resentments against minorities that would make the latter perpetual losers in the political process. Justice Scalia, by contrast, views minority groups as concentrated special interests that are particularly effective at gaining protection from the political process. (See, for example, his discussion of the Voting Rights Act in the oral argument to Shelby County v. Holder, supra.) See also Bertrall Ross, Democracy and Renewed Distrust: Equal Protection and the Evolving Judicial Conception of Politics, 101 Cal. L. Rev. 1565 (2013).

Protection of minorities was once the express aim of equal protection law; this understanding has changed over the succeeding decades, and as *Schuette* demonstrates, the Court's proper role in enforcing the Equal Protection Clause clearly divides the contemporary Court. See Reva B. Siegel, The Supreme Court Term October 2012 — Foreword: Equality Divided, 127 Harv. L. Rev. 1 (2013).

Insert on p. 1151 before the Note on American Indians and Affirmative Action:

FISHER v. UNIVERSITY OF TEXAS, 133 S. Ct. 2411 (2013): Fisher, who is white, was denied admission to the University of Texas at Austin in 2008. She sued the University, arguing that its admissions policies, which use race as a factor, violated the Equal Protection Clause. Following *Grutter*, Texas had added a race-conscious component to its admissions policies because it believed that its existing facially race-neutral policies produced inadequate educational diversity. The plaintiffs disagreed. The Court, in a 7-1 decision by Justice Kennedy (Justice Kagan not participating), held that the lower court had applied an incorrect standard of review.

Justice Kennedy explained that *Bakke, Grutter,* and *Gratz* require strict scrutiny of admissions policies that use race as a factor. Educational diversity can be a compelling state interest, and " 'the decision to pursue the educational benefits that flow from student body diversity,' that the University deems integral to its mission is, in substantial measure, an academic judgment to which some, but not complete, judicial deference is proper under *Grutter*. A court, of course, should ensure that there is a reasoned, principled explanation for the academic decision." However, "[t]he University must [also] prove that the means chosen by the University to attain diversity are narrowly tailored to that goal. On this point, the University receives no deference." "[I]t remains at all times the University's obligation to demonstrate, and the Judiciary's obligation to determine, that admissions processes 'ensure that each applicant is evaluated as an individual and not in a way that makes an applicant's race or ethnicity the defining feature of his or her application.' "

In addition, narrow tailoring "involves a careful judicial inquiry into whether a university could achieve sufficient diversity without using racial classifications. Although '[n]arrow tailoring does not require exhaustion of every *conceivable* race-neutral alternative,' strict scrutiny does require a court to examine with care, and not defer to, a university's 'serious, good faith consideration of workable race-neutral alternatives.' *Grutter*. Consideration by the university is of course necessary, but it is not sufficient to satisfy strict scrutiny: The reviewing court must ultimately be satisfied that no workable race-neutral alternatives would produce the educational benefits of diversity. If 'a nonracial approach . . . could promote the substantial interest about as well and at tolerable administrative expense,' then the university may not consider race. *Wygant v. Jackson Bd. of Ed.*, 476 U.S. 267, 280, n.6 (1986)."

The Fifth Circuit, Justice Kennedy explained, deferred to the good faith judgment of university administrators on the question of narrow tailoring and the adequacy of race-neutral alternatives. Therefore its judgment must be reversed, "but fairness to the litigants and the courts that heard the case requires that it be remanded so that the admissions process can be considered and judged under a correct analysis."

Justice Scalia, concurring, noted that "The petitioner in this case did not ask us to overrule *Grutter*'s holding that a 'compelling interest' in the educational benefits of diversity can justify racial preferences in university admissions." He reiterated his view that "The Constitution proscribes government discrimination on the basis of race, and state-provided education is no exception."

Justice Thomas, concurring, also stated that "I would overrule *Grutter v. Bollinger,* and hold that a State's use of race in higher education admissions decisions is categorically prohibited by the Equal Protection Clause." Justice Thomas asserted that the arguments for affirmative action—that it provides leadership opportunities for minorities, promotes racial harmony, and is a temporary measure—were the same as those offered by southern segregationists. "While the arguments advanced by the University in defense of discrimination are the same as those advanced by the segregationists, one obvious difference is that the segregationists argued that it was *segregation* that was necessary to obtain the alleged benefits, whereas the University argues that *diversity* is the key. Today, the segregationists' arguments would never be given serious consideration. . . . We should be equally hostile to the University's repackaged version of the same arguments in support of its favored form of racial discrimination." "There is no principled distinction between the University's assertion that diversity yields educational benefits and the segregationists' assertion that segregation yielded those same benefits." . . .

"Racial discrimination is never benign. '[B]enign' carries with it no independent meaning, but reflects only acceptance of the current generation's conclusion that a politically acceptable burden, imposed on particular citizens on the basis of race, is reasonable.' . . . The University's professed good intentions cannot excuse its outright racial discrimination any more than such intentions justified the now denounced arguments of slaveholders and segregationists."

Justice Thomas added: "I note that racial engineering does in fact have insidious consequences. There can be no doubt that the University's discrimination injures white and Asian applicants who are denied admission because of their race. But I believe the injury to those admitted under the University's discriminatory admissions program is even more harmful. Blacks and Hispanics admitted to the University as a result of racial discrimination are, on average, far less prepared than their white and Asian classmates."

Justice Ginsburg dissented: "The University of Texas at Austin . . . is candid about what it is endeavoring to do: It seeks to achieve student-body diversity through an admissions policy patterned after the Harvard plan referenced as exemplary in Justice Powell's opinion in *Bakke*. . . . And, like so many educational institutions across the Nation, the University has taken care to follow the model approved by the Court in *Grutter*. . . . Petitioner urges that Texas' Top Ten Percent Law [which grants automatic admission to any public state college to students in the top ten percent of their Texas high school class] and race-blind holistic review of each application achieve significant diversity, so the University must be content with those alternatives. I have said before and reiterate here that only an ostrich could regard the supposedly neutral alternatives as race unconscious."

"Texas' percentage plan was adopted with racially segregated neighborhoods and schools front and center stage. It is race consciousness, not blindness to race, that drives such plans. As for holistic review, if universities cannot explicitly include race as a factor, many may 'resort to camouflage' to 'maintain their minority enrollment.' . . . I remain convinced [that] 'those that candidly disclose their consideration of race [are] preferable to those that conceal it.' Accordingly, I would not return this case for a second look."

Discussion

1. *Fisher* appears to be a compromise opinion that sends the case back to the Fifth Circuit but does not purport to make new law. Note the Court's formulation of the narrow tailoring test, including its citation to *Wygant* (a plurality opinion from 1986). Will the Court's narrow tailoring test make it more difficult for colleges and universities to justify the use of race in admissions?

2. Justice Ginsburg criticizes the majority for treating ten-percent and class-based affirmative action programs as race-neutral, arguing that such plans are obviously race-conscious in purpose and design. *Fisher* suggests that the Court is willing to recognize a difference between benign and invidious race-consciousness in the creation of formally neutral programs and statutes (i.e., programs that do not overtly make racial classifications). The Court also seems to be willing to allow governments to use formally race-neutral means to achieve greater representation of minorities in colleges and universities.

In this respect, *Fisher* seems to follow Justice Kennedy's limiting concurrence in *Parents Involved*. On the other hand, is *Fisher* consistent with the plurality opinion in *Parents Involved*, which strongly opposed "racial balancing"? That depends on whether the plurality's analysis applies only to situations where the government employs explicit racial classifications or considers race in distinguishing among citizens. Is *Fisher* consistent with *Ricci*?

Chapter 8

Implied Fundamental Rights: The Constitution, the Family, and the Body

Insert the following after discussion note 5 on p. 1465:

GONZALES v. CARHART [*CARHART II*]
550 U.S. 124 (2007)

[Following the decision in *Stenberg v. Carhart*, Congress passed the Partial-Birth Abortion Act of 2003. The act bans a method of performing abortions, called "intact dilation and extraction" (intact D & E) or "dilation and extraction" (D & X), usually performed in the second and third trimesters of pregnancy. In the usual second-trimester procedure, "dilation and evacuation" (D & E), the doctor dilates the cervix and then inserts surgical instruments into the uterus and maneuvers them to grab the fetus and pull it back through the cervix and vagina. The fetus is usually ripped apart as it is removed, and the doctor may take 10 to 15 passes to remove it in its entirety. The federal act bans a variation of the standard D & E, intact D & E. To perform an intact D & E abortion, a doctor extracts the fetus intact or largely intact with only a few passes, pulling out its entire body instead of ripping it apart. In order to allow the head to pass through the cervix, the doctor typically pierces or crushes the skull.

The federal Partial Birth Abortion Act defines "partial-birth abortion," in §1531(b)(1), as a procedure in which the doctor: "(A) deliberately and intentionally vaginally delivers a living fetus until, in the case of a head-first presentation, the entire fetal head is outside the [mother's] body . . . , or, in the case of breech presentation, any part of the fetal trunk past the navel is outside the [mother's] body . . . , for the purpose of performing an overt act that the person knows will kill the partially delivered living fetus"; and "(B) performs the overt act, other than completion of delivery, that kills the fetus."

Congress found that, despite the district court's findings in *Stenberg* (accepted by the Supreme Court in that case), there was a moral, medical, and ethical consensus that partial-birth abortion is a gruesome and inhumane procedure that is never medically necessary and should be prohibited. The act contains an exception for situations where the mother's life is endangered: Section 1531(a) of the act prohibits "knowingly perform[ing] a partial-birth abortion . . . that is [not] necessary to save the life of a mother." It contains no exception for cases in which the mother's health would be endangered by using another method of abortion.

Physicians challenged the act on the ground that it imposed an undue burden on a woman's right to choose a second-trimester abortion, that the crime defined by the statute was unduly vague, and that it contained no health exception.]

Justice KENNEDY delivered the opinion of the Court.

. . .

II.

The principles set forth in the joint opinion in Planned Parenthood of Southeastern Pa. v. Casey, did not find support from all those who join the instant opinion. Whatever one's views concerning the *Casey* joint opinion, it is evident a premise central to its conclusion — that the government has a legitimate and substantial interest in preserving and promoting fetal life — would be repudiated were the Court now to affirm the judgments of the Courts of Appeals. . . . [W]e must determine whether the Act furthers the legitimate interest of the Government in protecting the life of the fetus that may become a child.

We assume the following principles for the purposes of this opinion. Before viability, a State "may not prohibit any woman from making the ultimate decision to terminate her pregnancy." It also may not impose upon this right an undue burden, which exists if a regulation's "purpose or effect is to place a substantial obstacle in the path of a woman seeking an abortion before the fetus attains viability." On the other hand, "[r]egulations which do no more than create a structural mechanism by which the State, or the parent or guardian of a minor, may express profound respect for the life of the unborn are permitted, if they are not a substantial obstacle to the woman's exercise of the right to choose."

III.

A

The Act does not restrict an abortion procedure involving the delivery of an expired fetus. The Act, furthermore, is inapplicable to abortions that do not involve vaginal delivery (for instance, hysterotomy or hysterectomy). The Act does apply both previability and postviability because, by common understanding and scientific terminology, a fetus is a living organism while within the womb, whether or not it is viable outside the womb. . . .

Second, the Act's definition of partial-birth abortion requires the fetus to be delivered "until, in the case of a head-first presentation, the entire fetal head is outside the body of the mother, or, in the case of breech presentation, any part of the fetal trunk past the navel is outside the body of the mother." §1531(b)(1)(A). The Attorney General concedes, and we agree, that if an abortion procedure does not involve the delivery of a living fetus to one of these "anatomical 'landmarks'" — where, depending on the presentation, either the fetal head or the fetal trunk past the navel is outside the body of the mother — the prohibitions of the Act do not apply.

Third, to fall within the Act, a doctor must perform an "overt act, other than completion of delivery, that kills the partially delivered living fetus." §1531(b)(1)(B). For purposes of criminal liability, the overt act causing the fetus' death must be separate from delivery. And the overt act must occur after the delivery to an anatomical landmark. This is because the Act proscribes killing "the partially delivered" fetus, which, when read in context, refers to a fetus that has been delivered to an anatomical landmark.

Fourth, the Act contains scienter requirements concerning all the actions involved in the prohibited abortion. To begin with, the physician must have "deliberately and intentionally" delivered the fetus to one of the Act's anatomical landmarks. §1531(b)(1)(A). If a living fetus is delivered past the critical point by accident or inadvertence, the Act is inapplicable. In addition, the fetus must have been delivered "for the purpose of performing an overt act that the [doctor] knows will kill [it]." *Ibid.* If either intent is absent, no crime has occurred. This follows from the general principle that where scienter is required no crime is committed absent the requisite state of mind.

B

[The Partial Birth Abortion Act is not vague.] Unlike the statutory language in *Stenberg* that prohibited the delivery of a "'substantial portion'" of the fetus, . . . [d]octors performing D & E will know that if they do not deliver a living fetus to an anatomical landmark they will not face criminal liability. . . . [Moreover] [b]ecause a doctor performing a D & E will not face criminal liability if he or she delivers a fetus beyond the prohibited point by mistake, the Act cannot be described as "a trap for those who act in good faith." [Nor should] the Act . . . be invalidated on its face because it encourages arbitrary or discriminatory enforcement. Just as the Act's anatomical landmarks provide doctors with objective standards, they also "establish minimal guidelines to govern law enforcement." The scienter requirements narrow the scope of the Act's prohibition and limit prosecutorial discretion. . . .

C

We next determine whether the Act imposes an undue burden, as a facial matter, because its restrictions on second-trimester abortions are too broad. . . . The Act excludes most D & Es in which the fetus is removed in pieces, not intact. If the doctor intends to remove the fetus in parts from the outset, the doctor will not have the requisite intent to incur criminal liability. A doctor performing a standard D & E procedure can often "tak[e] about 10-15 'passes' through the uterus to remove the entire fetus." Removing the fetus in this manner does not violate the Act because the doctor will not have delivered the living fetus to one of the anatomical landmarks or committed an additional overt act that kills the fetus after partial delivery.

The [Nebraska] statute in *Stenberg* prohibited "'deliberately and intentionally delivering into the vagina a living unborn child, or a substantial portion thereof, for the purpose of performing a procedure that the person performing such procedure knows will kill the unborn child and does kill the unborn child.' " The Court concluded that this statute encompassed D & E because "D & E will often involve a physician pulling a 'substantial portion' of a still living fetus, say, an arm or leg, into the vagina prior to the death of the fetus. The Court also rejected the limiting interpretation urged by Nebraska's Attorney General that the statute's reference to a "procedure" that " 'kill[s] the unborn child' " was to a distinct procedure, not to the abortion procedure as a whole.

Congress, it is apparent, responded to these concerns because the Act departs in material ways from the statute in *Stenberg*. It adopts the phrase "delivers a living fetus," instead of " 'delivering . . . a living unborn child, or a substantial portion thereof.' " . . . D & E does not involve the delivery of a fetus because it requires the removal of fetal parts that are ripped from the fetus as they are pulled through the cervix. . . . The Court in *Stenberg* interpreted " 'substantial portion' " of the fetus to include an arm or a leg. The Act's anatomical landmarks, by contrast, clarify that the removal of a small portion of the fetus is not prohibited. The landmarks also require the fetus to be delivered so that it is partially "outside the body of the mother." To come within the ambit of the Nebraska statute, on the other hand, a substantial portion of the fetus only had to be delivered into the vagina; no part of the fetus had to be outside the body of the mother before a doctor could face criminal sanctions. . . .

The Act makes the distinction the Nebraska statute failed to draw (but the Nebraska Attorney General advanced) by differentiating between the overall partial-birth abortion and the distinct overt act that kills the fetus. The fatal overt act must occur after delivery to an anatomical landmark, and it must be something "other than [the] completion of delivery." §1531(b)(1)(B). This distinction matters because, unlike intact D & E, standard D & E does not involve a delivery followed by a fatal act. . . .

If a doctor's intent at the outset is to perform a D & E in which the fetus would not be delivered to either of the Act's anatomical landmarks, but the fetus nonetheless is delivered past one of those points, the requisite and prohibited scienter is not present. When a doctor in that situation completes an abortion by performing an intact D & E, the doctor does not violate the Act. It is true that intent to cause a result may sometimes be inferred if a person "knows that that result is practically certain to follow from his conduct." Yet abortion doctors intending at the outset to perform a standard D & E procedure will not know that a prohibited abortion "is practically certain to follow from" their conduct. A fetus is only delivered largely intact in a small fraction of the overall number of D & E abortions.

The evidence also supports a legislative determination that an intact delivery is almost always a conscious choice rather than a happenstance. Doctors, for example, may remove the fetus in a manner that will increase the chances of an intact delivery. And intact D & E is usually described as involving some manner of serial dilation. Doctors who do not seek to obtain this serial dilation perform an intact D & E on far fewer occasions. This evidence belies any claim that a standard D & E cannot be performed without intending or foreseeing an intact D & E.

Many doctors who testified on behalf of respondents, and who objected to the Act, do not perform an intact D & E by accident. On the contrary, they begin every D & E abortion with the objective of removing the fetus as intact as possible. This does not prove, as respondents suggest, that every D & E might violate the Act and that the Act therefore imposes an undue burden. It demonstrates only that those doctors who intend to perform a D & E that would involve delivery of a living fetus to one of the Act's anatomical landmarks must adjust their conduct to the law by not attempting to deliver the fetus to either of those points. Respondents have not shown that requiring doctors to intend dismemberment before delivery to an anatomical landmark will prohibit the vast majority of D & E abortions. The Act, then, cannot be held invalid on its face on these grounds.

IV.

. . . The Act does not on its face impose a substantial obstacle [to late-term, but previability, abortions]. . . . Congress stated [its purposes] as follows: "Implicitly approving such a brutal and inhumane procedure by choosing not to prohibit it will further coarsen society to the humanity of not only newborns, but all vulnerable and innocent human life, making it increasingly difficult to protect such life." The Act expresses respect for the dignity of human life.

Congress was concerned, furthermore, with the effects on the medical community and on its reputation caused by the practice of partial-birth abortion. The findings in the Act explain:

> "Partial-birth abortion . . . confuses the medical, legal, and ethical duties of physicians to preserve and promote life, as the physician acts directly against the physical life of a child, whom he or she had just delivered, all but the head, out of the womb, in order to end that life."

There can be no doubt the government "has an interest in protecting the integrity and ethics of the medical profession." Washington v. Glucksberg. Under our precedents it is clear the State has a significant role to play in regulating the medical profession.

Casey reaffirmed these governmental objectives. The government may use its voice and its regulatory authority to show its profound respect for the life within the woman. A central premise of the opinion was that the Court's precedents after Roe had "undervalue[d] the State's interest in potential life." The plurality opinion indicated "[t]he fact that a law which serves a valid purpose, one not designed to strike at the right itself, has the incidental effect of making it more difficult or more expensive to procure an abortion cannot be enough to invalidate it." This was not an idle assertion. . . . [Casey's] third premise, that the State, from the inception of the pregnancy, maintains its own regulatory interest in protecting the life of the fetus that may become a child, cannot be set at naught by interpreting *Casey*'s requirement of a health exception so it becomes tantamount to allowing a doctor to choose the abortion method he or she might prefer. Where it has a rational basis to act, and it does not impose an undue burden, the State may use its regulatory power to bar certain procedures and substitute others, all in furtherance of its legitimate interests in regulating the medical profession in order to promote respect for life, including life of the unborn.

The Act's ban on abortions that involve partial delivery of a living fetus furthers the Government's objectives. No one would dispute that, for many, D & E is a procedure itself laden with the power to devalue human life. Congress could nonetheless conclude that the type of abortion proscribed by the Act requires specific regulation because it implicates additional ethical and moral concerns that justify a special prohibition. Congress determined that the abortion methods it proscribed had a "disturbing similarity to the killing of a newborn infant," and thus it was concerned with "draw[ing] a bright line that clearly distinguishes abortion and infanticide." The Court has in the past confirmed the validity of drawing boundaries to prevent certain practices that extinguish life and are close to actions that are condemned. *Glucksberg* found reasonable the State's "fear that permitting assisted suicide will start it down the path to voluntary and perhaps even involuntary euthanasia."

Respect for human life finds an ultimate expression in the bond of love the mother has for her child. The Act recognizes this reality as well. Whether to have an abortion requires a difficult and painful moral decision. While we find no reliable data to measure the phenomenon, it seems unexceptionable to conclude some women come to regret their choice to abort the infant life they once created and sustained. See Brief for Sandra Cano et al. as *Amici Curiae* in No. 05-380, pp. 22-24. Severe depression and loss of esteem can follow.

In a decision so fraught with emotional consequence some doctors may prefer not to disclose precise details of the means that will be used, confining themselves to the required statement of risks the procedure entails. From one standpoint this ought not to be surprising. Any number of patients facing imminent surgical procedures would prefer not to hear all details, lest the usual anxiety preceding invasive medical procedures become the more intense. This is likely the case with the abortion procedures here in issue. See, e.g *., Nat. Abortion Federation* [v. Ashcroft], 330 F. Supp. 2d [436,] 466, n.22 (S.D.N.Y. 2004) ("Most of [the plaintiffs'] experts acknowledged that they do not describe to their patients what [the D & E and intact D & E] procedures entail in clear and precise terms").

It is, however, precisely this lack of information concerning the way in which the fetus will be killed that is of legitimate concern to the State. The State has an interest in ensuring so grave a choice is well informed. It is self-evident that a mother who comes to regret her choice to abort must struggle with grief more anguished and sorrow more profound when she learns, only after the event, what she once did not know: that she allowed a doctor to pierce the skull and vacuum the fast-developing brain of her unborn child, a child assuming the human form.

It is a reasonable inference that a necessary effect of the regulation and the knowledge it conveys will be to encourage some women to carry the infant to full term, thus reducing the absolute number of late-term abortions. The medical profession, furthermore, may find different and less shocking methods to abort the fetus in the second trimester, thereby accommodating legislative demand. The State's interest in respect for life is advanced by the dialogue that better informs the political and legal systems, the medical profession, expectant mothers, and society as a whole of the consequences that follow from a decision to elect a late-term abortion.

It is objected that the standard D & E is in some respects as brutal, if not more, than the intact D & E, so that the legislation accomplishes little. What we have already said, however, shows ample justification for the regulation. Partial-birth abortion, as defined by the Act, differs from a standard D & E because the former occurs when the fetus is partially outside the mother to the point of one of the Act's anatomical landmarks. It was reasonable for Congress to think that partial-birth abortion, more than standard D & E, "undermines the public's perception of the appropriate role of a physician during the delivery process, and perverts a process during which life is brought into the world." There would be a flaw in this Court's logic, and an irony in its jurisprudence, were we first to conclude a ban on both D & E and intact D & E was overbroad and then to say it is irrational to ban only intact D & E because that does not proscribe both procedures. In sum, we reject the contention that the congressional purpose of the Act was "to place a substantial obstacle in the path of a woman seeking an abortion."

B

[T]he next question [is] whether the Act has the effect of imposing an unconstitutional burden on the abortion right because it does not allow use of the barred procedure where " 'necessary, in appropriate medical judgment, for [the] preservation of the . . . health of the mother.' " The prohibition in the Act would be unconstitutional, under precedents we here assume to be controlling, if it "subject[ed] [women] to significant health risks." Ayotte v. Planned Parenthood of Northern New Eng., 546 U.S. 320, 328 (2006). In *Ayotte* the parties agreed a health exception to the challenged parental-involvement statute was necessary "to avert serious and often irreversible damage to [a pregnant minor's] health." Here, by contrast, whether the Act creates significant health risks for women has been a contested factual question. The evidence presented in the trial courts and before Congress demonstrates both sides have medical support for their position.

Respondents presented evidence that intact D & E may be the safest method of abortion, for reasons similar to those adduced in *Stenberg*. Abortion doctors testified, for example, that intact D & E decreases the risk of cervical laceration or uterine perforation because it requires fewer passes into the uterus with surgical instruments and does not require the removal of bony fragments of the dismembered fetus, fragments that may be sharp. Respondents also presented evidence that intact D & E was safer both because it reduces the risks that fetal parts will remain in the uterus and because it takes less time to complete. Respondents, in addition, proffered evidence that intact D & E was safer for women with certain medical conditions or women with fetuses that had certain anomalies.

These contentions were contradicted by other doctors who testified in the District Courts and before Congress. They concluded that the alleged health advantages were based on speculation without scientific studies to support them. They considered D & E always to be a safe alternative.

There is documented medical disagreement whether the Act's prohibition would ever impose significant health risks on women. The three District Courts that considered the Act's constitutionality appeared to be in some disagreement on this central factual question.

The question becomes whether the Act can stand when this medical uncertainty persists. The Court's precedents instruct that the Act can survive this facial attack. The Court has given state and federal legislatures wide discretion to pass legislation in areas where there is medical and scientific uncertainty.

This traditional rule is consistent with *Casey,* which confirms the State's interest in promoting respect for human life at all stages in the pregnancy. Physicians are not entitled to ignore regulations that direct them to use reasonable alternative procedures. The law need not give abortion doctors unfettered choice in the course of their medical practice, nor should it elevate their status above other physicians in the medical community. In *Casey* the controlling opinion held an informed-consent requirement in the abortion context was "no different from a requirement that a doctor give certain specific information about any medical procedure." The opinion stated "the doctor-patient relation here is entitled to the same solicitude it receives in other contexts."

Medical uncertainty does not foreclose the exercise of legislative power in the abortion context any more than it does in other contexts. The medical uncertainty over whether the Act's prohibition creates significant health risks provides a sufficient basis to conclude in this facial attack that the Act does not impose an undue burden.

The conclusion that the Act does not impose an undue burden is supported by other considerations. Alternatives are available to the prohibited procedure. As we have noted, the Act does not proscribe D & E. . . . If the intact D & E procedure is truly necessary in some circumstances, it appears likely an injection that kills the fetus is an alternative under the Act that allows the doctor to perform the procedure.

The instant cases, then, are different from Planned Parenthood of Central Mo. v. Danforth, 428 U.S. 52 (1976), in which the Court invalidated a ban on saline amniocentesis, the then-dominant second-trimester abortion method. The Court found the ban in *Danforth* to be "an unreasonable or arbitrary regulation designed to inhibit, and having the effect of inhibiting, the vast majority of abortions after the first 12 weeks." Here the Act allows, among other means, a commonly used and generally accepted method, so it does not construct a substantial obstacle to the abortion right.

In reaching the conclusion the Act does not require a health exception we reject certain arguments made by the parties on both sides of these cases. On the one hand, the Attorney General urges us to uphold the Act on the basis of the congressional findings alone. Although we review congressional factfinding under a deferential standard, we do not in the circumstances here place dispositive weight on Congress' findings. The Court retains an independent constitutional duty to review factual findings where constitutional rights are at stake.

As respondents have noted, and the District Courts recognized, some recitations in the Act are factually incorrect. Whether or not accurate at the time, some of the important findings have been superseded. Two examples suffice. Congress determined no medical schools provide instruction on the prohibited procedure. The testimony in the District Courts, however, demonstrated intact D & E is taught at medical schools. Congress also found there existed a medical consensus that the prohibited procedure is never medically necessary. The evidence presented in the District Courts contradicts that conclusion. Uncritical deference to Congress' factual findings in these cases is inappropriate.

On the other hand, relying on the Court's opinion in *Stenberg,* respondents contend that an abortion regulation must contain a health exception "if 'substantial medical authority supports the proposition that banning a particular procedure could endanger women's health.' " As illustrated by respondents' arguments and the decisions of the Courts of Appeals, *Stenberg* has been interpreted to leave no margin of error for legislatures to act in the face of medical uncertainty.

A zero tolerance policy would strike down legitimate abortion regulations, like the present one, if some part of the medical community were disinclined to follow the proscription. This is too exacting a standard to impose on the legislative power, exercised in this instance under the Commerce Clause, to regulate the medical profession. Considerations of marginal safety, including the balance of risks, are within the legislative competence when the regulation is rational and in pursuit of legitimate ends. When standard medical options are available, mere convenience does not suffice to displace them; and if some procedures have different risks than others, it does not follow that the State is altogether barred from imposing reasonable regulations. The Act is not invalid on its face where there is uncertainty over whether the barred procedure is ever necessary to preserve a woman's health, given the availability of other abortion procedures that are considered to be safe alternatives.

V.

[T]hese facial attacks should not have been entertained in the first instance. In these circumstances the proper means to consider exceptions is by as-applied challenge. The Government has acknowledged that preenforcement, as-applied challenges to the Act can be maintained. This is the proper manner to protect the health of the woman if it can be shown that in discrete and well-defined instances a particular condition has or is likely to occur in which the procedure prohibited by the Act must be used. In an as-applied challenge the nature of the medical risk can be better quantified and balanced than in a facial attack. . . .

[R]espondents have not demonstrated that the Act would be unconstitutional in a large fraction of relevant cases. *Casey*. We note that the statute here applies to all instances in which the doctor proposes to use the prohibited procedure, not merely those in which the woman suffers from medical complications. It is neither our obligation nor within our traditional institutional role to resolve questions of constitutionality with respect to each potential situation that might develop. "[I]t would indeed be undesirable for this Court to consider every conceivable situation which might possibly arise in the application of complex and comprehensive legislation." United States v. Raines, 362 U.S. 17 (1960). For this reason, "[a]s-applied challenges are the basic building blocks of constitutional adjudication." Fallon, As-Applied and Facial Challenges and Third-Party Standing, 113 Harv. L. Rev. 1321, 1328 (2000).

The Act is open to a proper as-applied challenge in a discrete case. No as-applied challenge need be brought if the prohibition in the Act threatens a woman's life because the Act already contains a life exception. . . .

Justice THOMAS, with whom Justice SCALIA joins, concurring.

I join the Court's opinion because it accurately applies current jurisprudence. . . . I write separately to reiterate my view that the Court's abortion jurisprudence, including *Casey* and Roe v. Wade, has no basis in the Constitution. I also note that whether the Act constitutes a permissible exercise of Congress' power under the Commerce Clause is not before the Court. The parties did not raise or brief that issue; it is outside the question presented; and the lower courts did not address it.

Justice GINSBURG, with whom Justice STEVENS, Justice SOUTER, and Justice BREYER join, dissenting.

. . .

Today's decision is alarming. It refuses to take *Casey* and *Stenberg* seriously. It tolerates, indeed applauds, federal intervention to ban nationwide a procedure found necessary and proper in certain cases by the American College of Obstetricians and Gynecologists (ACOG). It blurs the line, firmly drawn in *Casey,* between previability and postviability abortions. And, for the first time since *Roe,* the Court blesses a prohibition with no exception safeguarding a woman's health. . . .

I.

A

As *Casey* comprehended, at stake in cases challenging abortion restrictions is a woman's "control over her [own] destiny." There was a time, not so long ago," when women were "regarded as the center of home and family life, with attendant special responsibilities that precluded full and independent legal status under the Constitution." Those views, this Court made clear in *Casey,* "are no longer consistent with our understanding of the family, the individual, or the

Constitution." Women, it is now acknowledged, have the talent, capacity, and right "to participate equally in the economic and social life of the Nation." Their ability to realize their full potential, the Court recognized, is intimately connected to "their ability to control their reproductive lives." Thus, legal challenges to undue restrictions on abortion procedures do not seek to vindicate some generalized notion of privacy; rather, they center on a woman's autonomy to determine her life's course, and thus to enjoy equal citizenship stature. See, e.g., Siegel, Reasoning from the Body: A Historical Perspective on Abortion Regulation and Questions of Equal Protection, 44 Stan. L. Rev. 261 (1992); Law, Rethinking Sex and the Constitution, 132 U. Pa. L. Rev. 955, 1002-1028 (1984).

[T]he Court has consistently required that laws regulating abortion, at any stage of pregnancy and in all cases, safeguard a woman's health. See, e.g., Ayotte ("[O]ur precedents hold . . . that a State may not restrict access to abortions that are necessary, in appropriate medical judgment, for preservation of the life or health of the [woman]."; Stenberg ("Since the law requires a health exception in order to validate even a postviability abortion regulation, it at a minimum requires the same in respect to previability regulation.").

We have thus ruled that a State must avoid subjecting women to health risks not only where the pregnancy itself creates danger, but also where state regulation forces women to resort to less safe methods of abortion. See Danforth, Stenberg. Indeed, we have applied the rule that abortion regulation must safeguard a woman's health to the particular procedure at issue here — intact dilation and evacuation (D & E).[a]

In Stenberg, we expressly held that a statute banning intact D & E was unconstitutional in part because it lacked a health exception. We noted that there existed a "division of medical opinion" about the relative safety of intact D & E, but we made clear that as long as "substantial medical authority supports the proposition that banning a particular abortion procedure could endanger women's health," a health exception is required. . . . Thus, we reasoned, division in medical opinion "at most means uncertainty, a factor that signals the presence of risk, not its absence." "[A] statute that altogether forbids [intact D & E] . . . consequently must contain a health exception."

---

a. Dilation and evacuation (D & E) is the most frequently used abortion procedure during the second trimester of pregnancy; intact D & E is a variant of the D & E procedure. Second-trimester abortions (i.e., midpregnancy, previability abortions) are, however, relatively uncommon. Between 85 and 90 percent of all abortions performed in the United States take place during the first three months of pregnancy.

Adolescents and indigent women, research suggests, are more likely than other women to have difficulty obtaining an abortion during the first trimester of pregnancy. Minors may be unaware they are pregnant until relatively late in pregnancy, while poor women's financial constraints are an obstacle to timely receipt of services. Severe fetal anomalies and health problems confronting the pregnant woman are also causes of second-trimester abortions; many such conditions cannot be diagnosed or do not develop until the second trimester.

B

In 2003, a few years after our ruling in *Stenberg,* Congress passed the Partial-Birth Abortion Ban Act — without an exception for women's health. See 18 U.S.C. §1531(a) (2000 ed., Supp. IV).[b] The congressional findings on which the Partial-Birth Abortion Ban Act rests do not withstand inspection, as the lower courts have determined and this Court is obliged to concede. See National Abortion Federation v. Ashcroft, 330 F. Supp. 2d 436, 482 (S.D.N.Y. 2004) ("Congress did not . . . carefully consider the evidence before arriving at its findings."), *aff'd sub nom.* National Abortion Federation v. Gonzales, 437 F.3d 278 (C.A.2 2006). See also Planned Parenthood Federation of Am. v. Ashcroft, 320 F. Supp. 2d 957, 1019 (N.D. Cal. 2004) ("[N] one of the six physicians who testified before Congress had ever performed an intact D & E. Several did not provide abortion services at all; and one was not even an obgyn. . . . [T]he oral testimony before Congress was not only unbalanced, but intentionally polemic."), *aff'd*, 435 F.3d 1163 (C.A.9 2006); Carhart v. Ashcroft, 331 F. Supp. 2d 805, 1011 (Neb. 2004) ("Congress arbitrarily relied upon the opinions of doctors who claimed to have no (or very little) recent and relevant experience with surgical abortions, and disregarded the views of doctors who had significant and relevant experience with those procedures."), *aff'd*, 413 F.3d 791 (C.A.8 2005).

Many of the Act's recitations are incorrect. . . . Congress claimed there was a medical consensus that the banned procedure is never necessary. . . . But the evidence "very clearly demonstrate[d] the opposite." Similarly, Congress found that "[t]here is no credible medical evidence that partial-birth abortions are safe or are safer than other abortion procedures." But the congressional record includes letters from numerous individual physicians stating that pregnant women's health would be jeopardized under the Act, as well as statements from nine professional associations, including ACOG, the American Public Health Association, and the California Medical Association, attesting that intact D & E carries meaningful safety advantages over other methods. No comparable medical groups supported the ban. In fact, "all of the government's own witnesses disagreed with many of the specific congressional findings."

C

In contrast to Congress, the District Courts made findings after full trials at which all parties had the opportunity to present their best evidence. The courts had the benefit of "much more extensive medical and scientific evidence . . . concerning the safety and necessity of intact D & Es."

---

b. The Act's sponsors left no doubt that their intention was to nullify our ruling in *Stenberg*. See, e.g., 149 Cong. Rec. 5731 (2003) (statement of Sen. Santorum) ("Why are we here? We are here because the Supreme Court defended the indefensible. . . . We have responded to the Supreme Court."). See also 148 Cong. Rec. 14273 (2002) (statement of Rep. Linder) (rejecting proposition that Congress has "no right to legislate a ban on this horrible practice because the Supreme Court says [it] cannot").

During the District Court trials, "numerous" "extraordinarily accomplished" and "very experienced" medical experts explained that, in certain circumstances and for certain women, intact D & E is safer than alternative procedures and necessary to protect women's health.

According to the expert testimony plaintiffs introduced, the safety advantages of intact D & E are marked for women with certain medical conditions, for example, uterine scarring, bleeding disorders, heart disease, or compromised immune systems. Further, plaintiffs' experts testified that intact D & E is significantly safer for women with certain pregnancy-related conditions, such as placenta previa and accreta, and for women carrying fetuses with certain abnormalities, such as severe hydrocephalus.

Intact D & E, plaintiffs' experts explained, provides safety benefits over D & E by dismemberment for several reasons: *First,* intact D & E minimizes the number of times a physician must insert instruments through the cervix and into the uterus, and thereby reduces the risk of trauma to, and perforation of, the cervix and uterus — the most serious complication associated with nonintact D & E. *Second,* removing the fetus intact, instead of dismembering it *in utero,* decreases the likelihood that fetal tissue will be retained in the uterus, a condition that can cause infection, hemorrhage, and infertility. *Third,* intact D & E diminishes the chances of exposing the patient's tissues to sharp bony fragments sometimes resulting from dismemberment of the fetus. *Fourth,* intact D & E takes less operating time than D & E by dismemberment, and thus may reduce bleeding, the risk of infection, and complications relating to anesthesia.

Based on thoroughgoing review of the trial evidence and the congressional record, each of the District Courts to consider the issue rejected Congress' findings as unreasonable and not supported by the evidence. The trial courts concluded, in contrast to Congress' findings, that "significant medical authority supports the proposition that in some circumstances, [intact D & E] is the safest procedure."[c]

The District Courts' findings merit this Court's respect. See, e.g., Fed. Rule Civ. Proc. 52(a). Today's opinion supplies no reason to reject those findings. Nevertheless, despite the District Courts' appraisal of the weight of the evidence, and in undisguised conflict with *Stenberg,* the Court asserts that the Partial-Birth Abortion Ban Act can survive "when . . . medical uncertainty persists." This assertion is bewildering. Not only does it defy the Court's longstanding precedent affirming the necessity of a health exception, with no carve-out for

---

c. Even the District Court for the Southern District of New York, which was more skeptical of the health benefits of intact D & E, recognized: "[T]he Government's own experts disagreed with almost all of Congress's factual findings"; a "significant body of medical opinion" holds that intact D & E has safety advantages over nonintact D & E; "[p]rofessional medical associations have also expressed their view that [intact D & E] may be the safest procedure for some women"; and "[t]he evidence indicates that the same disagreement among experts found by the Supreme Court in *Stenberg* existed throughout the time that Congress was considering the legislation, despite Congress's findings to the contrary."

circumstances of medical uncertainty, it gives short shrift to the records before us, carefully canvassed by the District Courts. Those records indicate that "the majority of highly qualified experts on the subject believe intact D & E to be the safest, most appropriate procedure under certain circumstances."

The Court acknowledges some of this evidence, but insists that, because some witnesses disagreed with the ACOG and other experts' assessment of risk, the Act can stand. In this insistence, the Court brushes under the rug the District Courts' well-supported findings that the physicians who testified that intact D & E is never necessary to preserve the health of a woman had slim authority for their opinions. They had no training for, or personal experience with, the intact D & E procedure, and many performed abortions only on rare occasions. Even indulging the assumption that the Government witnesses were equally qualified to evaluate the relative risks of abortion procedures, their testimony could not erase the "significant medical authority support[ing] the proposition that in some circumstances, [intact D & E] would be the safest procedure."[d]

II.

A

The Court offers flimsy and transparent justifications for upholding a nation-wide ban on intact D & E *sans* any exception to safeguard a women's health. Today's ruling, the Court declares, advances "a premise central to [*Casey's*] conclusion"—i.e., the Government's "legitimate and substantial interest in pre-serving and promoting fetal life." But the Act scarcely furthers that interest: The law saves not a single fetus from destruction, for it targets only a *method* of performing abortion. And surely the statute was not designed to protect the lives or health of pregnant women. In short, the Court upholds a law that, while doing nothing to "preserv[e] . . . fetal life," bars a woman from choosing intact D & E although her doctor "reasonably believes [that procedure] will best pro-tect [her]."

As another reason for upholding the ban, the Court emphasizes that the Act does not proscribe the nonintact D & E procedure. But why not, one might ask. Nonintact D & E could equally be characterized as "brutal," involving as it does "tear[ing] [a fetus] apart" and "ripp[ing] off" its limbs. "[T]he notion that either of these two equally gruesome procedures . . . is more akin to infanticide than the other, or that the State furthers any legitimate interest by banning one but not the other, is simply irrational."

---

d. The majority contends that "[i]f the intact D & E procedure is truly necessary in some circum-stances, it appears likely an injection that kills the fetus is an alternative under the Act that allows the doctor to perform the procedure." But a "significant body of medical opinion believes that inducing fetal death by injection is almost always inappropriate to the preservation of the health of women undergoing abortion because it poses tangible risk and provides no benefit to the woman." In some circumstances, injections are "absolutely [medically] contraindicated." The Court also identifies medical induction of labor as an alternative. That procedure, however, requires a hospital stay, ren-dering it inaccessible to patients who lack financial resources, and it too is considered less safe for many women, and impermissible for others.

Delivery of an intact, albeit nonviable, fetus warrants special condemnation, the Court maintains, because a fetus that is not dismembered resembles an infant. But so, too, does a fetus delivered intact after it is terminated by injection a day or two before the surgical evacuation, or a fetus delivered through medical induction or cesarean. Yet, the availability of those procedures — along with D & E by dismemberment — the Court says, saves the ban on intact D & E from a declaration of unconstitutionality. Never mind that the procedures deemed acceptable might put a woman's health at greater risk.

Ultimately, the Court admits that "moral concerns" are at work, concerns that could yield prohibitions on any abortion. Notably, the concerns expressed are untethered to any ground genuinely serving the Government's interest in preserving life. By allowing such concerns to carry the day and case, overriding fundamental rights, the Court dishonors our precedent. See, e.g., *Casey*; *Lawrence v. Texas*.

Revealing in this regard, the Court invokes an antiabortion shibboleth for which it concededly has no reliable evidence: Women who have abortions come to regret their choices, and consequently suffer from "[s]evere depression and loss of esteem."[e] Because of women's fragile emotional state and because of the

---

e. The Court is surely correct that, for most women, abortion is a painfully difficult decision. But "neither the weight of the scientific evidence to date nor the observable reality of 33 years of legal abortion in the United States comports with the idea that having an abortion is any more dangerous to a woman's long-term mental health than delivering and parenting a child that she did not intend to have. . . ." Cohen, Abortion and Mental Health: Myths and Realities, 9 Guttmacher Policy Rev. 8 (2006); see generally Bazelon, Is There a Post-Abortion Syndrome? N.Y. Times Magazine, Jan. 21, 2007, p. 40. See also, e.g., American Psychological Association, APA Briefing Paper on the Impact of Abortion (2005) (rejecting theory of a postabortion syndrome and stating that "[a]ccess to legal abortion to terminate an unwanted pregnancy is vital to safeguard both the physical and mental health of women"); Schmiege & Russo, Depression and Unwanted First Pregnancy: Longitudinal Cohort Study, 331 British Medical J. 1303 (2005) (finding no credible evidence that choosing to terminate an unwanted first pregnancy contributes to risk of subsequent depression); Gilchrist, Hannaford, Frank, & Kay, Termination of Pregnancy and Psychiatric Morbidity, 167 British J. of Psychiatry 243, 247-248 (1995) (finding, in a cohort of more than 13,000 women, that the rate of psychiatric disorder was no higher among women who terminated pregnancy than among those who carried pregnancy to term); Stodland, The Myth of the Abortion Trauma Syndrome, 268 JAMA 2078, 2079 (1992) ("Scientific studies indicate that legal abortion results in fewer deleterious sequelae for women compared with other possible outcomes of unwanted pregnancy. There is no evidence of an abortion trauma syndrome."); American Psychological Association, Council Policy Manual: (N)(I)(3), Public Interest (1989) (declaring assertions about widespread severe negative psychological effects of abortion to be "without fact"). But see Cougle, Reardon, & Coleman, Generalized Anxiety Following Unintended Pregnancies Resolved Through Childbirth and Abortion: A Cohort Study of the 1995 National Survey of Family Growth, 19 J. Anxiety Disorders 137, 142 (2005) (advancing theory of a postabortion syndrome but acknowledging that "no causal relationship between pregnancy outcome and anxiety could be determined" from study); Reardon et al., Psychiatric Admissions of Low-Income Women following Abortion and Childbirth, 168 Canadian Medical Assn. J. 1253, 1255-1256 (May 13, 2003) (concluding that psychiatric admission rates were higher for women who had an abortion compared with women who delivered); cf. Major, Psychological Implications of Abortion — Highly Charged and Rife with Misleading Research, 168 Canadian Medical Assn. J. 1257, 1258 (May 13, 2003) (critiquing Reardon study for failing to control for a host of differences between women in the delivery and abortion samples).

"bond of love the mother has for her child," the Court worries, doctors may withhold information about the nature of the intact D & E procedure.[f] The solution the Court approves, then, is *not* to require doctors to inform women, accurately and adequately, of the different procedures and their attendant risks. Instead, the Court deprives women of the right to make an autonomous choice, even at the expense of their safety.[g]

This way of thinking reflects ancient notions about women's place in the family and under the Constitution — ideas that have long since been discredited. Compare, e.g., Muller v. Oregon; Bradwell v. [Illinois] (Bradley, J., concurring) ("Man is, or should be, woman's protector and defender. The natural and proper timidity and delicacy which belongs to the female sex evidently unfits it for many of the occupations of civil life. . . . The paramount destiny and mission of woman are to fulfil[l] the noble and benign offices of wife and mother."), with United States v. Virginia; Califano v. Goldfarb, 430 U.S. 199 (1977) (gender-based Social Security classification rejected because it rested on "archaic and overbroad generalizations" "such as assumptions as to [women's] dependency" (internal quotation marks omitted)).

Though today's majority may regard women's feelings on the matter as "self-evident," this Court has repeatedly confirmed that "[t]he destiny of the woman must be shaped . . . on her own conception of her spiritual imperatives and her place in society." *Casey.*

B

In cases on a "woman's liberty to determine whether to [continue] her pregnancy," this Court has identified viability as a critical consideration. . . . Today,

---

f. Notwithstanding the "bond of love" women often have with their children, not all pregnancies, this Court has recognized, are wanted, or even the product of consensual activity. See *Casey,* 505 U.S., at 891, 112 S. Ct. 2791 ("[O]n an average day in the United States, nearly 11,000 women are severely assaulted by their male partners. Many of these incidents involve sexual assault.") See also Glander, Moore, Michielutte, & Parsons, The Prevalence of Domestic Violence Among Women Seeking Abortion, 91 Obstetrics & Gynecology 1002 (1998); Holmes, Resnick, Kilpatrick, & Best, Rape-Related Pregnancy; Estimates and Descriptive Characteristics from a National Sample of Women, 175 Am. J. Obstetrics & Gynecology 320 (Aug. 1996).

g. Eliminating or reducing women's reproductive choices is manifestly not a means of protecting them. When safe abortion procedures cease to be an option, many women seek other means to end unwanted or coerced pregnancies. See, e.g., World Health Organization, Unsafe Abortion: Global and Regional Estimates of the Incidence of Unsafe Abortion and Associated Mortality in 2000, pp. 3, 16 (4th ed. 2004) ("Restrictive legislation is associated with a high incidence of unsafe abortion" worldwide; unsafe abortion represents 13% of all "maternal" deaths); Henshaw, Unintended Pregnancy and Abortion: A Public Health Perspective, in A Clinician's Guide to Medical and Surgical Abortion 11, 19 (M. Paul, E. Lichtenberg, L. Borgatta, D. Grimes, & P. Stubblefield eds. 1999) ("Before legalization, large numbers of women in the United States died from unsafe abortions."); H. Boonstra, R. Gold, C. Richards, & L. Finer, Abortion in Women's Lives 13, and fig. 2.2 (2006) ("as late as 1965, illegal abortion still accounted for an estimated . . . 17% of all officially reported pregnancy-related deaths"; "[d]eaths from abortion declined dramatically after legalization").

the Court blurs that line, maintaining that "[t]he Act [legitimately] appl[ies] both previability and postviability because . . . a fetus is a living organism while within the womb, whether or not it is viable outside the womb." Instead of drawing the line at viability, the Court refers to Congress' purpose to differentiate "abortion and infanticide" based not on whether a fetus can survive outside the womb, but on where a fetus is anatomically located when a particular medical procedure is performed.

One wonders how long a line that saves no fetus from destruction will hold in face of the Court's "moral concerns." The Court's hostility to the right *Roe* and *Casey* secured is not concealed. Throughout, the opinion refers to obstetrician-gynecologists and surgeons who perform abortions not by the titles of their medical specialties, but by the pejorative label "abortion doctor." A fetus is described as an "unborn child," and as a "baby;" second-trimester, previability abortions are referred to as "late-term"; and the reasoned medical judgments of highly trained doctors are dismissed as "preferences" motivated by "mere convenience." Instead of the heightened scrutiny we have previously applied, the Court determines that a "rational" ground is enough to uphold the Act. And, most troubling, *Casey*'s principles, confirming the continuing vitality of "the essential holding of *Roe*," are merely "assume[d]" for the moment, rather than "retained" or "reaffirmed," *Casey*.

III.

A

The Court further confuses our jurisprudence when it declares that "facial attacks" are not permissible in "these circumstances," i.e., where medical uncertainty exists. This holding is perplexing given that, in materially identical circumstances we held that a statute lacking a health exception was unconstitutional on its face. *Stenberg*.

Without attempting to distinguish *Stenberg* and earlier decisions, the majority asserts that the Act survives review because respondents have not shown that the ban on intact D & E would be unconstitutional "in a large fraction of relevant cases." But *Casey* makes clear that, in determining whether any restriction poses an undue burden on a "large fraction" of women, the relevant class is *not* "all women," nor "all pregnant women," nor even all women "seeking abortions." Rather, a provision restricting access to abortion, "must be judged by reference to those [women] for whom it is an actual rather than an irrelevant restriction." Thus the absence of a health exception burdens *all* women for whom it is relevant—women who, in the judgment of their doctors, require an intact D & E because other procedures would place their health at risk.[h] It makes no sense to

---

h. There is, in short, no fraction because the numerator and denominator are the same: The health exception reaches only those cases where a woman's health is at risk. Perhaps for this reason, in mandating safeguards for women's health, we have never before invoked the "large fraction" test.

conclude that this facial challenge fails because respondents have not shown that a health exception is necessary for a large fraction of second-trimester abortions, including those for which a health exception is unnecessary: The very purpose of a health *exception* is to protect women in *exceptional* cases.

B

If there is anything at all redemptive to be said of today's opinion, it is that the Court is not willing to foreclose entirely a constitutional challenge to the Act. "The Act is open," the Court states, "to a proper as-applied challenge in a discrete case." But the Court offers no clue on what a "proper" lawsuit might look like. Nor does the Court explain why the injunctions ordered by the District Courts should not remain in place, trimmed only to exclude instances in which another procedure would safeguard a woman's health at least equally well. Surely the Court cannot mean that no suit may be brought until a woman's health is immediately jeopardized by the ban on intact D & E. A woman "suffer[ing] from medical complications," needs access to the medical procedure at once and cannot wait for the judicial process to unfold.

The Court appears, then, to contemplate another lawsuit by the initiators of the instant actions. In such a second round, the Court suggests, the challengers could succeed upon demonstrating that "in discrete and well-defined instances a particular condition has or is likely to occur in which the procedure prohibited by the Act must be used." One may anticipate that such a preenforcement challenge will be mounted swiftly, to ward off serious, sometimes irremediable harm, to women whose health would be endangered by the intact D & E prohibition.

The Court envisions that in an as-applied challenge, "the nature of the medical risk can be better quantified and balanced." But it should not escape notice that the record already includes hundreds and hundreds of pages of testimony identifying "discrete and well-defined instances" in which recourse to an intact D & E would better protect the health of women with particular conditions. Record evidence also documents that medical exigencies, unpredictable in advance, may indicate to a well-trained doctor that intact D & E is the safest procedure. In light of this evidence, our unanimous decision just one year ago in *Ayotte* counsels against reversal. See 546 U.S., at 331 (remanding for reconsideration of the remedy for the absence of a health exception, suggesting that an injunction prohibiting unconstitutional applications might suffice).

The Court's allowance only of an "as-applied challenge in a discrete case," jeopardizes women's health and places doctors in an untenable position. Even if courts were able to carve-out exceptions through piecemeal litigation for "discrete and well-defined instances," women whose circumstances have not been anticipated by prior litigation could well be left unprotected. In treating those women, physicians would risk criminal prosecution, conviction, and imprisonment if they exercise their best judgment as to the safest medical procedure for their patients. The Court is thus gravely mistaken to conclude that narrow as-applied challenges are "the proper manner to protect the health of the woman."

IV.

. . . Though today's opinion does not go so far as to discard *Roe* or *Casey,* the Court, differently composed than it was when we last considered a restrictive abortion regulation, is hardly faithful to our earlier invocations of "the rule of law" and the "principles of *stare decisis.*" Congress imposed a ban despite our clear prior holdings that the State cannot proscribe an abortion procedure when its use is necessary to protect a woman's health. Although Congress' findings could not withstand the crucible of trial, the Court defers to the legislative override of our Constitution-based rulings. A decision so at odds with our jurisprudence should not have staying power.

In sum, the notion that the Partial-Birth Abortion Ban Act furthers any legitimate governmental interest is, quite simply, irrational. The Court's defense of the statute provides no saving explanation. In candor, the Act, and the Court's defense of it, cannot be understood as anything other than an effort to chip away at a right declared again and again by this Court—and with increasing comprehension of its centrality to women's lives. When "a statute burdens constitutional rights and all that can be said on its behalf is that it is the vehicle that legislators have chosen for expressing their hostility to those rights, the burden is undue."

Discussion

1. *The fate of* Stenberg. Does the Court overrule *Stenberg v. Carhart* or merely distinguish it? If the latter, what part of *Stenberg* is still good law? If the former, does it satisfy the Court's analysis of when to overrule decisions in *Casey*?

2. *Changing justifications for the abortion right.* Note that Justice Ginsburg's dissent—joined by four Justices—no longer grounds the abortion right in "some generalized notion of privacy." Instead she bases the right on "a woman's autonomy to determine her life's course, and thus to enjoy equal citizenship stature." This is a shift to an equality-based model, foregrounded in *Casey.* (See the casebook discussion at pp. 1409-1419.) Meanwhile, Justice Kennedy's majority opinion notes that the principles stated in *Casey* "did not find support from all those who join the instant opinion," and merely "assume[s] the . . . principles for the purposes of this opinion." The views of Chief Justice Roberts and Justice Alito have yet to be determined.

3. *Facial and as-applied challenges.* The Court holds that respondents cannot challenge the PBAA facially but instead must make an "as-applied" challenge. Facial challenges claim that the language of a challenged statute is sufficient to demonstrate that it unconstitutionally burdens a constitutional right. When successful, facial challenges strike down the entire statute. As-applied challenges claim that the language of the statute has been unconstitutionally applied to the plaintiff. When successful, the law may not constitutionally be applied to a person in the plaintiff's situation.

Free speech doctrines have special rules for determining when courts will entertain facial or as-applied challenges, see Broadrick v. Oklahoma, 413 U.S.

601 (1973). Outside the free speech area, the Court has stated that as-applied challenges are preferred. In United States v. Salerno, 481 U.S. 739, 745 (1987), which challenged the 1984 federal Bail Reform Act, the Court stated that facial challenges "must establish that no set of circumstances exists under which the Act would be valid," but this has not always been the Court's consistent practice because of the different substantive tests prevailing in different areas of the law. See, e.g. Bowen v. Kendrick, 487 U.S. 589, 602 (1988), which determined facial validity under the Establishment Clause by asking whether a statute had a "primary effect" of advancing religion, or required "excessive entanglement" between church and state.

In *Casey* the Court considered facial challenges to abortion regulations in the context of its "undue burden" test. It argued that Pennsylvania's spousal notification law "must be judged by reference to those for whom it is an actual, rather than an irrelevant, restriction." The class relevant for determining whether a facial challenge was appropriate was "narrower . . . than the class of women seeking abortions identified by the State: it is married women seeking abortions who do not wish to notify their husbands of their intentions and who do not qualify for one of the statutory exceptions to the notice requirement." Defining the class in that way, the Court concluded that "in a large fraction of the cases in which [the spousal notification law] is relevant, it will operate as a substantial obstacle to a woman's choice to undergo an abortion" and was therefore facially invalid.

Casey seemed to suggest that if an abortion regulation was an undue burden with respect to a specific class of women, the court could strike down the entire statute even though it did not burden a far larger class. Similarly, in *Stenberg*, the Court had invalidated Nebraska's partial-birth abortion law on its face because of the lack of a health exception. In Ayotte v. Planned Parenthood of Northern New England, 546 U.S. 320, 328 (2006), the Court suggested a different approach. New Hampshire's parental notification law prohibited doctors from performing an abortion on a pregnant minor until 48 hours after written notification to the parent or guardian. The statute made exceptions for life-threatening emergencies, but no exception for medical emergencies that threatened a minor's health. The Court, in a unanimous opinion by Justice O'Connor, noted that "New Hampshire has conceded that . . . it would be unconstitutional to apply the Act in a manner that subjects minors to significant health risks." However, in *Ayotte*, the Court remanded the case to the New Hampshire courts to determine whether they could "issue a declaratory judgment and an injunction prohibiting the statute's unconstitutional application."

In *Carhart II*, Justice Kennedy upholds the federal statute on its face because he believes that there is a factual dispute about whether a health exception is necessary, but he provides for the possibility of a subsequent as-applied challenge. Is it realistic to think that a plaintiff in an actual medical emergency could make such a challenge? If not, who would have standing to bring an as-applied challenge? If, as Justice Ginsburg suggests, a preenforcement as-applied challenge is possible, what is the difference between it and the case that was actually before the Court in *Carhart II*?

Consider whether *Carhart II* changes *Casey*'s basic approach to facial challenges. And consider the consequences of requiring as-applied challenges to abortion regulations in the future. When states pass new abortion regulations, plaintiffs will have to bring challenges to each aspect of the law they object to and prove how the statute is unconstitutional as to their situation. Will this increase the cost of litigation or make injunctions against new abortion statutes harder to obtain?

Why didn't the Court simply interpret the federal statute to include a health exception and avoid the constitutional problem? One reason is that Congress did not want a health exception, thinking it would give doctors too much leeway to perform intact D & E abortions whenever they felt it would be medically indicated.

4. *Woman-protective arguments against abortion and "postabortion syndrome."* Although upholding the federal PBAA will affect only a few hundred women a year, another aspect of *Carhart II* may prove far more important. Justice Kennedy argues that the state may prevent women from having a particular abortion procedure because they may regret it later on. Can this be described as respecting a woman's choice or is it a thinly disguised form of paternalism? Could states prohibit other abortion procedures—or indeed all abortions—on the grounds that some percentage of women will later regret their choices?

In the middle of his argument for why the state may protect women from abortions they may later regret, Justice Kennedy cites an amicus brief by Sandra Cano—the original Mary Doe in *Doe v. Bolton*—who is now a pro-life advocate. He refers obliquely to the theory of "postabortion syndrome" (PAS), in which having an abortion can later cause women "[s]evere depression and loss of self esteem." Justice Kennedy states that "[w]hile we find no reliable data to measure the phenomenon, it seems unexceptionable to conclude some women come to regret their choice to abort the infant life they once created and sustained." Justice Ginsburg's dissent, citing numerous medical studies, accuses Justice Kennedy of promoting junk science in the United States Reports.

Justice Kennedy's argument is connected to a new class of pro-life arguments for abortion regulation. Early pro-life arguments focused on the fetus and fetal development. Beginning in the 1990s pro-life advocates began to argue that abortion hurts women because of women's natural propensities for bearing children and bonding with them. As Reva Siegel explains, this new class of "[g]ender-based arguments against abortion embed claims about protecting the unborn in an elaborate set of arguments about protecting women." Reva B. Siegel, The New Politics of Abortion: An Equality Analysis of Women-Protective Abortion Restrictions, 2007 Ill. L. Rev. 991. These new woman-protective arguments against abortion seek to turn the rhetoric of "choice" against the pro-choice movement; they argue that women do not freely choose abortion. That is either because women are misled by abortion providers who do not explain to them what they are actually doing to their unborn children, or because having an abortion poses risks to their physical and mental health that they do not fully understand. Hence abortion restrictions are necessary to prevent women from making choices that are not really theirs.

Are statutes that limit access to abortion based on this reasoning vulnerable to an equal protection challenge? Consider two possible theories. The first is that statutes motivated by these concerns embody stereotypical views about women's true natures and their natural bond of affection for their unborn children: Women will naturally choose to have children whenever they become pregnant unless they are misinformed or coerced. The second is that women-protective arguments embody stereotypical views about women's reasoning capacities, and particularly about their reasoning about reproductive issues: Women do not have the independence and judgment necessary to make responsible decisions about abortion and hence need protection from unscrupulous abortion doctors. Are these unconstitutional purposes under the 1970s sex equality decisions? Under *Feeney*? Under *Hibbs*?

5. *Informed consent and the protection of women.* A less restrictive alternative to prohibiting a procedure is to inform the woman about the nature of the procedure she is to undergo. *Casey* holds that states may express their preference for unborn life and attempt to persuade women not to have abortions as long as they provide women with information that is "truthful and not misleading." Does *Carhart II* give states more leeway in attempting to persuade women that they should not have abortions? After *Carhart II*, can states require that all women must pay for ultrasounds and view the ultrasounds of their fetus before having an abortion?

Consider South Dakota's 2005 informed consent statute. The legislative findings accompanying the bill state that "all abortions . . . terminate the life of a whole, separate, unique, living human being," and "that there is an existing relationship between a pregnant woman and her unborn child during the entire period of gestation." "[P]rocedures terminating the life of an unborn child impose risks to the life and health of the pregnant woman. . . . [A] woman seeking to terminate the life of her unborn child may be subject to pressures which can cause an emotional crisis, undue reliance on the advice of others, clouded judgment, and a willingness to violate conscience to avoid those pressures." "[P]regnant women contemplating the termination of their right to their relationship with their unborn children . . . are faced with making a profound decision most often under stress and pressures from circumstances and from other persons. [T]here exists a need for special protection of the rights of such pregnant women, and . . . the State of South Dakota has a compelling interest in providing such protection." S.D. Codified Laws §§34-23A-1.2 to 1.5. (2006).

The statute requires doctors to explain in detail the various risks of undergoing abortions, but not the risks of carrying a pregnancy to term. According to the statute, "voluntary and informed consent" to abortion requires that "in addition to any other information that must be disclosed under the common law doctrine, the physician provides th[e] pregnant woman with . . . a statement in writing" including "the following information":

> (b) That the abortion will terminate the life of a whole, separate, unique, living human being;
>
> (c) That the pregnant woman has an existing relationship with that unborn human being and that the relationship enjoys protection under the United States Constitution and under the laws of South Dakota;
>
> (d) That by having an abortion, her existing relationship and her existing constitutional rights with regards to that relationship will be terminated;
>
> (e) A description of all known medical risks of the procedure and statistically significant risk factors to which the pregnant woman would be subjected, including:
>
>> (i) Depression and related psychological distress;
>>
>> (ii) Increased risk of suicide ideation and suicide;
>>
>> (iii) A statement setting forth an accurate rate of deaths due to abortions, including all deaths in which the abortion procedure was a substantial contributing factor;
>>
>> (iv) All other known medical risks to the physical health of the woman, including the risk of infection, hemorrhage, danger to subsequent pregnancies, and infertility. . . .

S.D. Codified Laws §34-23A-10.1(b)-(e)(2006). The statute defines a "human being" "as an individual living member of the species of Homo sapiens, including the unborn human being during the entire embryonic and fetal ages from fertilization to full gestation." *Id.* at §34-23A-1. The South Dakota statute tries to combat misinformation and pressure that might lead women to choose abortions but not misinformation and pressure that might lead them to continue their pregnancies. The reason is that the state seeks to provide informed consent only where this might move women in the direction of its preferred moral choice, that women not have abortions. Moreover, section (b) suggests that state believes informed consent requires that doctors provide women with moral truths about the nature of the fetus.

Can informed-consent statutes in the abortion context avoid making some kinds of moral judgments or stating what the legislature regards as moral truths? If not, what kinds of moral judgments and statements may they properly make and not make? Is this statute consistent with women's rights under *Casey*?

6. *Informed consent requirements and postabortion syndrome: What is "medical uncertainty"?* Section (e)(i) and (e)(ii) of the South Dakota informed consent statute require, in effect, that women be informed about the dangers of the controversial phenomenon of "postabortion syndrome." Suppose that there is a consensus among the medical, psychiatric, and psychological communities that the disclosures in (e)(i) and (e)(ii) of the South Dakota informed statute are not in fact "statistically significant" risks of abortion, because "[t]he best

studies available on psychological responses to unwanted pregnancy terminated by abortion in the United States suggest that severe negative reactions are rare, and they parallel those following other normal life stresses." N.E. Adler et al., Psychological Factors in Abortion: A Review, American Psychologist, 1194-1204, 1202 (Oct. 1992). Therefore, according to these authorities, stating that the risks are significant is false and misleading. Nevertheless, advocates of post-abortion syndrome argue that these effects are quite frequent, and offer their own more recent studies to support it. Does the statute violate *Casey*? Does it violate the First Amendment rights of either doctors or their patients? See Robert Post, Informed Consent to Abortion: A First Amendment Analysis of Compelled Physician Speech, 2007 U. Ill. L. Rev. 939, 961-963.

In *Carhart II*, Justice Kennedy held that because Congress found medical experts who supported its view that intact D & E is never medically safer, the PBAA was constitutional because "state and federal legislatures [have] wide discretion to pass legislation in areas where there is medical and scientific uncertainty." After *Carhart II*, how many experts would South Dakota have to produce to establish "medical uncertainty" about the prevalence of postabortion syndrome?

Add the following after note 3 on p. 1536:

4. Dale *as a membership case.* In Rumsfeld v. FAIR, 547 U.S. 47 (2006), the Forum for Academic and Institutional Rights, Inc. (FAIR), an association of law schools and law faculties, challenged the Solomon Amendment — which provides that if any portion of an educational institution denies military recruiters access equal to that provided other recruiters, the entire institution will lose federal funding. Because FAIR's members had policies opposing sexual orientation discrimination, they sought to restrict military recruiting on campuses because the military discriminates against homosexuals. They raised several First Amendment challenges to the Solomon Amendment, including a claim that, under *Dale*, the Solomon Amendment interfered with their associational freedoms. The Supreme Court, in a unanimous opinion written by Chief Justice Roberts, rejected their claims: "To comply with the [Solomon Amendment], law schools must allow military recruiters on campus and assist them in whatever way the school chooses to assist other employers. Law schools therefore 'associate' with military recruiters in the sense that they interact with them. But recruiters are not part of the law school. Recruiters are, by definition, outsiders who come onto campus for the limited purpose of trying to hire students — not to become members of the school's expressive association. This distinction is critical. Unlike the public accommodations law in *Dale*, the Solomon Amendment does not force a law school '"to accept members it does not desire."' . . . FAIR correctly notes that the freedom of expressive association protects more than just a group's membership decisions. For example, we have held laws unconstitutional

that require disclosure of membership lists for groups seeking anonymity, Brown v. Socialist Workers '74 Campaign Comm. (Ohio), 459 U.S. 87, 101-102 (1982), or impose penalties or withhold benefits based on membership in a disfavored group, Healy v. James, 408 U.S. 169, 180-184 (1972). Although these laws did not directly interfere with an organization's composition, they made group membership less attractive, raising the same First Amendment concerns about affecting the group's ability to express its message."

"The Solomon Amendment has no similar effect on a law school's associational rights. Students and faculty are free to associate to voice their disapproval of the military's message; nothing about the statute affects the composition of the group by making group membership less desirable. The Solomon Amendment therefore does not violate a law school's First Amendment rights. A military recruiter's mere presence on campus does not violate a law school's right to associate, regardless of how repugnant the law school considers the recruiter's message."

Insert the following at the end of p. 1568:

UNITED STATES v. WINDSOR
133 S. Ct. 2675 (2013)

[Edith Windsor and Thea Spyer wed in Ontario, Canada in 2007. Both resided in New York, which recognized their marriage. When Spyer died in 2009, she left her entire estate to Windsor. Windsor sought to claim the federal estate tax exemption for surviving spouses, but was barred from doing so by §3 of the Defense of Marriage Act (DOMA). Section 3 of DOMA amended the Dictionary Act—a law providing rules of construction for over 1,000 federal laws and the whole realm of federal regulations—to define "marriage" and "spouse" as excluding same-sex partners. Windsor paid $363,053 in estate taxes and sought a refund. After the Internal Revenue Service denied her request, Windsor sued in federal court, arguing that §3 was unconstitutional. While the suit was pending, the Attorney General notified the Speaker of the House of Representatives that the Department of Justice would no longer defend §3's constitutionality but would continue to enforce the law until there was a final decision by the Supreme Court. In response, the Bipartisan Legal Advisory Group (BLAG) of the House of Representatives voted to intervene in the litigation to defend §3's constitutionality. The District Court permitted the intervention. On the merits, the court ruled against the United States, finding §3 unconstitutional and ordering the Treasury to refund Windsor's tax with interest. The Second Circuit affirmed, but the United States refused to comply with the judgment.]

Justice KENNEDY delivered the opinion of the Court.

[Justice Kennedy held that the Court had jurisdiction to hear the case because the petitioner U.S. government refuses to give Windsor her tax refund, and will do so only if it loses before the Supreme Court. Therefore it has a concrete stake in the outcome sufficient to provide standing under the minimum requirements of Article III. Nevertheless, prudential limits on standing would ordinarily weigh against hearing the suit because the United States agrees that DOMA is unconstitutional, and therefore is not really an adversary party. "[C]oncrete adverseness . . . sharpens the presentation of issues upon which the court so largely depends for illumination of difficult constitutional questions." However, Justice Kennedy explained, "BLAG's substantial adversarial argument for §3's constitutionality satisfies prudential concerns." Although "it is [not] appropriate for the Executive as a routine exercise to challenge statutes in court instead of making the case to Congress for amendment or repeal . . . this case is not routine [and] is of immediate importance to the Federal Government and to hundreds of thousands of persons."]

III

When at first Windsor and Spyer longed to marry, neither New York nor any other State granted them that right. After waiting some years, in 2007 they traveled to Ontario to be married there. It seems fair to conclude that, until recent years, many citizens had not even considered the possibility that two persons of the same sex might aspire to occupy the same status and dignity as that of a man and woman in lawful marriage. For marriage between a man and a woman no doubt had been thought of by most people as essential to the very definition of that term and to its role and function throughout the history of civilization. That belief, for many who long have held it, became even more urgent, more cherished when challenged. For others, however, came the beginnings of a new perspective, a new insight. Accordingly some States concluded that same-sex marriage ought to be given recognition and validity in the law for those same-sex couples who wish to define themselves by their commitment to each other. The limitation of lawful marriage to heterosexual couples, which for centuries had been deemed both necessary and fundamental, came to be seen in New York and certain other States as an unjust exclusion.

Slowly at first and then in rapid course, the laws of New York came to acknowledge the urgency of this issue for same-sex couples who wanted to affirm their commitment to one another before their children, their family, their friends, and their community. And so New York recognized same-sex marriages performed elsewhere; and then it later amended its own marriage laws to permit same-sex marriage. New York, in common with, as of this writing, 11 other States and the District of Columbia, decided that same-sex couples should have the right to marry and so live with pride in themselves and their union and in a status of equality with all other married persons. After a statewide deliberative process that enabled its citizens to discuss and weigh arguments for and against same-sex marriage, New York acted to enlarge the definition of marriage to correct what its citizens and elected representatives perceived to be an injustice that they had not earlier known or understood.

Against this background of lawful same-sex marriage in some States, the design, purpose, and effect of DOMA should be considered as the beginning point in deciding whether it is valid under the Constitution. By history and tradition the definition and regulation of marriage, as will be discussed in more detail, has been treated as being within the authority and realm of the separate States. Yet it is further established that Congress, in enacting discrete statutes, can make determinations that bear on marital rights and privileges. Just this Term the Court upheld the authority of the Congress to pre-empt state laws, allowing a former spouse to retain life insurance proceeds under a federal program that gave her priority, because of formal beneficiary designation rules, over the wife by a second marriage who survived the husband. *Hillman v. Maretta,* 569 U.S. ___ (2013). This is one example of the general principle that when the Federal Government acts in the exercise of its own proper authority, it has a wide choice of the mechanisms and means to adopt. See *McCulloch.* Congress has the power both to ensure efficiency in the administration of its programs and to choose what larger goals and policies to pursue.

Other precedents involving congressional statutes which affect marriages and family status further illustrate this point. In addressing the interaction of state domestic relations and federal immigration law Congress determined that marriages "entered into for the purpose of procuring an alien's admission [to the United States] as an immigrant" will not qualify the noncitizen for that status, even if the noncitizen's marriage is valid and proper for state-law purposes. And in establishing income-based criteria for Social Security benefits, Congress decided that although state law would determine in general who qualifies as an applicant's spouse, common-law marriages also should be recognized, regardless of any particular State's view on these relationships.

Though these discrete examples establish the constitutionality of limited federal laws that regulate the meaning of marriage in order to further federal policy, DOMA has a far greater reach; for it enacts a directive applicable to over 1,000 federal statutes and the whole realm of federal regulations. And its operation is directed to a class of persons that the laws of New York, and of 11 other States, have sought to protect.

In order to assess the validity of that intervention it is necessary to discuss the extent of the state power and authority over marriage as a matter of history and tradition. State laws defining and regulating marriage, of course, must respect the constitutional rights of persons, see, *e.g., Loving v. Virginia*; but, subject to those guarantees, "regulation of domestic relations" is "an area that has long been regarded as a virtually exclusive province of the States." *Sosna v. Iowa,* 419 U.S. 393 (1975).

The recognition of civil marriages is central to state domestic relations law applicable to its residents and citizens. The definition of marriage is the foundation of the State's broader authority to regulate the subject of domestic relations with respect to the "[p]rotection of offspring, property interests, and the enforcement of marital responsibilities." "[T]he states, at the time of the adoption of the

Constitution, possessed full power over the subject of marriage and divorce . . . [and] the Constitution delegated no authority to the Government of the United States on the subject of marriage and divorce." *Haddock v. Haddock,* 201 U.S. 562 (1906); see also *In re Burrus,* 136 U.S. 586 (1890) ("The whole subject of the domestic relations of husband and wife, parent and child, belongs to the laws of the States and not to the laws of the United States").

Consistent with this allocation of authority, the Federal Government, through our history, has deferred to state-law policy decisions with respect to domestic relations. In *De Sylva v. Ballentine,* 351 U.S. 570 (1956), for example, the Court held that, "[t]o decide who is the widow or widower of a deceased author, or who are his executors or next of kin," under the Copyright Act "requires a reference to the law of the State which created those legal relationships" because "there is no federal law of domestic relations." In order to respect this principle, the federal courts, as a general rule, do not adjudicate issues of marital status even when there might otherwise be a basis for federal jurisdiction. Federal courts will not hear divorce and custody cases even if they arise in diversity because of "the virtually exclusive primacy . . . of the States in the regulation of domestic relations."

The significance of state responsibilities for the definition and regulation of marriage dates to the Nation's beginning; for "when the Constitution was adopted the common understanding was that the domestic relations of husband and wife and parent and child were matters reserved to the States." Marriage laws vary in some respects from State to State. For example, the required minimum age is 16 in Vermont, but only 13 in New Hampshire. Likewise the permissible degree of consanguinity can vary (most States permit first cousins to marry, but a handful — such as Iowa and Washington — prohibit the practice). But these rules are in every event consistent within each State.

Against this background DOMA rejects the long-established precept that the incidents, benefits, and obligations of marriage are uniform for all married couples within each State, though they may vary, subject to constitutional guarantees, from one State to the next. Despite these considerations, it is unnecessary to decide whether this federal intrusion on state power is a violation of the Constitution because it disrupts the federal balance. The State's power in defining the marital relation is of central relevance in this case quite apart from principles of federalism. Here the State's decision to give this class of persons the right to marry conferred upon them a dignity and status of immense import. When the State used its historic and essential authority to define the marital relation in this way, its role and its power in making the decision enhanced the recognition, dignity, and protection of the class in their own community. DOMA, because of its reach and extent, departs from this history and tradition of reliance on state law to define marriage. "[D]iscriminations of an unusual character especially suggest careful consideration to determine whether they are obnoxious to the constitutional provision." *Romer v. Evans,* 517 U.S. 620 (1996).

The Federal Government uses this state-defined class for the opposite purpose — to impose restrictions and disabilities. That result requires this Court now to address whether the resulting injury and indignity is a deprivation of an essential part of the liberty protected by the Fifth Amendment. What the State of New York treats as alike the federal law deems unlike by a law designed to injure the same class the State seeks to protect.

In acting first to recognize and then to allow same-sex marriages, New York was responding "to the initiative of those who [sought] a voice in shaping the destiny of their own times." These actions were without doubt a proper exercise of its sovereign authority within our federal system, all in the way that the Framers of the Constitution intended. The dynamics of state government in the federal system are to allow the formation of consensus respecting the way the members of a discrete community treat each other in their daily contact and constant interaction with each other.

The States' interest in defining and regulating the marital relation, subject to constitutional guarantees, stems from the understanding that marriage is more than a routine classification for purposes of certain statutory benefits. Private, consensual sexual intimacy between two adult persons of the same sex may not be punished by the State, and it can form "but one element in a personal bond that is more enduring." *Lawrence v. Texas.* By its recognition of the validity of same-sex marriages performed in other jurisdictions and then by authorizing same-sex unions and same-sex marriages, New York sought to give further protection and dignity to that bond. For same-sex couples who wished to be married, the State acted to give their lawful conduct a lawful status. This status is a far-reaching legal acknowledgment of the intimate relationship between two people, a relationship deemed by the State worthy of dignity in the community equal with all other marriages. It reflects both the community's considered perspective on the historical roots of the institution of marriage and its evolving understanding of the meaning of equality.

IV

DOMA seeks to injure the very class New York seeks to protect. By doing so it violates basic due process and equal protection principles applicable to the Federal Government. See U.S. Const., Amdt. 5; *Bolling v. Sharpe,* 347 U.S. 497 (1954). The Constitution's guarantee of equality "must at the very least mean that a bare congressional desire to harm a politically unpopular group cannot" justify disparate treatment of that group. *Department of Agriculture v. Moreno,* 413 U.S. 528 (1973). In determining whether a law is motived by an improper animus or purpose, " '[d]iscriminations of an unusual character' " especially require careful consideration. *Romer.* DOMA cannot survive under these principles. The responsibility of the States for the regulation of domestic relations is an important indicator of the substantial societal impact the State's classifications have in the daily lives and customs of its people. DOMA's unusual deviation from the usual tradition of recognizing and accepting state definitions of marriage here operates to deprive same-sex couples of the benefits and responsibilities that come with the federal recognition of their marriages. This is strong evidence of a law having the purpose and effect of disapproval of that class. The avowed purpose and practical effect of the law here in question are to impose a disadvantage, a separate status, and so a stigma upon all who enter into same-sex marriages made lawful by the unquestioned authority of the States.

The history of DOMA's enactment and its own text demonstrate that interference with the equal dignity of same-sex marriages, a dignity conferred by the States in the exercise of their sovereign power, was more than an incidental effect of the federal statute. It was its essence. The House Report announced its conclusion that "it is both appropriate and necessary for Congress to do what it can to defend the institution of traditional heterosexual marriage. . . . H.R. 3396 is appropriately entitled the 'Defense of Marriage Act.' The effort to redefine 'marriage' to extend to homosexual couples is a truly radical proposal that would fundamentally alter the institution of marriage." The House concluded that DOMA expresses "both moral disapproval of homosexuality, and a moral conviction that heterosexuality better comports with traditional (especially Judeo-Christian) morality." The stated purpose of the law was to promote an "interest in protecting the traditional moral teachings reflected in heterosexual-only marriage laws." Were there any doubt of this far-reaching purpose, the title of the Act confirms it: The Defense of Marriage.

The arguments put forward by BLAG are just as candid about the congressional purpose to influence or interfere with state sovereign choices about who may be married. As the title and dynamics of the bill indicate, its purpose is to discourage enactment of state same-sex marriage laws and to restrict the freedom and choice of couples married under those laws if they are enacted. The congressional goal was "to put a thumb on the scales and influence a state's decision as to how to shape its own marriage laws." The Act's demonstrated purpose is to ensure that if any State decides to recognize same-sex marriages, those unions will be treated as second-class marriages for purposes of federal law. This raises a most serious question under the Constitution's Fifth Amendment.

DOMA's operation in practice confirms this purpose. When New York adopted a law to permit same-sex marriage, it sought to eliminate inequality; but DOMA frustrates that objective through a system-wide enactment with no identified connection to any particular area of federal law. DOMA writes inequality into the entire United States Code. The particular case at hand concerns the estate tax, but DOMA is more than a simple determination of what should or should not be allowed as an estate tax refund. Among the over 1,000 statutes and numerous federal regulations that DOMA controls are laws pertaining to Social Security, housing, taxes, criminal sanctions, copyright, and veterans' benefits.

DOMA's principal effect is to identify a subset of state-sanctioned marriages and make them unequal. The principal purpose is to impose inequality, not for other reasons like governmental efficiency. Responsibilities, as well as rights, enhance the dignity and integrity of the person. And DOMA contrives to deprive some couples married under the laws of their State, but not other couples, of both rights and responsibilities. By creating two contradictory marriage regimes within the same State, DOMA forces same-sex couples to live as married for the purpose of state law but unmarried for the purpose of federal law, thus diminishing the stability and predictability of basic personal relations the State has found it proper to acknowledge and protect. By this dynamic DOMA undermines both the public and private significance of state-sanctioned same-sex marriages; for it tells those couples, and all the world, that their otherwise valid marriages are unworthy of federal recognition. This places same-sex couples in an unstable position of being in a second-tier marriage. The differentiation demeans the couple, whose moral and sexual choices the Constitution protects, see *Lawrence*, and whose relationship the State has sought to dignify. And it humiliates tens of thousands of children now being raised by same-sex couples. The law in question makes it even more difficult for the children to understand the integrity and closeness of their own family and its concord with other families in their community and in their daily lives.

Under DOMA, same-sex married couples have their lives burdened, by reason of government decree, in visible and public ways. By its great reach, DOMA touches many aspects of married and family life, from the mundane to the profound. It prevents same-sex married couples from obtaining government healthcare benefits they would otherwise receive. It deprives them of the Bankruptcy Code's special protections for domestic-support obligations. It forces them to follow a complicated procedure to file their state and federal taxes jointly. It prohibits them from being buried together in veterans' cemeteries.

For certain married couples, DOMA's unequal effects are even more serious. The federal penal code makes it a crime to "assaul[t], kidna[p], or murde[r] . . . a member of the immediate family" of "a United States official, a United States judge, [or] a Federal law enforcement officer," with the intent to influence or retaliate against that official. Although a "spouse" qualifies as a member of the officer's "immediate family," DOMA makes this protection inapplicable to same-sex spouses.

DOMA also brings financial harm to children of same-sex couples. It raises the cost of health care for families by taxing health benefits provided by employers to their workers' same-sex spouses. And it denies or reduces benefits allowed to families upon the loss of a spouse and parent, benefits that are an integral part of family security. See Social Security Administration, Social Security Survivors Benefits 5 (2012) (benefits available to a surviving spouse caring for the couple's child).

DOMA divests married same-sex couples of the duties and responsibilities that are an essential part of married life and that they in most cases would be honored to accept were DOMA not in force. For instance, because it is expected that spouses will support each other as they pursue educational opportunities, federal law takes into consideration a spouse's income in calculating a student's federal financial aid eligibility. Same-sex married couples are exempt from this requirement. The same is true with respect to federal ethics rules. Federal executive and agency officials are prohibited from "participat[ing] personally and substantially" in matters as to which they or their spouses have a financial interest. A similar statute prohibits Senators, Senate employees, and their spouses from accepting high-value gifts from certain sources, and another mandates detailed financial disclosures by numerous high-ranking officials and their spouses. Under DOMA, however, these Government-integrity rules do not apply to same-sex spouses.

* * *

The power the Constitution grants it also restrains. And though Congress has great authority to design laws to fit its own conception of sound national policy, it cannot deny the liberty protected by the Due Process Clause of the Fifth Amendment.

What has been explained to this point should more than suffice to establish that the principal purpose and the necessary effect of this law are to demean those persons who are in a lawful same-sex marriage. This requires the Court to hold, as it now does, that DOMA is unconstitutional as a deprivation of the liberty of the person protected by the Fifth Amendment of the Constitution.

The liberty protected by the Fifth Amendment's Due Process Clause contains within it the prohibition against denying to any person the equal protection of the laws. See *Bolling*; *Adarand*. While the Fifth Amendment itself withdraws from Government the power to degrade or demean in the way this law does, the equal protection guarantee of the Fourteenth Amendment makes that Fifth Amendment right all the more specific and all the better understood and preserved.

The class to which DOMA directs its restrictions and restraints are those persons who are joined in same-sex marriages made lawful by the State. DOMA singles out a class of persons deemed by a State entitled to recognition and protection to enhance their own liberty. It imposes a disability on the class by refusing to acknowledge a status the State finds to be dignified and proper. DOMA instructs all federal officials, and indeed all persons with whom same-sex couples interact, including their own children, that their marriage is less worthy than the marriages of others. The federal statute is invalid, for no legitimate purpose overcomes the purpose and effect to disparage and to injure those whom the State, by its marriage laws, sought to protect in personhood and dignity. By seeking to displace this protection and treating those persons as living in marriages less respected than others, the federal statute is in violation of the Fifth Amendment. This opinion and its holding are confined to those lawful marriages.

The judgment of the Court of Appeals for the Second Circuit is affirmed.

It is so ordered.

Chief Justice ROBERTS, dissenting.

I agree with Justice Scalia that this Court lacks jurisdiction to review the decisions of the courts below. On the merits of the constitutional dispute the Court decides to decide, I also agree with Justice Scalia that Congress acted constitutionally in passing the Defense of Marriage Act (DOMA). Interests in uniformity and stability amply justified Congress's decision to retain the definition of marriage that, at that point, had been adopted by every State in our Nation, and every nation in the world.

The majority sees a more sinister motive, pointing out that the Federal Government has generally (though not uniformly) deferred to state definitions of marriage in the past. That is true, of course, but none of those prior state-by-state variations had involved differences over something—as the majority puts it—"thought of by most people as essential to the very definition of [marriage] and to its role and function throughout the history of civilization." That the Federal Government treated this fundamental question differently than it treated variations over consanguinity or minimum age is hardly surprising—and hardly enough to support a conclusion that the "principal purpose," of the 342 Representatives and 85 Senators who voted for it, and the President who signed it, was a bare desire to harm. Nor do the snippets of legislative history and the banal title of the Act to which the majority points suffice to make such a showing. At least without some more convincing evidence that the Act's principal purpose was to codify malice, and that it furthered *no* legitimate government interests, I would not tar the political branches with the brush of bigotry.

But while I disagree with the result to which the majority's analysis leads it in this case, I think it more important to point out that its analysis leads no further. The Court does not have before it, and the logic of its opinion does not decide, the distinct question whether the States, in the exercise of their "historic and essential authority to define the marital relation," may continue to utilize the traditional definition of marriage.

The majority goes out of its way to make this explicit in the penultimate sentence of its opinion. It states that "[t]his opinion and its holding are confined to those lawful marriages,"—referring to same-sex marriages that a State has already recognized as a result of the local "community's considered perspective on the historical roots of the institution of marriage and its evolving understanding of the meaning of equality." Justice Scalia believes this is a "'bald, unreasoned disclaime[r].'" In my view, though, the disclaimer is a logical and necessary consequence of the argument the majority has chosen to adopt. The dominant theme of the majority opinion is that the Federal Government's intrusion into an area "central to state domestic relations law applicable to its residents and citizens" is sufficiently "unusual" to set off alarm bells. I think the majority goes off course, as I have said, but it is undeniable that its judgment is based on federalism.

The majority extensively chronicles DOMA's departure from the normal allocation of responsibility between State and Federal Governments, emphasizing that DOMA "rejects the long-established precept that the incidents, benefits, and obligations of marriage are uniform for all married couples within each State." But there is no such departure when one State adopts or keeps a definition of marriage that differs from that of its neighbor, for it is entirely expected that state definitions would "vary, subject to constitutional guarantees, from one State to the next." Thus, while "[t]he State's power in defining the marital relation is of central relevance" to the majority's decision to strike down DOMA here, that power will come into play on the other side of the board in future cases about the constitutionality of state marriage definitions. So too will the concerns for state diversity and sovereignty that weigh against DOMA's constitutionality in this case.

It is not just this central feature of the majority's analysis that is unique to DOMA, but many considerations on the periphery as well. For example, the majority focuses on the legislative history and title of this particular Act; those statute-specific considerations will, of course, be irrelevant in future cases about different statutes. The majority emphasizes that DOMA was a "systemwide enactment with no identified connection to any particular area of federal law," but a State's definition of marriage "is the foundation of the State's broader authority to regulate the subject of domestic relations with respect to the '[p]rotection of offspring, property interests, and the enforcement of marital responsibilities.' " And the federal decision undermined (in the majority's view) the "dignity [already] conferred by the States in the exercise of their sovereign power," whereas a State's decision whether to expand the definition of marriage from its traditional contours involves no similar concern.

We may in the future have to resolve challenges to state marriage definitions affecting same-sex couples. That issue, however, is not before us in this case. . . . I write only to highlight the limits of the majority's holding and reasoning today, lest its opinion be taken to resolve not only a question that I believe is not properly before us—DOMA's constitutionality—but also a question that all agree, and the Court explicitly acknowledges, is not at issue.

Justice SCALIA, with whom Justice THOMAS joins, and with whom THE CHIEF JUSTICE joins as to Part I, dissenting.

I

This case is about power in several respects. It is about the power of our people to govern themselves, and the power of this Court to pronounce the law. Today's opinion aggrandizes the latter, with the predictable consequence of diminishing the former. We have no power to decide this case. And even if we did, we have no power under the Constitution to invalidate this democratically adopted legislation. The Court's errors on both points spring forth from the same diseased root: an exalted conception of the role of this institution in America. . . .

It may be argued that if what we say is true some Presidential determinations that statutes are unconstitutional will not be subject to our review. That is as it should be, when both the President and the plaintiff agree that the statute is unconstitutional. Where the Executive is enforcing an unconstitutional law, suit will of course lie; but if, in that suit, the Executive admits the unconstitutionality of the law, the litigation should end in an order or a consent decree enjoining enforcement. This suit saw the light of day only because the President enforced the Act (and thus gave Windsor standing to sue) even though he believed it unconstitutional. He could have equally chosen (more appropriately, some would say) neither to enforce nor to defend the statute he believed to be unconstitutional, see Presidential Authority to Decline to Execute Unconstitutional Statutes, 18 Op. Off. Legal Counsel 199 (Nov. 2, 1994) — in which event Windsor would not have been injured, the District Court could not have refereed this friendly scrimmage, and the Executive's determination of unconstitutionality would have escaped this Court's desire to blurt out its view of the law. The matter would have been left, as so many matters ought to be left, to a tug of war between the President and the Congress, which has innumerable means (up to and including impeachment) of compelling the President to enforce the laws it has written. Or the President could have evaded presentation of the constitutional issue to this Court simply by declining to appeal the District Court and Court of Appeals dispositions he agreed with. Be sure of this much: If a President wants to insulate his judgment of unconstitutionality from our review, he can. What the views urged in this dissent produce is not insulation from judicial review but insulation from Executive contrivance.

. . .

II

[G]iven that the majority has volunteered its view of the merits, however, I proceed to discuss that as well.

A

There are many remarkable things about the majority's merits holding. The first is how rootless and shifting its justifications are. For example, the opinion starts with seven full pages about the traditional power of States to define domestic relations — initially fooling many readers, I am sure, into thinking that this is a federalism opinion. But we are eventually told that "it is unnecessary to decide whether this federal intrusion on state power is a violation of the Constitution," and that "[t]he State's power in defining the marital relation is of central relevance in this case quite apart from principles of federalism" because "the State's decision to give this class of persons the right to marry conferred upon them a dignity and status of immense import." But no one questions the power of the States to define marriage (with the concomitant conferral of dignity and status), so what is the point of devoting seven pages to describing how long and well established that power is? . . .

Equally perplexing are the opinion's references to "the Constitution's guarantee of equality." Near the end of the opinion, we are told that although the "equal protection guarantee of the Fourteenth Amendment makes [the] Fifth Amendment [due process] right all the more specific and all the better understood and preserved"—what can *that* mean?—"the Fifth Amendment itself withdraws from Government the power to degrade or demean in the way this law does." The only possible interpretation of this statement is that the Equal Protection Clause, even the Equal Protection Clause as incorporated in the Due Process Clause, is not the basis for today's holding. But the portion of the majority opinion that explains why DOMA is unconstitutional (Part IV) begins by citing *Bolling v. Sharpe, Department of Agriculture v. Moreno,* and *Romer v. Evans*—all of which are equal-protection cases. And those three cases are the *only* authorities that the Court cites in Part IV about the Constitution's meaning, except for its citation of *Lawrence v. Texas* (not an equal-protection case) to support its passing assertion that the Constitution protects the "moral and sexual choices" of same-sex couples.

Moreover, if this is meant to be an equal-protection opinion, it is a confusing one. The opinion does not resolve and indeed does not even mention what had been the central question in this litigation: whether, under the Equal Protection Clause, laws restricting marriage to a man and a woman are reviewed for more than mere rationality. That is the issue that divided the parties and the court below. In accord with my previously expressed skepticism about the Court's "tiers of scrutiny" approach, I would review this classification only for its rationality. As nearly as I can tell, the Court agrees with that; its opinion does not apply strict scrutiny, and its central propositions are taken from rational-basis cases like *Moreno*. But the Court certainly does not *apply* anything that resembles that deferential framework. See *Heller v. Doe* (a classification " 'must be upheld . . . if there is any reasonably conceivable state of facts' " that could justify it).

The majority opinion need not get into the strict-vs.-rational-basis scrutiny question, and need not justify its holding under either, because it says that DOMA is unconstitutional as "a deprivation of the liberty of the person protected by the Fifth Amendment of the Constitution," that it violates "basic due process" principles, and that it inflicts an "injury and indignity" of a kind that denies "an essential part of the liberty protected by the Fifth Amendment." The majority never utters the dread words "substantive due process," perhaps sensing the disrepute into which that doctrine has fallen, but that is what those statements mean. Yet the opinion does not argue that same-sex marriage is "deeply rooted in this Nation's history and tradition," *Washington v. Glucksberg*, a claim that would of course be quite absurd. So would the further suggestion (also necessary, under our substantive-due-process precedents) that a world in which DOMA exists is one bereft of "ordered liberty." *Palko v. Connecticut*.

Some might conclude that this loaf could have used a while longer in the oven. But that would be wrong; it is already overcooked. The most expert care in preparation cannot redeem a bad recipe. The sum of all the Court's nonspecific hand-waving is that this law is invalid (maybe on equal-protection grounds, maybe on substantive-due-process grounds, and perhaps with some amorphous federalism component playing a role) because it is motivated by a "bare . . . desire to harm" couples in same-sex marriages. It is this proposition with which I will therefore engage.

B

As I have observed before, the Constitution does not forbid the government to enforce traditional moral and sexual norms. See *Lawrence v. Texas* (Scalia, J., dissenting). I will not swell the U.S. Reports with restatements of that point. It is enough to say that the Constitution neither requires nor forbids our society to approve of same-sex marriage, much as it neither requires nor forbids us to approve of no-fault divorce, polygamy, or the consumption of alcohol.

However, even setting aside traditional moral disapproval of same-sex marriage (or indeed same-sex sex), there are many perfectly valid—indeed, downright boring—justifying rationales for this legislation. Their existence ought to be the end of this case. For they give the lie to the Court's conclusion that only those with hateful hearts could have voted "aye" on this Act. And more importantly, they serve to make the contents of the legislators' hearts quite irrelevant: "It is a familiar principle of constitutional law that this Court will not strike down an otherwise constitutional statute on the basis of an alleged illicit legislative motive." *United States v. O'Brien,* 391 U.S. 367 (1968). Or at least it *was* a familiar principle. By holding to the contrary, the majority has declared open season on any law that (in the opinion of the law's opponents and any panel of like-minded federal judges) can be characterized as mean-spirited.

The majority concludes that the only motive for this Act was the "bare . . . desire to harm a politically unpopular group." Bear in mind that the object of this condemnation is not the legislature of some once-Confederate Southern state (familiar objects of the Court's scorn), but our respected coordinate branches, the Congress and Presidency of the United States. Laying such a charge against them should require the most extraordinary evidence, and I would have thought that every attempt would be made to indulge a more anodyne explanation for the statute. The majority does the opposite—affirmatively concealing from the reader the arguments that exist in justification. It makes only a passing mention of the "arguments put forward" by the Act's defenders, and does not even trouble to paraphrase or describe them. I imagine that this is because it is harder to maintain the illusion of the Act's supporters as unhinged members of a wild-eyed lynch mob when one first describes their views as *they* see them.

To choose just one of these defenders' arguments, DOMA avoids difficult choice-of-law issues that will now arise absent a uniform federal definition of marriage. Imagine a pair of women who marry in Albany and then move to Alabama, which does not "recognize as valid any marriage of parties of the same sex." When the couple files their next federal tax return, may it be a joint one? Which State's law controls, for federal-law purposes: their State of celebration (which recognizes the marriage) or their State of domicile (which does not)? (Does the answer depend on whether they were just visiting in Albany?) Are these questions to be answered as a matter of federal common law, or perhaps by borrowing a State's choice-of-law rules? If so, *which* State's? And what about States where the status of an out-of-state same-sex marriage is an unsettled question under local law? DOMA avoided all of this uncertainty by specifying which marriages would be recognized for federal purposes. That is a classic purpose for a definitional provision.

Further, DOMA preserves the intended effects of prior legislation against then-unforeseen changes in circumstance. When Congress provided (for example) that a special estate-tax exemption would exist for spouses, this exemption reached only *opposite-sex* spouses—those being the only sort that were recognized in *any* State at the time of DOMA's passage. When it became clear that changes in state law might one day alter that balance, DOMA's definitional section was enacted to ensure that state-level experimentation did not automatically alter the basic operation of federal law, unless and until Congress made the further judgment to do so on its own. That is not animus—just stabilizing prudence. Congress has hardly demonstrated itself unwilling to make such further, revising judgments upon due deliberation. See, *e.g.,* Don't Ask, Don't Tell Repeal Act of 2010, 124 Stat. 3515.

The Court mentions none of this. Instead, it accuses the Congress that enacted this law and the President who signed it of something much worse than, for example, having acted in excess of enumerated federal powers—or even having drawn distinctions that prove to be irrational. Those legal errors may be made in good faith, errors though they are. But the majority says that the supporters of this Act acted with *malice*—with *the "purpose"* "to disparage and to injure" same-sex couples. It says that the motivation for DOMA was to "demean," to "impose inequality," to "impose . . . a stigma," to deny people "equal dignity," to brand gay people as "unworthy," and to "*humiliat[e]*" their children (emphasis added).

I am sure these accusations are quite untrue. To be sure (as the majority points out), the legislation is called the Defense of Marriage Act. But to defend traditional marriage is not to condemn, demean, or humiliate those who would prefer other arrangements, any more than to defend the Constitution of the United States is to condemn, demean, or humiliate other constitutions. To hurl such accusations so casually demeans *this institution.* In the majority's judgment, any resistance to its holding is beyond the pale of reasoned disagreement. To question its high-handed invalidation of a presumptively valid statute is to act (the majority is sure) with *the purpose* to "disparage," "injure," "degrade," "demean," and "humiliate" our fellow human beings, our fellow citizens, who are homosexual. All that, simply for supporting an Act that did no more than codify an aspect of marriage that had been unquestioned in our society for most of its existence—indeed, had been unquestioned in virtually all societies for virtually all of human history. It is one thing for a society to elect change; it is another for a court of law to impose change by adjudging those who oppose it *hostes humani generis,* enemies of the human race.

* * *

The penultimate sentence of the majority's opinion is a naked declaration that "[t]his opinion and its holding are confined" to those couples "joined in same-sex marriages made lawful by the State." I have heard such "bald, unreasoned disclaimer[s]" before [in] *Lawrence*. When the Court declared a constitutional right to homosexual sodomy, we were assured that the case had nothing, nothing at all to do with "whether the government must give formal recognition to any relationship that homosexual persons seek to enter." Now we are told that DOMA is invalid because it "demeans the couple, whose moral and sexual choices the Constitution protects,"—with an accompanying citation of *Lawrence*. It takes real cheek for today's majority to assure us, as it is going out the door, that a constitutional requirement to give formal recognition to same-sex marriage is not at issue here—when what has preceded that assurance is a lecture on how superior the majority's moral judgment in favor of same-sex marriage is to the Congress's hateful moral judgment against it. I promise you this: The only thing that will "confine" the Court's holding is its sense of what it can get away with.

I do not mean to suggest disagreement with The Chief Justice's view . . . that lower federal courts and state courts can distinguish today's case when the issue before them is state denial of marital status to same-sex couples—or even that this Court could *theoretically* do so. Lord, an opinion with such scatter-shot rationales as this one (federalism noises among them) can be distinguished in many ways. And deserves to be. State and lower federal courts should take the Court at its word and distinguish away.

In my opinion, however, the view that *this* Court will take of state prohibition of same-sex marriage is indicated beyond mistaking by today's opinion. As I have said, the real rationale of today's opinion, whatever disappearing trail of its legalistic argle-bargle one chooses to follow, is that DOMA is motivated by " 'bare . . . desire to harm' " couples in same-sex marriages. How easy it is, indeed how inevitable, to reach the same conclusion with regard to state laws denying same-sex couples marital status. . . .

[T]hat Court which finds it so horrific that Congress irrationally and hatefully robbed same-sex couples of the "personhood and dignity" which state legislatures conferred upon them, will of a certitude be similarly appalled by state legislatures' irrational and hateful failure to acknowledge that "personhood and dignity" in the first place. As far as this Court is concerned, no one should be fooled; it is just a matter of listening and waiting for the other shoe.

By formally declaring anyone opposed to same-sex marriage an enemy of human decency, the majority arms well every challenger to a state law restricting marriage to its traditional definition. Henceforth those challengers will lead with this Court's declaration that there is "no legitimate purpose" served by such a law, and will claim that the traditional definition has "the purpose and effect to disparage and to injure" the "personhood and dignity" of same-sex couples. The majority's limiting assurance will be meaningless in the face of language like that, as the majority well knows. That is why the language is there. The result will be a judicial distortion of our society's debate over marriage—a debate that can seem in need of our clumsy "help" only to a member of this institution.

As to that debate: Few public controversies touch an institution so central to the lives of so many, and few inspire such attendant passion by good people on all sides. Few public controversies will ever demonstrate so vividly the beauty of what our Framers gave us, a gift the Court pawns today to buy its stolen moment in the spotlight: a system of government that permits us to rule *ourselves*. Since DOMA's passage, citizens on all sides of the question have seen victories and they have seen defeats. There have been plebiscites, legislation, persuasion, and loud voices — in other words, democracy. Victories in one place for some are offset by victories in other places for others. . . .

In the majority's telling, this story is black-and-white: Hate your neighbor or come along with us. The truth is more complicated. It is hard to admit that one's political opponents are not monsters, especially in a struggle like this one, and the challenge in the end proves more than today's Court can handle. Too bad. A reminder that disagreement over something so fundamental as marriage can still be politically legitimate would have been a fit task for what in earlier times was called the judicial temperament. We might have covered ourselves with honor today, by promising all sides of this debate that it was theirs to settle and that we would respect their resolution. We might have let the People decide.

But that the majority will not do. Some will rejoice in today's decision, and some will despair at it; that is the nature of a controversy that matters so much to so many. But the Court has cheated both sides, robbing the winners of an honest victory, and the losers of the peace that comes from a fair defeat. We owed both of them better. I dissent.

Justice ALITO, with whom Justice THOMAS joins as to Parts II and III, dissenting.

Our Nation is engaged in a heated debate about same-sex marriage. That debate is, at bottom, about the nature of the institution of marriage. Respondent Edith Windsor, supported by the United States, asks this Court to intervene in that debate, and although she couches her argument in different terms, what she seeks is a holding that enshrines in the Constitution a particular understanding of marriage under which the sex of the partners makes no difference. The Constitution, however, does not dictate that choice. It leaves the choice to the people, acting through their elected representatives at both the federal and state levels. I would therefore hold that Congress did not violate Windsor's constitutional rights by enacting §3 of the Defense of Marriage Act (DOMA), which defines the meaning of marriage under federal statutes that either confer upon married persons certain federal benefits or impose upon them certain federal obligations.

[Justice Alito argued that the case was justiciable. Although "the United States clearly is not a proper petitioner in this case," BLAG has standing.]

II

[S]ame-sex marriage presents a highly emotional and important question of public policy — but not a difficult question of constitutional law. The Constitution does not guarantee the right to enter into a same-sex marriage. Indeed, no provision of the Constitution speaks to the issue.

The Court has sometimes found the Due Process Clauses to have a substantive component that guarantees liberties beyond the absence of physical restraint. And the Court's holding that "DOMA is unconstitutional as a deprivation of the liberty of the person protected by the Fifth Amendment of the Constitution," suggests that substantive due process may partially underlie the Court's decision today. But it is well established that any "substantive" component to the Due Process Clause protects only "those fundamental rights and liberties which are, objectively, 'deeply rooted in this Nation's history and tradition,'" *Washington v. Glucksberg*; *Snyder v. Massachusetts,* 291 U.S. 97 (1934) (referring to fundamental rights as those that are so "rooted in the traditions and conscience of our people as to be ranked as fundamental"), as well as "'implicit in the concept of ordered liberty,' such that 'neither liberty nor justice would exist if they were sacrificed.'" *Glucksberg* (quoting *Palko v. Connecticut*).

It is beyond dispute that the right to same-sex marriage is not deeply rooted in this Nation's history and tradition. In this country, no State permitted same-sex marriage until the Massachusetts Supreme Judicial Court held in 2003 that limiting marriage to opposite-sex couples violated the State Constitution. Nor is the right to same-sex marriage deeply rooted in the traditions of other nations. No country allowed same-sex couples to marry until the Netherlands did so in 2000.

What Windsor and the United States seek, therefore, is not the protection of a deeply rooted right but the recognition of a very new right, and they seek this innovation not from a legislative body elected by the people, but from unelected judges. Faced with such a request, judges have cause for both caution and humility.

The family is an ancient and universal human institution. Family structure reflects the characteristics of a civilization, and changes in family structure and in the popular understanding of marriage and the family can have profound effects. Past changes in the understanding of marriage—for example, the gradual ascendance of the idea that romantic love is a prerequisite to marriage—have had far-reaching consequences. But the process by which such consequences come about is complex, involving the interaction of numerous factors, and tends to occur over an extended period of time.

We can expect something similar to take place if same-sex marriage becomes widely accepted. The long-term consequences of this change are not now known and are unlikely to be ascertainable for some time to come.[a] There are those who think that allowing same-sex marriage will seriously undermine the institution of marriage. Others think that recognition of same-sex marriage will fortify a now-shaky institution.

---

a. As sociologists have documented, it sometimes takes decades to document the effects of social changes—like the sharp rise in divorce rates following the advent of no-fault divorce—on children and society.

At present, no one — including social scientists, philosophers, and historians — can predict with any certainty what the long-term ramifications of widespread acceptance of same-sex marriage will be. And judges are certainly not equipped to make such an assessment. The Members of this Court have the authority and the responsibility to interpret and apply the Constitution. Thus, if the Constitution contained a provision guaranteeing the right to marry a person of the same sex, it would be our duty to enforce that right. But the Constitution simply does not speak to the issue of same-sex marriage. In our system of government, ultimate sovereignty rests with the people, and the people have the right to control their own destiny. Any change on a question so fundamental should be made by the people through their elected officials.

III

Perhaps because they cannot show that same-sex marriage is a fundamental right under our Constitution, Windsor and the United States couch their arguments in equal protection terms. They argue that §3 of DOMA discriminates on the basis of sexual orientation, that classifications based on sexual orientation should trigger a form of "heightened" scrutiny, and that §3 cannot survive such scrutiny. They further maintain that the governmental interests that §3 purports to serve are not sufficiently important and that it has not been adequately shown that §3 serves those interests very well. The Court's holding, too, seems to rest on "the equal protection guarantee of the Fourteenth Amendment," — although the Court is careful not to adopt most of Windsor's and the United States' argument.

In my view, the approach that Windsor and the United States advocate is misguided. Our equal protection framework, upon which Windsor and the United States rely, is a judicial construct that provides a useful mechanism for analyzing a certain universe of equal protection cases. But that framework is ill suited for use in evaluating the constitutionality of laws based on the traditional understanding of marriage, which fundamentally turn on what marriage is.

Underlying our equal protection jurisprudence is the central notion that "[a] classification 'must be reasonable, not arbitrary, and must rest upon some ground of difference having a fair and substantial relation to the object of the legislation, so that all persons similarly circumstanced shall be treated alike.'" *Reed v. Reed* (quoting *F.S. Royter Guano Co. v. Virginia,* 253 U.S. 412 (1920)). The modern tiers of scrutiny — on which Windsor and the United States rely so heavily — are a heuristic to help judges determine when classifications have that "fair and substantial relation to the object of the legislation."

So, for example, those classifications subject to strict scrutiny — *i.e.,* classifications that must be "narrowly tailored" to achieve a "compelling" government interest — are those that are "so seldom relevant to the achievement of any legitimate state interest that laws grounded in such considerations are deemed to reflect prejudice and antipathy." *Cleburne*; cf. *id.,* at 452-453 (Stevens, J., concurring) ("It would be utterly irrational to limit the franchise on the basis of height or weight; it is equally invalid to limit it on the basis of skin color. None of these attributes has any bearing at all on the citizen's willingness or ability to exercise that civil right").

In contrast, those characteristics subject to so-called intermediate scrutiny — *i.e.,* those classifications that must be "'substantially related'" to the achievement of "important governmental objective[s]," *United States v. Virginia* — are those that are *sometimes* relevant considerations to be taken into account by legislators, but "generally provid[e] no sensible ground for different treatment," *Cleburne.* For example, the Court has held that statutory rape laws that criminalize sexual intercourse with a woman under the age of 18 years, but place no similar liability on partners of underage men, are grounded in the very real distinction that "young men and young women are not similarly situated with respect to the problems and the risks of sexual intercourse." *Michael M. v. Superior Court, Sonoma Cty.* (plurality opinion). The plurality reasoned that "[o]nly women may become pregnant, and they suffer disproportionately the profound physical, emotional, and psychological consequences of sexual activity." In other contexts, however, the Court has found that classifications based on gender are "arbitrary," *Reed,* and based on "outmoded notions of the relative capabilities of men and women," *Cleburne,* as when a State provides that a man must always be preferred to an equally qualified woman when both seek to administer the estate of a deceased party, see *Reed.*

Finally, so-called rational-basis review applies to classifications based on "distinguishing characteristics relevant to interests the State has the authority to implement." We have long recognized that "the equal protection of the laws must coexist with the practical necessity that most legislation classifies for one purpose or another, with resulting disadvantages to various groups or persons." *Romer v. Evans.* As a result, in rational-basis cases, where the court does not view the classification at issue as "inherently suspect," "the courts have been very reluctant, as they should be in our federal system and with our respect for the separation of powers, to closely scrutinize legislative choices as to whether, how, and to what extent those interests should be pursued." *Cleburne.*

In asking the Court to determine that §3 of DOMA is subject to and violates heightened scrutiny, Windsor and the United States thus ask us to rule that the presence of two members of the opposite sex is as rationally related to marriage as white skin is to voting or a Y-chromosome is to the ability to administer an estate. That is a striking request and one that unelected judges should pause before granting. Acceptance of the argument would cast all those who cling to traditional beliefs about the nature of marriage in the role of bigots or superstitious fools.

By asking the Court to strike down DOMA as not satisfying some form of heightened scrutiny, Windsor and the United States are really seeking to have the Court resolve a debate between two competing views of marriage.

The first and older view, which I will call the "traditional" or "conjugal" view, sees marriage as an intrinsically opposite-sex institution. BLAG notes that virtually every culture, including many not influenced by the Abrahamic religions, has limited marriage to people of the opposite sex. And BLAG attempts to explain this phenomenon by arguing that the institution of marriage was created for the purpose of channeling heterosexual intercourse into a structure that supports child rearing. Others explain the basis for the institution in more philosophical terms. They argue that marriage is essentially the solemnizing of a comprehensive, exclusive, permanent union that is intrinsically ordered to producing new life, even if it does not always do so. While modern cultural changes have weakened the link between marriage and procreation in the popular mind, there is no doubt that, throughout human history and across many cultures, marriage has been viewed as an exclusively opposite-sex institution and as one inextricably linked to procreation and biological kinship.

The other, newer view is what I will call the "consent-based" vision of marriage, a vision that primarily defines marriage as the solemnization of mutual commitment — marked by strong emotional attachment and sexual attraction — between two persons. At least as it applies to heterosexual couples, this view of marriage now plays a very prominent role in the popular understanding of the institution. Indeed, our popular culture is infused with this understanding of marriage. Proponents of same-sex marriage argue that because gender differentiation is not relevant to this vision, the exclusion of same-sex couples from the institution of marriage is rank discrimination.

The Constitution does not codify either of these views of marriage (although I suspect it would have been hard at the time of the adoption of the Constitution or the Fifth Amendment to find Americans who did not take the traditional view for granted). The silence of the Constitution on this question should be enough to end the matter as far as the judiciary is concerned. Yet, Windsor and the United States implicitly ask us to endorse the consent-based view of marriage and to reject the traditional view, thereby arrogating to ourselves the power to decide a question that philosophers, historians, social scientists, and theologians are better qualified to explore. Because our constitutional order assigns the resolution of questions of this nature to the people, I would not presume to enshrine either vision of marriage in our constitutional jurisprudence.

Legislatures, however, have little choice but to decide between the two views. We have long made clear that neither the political branches of the Federal Government nor state governments are required to be neutral between competing visions of the good, provided that the vision of the good that they adopt is not countermanded by the Constitution. Accordingly, both Congress and the States are entitled to enact laws recognizing either of the two understandings of marriage. And given the size of government and the degree to which it now regulates daily life, it seems unlikely that either Congress or the States could maintain complete neutrality even if they tried assiduously to do so.

Rather than fully embracing the arguments made by Windsor and the United States, the Court strikes down §3 of DOMA as a classification not properly supported by its objectives. The Court reaches this conclusion in part because it believes that §3 encroaches upon the States' sovereign prerogative to define marriage. Indeed, the Court's ultimate conclusion is that DOMA falls afoul of the Fifth Amendment because it "singles out a class of persons deemed *by a State* entitled to recognition and protection to enhance their own liberty" and "imposes a disability on the class by refusing to acknowledge a status *the State finds* to be dignified and proper."

To the extent that the Court takes the position that the question of same-sex marriage should be resolved primarily at the state level, I wholeheartedly agree. I hope that the Court will ultimately permit the people of each State to decide this question for themselves. Unless the Court is willing to allow this to occur, the whiffs of federalism in the today's opinion of the Court will soon be scattered to the wind.

In any event, §3 of DOMA, in my view, does not encroach on the prerogatives of the States, assuming of course that the many federal statutes affected by DOMA have not already done so. Section 3 does not prevent any State from recognizing same-sex marriage or from extending to same-sex couples any right, privilege, benefit, or obligation stemming from state law. All that §3 does is to define a class of persons to whom federal law extends certain special benefits and upon whom federal law imposes certain special burdens. In these provisions, Congress used marital status as a way of defining this class—in part, I assume, because it viewed marriage as a valuable institution to be fostered and in part because it viewed married couples as comprising a unique type of economic unit that merits special regulatory treatment. Assuming that Congress has the power under the Constitution to enact the laws affected by §3, Congress has the power to define the category of persons to whom those laws apply.

* * *

For these reasons, I would hold that §3 of DOMA does not violate the Fifth Amendment. I respectfully dissent.

Discussion

1. *Faux federalism?* Justice Kennedy's opinion begins by invoking federalism principles but then veers off and notes that "[t]he State's power in defining the marital relation is of central relevance in this case quite apart from principles of federalism." What role does the state—and the balance between the states and the federal government—play in the majority opinion? Kennedy suggests that "the State's decision to give this class of persons the right to marry conferred upon them a dignity and status of immense import . . . [and] enhanced the recognition, dignity, and protection of the class in their own community." The federal government then demeaned (or sought to harm) that relationship by refusing to recognize it when the state does. Does this mean that same-sex relationships would lack either sufficient dignity or sufficient constitutional protection if states had not recognized them?

2. *Waiting for the other shoe to drop.* Justice Scalia mocks Justice Kennedy's federalism discussion, arguing that there is plenty of language in *Windsor* that a

future Court could use to require a state to recognize same-sex marriage. (In his dissent in *Lawrence v. Texas* in 2003, Scalia made a similar claim that the majority's reasoning would inevitably lead to constitutional recognition of same-sex marriage.) Chief Justice Roberts, by contrast, emphasizes the limited nature of the Court's holding, and argues that *Windsor* can easily be distinguished from a constitutional attack on state laws denying same-sex couples the right to marry. Roberts also argues that "it is undeniable that [the Court's] judgment is based on federalism." Is this clear? Is it possible that we will only know what *Windsor* means years later, and as a result of new Supreme Court appointments?

Why might Justice Kennedy have deliberately written a decision that is ambiguous on these questions? See Neil Siegel, Federalism as a Way Station: *Windsor* as Exemplar of Doctrine in Motion, __ J. Legal Analysis __ (forthcoming 2014).

3. *Mind reading.* Kennedy treats the case as falling within the rule that "'a bare congressional desire to harm a politically unpopular group cannot' justify disparate treatment of that group." How does Kennedy know that DOMA was based on a bare desire to harm a politically unpopular group? Is moral disapproval of homosexuality the same thing as a bare desire to harm homosexuals? Could somebody vote for DOMA in 1996 without animus against homosexuals?

Is Kennedy's argument a claim about the actual psychology of members of Congress, as well as President Clinton, who signed the bill? Or is it a judgment about the social meaning of DOMA? (Compare the previous discussion of *Plessy v. Ferguson* and *Brown v. Board of Education.*) Note that some liberal Democrats in Congress, and probably President Clinton himself, may have voted for the bill not because they had any animus against homosexuals, but because they feared that if they opposed DOMA, they would create an excellent wedge issue for Republicans in the 1996 election. How, if at all, should this affect Kennedy's analysis?

4. *Playing it safe.* Couldn't one argue, akin to Justice Alito, that Congress might simply have sought to protect an existing institution from an innovation that, in 1996, seemed particularly radical and dangerous and might have uncertain consequences? Is Kennedy's argument that the meaning of DOMA was demeaning in 1996 or that it is demeaning today? What if the social meaning changes yet again? What if there is no consensus in different parts of the country about the social meaning of opposition to same-sex marriage? Why doesn't Alito's argument that Congress wants to wait and see what develops provide an adequate rational basis for DOMA? Is it because the majority does not believe that this is the real basis for DOMA? If so, that would suggest that, whatever the opinion says, the Court is applying some form of heightened scrutiny.

5. *Standard of review?* The Court seems to base its decision on the rational basis test — supplemented by *Moreno* and *Romer v. Evans* — and does not take up the question whether classifications based on sexual orientation are subject to heightened scrutiny. Should it have? Heightened scrutiny for such classifications is now the official position of the Obama Justice Department. Is *Windsor* simply

an extension of the principle of *Romer v. Evans*? Or is it better understood as a deferral of the question, like *Reed v. Reed* in the area of gender discrimination? Note, however, that within five years of *Reed*, the Court had settled on intermediate scrutiny for sex classifications. It has now been 18 years since the Court broached the issue of sexual orientation and equal protection in *Romer*.

6. *Class legislation. Windsor* does not fit well into existing doctrinal categories. However, it does make sense as exemplifying the principles against class and caste legislation. These were among the original purposes of the Fourteenth Amendment's Due Process and Equal Protection Clauses, and the Reconstruction Framers assumed these principles also applied to the Due Process Clause of the Fifth Amendment.

7. *Dignity.* Kennedy's opinion repeatedly speaks of liberty. Sometimes he seems to mean that a guarantee of equal protection is contained within the Fifth Amendment's guarantee of liberty with due process. At other times he seems to speak of the liberty protected by the Fifth Amendment as more than simply a guarantee of equal protection. Thus, another possibility is that the Court has abandoned the tiered standards of review—as evidenced by *Casey*, *Romer*, and *Lawrence*—and will simply proceed on a case-by-case basis, relying on the unifying concept of dignity, which straddles liberty and equality concerns.

One reason for this development is that Justice Kennedy, the swing vote in all of these cases, prefers talking in these terms. If Kennedy is no longer the swing vote because of new appointments, however, the doctrine might evolve accordingly. How would you articulate the constitutional doctrine of dignity in *Casey*, *Romer*, *Lawrence*, and *Windsor*? Do these cases produce an easy to understand test of when dignity has been violated or undermined?

8. *We're not bigots.* Justices Scalia and Alito emphasize that it is perfectly reasonable to oppose same-sex marriage without being mean-spirited or bigoted, or without seeking to harm or humiliate homosexuals and their children. Why do you think they feel it necessary to make this point? Justice Scalia argues that the effect of the majority opinion in *Windsor* is to "adjudg[e] those who oppose [same-sex marriage as] *hostes humani generis,* enemies of the human race." Do you agree? Did *Romer* effectively adjudge the voters of the state of Colorado as bigoted?

Compare the current state of the constitutional debate over gay rights and same-sex marriage with the constitutional debate over racial equality and gender equality. What do you think of people who defended Jim Crow and "separate but equal" before *Brown* and the civil rights revolution; or people who believed, before the 1970s, that the Constitution does not guarantee women equality? Is it fair to view opponents of gay rights in the same way? Is the situation different? Or is this a judgment that can only be made in retrospect?

9. *Litigation in the states after* Windsor. When *Windsor* was decided, approximately 20 states had "super-DOMA" laws—either statutes or constitutional amendments. These not only prohibit same-sex marriage, but also civil unions, domestic partnerships, reciprocal benefits provisions, and other laws that might

give same-sex couples some of the traditional benefits of marriage. Under super-DOMA laws (which vary by jurisdiction), same-sex couples are generally in the same position as ordinary strangers who, of course, may make contracts with each other, but who may not take advantage of any of the incidents of marriage. Approximately ten other states had "mini-DOMA" laws, which, in general, simply prevent recognition of same-sex marriage but may allow the state to recognize other forms of partnership or reciprocal benefits that married couples enjoy.

Many challenges to state same-sex marriage bans or to lack of interstate recognition of same-sex marriages were filed in federal and state courts in the wake of *Windsor*. In this litigation, advocates of same-sex marriage have won repeated victories.[1] The rationales have been varied, involving liberty and equality justifications, and the application of both rational basis and heightened scrutiny. In general, post-*Windsor* decisions supporting same-sex marriage have not treated *Windsor* as merely a federalism case.

10. *Gay rights and racial justice*. *Windsor* is one of the "most striking statements of equality law the Court has handed down in decades."[2] It stands out in marked contrast to the Court's race cases of the last decades in "its determination to redress the dignitary and material injuries law inflicts on a minority group."[3] These cases are distinct not only in only outcome—minority claimants win when they are gay, racial minorities usually lose—but also in reasoning. For instance, in the race cases, the Court focuses on the presence or absence of classification, but in *Windsor* this language of classification—either based sexual orientation or sex—is missing.

While the Court does employ a standard akin to animus in its discriminatory purpose doctrine in race cases (see *Davis* and *Feeney*), racial minorities have consistently failed to demonstrate animus to courts' satisfaction. Indeed, as *Feeney* itself demonstrates, the Court's focus on whether a state pursues facially neutral action "because of," not merely "in spite of," its adverse effects upon an identifiable group is designed to limit the reach of the Equal Protection Clause. By contrast, the focus on animus in gay rights cases broadens the reach of equal protection. Compare the Court's skepticism about animus in the race cases with its treatment of animus in cases like *Romer* and *Windsor*. Do you think the Court

---

1. See, e.g., Love v. Beshear, 2014 WL 2957671 (W.D. Ky. July 1, 2014); Baskin v. Bogan, 2014 WL 2884868 (S.D. Ind. June 25, 2014); Wolf v. Walker, 2014 WL 2558444 (W.D. Wis. June 6, 2014); Whitewood v. Wolf, 2014 WL 2058105 (M.D. Pa. May 20, 2014); Geiger v. Kitzhaber, 13-1834, 2014 U.S. Dist. LEXIS 68171 (D. Or. May 19, 2014); Latta v. Otter, No. 13-482, 2014 WL 1909999 (D. Idaho May 13, 2014); DeBoer v. Snyder, No. 12-10285, 2014 WL 1100794 (E.D. Mich. Mar. 21, 2014); De Leon v. Perry, No. 13-982, 2014 WL 715741 (W.D. Tex. Feb. 26, 2014); Bostic v. Rainey, 970 F. Supp. 2d 456 (E.D. Va. 2014); McGee v. Cole, No. 13-24068, 2014 WL 321122 (S.D. W. Va. Jan. 29, 2014); Bishop v. U.S. ex rel. Holder, 962 F. Supp. 2d 1252 (N.D. Okla. 2014); Kitchen v. Herbert, 961 F. Supp. 2d 1181 (D. Utah 2013), aff'd, 2014 WL 2868044 (10th Cir. 2014). Many of these cases, however, are under appeal as this Supplement went to press.

2. Reva B. Siegel, Foreword: Equality Divided, 127 Harv. L. Rev. 1, 77 (2013).

3. *Id.*

would accept the same evidence of animus—for example, relying on the structure of the law, the impact on the victims, or the social meaning of the measure—in a case about racially discriminatory purpose?

Finally, in the race and sexual orientation cases, the Court is differently attentive to the way that members of burdened minority groups experience the law. In the race cases, empathy is typically extended to *majority* claimants (i.e., whites), and not to minority claimants. In contrast, the Court in *Windsor*, *Lawrence*, and *Romer* takes seriously the way that gay people experience law and its dignitary and material burdens. What do you think explains this divergence? For more on the difference between the Court's treatment of claims brought by gay people and by racial minorities, see Russell K. Robinson, Unequal Protection, 67 Stan. L. Rev. ___ (forthcoming 2015).

HOLLINGSWORTH v. PERRY, 133 S. Ct. 2652 (2013): After the California Supreme Court held that limiting marriage to opposite-sex couples violated the California Constitution, state voters passed a ballot initiative, Proposition 8, amending the State Constitution to define marriage as a union between a man and a woman. Respondents, a group of same-sex couples who sought to marry in California, challenged Proposition 8 in federal court, arguing that it violated the Due Process and Equal Protection Clauses of the Fourteenth Amendment. They named as defendants California's Governor and other state and local officials who are responsible for enforcing California's marriage laws. The officials refused to defend the law, so the District Court allowed petitioners—the initiative's official proponents—to intervene to defend it. After a bench trial, the court declared Proposition 8 unconstitutional under the federal Due Process Clause because it violated the fundamental right to marry, and under the Equal Protection Clause because it lacked a rational basis. The district court then issued an order "permanently enjoining [Proposition 8's] enforcement; prohibiting the official defendants from applying or enforcing Proposition 8 and directing the official defendants that all persons under their control or supervision shall not apply or enforce Proposition 8."

The state and local officials did not appeal, but the Proposition 8 proponents did. The Ninth Circuit then certified a question to the California Supreme Court: whether official proponents of a ballot initiative have authority to assert the State's interest in defending the constitutionality of the initiative when public officials refuse to do so. After the California Supreme Court held that the proponents had authority to defend the initiative, the Ninth Circuit concluded that petitioners had standing under federal law to defend Proposition 8's constitutionality, and, on the merits affirmed the District Court's order. According to Judge Reinhardt's opinion, "California had already extended to committed same-sex couples both the incidents of marriage and the official designation of 'marriage,' and Proposition 8's only effect was to take away that important and legally significant designation, while leaving in place all its incidents." This had no other purpose than to stigmatize same-sex couples and therefore violated *Romer v. Evans*.

Chief Justice Roberts, writing for Justices Scalia, Ginsburg, Breyer, and Kagan, held that proponents did not have standing to appeal the district court's order declaring the Proposition unconstitutional. This vacated the Ninth Circuit's decision.

Chief Justice Roberts argued that although the respondents initially had standing to challenge Proposition 8 at the district court level, "[a]fter the District Court declared Proposition 8 unconstitutional and enjoined the state officials named as defendants from enforcing it, . . . the inquiry under Article III changed. Respondents no longer had any injury to redress — they had won — and the state officials chose not to appeal." The petitioners had not been ordered to do anything by the court, and they had only a generalized grievance. "Petitioners have no role — special or otherwise — in the enforcement of Proposition 8. . . . They therefore have no 'personal stake' in defending its enforcement that is distinguishable from the general interest of every citizen of California."

Nor did the California Supreme Court's decision confer federal standing: "All that the California Supreme Court decision stands for is that, so far as California is concerned, petitioners may argue in defense of Proposition 8. This 'does not mean that the proponents become de facto public officials'; the authority they enjoy is 'simply the authority to participate as parties in a court action and to assert legal arguments in defense of the state's interest in the validity of the initiative measure.' That interest is by definition a generalized one, and it is precisely because proponents assert such an interest that they lack standing under our precedents."

Article III's "requirement that a party invoking the jurisdiction of a federal court seek relief for a personal, particularized injury serves vital interests going to the role of the Judiciary in our system of separated powers. 'Refusing to entertain generalized grievances ensures that . . . courts exercise power that is judicial in nature,' and ensures that the Federal Judiciary respects 'the proper — and properly limited — role of the courts in a democratic society.' States cannot alter that role simply by issuing to private parties who otherwise lack standing a ticket to the federal courthouse."

Justice Kennedy, joined by Justices Thomas, Alito, and Sotomayor, dissented: "The Court concludes that proponents lack sufficient ties to the state government. It notes that they 'are not elected,' 'answer to no one,' and lack 'a fiduciary obligation' to the State. But what the Court deems deficiencies in the proponents' connection to the State government, the State Supreme Court saw as essential qualifications to defend the initiative system. The very object of the initiative system is to establish a lawmaking process that does not depend upon state officials."

"Th[e] historic role for the initiative system 'grew out of dissatisfaction with the then governing public officials and a widespread belief that the people had lost control of the political process.' The initiative's 'primary purpose,' then, 'was to afford the people the ability to propose and to adopt constitutional amendments or statutory provisions that their elected public officials had refused or declined to adopt.'"

"The California Supreme Court has determined that this purpose is undermined if the very officials the initiative process seeks to circumvent are the only parties who can defend an enacted initiative when it is challenged in a legal proceeding. Giving the Governor and attorney general this de facto veto will erode one of the cornerstones of the State's governmental structure. And in light of the frequency with which initiatives' opponents resort to litigation, the impact of that veto could be substantial. As a consequence, California finds it necessary to vest the responsibility and right to defend a voter-approved initiative in the initiative's proponents when the State Executive declines to do so."

"[T]he Court today . . . leav[es] the law unclear and the District Court's judgment, and its accompanying statewide injunction, effectively immune from appellate review."

Discussion

1. *The aftermath.* Following the Supreme Court's decision in *Hollingsworth*, the Ninth Circuit dissolved its stay of the District Court's injunction against Proposition 8. That injunction extends to state and local officials and "direct[s] the official defendants that all persons under their control or supervision shall not apply or enforce Proposition 8." The practical effect is that the state of California will recognize same-sex marriages, although there is still some room for further litigation. The lower court decision was not in the context of a statewide class action, and some state officials may argue that the injunction was overbroad given the relief sought or that it does not otherwise apply to them.

2. *Strategy.* Note that although the decision is 5-4, the Justices do not line up along a conservative/liberal split. Why do you think this is so? What strategic considerations might have influenced the various Justices? Note that if the Court struck down Proposition 8 on the merits, it might be difficult to avoid striking down bans on same-sex marriage in other states (although this is still possible if the Court relied on *Romer v. Evans* and the special political context of Proposition 8). On the other hand, if the Court upheld Proposition 8 on the merits, it might have to decide that the ban on same-sex marriage did not involve a suspect classification or a fundamental right, thus dealing a serious blow to the gay rights movement.

It takes four Justices to grant certiorari in a case. Which Justices do you think voted to grant cert. in *Hollingsworth*? In *Windsor*?

3. *The reach of* Hollingsworth. After *Hollingsworth*, can California by statute create an office to defend initiatives and referenda in federal court that state officials are unwilling to defend, and would such an officer have Article III standing to defend a law like Proposition 8? If so, then the result in *Hollingsworth* is one that states can easily work around. If not, then *Hollingsworth* reveals important weaknesses in the initiative and referenda system in the states, because of the incentives it creates for state officials opposed to particular acts of popular lawmaking.

4. *Direct democracy.* Although direct democracy does not appear in the United States Constitution, it is present, in various forms, in 49 of the 50 state

constitutions. Is direct democracy, whether in the form of initiative, referendum, or otherwise, consistent with Article IV's guarantee of republican government? See Pacific States Telephone & Telegraph Co. v. State of Oregon, 223 U.S. 118 (1912) (rejecting a challenge to Oregon's adoption of initiative and referendum on the ground that the question of whether a state government is republican is a question for the political branches). Does the representation-reinforcement theory of *Carolene Products* have anything to say about judicial review of direct democracy?

Should the federal government adopt elements of direct democracy as a complement to representation by the President and Congress, especially if you think that the current system is increasingly dysfunctional?

Insert the following at the end of p. 1592:

DISTRICT ATTORNEY'S OFFICE FOR THE THIRD JUDICIAL DISTRICT v. OSBORNE, 557 U.S. 52 (2009): Osborne was convicted of sexual assault and other crimes in Alaska. Years later, he filed suit claiming a due process right to gain access to the evidence that had been used to convict him in order to subject it to DNA testing at his own expense in order to prove his innocence. The Ninth Circuit upheld his claim, arguing that the prosecution had a duty to disclose exculpatory evidence.

The Supreme Court, in a 5-4 opinion by Chief Justice Roberts, reversed, holding that Osborne had no constitutional right to obtain postconviction access to the State's evidence for DNA testing. Chief Justice Roberts rejected Osborne's claims as a matter of constitutional criminal procedure, as a matter of procedural due process, and as a matter of substantive due process. On the last theory, he argued: "Osborne seeks access to state evidence so that he can apply new DNA-testing technology that might prove him innocent. There is no long history of such a right, and '[t]he mere novelty of such a claim is reason enough to doubt that "substantive due process" sustains it.'" *Reno v. Flores,* 507 U.S. 292 (1993). "[Moreover,] [t]he elected governments of the States are actively confronting the challenges DNA technology poses to our criminal justice systems and our traditional notions of finality, as well as the opportunities it affords. To suddenly constitutionalize this area would short-circuit what looks to be a prompt and considered legislative response. The first DNA testing statutes were passed in 1994 and 1997. In the past decade, 44 States and the Federal Government have followed suit, reflecting the increased availability of DNA testing. As noted, Alaska itself is considering such legislation. 'By extending constitutional protection to an asserted right or liberty interest, we, to a great extent, place the matter outside the arena of public debate and legislative action. We must therefore exercise the utmost care whenever we are asked to break new ground in this field.' *Glucksberg.* '[J]udicial imposition of a categorical remedy . . . might pretermit other responsible solutions being considered in Congress and state legislatures.'

If we extended substantive due process to this area, we would cast these statutes into constitutional doubt and be forced to take over the issue of DNA access ourselves. We are reluctant to enlist the Federal Judiciary in creating a new constitutional code of rules for handling DNA."

"Establishing a freestanding right to access DNA evidence for testing would force us to act as policymakers, and our substantive-due-process rulemaking authority would not only have to cover the right of access but a myriad of other issues. We would soon have to decide if there is a constitutional obligation to preserve forensic evidence that might later be tested. If so, for how long? Would it be different for different types of evidence? Would the State also have some obligation to gather such evidence in the first place? How much, and when? No doubt there would be a miscellany of other minor directives."

"In this case, the evidence has already been gathered and preserved, but if we extend substantive due process to this area, these questions would be before us in short order, and it is hard to imagine what tools federal courts would use to answer them. At the end of the day, there is no reason to suppose that their answers to these questions would be any better than those of state courts and legislatures, and good reason to suspect the opposite."

Justice Stevens dissented: "The State of Alaska possesses physical evidence that, if tested, will conclusively establish whether respondent William Osborne committed rape and attempted murder. If he did, justice has been served by his conviction and sentence. If not, Osborne has needlessly spent decades behind bars while the true culprit has not been brought to justice. The DNA test Osborne seeks is a simple one, its cost modest, and its results uniquely precise. Yet for reasons the State has been unable or unwilling to articulate, it refuses to allow Osborne to test the evidence at his own expense and to thereby ascertain the truth once and for all."

"The fact that nearly all the States have now recognized some postconviction right to DNA evidence makes it more, not less, appropriate to recognize a limited federal right to such evidence in cases where litigants are unfairly barred from obtaining relief in state court." . . .

"Throughout the course of state and federal litigation, the State has failed to provide any concrete reason for denying Osborne the DNA testing he seeks, and none is apparent. Because Osborne has offered to pay for the tests, cost is not a factor. And as the State now concedes, there is no reason to doubt that such testing would provide conclusive confirmation of Osborne's guilt or revelation of his innocence. In the courts below, the State refused to provide an explanation for its refusal to permit testing of the evidence, and in this Court, its explanation has been, at best, unclear. Insofar as the State has articulated any reason at all, it appears to be a generalized interest in protecting the finality of the judgment of conviction from any possible future attacks."

"[W]hile we have long recognized that States have an interest in securing the finality of their judgments, finality is not a stand-alone value that trumps a State's overriding interest in ensuring that justice is done in its courts and secured to its citizens. Indeed, when absolute proof of innocence is readily at hand, a State should not shrink from the possibility that error may have occurred. . . . DNA evidence has led to an extraordinary series of exonerations, not only in cases where the trial evidence was weak, but also in cases where the convicted parties confessed their guilt and where the trial evidence against them appeared overwhelming. The examples provided by amici of the power of DNA testing serve to convince me that the fact of conviction is not sufficient to justify a State's refusal to perform a test that will conclusively establish innocence or guilt. . . . [P]owerful state interests . . . offset the State's purported interest in finality per se. When a person is convicted for a crime he did not commit, the true culprit escapes punishment. DNA testing may lead to his identification. Crime victims, the law enforcement profession, and society at large share a strong interest in identifying and apprehending the actual perpetrators of vicious crimes, such as the rape and attempted murder that gave rise to this case."

"[W]hile it is true that recent advances in DNA technology have led to a nationwide reexamination of state and federal postconviction procedures authorizing the use of DNA testing, it is highly unlikely that [recognizing a right] would significantly affect the use of DNA testing in any of the States that have already developed statutes and procedures for dealing with DNA evidence or would require the few States that have not yet done so to postpone the enactment of appropriate legislation. Indeed, a holding by this Court that the policy judgments underlying that legislation rest on a sound constitutional foundation could only be constructive."

Justice Alito wrote a concurring opinion. Justice Souter also dissented.

Discussion

1. *Tradition and new technologies.* Chief Justice Roberts argues that there can be no right to prove innocence using DNA because the technology is so new, and hence the claim is novel. Novel claims, by definition, are inappropriate for substantive due process protection. Doesn't this depend on how one characterizes the tradition or the principle involved? The technology or the circumstances might be new but the principle involved might be quite old. (Recall the discussion in *Michael M. v. Gerald D.*). Couldn't one have said with equal force that the First Amendment doesn't protect expression on the Internet because the medium is so new? Cf. Reno v. American Civil Liberties Union, 521 U.S. 844 (1997) (holding that Internet speech deserves full free speech protection); see also Kyllo v. United States 533 U.S. 27 (2001) (opinion of Scalia, J.) (holding that use of thermal imaging technology violated Fourth Amendment ban on unreasonable searches and seizures). Note, interestingly, that Justice Stevens (who dissents in *Osborne*), wrote the opinion in *Reno*, joined by Justice Scalia; while Justice Scalia (who joins the majority in *Osborne*) wrote the opinion in *Kyllo*, with Justice Stevens dissenting.

Could Chief Justice Roberts respond that the guarantees of freedom of speech and security against unreasonable searches and seizures are textually specific, while the constitutional guarantee against denials of liberty without due process of law is not? On the other hand, isn't Osborne's claim rather closely connected to the text? After all, he is invoking a right to prove one's innocence in order to regain one's liberty.

Note that much of the power of Osborne's argument stems from the fact that DNA tests are widely believed to be a highly accurate means of demonstrating innocence. If so, Alaska seems to be unreasonably denying him a right to prove his innocence conclusively. But what if the tests are complicated and their results inherently ambiguous? And what if we discover, after many years of experience, that DNA tests are not as reliable as we first thought? Should this affect whether courts should leave the question to the political process? Might this be a stronger way to restate Chief Justice Roberts' concerns about novelty?

2. *Bringing outliers in line.* In many of the Court's decisions, like *Griswold v. Connecticut* or *Lawrence v. Texas*, the Court waits until most states have recognized a right (or decriminalized an activity) and then brings the remaining outliers into line. By contrast, in *Glucksberg* and *Vacco*, very few states had modified their laws and the Court was not prepared to get very far ahead of the potential developing social consensus—at least as measured by state recognition. Along the same lines, a familiar criticism of *Roe v. Wade* is that the Court intervened too early, when only a small number of states had begun to reform their abortion laws, and the Court actually stuck down one of the abortion reform laws (in Georgia) as insufficient. In *Osborne*, however, 46 states and the federal government had recognized a right to use DNA to prove innocence before the Court was asked to decide the question. Can one defend *Osborne* on the ground that judicial recognition was unnecessary at this point? If so, why could one not say the same of *Griswold*?